DEUTS

DEUTSCH NA KLAR!

INSTRUCTOR'S EDITION

AN INTRODUCTORY GERMAN COURSE

Robert Di Donato — Miami University, Oxford, Ohio

Monica D. Clyde — College of San Mateo

Jacqueline Vansant — Miami University, Oxford, Ohio

McGRAW-HILL, INC.

NEW YORK • ST. LOUIS • SAN FRANCISCO • AUCKLAND • BOGOTÁ
CARACAS • HAMBURG • LISBON • LONDON • MADRID • MEXICO • MILAN • MONTREAL
NEW DELHI • PARIS • SAN JUAN • SÃO PAULO • SINGAPORE
SYDNEY • TOKYO • TORONTO

This is an ⌐BⅠ book.

Deutsch: Na klar!
An Introductory German Course

1 2 3 4 5 6 7 8 9 0 DOH DOH 9 5 4 3 2 1 0

ISBN 0-07-557031-9 (Student Edition)
ISBN 0-07-557029-7 (Instructor's Edition)

This book was set in Optima and New Aster by Graphic Typesetting Service.
The editors were Leslie Berriman and Marie Deer.
The art editor was Edie Williams.
The illustrators were Wolfgang Horsch, George Ulrich, and Lori Heckelman.
The photo researcher was Judy Mason.
The production supervisor was Tanya Nigh.

Production and editorial assistance was provided by Lorna Lo, Randie Miller, and Jane Parkinson.
The text designer was Wendy Calmenson.
The frontmatter designer was Martin Charles.
The backmatter designer was Paula Goldstein.
The cover was designed by BB & K Designs Inc.
This book was printed and bound by R. R. Donnelley & Sons Co.

Library of Congress Cataloging-in-Publication Data

Di Donato, Robert.
Deutsch, na klar! : an introductory German course / Robert Di Donato, Monica D. Clyde, Jacqueline Vansant. — Instructor's ed.
p. cm.
Includes index.
ISBN 0-07-557031-9 (student edition); ISBN 0-07-557029-7 (instructor's edition)
1. German language—Grammar—1950– 2. German language—Textbooks for foreign speakers—English. I. Clyde, Monica. II. Vansant, Jacqueline, 1954– . III. Title.
PF3112.D48 1991
438.2'421—dc20 90–43118 CIP

Grateful acknowledgment is made for use of the following:

Photographs *Page 2* © R. Hiller/Monkmeyer Press Photo Service; *3 (top)* © Beryl Goldberg; *3 (bottom)* © Ulrike Welsch; *23 (top and center)* © Peter Menzel/Stock, Boston; *23 (bottom)* © Ulrike Welsch; *25* © Bob Daemmrich/Stock, Boston; *27* © Peter Menzel/Stock, Boston; *45* © Henning Lülsdorf; *56* © Mike Mazzaschi/Stock, Boston; *63 (left)* © Ulrike Welsch/Photo Researchers, Inc.; *63 (right)* © Ulrike Welsch; *131* © Sam C. Pierson, Jr./Photo Researchers, Inc.; *171* © R. Hiller/Monkmeyer Press Photo Service; *196* © Eva M. Demjen/Stock, Boston; *233 (left)* © Ulrike Welsch; *233 (right)* © Beryl Goldberg; *239 (top left)* © Pierre Berger/Photo Researchers, Inc.; *239 (top right)* © Ulrike Welsch/Photo Researchers, Inc.; *239 (bottom left)* © Beryl Goldberg; *239 (bottom right)* © Ulrike Welsch; *250* © The Bettmann Archive; *271* © Michael E. Bry/Monkmeyer Press Photo Service; *272* © German Information Center; *283* © Peter Menzel; *302* © Andy Bernhaut/Photo Researchers, Inc.; *309* © German Information Center; *312* © Don Morgan/Photo Researchers, Inc.; *326* © Uta Hoffmann; *359* © Christa Armstrong/Photo Researchers, Inc.; *360* © Peter Menzel/Stock, Boston; *375* © Uta Hoffmann; *382* © Henning Lülsdorf; *384* © German Information Center; *390* © Owen Franken/Stock, Boston; *439* © Ulrike Welsch; *447* © Mike Mazzaschi/Stock, Boston; *470* © Ulrike Welsch; *475* © Topham/The Image Works; *476 (top)* © UPI/Bettmann Newsphotos; *476 (bottom)* © Keystone/The Image Works; *477 (top)* © The Bettmann Archive; *477 (bottom left)* © German Information Center; *477 (bottom right)* © UPI/Bettmann Newsphotos; *479 (top left)* © Reuters/Bettmann Newsphotos; *479 (top right)* © UPI/Bettmann Newsphotos; *479 (bottom left)* © UPI/Bettmann Newsphotos; *479 (bottom right)* © Topham/The Image Works; *482* © Lehnartz/Bundesbildstelle Bonn (German Information Center); *483 (top)* © AP/Wide World Photos; *483 (bottom)* © German Information Center

Realia, cartoons, and readings: *Page 4* Deutsche Bundespost; *6 (top left)* © Michel & Co.; *6 (top right)* © Eva Heller; *6 (bottom center)* Deutsche Chefaro Pharma GmbH; *6 (bottom right)* Jörg Rintelen, Horstedt; *8* © Funk Uhr; *10* Berliner Morgenpost; *11* Gelbe Seiten, Göttingen; *16 (top)* Tanzschule ADTV Wolfgang Kaschützke; *16 (bottom)* Musikhaus am Zoo, Berlin; *17* Reprinted with permission of Deutsches Theater in Göttingen; *20* Deutsches Jugendherbergswerk; *30* Universität Göttingen; *31* Agentur Hentschel, Munich; *33* Brenner Autobahn; *34* Pan-Creativ, Planegg; *36* © NASA and Franckh-Kosmos Verlags-GmbH; *39 (left)* Cartoon by Peter Gaymann. © Weitzdörfer/Wolf Editions; *39 (right)* © Bravo; *42* Cartoon by Peter Gaymann. © Weitzdörfer/Wolf Editions; *43* © Vincenth 19, Galerie der Töpferstube; *46 (left)* Familie Wischnewski, Bad Harzburg; *46 (right)* Familie Stock, Osnabrück; *48 (text)* Stern; *48 (photos)* Pellizoli/Stern; *57 (top left)* IKEA-Kamen; *57 (top center)* Möbel Hübner, Berlin; *57 (top right)* IKEA-Eching; *57 (bottom left)* IKEA-Kamen; *57 (bottom right)* BUNTE Magazin;
(continued on page 559)

CONTENTS

v

LESEN IM KONTEXT

KAPITEL 2

DAS TÄGLICHE LEBEN

WÖRTER IM KONTEXT

GRAMMATIK IM KONTEXT

KAPITEL

3

FAMILIE UND FREUNDE 82

KAPITEL

6

GRAMMATIK IM KONTEXT 266

LESEN IM KONTEXT 280

KAPITEL

10

UNTERWEGS 288

WÖRTER IM KONTEXT 290

KAPITEL 11

DAS LIEBE GELD — 318

LESEN IM KONTEXT

DIE VIER WÄNDE

WÖRTER IM KONTEXT

GRAMMATIK IM KONTEXT

KAPITEL 13

DER START IN DIE ZUKUNFT _____ 380

Kapitel 14

Wie Man auf dem Laufenden Bleibt — 414

APPENDIX 503

VOCABULARY 509

INDEX 551

ABOUT THE AUTHORS 559

TO THE INSTRUCTOR

Deutsch: Na klar! is a complete package of instructional materials for beginning German courses, geared to developing students' communication skills. It is designed for the instructor who wants a text that reflects current pedagogical theory while preserving many features instructors have come to trust. Thus, you will find that *Deutsch: Na klar!* offers a balance of original and standard features: it includes a rich array of authentic materials together with clear and succinct grammar explanations; it teaches particular strategies to develop the receptive skills of listening and reading while maintaining an emphasis on all four language skills; it is filled with communicative activities but not at the expense of controlled, skill-building exercises; it expands on the goal of systematic acquisition of vocabulary while continuing to recognize that students can profit from understanding the fundamental features of German morphology, syntax, and phonology.

Authenticity is of primary concern in *Deutsch: Na klar!* Authentic materials, whether they serve as the basis of student interaction or illustrate the communicative function of a grammar point, are chosen from real life. The readings also come from authentic sources and are made accessible to students by the manner in which they are approached. The goal in using the great variety of authentic materials and texts is to provide students with opportunities to relate their classroom learning to actual life experiences that they might encounter in German-speaking countries, either as students or later in their lives. Using authentic materials increases students' motivation and stimulates interest in the culture and language they are learning. Dialogues and listening comprehension materials simulate authentic discourse as closely as possible, and are often based on unrehearsed native speech.

Deutsch: Na klar! has been carefully developed for use in a proficiency-oriented classroom without dictating a particular methodology. It is compatible with a number of methodologies and approaches and with both theoretical and practical points of view regarding foreign language teaching and learning.

ORGANIZATION OF THE TEXT

Deutsch: Na klar! consists of sixteen chapters organized around major cultural themes. Each chapter begins with a piece of realia or a drawing that sets the stage for the chapter theme. The corresponding **Alles klar?**

section gets students thinking about the topic and encourages them to interact. Following this visually based opener, each chapter has three major parts:

Wörter im Kontext   This section presents thematically grouped vocabulary in context via authentic texts or dialogues. Students acquire and practice vocabulary by exploring the authentic materials in sections entitled **Analyse** that are followed by a variety of communicative activities. Listening comprehension skills are systematically developed through a series of activities entitled **Hören Sie zu.** The listening passages on which these activities are based appear on the Listening Comprehension Tapes that accompany *Deutsch: Na klar!* The scripts for these listening passages appear at the back of the *Instructor's Edition.* Additional listening practice is provided through the material in the section entitled **Dialog,** which also appears on the tapes. Marginal notes in the *Instructor's Edition* suggest additional activities for listening practice based on these dialogues. A cassette symbol next to an activity in the book indicates that corresponding listening material appears on tape for in-class listening practice. Cultural notes (**Kulturnotizen**) highlight special aspects of the chapter theme. Grammar tips in the form of **Sprachnotizen** give students just the right amount of information on a particular grammar point for them to complete an activity. Fuller explanations in the **Grammatik im Kontext** section expand on these functional grammar notes.

Grammatik im Kontext   Grammar structures are introduced by means of models demonstrating their communicative use. A characteristic feature of the grammar sections is **Analyse,** in which students take an active part in learning a new grammar item. Students analyze a brief text, a piece of realia, or a number of example sentences in order to discover on their own some of the characteristics of a particular grammar item before it is formally presented. Grammar, often already touched upon in the **Sprachnotizen** of the **Wörter im Kontext,** is presented in English with clear and succinct explanations and is then practiced in carefully sequenced contextualized exercises and activities. Vocabulary from **Wörter im Kontext** is reentered and practiced throughout the grammar section. Listening comprehension activities (**Hören Sie zu**) appear in this section in the early chapters. In addition, controlled, discrete-item practice drills are found in both the laboratory program and marginal notes in the *Instructor's Edition.*

Lesen im Kontext   This section provides students with a variety of authentic readings reflecting the chapter themes. With guidance from specific strategies, students learn to read unedited, authentic texts with increasing facility. Activities in the **Vor dem Lesen** section prepare students for the series of readings. The sections entitled **Auf den ersten Blick** ease students into the individual readings through contextual guessing based on skimming and scanning activities. In the **Zum Text**

sections, students work intensively on different elements of the reading text, including content, grammar, vocabulary, and text structure. These are often accompanied by communicative activities based on the reading. The reading section concludes with **Nach dem Lesen,** summarizing the chapter theme through activities such as interviews, role-playing, and writing.

In addition to the sixteen numbered chapters, a preliminary chapter, the **Einführung,** introduces students to the German language and German-speaking world. In this introductory chapter students get a preview of the activities they will encounter throughout *Deutsch: Na klar!* Student production in the **Einführung** is limited to carrying out a few everyday tasks, such as greeting, leavetaking, spelling, and counting numbers. To build motivation and to introduce students to the approach used in this text, carefully selected authentic materials appear and corresponding activities show students the value of cognate recognition and contextual guessing.

PROGRAM COMPONENTS

The *Deutsch: Na klar!* program consists of the following components:

- The *Student Text*, including realia, readings, vocabulary and grammar presentations, and activities for developing each of the four skills, plus a grammar appendix for reference and a comprehensive end vocabulary.

- The *Workbook*, containing controlled and open-ended writing activities together with additional authentic practice materials that reinforce the material in each chapter.

- A complete *Laboratory Program*, with systematic practice in German spelling and pronunciation, and practice with a variety of listening materials ranging from discrete-item drills to extended discourse passages for comprehension. Program components include a student *Laboratory Manual*, cassette or reel-to-reel tapes, and a full *Tapescript* of the laboratory material for the instructor's use.

- The annotated *Instructor's Edition*, containing everything in the student text plus:
  —On-page instructional ideas and answers to in-text listening comprehension activities.
  —Appendices, including scripts for the listening comprehension activities and realia support material that provides cultural information about realia in the text.

- The *Instructor's Manual*, including an explanation of the theoretical underpinnings of the text, course outlines for semester and quarter systems, and sample lesson plans.

- *Listening Comprehension Tapes*, containing the recorded material for the in-class listening activities. If the instructor prefers, he or she can read from the listening comprehension scripts that appear at the back of the *Instructor's Edition* in lieu of using the tapes. In addition to the **Hören Sie zu** listening comprehension passages, these tapes include dialogues from the **Dialog** sections.

- *Visual Materials and Activities*, tied to each chapter of the text and including optional activities, realia, and transparency masters.

- The *Testing Program,* with chapter tests and term exams, including testing for both receptive and productive skills.

- A video entitled *The McGraw-Hill Video Library of Authentic Materials: A German TV Journal,* accompanied by a *User's Guide* and including authentic segments from German television (ZDF). Topics relate directly to major topics in the text. The *User's Guide* contains a variety of activities that can be duplicated for students. Ordering information is available on request. Contact your McGraw-Hill representative.

- The *McGraw-Hill Electronic Language Tutor* (MHELT), computer materials containing the single-response exercises from the Student Text, available for the IBM PC, Macintosh, and Apple IIe and IIc.

- *Color Slides*, accompanied by a pamphlet of commentary and questions.

- *A Practical Guide to Language Learning: A Fifteen-Week Program of Strategies for Success* by H. Douglas Brown (San Francisco State University), a brief introduction to language learning written for beginning language students. Available free to adopters, this guide can be photocopied for students; it can also be made available through bookstores at a nominal price.

MAJOR FEATURES

Deutsch: Na klar! has six major characteristics:

- Emphasis on the development of strong receptive language skills
- Extensive use of authentic materials
- Acquisition of vocabulary through students' active participation in discovering the meaning of new words
- A full complement of exercises and activities to develop productive language skills
- A combination of inductive and deductive approaches to language together with the recycling of language functions
- Cultural contexts that reflect authentic use of German

The Development of Strong Receptive Language Skills

In contrast to many recent texts, *Deutsch: Na klar!* does not emphasize the development of productive language skills at the expense of the receptive skills. Rather, this text stresses the importance of learning language for recognition purposes in order to increase and enhance all communication skills. Readings and listening activities that promote recognition skills are designed to challenge students. These types of materials are pitched at a somewhat higher level than that at which the students themselves produce language. Thus, students familiarize themselves with new vocabulary and structures through listening and reading before they are asked to produce them. Students will generally take the step to production more comfortably because of the initial focus on recognition skills. These skills are developed in a variety of ways throughout the text, as further elaborated in the following section.

The Use of Authentic Materials

Authentic materials are the essence of *Deutsch: Na klar!* These materials come in many varieties: advertisements, announcements, flyers, headlines, brochures, tickets, menus, schedules, and so on. These materials appear throughout the text in their original form with occasional glosses. The realia are vehicles for presenting and practicing new vocabulary and grammar in authentic contexts; they are used to reinforce skimming and scanning skills, and student interaction with the realia forms the basis for follow-up activities.

The readings are also authentic texts, and they present material that students might encounter in a German-speaking environment. Readings include complete selections as well as excerpts from longer articles. Key words, phrases, or clauses are explained in marginal glosses. Unfamiliar language that is not essential to the total comprehension of a reading is not glossed, nor is guessable vocabulary glossed.

Each reading is accompanied by a wide variety of pre-reading, close reading, and post-reading activities designed to teach both extensive and intensive reading skills. Pre-reading activities (**Auf den ersten Blick**) include anticipating and predicting content, skimming, and scanning. These strategies, in conjunction with the activation of students' prior knowledge of a topic, contribute to the development of good guessing skills. Close reading activities (**Zum Text**) include comprehension checks, analysis at the word, text, and structural levels, paraphrasing, and summarizing. Post-reading activities (**Nach dem Lesen**) are points of departure for related reading, speaking, and writing practice.

Like the readings, the recorded materials for in-class use encourage the listening equivalents of skimming, scanning, and sensible guessing. These materials are generally based on interviews and conversations with native speakers.

Active Participation in the Acquisition of Vocabulary

As much as possible, students are encouraged to discover the meaning of new words from the context in which they are embedded. Recurring sections entitled **Alles klar** and **Analyse** pose questions about key words or expressions. The authors believe that students will generally find it easier to remember meanings that they have had to figure out for themselves. Words that are intended for active knowledge are summarized throughout the chapter in sections entitled **Neue Wörter.** Thus words are learned just a few at a time, and in meaningful contexts. The **Wortschatz** section at the end of each chapter summarizes the chapter's active vocabulary.

The Development of Productive Language Skills

In addition to many strategies for building receptive skills, *Deutsch: Na klar!* includes carefully sequenced activities designed to help students build productive skills, including guided role-playing situations that allow for student choices and simulate real communication in German. Activities are presented within a communicative context, even when the task performed is relatively mechanical.

Grammar structures and fixed phrases that students need in order to function within a given situation are presented in **Sprachnotizen** and in occasional short lists of **nützliche Wörter** or, in later chapters, **Redewendungen.** These items are presented where needed, regardless of where they might fit logically in the grammar sequence of the text. Thus, students learn phrases like **ich möchte** or **ich hätte gern** long before the subjunctive is formally presented in the actual grammar sections.

Recycling of Language Functions

Whenever feasible, grammar structures needed for active use are described and presented in terms of their language functions. These language functions are recycled throughout the text. Thus, the important language function of describing a person or an item is recycled in several chapters as students learn ever more complex manifestations of this language function, from simple descriptive statements with predicate adjectives, through attributive adjectives, to relative clauses.

Students are frequently encouraged to discover some of the characteristics of a new grammar item on their own by analyzing a short text or piece of realia before the grammar is formally presented. You will find these sections in the **Grammatik im Kontext** sections under the heading **Analyse.**

Culture in Authentic Contexts

One reason given by many students for studying a foreign language is to learn about the culture of the people who speak the language. In *Deutsch: Na klar!* we have made a major effort to meet this need. Authentic materials provide the basis for many insights into diverse aspects of daily life in German-speaking countries. In addition, cultural notes (**Kulturnotizen**) are interspersed throughout the text to provide information about important aspects of German culture.

ACKNOWLEDGMENTS

The authors would like to extend special thanks to Patricia Boylan and John A. Lett, Jr., of the Defense Language Institute, Dorothy Rissel of the University at Buffalo, and June K. Phillips of the Tennessee Foreign Language Institute. The first three, authors of the introductory Spanish text *¡En directo!*, and the last, main author of the introductory French text *Quoi de neuf?*, shared ideas and innovations from their texts, whose methodology is similar to that of *Deutsch: Na klar!*

The authors would also like to thank Renate Schulz of the University of Arizona, Tucson, for her contributions in the earliest stages of the book. Likewise, we would like to acknowledge the participation of John Lalande of the University of Illinois, Urbana-Champaign, and Ronald W. Walker of Colorado State University for their contributions to the earlier drafts and beginning chapters.

The authors and publisher would like to express their thanks to those instructors who responded to a series of surveys and reviews during the development of *Deutsch: Na klar!* The appearance of their names does not necessarily constitute their endorsement of the text or its methodology.

Veldon J. Bennett, Jacksonville State University
Robert Catura, California State University, Sacramento
Timothy Chamberlain, New York University
Lloyd Flanigan, Piedmont Virginia Community College
Brian A. Lewis, University of Colorado, Boulder
Michael Schultz, University of Pennsylvania
Elfriede W. Smith, Drew University
David A. Veeder, Drake University
Morris Vos, Western Illinois University

A very special word of thanks to Larry D. Wells of the State University of New York, Binghamton, whose careful and expert reading of the entire manuscript and whose insightful comments, reactions, and suggestions led to many improvements and new ideas. His keen eye for what works and what doesn't was of immeasurable value in shaping the final version of *Deutsch: Na klar!*

Because of the importance of authentic and up-to-date materials for the success of this book, we are indebted to innumerable people for their assistance in collecting and contributing interesting and exciting materials for the project, among them Brigitte Nikolai; Ellen Crocker; Ilsabeth Groetschel and her family in Kleve; Bloyken Haese and her family in Seevetal near Hamburg; Maria Weber and her family in Bonn; Marion Weber and her friends; David Fernandez for his continuous supply of the latest German newspapers through his connection with Lufthansa; and Dr. and Mrs. Richard Rutter, who contributed generously by sharing with us private letters from friends in the German Democratic Republic about the events in their country in November 1989. Last, but not least, the authors would like to thank Melissa Clyde for the many times she gave her critical input as a representative of the student audience for whom *Deutsch: Na klar!* is intended.

Our sincere thanks to Karen Judd and her excellent production staff at McGraw-Hill, foremost among them Marie Deer, who steered *Deutsch: Na klar!* through the various production stages with a keen eye for what is practical and sensible. Our thanks to Stacey Sawyer as well, for her important editorial contributions to the development of the manuscript. Another very special word of thanks goes to Wolfgang Horsch of Heidelberg, whose delightful and hilarious drawings enliven all chapters of *Deutsch: Na klar!*

Finally, the authors wish to thank the McGraw-Hill editorial staff, without whose expert guidance and encouragement *Deutsch: Na klar!* would not have gotten off the ground nor ever have been completed. A special word of thanks goes to Eirik Børve and Thalia Dorwick for their vision in beginning this project and for their unswerving faith and guidance throughout its development. We are also deeply grateful to Leslie Berriman, who came aboard in the middle of the project and whose constant help, guidance, and confidence kept the project on course.

TO THE STUDENT

Given the recent political events in Europe, a new and exciting perspective on Germany and its language is developing throughout the world. *Deutsch: Na klar!* (*German: You bet!*) affirms that new perspective in a fresh and lively approach to learning German.

You may have already studied a foreign language and may therefore be familiar with the different elements in language learning, such as vocabulary, grammar structures, readings, cultural information, photographs, and recorded listening materials, as well as activities to help you use what you have learned. In *Deutsch: Na klar!* you will find these and other familiar elements. What is different about this program is its approach to language learning. For one, *Deutsch: Na klar!* aims to stretch your thinking by asking you to participate actively in understanding and communicating what you want to say and write. For example, some of the language you see in *Deutsch: Na klar!* is not edited for beginning students, because to do so might tempt you to think that real people write or speak in that simplified way . . . and they do not! Instead, we will give you German as it really is. You are not expected to know and translate every word or phrase you see. In fact, we usually ask you just to get the gist and leave it at that, or to look for a few specific pieces of information. What sets *Deutsch: Na klar!* apart is that the language it uses is authentic and natural, and the topics it discusses are current.

Many of you have already had some experience with German, whether in the classroom, through travel, by meeting visitors to your country, or just through observing the world around you. After all, words like **Gesundheit, Delikatessen, Kindergarten,** and **Poltergeist** have long been a part of American English; even new words from German are beginning to be fashionable, such as **Fahrvergnügen** in Volkswagen ads. As you begin to work with *Deutsch: Na klar!*, you will be surprised by how much German you already know.

When you try to understand something in a foreign language, it is important that you draw on what you know in general, on all available clues (such as photos, headlines, or titles), and on your ability to predict what will probably come next, to make logical guesses about a text's meaning. You also bring to the task your skills from your native language; for example, you move back and forth among various sections of a reading text, using what comes later to make sense of the first parts of a passage. Keep these things in mind as you read the following descriptions of the various sections in your text and our hints on how to work with them.

Deutsch: Na klar! is organized around themes aimed at allowing you to function effectively in a German-speaking country. In the early chapters you will learn practical things such as how to identify yourself, shop for daily necessities, ask for directions, make reservations, arrange for transportation, and order at a restaurant. In the later chapters you will focus on issues and events that concern people from all cultures, and you will learn to express your opinions and ideas about them.

Each chapter of *Deutsch: Na klar!* begins with a piece or pieces of authentic material, such as a flyer from a university bulletin board, ads from a newspaper, or a schedule, to set the stage for the topic explored throughout the chapter. You will be asked to make some sense of these materials through creative guessing. Above all, don't be frustrated when you can't understand everything; no one expects you to be able to translate or even follow every word. What is important is that you try to guess the general meaning, for you will learn a great deal of German in the process. In most cases, the meaning of words in these authentic materials is not given to you, because we think you will find it easier to remember meanings that you have to figure out for yourself.

The chapter following this visual opener is divided into three sections. In **Wörter im Kontext,** many more words are presented through authentic materials, dialogues, and listening comprehension activities. New vocabulary is practiced in many different ways. Some activities simply guide you as you use the new words; others encourage you to be more creative, to stretch your ability in German by expressing your opinions, and to try out your versatility in role-playing situations with your classmates. Vocabulary intended for active use is summarized in short vocabulary lists (**Neue Wörter**) interspersed throughout the section. This allows you to learn manageable portions of vocabulary at a time. All of the chapter's active vocabulary is summarized in the **Wortschatz** list at the end of the chapter.

The middle section of each chapter, **Grammatik im Kontext,** deals with the German structures that you need to function in the specific situations suggested by the chapter theme. You are often asked to analyze the characteristics of a grammar item in sections entitled **Analyse,** before the formal presentation of the grammar. Doing these analytical exercises should help you focus on the essentials of a grammar item and strengthen your understanding of the way it functions. The grammar presented in *Deutsch: Na klar!* is not exhaustive and filled with innumerable exceptions to each and every rule. Instead, the grammar explanations are kept succinct and to the point, omitting detail that is not pertinent to the production of simple but correct German. Some structures are presented for recognition only in boxes marked **Sprachnotiz,** which you will find in all of the three major chapter sections.

The third part of each chapter is called **Lesen im Kontext,** and it focuses on reading, usually an article or portions of articles from a German-language publication on a topic related to the chapter theme. These readings are also authentic; that is, the originals are not edited, although sometimes they are shortened. Pre-reading activities and follow-up questions are designed to help you get the gist of a passage. The tasks expected of you get progressively more expansive over the course of the text, aiming in the later chapters at paraphrasing and summarizing a text and expressing your views about it. Finally, activities for group work and writing encourage you to use what you have learned throughout the chapter.

Like the authentic materials in the chapter opener, all other materials in *Deutsch: Na klar!* have been carefully chosen for their value in conveying a culturally authentic image. These materials will present you with a challenge because they are at a level higher than your speaking level. As you work with them, you will find that you not only learn to read in German but also learn by reading German.

So that's what's different about *Deutsch: Na klar!* The text and its accompanying materials rely on your willingness to be an active learner and to take risks, and to express your thoughts and ideas. We hope you enjoy working with it as much as the authors enjoyed creating it for you. **Viel Spaß!**

Der Watzmann, höchster Berg im Berchtesgadener Land (© Comstock)

Blumenpracht
in einem Park
in Mainz
(© Peter Menzel)

Morgens in einer
Kleinstadt
(© Peter Menzel)

Viktualien—ein altes Wort
für Lebensmittel

Der Viktualienmarkt im
Zentrum von München
(©Peter Menzel)

Abendstimmung in einer
mittelalterlichen Stadt (©Peter Menzel)

Volksfest in Süddeutschland
(©Monkmeyer, Edith Reichmann)

Eine Mahlzeit im Freien
(©Peter Menzel)

Stuttgart, die Metropole
Schwabens (©Comstock)

Öffentliche Verkehrsmittel in
der Großstadt—die Straßenbahn
(©Comstock, Hartman-DeWitt)

Wäsche im Hinterhof
(©Peter Menzel)

Schweizer Fahnen in Zürich
(©Comstock, A. J. Hartman)

Enge Gasse in einem
Städtchen am Rhein
(©Comstock, A. J. Hartman)

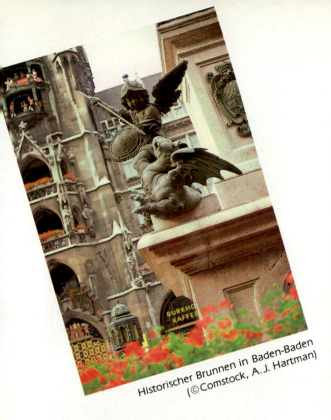

Historischer Brunnen in Baden-Baden
(©Comstock, A. J. Hartman)

Schlösser und Burgen wie im
Märchen gibt es viele.
(©Comstock)

Innsbruck im Winter (©Peter Menzel)

Das Matterhorn, einer
der höchsten und
eindrucksvollsten Berge
in den Schweizer Alpen
(©Comstock, A.J. Hartman)

Baden-Baden, ein
berühmtes Kurbad in
Baden-Württemberg
(©Peter Menzel)

(©Peter Menzel)

Menschen im Regen
(© Peter Menzel)

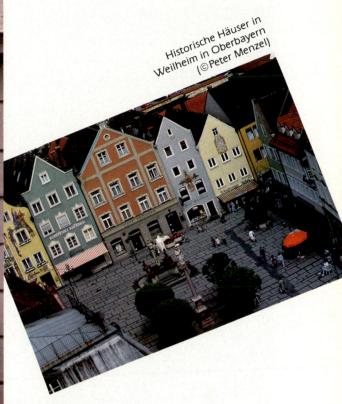

Historische Häuser in
Weilheim in Oberbayern
(© Peter Menzel)

Wohnen in der
Bundesrepublik
(© Peter Menzel)

Bei der Feldarbeit hilft
oft die ganze Familie.
(© Peter Menzel)

Ziegenherde in den
Schweizer Alpen
(©Comstock, A.J. Hartman)

Heidelberg am Neckar, eine alte Universitätsstadt (©Peter Menzel)

DEUTSCH ● NA KLAR!

EINFÜHRUNG

Einführung. The *Einführung* aims at familiarizing students with the diversity of activities they will encounter throughout the book. They will begin using the language in simple communicative situations. They will also be exposed to authentic texts to develop reading and listening comprehension. Communicative activities will focus mainly on sharing basic personal information.

Lernziele *In this chapter you will learn how to greet people in German, how to introduce yourself and someone else, and how to say where you're from. You'll also learn to ask people how they are and say how you are. Finally, you will learn some basic techniques for approaching a text in a foreign language.*

Hallo! Willkommen! Guten Tag!

Wie ist Ihr Name?
Mein Name ist _____. / Ich bin _____ .

Guten Tag. Mein Name ist Lindemann, Klaus Lindemann.
Und ich bin Ingrid Schlüter.

Hallo! **Suggestion:** Ask students if they already know some other greetings in German. Write them on the board.

Introduce yourself to students using the expressions on this page. Use the photos and their captions to convey the meanings of these phrases. Point out that it is customary in German-speaking countries to shake hands when greeting someone. Model both questions and responses for students before asking for individual responses.

Und woher sind Sie?
Ich bin aus _____. / Ich komme aus _____.

Woher sind Sie?
Ich bin aus Texas.
Ich komme aus
* Deutschland.*

▣ Alles klar?°

Alles... *Everything clear?*

Alles klar? Have students circulate around the class as they do this. Encourage them to shake hands.

Introduce yourself to several people in your class and ask them where they are from:

A: Guten Tag. Mein Name ist _____.
B: Guten Tag. Mein Name ist _____. / Ich bin _____.
A: Woher _____?
B: Ich bin aus _____. Und woher _____?
A: Ich komme aus _____.

Das ist Herr / Frau _____ aus _____. Start a chain, each person introducing a classmate in these more formal terms.

A: Das ist Herr _____ aus _____.
B: Und das ist Frau _____ aus _____.

Das ist Herr / Frau _____. Elaborate on the information provided in the *Kulturnotiz* on page 3 by pointing out that most German women now prefer to be addressed as *Frau*. Among more conservative groups and in some regions *Fräulein* is still used. You might also point out that whereas most young people address each other by first name, German adults do not address someone they have just met that way.

Das ist Herr Thompson aus
* Texas.*
Das ist Frau Roberts aus
* Washington.*

> ▢▢▢▢ *Kulturnotiz*
>
> In formal address, the title **Herr** means *Mr.* The title **Frau,** which generally refers to a married woman or to an older woman, married or not, is becoming the preferred mode of address for all women, particularly in a professional setting. The title **Fräulein,** however, is still used for the young, unmarried woman.

Neue Wörter

guten Tag *hello, good day*
Wie ist Ihr Name? *What is your name?*
mein Name ist *my name is*
ich bin *I am*
Woher sind Sie? *Where are you from?*

ich komme aus *I come from*
Deutschland *Germany*
das ist *this is*
Frau *Mrs.; Ms.; woman*
Fräulein *Miss*
Herr *Mr.; gentleman*

Kulturnotiz. This is a recurring feature. It introduces cultural information that relates to the activities or readings on the page. The material is kept very concise, giving the teacher a chance to add whatever he or she may consider pertinent.

Neue Wörter. This section will appear throughout the book. The words and expressions listed should become active vocabulary. At times the section will summarize vocabulary that has been introduced earlier; at others, it will preview new vocabulary.

Buchstabieren wir!°

In contrast to English, German follows fairly predictable spelling and pronunciation rules. You will gradually learn these rules throughout the course.

  The German alphabet has the same twenty-six letters as the English alphabet, plus four other letters of its own. The four special German letters are written as follows:

Ä ä   a-Umlaut: **Bär, Käse** (*may be typed* ae)
Ö ö   o-Umlaut: **böse, hören** (*may be typed* oe)
Ü ü   u-Umlaut: **müde, Süden** (*may be typed* ue)
ß   sz ("ess tsett"): **süß, Straße** (*used only in the middle or at the end of a word; may be typed* ss)

The following spelling chart (**Buchstabiertafel**) is distributed by the post office of the Federal Republic of Germany. You can use it to make sure of the spelling of a name or a word said over the phone.

Buchstabieren... *Let's spell!*

Buchstabieren wir! Point out: While we refer to letters with an umlaut as a-, o-, or u-Umlaut, these are distinct letters and sounds in German. Germans refer to them as *ä, ö,* and *ü.* Model these sounds carefully. Pronunciation rules and practice are covered in the Lab Manual.

Buchstabiertafel

A = Anton	G = Gustav	O = Otto	U = Ulrich
Ä = Ärger	H = Heinrich	Ö = Ökonom	Ü = Übermut
B = Berta	I = Ida	P = Paula	V = Victor
C = Cäsar	J = Julius	Q = Quelle	W = Wilhelm
Ch = Charlotte	K = Kaufmann	R = Richard	X = Xanthippe
D = Dora	L = Ludwig	S = Samuel	Y = Ypsilon
E = Emil	M = Martha	Sch = Schule	Z = Zacharias
F = Friedrich	N = Nordpol	T = Theodor	

For example, you could spell the name Linda as follows:

L wie (*as*) Ludwig, I wie Ida, N wie Nordpol, D wie Dora, A wie Anton.

In addition to the letters of the alphabet, the chart also lists such frequently used combinations as **ch** and **sch**. The letter **ß** is not listed because there are no words beginning with this letter.

Kulturnotiz

The telephone company is a state monopoly in Germany and is administered by the post office (**die Post**). If you need to find a public telephone in Germany, ask for the nearest post office.

Aktivität 1. Suggestion: Have students repeat in groups of three letters. It is best to write out and point to letters on the board as they are spoken.
Follow-up: Pass out a set of cards with a letter of the alphabet on each card. Say the letters at random. As each is said, the student with the corresponding card holds it up.

Aktivität 1. Das Alphabet

Repeat the letters of the German alphabet after your teacher.

Aktivität 2. Wie bitte?°

Introduce yourself and spell your name.

Wie... *How's that?*

Follow-up: Typewriter: Assign each student to play a letter of the alphabet; include the umlaut letters. Then call out a familiar word in German, e.g., *Name*. Students become a living typewriter. The student who is *N* stands up, says *N*, and remains standing. Then *A*, *M*, and *E* do the same. After the word is spelled, the whole class repeats the word.

Aktivität 2. Suggestion: Demonstrate this activity by referring to the accompanying drawing first. Students turn to each other to do the activity. Have them reverse roles.

A: Mein Name ist ____.
B: Wie bitte?
A: (*repeat your name; then spell it in German*)
B: Ah, so!

Aktivität 3. Suggestion: spot-check students' words by having several students spell the words they have written. Encourage them to come up with words other than the ones listed here.

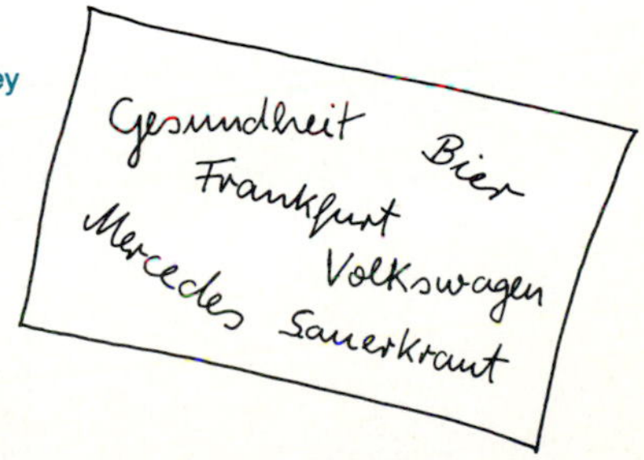

Aktivität 3. Buchstabieren Sie!

Think of a common German word, name, product, or company name. Without saying the word, spell it in German (**auf deutsch**) for a classmate who copies it down and reads the word back to you.

Hallo! Mach's gut!°

Mach's... *So long!*

How do people in German-speaking countries greet one another and say good-bye? Look at the following expressions and illustrations, and see if you can guess which ones are greetings and which are good-byes.

Germans use various formal and informal hellos and good-byes, depending on the situation and with whom they are speaking.

Saying hello:

FORMAL	CASUAL	USE
guten Morgen	Morgen	*until about 10:00 a.m.*
guten Tag	Tag	*generally between 10:00 a.m. and early evening*
guten Abend	'n Abend*	*from about 5:00 p.m. on*
grüß Gott†	grüß Gott	*Southern German and Austrian for* **guten Tag**
	grüß dich	*greeting among young people*
	hallo	*any time (emphatic)*

---

*The **'n** before **Abend** is short for **guten.**
†*Lit.* Greetings in the name of God.

Realia. See Realia Support Material (RSM) in the backmatter of the instructor's edition. The RSM gives additional information, such as source and other relevant information, about this item.

Hallo! Mach's gut!   Point out: Greetings differ from region to region; e.g., Austrians who know each other well say *Servus. Hallo* and *Hi* are becoming very popular among young people.

Saying good-bye:

FORMAL	CASUAL	USE
auf Wiedersehen	Wiedersehen	*any time*
	mach's gut	*among young people, friends, and family*
	tschüß*	*among young people, family*
gute Nacht	Nacht	*only when someone is going to bed at night*

▣ Aktivität 4. Was sagt man?

What would people say under the following circumstances? Match the expressions in the right-hand column with the situations described in the left-hand column. Several expressions may fit a particular situation.

1. Your German instructor entering the classroom
2. Two students saying good-bye
3. A person from Vienna greeting an acquaintance
4. Two students meeting at a café
5. A mother as she turns off the lights in her child's room at night
6. A student leaving a professor's office
7. A hostess and her guests saying good-bye in the evening
8. Family members greeting each other in the morning

a. Gute Nacht!
b. Grüß dich!
c. Tschüß!
d. Mach's gut!
e. Guten Tag!
f. (Auf) Wiedersehen!
g. (Guten) Morgen!
h. Grüß Gott!

Na, wie geht's?°

Na... So, how are you?

▣ Analyse

Look at the following two illustrations.

- What types of text are shown?
- How do both texts begin?
- Which sentence in the ad answers the question **Wie geht's?**

Sicherlich bald besser!

---

*This word is derived from the French word *adieu*.

German has formal and informal ways of asking *How are you?*

> Na, wie geht's? (*informal*)
> Wie geht es dir, Helga? (*informal*)
> Wie geht es Ihnen, Herr Lindemann? (*formal*)

You can respond to the question **Wie geht's?** or **Wie geht es Ihnen?** in a number of different ways.

phantastisch
prima
ausgezeichnet
sehr gut
danke, gut

es geht
nicht so gut
nicht besonders (gut)
schlecht
miserabel

⧈⧈⧈⧈ *Kulturnotiz*

Germans will ask someone **Na, wie geht's?** or **Wie geht es Ihnen?** only if they already know the person. When you meet a German for the first time, do not ask this question. When you do ask a friend, be prepared for a detailed answer, particularly if the person is not feeling great.

a. *I don't know! I feel so broken up this morning!*

▣ Aktivität 5. Reaktionen

Judging from the expressions on their faces, how would each of these people respond to the inquiry **Na, wie geht's?** or **Wie geht es Ihnen?** Match each drawing with an appropriate greeting and inquiry from the list below. Then have a partner give an appropriate response.

Aktivität 5.   **Suggestion:** As a variation have students do this activity with a partner. Then call on a pair at random for responses.

a.   b.   c.

d.   e.   f.

1. _____ Na, wie geht's, Thomas?
2. _____ Guten Tag, Frau Ebert. Wie geht es Ihnen?
3. _____ Hallo, Ursula, wie geht's?
4. _____ Grüß Gott, Herr Kümmerli. Wie geht es Ihnen?
5. _____ Grüß dich, Helmut! Wie geht's?
6. _____ Tag, Fräulein Engelhardt. Wie geht es Ihnen?

▣ Aktivität 6. Und wie geht es dir?

Start a chain reaction by asking one classmate how she or he is. That student responds and in turn asks someone else.

BEISPIEL: A: Na, Peter, wie geht's?
             B: Miserabel! Wie geht es dir, Kathy?
             C: Ausgezeichnet! Und wie geht's dir,... ?

Aktivität 6.   **Note:** Make sure that questions are directed to those across the room as well as to those next to the questioner.

Zahlen und Nummern

WIE ZÄHLT MAN AUF DEUTSCH?°

Wie... *How do you count in German?*

Eins,

zwei,

drei...

Zahlen und Nummern.   Suggestion: Model the numbers from 0 to 20 and have students repeat them. Write numbers on the board as you say them or hold up flash cards.
Follow-up: Pass out flash cards with numbers on them. Say numbers at random; student with the number called holds up the card.

0 null	11 elf	100 (ein)hundert
1 eins	12 zwölf	200 zweihundert
2 zwei	13 dreizehn	300 dreihundert
3 drei	14 vierzehn	1 000 (ein)tausend
4 vier	15 fünfzehn	2 000 zweitausend
5 fünf	16 sechzehn	
6 sechs	17 siebzehn	
7 sieben	18 achtzehn	
8 acht	19 neunzehn	
9 neun	20 zwanzig	
10 zehn		

The word **Zahl** (plural **Zahlen**) refers to numbers used by themselves. For example:

Sieben und elf sind Zahlen.   *Seven and eleven are numbers.*

The word **Nummer** refers to numbers in context. For example:

451-7368 ist meine Telefonnummer.

The numbers *one* and *seven* are written in the following manner:

$$1 \qquad 7$$

German uses a period or a space where English uses a comma:

$$1.000 \qquad 7\ 000$$

In German-speaking countries, telephone numbers generally have a varying number of digits and may be spoken as follows:

24 36 71 zwei, vier—drei, sechs—sieben, eins

▣ Aktivität 7. Wie ist Ihre Telefonnummer?

Exchange telephone numbers with three members of your class by asking: **Wie ist Ihre Telefonnummer?** Jot the numbers down.

▣ Aktivität 8. Wie ist die Telefonnummer, bitte?

Look at the list of frequently called numbers from a telephone book, on page 11. In most cases, you can tell from the visual clues what number you are calling. Work with a partner; one person says in English what information he or she needs, and the other person finds the appropriate telephone number and reads the number in German.

Farmers, lottery players, shoppers, and sports fans are some of the groups which have special numbers. Do you recognize the visual clues?

Aktivität 7.   Suggestion: Have students circulate in class for this activity. Spot-check the results by asking several students, *Wie ist die Telefonnummer von (Name)?*

Aktivität 8.   Point out: Two numbers are listed for each service. The first is for the city of Göttingen, the second for outlying areas near Göttingen. **Suggestion:** Make sure that students reverse roles so that each gets a chance to say the numbers in German.

Telefon-Ansagen		Ortsnetz Göttingen[1]	übrige Ortsnetze
	Fernsehprogramme	1 15 03	01 15 03
	Kinoprogramme	1 15 11	01 15 11
	Küchenrezepte	11 67	0 11 67
	Reisewettervorhersage, Wintersportwetterbericht	1 16 00	01 16 00
	Sportnachrichten	11 63	0 11 63
	Theater-und Konzert-veranstaltungen	1 15 17	01 15 17
	Verbraucher- und Einkauftips	1 16 06	01 16 06
	Wettervorhersage	11 64	0 11 64
	Witterungshinweise für die Landwirtschaft (bei Bedarf)	11 54	0 11 54
	Zahlenlotto	11 62	0 11 62
	Zeitansage	11 91	0 11 91

BEISPIEL: A: *I would like to find out what time it is.*
B: Die Telefonnummer ist eins eins, neun eins.

▣ Aktivität 9. Partnerarbeit°

Interview:

Working with a partner

A:	B:
Guten Tag. Wie ist Ihr Name, bitte?	→ Mein Name ist...
Woher sind Sie?	Ich bin aus...
Wie ist Ihre Telefonnummer?	Meine Telefonnummer ist... Und wie ist Ihre Telefonnummer?
	Danke schön.
...	
Bitte sehr.	

Aktivität 10. Hören Sie zu! Wichtige Telefonnummern°

Hören... Listen! Important phone numbers

You are calling German information for a list of important telephone numbers. Write the phone numbers you hear in the appropriate space.

Wie sind die Telefonnummern?

Polizei	012
Wetterbericht (*weather*)	03853
Zeitansage (*time*)	017468
Telegramme	072360
Konzert/Theater	019772

Neue Wörter

auf deutsch *in German*
bitte *please; you're welcome*
  bitte schön *please* (very polite)
  bitte sehr *please*
danke *thanks*
  danke schön *thanks a lot*
  danke sehr *thanks very much*

die Nummer *number*
die Telefonnummer *telephone number*
  meine Telefonnummer *my telephone number*
  Ihre Telefonnummer *your telephone number*
die Zahl *number*

Aktivität 10. This type of listening activity will appear regularly throughout the book. You may wish to play the tape that accompanies it, or you may simply want to read the script aloud. It is important to read at normal speed. Students may ask you to repeat by saying either *Wie bitte?* or *Wiederholen Sie bitte.*

Neue Wörter. These sections of *Neue Wörter* will appear throughout each chapter. They contain vocabulary and expressions which are to be memorized.

Adressen

Scan the addresses in the illustrations. How do addresses differ from the way they are written in the United States? Where do you find the zip code? Where is the house number?

    Look at the address of the Goethe-Institut in Munich. What do you think the word **Postfach** means?

Adressen. Point out that addresses in most European countries are written this way.

Goethe-Institut
Lenbachplatz 3 · Postfach 201009
D-8000 München 2
Tel. (089) 5999-200 · Telex 522940

Universitätsstraße 65–67
A-9020 Klagenfurt

Ferienträume?
Wir erfüllen sie!

TRAVELLER REISEN

Filiale Oerlikon
CH-8050 Zürich-Oerlikon, Ohmstrasse 14

Telefon 01-312 10 14
Telex 823 221
Telegramm: Travellerag Zürich

◻◻◻◻ *Kulturnotiz*

German zip codes (**Postleitzahl,** abbreviated **Plz.**) consist of four digits in front of the name of the city or town. Large cities have an additional number following the name of the city; this number refers to the postal district within the city. Sometimes you see **A, CH, D,** or **DDR** in front of the zip code. **A** stands for **Österreich** (Austria), **CH** for **die Schweiz** (Switzerland; CH stands for Confoederatio Helvetica, Latin for Swiss Federation), **D** for **(Bundesrepublik) Deutschland** (the Federal Republic), and **DDR** for **Deutsche Demokratische Republik.**

◙ **Aktivität 11. Straße und Hausnummer**

Say the following addresses.

Schillerstraße 9
Mozartstraße 3
Hauptstraße 14

Alexanderplatz 20
your own street address

◙ **Aktivität 12. Was ist die Postleitzahl, bitte?**

Working with a classmate, take turns asking each other for the zip codes of the places listed below. Read a zip code as follows:

8000 achttausend
8450 acht vier fünf null

BEISPIEL: A: Was ist die Postleitzahl von Hamburg?
B: Die Postleitzahl von Hamburg ist zweitausend.

1000 Berlin
5300 Bonn
6000 Frankfurt
2000 Hamburg
6900 Heidelberg

8000 München
8500 Nürnberg
8423 Ramsau
4155 Grefrath
2105 Seevetal

◙ **Aktivität 13. Adressen**

Find the addresses in the illustrations and read them, including the zip codes.

Wir heiraten heute, 27. Mai 1987

Günter Pradel
Gisela Goossens

Minkowskiweg 30, 3400 Göttingen

zum Uerige
Bergerstraße 1
Telefon (0211) 84455
4000 Düsseldorf (Altstadt)

Wilhelm Heyne Verlag
Türkenstr. 5–7
8000 München 2
Tel. (089) 231 71 70

Hueber
D-8045 Ismaning b. München
Max-Hueber-Str. 4

◻ **Aktivität 14. Was ist die Postleitzahl von... ?**

Start a chain asking a classmate for the zip code of his or her hometown.

Aktivität 14. Suggestion: Urge students to ask each other to repeat responses by asking *Wie bitte?*

> BEISPIEL: A: Susan, woher sind Sie?
> B: Aus Boston.
> A: Was ist Ihre Postleitzahl?
> B: ... Dan, woher sind Sie? usw.

Neue Wörter

die Adresse *address*
die Hausnummer *house number*
die Postleitzahl *zip code*
die Straße *street*

usw. (und so weiter) *and so forth, etc.*
von (Hamburg) *of (Hamburg)*
was *what*

Aktivität 15. Hören Sie zu! Die Adresse und Telefonnummer, bitte!

Aktivität 15. Point out to students that they are listening for only two pieces of information: the person's street number and telephone number. They will hear more than this, but should concentrate on the specific information requested.

Listen to the brief requests for street addresses and telephone numbers. Circle the correct street number and write the telephone number in the space provided.

1. Professor Hausers Adresse ist Gartenstraße 9 12 (19).
   Die Telefonnummer ist ____41 34 76____.
2. Die Adresse von McDonalds ist Frankfurter Straße 5 (15) 14.
   Die Telefonnummer ist ____20 86 73____.
3. Die Adresse von Autohaus Becker ist Hannoversche Straße (13) 12 17.
   Die Telefonnummer ist ____7 70 05 52____.
4. Die Telefonnummer von der Polizei ist ____020____.

Sie können schon etwas Deutsch!°

Sie... *You already know some German!*

Even if you have never studied German before, you will soon find that you know more German than you think. For example, look at the following ad taken from a German phone book's yellow pages (**gelbe Seiten**).

🔲 Analyse

- What is this ad for?
- Which words are *identical* in English?
- Which words in the ad look *similar* to words you use in English?

Words like **Motel, Hotel, Restaurant,** and **Sauna** are borrowed from other languages: **Motel** from American English, **Restaurant** and **Hotel** from French, and **Sauna** from Finnish. These words are used internationally.

Some words in the ad look similar to English words. Look more closely at one of those words: **Biergarten.** You may already have seen the word **Biergarten** in an English-language text. This word has been borrowed from German along with some other German words commonly used in English, such as **Kindergarten** or **Delikatessen.** You recognize the words *beer* and *garden* in **Biergarten. Bier** and *beer*, **Garten** and *garden* look similar, are pronounced similarly, and have the same meaning in both languages. These words are cognates. Cognates are related words; that is, they are descended from the same language or form. English and German are both Germanic languages, so they share many cognates. This common linguistic ancestry will help you a great deal in understanding German. Recognizing cognates is an important skill stressed throughout this textbook.

Cognates like **Bier** and **Garten** are easy to recognize. Understanding other words takes more imaginative guessing: for instance, what does **Hallenbad** mean? Other words in the ad probably look completely unfamiliar; they are not cognates or words that are used internationally. The word **Ruf,** for instance, is not easily recognizable when the word is by itself. However, the meaning can be guessed from the context, and you already know a synonym for this word. What is it?

PGH Foto-Zentrum Leipzig

7010 Leipzig, Thomasiusstr. 5   Ruf 28 17 21

🔲 Alles klar?

Now that you have analyzed in some detail what kind of place Zum Dorfkrug is, summarize what you have found out. Add any additional information you were able to extract from the ad by guessing.

🔲 Aktivität 16. Freizeitspaß°

Working with a partner or in small groups, find out as many things as possible about the ad at the top of page 16. You do not have to understand each word to get the gist of this ad. List any cognates or other words you recognize before answering the questions.

1. What is advertised here?
2. Which words do you recognize immediately?
3. What two cognates are in the word **Tanzschule?**
4. Where is the **Tanzschule** located?
5. Which words look familiar in the last sentence of this ad?
6. What do you think this sentence means?

□ **Aktivität 17.** **Musik**

Look for cognates and other clues in order to answer the questions about the following ad.

1. What is this ad for?
2. What is the name of the store?
3. In what city is the store located?
4. What is the street address?
5. What do the following words mean: **hören, kommen, sehen, testen?**

 ■ **Aktivität 18.** **Hören und Verstehen°**

Hören... *Listening and understanding*

Just as you are able to decode some written German without a dictionary, you can also decode some spoken German. You will hear some ads and news headlines read to you. You are not expected to understand them word for word, but try to recognize from a few clues what the content might be. Listen carefully for words that are similar in English. As you hear each item, write its number in front of the topics to which it refers. Some topics listed will have no text to go with them.

5	Bank	1	Tanz
2, 3	Musik	6	Restaurant
	Automobil		
4	Sport		
	Film		
2	Theater		

Aktivität 18. **Suggestion:** Ask students to scan the topics first. Then play the tape or read the ads and headlines at normal speed.

▣ Aktivität 19. Text Identifizieren°

Text... *Identifying a text*

An important step in developing good reading strategies in German is to identify at the outset the type of text you are going to read. Once you have identified a text, your expectations and what you already know about the subject will help you to figure out the meaning. Look for verbal as well as visual clues.

Look at the illustrations below and identify each. Write the letter of each item in front of the appropriate category. Some categories have no text to go with them, others have more than one.

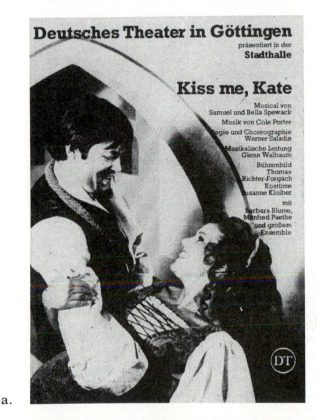

a.

Olympische Spiele Seoul '88
Vorletzter Tag: Noch einmal Medaillen-Glanz – Seiten 33–36

Tenniskönigin Steffi Graf schaffte den Golden Slam

b.

Restaurant **Waldhaus**
an der Havelchaussee
Unser Angebot:
Rieseneisbein
mit Sauerkraut
u. Kartoffeln **8,-**
Telefon: 304 05 95

c.

--Keese--
Jeden
SONNTAG
16.00 Uhr
TANZ TEE
Café Keese·
Ball Paradox·
Bismarckstr. 108

e.

d. **US-Bank kommt nach Berlin**
Merrill Lynch eröffnet im nächsten Jahr Repräsentanz

1. _____ an announcement for a play
2. _____ a letter
3. _____ a newspaper article headline
4. _____ an ad for a restaurant
5. _____ an announcement for a concert
6. _____ a concert ticket
7. _____ an ad for car equipment
8. _____ an ad for afternoon tea dancing

SYMPHONISCHES ORCHESTER BERLIN

Heute, 16 Uhr	**PHILHARMONIE**
Dirigent:	**László Kovács**
Solist:	**Boris Bloch**

Kodály: Tänze aus Galanta
Tschaikowsky: Konzert für Klavier und Orchester Nr. 2, G-Dur, op. 44
Rimsky-Korsakoff: „Scheherazade" Symphonische Suite aus „Tausend und eine Nacht"

f.

Wo spricht man Deutsch?°

Wo... *Where is German spoken?*

German is the official language of the Federal Republic of Germany (**Bundesrepublik Deutschland** or **BRD**), the German Democratic Republic (**Deutsche Demokratische Republik** or **DDR**), Austria (**Österreich**), and Liechtenstein. It is one of four languages spoken in Switzerland (**die Schweiz**). German is also spoken in some regions of Belgium, Luxembourg, France, Denmark, Italy, Yugoslavia, Poland, Rumania, Czechoslovakia, Hungary, and the Soviet Union. Altogether, approximately one hundred million Europeans speak German as their first language—more than the number of people in Europe who speak English as their first language.

German is also spoken in many areas outside of Europe, for instance Brazil, Argentina, Canada, and the United States (Pennsylvania Dutch). In Namibia, Africa, German is an official state language. It is estimated that outside of Europe an additional twenty million people speak German as their first language.

According to 1980 U.S. Department of Commerce figures, fifty-two million U.S. citizens claim German descent.

WORTSCHATZ

Substantive	**Nouns**
die Adresse	address
Frau; die Frau	Mrs., Ms.; woman
Fräulein; das Fräulein	Miss; young lady
Herr; der Herr	Mr.; gentleman
die Nummer	number
die Hausnummer	street address (number)
die Telefonnummer	telephone number
die Straße	street
die Zahl	number
die Postleitzahl	zip code

Hier spricht man Deutsch	**German is spoken here**
die Bundesrepublik Deutschland (BRD)	Federal Republic of Germany (FRG)
die Deutsche Demokratische Republik (DDR)	German Democratic Republic (GDR)
Österreich	Austria
die Schweiz	Switzerland

Zur Begrüßung	**Greetings**
grüß dich	hello (*among friends and family members*)
grüß Gott	hello, good day (*in Austria, Southern Germany*)
guten Abend	good evening
guten Morgen	good morning
guten Tag	hello, good day
hallo	hello
willkommen	welcome

Zum Abschied	**Saying good-bye**
auf Wiedersehen	good-bye
gute Nacht	good night
mach's gut	so long
tschüß	so long

Bekannt werden	**Getting acquainted**
Wie ist Ihr Name?	What is your name?
Mein Name ist...	My name is . . .
Woher sind Sie?	Where are you from?

Ich bin	I am
Ich komme aus...	I come from . . .
Das ist...	This is . . .
Wie ist Ihre Telefonnummer?	What is your telephone number?
Was ist die Postleitzahl von... ?	What is the zip code of . . . ?

Nach dem Befinden fragen

Asking about someone's well-being

Wie geht es dir?	How are you? (*informal*)
(Na) Wie geht's?	How are you? (*informal*)
Wie geht es Ihnen?	How are you? (*formal*)

Antworten

Answers

ausgezeichnet	excellent, great
Es geht.	It's all right.; OK.
(sehr) gut	(very) well, fine, good
miserabel	miserable, miserably
nicht besonders (gut)	not particularly (well)
phantastisch	fantastic
prima	great
schlecht	bad, poorly

Sonstiges

Other items

Ah, so! (*also:* **Ach, so!**)	Oh, I get it.
Alles klar	everything (is) all right
auf deutsch, bitte	in German, please
buchstabieren	to spell
Buchstabieren Sie!	Spell (it).

bitte	please; you are welcome
bitte schön	
bitte sehr	
danke	thanks
danke schön	
danke sehr	
und	and
Wie bitte?	How's that, please?

Zahlen von 0 bis 20

null	zero
eins	one
zwei	two
drei	three
vier	four
fünf	five
sechs	six
sieben	seven
acht	eight
neun	nine
zehn	ten
elf	eleven
zwölf	twelve
dreizehn	thirteen
vierzehn	fourteen
fünfzehn	fifteen
sechzehn	sixteen
siebzehn	seventeen
achtzehn	eighteen
neunzehn	nineteen
zwanzig	twenty

KAPITEL 1

ÜBER MICH UND ANDERE

Kapitel 1. You may preview the theme of this chapter by describing yourself and sharing some personal information (where you are from, where you live, etc.)

Alles klar? (Page 21) Beginning with this chapter, the *Alles klar?* section introduces the major chapter topic through illustrations and other visuals that set the tone and mood for the chapter. Students will be asked to react to them and to express their own opinions.

If this activity is done in class, give students time to scan the information requested as well as the documents. Then call on individuals for responses. Or have them work in pairs, allowing 3 to 4 minutes to complete the activity. Otherwise, have students do the activity as homework.

Lernziele   *In this chapter you will learn how to give more information about yourself, describe others, and ask questions.*

One of the things you will learn to do in German is to give information about people in many different contexts and situations. For example, people give information about themselves in personal documents—documents they use in everyday life. Here are some typical documents used by people in German-speaking countries.

UNIVERSITÄT GÖTTINGEN

a.

RSM

b.

▣ Alles klar?

Look for clues in these documents to find the following information. Which document is a:

- passport?
- youth hostel card?
- student ID card?
- driver's license?

Now scan the documents to find the words which mean:

- family name
- first name
- date of birth
- place of birth
- current residence
- street address and number

c.

FÜHRERSCHEIN

Permis de conduire
Kørekort
Ἄδεια Ὁδηγήσεως
Permiso de Conducción
Ceadúnas Tiomána
Patente di guida
Rijbewijs
Carta de Condução
Driving licence

Modell der
EUROPÄISCHEN GEMEINSCHAFTEN
A 6759999

1. Name	Tomkötter
2. Vorname	Karin
3. Geburtstag und -ort	05.07.1966 Münster
4. Wohnort	4400 Münster
5. Ausgestellt durch	Stadt Münster
6. in	4400 Münster
am	22.02.1988
7. Gültigkeit unbefristet	Ausnahmen siehe Seiten 5 und 6
8. Führerschein-Nr.	T 34/88

Unterschrift (Jeczyk) Stadtangestellter

Karin Tomkötter
Unterschrift des Inhabers

d.

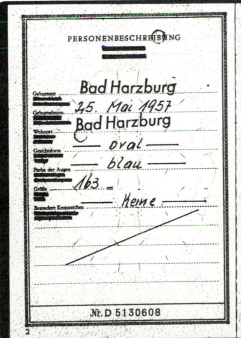

PERSONENBESCHREIBUNG

Geburtsort — Bad Harzburg
Geburtsdatum — 25. Mai 1957
Wohnort — Bad Harzburg
Gesichtsform — oval
Farbe der Augen — blau
Größe — 163 cm
Besondere Kennzeichen — Keine

Nr. D 5130608

2

Brigitte Nikolai
Unterschrift des Paßinhabers

Es wird hiermit bescheinigt, daß der Paßinhaber die im Lichtbild dargestellte Person ist und die Unterschrift darunter eigenhändig vollzogen hat.
It is hereby certified that the bearer is identical with the person on the photograph and that the signature has been given in his own hand.
Il est certifié que le titulaire est la personne représentée par la photographie ci-dessous et que la signature est autographe.

Bad Harzburg 1. Mai 1974
3388 Stadt Bad Harzburg 1
Paßamt
Unterschrift ... Angestellter

Nr. D 5130608

3

BUNDESREPUBLIK DEUTSCHLAND
FEDERAL REPUBLIC OF GERMANY
RÉPUBLIQUE FÉDÉRALE D'ALLEMAGNE

Gebührenmarke
Fiscal stamp
Droit de timbre

REISEPASS
PASSPORT
PASSEPORT

Nr. D 5130608

Nikolai
...habers / Name of bearer / Nom du titulaire

Irmgard
... / Christian names / Prénoms

... dieses Passes ist Deutscher
... of this passport is a German
... nt passeport est ressortissant allemand

... contains 32 pages / Ce passeport contient 32 pages

WÖRTER IM KONTEXT

Persönliche Angaben°

Persönliche... *Personal Information*

Let's take a closer look at one of the documents Germans use. This passport belongs to Brigitte.

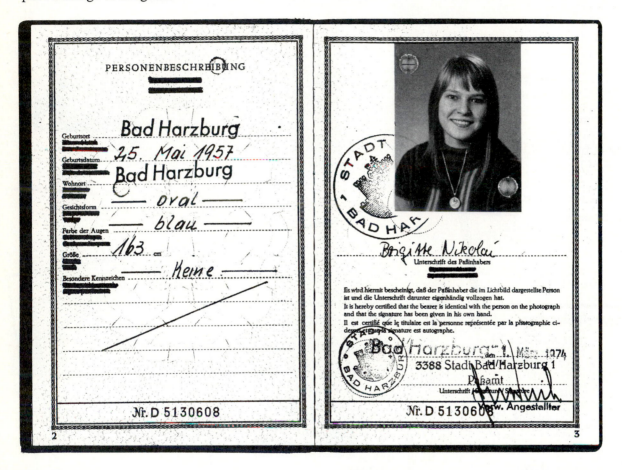

PERSONENBESCHREIBUNG

Geburtsort **Bad Harzburg**

Geburtsdatum **25. Mai 1957**

Wohnort **Bad Harzburg**

Gesichtsform **oval**

Farbe der Augen **blau**

Größe **163** cm

Besondere Kennzeichen **Keine**

Nr. D 5130608

Brigitte Nikolai
Unterschrift des Paßinhabers

Es wird hiermit bescheinigt, daß der Paßinhaber die im Lichtbild dargestellte Person ist und die Unterschrift darunter eigenhändig vollzogen hat.
It is hereby certified that the bearer is identical with the person on the photograph and that the signature has been given in his own hand.
Il est certifié que le titulaire est la personne représentée par la photographie ci-dessous, et que la signature est autographe.

Bad Harzburg, den 1. Mai 1974
3388 Stadt Bad Harzburg 1
Paßamt
Unterschrift (Behörde)/Signature
Verw. Angestellter

Nr. D 5130608

2   3

🖾 Analyse

Scan the passport for the following information.

- Where was Brigitte born?
- When was she born?
- What is listed as her place of residence?
- What color are her eyes?
- What must the word **oval** refer to?
- What does the word **Unterschrift** require someone to do?
- What information does the word **Größe** ask for?

Analyse. Analysis sections can be assigned ahead of time. In the first several chapters students may respond to the questions in English. You should supply the German response as each student answers, e.g., *Brigitte ist in Bad Harzburg geboren.* Later students will be encouraged to respond in German.

Wörter im Kontext. Each chapter is divided into three sections: *Wörter im Kontext, Grammatik im Kontext,* and *Lesen im Kontext.* The first section provides opportunities to acquire new vocabulary and expressions by exploring authentic materials. Students are asked to analyze the materials and figure out the meaning of words on their own. The activities of this section practice and recycle the vocabulary. Some grammar is previewed in short notes titled *Sprachnotiz.* Activities are targeted at getting students to interact.

🔲🔲🔲🔲 *Kulturnotiz*

In German-speaking countries, people sixteen years of age and over are required by law to carry an official ID. This may be a passport (**Reisepaß**) or a personal ID (**Personalausweis**).

🔲 **Aktivität 1. Wer sind diese Leute?°**

You see information about three different people in the accompanying charts. Complete the paragraphs about them.

Wer... Who are these people?

Aktivität 1. Let students work in pairs to check information. As for all such exercises, give them a moment to scan the information as well as the requests for information. Spot-check responses. **Suggestion:** three pairs of students, one for each item, can work at the board.

Vorname: Harald
Nachname: Lohmann
Straße und Hausnummer: Bahnhofstraße 20
Wohnort: Bonn
Beruf: Student
Land: Bundesrepublik Deutschland

Vorname: Daniela
Nachname: Lercher
Straße und Hausnummer: Mozartstraße 36
Wohnort: Wien
Beruf: Studentin
Land: Österreich

Vorname: Erich
Nachname: Koschel
Straße und Hausnummer: Lumumbastraße 13
Wohnort: Leipzig
Beruf: Architekt
Land: DDR

1. Ihr Name ist Daniela Lercher. Sie wohnt in ____. Das ist in ____ (Land). Daniela ist ____ von (*by*) Beruf.
2. Er ist Architekt von Beruf und heißt (*his name is*) ____. Er kommt aus ____ (Wohnort). Das Land heißt ____. Die Adresse ist ____ (Straße und Hausnummer).
3. Haralds Nachname ist ____. Er ist ____ von Beruf. Sein Wohnort ist ____. Das ist in der ____. Die Straße heißt ____.

▣ Aktivität 2. Auskunft, bitte°

Auskunft... *Information, please*

You're interested in studying at a German university. The application you must fill out asks you to provide, among other things, the following information.

Aktivität 2. Suggestion: Students can write this on a separate sheet of paper. Spot-check by calling on several students.

Nachname: ＿＿＿

Vorname: ＿＿＿

Straße und Hausnummer: ＿＿＿＿

Wohnort: ＿＿＿

Geburtsdatum: ＿＿＿＿

Geburtsort: ＿＿＿

▣ Aktivität 3. Interaktion

Aktivität 3. Suggestion: Have students move around the room interviewing a number of their classmates. Do the second part in one of two ways: (1) have students report their findings to another student, or (2) call on individuals to report on the person interviewed.

Sprachnotiz (below): This recurring feature focuses on an item of idiomatic usage of the language, or it briefly previews a grammar point that is explained in detail in the grammar section of the chapter or a later chapter.

Now find out some information from someone in your class by asking the following questions. Jot the answers down and then report the information to the class.

1. Wie ist Ihr Nachname, bitte?
2. Ihr Vorname?
3. Ihre Adresse?
4. Ihr Geburtsort?

To report your findings you say:

- Das ist... (Vorname und Nachname)
- Bobs / Sallys Adresse ist...
- Sein / Ihr Geburtsort ist...

Neue Wörter

der Beruf *occupation, profession*
  von Beruf *by occupation*
der Geburtsort *place of birth*
der Nachname *family name*

der Vorname *first name*
der Wohnort *place of residence*
er heißt *his name is*
sie wohnt *she lives*

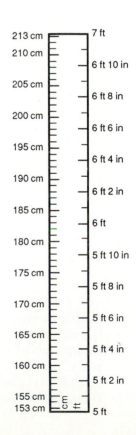

Sprachnotiz

In stating their height, Germans use the decimal system. If you are 1.63 m (163 cm) tall you can express it as follows: **Ich bin eins dreiundsechzig (groß).** In German, it's written 1,63 m.

1 cm (Zentimeter) = 0.39 in. (inch)	
1 in. (inch) = 2.54 cm (Zentimeter)	

Sie ist 1,56 m groß   Er ist 1,94 m groß

Neue Wörter

ZAHLEN VON ZWANZIG BIS HUNDERT

zwanzig *twenty*
einundzwanzig *twenty-one*
zweiundzwanig *twenty-two*
dreiundzwanzig *twenty-three*
dreißig *thirty*
vierzig *forty*

fünfzig *fifty*
sechzig *sixty*
siebzig *seventy*
achtzig *eighty*
neunzig *ninety*
hundert *one hundred*

Aktivität 4. Wie groß sind Sie? Wie alt sind Sie?

Figure out your height in meters with the help of the conversion chart. Then ask a partner to provide some information to you in German.

BEISPIEL: A: Wie groß sind Sie?
B: Ich bin 1,64 (eins vierundsechzig).
A: Wie alt sind Sie?
B: Ich bin dreiundzwanzig.

Report to the class what you know about your partner.

Information erfragen°

Listen to each of the following dialogues. Don't worry if you do not understand everything at first. The analysis questions following the dialogues will then help you to figure out what you might not have understood right away.

Information... Asking for information

Dialog 1

REPORTER: Guten Morgen. Mein Name ist Schneider. Ich bin Reporter für die *Berliner Abendpost.* Wie ist Ihr Name, bitte?
TOURISTIN: Savigny.
REPORTER: Woher kommen Sie, Frau Savigny?
TOURISTIN: Aus Frankreich; aus Paris.
REPORTER: Frau Savigny, was machen Sie hier in Berlin?
TOURISTIN: Wie bitte?
REPORTER: Was machen Sie hier in Berlin?
TOURISTIN: Ach so! Ich bin hier nur zu Besuch.
REPORTER: Wie finden Sie Berlin?
TOURISTIN: Sehr interessant, faszinierend.
REPORTER: Danke sehr, Frau Savigny.
TOURISTIN: Bitte schön.

☐☐☐☐ *Kulturnotiz*

When introducing themselves, German speakers usually give their last names only, particularly under formal conditions.

Dialog 2

REPORTER:	Guten Tag!
HERR UND FRAU MEIER:	Grüß Gott!
REPORTER:	Ich heiße Schneider. Wie heißen Sie, bitte?
HERR MEIER:	Meier. Und das ist meine Frau.
REPORTER:	Woher sind Sie, Herr Meier?
HERR MEIER:	Wir kommen aus München.
REPORTER:	Und was machen Sie in Berlin?
FRAU MEIER:	Wir besuchen Freunde.
REPORTER:	Wie finden Sie Berlin?
HERR MEIER:	Berlin ist ja ganz interessant, aber München ist schöner.
REPORTER:	Viel Spaß in Berlin.

Note: The dialogues throughout the book lend themselves to a variety of activities besides the ones suggested in the book. They can be used for role-playing situations and practicing reading out loud to acquire good pronunciation and intonation.

Neue Wörter

der Freund *friend*
besuchen *to visit*
machen *to make, do*
aber *but*
schön *beautiful*

Ich bin zu Besuch. *I am (here) for a visit.*
viel Spaß *have fun*
Wie finden Sie...? *What do you think of . . . ?*

☐ Analyse

Working with a partner, read through the preceding dialogues in order to supply the following information.

- Dieter Schneider says "My name is . . ." in two ways. What are they?
- How does he greet people?
- How do Herr and Frau Meier respond to the reporter's greeting? Why is their greeting different?
- To find out where people come from, what does Dieter Schneider ask?
- What does he ask to find out why Frau Savigny and the Meiers are visiting Berlin?
- Frau Savigny does not understand what the reporter wants to know at one point. How does she let him know that?

- How does the reporter ask Frau Savigny and the Meiers what they think of Berlin?
- How does the reporter express his appreciation to Frau Savigny for answering his questions?
- The reporter wishes the Meiers a lot of fun in Berlin. What words does he use?

▣ Aktivität 5. Ergänzen Sie

Locate the missing information in the interviews with the tourists.

1. Frau Savigny kommt aus _____ .
2. Herr und Frau Meier sind aus _____ .
3. Herr Schneider ist _____ von Beruf.
4. Frau Savigny findet Berlin _____ .
5. Herr Meier findet Berlin _____ , aber er findet München _____ .

 ## Dialog 3. Ein Gespräch

Dialog 3. Suggestion: Approach *Dialog 3* in the same way as 1 and 2.

Two students strike up a conversation in a café in Berlin.

HELMUT: Tag! Mein Name ist Helmut, Helmut Sachs.
WENDY: Tag! Ich heiße Wendy Harrison.
HELMUT: Woher kommst du?
WENDY: Ich komme aus Ohio, aus Cincinnati.
HELMUT: Ohio, wo ist denn das?
WENDY: In den USA, im Mittelwesten.
HELMUT: Was machst du hier in Berlin?
WENDY: Ich lerne Deutsch hier. Und du?
HELMUT: Ich studiere hier.
WENDY: Was studierst du?
HELMUT: Physik.

Das macht Spaß: mit Freunden im Straßencafé

▣ Analyse

Analyze the conversation between Wendy and Helmut and answer the following questions.

- How do Helmut and Wendy greet each other?
- How does Helmut introduce himself?
- What phrase does he use to find out where Wendy is from?
- Helmut doesn't know where Ohio is. How does he get that information?
- What phrase does Helmut use to find out what Wendy is doing in Berlin?

> ## Sprachnotiz
>
> To say you are studying at a university or to state your major subject, use the verb **studieren.**
>
> > Ich studiere Physik in Berlin.
>
> To say you are learning or studying a language, use the verb **lernen.**
>
> > Ich lerne Deutsch.

▣ Aktivität 6.   Richtig oder falsch?°

Richtig... *True or false?*

1. _____ Helmut ist Professor.
2. _____ Wendy kommt aus Amerika.
3. _____ Wendy studiert in Berlin.
4. _____ Helmuts Nachname ist Sachs.
5. _____ Helmut besucht Freunde in Berlin.

▣ Aktivität 7.   Fragen und Antworten

Match each question in the left-hand column with a possible answer from the right-hand column.

Aktivität 7.   Suggestion: Students can work in pairs. Call on individuals to supply responses. After the exercise has been completed, students can act out the dialogue.

1. Wie heißen Sie?
2. Woher kommst du?
3. Was machen Sie hier?
4. Wo ist das?

a. Ich studiere hier.
b. Das ist im Mittelwesten.
c. Mein Name ist Meier.
d. Ich heiße Keller.
e. Wir besuchen Freunde.
f. Ich komme aus Deutschland.
g. Ich bin aus Kalifornien.

> ## Sprachnotiz
>
> In the various conversations in this chapter, you have probably noticed that people address each other in different ways. In German, people are addressed either formally, with **Sie,** or informally, with **du.**
>
> > **du** (*you*): informal, one person
> > **Sie** (*you*): formal, one or more people, always capitalized
>
> | USE **DU** FOR | USE **SIE** FOR |
> | --- | --- |
> | a family member | strangers |
> | a close friend | acquaintances |
> | a fellow student | anyone you address as |
> | a child | **Herr, Frau,** or **Fräulein** |

▣ Aktivität 8. Was sagen diese Leute zueinander?°

Determine whether the following phrases and questions would be used by two students talking to each other, or by a professor and a student, or could be used in either situation.

	ZWEI STUDENTEN	PROFESSOR(IN) UND STUDENT(IN)
1. Was machen Sie hier?	——	——
2. Grüß dich!	——	——
3. Auf Wiedersehen.	——	——
4. Wie heißt du?	——	——
5. Guten Tag!	——	——
6. Wie heißen Sie?	——	——
7. Was machst du hier?	——	——
8. Was studieren Sie?	——	——
9. Tschüß!	——	——

Aktivität 8.   Suggestion: Have students work in pairs, taking turns saying a sentence and marking an X in the appropriate column. Check responses to several items or to all.

▣ Aktivität 9. Konversation

When rearranged, the following sentences will form a short conversation between Herr Brinkmann and Frau Garcia, who are just getting acquainted. Create the conversation. Then act it out with a partner.

    Ich finde Hamburg interessant.
    Und was machen Sie hier?
    Wie bitte?
    Guten Tag. Mein Name ist Brinkmann.
    Ich komme aus Florida.
    Brinkmann.
1 Guten Tag. Ich heiße Garcia.
    Ach so!
    Wie finden Sie Hamburg?
    Ich besuche Freunde.
    Woher kommen Sie?

▣ Aktivität 10. Hören Sie zu.

Listen to the brief conversational exchanges and indicate whether the response to each question or statement is logical or illogical.

Aktivität 10.   Suggestion: Play tape twice or say each item twice. When checking responses, replay each item on tape or read it out loud. Then ask students to give the correct response to all items marked illogical.

	LOGISCH	UNLOGISCH			LOGISCH	UNLOGISCH
1.	✓	——		6.	✓	——
2.	——	✓		7.	——	✓
3.	✓	——		8.	✓	——
4.	✓	——		9.	——	✓
5.	——	✓		10.	✓	——

▣ Aktivität 11. Interaktion

Find your major in the accompanying list of subjects taught at a German university. Then take turns with a classmate asking and answering questions about it.

BEISPIEL: A: Woher kommst du?
B: Ich komme aus Texas.
A: Was studierst du?
B: Ich studiere Englisch. Und du?
A: Ich studiere Physik.

Kombinationsmöglichkeiten an der Universität Göttingen   **RSM**

1. oder 2. Unterrichtsfach	Biologie	Chemie	Deutsch	Englisch	Erdkunde	Evangelische Religion	Französisch	Geschichte	Griechisch	Latein	Mathematik	Philosophie	Physik	Russisch	Sozialkunde/Gemeinschaftsk.	Spanisch	Sport
Biologie		x	x	x		x	x			x	x		x				x
Chemie	x		x	x		x	x			x	x		x				
Deutsch	x	x		x	x	x	x	x	x	x	x	x	x	x	x	x	x
Englisch	x	x	x		x	x	x	x	x	x	x	x	x	x	x	x	x
Erdkunde			x	x		x	x			x	x						
Evangelische Religion	x	x	x	x	x		x	x		x	x		x				
Französisch	x	x	x	x	x	x		x	x	x	x	x	x	x	x	x	x
Geschichte			x	x		x	x			x	x						
Griechisch			x	x			x			x	x						
Latein	x	x	x	x	x	x	x	x	x		x	x	x	x	x	x	x
Mathematik	x	x	x	x	x	x	x	x	x	x		x	x	x	x	x	x
Philosophie			x	x			x			x	x						
Physik	x	x	x	x		x	x			x	x						
Russisch			x	x			x			x	x						
Sozialkunde/Gemeinschaftsk.			x	x			x			x	x						
Spanisch			x	x			x			x	x						
Sport	x		x	x			x			x	x						

x Es besteht eine Kombinationsmöglichkeit
   Felder ohne Zeichen weisen ein Kombinationsverbot aus.

Meine Eigenschaften°

Look at this personal ad from a German magazine. You will be able to understand much of the ad by recognizing some words as cognates and by guessing the meaning of others from the context.

Meine... My characteristics

Meine Eigenschaften. Explain that personal ads have been an acceptable way to find a partner in German-speaking countries for a long time. They are growing in popularity in the U.S. as well.

SCHON BALD ZU ZWEIT?
Zu zweit ist's schöner!
..."Ich bin allein. Und schon so lange."

personality-coupon

Persönliche Angaben	So sollte mein Partner sein:	Das macht mir besonders Spaß:
○ Frl. ○ Frau ○ Herr	Alter: von_____ bis_____	○ Natur und Tiere
Name_____	Größe: von_____ bis_____	○ Schnee, Wassersport
Vorname_____		○ Fotografieren, Filmen
Straße Nr._____	○ zärtlich ○ fröhlich	○ Literatur, Kunst
PLZ Ort_____	○ häuslich ○ romantisch	○ Theater, Konzerte, Musik
Tel.-Priv._____	○ gefühlvoll ○ gesellig	○ Wissenschaft, Politik
Geb.-Jahr_____	○ dynamisch ○ treu	○ Reisen
Beruf_____	○ ruhig ○ tolerant	○ Handarbeiten, Basteln
○ led. ○ gesch. ○ getr. lebend	○ kinderlieb ○ natürlich	○ Kochen, Essen
Unterschrift_____		○ Diskussionen, Gespräche

RSM

▣ Analyse

Refer to the section "So sollte mein Partner sein:" (*My partner should be like this:*). Which adjectives are you able to guess? Now look at the section "Das macht mir besonders Spaß:" (*What I particularly enjoy / have fun doing*). Which words do you know immediately?

You probably understood quite a few of the characterstics and interests listed in the ad. The vocabulary section lists some important ones you might not have been able to figure out, along with several characteristics not on the list.

Analyse. Suggestion: Students need not understand the meaning of all words in the ads. First have them identify words they recognize, e.g., *(Dynamisch) heißt* (dynamic). To learn the meaning of other words that might interest them, they may ask you *Was heißt (treu)?*

Neue Wörter

EIGENSCHAFTEN

fleißig *hardworking*
freundlich *friendly*
fröhlich *cheerful*
nett *nice*
ruhig *calm*
treu *faithful*

INTERESSEN

Essen *eating*
Reisen *traveling*
Tanzen *dancing*

▣ Aktivität 12. Was sind meine Eigenschaften? Was macht mir Spaß?

Choose two adjectives that describe you, and one interest that you have. Turn to your neighbor and describe yourself.

> BEISPIEL: Ich bin tolerant und ruhig. Essen macht mir Spaß.

Take turns doing this with several class members.

Aktivität 12. This activity allows students to link bits of information together. It prepares them for constructing longer sentences later on.

▣ Aktivität 13. Was sind ihre Eigenschaften?

Which qualities do you associate with the following people?

> BEISPIEL: Mein Freund ist dynamisch.

If you want to state something negative, add **nicht** (*not*) before the adjective.

> BEISPIEL: Mein Freund ist nicht tolerant.

1. Mein Freund
2. Meine Freundin (*girlfriend or female friend*)
3. Mein Zimmergenosse (*male roommate*)
4. Meine Zimmergenossin (*female roommate*)
5. Tom Cruise
6. Michael Jackson
7. Madonna
8. ?

Aktivität 13. Suggest additional names of well-known personalities and ask students to do the same: *der Präsident, die Königin von England, der Bundeskanzler, Raisa Gorbachev,* etc.

▣ Aktivität 14. Komplimente

Use some of the adjectives you know to pay compliments to several people in your class. Here is what you might say:

> BEISPIEL: A: Julie, du bist dynamisch.
> B: Findest du? (*You think so?*) Danke. Und du bist nett.
> A: Wirklich?

Aktivität 14. Point out that German speakers often respond to a compliment by deflecting: *Findest du?* English speakers frequently do the same: "Do you think so?" A simple *danke* is also acceptable.

GRAMMATIK IM KONTEXT

Nouns and Definite Articles

Substantive und bestimmte Artikel

You have already seen and used German nouns in many different contexts. Nouns in German are easily recognized in writing because they are always capitalized.

German nouns are classified by gender as either masculine, feminine, or neuter. The definite articles **der, die,** and **das** (all meaning *the* in German) signal the gender of nouns.

Dort ist die Straße.

Hier ist die Autobahn.

MASCULINE: **der**	FEMININE: **die**	NEUTER: **das**
der Mann	die Frau	das Land
der Student	die Studentin	das Mädchen
der Name	die Straße	das Auto
der Beruf	die Hausnummer	das Buch

Nouns that refer to living beings generally have natural gender; that is, a male being is masculine, a female being is feminine. Most other German nouns, however, have unpredictable grammatical gender.

Even words borrowed from other languages have a grammatical gender in German, as you can see from the following newspaper headline.

Fußball ist der Hit

Since the gender of a noun is generally unpredictable, you should make it a habit to learn the definite article with each noun.

Sometimes gender is also signaled by the ending of the noun. The suffix **-in,** for instance, always signals a feminine noun:

> der Student, die Student**in**
> der Freund, die Freund**in**
> der Amerikaner, die Amerikaner**in**

The suffixes **-chen** and **-lein** always signal a neuter noun.

> das Mädchen (*girl*)
> das Fräulein (*young lady*)

Compound nouns that combine two or more nouns in one word always take the gender of the last noun in the compound.

> die Telefonnummer = das Telefon + die Nummer
> der Biergarten = das Bier + der Garten
> das Telefonbuch = das Telefon + das Buch

Übung 1. Hören Sie zu.

You will hear eight short questions and statements with nouns and definite articles. For each sentence, circle the definite article you hear.

1. (der) die das
2. (der) die das
3. der (die) das
4. der die (das)
5. der (die) das
6. der die (das)
7. der (die) das
8. (der) die das

⊡ Übung 2. Fragen und Antworten°

Fragen... *Questions and Answers*

Übung 2. Suggestion: Have students work in pairs. One student asks *Wie ist_____?*, choosing an item from the second column. Though students' responses will be limited, have them answer as precisely as possible.

BEISPIEL: A: Wie ist der Film *Indiana Jones*?
            B: Der Film ist sehr interessant.

Wie ist _____ ?

Wo wohnt _____ ?

Woher kommt _____ ?

Wie heißt _____ ?

Adresse von _____

Auto

Biergarten

Film

Professor

Stadt

Student

Studentin

Telefonnummer von _____

Personal Pronouns

Personalpronomen

A personal pronoun stands for a person or a noun.

Du bist nett, Ilse.   *You are nice, Ilse.*

Ich bin praktisch.   *I am practical.*

Der Mercedes—ist **er** neu?   *That Mercedes—is it new?*

The following personal pronouns function as subjects in a sentence.

	Singular		Plural	
1. Person	ich	*I*	wir	*we*
2. Person	Sie	*you (formal)*	Sie	*you (formal)*
	du	*you (informal)*	ihr	*you (informal)*
3. Person	er	*he; it*	sie	*they*
	sie	*she; it*		
	es	*it*		

Ich bin rundum Spitzeᵃ
mit pan-ADRESS

a. Ich... *I am really sharp. (I am great in every way.)*

RSM

Harald und Elke sind Europäer.   *Harald and Elke are Europeans.*

Er kommt aus Bonn. Sie kommt aus Wien.   *He comes from Bonn. She comes from Vienna.*

Wie ist der Film?   *How is the movie?*

Er ist interessant.   *It is interesting.*

Wo ist die Zeitung?   *Where is the newspaper?*

Sie ist hier.   *It is here.*

Wo ist das Buch?   *Where is the book?*

Es ist nicht hier.   *It is not here.*

The third-person singular pronouns **er, sie,** and **es** reflect the grammatical gender of the noun for which they stand.

The pronoun **ich** is not capitalized unless it is the first word in the sentence. Note that the formal second-person pronoun **Sie** is always capitalized.

The pronoun **du** is used for a family member, a close personal friend, or a child. **Ihr** is used for addressing two or more people whom you would individually address with **du.** Use **Sie** for anyone else.

▣ **Übung 3.** **Ergänzen Sie. Du, ihr** *or* **Sie?**

How would you address these people?

1. Herr Professor Dr. Rauschenbach: Woher kommen _____?
2. Christian, Karin und Andreas: Was macht _____ heute?
3. Michael: Woher kommst _____?
4. Ihre Mutter: Was machst _____ da?
5. Ein Tourist aus Amerika: Wie finden _____ Berlin?
6. Zehn Touristen aus Kanada: Wie finden _____ Berlin?
7. Ihr Vater und Ihr Bruder: Woher kommt _____?

▣ **Übung 4.** **Ergänzen Sie. Er, es** *or* **sie?**

1. Herr und Frau Meier sind aus München. _____ besuchen Berlin. Herr Meier ist sehr kritisch. _____ findet Berlin interessant, aber _____ findet München schöner. Frau Meier ist nicht so kritisch. _____ findet Berlin sehr schön.
2. Daniela Lercher ist Studentin. _____ kommt aus Österreich.
3. Jürgen Prochnow ist Schauspieler (*actor*). _____ ist groß und dynamisch. _____ kommt aus Deutschland.
4. Jürgen und Sabine studieren in Tübingen. _____ sind aus Köln.
5. Der Film kommt aus Deutschland. _____ ist sehr kompliziert und lang.

▣ **Übung 5.** **Wie ist das?**

BEISPIEL: A: Wie ist der Film *Bagdad Cafe*?
           B: Er ist ausgezeichnet.

der Film _____	ausgezeichnet
das Buch _____	interessant
das Wetter in _____	prima
die Zeitung _____	nicht besonders gut
das Essen (im	langweilig (*boring*)
Studentenheim)	schön
die Uni (Universität)	
?	

The Verb: Infinitive and Present Tense

Das Verb: Infinitiv und Präsenz

A verb expresses an action or describes a situation. The basic form of a verb is the infinitive, the form that you find listed in the dictionary.

In German, the infinitive consists of the verb stem plus the ending **-en** or just **-n.**

VERB STEM	ENDING	INFINITIVE	ENGLISH
wohn-	-en	wohnen	*to live*
wander-	-n	wandern	*to hike*

To express a situation or an action that is going on right now, a verb requires special endings. These endings depend on the subject of the sentence.

RSM

Kommt
die Inflation
wieder?

*FLORIDA,
ICH KOMME!*

▣ Analyse

- How many different verb endings can you find in the above items?
- What are the subjects in each of the sentences? Are they in the singular or in the plural?
- What are the infinitive forms of these verbs?

Analyse exercises in the grammar are intended to make students draw some conclusions on their own about a particular grammatical point before a rule or explanation is given. It is important, therefore, that students do not read ahead in the text before doing each *Analyse.*

Here are the complete present-tense forms:

INFINITIVE: **wohnen** STEM: **wohn-**		INFINITIVE: **finden** STEM: **find-**	
Singular	*Plural*	*Singular*	*Plural*
ich wohn**e**	wir wohn**en**	ich find**e**	wir find**en**
Sie wohn**en**	Sie wohn**en**	Sie find**en**	Sie find**en**
du wohn**st**	ihr wohn**t**	du find**est**	ihr find**et**
er sie es } wohn**t**	sie wohn**en**	er sie es } find**et**	sie find**en**

In German, four different personal endings can be added to the infinitive stem: **-e, -en, -(e)t,** and **-(e)st.** In contrast, English has only one ending added to the infinitive stem, *-s,* for the third-person singular (*comes, finds, lives*).

The **e** inserted before the **-t** or **-st** is used for all verbs whose stem ends in **d** or **t** (such as **finden, antworten,** *to answer,* and **arbeiten,** *to work*). The added **e** makes them easier to pronounce.

Note that verbs whose stem ends in **ß, s, ss,** or **z** (such as **heißen**) just take **-t** in the **du** form (**du heißt**).

Using the Present Tense

The present tense in German expresses either something going on at the moment or a recurring action.

Sie lernen Deutsch.   *You are learning German.*

It can also express future action.

Nächstes Jahr lerne ich   *Next year I'm going to learn*
    Chinesisch.   *Chinese.*

German has only one form of the present tense, whereas English has three different forms:

Hans tanzt gut.
{
Hans dances well. (*simple*)
Hans is dancing well.
    (*progressive*)
Hans does dance well.
    (*emphatic*)
}

▣ Übung 6. Wer sind sie? Was machen sie?

You read about the following people earlier in this chapter. What do you remember about them?

BEISPIEL: Herr und Frau Meier wohnen in München.

Herr und Frau Meier	arbeiten	München
Frau Savigny	besuchen	Frankreich
Herr Meier	finden	Deutsch
Dieter Schneider	kommen	Berlin
Helmut	lernen	Amerika
Wendy	studieren	Physik
	wohnen	

Übung 6. Suggestion: This activity picks up on previous dialogues in this chapter. Ask students to recall who the characters are, where they are from, etc. Sentence-builder activities work best when students are given a few minutes to scan the entire range of possibilities before formulating sentences.

▣ Übung 7. Ergänzen Sie.

Complete these short dialogues with the appropriate verb endings.

1. Herr Meier, ich höre, Sie komm_____ aus Wien?
    Nein, ich komm_____ aus München.

Übung 7, 8. Suggestion: These short conversations focus on verb endings. Personalize the material by asking students directly *Wie finden Sie / findest du* (name of the university / college town / city)? Also vary the person through questions such as *Wie findet Frau Savigny Berlin? Wo arbeitet Peter?*

2. Wendy, du studier_____ Deutsch hier in Berlin?
   Nein, ich lern_____ Deutsch am Sprachinstitut (*language institute*).
   Nächstes Jahr studier_____ ich an der Uni.
3. Woher komm_____ du, Helmut?
   Ich komm_____ aus Köln. Meine Familie wohn_____ da.
4. Frau Savigny, wie find_____ Sie Berlin?
   Ich find_____ Berlin sehr interessant.
5. Wendy und Helmut, ihr arbeit_____ in Berlin?
   Nein, wir studier_____ in Berlin. Wendy lern_____ Deutsch. Ich studier_____ Physik an der FU (= Freie Universität, *Free University in Berlin*).

Neue Wörter

das Geld *money*

seit wann *since when*

bleiben *to stay*

brauchen *to need*

sagen *to say*

suchen *to look for*

⊡ Übung 8. Situationen und Konversationen im Alltag

Everyday situations and conversation: complete the following brief conversations.

1. REISEFÜHRER:° Guten Morgen, meine Damen und Herren. Ich   *tour guide*
                heiß_____ Andreas Siebert. Wir besuch_____ heute
                das Museum in Berlin-Dahlem.
      TOURIST: Bleib_____ wir lange da?

2.   ANDREA: Grüß dich, Peter! Was mach_____ du denn hier bei
                McDonald's?
         PETER: Ich arbeit_____ hier.
       ANDREA: Du arbeit_____ hier? Studier_____ du nicht mehr°?   nicht... *not any more*
         PETER: Doch, aber ich brauch_____ Geld.

3.   REPORTER: Und woher komm_____ Sie, Herr... eh?
   HERR MEIER: Meier. Wir komm_____ aus München.

4.   NICOLA: Tag, Daniela! Grüß dich, Uwe. Was mach_____ ihr
                denn in Bonn?
       DANIELA: Ich studier_____ jetzt hier Biologie. Uwe studier_____
                Physik.

5.   HEIDI: Daniela und Uwe studier_____ jetzt in Bonn. Und
                Peter arbeit_____ bei McDonald's. Er sag_____, er
                brauch_____ Geld.
            KAI: Ich such_____ auch Arbeit. Die Tanzschule Keller
                such_____ Studenten für Tanzkurse. Ich
                tanz_____ gut. Tanzen mach_____ Spaß!
          HEIDI: Du tanz_____ gut? Seit wann?

The Verbs *sein* and *heißen*

The verb **sein** is used to describe or identify someone or something:

> Ich **bin** Studentin.
> Sie **ist** freundlich.
> Der Film **ist** ausgezeichnet.

*Ich bin ein Adler*ª*!*
Ich bin ein Adler!
Ich bin ein Adler!

RSM   a. *eagle*

Here are the present-tense forms of **sein.**

Singular	Plural
ich bin *I am*	wir sind *we are*
Sie sind *you are (formal)*	Sie sind *you are (formal)*
du bist *you are*	ihr seid *you are*
er ⎫ he ⎫	
sie ⎬ ist she ⎬ *is*	sie sind *they are*
es ⎭ it ⎭	

Wie heißt der Film?

The verb **heißen** is used to give or ask for the name of a person or object.

▣ Übung 9. Zwei Menschen°

Zwei... *Two human beings*

Read the descriptions of Jürgen and Petra. You will find the information to answer the following questions in the texts.

1. Wie heißt der Mann?
2. Wie heißt die Frau?
3. Wie alt ist die Frau?
4. Wie alt ist der Mann?
5. Wie groß ist der Mann?
6. Wie groß ist die Frau?
7. Wie ist der Mann? (drei Adjektive)
8. Was macht Petra?

> **Ich heiße Petra,** bin 28 Jahre alt, 168 cm groß und arbeite in einem Ingenieurbüro.

> **Jürgen** ist 25 Jahre alt, 185 cm groß, blond, sportlich-schlank, gut aussehend und sympathisch.

Übung 9. Suggestion: First have students scan questions to be answered; then ask them to look at descriptions. The activity can be done as *Partnerarbeit* or by the whole group. Complete-sentence answers are not necessary.

RSM

▣ Übung 10. Ich bin, wer ich bin!

Complete the sentences with the appropriate form of **sein.**

1. Ich sage: Du _____ immer so konservativ, Thomas.
2. Thomas sagt: Wie bitte? Ich _____ liberal!
3. Sein Vater sagt: Thomas _____ nicht praktisch.
4. Seine Mutter sagt: Wir _____ zu kritisch. Thomas _____ sehr jung. Er _____ sehr intelligent und fleißig.
6. Sein Boss: Herr Berger, Sie _____ nicht dynamisch.
7. Thomas denkt (*thinks*): Ihr _____ alle unfair. Ich _____, wer ich _____: ein Genie!

Übung 10. Suggestion: Ask several students to describe themselves first. Then ask how other people would describe them, e.g., *Was sagt Ihre Mutter? Was sagen Ihre Freunde? Ihr Professor?*

▣ Übung 11. Wie heißen Sie?

Introduce yourself in German to several fellow students. Pay each other a compliment, thank each other for the compliments, and say good-bye.

A:	B:
Ich heiße _____. Wie _____ du?	Ich _____.
Woher _____?	Ich _____ aus _____.
Du _____ wirklich _____.	Danke, wie nett.
Tschüß.	_____

Übung 11. Suggestion: These guided conversations allow students to provide their own information. Give them time to complete the activity in pairs; then call on several pairs to perform the role-play for the class. Have students practice this with several partners.

The Sentence

Der Satz

The Declarative Sentence

A declarative sentence is a sentence that makes a statement. In a German declarative sentence, the finite verb (the verb with the personal ending) always stands in the second position.

1	2	3	4...
Meine Familie	wohnt	in Österreich.	
Ich	studiere	in Deutschland.	
Manchmal	besuche	ich	Freunde.
Heute	spielen	wir	Karten.

The subject of the sentence usually stands at the beginning of the sentence.

> **Meine Familie** wohnt in Österreich.
> **Ich** studiere in Deutschland.

If another sentence element, such as an adverb, stands at the beginning of the sentence, however, the verb stays in the second position and the subject follows the verb in the third position. This is referred to as inverted word order.

1	2	3	4...
Manchmal	besuche	**ich**	Freunde.
Heute	spielen	**wir**	Karten.

▣ Übung 12. **Was machen sie?**

Choose an item from each of the four columns and create sentences. Remember to use the proper ending for the verb.

BEISPIEL: Jetzt studiert mein Freund Medizin.

Heute	besuchen	wir	in Deutschland
Morgen	studieren	mein Freund	Karten
Nächstes Jahr	spielen	ich	Freunde
Jetzt	lernen		Deutsch
Manchmal			Medizin
			?

▣ Übung 13. **Interaktion**

Tell a partner some of the things you will do today, tomorrow, or next year (**heute, morgen,** or **nächstes Jahr**). Make a list of what your partner will do and be prepared to tell the class about his or her plans.

BEISPIEL: Heute spiele ich Karten. Morgen arbeite ich. Und nächstes Jahr studiere ich in Deutschland.

Übung 13. This exercise requires students to link pieces of information. It is a speaking, listening, and note-taking exercise. Encourage students to ask for clarification if they want someone to repeat what they did not understand by saying *Wie bitte?* or *Wiederholen Sie bitte!*

Questions

You have already used questions in many different contexts, for example:

> Wie heißen Sie? (Meier)
> Woher kommt Herr Meier? (aus München)

An interrogative pronoun (**wie, woher, was**) at the beginning of a question asks for specific information. The finite verb again stands in the second position, now following the interrogative pronoun.

RSM

a. am... *on the weekend*

1	2	3	4...
Interrogative Pronoun	*Finite Verb*	*Subject*	*Other Elements*
Was	machen	wir	heute?
Woher	kommst	du?	
Wer	ist		aus Berlin?

Here are some common interrogative pronouns:

wann *when*	wie *how*
warum *why*	wo *where*
was *what*	woher *from where*
wer *who*	

A question that requires either a *yes* or a *no* for an answer begins with the finite verb. The subject immediately follows the verb. This is yet another example of inverted word order.

Verb	*Subject*	*Other Elements*
Kommst	du	bald?
Heißen	Sie	Martina Seghers?
Studierst	du	Deutsch?
Ist	Herr Schneider	aus Berlin?

KOMMST DU BALD ?

RSM

Questions in English use either the progressive form of the verb or the auxiliary verb *to do*. Note that German has only the one form shown below.

Was studierst du? $\begin{cases} \textit{What are you studying?} \\ \quad (\textit{present progressive}) \\ \textit{What do you study?} \\ \quad (\textbf{\textit{auxiliary}} \text{ to do}) \end{cases}$

Woher kommen Sie? $\begin{cases} \textit{Where are you coming from?} \\ \quad (\textit{present progressive}) \\ \textit{Where do you come from?} \\ \quad (\textbf{\textit{auxiliary}} \text{ to do}) \end{cases}$

Particles

Partikeln

Germans often add particles (intensifiers) to a statement or a question to convey their attitude toward what they are saying. In questions, the particle **denn** indicates surprise or strong interest.

Was machst du denn hier, Hans?   *What are you doing here, Hans?*

Wie geht es dir denn?   *How are you?*

In short questions, **denn** is usually placed at the end of the sentence.

▣ Übung 14. Fragen und Antworten

Ergänzen Sie die Interrogativpronomen.

1. _____ heißen Sie, bitte?
2. _____ kommen Sie denn?
3. _____ studieren Sie?
4. _____ wohnen Sie denn?

5. ____ machen Sie morgen?
6. ____ studieren Sie in Deutschland?
7. ____ wohnt in Berlin?
8. ____ ist Ihre Adresse, bitte?

⊡ Übung 15. Wie bitte?

Imagine that you are having some difficulty understanding what someone is saying to you. Ask him or her to repeat the information.

> BEISPIEL: A: Ich heiße Karl-Heinz Rüschenbaum.
>   B: Wie bitte? Wie heißen Sie?
>   A: Karl-Heinz Rüschenbaum.
>   B: Ach so!

1. Ich heiße ____ .
2. Ich komme aus ____ .
3. Das ist in ____ .
4. Ich studiere ____ .
5. ____ ist sehr interessant.
6. Professor ____ ist auch sehr interessant.
7. Nächstes Jahr studiere ich in Heidelberg.

Übung 15. This activity is specifically designed to practice asking for clarification and demonstrating understanding. Model the activity with a student so that the class hears the proper intonation patterns. Have students reverse roles in this activity.

⊡ Übung 16. Partnerarbeit

Ask a partner several questions; take turns asking questions and answering them.

> BEISPIEL: A: Wann gehst du tanzen?
>   B: Ich gehe morgen tanzen.

Was	spielen... Karten
Wo	machen
Wie	gehen... tanzen (*to go dancing*)
Wann	wohnen
Wer	heißen
Woher	kommen
	lernen
	?

Übung 16. Give students several minutes to formulate questions from the list. They need not form questions with all interrogative pronouns, but insist that they use at least three.

⊡ Übung 17. Ja oder nein?

Start a chain by asking one person in your class a yes or no question. Create the question with the help of some of the verbs listed, or using others you remember.

> BEISPIEL: A: Spielst du gut Karten?
>   B: Nein. Tanzt du gut?
>   C: Ja...

Übung 17. This activity will help students initiate questions. Although it is a chain exercise, have students direct their questions randomly to other class members. Encourage them to go beyond the verb list given.

Ich studiere jetzt hier. Und du? Was machst du?

Übung 18.   Suggestion: Have students scan the questions before listening to the conversation. Tell them they will not understand every word and should only focus on information elicited by the questions.
Note: Exploit the conversation by asking further questions: *Was macht Sabine in Tübingen? Wie findet Hans seine Arbeit?*

arbeiten	kommen	studieren
finden	sein	tanzen
heißen	spielen	wohnen

Übung 18.   Hören Sie zu! Ein Gespräch° auf der Straße   *conversation*

Sabine and Christian meet in the southern German university town of Tübingen.

Richtig oder falsch?

1. __F__ The speakers are just getting acquainted.
2. __F__ Christian is working for a bank.
3. __R__ Sabine is a student.
4. __R__ Christian is sharing a place with his brother.
5. __R__ Sabine enjoys playing cards.
6. __F__ Christian invites Sabine to play cards with him.

Lesen im Kontext.   These sections focus on developing effective reading strategies. The selections in this chapter introduce basic techniques such as skimming and scanning. You should stress recognizing cognates and guessing from context. The texts are not meant to be read aloud in class. Students will need a lot of reassurance and encouragement to develop a positive attitude toward reading authentic material. The text titled *Menschen* will seem daunting if approached word for word, but with proper application of the strategies suggested here, students will learn to enjoy taking risks when exploring an unknown text.
Prereading activities, called *Auf den ersten Blick*, will require students to brainstorm and speculate about the text. In the section titled *Zum Text*, students work with the text to acquire vocabulary and gather more detailed information. When there is more than one reading, the

LESEN IM KONTEXT

Auf den ersten Blick and *Zum Text* sections are numbered in order to clearly differentiate the readings. The section titled *Nach dem Lesen* sums up the theme through communicative activities. Writing activities are also suggested in this section.

This section of each chapter will introduce you to reading in German through a variety of authentic texts, texts written by and for native speakers of German. The texts in this chapter include newspaper announcements and an excerpt from a magazine article about young people in Germany.

Vor dem Lesen

You will be concentrating on skimming (reading superficially) and scanning (reading to find specific information). Here are some guidelines to help you to develop efficient reading strategies:

- Establish what type of text you are about to read.
- Ask yourself what you expect to find out from this text.

Do not read word for word or reach for the dictionary when you come across a word you don't know. Look for cognates and words you do know instead. Try guessing meaning from context. **Viel Spaß!**

Auf den ersten Blick° 1

Auf... *At first glance*

1. Look at the two texts below. What type of texts do you think they are? What leads you to believe this?
2. Now that you have established what kind of text you are reading, scan the text and give the following information.

Fabians Eltern heißen ＿＿＿ .   Jennifers Eltern sind ＿＿＿
Sie wohnen in ＿＿＿ .   Sie wohnen in ＿＿＿ .
Ihre Adresse ist ＿＿＿ .   Ihre Adresse ist ＿＿＿ .

Auf den ersten Blick. **Note:** In this section students will get a first glance at the reading(s). Tell them to use all clues, including pictures, to figure out the basic meaning of the texts. Stress that in all such texts they are not expected to understand every word. If you assign the text to be read outside of class, this section provides a useful preview.

Hallo! Ich bin da!

Hallo! Ich bin da!

Fabian * 16. 4. 1987

Meine Eltern
Ilona und Hermann Wischnewski
freuen sich riesig.

Bad Harzburg 3, Am Stadtstieg 9

Hurra! **Jennifer** ist da.
27. Mai 1987, 54 cm, 3730 Gramm.

Wir freuen uns mit Jessica über die Geburt unseres 2. Kindes

Manuela Stock, geb. Exner
Udo Stock

4500 Osnabrück, Schweriner Straße 9
Z. Z. Paracelsusklinik, Dr. Schallenberg, Dr. Quade

RSM

Zum Text 1

The two families have to register their new offspring and are asked to provide the following information on a form:

Familienname: ＿＿＿
Vorname: ＿＿＿
Geburtsdatum: ＿＿＿
Wohnort: ＿＿＿
Straße und Hausnummer: ＿＿＿

Zum Text. In this section students will do various activities with the text, such as vocabulary practice, extracting more detailed information, summarizing, and paraphrasing. In the early readings, answers may be given in English.

Auf den ersten Blick 2

1. Skim the following four short texts from German newspapers. Which words do you recognize?
2. The texts are:
   a. birth announcements
   b. anniversary announcements
   c. birthday greetings

   What led you to your decision?
3. Scan the texts again and provide the following information.

Congratulations sent by	*meant for*	*person's age*
1.		
2.		
3.		
4.		

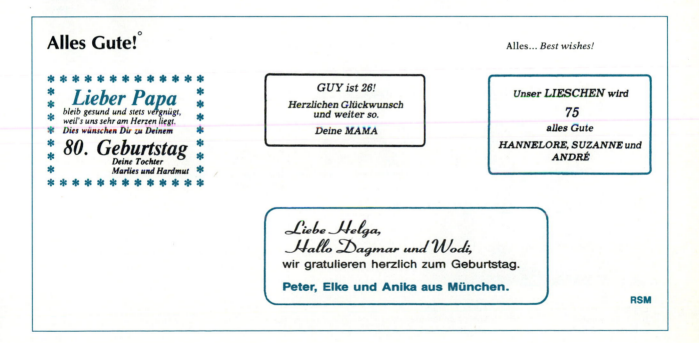

Alles Gute!°

Alles… *Best wishes!*

* * * * * * * * * * *
Lieber Papa
bleib gesund und stets vergnügt,
weil's uns sehr am Herzen liegt.
Dies wünschen Dir zu Deinem
80. Geburtstag
Deine Tochter
Marlies und Hardmut
* * * * * * * * * * *

GUY ist 26!
Herzlichen Glückwunsch
und weiter so.
Deine MAMA

Unser LIESCHEN wird
75
alles Gute
HANNELORE, SUZANNE und
ANDRÉ

Liebe Helga,
Hallo Dagmar und Wodi,
wir gratulieren herzlich zum Geburtstag.

Peter, Elke und Anika aus München.

RSM

Zum Text 2

Herzlichen Glückwunsch! (*Congratulations!*) Using the language and format of the preceding texts, write a simple birthday greeting for a friend or a relative.

Auf den ersten Blick 3

1. Look at the pictures in the article and then at the article's heading.
   What do you think is the meaning of the word **Ausländer?**
   a. outlandish
   b. foreign country
   c. foreigners
   What are the reasons for your choice? How do the other words in the heading and the pictures support your choice?
2. Judging from the heading and the pictures, what do you expect to find out by reading this article?

Menschen°

People

Junge Ausländer über Deutsche.

Njeri Kinyantui, 24, stammt aus Kenia und studiert in West-Berlin Volkswirtschaft.[a] "Das Leben hier ist freier als in meiner Heimat.[b] Ich kann studieren, was ich will, kann leben, wie ich will."

Cengiz Temur, 16, Türke, kam als Zwei-jähriger nach Essen-Stoppenberg, wo er zur Schule geht:"Hier kann man besser einkaufen[c] als in der Türkei. Auch die Schule ist hier besser."

Canndy John, 19, Japaner, arbeitet zur Zeit als Chemielaborant[d] in West-Berlin: "Mir gefallen meine Freunde in Berlin total. Und auch die Musik hier finde ich ganz gut."

Nicholaas Solaiman, 33, Indonesier, zur Zeit Student der Betriebs-wirtschaft[e] in West-Berlin. "Mir gefällt nicht,[f] daß viele Deutsche so überheblich[g] sind. Und so materialistisch... Mir gefällt, daß man hier tatsächlich eine gewisse Demokratie hat und daß man auch als Ausländer demokratische Rechte hat."

a. *economics*
b. *native country*
c. *besser... shop better*
d. *business management*
e. *lab technician*
f. *Mir... I do not like*
g. *arrogant*

RSM

Zum Text 3

The article talks about four young people in the Federal Republic of Germany. Do not read word for word. It would be frustrating and inefficient at this time. You are not expected to understand everything. Look for cognates and words you know already to find out something about the people in this article.

1. Look at the beginning of each segment. How does each section begin?
2. Scan each section and provide the following information for each person:

   Name: _____
   Heimat (*native country*): _____
   Beruf: _____
   Wohnort in Deutschland: _____

3. Now take a closer look at the texts and try to find out what these people like, or dislike, about Germany. Remember to look for words that you know or recognize as similar in English.

Nach dem Lesen°

Nach... *After reading*

▣ **Aktivität 1. So ist das Leben hier!°**

With a partner, describe the life of the people around you. Use some of the following adjectives, or others you have already learned in this chapter.

So... That's life around here!

Nach dem Lesen. This section encourages students to synthesize all chapter material in communicative speaking and writing activities.

arrogant	gut	praktisch
faul (*lazy*)	(un)kompliziert	schlecht
fleißig	materialistisch	schön
freundlich	nett	tolerant

BEISPIEL: A: Ich finde das Leben hier gut. Die Studenten sind fleißig.

B: Findest du? Die Studenten hier sind so materialistisch.

Report back to the class what your partner had to say about life and the people around you.

BEISPIEL: Craig findet das Leben hier gut. Er findet die Studenten fleißig.

▣ **Aktivität 2. Persönliche Angaben**

Write a personal profile of a classmate. You should include the following information:

- wie er/sie heißt
- woher er/sie kommt
- was er/sie studiert
- wie er/sie ist
- wie er/sie _____ findet (zum Beispiel: die Universität, das Leben, die Menschen hier)

WORTSCHATZ

Substantive

Länder und Leute

der Amerikaner, die Amerikanerin	American
der Ausländer, die Ausländerin	foreigner
die Eltern	parents
Frankreich	France
der Freund, die Freundin	friend
das Land	country, land
das Mädchen	girl
der Mann	man
der Mensch (pl. Menschen)	human being
der Professor, die Professorin	professor
der Reporter, die Reporterin	reporter
der Schauspieler, die Schauspielerin	actor, actress
der Student, die Studentin	student
der Tourist, die Touristin	tourist
die USA (pl.)	the United States
aus den USA	from the United States
der Zimmergenosse, die Zimmergenossin	roommate

Persönliche Angaben

Countries and people

Personal information

der Ausweis	ID card
der Beruf	occupation, profession
von Beruf	by occupation
das Geburtsdatum	date of birth
der Geburtsort	place of birth
der Name	name
der Familienname	family name
der Nachname	family name
der Vorname	given name
der Reisepaß	passport
der Wohnort	place of residence

Andere Substantive

Other nouns

die Arbeit	work, job
das Auto	car, automobile
das Buch	book
das Essen	food; eating
der Film	film, movie
das Geld	money
das Haus	house
das Jahr	year
nächstes Jahr	next year
das Leben	life
die Stadt	city
die Zeitung	newspaper

Verben

Verbs

antworten	to answer
arbeiten	to work
besuchen	to visit
bleiben	to stay
brauchen	to need
finden	to find
gehen	to go
kommen	to come
lernen	to learn
Ich lerne Deutsch.	I'm learning German.
heißen	to be named; to mean; to be called
machen	to do, make
reisen	to travel
das Reisen	traveling
sagen	to say
sein	to be
spielen	to play
Karten spielen	to play cards
studieren	to study (a subject at a university)
suchen	to look for
tanzen	to dance
das Tanzen	dancing
wandern	to hike
wohnen	to live

Adjektive

Adjectives

alt	old
falsch	false
faul	lazy
fleißig	hardworking, diligent
freundlich	friendly
fröhlich	cheerful
groß	big; tall

interessant	interesting
jung	young
kritisch	critical
langweilig	boring
natürlich	natural
nett	nice
neu	new
praktisch	practical
richtig	right, correct
ruhig	calm; quiet
schön	beautiful
sympathisch	nice, pleasant
treu	loyal

Sonstiges — Other items

aber	but
auch	also
da	there
doch	yes
heute	today
hier	here
ja	yes
jetzt	now
manchmal	sometimes
morgen	tomorrow
nein	no
nicht	not
sehr	very
wirklich	really

Fragewörter — Question words

wann	when
seit wann	since when
warum	why
was	what
wer	who
wie	how
wo	where
woher	from where

Zahlen (30–100) — Numbers

dreißig	thirty
vierzig	forty
fünfzig	fifty
sechzig	sixty
siebzig	seventy
achtzig	eighty
neunzig	ninety
(ein) hundert	one hundred

Ausdrücke — Expressions

Wie finden Sie Berlin?	What do you think of Berlin?
Ich finde Berlin schön.	I think Berlin is beautiful.
Das macht (mir) Spaß.	That's fun, I enjoy that.
Viel Spaß!	Have fun!
zum Beispiel (*abbr.* **z.B.**)	for example

KAPITEL 2

DAS TÄGLICHE LEBEN

Kapitel 2. Introduce the theme of this chapter by focusing briefly on students' concern for housing. State in simple German where you live, and ask where they live. Be tolerant if their answers are only partially in German.

Lernziele   *In this chapter you will learn how to ask for things you need and how to express an opinion about things you want to buy. You'll also learn how to accept or reject something offered to you. You will talk about the things you enjoy doing.*

Was suchen sie?

Where would you find a flyer like the one you see here?

▣ Alles klar?

- Was suchen die vier Studentinnen?
  - a. einen Regenschirm

  - b. eine Wohnung
  - c. ein Dach

  - d. ein Zimmer

- Wie viele Zimmer brauchen sie?
  - a. ein bis zwei Zimmer
  - b. zwei bis drei
  - d. vier bis fünf
- Was heißt **mit Küche und Bad?**
- Was heißt **zentrale Lage?**
- **100 DM Belohnung:** was heißt das?

RSM

Wörter im Kontext.   Each chapter is divided into three sections: *Wörter im Kontext, Grammatik im Kontext,* and *Lesen im Kontext.* The first section provides opportunities to acquire new vocabulary and expressions by exploring authentic materials. Students are asked to analyze the materials and figure out the meaning of words on their own. The activities of this section practice and recycle the vocabulary. Some grammar is previewed in short notes titled *Sprachnotiz.* Activities are targeted at getting students to interact.

WOHNUNGS-ANGEBOTE
Möbl. 2 Zi-Mans.-Whg. in Bft., ca. 60 m², ZH, für 400 DM incl. NK, außer Strom ab sof. zu verm. Zuschriften unter RZ 00359
Schönes möbl. Zimmer ab 1.1.88 in Zussdorf zu verm. DM 200 warm Tel. (07503) 1397
Sonnige 3 Zi-Whg. RV Süd an ruh. Ehepaar zu verm. Zuschriften unter RZ 00407
Zimmer in WG in Bft. f. 3 Mo. zu verm. (0751) 49922
1 Zi.-Appartement in Wgt., 35 m², 320 DM zum 1.2.88 zu verm. (0751) 14644 gewerblich
1 Zi-Appartement 34 m² EBK, an Nichtraucherin zu verm., Kaltm. DM 300 (0751) 51716

Zi	= Zimmer
Mans.	= die Mansarde *=under the roof*
Whg.	= die Wohnung
WG	= Wohngemeinschaft = *shared housing*
möbl.	= möbliert
warm	= *heating included*
kalt	= *heating excluded*
zu verm.	= zu vermieten = *for rent*

WÖRTER IM KONTEXT

Was Studenten brauchen

▣ Dialog 1

Dialog 1.   Preview dialogue contents for the students in a general way. Go over the *Neue Wörter* to prepare them for listening to the dialogue. Play the tape once, asking students what they have understood. Then have students read the dialogue as a role-play. The *Analyse* can be done in pairs.

Eine Studentin hat ein Problem. Was ist das Problem?

STEFAN: Tag, Ulla, wie geht's?

ULLA: Ach, nicht besonders.

STEFAN: Was ist denn los?

ULLA: Ich suche eine Wohnung oder ein Zimmer. Die Wohnungen sind alle so teuer.

STEFAN: Hier ist die Zeitung. Wohnungsangebote. Da, schau mal: Schönes möbliertes Zimmer.

ULLA: Wie hoch ist die Miete?

STEFAN: Nur DM 200, -.

◙ Analyse

- Why is Ulla responding negatively to Stefan's greetings?
- How does Stefan ask Ulla about her problem? What would the English equivalent of this phrase be?
- How is Stefan able to help Ulla?
- How does Ulla ask for the rental price?

◻◻◻◻ *Kulturnotiz*

DM = Deutsche Mark. Read **DM 200, -** as **zweihundert Mark.** The notation **DM** can come before or after the price (**200,- DM** or **DM 200,-**).

Kulturnotiz. If possible, bring in the foreign exchange page from a newspaper to give students the most current rates.

Neue Wörter

das Bad *bath, bathroom*   **hoch** *high*
die Küche *kitchen*   **möbliert** *furnished*
die Miete *rent*   **teuer** *expensive*
die Wohnung *apartment*
das Zimmer *room*

■ Dialog 2

Wie geht es Ulla jetzt?

Dialog 2. Approach this dialogue in the same way as *Dialog 1*. It is a follow-up to *Dialog 1*.

KARIN: Tag, Ulla. Wie geht's dir denn?
ULLA: Tag, Karin. Es geht mir prima. Ich habe jetzt endlich ein Zimmer.
KARIN: Wo denn?
ULLA: Schillerstraße 13.
KARIN: Toll, in zentraler Lage. Ist das Zimmer möbliert?
ULLA: Ja. Es hat ein Bett, einen Schreibtisch, einen Stuhl, einen Tisch und einen Sessel. Ich brauche nur noch eine Lampe für den Schreibtisch und ein Bücherregal.
KARIN: Wie hoch ist die Miete?
ULLA: Nur DM 200, -.
KARIN: Hast du Telefon?
ULLA: Nein, noch nicht.

◙ Analyse

- Ulla is feeling **"prima"** now. What words does she use to explain why she feels this way?
- How does her friend indicate that Ulla is lucky, and why does she think so?

- How does Ulla express her needs?
- How does Ulla indicate that she considers the rent low?

 Aktivität 1.   Hören Sie zu. Wir brauchen eine Wohnung / ein Zimmer! Follow-up: Ask students questions about the ads to check under-standing: "What is the musician looking for?"

Scan the five circled ads from people looking for housing. Label the ads from one to five in the order in which they are read to you.

a. ___4___   d. ___1___
b. ___5___   e. ___3___
c. ___2___

Aktivität 1.   Suggestion: Let students scan the circled ads before listening to the tape. Tell them they will hear and see unfamiliar words but that they need only recognize which ad is being read.

Aktivität 2.   Encourage students to give as much information as possible. Accept a wide variety of responses.

☐ **Aktivität 2.   Wer braucht eine Wohnung?**

Skim the housing ads and choose three. Tell the class who the people looking for housing are and what they are looking for.

BEISPIEL: Eine Studentin und ein Koch (*cook*) suchen ein Zimmer. Die Studentin heißt Uschi, der Koch heißt Emanuele. Uschi ist 21, Emanuele ist 29.

Sprachnotiz

The indefinite articles **ein** and **eine** (*a, an*) are used with the subject of a sentence.

der Student	die Studentin	das Zimmer
ein Student	eine Studentin	ein Zimmer

With a masculine noun functioning as direct object, the indefinite article is changed to **einen,** whereas it remains unchanged with a neuter or feminine direct object noun.

einen Sessel	eine Lampe	ein Zimmer

☐ **Aktivität 3.   Eine Anzeige schreiben**

Using the newspaper ads as models, create a simple ad with the help of the following expressions. Trade ads with another person who will read yours to the class.

Student/Studentin sucht
  in zentraler Lage
  möbliertes/ruhiges/großes/kleines Zimmer
  mit Telefon/Küche/Bad
  Miete bis zu DM _____
  in Wohngemeinschaft

RSM

Freundl. junger 37-jähriger Englischlehrer su. 1 Zi. in WG um mit Euch Deutsch zu sprechen und es besser zu lernen. ☎ 570 56 39   **a.**

Studentin und italienischer Koch (22/29) suchen Zimmer in WG. Gemeinsam wäre schön, ist aber nicht Voraussetzung. Uschi und Emanuele ☎ 42 33 26

Musiker (24) sucht Zimmer oder Raum in WG o.ä. zum 1.6. oder etwas früher. ☎ 040/439 84 20 Markus (rufe zurück) PS.: Zahle bis 500 DM incl.   **b.**

Roland, 30, WG-erfahren, sucht ab sofort ein großes, ruhiges Zimmer bei aufgeschlossenen Mitmenschen. Bevorzugt zentral u. gute S-Bahn-Verb. ☎ 77 49 70

Freundlicher Schauspieler aus Hamburg sucht Zi in WG vom 1. Mai bis 1. August in München. ☎ 637 88 78, ♂Manfred   **c.**

Fotodesigner, 22, sucht preiswertes Zimmer in junger WG, mögl. zentral zum 1.7.87. Kischel Benno, Westendstr. 237, 8 Mü 21 (telefonisch schlecht erreichbar)   **d.**

Ronald, 24, z.Z. in Berlin (kein Preuße) sucht ab Juli nettes Zi. in ebensolcher WG in Schwabing oder Norden Münchens. ☎ 030/333 12 45 abends

Architekturstudent (TU) sucht Zimmer in mögl. zentral gelegener WG ab sofort für länger. Ich, Nichtraucher bin 23 Jahre alt. ☎ 080 92/20 415 Gerd

Architekturstudentin (25) sucht zum 1. od. 15.5. ruhiges Zim. bis 400,— incl. in WG ☎ 857 63 90 (evtl. 50 72 58)   **e.**

Toni 25 J., Industriekfm. ab Sept. 87 Schule (Abi) sucht ab sofort ruhiges Zimmer bis DM 420,— incl. in netter WG, mind. 4 Leute, bin WG-erfahren, ☎ 260 48 96

Home is where the heart is. Studentin sucht schönes Zimmer in unkomplizierter WG, ☎ 814 22 04

Sprachnotiz. This is a brief introduction to a grammar point that will be explained more fully later.

Sprachnotiz

In German, attributive adjectives—that is, adjectives in front of nouns—take endings.

> Ich suche ein möbliert**es** Zimmer.　　*I'm looking for a furnished room.*

Predicate adjectives—that is, adjectives used after the verb **sein**—do not take endings.

> Das Zimmer ist möbliert.　　*The room is furnished.*

You will learn about attributive adjective endings in a later chapter.

Einkäufe im Kaufhaus°

Einkäufe... *Shopping at a department store*

 **Dialog**

Ein Gespräch im Kaufhaus

VERKÄUFER: Bitte sehr?
ULLA: Ich suche eine Lampe für meinen Schreibtisch.
VERKÄUFER: Hier haben wir Lampen.
ULLA: Was kostet die Lampe hier?
VERKÄUFER: DM 350, -. Die ist aus Italien.
ULLA: Die ist sehr schön, aber zu teuer.
VERKÄUFER: Hier ist eine Lampe für DM 50, sehr preiswert und modern. Ein Sonderangebot.
ULLA: Gut, die nehme ich. Und wo finde ich hier Bücherregale?
VERKÄUFER: Tut mir leid. Wir haben keine° Bücherregale.

no

Dialog. Suggestion: Go over the *Neue Wörter* with students as a way of previewing the dialogue. Then let students listen to it. Ask several general questions about it. Let them read dialogue before doing the activity that follows.

Aktivität 4. Richtig oder falsch?

Correct any false statements.

1. Ulla braucht nur eine Lampe.
2. Ulla findet eine italienische Lampe schön.
3. Die Lampe aus Italien ist nicht teuer.
4. Ulla kauft die Lampe für DM 50, -.
5. Ulla findet auch ein Bücherregal für ihr Zimmer.

Aktivität 4. Suggestion: Teach the following expressions for agreement or disagreement: *Das stimmt* and *Das stimmt nicht / Quatsch!* Read statements aloud; students can respond either individually or as a group, using these expressions.

Neue Wörter

das Sonderangebot *special offer*
der Verkäufer *salesman*
nehmen *to take*

preiswert *a bargain; inexpensive*
zu *too*
Tut mir leid. *I'm sorry.*

Einkaufszentrum: Hier findet man alles, was man braucht.

> ### *Sprachnotiz*
>
> Was kostet die Lampe? **Die** kostet DM 350, - (Sie kostet...)
> Der Sessel hier ist preiswert. **Der** kostet nur DM 100, - (Er
> kostet...)
>
> Germans often just use the definite article without the noun instead
> of a personal pronoun (**er, sie, es**), particularly in conversation.

▣ **Aktivität 5.   Partnerarbeit. Wie findest du das?**

ALINGSÅS 2er-Sofa. Massivholz. Polsterkissen 60 % Polyätherflocken, 40 % Federn. Baumwollbezug, grau. 157 x 84 cm. 354.-

Schreibtisch
*Korpus Kiefer furniert,
Front Kiefer massiv,
B 135, H 75, T 64 cm.*

498.-

ASPIRANT
Bücherregal.
1 fester und
3 verstellbare
Einlegeböden.
75 x 24 cm,
176 cm hoch.

59.-

IKEA®

STUDENT Arbeitsleuchte. Schwarz oder weiß lakkiertes Metall. Mit Klemmfuß. 17.50

17.50

Traumsessel. Er soll den alten Studentensessel im Erker (großes Foto) ersetzen. Der lederne Ohrensessel („unübertroffen gemütlich") stammt aus England, ist aufgearbeitet, soll 3500 Mark kosten

BEISPIEL: A: Wie findest du den Traumsessel?
            B: Sehr schön. Und wie findest du _____ ?

	A:		B:
	die Lampe		teuer
	das Bücherregal	zu	häßlich
Wie findest du	den Schreibtisch	sehr	schön
	den Sessel	nicht	preiswert
	das Sofa		praktisch
			bequem

Was macht Spaß? Was machen Sie gern?

In chapter one you learned to say what you liked to do by using such expressions as

Essen macht Spaß.
Fotografieren macht Spaß.

Now you will learn yet another simple way of expressing your likes and dislikes. Take a look at the ad and the headline below. What word do they have in common?

Warum ich so gern in Hamburg arbeite

Von WOLFGANG JOOP, Hamburg

Ich lebe und arbeite in Hamburg.

Realia. Encourage students to guess what each of the lines means by using the pictures as well as the verbal cues.

▣ Analyse. Was macht Spaß?

Ergänzen Sie. What activities are described in the ad and headline?

- Wandern macht Spaß. Ich _____ gern.
- In Hamburg arbeiten macht Spaß. Ich _____ gern in Hamburg.

▣ Aktivität 6. Was machen diese Leute gern?

Match the captions and the pictures.

1. _____ Herr Wurm liest gern.
2. _____ Frau Schlemmer ißt gern.
3. _____ Ernst Immermüd schläft gern.

4. _____ Uschi und Kurt Strauß tanzen gern.
5. _____ Frau Renner läuft gern.
6. _____ Herr Becher trinkt gern.

Aktivität 6.   Suggestion: Give students time, individually or in pairs, to complete the matching exercise. Personalize the items by asking, e.g., *Wer schläft gern? Wer läuft gern?* Ask students to raise hands in response.

a.

b.

c.

d.

e.

f.

Sprachnotiz

Some verbs change their stem vowel in the **du** and **er/sie/es** forms. Four important verbs that do this are:

Ich esse gern. Er **ißt** gern.
Ich laufe gern. Er **läuft** gern.
Ich lese gern. Er **liest** gern.
Ich schlafe gern. Er **schläft** gern.

Neue Wörter

essen *to eat*
faulenzen *to be lazy*
hören *to listen to*
kochen *to cook*
laufen *to run*
lesen *to read*
rauchen *to smoke*
schlafen *to sleep*
schreiben *to write*

▣ Aktivität 7. Machen Sie das sehr gern oder nicht gern?

Use verbs from the vocabulary above as well as from the following list to say what you like and dislike doing:

arbeiten	schwimmen
fotografieren	singen
reisen	tanzen

BEISPIEL: Ich schlafe sehr gern, aber ich koche nicht gern.

Sprachnotiz

The adverb **gern** usually precedes objects.

Ich spiele gern Tennis.
Georg hört gern Musik.
Frau Schlemmer ißt gern Spaghetti.

▣ Aktivität 8. Ein Interview

Ask three people in your class, "Was machst du gern, und was machst du nicht gern?" Report your findings to the class.

BEISPIEL: Jeff reist gern, aber er tanzt nicht gern.
Sharon spielt gern Karten, aber sie kocht nicht gern.
Dave fährt gern Motorrad, aber er arbeitet nicht gern.

Aktivität 8. Suggestion: You might jot down a number of student responses. When activity is completed, ask students to identify who likes or dislikes certain activities, e.g., *Wer fährt gern Motorrad?*

Neue Wörter

der Brief *letter*
der Witz *joke*
  Witze erzählen *to tell jokes*
erzählen *to tell*

⊡ **Aktivität 9.** **Zwei deutsche Politiker: Helmut Kohl und Johannes Rau**

Im Jahre 1987 waren Kohl und Rau Kandidaten in den Wahlen (*elections*) in der Bundesrepublik. Kohl wurde Bundeskanzler.

1. Was macht Helmut Kohl gern? (Hobby)
2. Was macht Johannes Rau gern?
3. Was essen sie gern?
4. Was trinken sie gern?
5. Was für (*What kind of*) Musik hören sie gern?

Aktivität 9. Go over the *Neue Wörter* with students before answering the questions.
Follow-up: Ask students to create a similar profile for George Bush or other prominent figures.

RSM

BUNTE-STECK-BRIEF DER KANZLER-KANDIDATEN	Helmut Kohl	Johannes Rau
Alter	56 (3. 4. 1930)	56 (16. 1. 1931)
Sternzeichen	Widder	Steinbock
Vater	Hans, Steuerobersekretär	Ewald, Prediger
Bildung/Beruf	Dr. phil., Referent „Industrieverband Chemie"	Doktor ehrenhalber, Verlagsdirektor
Größe	193 cm	180 cm
Gewicht	um 110 kg	um 85 kg
Haarfarbe	grau-meliert	grau-blond
Konfession	römisch-katholisch	evangelisch
Verheiratet mit	Hannelore Renner	Christina Delius
Kinder/Alter	Walter (23), Peter (21)	Anna-Christina (3), Philip-Immanuel (2), Laura-Helena (3 Monate)
Monatseinkommen	26 020 DM brutto	20 754 DM brutto
Hobbys	Wandern, Schwimmen, Lesen, klassische Musik	Lesen, Briefe schreiben, Skat,[a] Witze[b] erzählen, klassische Musik, Jazz
Vorbild	Vater Hans, Konrad Adenauer, Priester Johannes Fink, Lehrer Prof. Otto Stamfort (Marxist)	Vater Ewald, Gustav Heinemann, Soziologe Johannes Harder
Lieblingsautor	Golo Mann	Siegfried Lenz, Heinrich Böll, Manfred Hausmann
Lieblingsmaler	Lovis Corinth, moderne Maler	Wilfried Reckewitz (aus Wuppertal)
Getränk	Pfälzer Wein	Bier (Pils)
Lieblingskomponist[c]	Mozart, Bach	Bach
Tabak	Navy Cut (Pfeife)	Stuyvesant, Pfeifentabak
Essen	Pfälzische Hausmannskost, italienische Gerichte, Karamelpudding	Heringsstip mit Bratkartoffeln
Privat-Auto	Audi 200 mit Kat.	Mercedes 230TE mit Kat.
Kleidung	dezente Farben, Marke Volkmar Arnulf (Berlin), Cordhose für die Freizeit	dunkelblau mit Weste, neuerdings Zweireiher, Cordhose für die Freizeit
Traumberuf	Förster	Dichter
Berufsziel	bleiben, was er ist	Bundespräsident

a. *a card game*
b. *jokes*
c. *favorite composer*

Immer diese Ausreden°

Immer... Excuses, excuses

In order to turn down an invitation, you could offer the following excuses.

A: Wir gehen ins Konzert.   *We're going to the concert. Will*
    Kommst du mit?   *you come along?*
B: Nein, ich habe keine Zeit.   *No, I don't have the time.*
    or
B: Nein, ich habe keine Lust.   *No, I don't feel like it.*
    or
B: Nein, ich habe kein Geld.   *No, I don't have any money.*

Aktivität 10. Hören Sie zu. Sie hören zwei kurze Dialoge.

Aktivität 10.   Suggestion: Preview content of dialogues with students by having them scan questions before listening.

1. The topic of the first conversation is
   a. work   b. dance   c. music
2. The topic of the second conversation is
   a. music   b. dance   c. walking
3. In the first conversation the invitation to come along is
   a. accepted   b. not accepted
4. In the second conversation the invitation is
   a. accepted   b. not accepted

Aktivität 11. Interaktion

Aktivität 11.   Suggestion: Students should circulate to do this activity. They should extend at least three invitations and be able to either accept or reject invitations extended to them.

You receive invitations from several people. Do you want to accept or reject the invitations?

BEISPIEL: A: Wir gehen heute tanzen. Kommst du mit?
             B: Schön. Ich komme mit. Ich tanze sehr gern.
                 or
             B: Ich habe keine Lust.

EINLADUNG (A)	REAKTION (B)
Ich gehe / Wir gehen heute	Ja, schön
in ein Rockkonzert	gut
ins Kino (*to a movie*)	Tut mir leid.
ins Theater	Ich habe
schwimmen	keine Zeit.
Tennis/Fußball spielen	keine Lust.
	kein Geld.

Ich spiele heute Fußball. Kommst du mit?

Wir gehen in ein Rockkonzert. Kommt ihr mit?

GRAMMATIK IM KONTEXT

Cases: The Nominative and the Accusative

Kasus: der Nominativ und der Akkusativ

In English, the subject and object in a sentence are indicated by their positions. The subject usually comes first and always precedes the verb. If another element, such as an adverb, is at the beginning of the sentence, the subject will be the second element. Objects follow the verb.

(Adverb)	*Subject*	*Verb*	*Direct Object*
	I	need	a new car.
Tomorrow	I	will buy	a new car.

German, unlike English, does not rely on position to differentiate between subject and object. They are indicated instead by different forms called cases.

There are four cases in German: 1. nominative (**der Nominativ**), 2. accusative (**der Akkusativ**), 3. dative (**der Dativ**), and 4. genitive (**der Genitiv**). In this chapter you will learn about the nominative and the accusative cases.

Grammatik im Kontext. This section aims to give students a concise explanation of grammar. Specific points brought up previously in a *Sprachnotiz* are elaborated. Exercises reinforce specific grammar points and incorporate them into meaningful contexts. Listening exercises in this section focus on grammar rather than on information. Whenever possible, grammar points are illustrated by authentic texts. Students are asked to analyze the texts and illustrations and to draw their own conclusions concerning a particular grammar point. Grammar sections should be previewed in class and then assigned for homework.

The nominative case is used for the subject; the accusative case is used for the direct object. You will be learning additional uses for the accusative case in later chapters.

The most important way to tell the case of a noun is by looking at the article preceding it.

▣ Analyse

Look over the following excerpt from an imaginative ad for the chain of IKEA stores and answer the questions.

Analyse. **Suggestion:** Preview in class; then assign explanation and *Analyse* for homework. Discuss the *Analyse* in class the following day.
Exploit the excerpt from the IKEA ad by personalizing it: *Was brauchst du?* Correct wrong articles in responses by modeling correctly: *Aha, Sie brauchen* _____.

Der Mensch braucht alles, der Mensch braucht nichts. Der Mensch braucht Licht[a] und Luft,[b] Liebe, Gesundheit, Glück.[c] Die Sonne.

Der Mensch braucht Geld.

Der Mensch braucht dringend Bücher. Wenigstens das Buch der Bücher.[d] Und das Telefonbuch. Und den IKEA-Katalog Der Mensch braucht eine Uhr. Die Normal-uhr, die Standuhr, die Armbanduhr. Die Eieruhr.

Der Mensch braucht Radio, Video-Recorder, HiFi-Anla-gen, Fernseher,[f] Schall-platten[g]

Was der Mensch so braucht.

Der Mensch braucht sich selbst, den Geliebten,[h] den Vater, die Mutter, den Freund. Die Kinder.

Klapptisch **SÖRGÅRDEN** Kiefer massiv, unbehandelt. Ausgeklappt: 166 x 80 cm **250.–**

Stuhl **OLOF** Kiefer massiv, klarlack-behandelt Stoffbezug **GALLAS,** braun. **69.–**

Bett **BONUS,** Kiefer, klarlackbehandelt. 90 x 200 cm, incl. Lattenrost **214.–**

Matratze **SENCELLO FAVORIT**
90 x 200 cm **109.–**
Steppdecke ASP, 150 x 200 cm **35.–**
Kopfkissen ASP, 50 x 60 cm **14.–**
Leintuch SOVA, weiß, 150 x 250 cm **19.–**

a. *light*
b. *air*
c. *happiness*
d. Wenigstens... *At least the book of books.*
e. *watch*
f. *T.V.*
g. *records*
h. *beloved*   RSM

- What is the subject in these sentences?
- What are the direct objects in this text?
- What are the definite articles preceding the direct objects?
- Several direct object nouns are preceded by a definite article that is different from **der, die, das.** What is this article? What is the gender of these nouns?

- Find two nouns in the plural. What is the definite article preceding one of them?

The Definite Article: Nominative and Accusative

	SINGULAR			PLURAL
	Masculine	*Neuter*	*Feminine*	*all genders*
Nominative	**der**	**das**	**die**	**die**
Accusative	**den**	**das**	**die**	**die**

Note that only in the masculine singular form does the accusative differ from the nominative. In the plural, there is only one article for all three genders.

To ask for the subject of a sentence, ask **wer** (*who*) or **was** (*what*). To ask for the direct object, ask **wen** (*whom*) or **was.**

Wer sucht ein Zimmer? *Who is looking for a room?*
Wen besucht Frau Martin? *Whom is Mrs. Martin visiting?*

Special Masculine Nouns

Most nouns do not change in the accusative case. A few masculine nouns, however, have a special ending in the accusative.* Three important nouns of this type are:

	Singular		
Nominative	der Mensch	der Student	der Herr
Accusative	den Mensch**en**	den Student**en**	den Herr**n**

These masculine nouns are listed in the vocabulary section as follows: **der Mensch (-n** masc.).

▣ Übung 1. Fragen und Antworten

Wie findest du das? Wie heißt das?

BEISPIEL: A: Wie heißt der Deutschprofessor?
B: Er heißt Hartung.

Übung 1. **Suggestion:** Have students alternate asking questions and responding.

---

*These so-called **-n** masculine nouns take an **-en** or **-n** ending in all cases except for the nominative.

A: Wie findest du den Professor?
B: Ich finde den Professor interessant.

A:
Wie heißt _____
Wie findest du _____
   der Film mit (*with*) _____
   das Buch von (*by*) _____
   das Restaurant in _____
   der Student
   die Studentin

B:
interessant/langweilig
modern/unmodern
teuer/billig/preiswert
praktisch/unpraktisch
tolerant/intolerant
sympathisch/unsympathisch

▣ Übung 2. Was kaufen Sie?

Sie brauchen Möbel für Ihr Zimmer und haben nur DM 500, -. Was kaufen Sie?

TARPAN
Kinderstuhl.
Unbehandeltes
Massivholz. Sitzhöhe 31 cm. 15.–

a. *Take a break!* **RSM**

Check pages 57 and 64 for additional suggestions. Which of the items in the ads would you buy? Compare how you and your classmates would spend your money.

BEISPIEL: Ich kaufe den Fernsehsessel für DM 398, -.

The Indefinite Article: Nominative and Accusative   Der unbestimmte Artikel

The indefinite article **ein/eine** (*a, an*) indicates that the person or object being referred to is representative of a class.

> Österreich ist ein Land. Wien ist eine Stadt.

	Masculine	Neuter	Feminine
Nominative	**ein**	**ein**	**eine**
Accusative	**einen**	**ein**	**eine**

Note that the masculine and neuter nominative forms of the indefinite article are the same. As with the definite article, only the masculine accusative form differs from the nominative form. The indefinite article has no plural.

Was ist das?

ein Fussballspieler

Sprachnotiz

Germans normally state their occupation and nationality without using an indefinite article.

> Was sind Sie von Beruf, Herr Schneider? Ich bin Journalist.
> Sind Sie Engländerin, Frau Roberts? Nein, ich bin Amerikanerin.

Übung 3. Identifizieren Sie diese Dinge.°

Identifizieren... *Identify these items.*

BEISPIEL: Was ist Nummer sieben?
　　　　　　 Das ist ein Kugelschreiber.

_____ das Buch
_____ der Kugelschreiber
_____ die Lampe
_____ das Radio
_____ der Regenschirm
_____ der Sessel
_____ der Stuhl
_____ das Telefon
_____ der Tisch
_____ die Uhr

1.　2.　3.　4.　5.

6.　7.　8.　9.　10.

☑ Übung 4. **Was haben Sie in Ihrem Zimmer?**

BEISPIEL: Ich habe ein Bücherregal und ein Bett.

Nützliche Wörter:
  der Computer
  der Fernsehapparat (*TV*)
  der Wecker (*alarm clock*)

☑ Übung 5. **Was brauchen Sie dringend°?**

Indicate several things that you really need.

The Plural of Nouns

Substantive im Plural

German forms the plural of nouns in several different ways. Some nouns stay the same in the plural, others add one of a number of different endings. Certain nouns change their stem vowel in the plural. Since, in most cases, you cannot predict what the plural will be, make it a habit to memorize each noun with its plural form. Following are some examples of different noun plurals and the way each plural pattern will be listed in the vocabulary sections, beginning with this chapter.

Noun	Plural	Plural Pattern	Notation
das Zimmer	die Zimmer	*no change*	(-)
der Stuhl	die Stühle	*stem vowel is umlauted; ending* **-e** *is added*	(¨e)
die Frau	die Frauen	*ending* **-en** *is added*	(-en)
der Mann	die Männer	*stem vowel is umlauted; ending* **-er** *is added*	(¨er)
das Auto	die Autos	*ending* **-s** *is added*	(-s)

A couple of simple rules will help you form the plurals of some nouns.

1. The plural of masculine nouns denoting nationality or a profession and ending in **-er** is identical to the singular.

SINGULAR	PLURAL
der Amerikaner	die Amerikaner
der Reporter	die Reporter

2. Feminine nouns ending in **-in** form the plural by adding **-nen** to the singular.

SINGULAR	PLURAL
die Amerikanerin	die Amerikanerinnen
die Journalistin	die Journalistinnen

□ **Übung 6. Wie viele?°**

Wie... How many?

List items in your classroom, students in your class, and things that you and your friends own.

BEISPIEL: **Das Klassenzimmer hat 25 Stühle und 27 Studenten!**

das Klassenzimmer
die Deutschklasse
ich
mein Freund / meine Freundin

Fenster (-)
Tür (-en)
Stuhl (¨e)
Tisch (-e)
Student (-en)
Studentin (-nen)
Buch (¨er)
Freund (-e)
Freundin (-nen)
Uhr (-en)
Problem (-e)

☐ Übung 7. Rollenspiel. Was brauchen Sie noch?

You are shopping for several items. Think of at least five different items you could use.

Übung 7.   This activity will be more successful if you take a few moments beforehand to brainstorm what items students could use.

> BEISPIEL: A: Haben Sie Lampen? Ich brauche eine Lampe für mein Zimmer.
> B: Hier haben wir Lampen.
> A: Was kosten die Lampen?
> B: 250 Mark pro Stück.
> A: Das ist aber teuer.

Here are some additional noun plurals:

Betten	Uhren
Radios	Videorecorder
Sessel	Wecker
Sofas	

The Negative Article: *kein*

Der Negativartikel

In chapter one you learned to negate a simple statement by adding the word **nicht** (*not*) before a predicate adjective.

> Die Lampe ist **nicht** billig.   *The lamp is not inexpensive.*

You can also use **nicht** to negate an entire statement, or just an adverb.

> Karin kauft die Lampe **nicht.**   *Karin is not buying the lamp.*
> Sie findet die Lampe **nicht** schön.   *She doesn't think the lamp is nice.*

You will learn more about the placement of **nicht** later on.

One other important way to express negation is by using the negative article **kein.**

Use **kein** (*no, not a, not any*) to negate a noun that would normally be preceded by an indefinite article or no article at all.

Hast du Geld? —Nein, ich habe **kein** Geld.	*Do you have money? —No, I have no money.*
Ist das ein Problem? —Nein, das ist **kein** Problem.	*Is that a problem? —No, that is not a problem.*
Hast du Zeit, Uschi? —Nein, ich habe **keine** Zeit.	*Do you have time, Uschi? —No, I don't have any time.*

In the singular, the negative article **kein** takes the same endings as the indefinite article. Unlike **ein,** however, **kein** has plural forms that take their endings from the plural forms of the definite article.

	SINGULAR			PLURAL
	Masculine	*Neuter*	*Feminine*	*all genders*
Nominative	kein	kein	keine	keine
Accusative	keinen	kein	keine	keine

◻ **Übung 8. Ergänzen Sie:** *kein*

1. A: Ich gehe ins Kino. Kommst du mit?
   B: Nein, ich habe heute _____ Zeit.
2. A: Hast du Hunger?
   B: Nein, ich habe _____ Hunger.
3. A: Ich brauche eine Lampe.
   B: Wir haben _____ Lampen hier.
4. A: Brauchst du einen Regenschirm?
   B: Nein, ich brauche _____ Regenschirm.
5. A: Braucht Ulla ein Zimmer?
   B: Nein, sie braucht _____ Zimmer.
6. A: Hat Ulla einen Freund?
   B: Im Moment hat sie _____ Freund.
7. A: Ich brauche dringend Geld.
   B: Ich habe _____ Geld im Moment.
8. A: Ich gehe jetzt essen. Kommst du mit?
   B: Nein, ich habe _____ Lust und _____ Geld.
9. A: Es ist wirklich ein Problem. Es gibt hier _____ Wohnungen für Studenten.

Übung 8. Suggestion: Pair students to do these question-and-answer exchanges, alternating as they proceed. Spot-check several responses by repeating question or statement and letting individuals respond.

◻ **Übung 9. Partnerarbeit: Was ich habe, und was ich nicht habe**

Take turns asking each other what you have and giving answers.

BEISPIEL: A: Hast du einen Wecker?
           B: Nein, ich habe keinen Wecker.

Übung 9. Suggestion: Turn the results of this exercise into a listening activity for the whole group, e.g., *Wer hat keinen Videorecorder?* Students demonstrate their comprehension by raising their hands when they have the item.

das Auto   das Haus
der CD Player   das Motorrad
der Fernsehapparat   der Videorecorder
der Freund   eine Villa in Spanien
die Freundin   der Wecker
das Geld

The Verb *haben*

Ein Gespräch zwischen zwei Studenten. Es ist Mittagszeit (noon).

JÜRGEN: Grüß dich, Petra. Hast du Hunger?

PETRA: Warum fragst du?

JÜRGEN: Ich gehe jetzt essen. Ich habe Hunger. Kommst du mit?

PETRA: Na gut. Da kommt übrigens der Hans. Der hat bestimmt auch Hunger. Ich hab' aber nicht viel Zeit. Um zwei haben wir eine Vorlesung.

HANS: Habt ihr zwei vielleicht Hunger?

▣ Analyse

- What different forms of the verb **haben** do you find in the dialogue?
- The **ich** form of **haben** appears in two different ways. What are they? One is the traditional way, the other a more conversational way that reflects the way Germans usually speak.* Which do you think is the traditional form, which the conversational form? Explain your choice.

Here are the present tense forms of **haben.**

Singular	Plural
ich habe	wir haben
Sie haben	Sie haben
du hast	ihr habt
er ⎫	
sie ⎬ hat	sie haben
es ⎭	

The Verb *haben*. Suggestion: Have students first scan the *Analyse* to familiarize themselves with the information requested. Then let them read the text. Have them work in pairs to complete the *Analyse*.

---

*In informal spoken German, the **-e** of the **ich** form is dropped for nearly all verbs.

Ich geh' jetzt nach Hause.   *I am going home now.*

The verb **haben,** like many other verbs, needs an accusative object (a direct object).

Ich habe **Hunger.**	*I am hungry.*
Wir haben **eine Vorlesung** um zwei Uhr.	*We have a lecture at two o'clock.*
Die Wohnung hat **vier Zimmer.**	*The apartment has four rooms.*

Verbs like **haben**—verbs that need an accusative object—are called transitive verbs. Some other transitive verbs you already know are **brauchen, finden, kaufen,** and **suchen.**

Verbs that need no accusative (direct) object are called intransitive verbs. Besides **sein** and **heißen,** some other intransitive verbs you already know include **bleiben, kommen, wandern,** and **wohnen.**

▣ Übung 10. Kommst du mit?

Everyone has a different excuse for not coming.

Übung 10. Suggestion: Personalize this activity by having half the class make up invitations and the other half excuses. Call on one individual to invite another to do something. The other must give an excuse.

1. A: Kommt ihr mit ins Kino?
    B: Wir _____ kein Geld.
2. A: Kommst du mit ins Museum, Jens?
    B: Ich _____ keine Lust.
3. A: Herr Becher, _____ Sie jetzt Zeit für eine Tasse Kaffee?
    B: Tut mir leid, ich _____ im Moment keine Zeit.
4. A: Peter, _____ du Lust, ins Kino zu gehen?
    B: Ich _____ keine Zeit, aber vielleicht _____ die Inge Zeit.
5. A: Was meinst du, _____ Karin und Annemarie jetzt Zeit für eine Tasse Kaffee?
    B: Sie _____ morgen eine Prüfung. Die _____ bestimmt keine Zeit.

▣ Übung 11. Hast du Hunger?

Ergänzen Sie: **haben** oder **sein**

Jürgen, Petra und Hans _____[1] Studenten. Es _____[2] gerade Mittagszeit. Jürgen _____[3] Hunger. Er fragt Petra: "_____[4] du Hunger?" Hans _____[5] Petras Freund. Hans und Petra _____[6] um zwei eine Vorlesung. Sie _____[7] nicht viel Zeit. Und Jürgen _____[8] nicht viel Geld. Er fragt Hans: "_____[9] du etwas Geld?"

Verbs with Stem-Vowel Changes

A number of verbs have important vowel changes in the second- and third-person singular of the present tense.

1. a → ä   fahren: du **fährst,** er/sie/es **fährt**
              schlafen: du **schläfst,** er/sie/es **schläft**
2. au → äu   laufen: du **läufst,** er/sie/es **läuft**
3. e → i   nehmen: du **nimmst,** er/sie/es **nimmt**
              essen: du **ißt,** er/sie/es **ißt**
4. e → ie   lesen: du **liest,** er/sie/es **liest**
              sehen: du **siehst,** er/sie/es **sieht**

Here are the present-tense forms of **nehmen,** which has not only stem vowel changes, but some other changes as well.

Singular	Plural
ich nehme	wir nehmen
Sie nehmen	Sie nehmen
du nimmst	ihr nehmt
er sie } nimmt es	sie nehmen

Note that the vowel changes occur in the second-person and third-person singular forms only. All the other verb forms are based on the stem of the infinitive. Verbs with vowel changes will be indicated as such in the vocabulary sections of each chapter (**schlafen, schläft**).

▣ Übung 12.   Was machen sie gern?

Ergänzen Sie den Text.

Übung 12.   Note: This activity recycles *gern* in addition to practicing stem-vowel-change verbs.

1. Ich _____ gern italienisch, Karin _____ gern chinesisch. (essen)
2. Klaus und Petra essen heute im Restaurant. Petra _____ Fisch und Klaus _____ ein Wienerschnitzel. (nehmen)
3. Hans braucht eine Lampe. Er _____ eine supermoderne Lampe im Kaufhaus. (sehen)
4. Ilse _____ gern Auto. Morgen _____ wir nach Berlin. (fahren)
5. Herr Renner _____ jeden Tag im Park. Dort _____ viele Jogger. (laufen)
6. Was _____ du gern? Ich _____ gern Detektivromane. (lesen)

Neue Wörter

nie *never*
oft *often*
viel *a lot*

◫ **Übung 13.** **Partnerarbeit: Was machen Sie gern, oft, viel, manchmal, nie?**

Tell a partner several things you do or don't like to do: **gern, manchmal,** etc. Report to the class what your partner has been doing.

> BEISPIEL: A: Ich esse gern, ich tanze manchmal, ich laufe nie.
>   B: John ißt gern, tanzt manchmal und läuft nie.

Übung 13.   **Suggestion:** As students tell each other several things they like to do, have them jot down the activities. This will facilitate reporting them to the class.

arbeiten	reisen
Auto/Motorrad fahren	schlafen
essen	schwimmen
faulenzen	tanzen
Karten/Tennis/Fußball spielen	trinken
laufen	wandern
lesen	

Demonstrative Pronouns

Demonstrativpronomen

ROBERT: Was kostet der Schreibtisch hier?

VERKÄUFERIN: **Der** kostet 1.000 Mark.

ULLA: Wie findest du meine neue Lampe?

ROBERT: **Die** finde ich prima.

HERR HOLZ: Was kostet der Tisch hier?

VERKÄUFER: **Der** kostet nur 250 Mark.

FRAU HOLZ: Gut, **den** nehmen wir.

In the preceding dialogues, a definite article sometimes appears without a noun at the beginning of a sentence. The article refers to a previously mentioned noun. In such a situation, the definite article becomes a demonstrative pronoun and the noun is understood. The demonstrative pronoun is used for emphasis. It is usually placed at the beginning of the sentence.

◫ **Übung 14.** **Was machen diese Leute?**

Kombinieren Sie.

> BEISPIEL: A: Was macht Herr Renner?
>   B: Der läuft schon wieder im Park.

Übung 14.   **Suggestion:** Give students time to scan the sentence builder. Have them alternate asking and responding.

Frau Schlemmer	lesen	den ganzen Tag
Herr Wurm	essen	schon wieder einen Detektivroman
mein Freund	faulenzen	schon wieder Spaghetti
mein Zimmergenosse	schlafen	gern Motorrad
meine Freundin	fahren	im Park
Herr Renner	laufen	immer in der Klasse

▣ Übung 15. Partnerabeit

Wie findest du das? Wie findest du diese Person?

> BEISPIEL: A: Wie findest du das Buch?
> B: Das finde ich interessant.

der Film (*Name*)	phantastisch
die Musik von ____	toll
der Schauspieler (*Name*)	langweilig
die Schauspielerin (*Name*)	prima
der Sänger, die Sängerin	miserabel
eine Person (*Name*)	ausgezeichnet
die Leute hier	sehr gut
	nicht besonders gut
	schlecht

Übung 15. Suggestion: Have students alternate asking and answering. Students respond by using the demonstrative pronoun. Pay attention to the intonation pattern, emphasizing the demonstrative pronoun at the beginning of each response.

LESEN IM KONTEXT

Wie und wo wohnen junge Leute in Deutschland? In this section you will look at texts focusing on housing possibilities for young people in the Federal Republic of Germany.

Vor dem Lesen

▣ Aktivität. Wie wohnen Sie?

Arbeiten Sie zu zweit. Welche Information trifft auf Sie zu?

1. Ich wohne ____.
   a. in einem Studentenheim
   b. in einer Wohnung
   c. bei meinen Eltern
   d. in meinem eigenen Haus
   e. privat in einem Zimmer
   f. ?

Lesen im Kontext. These sections focus on developing effective reading strategies. The selections in this chapter introduce basic techniques such as skimming, scanning, and reading for specific information. You should stress recognizing cognates and guessing from context. The texts are not meant to be read aloud in class. Students will need a lot of reassurance and encouragement to develop a positive attitude toward reading authentic material. The texts will seem daunting if approached word for word, but with proper application of the strategies suggested here, students will learn to enjoy taking risks when exploring an unknown text.

2. Ich teile (*share*) mein Zimmer / meine Wohnung / mein Haus mit
   _____ .
   a. einer anderen Person
   b. zwei, drei, vier, ... Personen
   c. niemand anderem. Ich wohne allein.
3. Ich habe _____ .
   a. eine Katze
   b. einen Hund
   c. einen Goldfisch
   d. andere Haustiere (eine Kobra, einen Kanarienvogel, ...)
   e. keine Haustiere
4. Ich wohne gern / nicht gern _____ .
   a. in einer Großstadt
   b. in einer Kleinstadt
   c. auf dem Land
5. Als Student hat man hier _____ Probleme, eine Wohnung zu finden.
   a. keine
   b. manchmal
   c. große
6. Die Mieten sind _____ hier.
   a. niedrig (*low*)
   b. hoch

Report to the class what you found out about your partner.

Auf den ersten Blick

The pictures and excerpts from German newspapers in this reading illustrate some of the difficulties faced by students in Berlin and Bonn. They are typical of other popular German university cities as well. Familiarize yourself with the vocabulary before reading the texts.

Neue Wörter

die Bibliothek *library*
die Bude *room (slang term used by students)*
die Mensa *student cafeteria*
der Platz (¨e) *space, place*
das Seminar *university department*

übernachten *to stay overnight*

1. Scan the headlines and boldfaced texts as well as the pictures. Judging from these, what are the most pressing needs of German students?
2. Find information that talks about numbers: enrollment figures, over-enrollment, number of applicants, etc.

Wir brauchen ein Dach! Studenten und ihre Probleme

Berliner Hochschulen platzen aus allen Nähten

Neue Rekordmarke: An der FU gibt's 59 000 Studenten

„Wir haben 5000 Studenten, aber nur 1000 Plätze", stöhnt Björn Loeser (22) von der Fachschaft Jura.

Fünf Mark fürs Bett
Studenten bezahlen fünf Mark für ein Bett in einer Notunterkunft.[a]

Bonner Uni–38 500 Studenten

Für Gwenola Le Martelot (21) aus Paris sind die Mietpreise einfach zu hoch. Die Germanistik-Studentin kann 300 Mark ausgeben.

„Rund 1000 Mark brauchst du als Student", rechnet mir Jura-student Björn Loeser (23) vor. Unter 280 Mark findest du keine Bude im Anzeigenteil oder am Schwarzen Brett.

Rund 1000 Mark brauchst du als Student

Viele müssen schon in ihren Autos schlafen

Kamal Louh (19), Zahnmedizin-Student an der FU:„Bislang haben alle Vermieter gesagt, daß sie nicht an Ausländer vermieten." Seit zwei Monaten schläft er bei Freunden.

Studenten sind faul, demonstrieren gern, finden nach dem Examen keine Jobs.

Am wildesten aber geht's bei den Germanisten[c] zu—5292 studieren Deutsch.

Halbes Jahr auf Budensuche
300 Mark Belohnung für die Vermittlung einer Wohnung"- Zettel[e] von Studenten, die eine Bude suchen, hängen am Schwarzen Brett der Mensa. Klaus Wardenbach (24) sucht schon ein halbes Jahr.   Fotos: Karin Knobloch

Schlaue[d] übernachten in der Bibliothek
„Ganz Schlaue haben sich sogar schon im Seminar einschließen lassen und im Schlafsack zwischen den rund 100 000 Büchern der Bibliothek übernachtet", erzählt Examenskandidatin Roswitha Wensel (26).

Billige Wohnungen sind rar

a. *emergency housing*
b. *So far*
c. *German majors*
d. *Clever ones*
e. *notes*
f. *bulletin board at a university (literally "black board")*

RSM

Zum Text

1. **Wo übernachten die Studenten?** Place a check mark by those places that are mentioned in the texts.
   _____ in der Mensa
   _____ in Vorlesungsräumen
   _____ in Hotels
   _____ im Park
   _____ im Auto
   _____ in der Bibliothek
   _____ in einer Notunterkunft
   _____ bei Freunden
   _____ auf der Straße

2. Zwei ausländische Studenten haben Probleme. Wer sind sie? Was sind ihre Probleme?

3. Wieviel Geld braucht man als Student pro Monat laut (_according to_) Björn Loeser?

Zum Text, #3. Personalize by asking _Wieviel Geld brauchen Sie hier an dieser Uni / an diesem College?_

Nach dem Lesen

☐ **Aktivität 1.** **Sie schreiben eine Anzeige.°**

_ad_

One of your housemates has moved out, and you and your other housemate want to advertise your new vacancy. Using the advertisements in this chapter as guides (pages 53 and 55), create your own.
   Start with these words: **Haus/Zimmer zu vermieten...**

☐ **Aktivität 2.** **Ein Interview**

Aktivität 2. Encourage students to go beyond this list to think up further questions.

You have received some answers in response to your ad. Work in pairs and interview each other to see if you would be suited as roommates or housemates. Here are some possible questions:

VERMIETER:	MIETER:
Rauchen Sie?	Wie groß ist _____ ?
Haben Sie Haustiere?	Wie hoch ist die Miete?
Haben Sie ein Auto?	Haben Sie Telefon?
Telefonieren Sie viel?	Haben Sie einen Garten?
Haben Sie oft Freunde zu Besuch?	Haben Sie eine Garage?
Spielen Sie laute Musik?	Ist das Zimmer möbliert?

After you've interviewed several prospective housemates, report back to the class about whom you chose.

   BEISPIEL: Wir vermieten das Zimmer an Jeanine. Sie ist sehr nett und sympathisch. Sie spielt keine laute Musik.

WORTSCHATZ

Substantive

Möbel / Furnishings

das Bett (-en)	bed
das Bücherregal (-e)	bookshelf
der Fernsehapparat (-e)	TV
die Lampe (-n)	lamp
das Radio (-s)	radio
der Schreibtisch (-e)	desk
der Sessel (-)	easy chair
das Sofa (-s)	sofa, couch
der Stuhl (¨e)	chair
der Tisch (-e)	table

Andere Substantive

die Anzeige (-n)	advertisement
das Bad (¨er)	bathroom; bath
die Bibliothek (-en)	library
der Brief (-e)	letter
die Bude (-n)	room (*slang term used by students*)
das Dach (¨er)	roof (fig. *a roof over one's head, a place to live*)
das Ding (-e)	thing, object
das Gespräch (-e)	conversation
das Kaufhaus (¨er)	department store
das Kino (-s)	movie house
ins Kino	to the movies
die Küche (-n)	kitchen
der Kugelschreiber (-)	ballpoint pen
die Mark	mark (*German money*)
die Deutsche Mark	German mark
die Mensa	student cafeteria
die Miete (-n)	rent
der Platz (¨e)	place, space
das Problem (-e)	problem
die Prüfung (-en)	exam
der Regenschirm (-e)	umbrella
das Seminar (-e)	university department, seminar
das Sonderangebot (-e)	special offer (*at a store*)
das Stück (-e)	piece
pro Stück	each, per piece
das Telefon (-e)	telephone
die Uhr (-en)	watch, clock
der Verkäufer (-), die Verkäuferin (-nen)	salesperson
die Vorlesung (-en)	lecture
der Wecker (-)	alarm clock
der Witz (-e)	joke
die Wohnung (-en)	apartment
die Zeit	time
das Zimmer (-)	room

Adjektive und Adverbien

bequem	comfortable
bestimmt	to be sure, for certain
billig	cheap, inexpensive
dringend	urgent
endlich	finally
gern(e)	gladly
häßlich	ugly
hoch	high
immer	always
klein	little, small
möbliert	furnished
nie	never
niedrig	low
oft	often
preiswert	a bargain, inexpensive
teuer	expensive
toll	great (*colloquial*)
übrigens	by the way
viel	much, a lot
vielleicht	perhaps
wieder	again
schon wieder	yet again (*emphatic*)

Verben

erzählen	to tell, narrate
essen (ißt)	to eat
fahren (fährt)	to drive
faulenzen	to be lazy
fragen	to ask
haben	to have
Hunger haben	to be hungry
Lust haben	to feel like doing something
hören	to listen to; hear
kochen	to cook
kosten	to cost
laufen (läuft)	to run
lesen (liest)	to read

mieten	to rent		
nehmen (nimmt)	to take		
rauchen	to smoke		
schlafen (schläft)	to sleep		
schreiben	to write		
schwimmen	to swim		
sehen (sieht)	to see		
trinken	to drink		
übernachten	to stay overnight		

Sonstiges

Bitte sehr?	May I help you? (*in a store*)
Es geht mir (prima).	I'm fine.
Kommst du mit?	Are you coming along?
Schau mal!	Look!
Tut mir leid.	I'm sorry.
Was ist denn los?	What's the matter?
wieviel	how much
wie viele	how many
zu	too
zu vermieten	for rent

KAPITEL 3

FAMILIE UND FREUNDE

Lernziele *In this chapter you'll be talking about family and friends, special events in your life, inviting someone to a party, and wishing someone a happy birthday.*

Kapitel 3. Introduce the chapter theme (family, friends, special events) by talking about your own experiences. Discuss cultural differences by mentioning that Germans consider fewer people to be their friends than we do in the U.S. Germans distinguish carefully between friends and acquaintances. The use of *du* and *Sie* emphasizes this distinction.

Aus dem Familienalbum: Meine Familie

Das ist meine Familie. Das sind meine Eltern, mein Bruder Klaus und meine Schwester Heike. Und das bin ich. Meine Schwester Heike wird im April 21. Mein Bruder Klaus ist 15, und ich bin 22 Jahre alt.

Mein Vater ist Ingenieur von Beruf und meine Mutter ist Lehrerin. Wir haben ein Einfamilienhaus mit Garten und Garage in Düsseldorf. Ich studiere Architektur in Berlin und komme nur ab und zu nach Hause.

Aus dem Familienalbum. Suggestion: Focus students' attention on the picture. You can read the text aloud as students look at it.
Follow-up: Ask students about their own family members. Begin with cognate items: *Haben Sie einen Bruder? Wie heißt er? Wie alt ist er?*

Meine Familie: Klaus, Heike, meine Eltern, und ich

Familie Fischer: ein Porträt. Ergänzen Sie die Information.

Familie Fischer wohnt in _____. Herr und Frau Fischer haben _____ Kinder: _____ Söhne und _____ Tochter.

    Ihre Tochter heißt _____. Sie ist _____ Jahre alt. Im April wird sie _____.

    Ein Sohn ist 15 Jahre alt und heißt _____. Der andere heißt Horst, ist 22 und studiert in Berlin. Familie Fischer hat ein Einfamilienhaus mit _____ und _____.

Alles klar? Have students work in pairs to complete the text. Check accuracy of responses by having several students read segments aloud.

Ein Familienstammbaum. Suggestion: You can begin by asking general questions on the illustration, e.g., *Wie heißen die Kinder von Herrn Fischer?*

WÖRTER IM KONTEXT

Ein Familienstammbaum

Aktivität 1: **Suggestion:** Before doing *Aktivität 1*, bring up the *Sprachnotiz* on page 84. Point out that the preposition *von* plus a name can also be used to express a relationship and is, in fact, preferred when a proper name ends in *s* (*der Vater von Hans*). Assign as homework for reinforcement or have students complete the activity in pairs.

◨ **Aktivität 1.** **Horst Fischers Familie**

1. Horst hat vier Großeltern. Wer sind sie? Was heißt mütterlicherseits und väterlicherseits?
2. Wie heißt Horsts Großmutter mütterlicherseits? Und väterlicherseits?
3. Wie viele Kinder haben seine Großeltern väterlicherseits?
4. Horsts Mutter hat einen Bruder. Er ist Horsts _____.
5. Horsts Vater hat eine Schwester. Sie ist Horsts _____.
6. Tante Elfriede und ihr Mann haben nur eine Tochter. Sie heißt Anneliese und ist Horsts _____.
7. Horsts Onkel Heinz und seine Frau Karin haben zwei Kinder. Hans ist Horsts _____, und Helga ist seine _____.

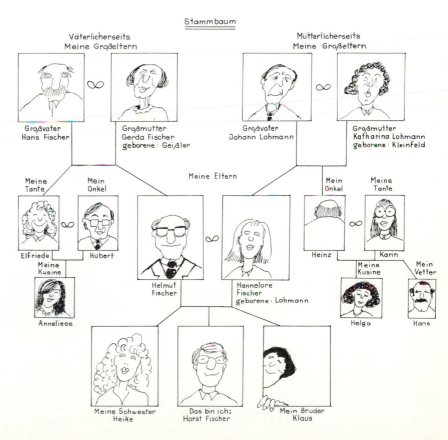

Stammbaum

Väterlicherseits Meine Großeltern

Mütterlicherseits Meine Großeltern

Großvater Hans Fischer — Großmutter Gerda Fischer geborene: Geißler

Großvater Johann Lohmann — Großmutter Katharina Lohmann geborene: Kleinfeld

Meine Eltern

Meine Tante Elfriede — Mein Onkel Hubert

Meine Kusine Anneliese

Helmut Fischer — Hannelore Fischer geborene: Lohmann

Mein Onkel Heinz — Meine Tante Karin

Meine Kusine Helga — Mein Vetter Hans

Meine Schwester Heike

Das bin ich: Horst Fischer

Mein Bruder Klaus

Sprachnotiz

To indicate a person's family relationships or possessions when a proper name is used, just add an *s* to the person's name, without an apostrophe.

> Das ist Horsts Familie.
> Helgas Mutter ist Horsts Tante.
> Das ist Familie Fischers Haus.

▣ Aktivität 2. Ein Interview

Fragen Sie eine Person in Ihrer Klasse nach seiner/ihrer Familie. Berichten Sie dann in der Klasse (*Report in class about your partner's family*).

1. Wo wohnt deine Familie?
2. Wie viele Geschwister (Brüder und Schwestern) hast du?
3. Wie heißen deine Geschwister?
4. Wie heißen deine Eltern mit Vornamen?
5. Wie alt sind deine Geschwister?
6. _____ (sonstige Fragen)?

Aktivität 2.   Suggestion: Before doing this activity, brainstorm possible questions with students for #6. Then have students work in pairs to interview each other, taking notes. Ask several students to report their findings.

▣ Aktivität 3. Generationen: Wer ist wer?

1. Wie viele Generationen sind auf diesem Bild?
2. Wie heißen die Frauen mit Vornamen?
3. Wie heißen die zwei jüngsten (*youngest*) Frauen? Wie alt sind sie?
4. Wer ist die älteste (*oldest*) Frau? Wie alt ist sie?
5. Wer ist die Mutter von Susanne und Nicole?
6. Wer ist die Großmutter von Frauke?
7. Wer ist die Tochter von Pauline?
8. Wer ist die Großmutter von Frauke?

Aktivität 3.   Suggestion: Students can work in pairs to ask and answer the questions.

RSM

Landeskinder: Tochter Susanne, 18, Großmutter Alma, 63, Tochter Nicole, 19, Urgroßmutter Pauline, 87, Mutter Frauke, 40

▣ Aktivität 4. Eine Familie

Ergänzen Sie die fehlende Information.

1. Susanne und Nicole sind Fraukes _____ .
2. Pauline ist Susannes und Nicoles _____ und Fraukes _____ .
3. Alma ist Paulines _____ und Susannes und Nicoles _____ .
4. _____ spielt gern Fußball. Sie ist Paulines Enkelin.
5. Alma hat zwei Enkelinnen, _____ und _____ . Und wer ist das in der Mitte? Sie gehört (*belongs*) auch zur Familie.

Aktivität 4. Suggestion: This activity is a summary of *Aktivität 3*. To reinforce new vocabulary, it can be done as a whole-group activity or as a homework assignment.

Neue Wörter

der Enkel *grandson*
die Enkelin *granddaughter*
der Geburtstag *birthday*
der Neffe (-n *masc.*) *nephew*
die Nichte *niece*
die Urgroßmutter *great-grandmother*

merkwürdig *peculiar, strange*
feiern *to celebrate*
es gibt *there is/there are*
kennen *to know* (a person)

▣ Aktivität 5. Ein merkwürdiger Stammbaum

RSM

1. Eine ganze Familie feiert Geburtstag. Wie heißt diese Familie?
2. Wen gibt es, und wen gibt es nicht in diesem Stammbaum? **Beispiel:** Es gibt einen Großvater, aber es gibt keine Großmutter.
3. Wie alt ist der Großvater? Was meinen Sie?
   a. 80 Jahre alt
   b. 100 Jahre alt
   c. 50 Jahre alt
4. Welche Namen dieser Familie kennen Sie? Welche Namen kennen Sie nicht?
5. Wie heißt der **Käfer** auf englisch?

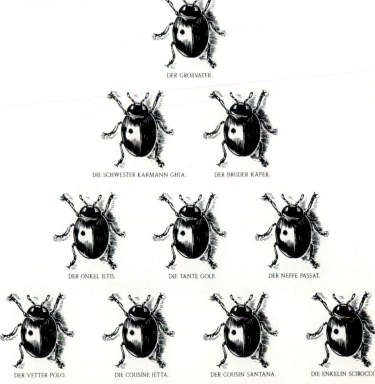

DER GROSSVATER.

DIE SCHWESTER KARMANN GHIA.   DER BRUDER KÄFER.

DER ONKEL ILTIS.   DIE TANTE GOLF.   DER NEFFE PASSAT.

DER VETTER POLO.   DIE COUSINE JETTA.   DER COUSIN SANTANA.   DIE ENKELIN SCIROCCO.

Wir gratulieren der ganzen Familie.

Aktivität 5. Suggestion: Students should first scan the realia as well as the accompanying questions. Then ask them to complete the activity, asking each other the questions. Elicit responses from students as a whole group.

Familienangelegenheiten°

 **Dialog**

Family matters

Frau Fischer und Herr Schmidt reden über ihre Familien.

HERR SCHMIDT: Guten Tag, Frau Fischer.
FRAU FISCHER: Ja, guten Tag, Herr Schmidt. Wie geht es Ihnen denn?
HERR SCHMIDT: Danke, gut. Und Ihnen?
FRAU FISCHER: Danke, auch gut.
HERR SCHMIDT: Und was macht Ihre Familie?
FRAU FISCHER: Unser Horst ist jetzt in Berlin an der Technischen Universität.
HERR SCHMIDT: So? Was studiert er denn?
FRAU FISCHER: Architektur.
HERR SCHMIDT: So. Das ist ja schön. Unser Andreas geht jetzt für ein Semester nach Texas als Austauschstudent. Und was macht Ihre Tochter?
FRAU FISCHER: Die Heike wird jetzt 21. Sie hat endlich einen Studienplatz ... in Münster. Jetzt braucht sie noch eine Wohnung. Das ist wirklich ein Problem.
HERR SCHMIDT: Unsere Helga heiratet übrigens im April ... ihren alten Schulfreund, den Oliver Reich.
FRAU FISCHER: Ach ja? Na, das wird ja sicher ein großes Familienfest.

Dialog. Suggestion: Preview the statements in *Aktivität 6* before students hear the dialogue. They should listen once and try to answer as many questions as possible in *Aktivität 6*. Then let them hear the dialogue a second time as they read along, completing any unanswered questions.

◱ Aktivität 6. Richtig oder falsch?

Correct statements that are wrong.

1. Herr Schmidt kennt die Familie Fischer gut.
2. Frau Fischer geht es nicht so gut.
3. Frau Fischers Sohn studiert Medizin in Berlin.
4. Heike Fischer hat einen Studienplatz in Münster, aber keine Wohnung.
6. Herrn Schmidts Sohn geht für ein Jahr als Austauschstudent nach Amerika.
7. In der Familie Schmidt gibt es im April einen Geburtstag.
8. Helga Schmidt heiratet einen Schulfreund.

Neue Wörter

der Austauschstudent *exchange student*
das Familienfest *family celebration*
heiraten *to get married*
reden über *to talk about*
Was macht _____?
How is _____?

Sprachnotiz

Die Heike, unsere Heike, der Horst, unser Andreas: When Germans talk casually about family members or friends, they sometimes add the definite article or a possessive adjective (**mein, unser**) before the proper name.

Ich bin die Jutta und bin im Service für Sie da!

Hotel Braam
Emmericher Straße 161 (B 220)
4190 Kleve-Kellen

RSM

▢▢▢▢ *Kulturnotiz*

Space at German universities is at a premium. Overcrowded universities and over-enrolled fields of study have led to a system of distributing the limited spaces (**Studienplätze**) available for specific majors through a national distribution agency. High-school grades and the prospective university major play a role in how long a student will have to wait for a **Studienplatz.** Often the choice of where to study is very limited. The distributing agency will assign a place to a student. It has become popular among students to trade places in order to study at the university of their choice, if only for one semester.

Here you see a form students use to put an ad in the *Uni-Journal* to exchange **Studienplätze.**

✂ - - -

Meine Tauschanzeige

Einsenden an: UNI JOURNAL, Aktion Studienplatztausch, Westfalenstraße 98, 4300 Essen 1

Fachrichtung: _____

Biete[a]: _____   _____ Sem.

Suche: _____   _____ Sem.

Vorname: _____   Name: _____

Straße: _____

Ort: _____   Telefon: _____

DM 2,-- in Briefmarken[b] habe ich beigefügt.

_____
Unterschrift

a. *offer*
b. *stamps*

Ein Familienfest

Diese Anzeigen gibt es in deutschen Tageszeitungen, meistens in kleinen Wohnorten.

Heike
wird heute
„21"
Herzlichen Glückwunsch

Hallo, Belinda!
Viel Glück und alles Gute
zum 18.
wünschen Mutti und Papa
und der ganze Clan.
**W. W. B. U. S. U. J. D. M.
S. W. P. S. W. und Chris**

0725-1785 30.07 030-070

**Ralf hatte
Geburtstag!**
Alles Gute!

Liebe Oma *Marie Sudhoff*
zu Deinem **80. Geburtstag** wünschen Dir
Deine Kinder, Enkel und Urenkel alles
Liebe und Gute.

Lieber Vater und Opa!
Zu Deinem 85. Geburtstag gratulieren
*Hansi — Waltraud — Angela — Torsten — Birgit —
Peter — Jan und Marco*

▣ Analyse. Geburtstagswünsche

Germans express their birthday wishes in several ways.

1. Find two different expressions of good wishes in the announcements.
2. Who are the family members sending birthday greetings to Belinda and Marie Sudhoff?
3. Frau Sudhoff is being addressed as **liebe Oma.** Which family member is most likely called that way?
4. One birthday greeting gives no name, only **lieber Vater und Opa.** What do you think the word **Opa** means? Who probably put this birthday ad in the paper?

Analyse. Suggestion: Preview realia by going over the *Neue Wörter* section on p. 88 with students. Then have students work in pairs to complete the *Analyse.*

Neue Wörter

gratulieren *to congratulate*
werden (wird) *to become*
wünschen *to wish*

herzlichen Glückwunsch zum
    Geburtstag *happy birthday*
viel Glück *lots of luck*
alles Gute *best wishes*

DIE WOCHENTAGE

der Montag *Monday*
der Dienstag *Tuesday*
der Mittwoch *Wednesday*
der Donnerstag *Thursday*

der Freitag *Friday*
der Samstag (der
    Sonnabend) *Saturday*
der Sonntag *Sunday*

Days of the week: Suggestion: State your own schedule for the coming week, beginning each sentence with *Am...* Write the days of the week on the board, asking students to repeat. Accustom students to hearing the combination *am Mittwoch, am Freitag,* etc.

die Monate:

der Januar	der Februar	der März
1 2 3 4 5 6	1 2 3	1 2 3
7 8 9 10 11 12 13	4 5 6 7 8 9 10	4 5 6 7 8 9 10
14 15 16 17 18 19 20	11 12 13 14 15 16 17	11 12 13 14 15 16 17
21 22 23 24 25 26 27	18 19 20 21 22 23 24	18 19 20 21 22 23 24
28 29 30 31	25 26 27 28	25 26 27 28 29 30 31

der April	der Mai	der Juni
1 2 3 4 5 6 7	1 2 3 4 5	1 2
8 9 10 11 12 13 14	6 7 8 9 10 11 12	3 4 5 6 7 8 9
15 16 17 18 19 20 21	13 14 15 16 17 18 19	10 11 12 13 14 15 16
22 23 24 25 26 27 28	20 21 22 23 24 25 26	17 18 19 20 21 22 23
29 30	27 28 29 30 31	24 25 26 27 28 29 30

der Juli	der August	der September
1 2 3 4 5 6 7	1 2 3 4	1
8 9 10 11 12 13 14	5 6 7 8 9 10 11	2 3 4 5 6 7 8
15 16 17 18 19 20 21	12 13 14 15 16 17 18	9 10 11 12 13 14 15
22 23 24 25 26 27 28	19 20 21 22 23 24 25	16 17 18 19 20 21 22
29 30 31	26 27 28 29 30 31	23 24 25 26 27 28 29
		30

der Oktober	der November	der Dezember
1 2 3 4 5	1 2	1 2 3 4 5 6 7
6 7 8 9 10 11 12	3 4 5 6 7 8 9	8 9 10 11 12 13 14
13 14 15 16 17 18 19	10 11 12 13 14 15 16	15 16 17 18 19 20 21
20 21 22 23 24 25 26	17 18 19 20 21 22 23	22 23 24 25 26 27 28
27 28 29 30 31	24 25 26 27 28 29 30	29 30

Sprachnotiz

Use the following time phrases to say when something is taking place.

Wann wirst du 21? Ich werde **im Mai** 21.
Wann hast du Geburtstag? Ich habe **im Dezember** Geburtstag.
Wann feierst du deinen Geburtstag? **Am Samstag.**

B☼nn wird 2000

⊡ Aktivität 7. Interaktion

Wie alt bist du? Wann wirst du _____?

BEISPIEL: A: Wie alt bist du?
B: Ich bin 23.
A: Wann wirst du 24?
B: Ich werde im August 24. Und du?

Aktivität 8.   Hören Sie zu. Eine Einladung zum Geburtstag

1. Wer hat Geburtstag? _{Heike}
2. Wann ist der Geburtstag (Tag)? _{Samstag}
3. Wo ist die Party? _{bei Heike zu Hause}
4. Wer kommt sonst noch (*else*)? _{Gabi, Jürgen, Heikes Eltern and Geschwister}
5. Kommt die Person am Telefon, oder nicht? _{ja, sie kommt}

Aktivität 8.   Suggestion: Students should scan the questions before listening to the dialogue. Play the tape once; students answer as many questions as they can based on one listening. Play it a second time and have them complete any unfinished questions.

Dialog.   Eine zweite Einladung zum Geburtstag

Hören Sie den Dialog zuerst.

Dialog.   Suggestion: Students should look over the *Analyse* before listening to the dialogue. Let them read along in the text as they listen. You may want to use this as a role-play.

> HEIKE: Tag, Andreas.
> ANDREAS: Hallo, Heike. Wie geht's?
> HEIKE: Danke, es geht. Gut, daß ich dich treffe. Hast du am Samstag Zeit? Ich feiere nämlich Geburtstag. Ich möchte dich einladen.
> ANDREAS: Vielen Dank für die Einladung, Heike. Leider kann ich nicht kommen. Ich fahre nämlich nach Hamburg.
> HEIKE: Schade.

⊡ Analyse

- How does Heike state the reason for her party?
- How does Andreas thank Heike for the invitation?
- How does he decline the invitation, and what is his reason?
- How does Heike respond?

Neue Wörter

nach (Hamburg) *to (Hamburg)*
nach Hause *(going) home*
zu Hause *at home*

einladen *to invite*

Ich möchte... *I would like . . .*
treffen (trifft) *to meet*

leider *unfortunately*
schade *too bad*

Sprachnotiz

When stating your reason for an action, use the adverb **nämlich** in the explanation.

> Ich kann nicht kommen. Ich fahre **nämlich** nach Hamburg.
>
> *I cannot come. The reason is, I am going to Hamburg.*

Note that there is no particular equivalent for **nämlich** in English.

▣ Aktivität 9. Interaktion

Eine Einladung zu einer Party.

BEISPIEL: A: Ich mache am Sonntag eine Party. Ich möchte dich einladen.

B: Am Sonntag? Vielen Dank. Ich komme gern.

B: Vielen Dank. Leider kann ich nicht kommen. Ich muß nämlich arbeiten.

Other excuses:

Es tut mir leid.
Ich bin leider nicht zu Hause.
Ich fahre nämlich nach _____.
Meine Mutter hat nämlich auch Geburtstag.

GRAMMATIK IM KONTEXT

Possessive Adjectives

Use possessive adjectives (*my, his, our*) to express ownership or belonging.

Possessivpronomen

> **Hallo Maus!**
> Nun ist es doch schon das 4. Jahr!
> **In Liebe Deine Katze**
> GE90558

> **Liebe Christina**
> Zum Valentinstag herzliche Grüße
> und alles Liebe und Gute wünscht
> Dir **Dein Vater**
> GC114748

Herzliche Grüße
auch an Ihre Tochter

Ihre

Ute Oswald

Ute Oswald

▣ Analyse

Analyse. Suggestion: Guide students by saying examples aloud.

- Scan the illustrations for possessive adjectives.
- Two examples demonstrate closings in a letter or postcard. What possessive adjectives are used?

You have already used a number of possessive adjectives in many different contexts.

> Wie ist **Ihr** Name? **Mein** Name ist Hermsen.
> Wer hat Geburtstag? **Meine** Schwester hat Geburtstag.

Here is the complete list of possessive adjectives:

*Herzliche Grüße
Eure Bloyhen*

Eure Saskia und Nicholas

RSM

Singular	Plural
mein *my*	unser *our*
Ihr *your (formal)*	Ihr *your (formal, pl.)*
dein *your (informal)*	euer *your (informal, pl.)*
sein *his*	
ihr *her*	ihr *their*
sein *its*	

The formal possessive adjective **Ihr** (*your*) is capitalized, just like the formal personal pronoun **Sie** (*you*). In a letter all forms of *you* and *your* are capitalized (**Du, Dein, Euer**). The possessive adjective **ihr** (not capitalized) can mean either *her* or *their*.

Possessives—short for possessive adjectives—take the same endings as the indefinite article. Unlike **ein,** however, they also have plural forms. They agree in gender, case, and number with the nouns they modify.

Here are the nominative and accusative forms of **mein** and **unser** to illustrate the pattern for all possessives.

	SINGULAR			PLURAL
	Masculine	*Neuter*	*Feminine*	
Nominative	mein	mein	meine	meine
	unser	unser	unsere	unsere
Accusative	meinen	mein	meine	meine
	unseren	unser	unsere	unsere

Note that the only accusative form that differs from the nominative case is the masculine singular.

▣ Übung 1. Das bin ich!

Complete the personal profile of yourself.

_____ Name ist _____.   _____ Familie wohnt in _____.
_____ Adresse ist _____.   _____ Mutter heißt _____.
_____ Beruf ist _____.   _____ Vater heißt _____.
_____ Telefonnummer ist _____. _____ Auto ist ein _____.

Übung 1. **Follow-up:** Encourage students to be creative by making up personal profiles of fictional characters or of famous people.

▣ Übung 2. Persönliche Angaben

Exchange personal profiles with someone else in your class and report about this person to the class.

> BEISPIEL: Sein Name ist Lee. Seine Telefonnummer ist _____. Und sein Auto ist ein Maserati!
> usw.

▣ Übung 3. Kleine Gespräche im Alltag

Ergänzen Sie die fehlenden Possessivpronomen.

1. CLAUDIA: Hast du _____ Telefonnummer?
   STEFAN: Ja, und wie ist _____ Adresse?
   CLAUDIA: Hier ist _____ neue Adresse.

Übung 3. **Suggestion:** Have students work in pairs, assigning one conversation per pair. Then have each pair act out its conversation. For the remainder of the conversations, (1) have students fill them in as other students act them out or (2) assign them for homework.

2. LILO: Und dies hier ist _____ Freund.

    HELGA: Wie heißt _____ Freund denn?

    LILO: _____ Name ist Max.

    HELGA: Max? Na, so was! So heißt nämlich _____ Hund.

3. HERR WEIDNER: Und was sind Sie von Beruf, Frau Rudolf?

    FRAU RUDOLF: Ich bin Automechanikerin.

    HERR WEIDNER: Und was ist _____ Mann von Beruf?

    FRAU RUDOLF: _____ Mann ist Hausmann.

    HERR WEIDNER: Wie bitte? Hausmann?

4. FRAU SANDERS: Ach, wie niedlich! Ist das _____ Tochter?

    FRAU KARSTEN: Ja, das ist _____ Tochter.

    FRAU SANDERS: Und ist das _____ Hund?

    FRAU KARSTEN: Ja, das ist _____ Hund. Das ist der Caesar.

5. POLIZIST: Ist das _____ Wagen?

    FRAU KUNZE: Ja, leider ist das _____ Wagen.

6. INGE: Kennst du _____ Freund Klaus?
    ERNST: Ich kenne Klaus nicht, aber ich kenne _____ Schwester.
    INGE: Morgen besuchen wir _____ Eltern in Stuttgart.
7. KLAUS: Morgen fahren wir nach Stuttgart.
    KURT: Wie fahrt ihr denn?
    KLAUS: Wir nehmen _____ Wagen.

Personal Pronouns in the Accusative

Personalpronomen im Akkusativ

▣ Analyse

Scan the illustrations and determine which of the pronouns are subjects and which are objects.

> Er sucht Sie

> Sie sucht Ihn

Mein Schatz,
Ich liebe Dich.
Deine Jutta
GA140650

Gourmets lieben ihn.

RSM

Here are the accusative forms of the personal pronouns.

Singular		Plural	
mich	*me*	uns	*us*
Sie	*you*	Sie	*you*
dich	*you*	ihr	*you*
ihn	*him, it*		
sie	*her, it*	sie	*them*
es	*it*		

Ich brauche Dich.

Note that **ihn, sie,** and **es** must agree in gender with the noun to which they refer.

> Hast du **meinen Autoschlüssel**?
>
> Ja, ich habe **ihn**.
> Haben Sie **meine Telefonnummer**?
>
> Ja, ich habe **sie**.

▣ Übung 4.

Ergänzen Sie die Sätze durch Personalpronomen.

1. Wo ist mein Buch? Ich brauche _____.
2. Die Lampe ist praktisch. Ich kaufe _____.

3. Wo ist der Autoschlüssel? Ich glaube, _____ ist noch im Auto.
4. Wo sind unsere Kinder? _____ sind im Garten.
5. Wo ist mein Bruder? Ich suche _____.
6. Ist Petra zu Hause? Ja, ich rufe (*call*) _____.
7. Wie möchten Sie Ihren Kaffee? Schwarz oder mit Milch?
   Ich trinke _____ schwarz.
8. Ach, hier ist meine Kamera. Ich suche _____ schon drei Tage.

🔲 **Übung 5.** **Interaktion**

Kennst du ihn? Wie findest du ihn?

> BEISPIEL: A: Kennst du meinen Freund, den Toni?
> B: Ja, ich kenne ihn.
> A: Wie findest du ihn denn?
> B: Sehr sympathisch.

der Film _____ (Name)
der Professor _____ (Name)
meine Freundin
mein Freund
unsere Stadt
das Buch _____ (Titel)

Prepositions with the Accusative

Präpositionen mit dem Akkusativ

In German, some prepositions govern the accusative case, others the dative or the genitive case. That means that articles, nouns, and pronouns following a given preposition have to be in a particular case.

🔲 **Analyse**

- List the words in the illustrations that are prepositions.
- In what case does the definite article following each preposition appear?
- What does the ad **Fit durch den Winter** suggest?

The following prepositions always take the accusative case.

durch *through, across*
für *for*
gegen *against*
ohne *without*
um *around*

The way these prepositions are used in German does not always coincide with the way they are used in English. Compare the following sentences.

Herr Hübner fährt jeden Tag **durch** die Stadt.	*Mr. Hübner drives through (across) the city every day.*
Tom kauft ein Geburtstagsge-schenk **für** seinen Bruder.	*Tom is buying a birthday gift for his brother.*
Was ist gut **gegen** Schnupfen?	*What is good for a cold?*
Ich trinke meinen Kaffee **ohne** Milch.	*I drink my coffee without milk.*
Kennst du den Film, *In 80 Tagen* **um** *die Welt*?	*Do you know the movie* Around the World in 80 Days?
Der Film beginnt **um** drei Uhr.	*The movie begins at three o'clock.*

Some prepositions combine with the definite article that follows them to form one word.

durch das → durchs Zimmer
für das → fürs Auto
um das → ums Haus

⊡ Übung 6. Informationen

Ergänzen Sie die Präpositionen.

1. Frau Kortenkamp, trinken Sie Ihren Tee mit oder _____ Zucker?
2. Herr Dr. Hungerknobel, haben Sie etwas _____ Schnupfen?
3. Ich brauche noch einen Sessel _____ mein Zimmer.
4. Frau Storch fährt leider immer zu schnell _____ die Stadt.
5. Wann beginnt der Film? _____ vier Uhr?
6. Du bist so unfreundlich. Hast du etwas _____ mich?
7. Kennen Sie den Film *In 80 Tagen* _____ *die Welt*?

⊡ Übung 7. Interaktion

Für wen sind diese Dinge?

BEISPIEL: A: Für wen ist die Uhr?
          B: Die Uhr ist für meinen Bruder.

die Armbanduhr

die Kuckucksuhr

der Blumenstrauß

die Krawatte

das Buch

die Ohrringe

das Armband

der Fotoapparat

das Fotoalbum

Freund	Bruder	Mutter
Onkel	Tante	Urgroßmutter
Freundin	Großmutter	Vater

The Verb *werden*

The irregular verb **werden** means *to become*. Here are its present-tense forms:

Singular	Plural
ich werde	wir werden
Sie werden	Sie werden
du wirst	ihr werdet
er sie } wird es	sie werden

*Prinz Charles
wird 40 Jahre*

Serie
FOLGE 2

▣ Übung 8. Geburtstage

Ergänzen Sie die Sätze durch eine Form von **werden.**

1. Ulrike hat im September Geburtstag. Sie _____ 23 Jahre alt. Ihre Brüder Achim und Mathias _____ im März 18.
2. Unser Auto _____ dieses Jahr 10.
3. Wann _____ du 21, Mathias?
   —Ich _____ im Februar 21.
4. Meine Großmutter? Ich glaube, sie _____ im Juli 85.
5. Ach, ihr seid Zwillinge (*twins*)? Und wie alt seid ihr denn?
   —Wir haben am Samstag Geburtstag. Wir _____ 13.

◙ **Übung 9.** **Wer wird wann wie alt?**

Fragen Sie in der Klasse:

1. Wer _____ dieses Jahr _____ (z.B. 21 oder 30)?
2. Wie viele Leute _____ dieses Jahr 18?
3. Wann _____ du 50? 100? (z.B. Ich werde in 30 Jahren 50.)
4. Wann _____ dein Freund oder deine Freundin _____?

LESEN IM KONTEXT

This section focuses on a text dealing with relationships between
generations.

Vor dem Lesen

◙ **Aktivität.** **Eine Umfrage**

Fill out the questionnaire and compare answers in class.

1. **Was haben Sie gern zu Hause?** Antworten Sie mit Ja oder Nein.

	JA	NEIN
Familie	_____	_____
gutes Essen	_____	_____
viel Freiheit (*freedom*)	_____	_____
Hund/Katze	_____	_____
Auto	_____	_____
Arbeit im Haus und Garten	_____	_____
viel Spaß	_____	_____
Sonstiges (*other things*)	_____	_____

2. **Was nervt Sie** (*gets on your nerves*) **zu Hause?**

	JA	NEIN
Konflikte mit Geschwistern	_____	_____
laute Musik	_____	_____
zuviele Menschen um mich	_____	_____
zuviel Fernsehen	_____	_____
Eltern zu autoritär	_____	_____
zuviel Arbeit	_____	_____
nichts—alles ist perfekt	_____	_____
Sonstiges	_____	_____

Auf den ersten Blick

Guessing the theme. Scan the introductory paragraph of the reading below and answer the following questions. Explain the reasons for your answer.

1. What contrasts does the introductory paragraph mention?
2. **Trau keinem über dreißig** means:
   a. don't trust anybody under thirty
   b. people over thirty don't trust anybody
   c. don't trust anyone over thirty
3. The theme of the article is probably
   a. the generation of the 60s
   b. conflicts among generations of today
   c. trust no one over thirty

Auf den ersten Blick. Suggestion: Have students scan the questions before reading the paragraph silently. They then answer the questions that follow. The remainder of the article can be assigned for homework.

Neue Wörter

Das nervt mich *That gets on my nerves (colloquialism used mostly by young people to express:* **Das geht mir auf die Nerven.***)*

der Unterschied *difference*
aktuell *current*

Was nervt euch? Oder auch nicht?

Alt und Jung. Eltern und Kinder. Ist das nicht ein Unterschied wie Tag und Nacht? Oder wie Feuer und Wasser? „Trau° keinem über dreißig", hieß ein Spruch° der legendären Generation von 1968. Das Argument der Gegenseite:° „Solange du deine Füße unter unseren Tisch stellst, mußt du gehorchen.°" Sind die Gegensätze heute noch aktuell? Jugendscala wollte es wissen° und fragte Eltern und Kinder.

Trust

saying

opposite side

obey

wollte... *wanted to know*

The text goes on. Before reading it, familiarize yourself with some important new words.

Neue Wörter

das Fahrrad *bicycle*
das Gymnasium *secondary school, college preparatory school*
das Lieblingsfach *favorite subject*

das Pferd *horse*
ordentlich *neat(ly)*
streng *strict*
reiten *to ride (on horseback)*
verstehen *to understand*

Anja wohnt mit ihrer Mutter Ursula, ihrem Vater Hermann, ihrer älteren Schwester Martina und dem Hund Cora in einem Haus mit großem Garten. Anja geht aufs Gymnasium: „Meine Lieblingsfächer sind Biologie, Mathematik und natürlich Sport." Auch in ihrer Freizeit ist sie sportlich aktiv: Sie reitet—auf ihrem eigenen Pferd, sie fährt gerne Fahrrad und macht Karate. Mit ihren Eltern versteht sie sich „eigentlich ganz gut". Anja findet es toll, daß Ursula und Hermann so tolerant sind. Sie darf in Discos, Freunde besuchen und im nächsten Jahr (wahrscheinlich) auch allein in den Urlaub° fahren. „Der Vater meiner Freundin ist viel strenger."…

vacation

Doch es gibt auch Probleme. „Anja ist nicht so ordentlich", ärgert sich° ihre Mutter. Vater Hermann kann das nur bestätigen…

ärgert... complains

Anja hat auch einen Wunsch. Sie möchte gern mehr Ausflüge° mit der Familie machen, mal an den Ozean fahren oder gemeinsam spazierengehen.° „Wir unternehmen zu wenig." Da muß Hermann lachen° „Du gehst doch sowieso nicht mit uns." Und Ursula meint: „Wir arbeiten beide. Darum sind wir froh, wenn wir am Wochenende zu Hause bleiben können. Es gibt immer was zu tun, zum Beispiel im Garten."

excursions

go for walks / laugh

Und was ist Anjas größtes Problem mit den Eltern? „Die beiden rauchen zu viel." Dazu sagen Hermann und Ursula nichts mehr…

Jugendscala, Dezember 1988

Zum Text

1. **Familie Schroeter.** Hier ist der Stammbaum der Familie Schroeter, aber ohne Namen. Setzen Sie die Namen ein.

Zum Text, #1. Suggestion: Have students do as a homework assignment. Review family members in class.

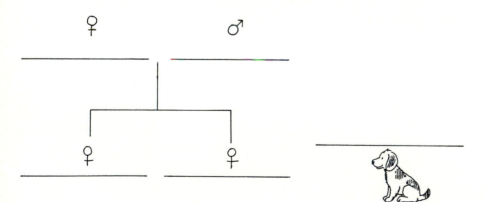

2. **Richtig oder falsch?** If the answer is false, give the right information.

Zum Text, #2. Suggestion: Have students work in pairs, saying each statement in alternation. Students can respond *das stimmt* or *das stimmt nicht.*

a. _____ Anja hat eine große Familie.
b. _____ In ihrer Freizeit liest Anja gern über Sport.
c. _____ Herr und Frau Schroeter sind autoritäre Eltern.
d. _____ Anja ist sehr ordentlich.
e. _____ Anja raucht zuviel.

3. **Anja.** What do you know about Anja?

   Anja ist _____ Jahre alt. Ihre Lieblingsfächer sind _____ . Sie wohnt in _____ . Anja ist sportlich aktiv. Sie _____ . Anja ist Schülerin. Sie geht aufs _____ .

4. **Genau lesen** (*Reading carefully*). Reread the second part of the text, locating and listing sentences that describe the kind of relationship Anja has with her parents. What do they tell you about the relationship?

5. **Wortschatzübung.** Match the opposites.

1.	Tag	a.	Eltern
2.	Feuer	b.	Pfeffer
3.	Kinder	c.	Wasser
4.	Salz	d.	Nacht

Nach dem Lesen

▣ Aktivität 1. Eine Person vorstellen°

Work in small groups. Bring in a picture of your family, a family member, or a friend and describe the person or people in the picture to your group.

> BEISPIEL: Das ist meine Mutter. Sie heißt Barbara. Sie ist 44 Jahre alt. Sie ist sehr aktiv. Sie kocht gern and läuft gern.

▣ Aktivität 2. Ein Bericht°

Write a short report about yourself and your family or write about a friend and his or her family. Include in your report:

- wie groß die Familie ist
- wo sie wohnt
- was Sie nervt
- wen Sie besonders nett finden
- wann Sie Geburtstag haben (Monat: im Dezember)
- was Sie und andere Familienmitglieder (*family members*) gern machen (kochen, tanzen, usw.)
- Lieblings... (-sport, -komponist, -musiker)
- Probleme (kein Geld, zuviel Geld...)

Eine... *Introducing someone*

Aktivität 1. Suggestion: As each student describes his or her picture, the others take notes. One student in each group should be called on to report on one of the photos described.

Ein... *A report*

Aktivität 2. Suggestion: Have students form groups of five. One narrates the report he or she wrote to the group; the others take notes, and one of them reports to the whole class.

WORTSCHATZ

Substantive

Familie — Family

der Bruder (¨)	brother
die Eltern (*pl.*)	parents
der Enkel (-), die Enkelin (-nen)	grandson, granddaughter
die Familie (-n)	family
das Familienfest (-e)	family celebration
die Geschwister (*pl.*)	siblings
die Großeltern (*pl.*)	grandparents
die Großmutter (¨)	grandmother
der Großvater (¨)	grandfather
das Kind (-er)	child
die Kusine (-n)	female cousin
die Mutter (¨)	mother
der Neffe (-n *masc.*)	nephew
die Nichte (-n)	niece
die Oma (-s) (*coll.*)	grandma
der Onkel (-)	uncle
der Opa (-s) (*coll.*)	grandpa
die Schwester (-n)	sister
der Sohn (¨e)	son
der Stammbaum (¨e)	family tree
die Tante (-n)	aunt
die Tochter (¨)	daughter
die Urgroßmutter (¨)	great-grandmother
der Urgroßvater (¨)	great-grandfather
der Vater (¨)	father

Andere Substantive

der Austauschstudent (-en)	exchange student
das Bild (-er)	picture
die Einladung (-en)	invitation
das Fahrrad (¨er)	bicycle
das Familienfest (-e)	family celebration
die Garage (-n)	garage
der Garten (¨)	garden
der Geburtstag (-e)	birthday
das Gymnasium (Gymnasien)	secondary school
der Hund (-e)	dog
der Kaffee	coffee
der Lehrer (-), die Lehrerin (-nen)	teacher

das Lieblingsfach (¨er)	favorite subject (in school)
die Milch	milk
die Party (-s)	party
das Pferd (-e)	horse
der Schlüssel (-)	key
der Wagen (-)	car

Verben

einladen	to invite
feiern	to celebrate
geben (gibt)	to give
es gibt	there is, there are
gratulieren	to congratulate
heiraten	to marry, to get married
kaufen	to buy
kennen	to know, to be acquainted with someone
(ich) möchte	(I) would like
reden über	to talk about
rufen	to call
treffen (trifft)	to meet
verstehen	to understand
werden (wird)	to become
wünschen	to wish

Sonstige Wörter

ab und zu	now and then
aktuell	current
dieser	this
leider	unfortunately
merkwürdig	strange, peculiar
nach	to (*place name*)
nach Hause	home (*indicating going home*)
natürlich	of course, naturally
niedlich	cute
nur	only
ordentlich	neat
schade	too bad
schon	already
sicher	certainly, for sure
sonst (noch)	otherwise
streng	strict

wie lange	(for) how long
zu Hause	at home

Präpositionen

durch	through
für	for
gegen	against
ohne	without
um	around; at
um 10.00	at 10:00

Ausdrücke

alles Gute	best wishes
herzlichen Glückwunsch	congratulations
herzlichen Glückwunsch zum Geburtstag	happy birthday
vielen Dank	many thanks
viel Glück	much luck
Was macht _____?	How is _____?

Wochentage / Days of the Week

der Montag	Monday
der Dienstag	Tuesday
der Mittwoch	Wednesday
der Donnerstag	Thursday
der Freitag	Friday
der Samstag	Saturday
der Sonnabend	Saturday
der Sonntag	Sunday

Monate / Months

der Januar	January
der Februar	February
der März	March
der April	April
der Mai	May
der Juni	June
der Juli	July
der August	August
der September	September
der Oktober	October
der November	November
der Dezember	December

PLÄNE MACHEN

Kapitel 4. Introduce this chapter by talking about plans for the coming week, month, etc., as well as about daily schedules, incorporating adverbs of time and modal verbs.

Lernziele *In this chapter you will learn to make plans with someone, talk about your daily schedule, and tell time.*

In diesem  sehen Sie fünf (Bilder). Die Bilder stehen für fünf Wörter oder Ausdrücke (*expressions*). Die Ausdrücke sind in alphabetischer Ordnung:

RSM

Fahrrad
Haus(e)
Herz
Sonntag
Tasse Kaffee

Lesen Sie den Brief nun mit den Wörtern!

Realia. **Suggestion:** Have students scan the note to determine (1) what kind of text it is and (2) what it might be about.
Follow-up: Do the *Alles klar* activity as a whole group.

- Dies ist ein Brief
  a. zum Muttertag
  b. zum Geburtstag
  c. für Freunde
- Am Wochenende wollen Susanne und Peter
  a. Kaffee trinken
  b. zu Hause bleiben
  c. Freunde besuchen
- Sie wollen nur ____ bleiben.
  a. einen Tag
  b. ungefähr eine Stunde (60 Minuten)
  c. ein Wochenende

The writer ends the letter with a standard closing, **Herzliche Grüße,** which is used in letters or postcards to family and friends. What would be the English equivalent?

WÖRTER IM KONTEXT

Was machst du am Wochenende?

☑ **Aktivität 1. Wann möchten Sie das machen?**

	HEUTE	MORGEN	WOCHENENDE
8.00 Uhr	heute morgen	morgen früh	Samstag morgen
12.00 Uhr	heute mittag	morgen mittag	Samstag mittag
15.00 Uhr	heute nachmittag	morgen nachmittag	Sonntag nachmittag
20.00 Uhr	heute abend	morgen abend	Sonntag abend

BEISPIEL: A: Samstag morgen möchte ich lange schlafen.
B: Morgen früh möchte ich Tennis spielen.

ins Kino gehen	mein Zimmer / meine Wohnung aufräumen
lange schlafen	
in ein Rockkonzert gehen	faulenzen
Tennis spielen	im Garten arbeiten
gemütlich frühstücken	ins Café gehen
die Zeitung lesen	
Freunde besuchen	
einkaufen	

Aktivität 1. Note: The specific times to the left exemplify the general times of day. They are not part of the exercise. **Suggestion:** Have students work in pairs. They should first scan the possibilities. Then they take turns stating what they would like to do and when.
Suggestion: Have students circulate in class and ask several questions of a number of classmates; e.g. *Was machst du morgen nachmittag?*

> ## Sprachnotiz
>
> | | |
> |---|---|
> | Ich **komme** auf eine Stunde **vorbei.** | *I am* coming by *for an hour.* |
> | Morgen **möchten** wir Tennis **spielen.** | *Tomorrow we* would like to play *tennis.* |
>
> In German main clauses with two-part verbs, the second part stands at the end of the sentence.

Neue Wörter

die Minute *minute*
  (auf) ein paar Minuten (*for*)
   a few minutes
die Stunde *hour*
die Tasse Kaffee *cup of coffee*
  (auf) eine Tasse Kaffee (*for*)
   a cup of coffee

aufräumen *to straighten up*
frühstücken *to eat breakfast*
Ich komme vorbei (*I am coming by*)

gemütlich *leisurely, comfortable*
kurz *for a short while*
leider *unfortunately*

▣ Aktivität 2. Bist du zu Hause?

Invite yourself to a friend's house for a brief visit. Say when you would like to come and for how long you are planning to stay.

A: Bist du _____ zu Hause?

B: Ja, ich bin zu Hause.
A: Gut. Ich komme _____ vorbei.
B: Schön, ich sehe dich _____ .

B: Nein, da bin ich leider nicht zu Hause.
A: Schade.
B: Ja, es tut mir auch leid. Kannst du _____ kommen?
A: (ja, nein)

Aktivität 2. **Suggestion:** To introduce this activity, go over the *Neue Wörter* first. Let students do the exchange with several different partners, encouraging them to respond positively to some and negatively to others.

Wieviel Uhr ist es?

Es ist eins. / Es ist ein Uhr.

Es ist zehn (Minuten) nach eins.

Wieviel Uhr ist es? **Suggestion:** Present times using an actual clock (or one made from a paper plate), moving the hands to correspond to the times in the examples. Students repeat the times. Check students' comprehension by reviewing the examples in random order, using the clock, and asking them to say what time it is.

Es ist Viertel nach eins.

Es ist halb zwei. /
Es ist ein Uhr dreißig.

Es ist zwanzig (Minuten) vor zwei.

Es ist Viertel vor zwei.

In official timetables—for instance, in radio, television, movie, and theater guides—time is expressed according to the twenty-four-hour system.

1.00–12.00 Uhr	*1:00 a.m. to 12:00 noon*
13.00–24.00 Uhr	*1:00 p.m. to midnight*

Midnight may also be referred to as **0 (null) Uhr.**

When writing time in numbers, Germans separate hours and minutes by a period, instead of a colon as in English.

Aktivität 3. **Hören Sie zu.**

You are calling for the time (**die Zeitansage**) on the phone. Circle the time you hear.

1. a. 7.38   b. 17.35   c. 17.30
2. a. 3.06   b. 2.06   c. 20.16
3. a. 14.00   b. 14.15   c. 14.05
4. a. 12.25   b. 10.24   c. 11.25
5. a. 19.45   b. 9.45   c. 19.40
6. a. 13.00   b. 3.40   c. 13.40
7. a. 0.15   b. 0.05   c. 0.45
8. a. 20.05   b. 20.50   c. 21.50

Aktivität 4. **Wieviel Uhr ist es? Wie spät ist es?**

BEISPIEL: Wieviel Uhr ist es? (Wie spät ist es?)
Es ist Viertel nach zwölf.

Sprachnotiz

To give the exact time when something begins or ends, use the preposition **um** with the time.

Wann fängt das Kino an? Um acht (20.00) Uhr.
Wann ist es zu Ende? Um zehn (22.00) Uhr.

 Aktivität 5. **Interaktion. Was läuft denn im Kino?**

Scan the movie guide for titles, places, and times.

RSM

 Esplanade 2
T. 28 57 89
Zeil 125

12.15, 14.15, 16.15, 18.15, 20.15 Uhr, Fr./Sa. auch 22.15 Uhr   ab 6 J.
Ganz Deutschland lacht über die Superkomödie des Jahres.
TOM HANKS in
BIG ⊠ DOLBY STEREO   **16. Woche**
Was passiert, wenn ein 12jähriger über Nacht das Aussehen eines 30jährigen hat?   **Prädikat: wertvoll**

ESPRIT 1
T. 28 52 05
Zeil 125

12.30, 14.30, 16.30, 18.30, 20.45 Uhr, Fr./Sa. auch 23 Uhr   ab 12 J.
STEVEN SPIELBERG präsentiert einen ROBERT-ZEMECKI-Film: Menschen und Zeichentrickfiguren leben in Hollywood in schöner Eintracht zusammen, bis es zu einem Mord kommt . . .
Falsches Spiel mit Roger Rabbit   **12. Woche**

ESPRIT 2
T. 28 52 05
Zeil 125

12.15, 14.15, 16.15, 18.15, 20.15 Uhr, Fr./Sa. auch 22.15 Uhr   ab 16 J.
Der neue Film von DORIS DÖRRIE. GRIFFIN DUNNE in
Ich und er   **18. Woche**
Eine Komödie über Männer und Frauen und den kleinen Unterschied zwischen ihnen.

EUROPA **Palast**
T. 28 52 05
Zeil 125

12.45, 15.15, 17.45, 20.15 Uhr, Fr./Sa. auch 22.45 Uhr   ab 12 J.
Die brillante Verfilmung des erfolgreichen Romans von HANS HELMUT KIRST — „Von Soldaten und Menschen"
Fabrik der Offiziere ⊠ DOLBY STEREO

Vorverkauf und Kartenreservierung mit Computer-Kasse im Olympia-Center

olympia
Telefon 28 31 28
Weißfrauenstr. 12-16
⊠ DOLBY STEREO

14.00, 17.00, 20.00 Uhr · Fr./Sa. 23.00 Uhr   ab 12 J.
MERYL STREEP und JACK NICHOLSON interpretieren die Personen zweier Clochards auf geniale Art. (France-Soir)
WOLFSMILCH   **4. Woche**
Francis Phelan und seine Weggefährtin Helen ziehen durch Amerika, den Kopf voller Schnaps und schuldgetränkter Halluzinationen.

alpha
Telefon 28 31 28
Weißfrauenstr. 12-16

13.45, 17.00, 20.30 Uhr   ab 16 J.
„Ein Meisterwerk! Einer der ambitioniertesten Filme seit langer Zeit — eine Atmosphäre, die Herz und Kopf gleichermaßen in Aufruhr versetzt."   (Washington Post)
Die unerträgliche Leichtigkeit des Seins ⊠ DOLBY STEREO   **40. Woche**
Ein Film von PHILIP KAUFMANN nach dem Bestseller von MILAN KUNDERA mit DANIEL DAY-LEWIS, ERLAND JOSEPHSON u. a.   **Prädikat: wertvoll**

BEISPIEL: A: Wollen wir heute ins Kino?
               B: Na, gut. Was läuft denn im Olympia?
               A: *Wolfsmilch.*
               B: Um wieviel Uhr denn?
               A: Es gibt eine Vorstellung um zwei (14.00) Uhr.

Neue Wörter

die Vorstellung *performance*

Um wieviel Uhr? *At what time?*

Was läuft denn? *What is playing?*

Sprachnotiz

When you do something on a regular basis, use the following adverbs to express the day or the time:

montags	morgens
dienstags	mittags
mittwochs	nachmittags
donnerstags	abends
freitags	nachts
samstags/sonnabends	
sonntags	

⊡ Aktivität 6. Interaktion. Jankas Stundenplan

Aktivität 6. Suggestion: First go over the subjects in the *Stundenplan* with students. Then have students do the activity in pairs, taking turns asking questions.

Janka ist 18 Jahre alt und geht aufs Gymnasium. So sieht ihr Stundenplan aus. Was macht sie jeden Tag?

Neue Wörter

die Erdkunde *geography*
die Sozialkunde *social science*
der Stundenplan *class schedule*
alle zwei Wochen *every other week*

Note: the abbreviation GK in the *Stundenplan* means *Grundkurs;* LK is for *Leistungskurs. Leistungskurse* are more demanding than *Grundkurse.* The subjects of *Leistungskurse* are those in which students are examined in the *Abitur,* the final examination at the *Gymnasium.*

RSM

a. Mathematik
b. Religion

STUNDENPLAN

Zeit	Montag	Dienstag	Mittwoch	Donnerstag	Freitag	Sonnabend
8 - 8⁴⁵	Sozialkunde ᴳᵏ	—	Englisch ᴸᵏ	Physik ᴳᵏ	—	Erdkunde ᴳᵏ
8⁵⁰ - 9³⁵	Sozialkunde ᴳᵏ	—	Deutsch ᴸᵏ	Physik ᴳᵏ	—	Erdkunde ᴳᵏ
9⁵⁵ - 10¹⁰	Deutsch ᴸᵏ	Literatur ᴳᵏ	Mathe ᵃ ᴳᵏ	—	Englisch ᴸᵏ	
10⁴⁵ - 11³⁰	Deutsch ᴸᵏ	Mathe ᴳᵏ	Mathe ᴳᵏ	—	Englisch ᴸᵏ	—
11⁴⁵ - 12³⁰	Englisch ᴸᵏ	Erdkunde ᴳᵏ	—	Reli ᵇ ᴳᵏ	Deutsch ᴸᵏ	Reli ᴳᵏ
12³⁵ - 13²⁰	Englisch ᴸᵏ	Erdkunde ᴳᵏ	—	Reli ᴳᵏ	Deutsch ᴸᵏ	Reli ᴳᵏ
15 - 16³⁰	Sport ᴳᵏ		Literatur ᴳᵏ	Sport ᴳᵏ ↑	Physik ᴳᵏ ↑	
16³⁰ - 18⁰⁰				nur alle 2 Wochen		

BEISPIEL: A: Was macht Janka donnerstags um 8.00 Uhr?
               B: Donnerstags um 8 Uhr hat sie Physik.

◻ **Aktivität 7.** **Interaktion. Was ist dein Stundenplan?**

BEISPIEL: A: Was machst du donnerstags um 9.00 Uhr?
B: Morgens um 9.00 Uhr habe ich Deutsch.

Aktivität 7. **Suggestion:** Assign students to create a *Stundenplan* such as Janka's. Students then interview one other person regarding his or her schedule. The interviewers can write the information in a blank schedule as they interview.

Am Wochenende

◻ **Aktivität 8.** **Bildgeschichte. Dieters Wochenende**

Aktivität 8. **Suggestion:** Go over the *Neue Wörter* with students before doing this activity, which can be done in pairs or as a group.

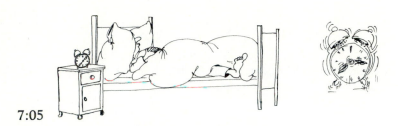

7:05

7:20

7:45 – 8:30

9:30

11:20

12:15

15:00

19:15

Complete Dieter's weekend schedule.

1. Um _____ schläft Dieter noch. Dann klingelt der Wecker.
2. _____ steht er endlich auf.
3. Von _____ bis _____ geht er joggen.
4. _____ frühstückt er und liest die Zeitung.
5. _____ ruft er einen Freund an.
6. _____ trifft er eine Freundin im Café.
7. _____ spielt Dieter Fußball auf dem Sportplatz.
8. _____ ist er mit Freunden im Kino.

Neue Wörter

anrufen (ruft an) *call up*
aufstehen (steht auf) *get up*

von _____ bis _____
from _____ to _____

▣ **Aktivität 9. Partnerarbeit. Was machst du so° am Wochenende?**

generally

Tell a partner three or four things you enjoy doing. Report back to the class what you found out.

> BEISPIEL: A: **Was machst du gern am Wochenende?**
> B: **Ich gehe gern schwimmen.**

Aktivität 9. Suggestion: Students work in pairs. As one tells the other what he or she enjoys doing, the other takes notes in order to report back to the class.

Ich gehe _____. (tanzen, spazieren, einkaufen, laufen,
schwimmen, wandern)
Ich stehe _____ auf. (früh, spät)
Ich spiele _____. (Karten, Tennis, usw.)

 Aktivität 10. Hören Sie zu. Eine Einladung

DIALOG 1

1. Die Sprecher sind
   a. ein Professor und ein Student
   b. zwei Studentinnen
   c. eine Studentin und ein Freund
2. Der eine Sprecher möchte
   a. zu Hause arbeiten
   b. ins Kino
   c. ins Konzert
3. Der andere Sprecher muß leider
   a. arbeiten
   b. in eine Vorlesung
   c. einen Brief schreiben

DIALOG 2

1. Die Sprecher sind
   a. zwei Studenten
   b. zwei Professoren
   c. ein Student und eine Studentin
2. Der eine Sprecher möchte
   a. ins Kino
   b. in eine Vorlesung
   c. Karten spielen
3. Der andere Sprecher
   a. hat eine Vorlesung
   b. hat Labor
   c. muß in die Bibliothek

> *Sprachnotiz*
>
> To say where you are going use the following expressions.
>
> | | |
> |-----------|-------------|
> | | ins Kino |
> | | ins Theater |
> | Ich gehe | ins Konzert |
> | | in die Oper |
> | | in die Disko|

Aktivität 11. Interaktion. Was hast du vor?

A: Was hast du am Samstag vor?
B: Ich gehe _____.
   Willst du mitgehen?
A: Was gibt es denn?
B: _____ (*Titel*).

A: Gut. Wann fängt es denn an?
B: _____

A: Ach, ich bleibe lieber zu
   Hause.
B: Schade.

NEU IM KINO

Beetlejuice
Gloria-Palast (Premiere am 4. November, 23.00 – ab 10. November: 15.30, 18.00, 20.30, Fr., Sa. u. Mi. a. 22.45)
Bestseller
Film-Bühne Wien (15.15, 17.45, 20.15, 22.45, So. a. 11.00)
Der Blob
Zoo-Palast (Kino Sieben) (15.30, 18.00, 20.30, Fr., Sa. u. Mi. a. 22.45)
Buster
Royal-Palast (14.45, 17.30, 20.15, Fr. a. 23.00)
Marmorhaus (10.15, 12.15, 14.30, 17.15, 20.00, Mi. a. 22.30)
Die Kurbel (16.00, 18.15, 20.30, 22.45)
Einer trage des anderen Last
Film-Bühne Wien (15.15, 17.45, 20.15, 23.00, So. a. 11.00)
Filmbühne am Steinplatz (18.00)
Falsches Spiel mit Roger Rabbit
Royal-Palast 1 (14.30, 17.15, 20.00, Fr., Sa. u. So. a. 22.45)
Zoo-Palast (Atelier) (14.00, 16.15, 18.30, 20.45, Fr., Sa. u. Mi. a. 23.00)

Film-Bühne Wien (15.30, 18.00, 20.30, 23.00, So. a. 11.00)
Marmorhaus (10.00, 12.30, 14.45, 17.30, 20.15, Do. bis So. u. Mi. a. 22.45)
Odeon (18.00, 20.30, 23.00, Sa. u. So. a. 16.00 – O.m.U)
Die Kommissarin
Filmbühne am Steinplatz (20.30, 23.00 – O.m.U)
Graffiti (18.00, 20.00, Do. – Sa. a. 22.00)
Killing Blue
Royal-Palast (15.00, 17.30, 20.00, Fr. u. Sa. a. 22.45)
Marmorhaus (18.00, 20.30, Mi. a. 23.00)
Stirb langsam (Die Hard)
(ab 10. 11., Aufführungsorte standen bei Redaktionsschluß noch nicht fest)
Traumdämon – Dream Demon
Film-Bühne Wien (15.15, 17.45, 20.15, 22.45, So. a. 11.00)
In Rixdorf is Musike und
Einmal Mittenwalde und zurück
Gemeinschaftsh. Gropiusstadt
(Di., 8. Nov., 15.00, 17.00 u. 19.00)

UND WAS NOCH?

JAZZ-ROCK-POP

Sonntag
6. November

Aue ☎ 87 49 76
13.00: Jürgen-Benzin-Quartett (Bebop – Jazz)
BKA-Kabarett ☎ 251 01 12
20.30: Zuckerbrot und Peitsche (Georgette Dee & Terry Truck, Chansons)
Blisse 14 ☎ 821 10 91
11.00: Helmut-Brandt-Combo
Delphi ☎ 312 10 26
Jazz-Fest Berlin '88
15.00: Compagnie Lubat and Marc Perrone, Quartette Indigo mit John Blake, Melvyn Roundtree, Gayle Dixon, Akua Dixon-Turre

17.00: Total Music Meeting '88 mit Curtis Clark, Keith Tippelt
Go in ☎ 881 72 18
21.30: Christiane Wegerle
Jazz For Fun ☎ 262 45 56
22.00: Session on Sunday
Joe am Kudamm ☎ 883 62 73
16.00: Western Union
Joe am Wedding ☎ 454 19 06
9.00: Heartbeat (Rock 'n' Roll)
LabSaal Lübars ☎ 402 90 13
17.00: Duo Pararayos (Flamenco)
Loft im Metropol ☎ 216 10 20
20.30: The Lurkers
Lützower Lampe
20.30: Hanne Wieder u. Aljoscha Zimmermann (Piano) Witzlebenstraße 38, Charlottenburg

OPERNHAUS

Sa 7. 11. 19.30–23.00 beschr. FV	**DIE ZAUBERFLÖTE** Oper von Wolfgang Amadeus Mozart Harnoncourt; Bonney, Goetze, Rohner, Maclean, Gjevang; Ryhänen, Protschka, Scharinger, Keller, Hermann, Rohr, Peter, Zürcher Sängerknaben Gesponsert von Mercedes-Benz (Schweiz) AG
So 8. 11. 14.00–17.00 VV FV Fr. 7.–/28.–	**DIE FLEDERMAUS** Operette von Johann Strauss Ch. Schneider; Coburn, Steinsky, Kaluza; Boesch, Offczarek, Protschka, Hartmann, Keller, J. Schneider Gesponsert von Jacobs Suchard
20.00–22.45 Freier Verkauf	**Gala** mit den Stars des Stuttgarter Balletts **Marcia Haydée und Richard Cragun** ROMEO UND JULIA Ballett in 3 Akten nach William Shakespeare Musik von Sergei Prokofiew Choreographie John Cranko Presser; McBeth, Newburger, Gabriel, Lopez, Muri; Dadey, Harris, Cruz Martinez, Candeloro, Dalle, Stripling, Miedzinski und das Corps de ballet
Fr. 22.–/134.–	

RSM

Neue Wörter

anfangen (fängt an) *to begin*
mitgehen (geht mit) *to come along*

vorhaben (hat vor) *to plan*
lieber *rather*

▣ Aktivität 12. Mein Zeitbudget

Wieviel Zeit verbringen (*spend*) Sie mit diesen Dingen?

Tätigkeit	Montag	Dienstag	Mittwoch	Donnerstag	Freitag	Samstag	Sonntag	insgesamt[b]

Arbeiten:
  Vorlesungen
  Labor
  Lesen
  Schreiben								

Nebenarbeit[a]								

Essen:
  Frühstück
  Mittagessen
  Abendessen								

Einkaufen								
Sport								
Schlafen								

Zeit für mich
  Fernsehen
  Zeitung lesen
  Freunde besuchen								

Aktivität 12. Have students follow the format of the *Tabelle*, jotting down their own and their partner's answers in the various categories. Students should use their notes when sharing information with the class.

a. *job on the side*
b. *total*

1. Tragen Sie die Zeit in die Tabelle ein.
2. Fragen Sie dann einen Partner / eine Partnerin.
   a. Wieviel Zeit verbringst du mit Essen, mit Arbeiten (Studium), mit Nebenarbeit, mit Schlafen, usw.?
   b. Wieviel Zeit hast du für dich?

Berichten Sie, wie Ihr Partner seine Zeit verbringt.

GRAMMATIK IM KONTEXT

Separable-Prefix Verbs

Verben mit trennbaren Präfixen

You have already used sentences like

Ich rufe an.... (Telefonieren ist einfach)

RSM

Susanne und Peter **kommen** per Fahrrad **vorbei.**	Susanne and Peter are coming by on their bikes.
Ich gehe heute tanzen. **Kommst** du **mit?**	I am going dancing today. Will you come along?

German has many two-part verbs that consist of a verb and a short complement that alters or in some way affects the meaning of the main verb. Examples of such two-part verbs in English are

to come by, to come along, to call up, to get up

Wüstenrot-Rendite[a]-Programm mit 936 Mark pro anno.

Jede Million fängt klein an.

RSM

a. *yield on investment*

Kommen ____ **vorbei,** and **kommst** ____ **mit** are examples of such two-part verbs in German. They are called separable-prefix verbs. In the infinitive, the separable part of these verbs forms the verb's prefix. The prefixes are always stressed:

ánrufen   ánfangen   vorbéikommen   mítkommen

In a declarative sentence or in a question in the present tense, the prefix is separated from the finite verb and placed at the end of the sentence.

> **Kommst** du heute abend **vorbei?**
> Ja, aber ich **rufe** vorher **an.**

Here are examples of frequently used separable-prefix verbs.

Infinitiv	3. Pers. Sg.	Beispiel
anfangen (*to begin*)	fängt an	Wann fängt die Vorlesung an?
anrufen (*to call*)	ruft an	Ich rufe dich morgen an.
aufstehen (*to get up*)	steht auf	Er steht um 9 Uhr auf.
einkaufen (*to go shopping*)	kauft ein	Frau Lerche kauft immer im Supermarkt ein.
einladen (*to invite*)	lädt ein	Ich lade dich zum Geburtstag ein.
mitkommen (*to come along*)	kommt mit	Kommst du mit?
mitnehmen (*to take along*)	nimmt mit	Nimmst du einen Regenschirm mit?
spazierengehen (*to go for a walk*)	geht spazieren	Ich gehe oft spazieren.
vorbeikommen (*to come by*)	kommt vorbei	Wir kommen Sonntag vorbei.
vorhaben (*to plan to do*)	hat vor	Was hast du heute vor?
zurückkommen (*to come back*)	kommt zurück	Wann kommst du zurück?

Separable-prefix verbs will be listed in the vocabulary as follows:

> einladen (lädt ein)
> vorhaben (hat vor)

When the main verb shows stem-vowel changes or other irregularities in the present tense (**nehmen, nimmt**), the separable-prefix verb will also have these changes.

anfangen	Der Film **fängt** um 20.00 Uhr **an.**
mitnehmen	{ **Nimmst** du einen Schirm **mit?**
	Ich **nehme keinen Schirm **mit.**

The Sentence Bracket

Die Satzklammer

Separable-prefix verbs show a sentence structure that is characteristic for German: the predicate (the finite verb and its complement) forms a bracket around the core of the sentence. The finite verb (the verb with the personal ending) is the second element of the sentence, and the separable prefix is the last element.

> Ich **fange** jetzt ein neues Leben **an.**

Another example of the sentence bracket can be seen in such sentences as:

> Klaus und Erika **gehen** Sonntag mit Freunden **tanzen.**

The finite verb **gehen** and the infinitive **tanzen** form a bracket around: **Sonntag mit Freunden. Tanzen** is a necessary verbal complement. You will learn yet another type of verb that uses the sentence bracket in the following section on modal auxiliaries (**müssen, möchte,** etc.).

▣ **Übung 1. Was haben sie vor? Und wann?**

Bilden Sie Sätze.

> BEISPIEL: Ich gehe morgen früh spazieren.

ich	einkaufen
Herr Einsam	einladen
Herr und Frau Klinger	vorbeikommen
Jürgen	tanzen gehen
mein Freund / meine	spazierengehen
Freundin	anrufen

Übung 1.   Suggestion: Review adverbs of time with students beforehand, and remind them to add them when doing the exercise.

▣ **Übung 2. Eine Verabredung°**

Eine... *A date*

Fill in the appropriate prefixes. Then arrange the sentences in a sequence (1–5) to make a date.

> _____ Wie nett. Wann fängt der Film denn _____?
> _____ Ich gehe heute abend ins Kino. Kommst du _____?

Übung 2.   Point out: *Verabredung* can mean a casual meeting with someone as well as a formal date.

_____ Was hast du heute abend _____?
_____ Ich lade dich _____.
_____ Um sieben Uhr. Ich komme um halb sieben bei dir _____?

Suggestion: Have students fill in the prefixes, working alone. Then have them work in pairs to rearrange the sentences and practice "making a date" in German.

Übung 3. Familie Bauer macht ein Picknick

Wer nimmt was mit?

Übung 3. Suggestion: Personalize this activity by asking *Was nehmen Sie mit, wenn Sie ein Picknick machen?* Students need only respond *Ich nehme _____ mit.*

BEISPIEL: Thomas nimmt sein Kofferradio mit.

Frau Bauer (39)
Herr Bauer (42)
Inge Bauer (7)
Erika Bauer (15)
Thomas Bauer (12)

Bier und Wurst
das Buch
der Fotoapparat
Freundin
der Fußball
der Kassettenrecorder
das Kofferradio (*portable radio*)
der Picknickkorb
der Regenschirm
die Zeitung
?

Übung 4. Was machen diese Leute am Wochenende?

Bilden Sie Sätze.

Übung 4. Follow up: Encourage students to talk about their family and friends using these expressions.

1. Herr Weidner: lange schlafen, spät aufstehen
2. Frau Weidner: mit einer Freundin spazierengehen
3. Familie Schmidt: manchmal Freunde einladen, ins Theater gehen, die Wohnung aufräumen
4. Inge, Studentin in Würzburg: ihre Eltern in Fürth anrufen, manchmal Tennis spielen gehen; abends mit Freunden ausgehen
5. Hans-Peter, Student in Berlin: sehr spät aufstehen, Zeitung lesen, im Restaurant frühstücken; abends oft fernsehen (*watch TV*), ins Kino gehen, Freunde einladen

Übung 5. Interaktion

Und Sie? Was machen Sie am Wochenende? Fragen Sie einen Partner oder eine Partnerin, was sie oder er am Wochenende macht. Berichten Sie der Klasse, was Ihr Partner macht.

Übung 5. Point out: Students should be jotting down each other's responses during this activity.

BEISPIEL: A: Was machst du am Wochenende?
            B: Ich stehe um 11 Uhr auf. Dann frühstücke ich. Dann kaufe ich ein.

Modal Auxiliary Verbs

Modalverben

Modal auxiliary verbs (for example, *must, can, may*) express an attitude toward an action.

⊡ Analyse

Modal Auxiliary Verbs. Encourage students to guess the meaning of the headlines illustrating modals.

- Name the modal auxiliary verbs you see in the headlines. What are their English equivalents?
- What verbs express the action in those sentences? Where are these action verbs placed in each sentence?

Die Studenten wollen streiken

Protest gegen Studienbedingungen / Heute Vollversammlungen

Viele müssen schon in ihren Autos schlafen

„Biete[a] Freibier für die Vermittlung einer Wohnung."

a. *[I'm] offering*

Let's summarize. The examples show:

1. The modal auxiliary verb is the finite verb and stands in the second place in a statement.
2. The verb that expresses the action is in the infinitive form and stands at the end of the sentence.
3. The modal verb and infinitive form a sentence bracket (**Satzklammer**) like other verbs with fixed complements.

Viele Studenten **müssen** schon in ihren Autos **schlafen.**

In German, as well as in English, modal auxiliary verbs differ from regular verbs. The first- and third-person singular are identical and have no personal ending. Here are the present-tense forms of the modals together with the meaning of each verb.

1. wollen (*to want, wish, desire*)

The modal verb **wollen** expresses an intention or a desire.

Willst du ins Kino gehen?   *Do you want to go to the movies?*

Singular	Plural
ich will	wir wollen
Sie wollen	Sie wollen
du willst	ihr wollt
er ⎫ sie ⎬ will es ⎭	sie wollen

2. mögen (*to like*)

Großer Buchmarkt

Vom 2. bis 5. November 88

Mögen Sie Bücher? Und lesen Sie gern? Dann dürfen Sie nicht versäumen, einen Kulturbummel durchs Isenburg Zentrum zu machen. Bücher sind jetzt bei uns ein hochaktuelles Thema.

ISENBURG ZENTRUM

shopping mit Flair

The modal verb **mögen** expresses liking. It is nearly always used without a dependent infinitive.

Mögen Sie Bücher?	*Do you like books?*

You have already been using a form of **mögen: möchte** (*would like*). **Möchte** is normally used with an infinitive, unless the infinitive is implied. Use **möchte** to express your wishes politely.

Möchtest du heute abend ins Kino gehen?	*Would you like to go to the movies tonight?*

Here are the complete forms of **mögen** and **möchte.**

Singular	Plural	Singular	Plural
ich mag	wir mögen	ich möchte	wir möchten
Sie mögen	Sie mögen	Sie möchten	Sie möchten
du magst	ihr mögt	du möchtest	ihr möchtet
er		er	
sie } mag	sie mögen	sie } möchte	sie möchten
es		es	

3. müssen (*must, to have to*)

The modal auxiliary **müssen** expresses necessity.

Ich **muß** heute abend zu Hause bleiben und arbeiten.	*I have to stay home tonight and work.*

Singular		Plural
ich muß		wir müssen
Sie müssen		Sie müssen
du mußt		ihr müßt
er		
sie } muß		sie müssen
es		

Übung 6. **Suggestion:** This activity can be done either with students taking turns in pairs or as a whole-group activity.

1104 S. (1731) DM 12,–

RSM

◻ **Übung 6.** **Wer mag das?**

Mögen die Schuberts Eisbein (*pigs' feet*) mit Sauerkraut? Mögen Sie Eisbein mit Sauerkraut?

BEISPIEL: Herr und Frau Schubert mögen Eisbein mit Sauerkraut, ihre Kinder mögen kein Eisbein mit Sauerkraut. Und ich mag Sauerkraut und Eisbein.

	Herr Schubert	Frau Schubert	ihre Kinder	Sie
der Fisch	+	+	−	?
die Pommes frites	−	−	+	?
das Eisbein mit Sauerkraut	+	+	−	?
das Bier	+	−	−	?
die Schnecken (*escargot*)	−	+	−	?
die Pizza	+	+	+	?

◻ **Übung 7.** **Was möchtest du lieber machen?**

Ask a classmate what she or he would prefer to do?
   The adverb **lieber** means *rather* (as in *I would rather . . .*).

BEISPIEL: A: Was möchtest du lieber machen: lange schlafen oder Tennis spielen?
   B: Ich möchte lieber Tennis spielen.

1. Zeitung lesen oder fernsehen?
2. lange schlafen oder einkaufen gehen?
3. ins Konzert oder ins Kino gehen?
4. deine Familie anrufen oder einen Brief schreiben?
5. ein Picknick machen oder spazierengehen?
6. eine Party zu Hause machen oder ausgehen?

Übung 7. **Suggestion:** Model the example with a student to convey the meaning of *lieber*. Point out that *lieber* is the comparative form of *gern*. Have students take turns initiating questions.

7. zu Hause bleiben oder Freunde besuchen?
8. Deutsch lernen oder faulenzen?

⊡ **Übung 8. Familie Webers Picknick**

Für Samstag plant Familie Weber ein Picknick im Grünen. Was müssen
sie noch machen?

> BEISPIEL: Sie **müssen** früh aufstehen.

1. Um sieben Uhr _____ wir alle aufstehen.
2. Andrea _____ Kaffee kochen.
3. Die Kinder _____ ihre Betten machen.
4. Herr Weber _____ das Auto volltanken.
5. Wir _____ den Wetterbericht im Radio hören.
6. Dann _____ du noch den Picknickkorb packen.
7. Um acht _____ wir fertig sein.
8. Unser Hund _____ heute allein bleiben.
9. Und ich _____ noch die Zeitung lesen.

⊡ **Übung 9. Unser Picknick**

Was nehmen wir mit?

ich	wollen	Kofferradio
Herr Bauer	müssen	Fotoapparat
Inge Bauer (8)	möchten	Zeitung
Erika Bauer (22)		Picknickkorb
Frau Bauer		Buch
Thomas Bauer (12)		Frisbee
		Fußball

Übung 9.   Give students time to
scan the possibilities before doing
the activity.

4. können (*can, to be able to*)

Können expresses ability or possibility. It is also used to ask for
permission.

Ich **kann** schon etwas   *I can already speak some*
  Deutsch (sprechen).   *German.*

Singular	Plural
ich kann	wir können
Sie können	Sie können
du kannst	ihr könnt
er ⎫	
sie ⎬ kann	sie können
es ⎭	

⊡ Übung 10. Was kann man da machen?

BEISPIEL: in der Bibliothek: Da kann man Bücher lesen.

1. im Restaurant
2. im Kino
3. im Café
4. im Bett
5. im Kaufhaus
6. im Park
7. in der Bibliothek

a. Filme sehen
b. einkaufen
c. schlafen
d. Kaffee trinken
e. Bücher lesen
f. essen
g. spazierengehen

Übung 10. Suggestion: Have students do this matching exercise in pairs, alternating questions and responses.

⊡ Übung 11. Interaktion. Wer kann das?

BEISPIEL: A: Kannst du Trompete spielen?
B: Nein, das kann ich nicht.

du
dein Freund
deine Freundin
dein Zimmergenosse
deine Zimmergenossin
deine Mutter
dein Bruder
deine Eltern

Klavier (*piano*) spielen
Bridge spielen
Schach spielen
gut kochen
schön (oder laut) singen
gut tanzen

Übung 11. Follow-up: Make a list of questions that apply to students, e.g., *Wer kann Tennis spielen? Wer kann gut fotografieren?* Say each question aloud. Students demonstrate their comprehension by signaling (raising their hands, clapping, etc.) if they can do the activity.

5. sollen (*to be supposed to, shall*)

The modal **sollen** expresses that someone is either obligated or requested to do something. It often expresses a suggestion (*shall, should*).

Du sollst zu Hause bleiben.   *You are supposed to stay home.*

Singular	*Plural*
ich soll	wir sollen
Sie sollen	Sie sollen
du sollst	ihr sollt
er ⎫ sie ⎬ soll es ⎭	sie sollen

6. dürfen (*may, to be allowed to*)

The modal **dürfen** expresses permission. It is also used to make questions more polite.

Darf ich einmal Ihren   *May I see your ticket?*
Fahrschein sehen?

Singular	Plural
ich darf	wir dürfen
Sie dürfen	Sie dürfen
du darfst	ihr dürft
er	
sie } darf	sie dürfen
es	

„Darf ich einmal Ihren Fahrschein[a] sehen!"

a. ticket

□ **Übung 12.** **Wer soll das machen? Und wann?**

ich	morgen	zu Hause bleiben
wir	heute abend	einen Brief schreiben
Fräulein Klecks	jetzt	endlich aufstehen
ihr		arbeiten
du		Deutsch lernen
		nicht soviel trinken

□ **Übung 13.** **Was darf man hier und was darf man hier nicht machen?**

BEISPIEL: **Hier darf man nicht parken.**

 1.

 2.

 3.

 4.

 5.

 6.

fahren
parken
rauchen
schwimmen
spielen
zelten

□ **Übung 14.** **Interaktion. Kommst du mit?**

Tell a friend what you plan to do and invite him or her to join you. Your friend has to decline and states a reason. Look at page 124 for suggestions.

BEISPIEL: A: **Ich will heute Tennis spielen. Möchtest du mitkommen?**
B: **Nein, leider kann ich nicht. Ich muß nämlich arbeiten.**

heute abend ins Rockkonzert gehen
tanzen gehen
nach _____ (Ort) fahren
arbeiten
ins Grüne fahren
Tennis spielen
Karten spielen
meine Familie besuchen
mein Zimmer aufräumen
eine Party machen

 Übung 15. Hören Sie zu.

Studenten und ihre Probleme: Welche Information stimmt?

Übung 15. Students should first look over the questions before listening to the texts.

1. Viele Studenten können __c__ finden.
   a. keinen Studienplatz
   b. keine Freunde
   c. keine Wohnung
2. Die drei Studenten wollen in __b__ studieren.
   a. Heidelberg
   b. Berlin
   c. München
3. Eine Studentin aus Paris kann nur __c__ Mark für Miete ausgeben.
   a. 100
   b. 500
   c. 300
4. Viele Studenten schlafen __c__.
   a. in Parks
   b. in der Universität
   c. in Autos
5. Kamal Louh darf __c__ schlafen.
   a. im Park
   b. in der Bibliothek
   c. bei Freunden

The Verbs *wissen* and *kennen*

The verbs **wissen** and **kennen** both mean *to know*. However, **wissen** means *to know facts*, whereas **kennen** means *to know a person* or *to be acquainted with something*. **Kennen** is a regular verb; **wissen** is irregular. As with the modals, the first- and third-person singular of the present tense of **wissen** are identical.

Realia. Focus on Goethe button. Elicit what students know about Goethe.

ZEITUNGSLESER
    WISSEN MEHR!

1832-1982
Wer kennt Goethe?

RSM

Singular	Plural
ich weiß	wir wissen
Sie wissen	Sie wissen
du weißt	ihr wißt
er sie es } weiß	sie wissen

▣ **Übung 16. Kennen oder wissen?**

Ergänzen Sie.

1. _____ Sie Goethe? Nein, ich _____ ihn nicht, aber ich _____, wer er ist.
2. _____ du, wo er gelebt hat? Nein, das _____ ich leider nicht.
3. _____ du seinen Roman *Die Leiden des jungen Werther?*
4. Was willst du später mal machen? Das _____ ich noch nicht.
5. _____ ihr was? Ich mache Schluß für heute (*I'm quitting*).

LESEN IM KONTEXT ▣▣▣▣▣▣▣▣▣▣▣▣▣▣▣

In this section, you will explore texts with information about entertainment opportunities, leisure time, and cultural activities. The objective is to read for specific information without going into the details.

Vor dem Lesen

▣ **Aktivität. Was machen Sie gern am Wochenende?**

Füllen Sie den Fragebogen aus!

	SEHR GERN	GERN	NICHT BESONDERS GERN	GAR NICHT GERN
1. ins Kino gehen	____	____	____	____
2. ins Theater gehen	____	____	____	____
3. in die Oper gehen	____	____	____	____
4. Freunde besuchen	____	____	____	____
5. ins Restaurant gehen	____	____	____	____
6. zu einer Party gehen	____	____	____	____
7. ein gutes Buch lesen	____	____	____	____
8. Sport treiben	____	____	____	____
9. fernsehen	____	____	____	____
10. arbeiten	____	____	____	____

Vor dem Lesen.   Suggestion: Students should fill out *Fragebogen* at home. In class, have them compare results and report five points on which they differ from a partner, e.g., *Linda spielt gern Karten, aber ich spiele gar nicht gern Karten.*
To obtain a class profile of students' favorite activities, you can read items aloud. Students raise their hands if they have responded *sehr gern.*

Was machen die Studenten in Ihrer Klasse gern? Was sind die Lieblings-
beschäftigungen (*favorite activities*)?

Text Collage

You see here a collage of six different types of texts. Even though you are
getting only a few snippets of information, you will be able to find out quite
a bit about the content without knowing the entire text.

Zum Text 1

1. Welcher Text paßt (*fits*) thematisch nicht zu den anderen Texten?
2. Welcher Text (a–f) paßt zu welcher Kategorie? Es gibt sieben Kategorien, aber nur sechs Texte! Für eine Kategorie gibt es keinen Text.

Zum Text 1.   Suggestion: #1 and #2 can be done as a pair activity. For #2, students should alternate reading items in the list; #3 can be done individually, either silently in class or as homework.

TV Magazin   _____
Was ist los in Wien?   _____
Kultur in Berlin   _____
Kinoprogramm   _____
Theaterprogramm   _____
Rezept zum Backen   _____
Kalender   _____

3. In welchen Texten finden Sie diese Information? (*Just place a check-mark when information is provided. Leave the space blank if no information is given.*)

TEXT	STADT (WO)	DATUM (MONAT)	ANFANGSZEIT (WANN)
a.	_____	_____	_____
b.	_____	_____	_____
c.	_____	_____	_____
d.	_____	_____	_____
e.	_____	_____	_____

You have just practiced scanning a text for specific information. You do not need to read every word of certain types of texts. When you need information about a particular movie you want to see, for example, you don't usually read every word of a movie ad or announcement.

Kinoanzeigen°

Movie announcements

RSM

„ES IST SCHON EIN KLEINES GLÜCK, DIESEN FILM SEHEN ZU KÖNNEN." *ZDF*

MALCOLM

DAS SYMPATHISCHSTE ORIGINAL SEIT BUSTER KEATON

Ausgezeichnet mit 8 australischen Oscars (bester Film, beste Regie, beste Darsteller).

Malcolm (30), ein kauziger Bastelfreak, schickt Miniautos zum Milchholen und zum Überfall auf Geldboten, fährt nachts mit einer Ein-Mann-Straßenbahn spazieren und landet den abenteuerlichsten Bankraub der Filmgeschichte.

„Eine liebenswerte Komödie um einen jener hinreißenden Spinner, die mehr draufhaben als so viele Macher und Macker drumherum. Sehenswert."
Tip, Berlin

„»Malcolm« ist eine ungeheuer witzige Komödie, die das gewisse Etwas hat, worüber man später noch schmunzeln muß." *Stadtzeitung, München*

„Ein Fundstück von verblüffendem Spinner-Charme: Sowohl als naiv-krimineller Geniestreich wie auch als liebenswertes Bastlermärchen ein überaus originelles Produkt blühender Phantasie – der reinste Bussifilm." *Ponkie, AZ*

5. WOCHE

FILM-CASINO Odeonspl. 8, Tel. 220818
Tägl. 15.30, 18.00, 20.30 U.

RSM

Zum Text 2

1. Sie möchten einen bestimmten Film sehen. Was möchten Sie wissen? Lesen Sie die Fragen und antworten Sie: wichtig, interessant oder unwichtig.

   BEISPIEL: Wo läuft der Film? → wichtig

   a. Wo läuft der Film?
   b. Wieviel kosten die Kinokarten?
   c. Wann fängt der Film an?
   d. Bekommt der Film einen Filmpreis (z.B. einen Oscar)?
   e. Wer ist der Regisseur (*director*)?
   f. Wer sind die Schauspieler?
   g. Wo war der Film erfolgreich (*successful*)?

2. **Welche Filme möchten Sie sehen?** Choose three films you would like to see from the movie ads on this and the previous page and look for relevant information in the ads.

FILM	ANFANGSZEIT	KINO
BEISPIEL: *Top Gun*	17.00 Uhr	Stachus Kino Center, Kino 4
a. ____	____	____
b. ____	____	____
c. ____	____	____

Was ist los in Wien?

Veranstaltungen

Österreichisches Rotes Kreuz: 9 bis 12.30 Uhr und 13.30 bis 15 Uhr, Blutspendeaktion (Flohmarkt / Naschmarkt, 6, Linke Wienzeile).

Dornbacher Annen-Kirtag: 23. 7., 14 Uhr, Platzkonzert, 17 Uhr, Ernst Farkas, „Evergreens und Schlager" (Schwarzenberg-Meierei, 17, Endstation Linie 43).

Pfarrkirche St. Hubertus (13, Dr.-Schober-Straße 96): 23. 7., 18 Uhr, „Christophorus-Sonntag", Fahrzeugweihe nach den Hl. Messen.

Filmhaus Stöbergasse: 23. 7., 18.30 und 21 Uhr, „2001: Odyssee im Weltraum", Regie: Kubrick.

Sommerkino-Festival (Artis-Kino, 1, Schultergasse/Jordangasse): 23. 7., 17.45 Uhr, „Otto – der neue Film"; 20 Uhr, „Maccaroni"; 22.15 Uhr, „Angel Heart".

Konzerte

Kleiner Redoutensaal: 23. 7., 20.30 Uhr, Haydn-Sinfonietta, Dirigent: Manfred Huss, Werke von Mozart, Haydn, Beethoven.

Konzerthaus: 23. 7., 20.30 Uhr, Wiener Hofburg-Orchester und internationale Gesangssolisten, Dirigent: Gert Hofbauer.

Votivkirche: 23. 7., 19.30 Uhr, Synthesizerkonzert Romayne Wheeler, Werke von Grieg, Liszt, Debussy, Wheeler.

Wiener Musiksommer

Schrammelmusik: 22. 7., 17 Uhr, Philharmonia-Schrammeln (Haydn-Haus, Hof).

Promenadenkonzert: 22. 7., 17 Uhr, Militärmusik des Gardebataillons Wien, Leitung: Obstlt. Hans Schadenbauer (Rathausplatz).

Festival Orgelkunst, Augustinerkirche: 22. 7., 19.30 Uhr, Monika Lenz, Sopran, Peter Frankenberg, Oboe, Martin Haselböck, Orgel und Leitung, Wiener Akademie, Werke von Händel und Mozart (Drei Kirchensonaten für Orgel und Orchester KV 328, 244, 336, Motette).

Für Kinder

Peter Schafler's Puppentheater: 23. und 24. 7., 15 und 16.30 Uhr, Vorstellungen bei Schönwetter im Böhmischen Prater (10, Laaerberg).

Kasperl am Kanal: 23. 7., 16 Uhr, Sandkorntheater Berlin, „Die Reise ans Ende der Welt" (Donaukanal, bei der Salztorbrücke/U-Bahn Schwedenplatz).

„Kunterbunter Bäderspaß": 22. 7., (Arbeiterstrandbad) und 23. 7., (Kongreßbad).

Flohmärkte

Kunst- und Antik-Markt (an der Donaukanalpromenade zwischen Salztorbrücke und Schwedenbrücke): 23. 7., 14 bis 20 Uhr, 24. 7., 10 bis 20 Uhr.

SPÖ-Bezirksorganisation Döbling: 22. bis 24. 7., 10 bis 18 Uhr, Flohmarkt am Kahlenberg.

Musik

Jazzland: 23. 7., 21 Uhr, „Wiener Jazz-Spezialität", Hodina, Bienert, Hansen, Henkes.

Andino (6, Münzwardeing. 2): 23. 7., 21.30 Uhr, „Mato Grosso".

Papa's Tapas (4, Schwarzenbergplatz 10): 23. 7., 22 Uhr, Christoph Rois – Boogie-Piano.

Wanderung

Österreichischer Alpenverein: 23. bis 24. 7., 6.50 Uhr, Maria Schutz–Sonnwendstein–Wetterkoglerhaus, Treffpunkt: Südbahnhof.

Freitag

22 Juli

Namenstag: Maria Magdalena, Marlene, Verena

Zum Text 3

Kann man diese Information im Kulturkalender *Was ist los in Wien?* finden?

Zum Text 3. Students can do this in pairs or individually. When working in pairs, they should alternate reading the items (followed by the question *Steht das im Text?*) and responding.

	JA	NEIN	INFORMATION
1. Datum	X	_____	Freitag, 22. Juli
2. Information über ein Museum	_____	_____	_____
3. Wo findet man einen Floh-markt (*flea market*)?	_____	_____	_____
4. Was macht Kindern Spaß?	_____	_____	_____
5. Jazzkonzerte	_____	_____	_____
6. Filmprogramm	_____	_____	_____
7. Restaurants	_____	_____	_____
8. Wiener Oper	_____	_____	_____
9. Sport	_____	_____	_____
10. Konferenzen	_____	_____	_____

Nach dem Lesen

☐ Aktivität. Interaktion

Aktivität. Note: This is an information gap activity, in which one student has information that the other lacks. The purpose is to get the missing information from each other. These activities are designed to help students initiate questions and respond in detail. Make sure students cover up either the A or B section so they will not see what the other information is that they need.

You would like information about different museums and entertainment possibilities in Vienna in order to make up your mind where to go and when.

One student looks at part A of this activity, the other at part B. Section A contains information that is missing in the B section and vice versa. Ask questions of each other to get the missing information about the location, opening times, and dates.

BEISPIEL:

A

Name:	Zirkus- und Clownmuseum
Straße:	Karmelitergasse 9
Telefon:	_____
geöffnet:	Mittwoch, 17.30–19.00
	Samstag, 14.30–17.00
	Sonntag, 10–12

B

Name:	Zirkus- und Clownmuseum
Straße:	_____
Telefon:	34 68 615
geöffnet:	_____

B: Wie ist die Adresse vom Zirkus- und Clownmuseum?
A: Die Adresse ist Karmelitergasse 9. Wie ist die Telefonnummer?
B: Die Telefonnummer ist 34 68 615. Wann ist das Museum geöffnet?
A: Mittwoch, 17.30–19.00 Uhr.

A

Name:	_____ Museum	Museum Moderner Kunst	Riesenrad (*ferris wheel*)
Straße:	Berggasse 19	_____	Prater
Telefon:	31 15 96	34 12 59	_____
geöffnet:	_____	Täglich außer Dienstag 10–18	März und Oktober 10–12, April bis September 9–12

B

Name:	Sigmund Freud Museum	Museum Moderner Kunst	Riesenrad
Straße:	Berggasse 19	Fürstengasse 1	_____
Telefon:	_____	_____	512 83 14
geöffnet:	Mo–Fr 9–13, Sa, So 10–12	_____	

Das Riesenrad im Prater in Wien

WORTSCHATZ

Zeitausdrücke / Time Expressions

Substantive

das Jahr (-e)	year
die Minute (-n)	minute
die Mittagszeit (-en)	noontime
der Monat (-e)	month
der Nachmittag (-e)	afternoon
die Stunde (-n)	hour
der Tag (-e)	day
die Woche (-n)	week
das Wochenende (-n)	weekend
am Wochenende	on the weekend
die Uhr (-en)	watch; clock
um ein Uhr	at one o'clock
Wieviel Uhr ist es? / Wie spät ist es?	What time is it?
Es ist ein Uhr.	It is one o'clock.

Adverbien

abends	in the evenings
früh	early
heute abend	tonight
heute mittag	today at noon
heute morgen	this morning
morgen früh	early tomorrow morning
morgens	in the mornings
mittags	at noon
nachmittags	in the afternoon
nachts	at night
spät	late

Andere Substantive

das Bier (-e)	beer
die Erdkunde	geography
die Geschichte (-n)	history; story
das Kofferradio	portable radio
die Nebenarbeit (-en)	job on the side
das Picknick (-s)	picnic
der Picknickkorb (-̈e)	picnic basket
die Sozialkunde	social science
der Stundenplan (-̈e)	hourly schedule
die Tasse (-n)	cup
Tasse Kaffee	cup of coffee
die Verabredung (-en)	date
der Wetterbericht (-e)	weather report
die Wurst (-̈e)	sausage

Verben

anfangen (fängt an)	to start, begin
anrufen (ruft an)	to call (on the phone)
aufräumen (räumt auf)	to straighten up (a room)
aufstehen (steht auf)	to get up
ausgehen (geht aus)	to go out
aussehen (sieht aus)	to look
beginnen	to begin
bekommen	to get, receive
einkaufen (kauft ein)	to shop, go shopping
fernsehen (sieht fern)	to watch TV
frühstücken	to have breakfast
klingeln	to ring
kochen	to cook
leben	to live, reside
mitgehen (geht mit)	to come along
spazierengehen (geht spazieren)	to go for a walk
sprechen (spricht)	to speak
stehen	to stand
(Zeit) verbringen	to spend time
volltanken (tankt voll)	to get gasoline, to fill up
vorbeikommen (kommt vorbei)	to come by
vorhaben (hat vor)	to plan
wissen (weiß)	to know
zurückkommen (kommt zurück)	to come back

Modalverben

dürfen (darf)	may, to be allowed to
können (kann)	can, to be able to
mögen (mag)	to like
möchte	would like to
müssen (muß)	must, to have to
sollen	to be supposed to, shall
wollen (will)	to want, wish, desire, intend

Sonstiges

allein	alone
fertig	ready
gemütlich	comfortable, leisurely
jeder	every
jeden Tag	every day

kurz — for a short time
laut — loud(ly)
lieber — rather
man (*indef. pronoun*) — one; you; they; people
sonst — otherwise
ungefähr — approximately
verboten — forbidden
von... bis — from . . . to

Ausdrücke

alle zwei Wochen — every other week
herzliche Grüße — greetings, regards
ins Grüne fahren — to go on an outing (to where it is green)

(das) stimmt — that's correct
viel Glück — lots of luck
Der Film läuft im... — The film is playing at . . .
Es ist zu Ende. — It is over.

KAPITEL 5

EINKAUFEN

Einkaufen. Approach the material in this chapter by talking about things you need and where you will go to buy them. Be sure to recycle material from previous chapters, e.g., *Kapitel 2,* in which shopping was first introduced.

Lernziele *In this chapter you will learn what to say when going shopping for food and clothing. You will be describing where something is located and where you are going. You will also learn to make requests and suggestions.*

RSM

Profil einer Straße

Einkaufen *mit Spaß* im Uni-Viertel

a. die Vollkornbäckerei *whole-grain bakery*
b. auf... *on quiet soles*
c. das Fachbuch(-̈er) *specialty book*
d. das Geschenk(-e) *gift*
e. der Sekt *champagne*
f. die Mitfahrzentrale *ride-sharing agency*

▣ Alles klar?

Was kann man in dieser Straße kaufen?

	JA	NEIN	WO?
Bücher	X		bei Mandala
Bekleidung (*clothing*)	___	___	_____
Sportartikel	___	___	_____
Papier	___	___	_____
Getränke (trinken)	___	___	_____
Lebensmittel (*groceries*)	___	___	_____
Schuhe	___	___	_____
Geschenke	___	___	_____
Brot	___	___	_____

The shops in this street appeal to people interested in particular products and materials. What clues can you find for this?

Alles klar? Suggestion: This activity can be done as homework to introduce the chapter, or in class, with students working in pairs. Students should take turns asking each other *Kann man _____ in dieser Straße kaufen?* and responding.

Aktivität 1 (*below*). **Suggestion:** Encourage students to include in their responses new items listed in the exercise and items shown in the drawings. **Point out:** *Sakko* is either masculine or neuter.
Point out: *0 Grad Celsius* is 32 degrees Fahrenheit. Brainstorm other possibilities with students.

WÖRTER IM KONTEXT

Mode und Bekleidung

Suggestion: Let students look over the vocabulary for clothing items in the drawings. Then ask questions such as *Wer trägt heute einen Rock?* or *Wer trägt ein Hemd?* Students raise their hand when a question applies to them.

▣ Aktivität 1. Was tragen Sie gewöhnlich°?

usually

BEISPIEL: Ich trage gewöhnlich Jeans und ein T-Shirt zur Uni.° Zur Arbeit trage ich ein Sporthemd, eine Hose und ein Sakko.

Universität

1. zur Arbeit
2. zur Uni
3. im Winter bei 0 Grad Celsius
4. am Wochenende
5. im Konzert oder in der Oper
6. zu einem Rockkonzert

    der Anzug (*suit*)
    die Jeans
    der Jeansrock
    die Lederjacke
    der Parka
    der/das Sakko (*sports jacket*)
    der Schal
    die Skihose
    das T-Shirt
    der Wintermantel

🔲 Analyse

Schauen Sie sich die Anzeigen an. Beantworten Sie dann die Fragen.

machen's möglich[a]
Über 10 000 Konfektionsteile[b]
in allen Größen für Damen und Herren.
Spezial-Abteilungen:[c]
Braut- u. Abendgarderobe, Schwarz/Weiß

BEKLEIDUNGSHAUS MARTENS
Einkaufsziel vieler Niederrheiner
Goch-Pfalzdorf, an der alten B 9
(zwischen Goch und Kleve)

a. *possible*
b. die Konfektion *ready-made clothes*
c. die Abteilung *department*

RSM

Hemden, Hosen,
Sakkos, Anzüge[a]
T-Shirts, Pullover
und, und, und ...

Viele Einzelteile unserer hochwertigen Sommer-
Collectionen sind drastisch preisreduziert. Über-
zeugen Sie sich von der Auswahl unserer
Angebote - es lohnt sich![b]

Leyendeckers
herrenmoden
Inhaber Rolf Kaspers · BONN-BAD GODESBERG
· Konfektion: Fronhof · Herrenartikel: Theaterplatz
Tel.: (0228) 36 45 93

a. das Sakko, der Anzug(-̈e) *sports
jacket/men's suit*
b. es... *it's worth it!*

Schön, chic und auch ein bißchen frech:[a]

neue mode
Die vielseitige Frauenzeitschrift

a. *naughty*

1. Die Texte haben ein Wort gemeinsam (*in common*). Wie heißt das
   Wort? Wie heißt dieses Wort auf englisch?
2. Welches Geschäft (*store*) hat Bekleidung nur für Männer?
3. Welches Geschäft hat Bekleidung für Männer und Frauen?
4. Welches Geschäft hat Ausverkauf? (Das heißt, die Preise sind reduziert.) Welche Wörter im Text sagen etwas über einen Ausverkauf aus?

Sprachnotiz

The impersonal expression **es gibt** means *there is* or *there are*. It can also be used to say where you can get something. The object of **es gibt** is always in the accusative case.

Schicke Blusen
Wo?
bei
Gisie
Papendiek 29

Gibt es in dieser Stadt einen Markt?
Is there a market in this town? (Does it exist?)

Wo gibt es schicke Blusen?
Where can you get stylish blouses?

Blusen gibt es bei Gisie.
You can get blouses at Gisie's (shop).

Use the preposition **bei** and the name of the place to say where you can get something.

Wo gibt es Hamburger? Bei McDonald's.

Aktivität 2. Interaktion

Was brauchen Sie, und wo gibt es das zu kaufen? Was kostet das?

Das neue Jahr fängt preiswert an...

Für die Dame

Pullover
viele Farben und Formen
40,-/60,-/80,-

Röcke *70,-/90,-*

Jacken
Thermo und Wolle
80,-/120,-/150,-

Mäntel
Popeline- und Wollqualitäten
90,-/120,-/250,-

Für den Herrn

Pullover
40,-/60,-/90,-

Hosen
Cord- und Wollqualitäten
60,-/90,-

Sakkos
180,-/240,-

Anzüge
IWS und Mischgewebe
250,-/350,-

... und vieles mehr

SONDERANGEBOTE IN DER HERRENABTEILUNG!!

ab **65.-**

Modellbeispiel
Stiefel reduziert ab **69.-**

Moon Boots und gefütterte Gummistiefel ab **25.-**

Schuhkauf = ohne Parkprobleme

Otten & Leenders
Ihr Schuhzentrum in Kleve
Mittelweg 48

BEISPIEL:
A: Ich brauche dringend einen Anzug. Wo gibt es hier Anzüge?
B: Anzüge gibt es bei Straub.
A: Weißt du, wieviel ein Anzug da kostet?
B: Es gibt Anzüge für 250 Mark.

Pullover (Pulli)
Stiefel
Jacke
Hose

Bluse
Sakko
Rock
Anzug

▣ Aktivität 3. Koffer-Memo

The following **Koffer-Memo** lists clothing items a family might buy and pack when going on a vacation.

1. Welche Bekleidungsstücke sind nur für Mädchen? Welche sind für Mädchen und für Jungen?
2. Welche Sachen auf dieser Liste tragen Sie besonders gern? Welche tragen Sie nie?

Sprachnotiz

Trainings- und Jogginganzüge = Trainingsanzüge und Jogginganzüge

The hyphen after **Trainings-** stands for the word shared with the following compound noun (**Anzüge**).

▣ Aktivität 4. Kofferpacken!

Spielen Sie in Gruppen von vier bis fünf Personen. So spielt man es:

A: Ich packe fünf Bikinis in meinen Koffer.
B: Ich packe fünf Bikinis und Sportschuhe.
C: Ich packe fünf Bikinis, Sportschuhe und Ledersandalen.

Wer etwas vergißt oder falsch sagt, scheidet aus (*drops out*).

Neue Wörter

die Farbe (-n) *color*

beige *beige*
blau *blue*
braun *brown*
gelb *yellow*
grau *gray*
grün *green*
lila *purple*
orange *orange*
rot *red*
schwarz *black*
weiß *white*

dunkel *dark*
    dunkelgrün *dark green*

hell *light*
    hellblau *light blue*

gestreift *striped*
kariert *checkered*

RSM

Koffer-Memo
Alles zu Erholungspreisen

Für Kleinkinder

◯ T-Shirts	**4.-**
◯ Shorts	**6.-**
◯ Boxer-Shorts	**6.50**
◯ Cordhosen	**12.-**
◯ Kleidchen[a]	**15.-**
◯ Lack-Regenmäntel	**9.-**
◯ Leder-Sandalen	**18.-**

Für Schüler und Teener

◯ Badeanzüge und Bikinis	**12.-**
◯ Shorts	**8.-**
◯ Blusen	**14.-**
◯ Röcke	**16.-**
◯ Kleider	**20.-**
◯ Hemden	**10.-**
◯ Sweatshirts	**10.-**
◯ Baumwollhosen	**17.-**
◯ Trainings- und Jogginganzüge	**27.-**
◯ Sportschuhe	**12.-**
◯ Wäsche-Garnituren[b]	**6.-**
◯ Shorty-Schlafanzüge	**10.-**

C&A

...wo Mode so wenig kostet

a. *child's dress*
b. *sets of underwear*

⊡ Aktivität 5. Bekleidung

Beschreiben Sie, was und welche Farben eine Person in der Klasse trägt.

> BEISPIEL: Karin trägt eine Bluse. Die Bluse ist rot-weiß gestreift. Sie trägt auch Jeans; die sind natürlich blau. Und ihre Schuhe sind, hm, lila.

RSM

Sprachnotiz

Welche Größe brauchen Sie?

FÜR DAMEN: KLEIDER, MÄNTEL, JACKEN, BLUSEN

in USA	6	8	10	12	14	16
in Deutschland	34	36	38	40	42	44

FÜR HERREN: MÄNTEL, ANZÜGE, SAKKOS

in USA	36	38	40	42	44
in Deutschland	46	48	50	52	54

HERRENHEMDEN

in USA	14	14½	15	15½	16	16½
in Deutschland	36	37	38	39	40	42

SCHUHGRÖßEN (DAMEN UND HERREN)

in USA	5½	6½	7½	8½	9½	10½	11½	12½
in Deutschland	37	38	39/40	41	42	43	44	45

Kleine Preise auch für große Größen! Tolle Angebote, wie z. B. sportliche Pullover in modischen Dessins

ab **90,–**

🔲 Aktivität 6. Hören Sie zu. Gespräche im Geschäft

Was brauchen die Leute? In welcher Größe und in welcher Farbe?

	was?	*welche Größe?*	*welche Farbe?*
A.	Schuhe	44	schwarz
B.	Hose	38	blau-weiß
C.	Bluse	38	rot
D.	Wintermantel	44	dunkelblau

Neue Wörter

die Baumwolle *cotton*
die Kasse *cash register*
  vorne an der Kasse *at the*
    cash register in the front
der Kunde *customer*

anprobieren (probiert an)
  to try on
helfen (hilft) *to help*

zahlen *to pay*

Das gefällt mir. *I like it (lit. that*
  pleases me)
Das macht zusammen... *The total*
  is...
Das paßt mir. *That fits me.*

nötig *necessary*

Sprachnotiz

Gefällt Ihnen das Hemd?	*Do you like the shirt?*
Ja, es gefällt mir.	*Yes, I like it.*
Das Hemd paßt ihm.	*The shirt fits (him).*

The verbs **gefallen** (*to like*) and **passen** (*to fit*) require a dative object. The words **Ihnen** (*you*), **mir** (*me*), and **ihm** (*him*) are personal pronoun objects in the dative case.

Dialog. Beim Einkaufen im Kaufhaus

VERKÄUFER: Bitte schön. Kann ich Ihnen helfen?
    KUNDE: Ich brauche ein paar Sporthemden.
VERKÄUFER: Welche Größe brauchen Sie?
    KUNDE: Größe 42.

VERKÄUFER: Und welche Farbe?

KUNDE: Grün oder blau.

VERKÄUFER: Wie gefällt Ihnen dieses Hemd in Marineblau?

KUNDE: Die Farbe ist mir zu dunkel. Haben Sie das in Hellblau?

VERKÄUFER: Ja, hier ist ein Hemd in Hellblau.

KUNDE: Ist das aus Baumwolle oder Synthetik?

VERKÄUFER: Das ist 100 Prozent Baumwolle. Möchten Sie es anprobieren?

KUNDE: Nein, das ist nicht nötig. Größe 42 paßt mir bestimmt. Wieviel kostet dieses Hemd?

VERKÄUFER: 45 Mark.

KUNDE: Gut. Ich nehme drei Hemden.

VERKÄUFER: Alle in Hellblau?

KUNDE: Nein, geben Sie mir bitte zwei in Blau und ein Hemd in Weiß.

VERKÄUFER: Das macht zusammen 135 Mark. Bitte, zahlen Sie vorne an der Kasse!

KUNDE: Danke schön.

VERKÄUFER: Bitte sehr.

▣ Aktivität 7. Zum Dialog im Kaufhaus

Ergänzen Sie die fehlende Information.

1. Der Kunde braucht _____.
2. Der Verkäufer möchte _____ und _____ wissen.
3. Der Kunde braucht _____ 42.
4. Größe 42 _____ ihm.
5. Das Hemd in Marineblau _____ ihm nicht.
6. Das Hemd ist aus _____.
7. Der Kunde _____ 135 Mark für drei Hemden.

▣ Aktivität 8. Rollenspiel

Ein Gespräch im Geschäft: Was brauchen Sie?

VERKÄUFER/VERKÄUFERIN	KUNDE/KUNDIN
Guten Tag. Kann _____? ⟶	Ich möchte gern _____.
Größe?	_____
Farbe?	_____
Wie gefällt Ihnen _____?	paßt mir (nicht)
	gefällt mir (nicht)
anprobieren?	_____
_____ Mark.	kostet?
	zu teuer, preiswert
	nehmen

Aktivität 8. **Suggestion:** Have students act out the role-play several times with different partners. **Point out:** Students choose expressions appropriate for their dialogue. Not every expression will be used. **Follow-up:** Role-plays can be assigned as a partner homework activity to be presented in class the next day.

Essen und Trinken

Schauen Sie sich die Anzeige für den Supermarkt an. Was gibt es zu kaufen?

a. aus Griechenland
b. *asparagus*
c. aus Holland
d. *beef roast*
e. aus Spanien
f. *strawberries*
g. aus Frankreich
h. *cauliflower*
i. *onion*
j. Gurken *pickles, cucumbers*
k. *cheese*
l. *cold cuts*
m. *meat*
n. Wurst *sausage*
o. *granola bar*
p. *pastry made with nuts*
q. *pastry made with strawberries*
r. Zitrone *lemon*

☐ **Analyse**

Analyse. **Suggestion:** This activity is geared toward list making and can be approached in various ways: (1) preview the ad with students, then assign the *Analyse* for homework; (2) have students work in pairs, assigning one question to each pair. When results are reported to the class, have other students take notes. **Point out** abbreviations in the ad: *franz. = französisch; holl. = holländisch; span. = spanisch; griech. = griechisch.* Write the German names for these countries on the board.

1. Welche Getränke bietet der Supermarkt an? Welche kennen Sie? Welche kennen Sie nicht?
2. Aus welchen Ländern kommen das Gemüse und das Obst?
3. Gibt es Fleischwaren?
4. Gibt es Milchprodukte?

Sprachnotiz

The metric system is used in German-speaking countries. The following abbreviations for weights and measures occur in the supermarket ad:

> 1 kg = 1 Kilogramm = 1000 Gramm = 2 Pfund
> 500 g = 500 Gramm = 1 Pfund
> 1000 ml = 1000 Milliliter
> 0,75 l = 0,75 Liter
> 1 l = 1 Liter

Other abbreviations used in the supermarket ad are:

> Kl. I = Klasse I *top quality*
> Stck. = Stück *piece*

To read prices out loud:

> DM 11,99 = elf Mark neunundneunzig *or* elf
>   neunundneunzig
> DM 1,49 = eine Mark neunundvierzig *or* eins
>   neunundvierzig
> 0,75 = fünfundsiebzig Pfennig

▣ Aktivität 9. Interaktion

Schauen Sie sich die Liste mit Waren aus dem Supermarkt an. Was kosten diese Waren? Für wieviel? Woher sind sie?

> BEISPIEL: A: Was kosten Erdbeeren?
> B: Erdbeeren kosten eins neunundvierzig.
> A: Für wieviel?
> B: Für 250g.
> A: Woher sind die Erdbeeren?
> B: Aus Spanien.

▣ Aktivität 10. Interaktion

Sie haben nur 20 Mark für Essen und Trinken übrig und müssen damit ein ganzes Wochenende auskommen.

Wählen Sie Waren aus den Anzeigen auf Seite 142 und auf der nächsten Seite aus. Vergleichen Sie (*Compare*) Ihre Listen in der Klasse.

> BEISPIEL: Wir kaufen ein Bauernbrot für DM 1,79, 200 g Kalbsleberwurst für DM 2,56, 1 Kilo Tomaten für DM 2,98 und eine Schwarzwälder Kirsch-Torte für DM 9,95.

RSM

Mühlbacher Bauernbrot,[a]
täglich frisch bei Tengelmann.

Alle guten Sorten
sind jetzt 4!
Probieren Sie mal!

MÜHLBACHER
Bauernbrot
herzhaft, gewürzt,
Sonnenblume
oder Kornlaib
je 500 g

1,79

Vollwert-Dreikorn Toast
500 g Packung

1,79

BATSCHEIDER
Katenbrot
500 g

1,99

a. *farmer's bread*

Langnese Eiscreme
„Maxim's", 3 Sorten
je 750 ml

3.99

Goldstein
Schwarzwälder
Kirsch-Torte[a]
tiefgekühlt   1150 g-Pkg.

9.95

a. *Black Forest cherry tart*

NeuKauf

Unser Metzgermeister empfiehlt:

vm
vinzenzmurr

1a Rinderrouladen 100 g		**1.39**
Delik. Kalbsleberwurst extra i. Fettdarm, DLG-präm. 100 g		**1.28**

Aus den Obst- und Gemüsegärten der Welt

Spanische Navel-Orangen HKL II	3 kg	**3.98**
Spanische Satsumas HKL II	1 kg	**1.58**
Italienische Kiwi	Stück	**-.48**
Spanische Tomaten HKL I	1 kg	**2.98**
Griechische Gurken HKL I	350-450-g-Stück	**-.98**
Holländischer Kopfsalat HKL. I	Stück	**-.98**

Neue Wörter

der Aufschnitt *cold cuts*
die Bäckerei *bakery*
das Brot *bread*
  das Bauernbrot *farmer's bread*
das Brötchen *roll*
die Erdbeeren *strawberries*
das Gemüse *vegetable*
der Kuchen *cake*
die Leberwurst *liverwurst*
die Metzgerei *butcher shop*

das Obst *fruit*
die Ware *goods*
das Würstchen *small sausage (hot dog)*
sonst noch (et)was? *anything else?*

4,99

⊡ **Aktivität 11.** **Eine Bildgeschichte: Einkaufstag für Jutta**

Jutta gibt eine Party. Deshalb muß sie einkaufen. Schreiben Sie einen Text für die Bilder. So beginnt die Geschichte: Jutta gibt am Wochenende eine Party. Deshalb geht sie heute einkaufen. (*Match elements from columns A and B to form your sentences.*)

A:	B:
Dort kauft sie	Obst und Gemüse—alles ganz frisch.
Zuletzt geht sie	Brot, Brötchen und Käsekuchen.
Zuerst geht sie	und geht nach Hause.
Da gibt es	zur Bäckerei.
Dann geht sie	zum Lebensmittelgeschäft.
Jutta braucht auch	zur Metzgerei.
Deshalb geht sie auch	Würstchen zum Grillen.
Jetzt hat sie alles	Kaffee, Zucker, Milch und Käse.
	zum Markt.

> ## Sprachnotiz
>
> The suffixes **-chen** and **-lein** usually indicate a small version of an item. Nouns ending in **-chen** or **-lein** are always neuter. The plural form is identical with the singular form.
>
> das Brot (*bread*) → das Brötchen (*roll*)
>
> die Wurst (*sausage*) → das Würstchen (*small sausage*)

Aktivität 12. Hören Sie zu.

Sie hören drei Dialoge: in einer Bäckerei, auf dem Markt und in einer Metzgerei.
Schreiben Sie die Information in die Tabelle (kreuzen Sie das richtige Geschäft an).

	Markt	*Bäckerei*	*Metzgerei*	*Was?*	*Preis?*
Dialog 1			✓	Würstchen Aufschnitt	DM 13, –
Dialog 2		✓		Brötchen Schwarzbrot	DM 6, 50
Dialog 3	✓			Erdbeeren Tomaten	DM 11, 75

Aktivität 12. Suggestion: Make sure students understand how to work with the chart: place check marks under correct store and write in what the item is and its price. Play each dialogue once. Then let students listen a second time, pausing after each to let them write down the information.

Neue Wörter

die Kartoffel (-n) *potato*
der Nachtisch *dessert*
das schmeckt gut *that tastes good*

vorschlagen (schlägt vor) *to suggest*
lieber *rather*
ich möchte lieber... *I would rather . . .*

Aktivität 13. Interaktion

Sie planen mit einem Freund oder mit einer Freundin ein Menü für eine Party. Was wollen Sie servieren? Hier sind einige Vorschläge. Wählen Sie Dinge aus jeder Gruppe aus.

zum Essen: Würstchen, Steaks, Hamburger, Kartoffelsalat, Kartoffelchips, Pommes frites, Salat, Gemüse
zum Nachtisch: Eis, Pudding, frische Erdbeeren, Käsekuchen
zum Trinken: Mineralwasser (Sprudel), Bier, Wein, Limonade

Aktivität 13. Note: This interactive activity again allows for personal choices. Review the vocabulary first; then have students do the activity with several different partners. Call on several pairs to role-play a dialogue for the whole class.

A: Wollen wir ＿＿＿ grillen?

B: Gut. Machen wir ＿＿＿ mit ＿＿＿
und ＿＿＿.

B: Nein, ich möchte lieber ＿＿＿
mit ＿＿＿ und ＿＿＿.

A: Und zum Nachtisch ＿＿＿.

A: Na, gut. Und ＿＿＿.

B: Was sollen wir dabei trinken?

A: ＿＿＿.

B: Na gut.

B: Also, ＿＿＿ schmeckt doch nicht
dabei. Ich schlage vor, wir
trinken ＿＿＿.

GRAMMATIK IM KONTEXT ▫▫▫▫▫▫▫▫▫▫▫▫

der-Words: *dieser, jeder,* and *welcher*

The demonstrative adjectives **dieser** (*this*), **jeder** (*every*), and the interrogative adjective **welcher** (*which*) have the same endings as the definite article. Like the definite article, they signal the gender, case, and number of the following noun. For this reason they are frequently called **der-**words.

Welches Hemd möchten Sie?	*Which shirt would you like?*
Welche Farbe möchten Sie?	*Which color would you like?*
Dieser Mantel paßt gut.	*This coat fits well.*
Ich kann nicht **jede** Farbe tragen.	*I cannot wear every color.*

The forms of **dieser** exemplify the declension of all **der-**words.

	Masculine	*Neuter*	*Feminine*	*Plural*
Nominative	dieser	dieses	diese	diese
Accusative	diesen	dieses	diese	diese

▫ Übung 1. Im Geschäft

Was kostet das? Ergänzen Sie die passende Form von **dieser, jeder** oder **welcher.**

    BEISPIEL: **Was kostet diese Krawatte?**

Übung 1. **Suggestion:** Students can do this exercise in pairs, alternating asking and answering questions. Add on to this exercise by suggesting other items, using magazine ads or other visuals.

1. Was kosten _____ Cowboystiefel?
2. _____ Stiefel meinen Sie?
3. Wie finden Sie _____ Mantel?
4. _____ Mantel meinen Sie?
5. Wieviel kosten _____ Hemden?
6. _____ Hemd kostet 52 Mark.
7. Was kostet _____ Anzug?
8. Wir haben _____ Woche ein Sonderangebot.
   _____ Anzug im Laden kostet nur DM 230, -.

The Dative Case

The dative case is used as an object case with specific verbs and prepositions.

In chapter two you learned that the accusative case is used for the direct object of a sentence. Most German verbs that need a complement to make a sentence take an object in the accusative case.

> Peter braucht einen Regenmantel.
> Er findet einen Mantel bei Hertie.

A number of common verbs, however, always take an object in the dative case. Other verbs can take two objects: one object in the accusative case (direct object) and the other in the dative case (indirect object). The object in the dative case nearly always indicates a person—but occasionally an animal or a thing—toward whom the action of the verb is directed.

Wir wünschen unseren Gästen und Bekannten[a]
ein gesundes Neues Jahr.

*Ab Januar 1989 möchten wir Ihnen unsere
neue Speiseauswahl*[b] *anbieten.*[c]

**Restaurant
Haus Kuckuck**
Bedburg-Hau

Horst und Christine Schmidt

a. *acquaintances*
b. *menu*
c. *offer*

Liebe Mutti,

Zum Geburtstag
wünschen wir dir alles,
alles Gute
*Vati
und die
ganze Bande*[a]

a. die ganze Bande *the whole gang*

**Herr Professor, bitte
helfen Sie mir!**

RSM

◻ Analyse

- Look at the texts above and find the dative object by asking yourself for whom the action indicated by the verb is intended.
- Find several personal pronoun objects in the dative. What is the nominative of these pronouns?
- Find several noun objects in the dative case.

Analyse. Suggestion: Review accusative case endings and personal pronouns before approaching dative objects through the *Analyse*. Do this as a whole group.

PERSONAL PRONOUNS IN THE DATIVE			
Singular		*Plural*	
mir	*me*	uns	*us*
Ihnen (*formal*)	*you*	Ihnen (*formal*)	*you*
dir	*you*	euch	*you*
ihm	to/for *him*		to/for
ihr	*her*	ihnen	*them*
ihm	*it*		

der- AND **ein-**WORDS IN THE DATIVE			
Masculine	*Neuter*	*Feminine*	*Plural*
dem	dem	der	den
diesem	diesem	dieser	diesen
(k)einem	(k)einem	(k)einer	keinen
meinem	meinem	meiner	meinen

Nouns in the Dative

Nouns do not take an ending in the dative singular, except for those special masculine nouns that take **-n** or **-en** in the accusative singular (chapter two). These irregular masculine nouns also take **-n** or **-en** in the dative singular.

-**(e)n** MASCULINE NOUNS			
Nominative	der Herr	der Student	der Kunde
Accusative	den Herrn	den Studenten	den Kunden
Dative	dem Herrn	dem Studenten	dem Kunden

In the dative plural, all nouns add **-n** to the nominative plural ending, unless the plural already ends in **n.** Nouns of foreign origin whose plural ends in **s** are unchanged in the dative plural.

Nominative Singular	die Dame	der Mann	das Auto
Nominative Plural	die Damen	die Männer	die Autos
Dative Plural	den Damen	den Männern	den Autos

Verbs with Accusative and Dative Objects

In the case of verbs that can take two objects, the object in the accusative case (the direct object in English) will usually be a thing; the object in the dative case (the indirect object in English) will normally be a person. Verbs that can take an accusative and a dative object in German include:

empfehlen (empfiehlt)	*to recommend*
geben (gibt)	*to give*
kaufen	*to buy*
schenken	*to give as a gift*
schreiben	*to write*
wünschen	*to wish*
zeigen	*to show*

	DATIVE OBJECT	ACCUSATIVE OBJECT	
Wir wünschen	dir	alles Gute	zum Geburtstag.
Herr Schmidt schenkt	seiner Frau	einen Ring	zum Geburtstag.
Der Verkäufer zeigt	Herrn Schmidt	drei Ringe.	
Er empfiehlt	ihm	einen Ring	aus Platin.

Note the position of the dative object: it precedes the accusative object. If the accusative object is a pronoun, however, the accusative object precedes the dative object.

	ACCUSATIVE OBJECT	DATIVE OBJECT	
Herr Schmidt schenkt	ihn (den Ring)	seiner Frau	zum Geburtstag.
Herr Schmidt schenkt	ihn	ihr	zum Geburtstag.

The dative object answers the question **wem** (*for whom, to whom*).

Wem schenkt Herr Schmidt einen Ring zum Geburtstag?	*To whom does Mr. Schmidt give a ring for a birthday gift?*
Wem gehört der Ring?	*To whom does the ring belong?*

▣ **Übung 2. Wem schenkst du diese Dinge?**

das Buch · die Ohrringe · der Schal · die Flasche Wein · die Krawatte · ein Aquarium mit zwei Goldfischen · der Gürtel

BEISPIEL: A: Wem schenkst du die Krawatte?
B: Die schenke ich meinem Vater.

Verbs with a Dative Object Only

A number of German verbs take an object in the dative case only. Several of these verbs are impersonal expressions. Two of them you have already learned in previous chapters.

Wie geht es dir?	*How are you?*
Es geht mir nicht gut.	*I am not well.*
Das tut mir leid.	*I am sorry.*

Here are several other important verbs with dative objects.

danken	Ich danke **Ihnen** für Ihre Hilfe.
	I thank you for your help.
gefallen	Wie gefällt **Ihnen** dieses Hemd?
	How do you like this shirt?
gehören	Der Mercedes gehört **meinem Bruder.**
	The Mercedes belongs to my brother.
helfen	Der Verkäufer hilft **dem Kunden.**
	The salesman helps the customer.
passen	Größe 48 paßt **mir** bestimmt.
	Size 48 fits me for sure.
schmecken	Der Kuchen schmeckt **mir** gut.
	The cake tastes good (to me).
stehen	Das Hemd steht **dir** gut.
	The shirt looks good on you.

Verbs that take only a dative object will be listed in the end vocabulary of each chapter and in the vocabulary section at the end of the book as follows:

helfen (hilft, *dat.*)

Dative Case with Adjectives

The dative case is used in conjunction with many predicate adjectives.

1000 Mark für dieses Kleid?	*1000 marks for this dress?*
Das ist **mir** zu teuer.	*That's too expensive (for me).*
Das Kleid ist **dir** zu eng.	*The dress is too tight (on you).*
Das ist **mir** egal.	*I don't care.*
Dieser Mantel ist **ihm** zu groß.	*This coat is too big for him.*

Übung 3. Suggestion: Review the meanings of the verbs first. Then let students work in pairs to complete the exercise. Have several pairs role-play the completed dialogue for the class.

□ **Übung 3. Ein schwieriger° Kunde**

difficult

Ergänzen Sie die Sätze. Wählen Sie ein Verb aus der Liste, und setzen Sie ein passendes Pronomen im Dativ ein.

danken, empfehlen, gefallen, helfen, passen, stehen, zeigen

VERKÄUFER: Kann ich _____[1]?

KUNDE: Ich brauche ein Geburtstagsgeschenk für meine Freundin. Können Sie _____ vielleicht etwas _____[2]?

VERKÄUFER: Wie wäre es mit einer Bluse?

KUNDE: Können Sie _____ vielleicht eine schicke Bluse in Größe 40 _____[3]?

VERKÄUFER: Hier habe ich eine Seidenbluse (*silk blouse*).

KUNDE: In Schwarz? Nein, schwarz _____[4] nicht.

VERKÄUFER: _____[5] diese Bluse in Rot?

KUNDE: Rot? Nein, die Farbe _____[6] nicht.

VERKÄUFER: Hier habe ich ein Modell aus Paris für 1250 Mark.

KUNDE: Wie bitte? 1250 Mark! Das ist zu teuer.

VERKÄUFER: Kann ich _____ etwas anderes (*different*) _____[7]?

KUNDE: Können Sie _____ vielleicht einen Hut _____[8]?

VERKÄUFER: Ja natürlich. Hier habe ich...

KUNDE: Ich muß jetzt gehen. Ich _____[9].

▣ Übung 4. **Fragen und Antworten**

Übung 4. Suggestion: Students should take turns initiating questions and responding.

Wem gehört das?

BEISPIEL: die Uhr
A: Wem gehört diese Uhr?
B: Die gehört meinem Vater.

das Fotoalbum	meine Schwester
die Schuhe	ich
die Kamera	Herr Hansen
der BMW	unser(e) Deutschprofessor(in)
der Mantel	meine Eltern
der Hut	unser Onkel Egon
das Kleid	unsere Oma
der Fußball	mein Bruder

▣ Übung 5. **Partnerarbeit**

Fragen Sie einen Partner in der Klasse: „Wie gefällt dir das?"

Übung 5. Follow up: Expand this activity by bringing a number of clothing items to class. Each pair of students receives one item, which they describe either positively or negatively, according to their opinion. Spot-check by having several pairs role-play the activity.

Michael

Jutta

Mark

Sabine

A: Wie gefällt dir Juttas Hut?

B: Er gefällt mir gut.

B: Er ist ihr zu groß.

POSITIV:

gefällt mir
ich finde _____
nicht schlecht
sehr schick
prima

NEGATIV:

gefällt mir nicht
_____ paßt ihm/ihr nicht.
Das ist ihm/ihr _____
   zu eng, groß, weit (*big*),
   kurz (*short*), lang
   ein bißchen komisch

Prepositions with the Dative

A number of common prepositions that require the dative case of nouns and pronouns are:

aus	*from, out of*	Richard kommt gerade aus dem Haus.
	(made) of	Das Hemd ist aus Baumwolle.
bei	*near*	Die Bäckerei ist beim (bei dem) Marktplatz.
	at (the place of)	Schicke Blusen bei Gisie
	for, at (a company)	Manfred arbeitet bei VW.
mit	*with*	Herr Schweiger geht mit seiner Frau einkaufen.
	by (means of)	Wir fahren mit dem Bus.

nach	*to (place name)*	Der Bus fährt nach Frankfurt.
		Ich fahre jetzt nach Hause.
	after	Nach dem Essen gehen wir einkaufen.
seit	*since*	Seit gestern haben wir schönes Wetter.
	for (time)	Seit einem Monat kauft sie nur noch Bio-Brot.

von	*from*	Das Brot ist vom (von dem) Bäcker.
		Frank kommt gerade vom Markt.
	by (origin)	Dieses Buch ist von Peter Handke.
zu	*to*	Wir gehen heute zum (zu dem)
		Supermarkt.
		Er ist jetzt wieder zu Hause.

Several of these prepositions are nearly always combined with the following definite article.

bei dem → beim	Jürgen kauft sein Brot nur **beim** Bäcker.
von dem → vom	Er kommt gerade **vom** Markt.
zu dem → zum	Er muß jetzt noch **zum** Bäcker.
zu der → zur	Dann geht er **zur** Bank.

The expressions **nach Hause** and **zu Hause** show an old dative ending (**e**) that is retained in writing but is often dropped in conversational German.

Wohin gehst du? Ich gehe jetzt nach Haus(e).
Wo ist Ilse? Sie ist zu Haus(e).

Vom Korn zum Brot[a]

Mühlenbäckerei
BORGMANN
Mühlenstraße 11 • Kranenburg
Inh. Ralf Borgmann
Telefon 0 28 26 / 2 65

a. Vom... *From grain to bread*

RSM

▣ Übung 6. Auskunft geben

Ergänzen Sie die Präpositionen.

1. Sag mal, wo gibt es hier denn schicke Blusen? _____ Gisie.
2. Die Bluse steht dir gut. Ist sie _____ Leinen oder Synthetik?
3. Ich brauche eine neue Kamera. _____ welcher Kamera kann man gut fotografieren?
4. Das Brot schmeckt ausgezeichnet. Woher hast du es? Ich bekomme es täglich frisch _____ der Bäckerei.
5. Ich muß heute noch für die Party einkaufen. Ich fahre _____ dem Wagen zum Supermarkt.
6. Bitte, komm _____ dem Einkaufen sofort _____ Hause.
7. Ich plane schon _____ drei Monaten eine Grillparty.
8. Wollen wir die Party _____ dir oder _____ mir _____ Hause machen?

Übung 6. **Suggestion:** Students can work in pairs, taking turns saying each sentence or question and giving the response. Check by calling on individuals to provide answers.

▣ Übung 7. Einkaufen

Beantworten Sie die Fragen. Benutzen Sie Wörter aus der Liste.

Bäckerei, Schwester, Haus, zwei Monate, Markt, Supermarkt, Wagen

1. Woher hat Christine die frischen Brötchen?
2. Wo ist diese Bäckerei?
3. Seit wann kauft sie bei diesem Bäcker ein?
4. Wohin muß sie dann noch gehen?

Übung 7. **Suggestion:** Have students work in pairs, taking turns asking questions and responding. Accept phrase-only responses: *Aus der Bäckerei.* Spot-check by asking several students to come up with different answers, whenever possible.

5. Fährt sie oder geht sie zu Fuß einkaufen?
6. Wohin geht sie dann?

▣ Übung 8. **Partnerarbeit**

Stellen Sie Fragen. Seit wann machst du das?

> BEISPIEL: A: Seit wann studierst du?
> B: Ich studiere seit einem Jahr.

1. Deutsch lernen
2. Auto fahren
3. ein Auto haben
4. arbeiten
5. ?

Two-Way Prepositions

A number of prepositions can be used with either the dative case or the accusative case. They take the dative case when answering the question **wo** (*where:* in reference to stationary location), but they take the accusative case when answering the question **wohin** (*where:* in reference to direction to a location).

Here are three common two-way prepositions. You will learn other two-way prepositions in chapter six.

in	*in (an enclosed space, or limited area)*
an	*at, by (bordering a place)*
auf	*on, on top of, at (a horizontal place)*

WO: *STATIONARY LOCATION (DATIVE)*

Wo kauft man Brot?	**In der** Bäckerei.
Wo zahlt der Kunde?	**An der** Kasse.
Wo kauft man frisches Gemüse?	**Auf dem** Markt.

WOHIN: *DIRECTION TO A LOCATION (ACCUSATIVE)*

Wohin fährt der Bus?	**In die** Stadt.
Wohin geht der Kunde?	**An die** Kasse.
Wohin gehst du?	**Auf den** Markt.

The prepositions **in, an,** and **auf** are usually contracted with the definite article.

in dem → im Garten
in das → ins Geschäft
an dem → am Markt
an das → ans Haus
auf das → aufs Haus

▣ Übung 9. Wo kauft Mark ein?

Mark muß heute einkaufen. Hier ist sein Einkaufszettel. Wo bekommt er diese Sachen?

BEISPIEL: Käsekuchen bekommt er in der Bäckerei.

der Supermarkt
die Metzgerei
der Buchladen
der Markt
das Schuhgeschäft
die Bäckerei
die Konditorei (*pastry shop*)

Übung 9. **Suggestion:** Review items on the shopping list before beginning the activity. Have students work in pairs taking turns asking, e.g., *Wo bekommt Mark Aufschnitt?* and responding *Aufschnitt bekommt er in der Metzgerei.*
Follow-up: Have students draw up a shopping list with at least five items. Then have them say to each other, *Ich brauche Leberwurst. Wo kann ich die bekommen?* Students can respond with *im / in der* or by using *bei* plus the store's name.

> Einkaufzettel
> 250 g Aufschnitt
> Käsekuchen
> 150 g Emmentaler Käse
> 6 Brötchen
> 12 Würstchen zum Grillen
> 1 Pfund Kaffee
> Schwarzbrot
> 2 Flaschen Sprudel
> 4 Tomaten
> nicht vergessen:
> Wörterbuch
> Tennisschuhe

▣ Übung 10. Ein Einkaufszentrum

Wie kommt man dahin, und was kann man dort machen? Schauen Sie sich die Werbung an, und beantworten Sie die Fragen.

1. Wie kommt man zu dem Einkaufszentrum (Spahn)?
2. Mit welcher Buslinie kann man dahin fahren?
3. Wo kann man dort essen?
4. Wo kann man Lampen kaufen?
5. Wo kann man parken?
6. Wo kann man Geschenke kaufen?
7. Wohin kann eine Mutter ihre Kinder bringen?

Übung 10. **Point out:** Students should rely on visual as well as written cues when working with this drawing.
Suggestion: Have students work in pairs, taking turns asking questions and responding.
Follow-up: As a homework assignment, have students create a similar shopping center plan with different stores. They should also provide questions, as in this exercise. Students can answer each other's questions in class the next day.

The Imperative

The imperative is a verb form used to make requests and recommendations and to give instructions, advice, or commands.

Bitte nehmen Sie Platz

HERTIE
BONN - Poststraße
BAD GODESBERG
Am Fronhof
Komm zu uns

▣ Analyse

- Finden Sie den Imperativ auf jedem Bild!
- Was sollen Sie tun oder kaufen?
- Wo steht das Verb in diesen Imperativsätzen?
- Gibt es ein Subjekt oder nicht? Wo steht es im Satz?

German uses several different imperative forms. You saw a few of them in the accompanying ads.

Formal Imperative

The formal imperative is used for anyone you address with the polite form **Sie.**

GENIESS DIE KLEINE PAUSE.
SAG JA ZU YES.
Leicht wie Biscuit.
Locker wie frische Torte.

Nehmen Sie Platz!	*Have a seat.*
Probieren Sie: Bitter-Bio-Brot!	*Try: Bitter-Bio-Brot!*
Bitte **geben Sie** mir zwei Pfund Kaffee!	*Please give me two pounds of coffee.*

The verb, identical with the infinitive, appears at the beginning of the sentence and is followed by the pronoun **Sie.** The word **bitte** may stand in front of the verb. An exclamation point is generally used at the end of the sentence.

The formal imperative has the same word order as a formal yes or no question. The exclamation point and the question mark at the end of the sentence make it clear whether it's an imperative or a question.

Probieren Sie Bio-Brot!	*Try some Bio-Brot!*
Probieren Sie Bio-Brot?	*Are you going to try some Bio-Brot?*

The Imperative. Introduce imperatives through Total Physical Response (TPR) techniques. Have students carry out several typical classroom actions: *Machen Sie das Fenster auf! Gehen Sie an die Tafel! Öffnen Sie Ihr Buch! Geben Sie es mir! Stehen Sie auf! Setzen Sie sich!*, etc. You should act out the exercise along with the students. **Follow-up:** Either in class or as a homework assignment, have students compare their answers to the *Analyse.*

In spoken German, only intonation indicates whether the speaker is requesting something or asking a question. In the case of a request or command, the speaker's voice falls at the end. In the case of a question, the speaker's voice rises at the end.

The German equivalent for English "Let's . . . (do something)" also has the word order of a request or a question.

Probieren wir Bio-Brot!	*Let's try Bio-Brot!*

Verbs with separable prefixes place the prefix at the end of the sentence in the imperative form.

Bringen Sie mir ein paar Brötchen **mit.**	*Pick up a few rolls for me.*

Singular Informal Imperative

The informal imperative is used for anyone you address with **du.**

Komm zu uns!	*Come to us (our house).*
Genieß die kleine Pause!	*Enjoy the short break.*
Sag ja!	*Say yes.*
Gib mir eine Tasse Kaffee!	*Give me a cup of coffee.*

The singular informal imperative is formed from the present tense **du** form of the verb; just omit the pronoun **du** and drop the **-st** ending.

INFINITIVE	**du** FORM	STEM OF **du** FORM	IMPERATIVE
kommen	du kommst	komm-	Komm!
geben	du gibst	gib-	Gib!
nehmen	du nimmst	nimm-	Nimm!
anrufen	du rufst an	ruf- an	Ruf an!

Verbs that show a vowel change from **a** to **ä** (**au** to **äu**) in the present tense **du** form have no umlaut in the imperative.

fahren	(du fährst)	**Fahr!**
laufen	(du läufst)	**Lauf!**

Sometimes, the informal (**du**) imperative ends in **-e**. This **e**—once a required ending—has generally become optional, particularly in conversational German. It is still used when a verb stem ends in **d** or **t**, and when it is needed to facilitate pronunciation.

füttern	**Fütter(e)** mich!	Feed me!
finden	**Finde** mal gutes Brot!	Try to find good bread!
reden	**Rede** nicht so viel!	Don't talk so much!

Plural Informal Imperative

The plural informal imperative is used to request something from several persons whom you individually address with **du.**

Kommt zu uns!	*Come see us. (lit., Come to us.)*
Fahrt jetzt nach Hause!	*Drive home now.*
Gebt mir bitte etwas zu essen!	*Give me something to eat, please.*

This imperative form is identical to the **ihr** form of the present tense, but without the pronoun **ihr.**

Particles and *bitte* with the Imperative

Requests or commands are often softened by adding the word **bitte** and particles such as **doch** and **mal**. **Bitte** can stand at the beginning, in the middle, or at the end of the sentence. The particles **doch** and **mal** follow the imperative form. They have no English equivalent.

Probier mal wieder!
Am 12. u. 13. Januar
kostenlose Probieraktion
von Pizza-Schnitte und
Fleischrollen

Kommen Sie **doch mal** in unser Geschäft!	*Why don't you visit our store?*
Bitte nehmen Sie **doch** Platz!	*Please, have a seat.*
Probier **mal** wieder Bio-Brot!	*Why don't you try Bio-Brot again?*
Zeigen Sie mir **bitte** ein Hemd in Marineblau!	*Show me a shirt in navy blue, please.*

Neue Wörter

der Braten *roast*
die Rechnung *the bill*
bestellen *to order*
holen *to get*

mitbringen (bringt mit) *to bring along*
schicken *to send*
vergessen (vergißt) *to forget*

☐ **Übung 11.** **Partysachen**

Herr Berger von der Firma Lustig organisiert eine Party für Sie. Sie schicken ihn zum Einkaufen. Was sagen Sie ihm?

BEISPIEL: Kaufen Sie bitte für uns ein.

1. Gemüse und Obst / kaufen / auf dem Markt
2. beim Metzger / Fleisch / holen / für die Party
3. einen guten Wein / mitbringen
4. am Markt / Brot / kaufen / in der Bäckerei
5. bestellen / einen Käsekuchen / uns / auch
6. mit dem Wagen / fahren / zum Markt
7. die Rechnung / mir / schicken

▣ Übung 12. Einkaufswünsche

Sie schicken einen Freund in Ihrer Wohngemeinschaft zum Einkaufen.
Bilden Sie Sätze im Imperativ.

BEISPIEL: Geh jetzt bitte einkaufen.

1. gehen / jetzt / einkaufen / bitte
2. Supermarkt / nicht / gehen
3. Brot / kaufen / Bäckerei
4. nur / nehmen / Schwarzbrot
5. holen / auch / Brötchen
6. Metzger / dann / gehen
7. mitbringen / Leberwurst
8. für Samstag / bestellen / einen Braten
9. etwas Obst / Markt / kaufen
10. das Geld / nicht / vergessen

Übung 11. **Point out:** Students
should add *bitte* to make their
request more polite.
Follow-up: *Rat geben.* Put students
in groups of four. Assign one to be
the advisor (*Ratgeber/Ratgeberin*).
The others each write down one or
two problems or tasks for which they
would like advice, e.g., *Mathematik
gefällt mir nicht. Ich muß meinem
Freund ein Geschenk zum Geburtstag kaufen.* The advisor makes a
recommendation using the imperative. Students jot down the advice
they are given. Ask several students
to report to the whole group.

Imperative of *sein*

Formal:	**Seien Sie** bitte um 10 Uhr hier!
Informal Singular:	Bitte, **sei** doch so nett und kauf mir ein Brot!
Informal Plural:	**Seid** bitte freundlich!

The Impersonal Imperative

In written German, but rarely in spoken German, an impersonal imperative is used to give general directions.

RSM

▣ Analyse

• Look at the card on the next page, from a German parking garage
  What is the cardholder asked to do?
• Where do you find the impersonal imperative in the sentence?
• What verb form is identical to the impersonal imperative?

> **Bitte erst zahlen, dann den**
> **Wagen holen. Kasse bei der Einfahrt.**
>
> Gutschein DM 0,50
> zur Anrechnung
> beim Kauf.
>
> 04.08.88 17:39 001502 P1 00
>
> **PARKHAUS ALTSTADT**
> Parkhausgesellschaft Limburg mbH
> Sackgasse, Tel.: 06431/8123
> **6250 LIMBURG / LAHN**

Typically, you find the impersonal imperative form in advertisements and in written instructions, as for instance in recipes.

Die Kartoffeln schälen, waschen und in feine Scheiben schneiden. Mit Salz und Pfeffer würzen.

Peel the potatoes, wash and slice thinly. Season with salt and pepper.

◉ Übung 14.

Schauen Sie sich das Rezept für ein Butterbrot an. Was braucht man, und wie macht man es?

BEISPIEL: **Nehmen Sie (Nimm) zwei Scheiben Brot.**

Übung 14. Suggestion: Students should scan the recipe first to clarify unfamiliar words. Stress contextual guessing.
Follow-up: Have students bring an easy recipe to class and tell other students how to make it.

Schon probiert?

a. *fold together*

Doppeldecker mit Käse und Salat

2 Scheiben (100 g) Weizenvoll-
kornbrot
3 Teelöffel (15 g) Butter oder
Margarine
1 dünne Scheibe (30 g) Emmentaler
4 Salatblätter
Das Brot mit Butter oder Margarine bestreichen. Jeweils 2 Salatblätter und den Käse auf die
Brotseiten legen, dann zusam-
menklappen[a]
Energiegehalt: 442 kcal, 1853 kJ.

LESEN IM KONTEXT

In diesem Teil lesen Sie, was einige Deutsche zum Frühstück essen. Ein typisch deutsches Frühstück, das heißt frische Brötchen mit Butter, Marmelade oder Aufschnitt, ein Ei und eine Tasse Kaffee. Das gibt es noch, aber die Eßgewohnheiten (*eating habits*) zeigen heute viele individuelle Unterschiede (*differences*). Das Mittagessen ist die Hauptmahlzeit (*main meal*) des Tages. Das Abendessen ist meistens nur leicht (*light*) und kalt.

Lesen im Kontext. Suggestion: You can summarize contents of this introduction in German or have students read silently and ask them to summarize in English.

◻◻◻◻ *Kulturnotiz*

Brötchen, Semmeln oder Schrippen?
Each geographical area has its own word for the fresh, crisp rolls people enjoy eating for breakfast. The three words represent three geographical areas: **Brötchen** is more common in northern Germany, **Schrippen** in Berlin, and **Semmeln** in southern Germany and in Austria.

Vor dem Lesen

◻ **Aktivität. Wie sind Ihre Eßgewohnheiten?**

Stellen Sie einem Partner folgende Fragen. Berichten Sie in der Klasse.

1. Was ist deine Hauptmahlzeit?
   a. das Frühstück
   b. das Mittagessen
   c. das Abendessen
   d. keine Hauptmahlzeit
2. Was ißt du gewöhnlich zum Frühstück?
   a. Eier mit/ohne Speck (*bacon*)
   b. Toast, Butter und Marmelade
   c. Müsli mit Milch
   d. Pfannkuchen (*pancakes*) mit Butter und Sirup
   e. nichts
   f. etwas anderes (was?)
3. Was trinkst du zum Frühstück?
   a. Kaffee mit/ohne Milch und Zucker
   b. Tee
   c. Saft
   d. Milch
   e. etwas anderes
4. Wie oft ißt du am Tag?
   a. eine oder zwei Mahlzeiten
   b. drei oder vier Mahlzeiten

Auf den ersten Blick

Schauen Sie sich die Bilder und Überschriften (*headings*) an. Überfliegen Sie die Texte. Welche Überschrift paßt zu welchem Text?

Neue Wörter

der Quark *curd cheese*
der Schonkaffee *low-acid decaffeinated coffee*
die Vollmilch *whole milk*

Durst haben *to be thirsty*
gesund *healthy*

Wie frühstücken Sie eigentlich?

Erst ein Steak – und dann aufs Dach
a.

1 Christina Dinné (18) trainiert fürs Ballett – wenn's sein muß, auch zu Hause: „Vor dem Sport frühstücke ich nie – höchstens mal ein Glas Milch vor dem Training; oder wenn ich zwischendurch mal Durst habe." Auch sonst ist sie sehr ernährungsbewußt.[a] „Diese Fetternährung[b] finde ich einfach widerlich.[c] Es ist eine Art Selbstmord[d] mit Messer und Gabel. Ich achte immer auf Kalorien – esse jeden Morgen das gleiche: Eine kleine Schüssel[e] Müsli mit Milch drüber und gemahlene[f] Körner obendrauf."

a. *conscious of nutrition*
b. *fatty foods*
c. *disgusting*
d. *suicide*
e. *bowl*
f. *ground*

c.

In der WG gibt's Müsli und Tee

3 Maik (25), Maria (25), Christine (20), Nicolas (19) und Christian (26) wohnen miteinander in einer Fünf-Zimmer-Altbauwohnung in Hamburg. Christine: „Wir versuchen möglichst gemeinsam zu frühstücken und besprechen Dinge, die uns alle angehen: Wohnung putzen, Miete bezahlen, einkaufen." Gegessen wird[a] ganz gesund: Vollkornsachen,[b] Müsli und Tee. „Ich kriege morgens nur eine Tasse Kaffee mit Milch und Zucker herunter[c] richtig was essen kann ich erst später", gesteht Christian.

a. Gegessen... *they eat*
b. *food made from whole grains*
c. Kriege... herunter *get down*

2 Stefan Buhk (21) ist Gärtner. Er verkauft Importware aus Holland, Kolumbien, Israel, Spanien und Brasilien auf dem Blumengroßmarkt in Hamburg. „Wir beginnen schon nachts um ein Uhr mit dem Aufbau. In Stapelfeld hat meine Familie eine eigene Gärtnerei.[a]" Um 3 Uhr beginnt der Verkauf an die Großhändler.[b] Stefan: „Da bleibt kaum[c] Zeit zum Frühstücken. Bis 9 Uhr ist hier die Hölle los.[d] Wir essen höchstens mal zwischendurch auf die schnelle ein Brötchen am Stand." Ruhiger[e] wird's erst so gegen 10: „Endlich ist dann Zeit für eine Tasse Kaffee und die Zeitung."

a. *nursery*
b. *wholesalers*
c. *hardly*
d. ist... *all hell is loose*
e. *Calmer*

Sonntags ein Ei
d.

4 Der 27jährige Schornsteinfeger[a] Jochen Meyl aus Bergisch Gladbach treibt mindestens zwei Stunden am Tag Sport – Bodybuilding, Boxen, Radfahren. „Ein Frühstück am Tag reicht da nicht aus.[b] Deshalb frühstücke ich zweimal täglich – um 7 und um 11 Uhr: entweder ein 250-Gramm-Steak mit Kartoffeln oder[c] Eiern, Toast mit Marmelade und Vollkornbrot mit Rübenkraut[d] und Quark – möglichst alles naturbelassen." Außerdem nimmt er Zusatzpräparate wie Hefeextrakt,[e] Vitamin E mit Pollenzusatz und Kohlenhydratkonzentrat.

a. *chimney sweep*
b. reicht... *is not sufficient*
c. entweder... oder *either . . . or*
d. *beet syrup*
e. *yeast extract*

Vor dem Tanz trinke ich ein Glas Milch

b.

Auf die schnelle ein Brötchen am Stand
e.

5 Das Rentnerehepaar[a] Grete (72) und Wilhelm G. (82) lebt auf dem Land, in Müden an der Aller. Da gibt's natürlich alles frisch. „Mittwochs und sonntags gibt's auch mal ein Ei", sagt Grete G. Ihr Mann ist zuckerkrank, frühstückt Diätwurst, Diätmargarine mit Dreikornbrot: „Aber den Kaffee, den trinke ich mit Vollmilch vom Bauernhof![b]" Sie ißt frisches Brot mit Quark, trinkt dazu eine Tasse Schonkaffee: „Bei uns geht's gemütlich zu. Mann muß den Tag ja schön beginnen. Und wir haben uns morgens immer viel zu erzählen – da planen wir nämlich den ganzen Tagesablauf."

a. *retired couple*
b. *farm*

Zum Text

1. Welche Information steht über diese Personen in den Texten?

TEXT	PERSON	ALTER	WOHNORT	BERUF
_____	Maik	_____	_____	keine Information
_____	Grete G.	_____	_____	_____
_____	_____	_____	Bergisch-Gladbach	Gärtner
_____	_____	18	_____	_____
_____	Christine	_____	_____	_____

Zum Text #1. **Suggestion:** Have students work in pairs or groups of three to fill in the grid. Call on individuals to give information about each person.
Note: This activity is designed to get students to link information when reporting to the class.

2. Wer ißt und trinkt folgende Sachen?

Stefan Buhk
Christina Dinné
Jochen Meyl
Grete G.

Diätmargarine mit
   Dreikornbrot
Müsli
Toast und Marmelade
Steak mit Kartoffeln
Kaffee/Schonkaffee
Brot mit Rübenkraut
Tee
Orangensaft
Milch
Brot mit Quark
ein Ei (Eier)
Brötchen

Zum Text #2. **Suggestion:** Give students time to scan the possibilities before doing the activity.
Follow-up: Personalize the activity by asking students which of these items they eat for breakfast.

3. Fassen Sie die Information zusammen. Bilden Sie Sätze mit Elementen aus jeder Spalte.

WER?	WAS?	WARUM?
Christina Dinné	ißt nur schnell ein Brötchen,	denn er treibt zwei Stunden Sport.
Stefan Buhk	frühstückt zweimal,	denn er ist zuckerkrank.
Wilhelm G.	trinkt manchmal nur Milch,	denn sie muß trainieren.
Jochen Meyl	ißt Diätwurst und Diätmargarine,	denn er hat keine Zeit.

Nach dem Lesen

▣ Aktivität 1. Eine Umfrage in der Klasse

Wer ißt was? Schreiben Sie die Namen auf, und berichten Sie.

Aktivität 1. **Suggestion:** Give students 5 minutes to interview as many students in class as possible. Call on several students to report the results of their interviews.

1. Wer ißt gern: Spinat? Fisch? Süßigkeiten (*sweets*)?
2. Wer ist Vegetarier? Seit wann?
3. Wer ißt gewöhnlich kein Frühstück?
4. Wer mag keine Süßigkeiten?

▣ Aktivität 2. Eine Umfrage: Was essen Sie gewöhnlich zum Frühstück?

Fragen Sie vier oder fünf Leute (keine Studenten aus Ihrer Klasse), was sie morgens zum Frühstück essen. Schreiben Sie dann kurze Berichte (auf deutsch natürlich) über diese Leute: nicht nur, was sie essen, sondern auch wer sie sind, wie alt sie sind, und was sie machen.

WORTSCHATZ

Substantive

Essen und Trinken

der Aufschnitt	cold cuts
der Braten (-)	roast
das Brot (-e)	bread
das Butterbrot (-e)	sandwich
das Brötchen (-)	roll
das Fleisch	meat
das Getränk (-e)	drink
der Käse	cheese
der Kuchen (-)	cake
die Lebensmittel (*pl.*)	food, groceries
die Leberwurst	liverwurst
die Limonade	soda, soft drink
das Mineralwasser	mineral water
der Pfeffer	pepper
der Quark	curd cheese
der Saft (¨e)	juice
das Salz	salt
der Schonkaffee	low-acid decaffeinated coffee
der Speck	bacon
der Sprudel	carbonated water
der Wein (-e)	wine
eine Flasche Wein	a bottle of wine
das Würstchen (-)	small sausage, hot dog
der Zucker	sugar

Food and Drinks

Obst und Gemüse

der Blumenkohl	cauliflower
die Erdbeere (-n)	strawberry

Fruit and Vegetables

das Gemüse	vegetable
die Gurke (-n)	cucumber; pickle
die Kartoffel (-n)	potato
das Obst	fruit
die Orange (-n)	orange
der Salat (-e)	lettuce, salad
der Kartoffelsalat	potato salad
der Spargel	asparagus
die Tomate (-n)	tomato
die Zwiebel (-n)	onion

Geschäfte

die Bäckerei (-en)	bakery
das Einkaufszentrum (Einkaufszentren)	shopping center
das Geschäft (-e)	store
die Konditorei (-en)	pastry shop
der Laden (¨)	store
der Markt (¨e)	market, marketplace
die Metzgerei (-en)	butcher store
der Supermarkt (¨e)	supermarket

Stores

Bekleidung

der Anzug (¨e)	suit
die Bekleidung	clothing
die Bluse (-n)	blouse
der Gürtel (-)	belt
das Hemd (-en)	shirt
die Hose (-n)	slacks, trousers
der Hut (¨e)	hat
die Jacke (-n)	jacket
das Kleid (-er)	dress

Clothing

die Krawatte (-n)	tie
der Mantel (¨)	coat
der Pullover (-)	pullover
der Rock (¨e)	skirt
der/das Sakko (-s)	man's jacket, coat
der Schal (-s)	scarf, shawl
der Schlips (-e)	tie
der Schuh (-e)	shoe
der Stiefel (-)	boot

Andere Substantive

der Ausverkauf (¨e)	sale
die Baumwolle	cotton
die Dame (-n)	lady
der Durst	thirst
Durst haben	to be thirsty
die Farbe (-n)	color
das Frühstück (-e)	breakfast
das Geschenk (-e)	gift
die Größe (-n)	size
die Kasse (-n)	cash register
vorne an der Kasse	up front at the cash register
der Kunde (-n masc.), die Kundin (-nen)	customer
die Mode (-n)	fashion
das Papier (-e)	paper
der Preis (-e)	price
die Rechnung (-en)	bill
die Sache (-n)	thing
die Seide (-n)	silk
die Ware (-n)	goods, product

Verben

anbieten (bietet an)	to offer
anprobieren (probiert an)	to try on
bestellen	to order
danken (dat.)	to thank
empfehlen (empfiehlt)	to recommend
füttern	to feed
gefallen (gefällt, dat.)	to like
Das gefällt mir.	I like that.
gehören (dat.)	to belong
genießen	to enjoy
grillen	to grill, barbecue
helfen (hilft, dat.)	to help
holen	to get, to fetch
kaufen	to buy
mitbringen (bringt mit)	to bring along

mitnehmen (nimmt mit)	to take along
passen (paßt, dat.)	to fit
Das paßt mir.	That fits (me).
probieren	to try, sample
schenken	to give (a gift)
schicken	to send
schmecken (dat.)	to taste
Das schmeckt gut.	That tastes good.
tragen (trägt)	to wear
vergessen (vergißt)	to forget
vorschlagen (schlägt vor)	to suggest
zahlen	to pay
zeigen	to show

Adjektive und Adverbien

Die Farben	Colors
blau	blue
hellblau	light blue
dunkelblau	dark blue
marineblau	navy blue
in Blau	in blue
braun	brown
gelb	yellow
grau	gray
grün	green
lila	purple
rot	red
schwarz	black
weiß	white

Andere Adjektive und Adverbien

eng	tight
dunkel	dark
frisch	fresh
gemeinsam	together; in common
gestreift	striped
gesund	healthy
gewöhnlich	usually
hell	light, bright
kariert	checkered
komisch	funny; strange
lieber (adv.)	preferably
ich möchte lieber	I would prefer; I would rather
nötig	necessary
zusammen	together

Präpositionen

an	at; near
auf	on, on top of
aus	out of
bei	with; at
mit	with
nach	to; after
seit	since
von	from; by
zu	to

Ausdrücke

Das ist alles.	That is all.
Das ist mir egal.	I don't care.
Das macht zusammen...	That comes to . . .
Das steht dir gut.	that looks good on you.
etwas anderes	something different
Sonst noch was?	Anything else?

KAPITEL 6

WIR GEHEN AUS

BEI UNS
WAREN SCHON MOZARTS
ZU GAST![a]
GENIESSEN SIE
EINEN SCHÖNEN ABEND
IN MOZARTS GEBURTSHAUS-
„BEI TRADITIONELLER KÜCHE".

DER „IN-TREFF"[b]—
BESONDERS AUCH NACH DEM THEATER

„Hagenauerstuben"[c]

MONTAG-SAMSTAG VON 9.00 BIS 24.00 UHR GEÖFFNET
WARME KÜCHE BIS 23.00 UHR

SALZBURG · UNIVERSITÄTSPLATZ 14
TISCHRESERVIERUNG ERBETEN UNTER TELEFON 84 26 57

Wir gehen aus. **Suggestion:** Introduce this chapter by describing a recent visit to a restaurant, to the movies, or to the theater, incorporating the present perfect tense. Check comprehension by asking students to summarize in English.

Lernziele *In this chapter you will learn to talk about going to a restaurant, ordering meals, and going to the theater. You will also learn to talk about events that happened in the past.*

RSM

a. der Gast *guest*
b. treffen *to meet*
c. die Stube *room, lounge*

▣ Alles klar?

- Hagenauerstuben ist _____.
  - a. ein Museum
  - b. Mozarts Geburtshaus
  - c. ein Restaurant
- Das Haus steht in _____ (Stadt).
- In dem Haus hat früher die Familie _____ gewohnt.
- Die Salzburger gehen gern _____ Theater in die Hagenauerstuben.
- Die Hagenauerstuben sind Montag bis _____ geöffnet.
- „Bei traditioneller Küche" heißt _____.
  - a. die Küche ist altmodisch
  - b. das Essen ist typisch für Österreich (Salzburg)
  - c. das Essen schmeckt gut
- „Warme Küche" heißt _____.
  - a. das Restaurant ist sehr gemütlich
  - b. die Küche ist schön warm
  - c. man kann da warmes Essen bekommen

WÖRTER IM KONTEXT ▣▣▣▣▣▣▣▣▣▣▣▣

Wir gehen zum Essen aus.

Gaststätte Leopold

Gemütliche Gastlichkeit[a] im Herzen Schwabings.[b] Bayerische und internationale Spezialitäten, tgl. frische Weißwürste,[c] warmer Leberkäs[d] Eigene Metzgerei.

9.30—24.00 warme Küche.
Leopoldstr. 50, 8 München 40, Tel. 0 89 / 39 94 33

a. gemütliche... *cozy hospitality*
b. Schwabing *area in Munich*
c. *veal sausages*
d. *type of meatloaf (traditional in Bavaria)*

Dienstag–Samstag 16.00–1.00 Uhr
Sonn- und Feiertags 11.00–1.00 Uhr
Montags Ruhetag

Ehrwalderstraße 77
8000 München 70
Tel. 0 89 / 7 14 58 85

**Restaurant · Pilsbar
Biergarten**

Gasthaus „Bärenwirt"

8451 Rieden, Tel. 09624/3 88

Täglich reichhaltiger Mittag- u. Abendtisch.[a]
Hausgemachte Brotzeiten[b] – große Eiskarte.
Für Muttertag bitten wir um Tischreservierung
Ihre Familie RICHTHAMMER

a. *extensive*
b. hausgemachte... *homemade bread (sandwiches)*

a. Kloster... *brand of beer*
b. vom... *on tap*

a. Stüberl *small lounge, room*
  (*Bavaria*)

▣ Analyse

1. German has many different words for a place where one can eat or drink something: for instance, **das Restaurant**, **das Café**. What other words can you find in the accompanying ads?
2. How does a restaurant indicate that it is open daily?
3. Ehrwalder Stuben is closed on one particular day of the week. What word indicates this?

▣ Aktivität 1. Geben Sie Auskunft über diese Restaurants.

1. Bärenwirt ist ein ＿＿＿.
2. Altstadtstüberl ist ein ＿＿＿.
3. Die ＿＿＿ Leopold ist in München.
4. Krümelstübchen ist ein ＿＿＿, ein ＿＿＿ und eine ＿＿＿.
5. Pipusch ist ein ＿＿＿ und eine ＿＿＿ in ＿＿＿ (Stadt). Es gibt auch eine ＿＿＿ im Pipusch.
6. Ehrwalder Stuben ist ein ＿＿＿. Bei schönem Wetter kann man im ＿＿＿ sitzen.

Neue Wörter

Bier vom Faß *beer on tap*
der Gast *guest*
das Gasthaus *inn*
die Gaststätte *restaurant*
die Kneipe *pub*
die Küche here: *food, cuisine;* otherwise: *kitchen*

der Ruhetag *day when restaurant is closed (lit. day of rest)*
geöffnet *open*
täglich (*abbreviated* tgl. *or* tägl.) *daily*

a. nichts... *nothing decent*
b. *to chat*

Hier kann man schnell etwas essen und trinken.

▣ Aktivität 2. Interaktion

Ich habe Hunger. Ich habe Durst. Wo gibt es was zu essen und zu trinken? Die Information für Ihre Antworten finden Sie in den Restaurant-Anzeigen.

Vorschläge für Essen und Trinken: Pizza, Bier (vom Faß), griechische Küche, bayerische Spezialitäten (z.B. Weißwurst), internationale Küche, ein Eis, eine Tasse Kaffee.

A:		B:
Ich habe Hunger.	⟶	Magst du ____?
Ich habe Durst.		Ißt du gern ____?
		Möchtest du ____?
Ja. Wo kann man das bekommen?		Im ____.
Wann ist es geöffnet?		Ich weiß es nicht genau.
Ist es heute geöffnet?		Täglich von ____ bis ____.

Im Restaurant

Käuzchen

Inh. Jochen Valta

Telefon 5 47 19
Gesandtenstr. 2

Falls[a] Sie in der Uni-Bibliothek keinen Platz mehr finden sollten – wir halten immer einen für Sie reserviert. B2 ⑮

Öffnungszeiten: 12.00 mittags – 1.00 nachts

a. *In case*

Dialog. Zwei Freunde, Jens und Stefanie, suchen einen Platz im Restaurant Käuzchen.

STEFANIE: Hier ist es aber ziemlich voll. Hoffentlich finden wir noch Platz.

JENS: Da drüben sehe ich noch etwas frei. Da sitzen nur zwei Leute am Tisch. Ich gehe mal dahin und frage. (*Jens redet zwei Leute am Tisch an.*)

JENS: Entschuldigen Sie bitte! Ist hier noch frei?

HERR AM TISCH: Nein, hier ist besetzt.

JENS: (*an einem anderen Tisch*) Entschuldigen Sie. Ist hier noch frei?

DAME AM TISCH: Ja, hier ist noch frei. Bitte sehr.

JENS: Danke schön.

Ist hier noch frei?

▢▢▢▢ *Kulturnotiz*

In all but the most exclusive restaurants in German-speaking countries, it is acceptable for strangers to ask to share a table at a restaurant if it is very crowded.

Simply ask: **Ist hier noch frei?** The answer might be: **Ja, hier ist noch frei.** Or: **Nein, hier ist besetzt.**

Neue Wörter

der Platz *seat, place*
entschuldigen *to excuse*
sitzen *to sit*

besetzt *taken, occupied*
da *there*
   da drüben *over there*

dahin *there*
frei *free*
  Ist hier noch frei? *Is there a
  free place here?*
hoffentlich *I hope*

noch *still, yet*
voll *here: crowded, full*
ziemlich *rather*

Sprachnotiz

The adverbs **da** and **dahin** both mean *there*. **Da** refers to stationary location, answering the question **wo**; **dahin** (also just **hin**) refers to movement away from the speaker toward a place, answering the question **wohin**.

> **Da** sitzen nur zwei Leute am Tisch. —**Wo** denn?
> —**Da** drüben. Ich gehe mal **dahin** (**hin**).

The particle **aber** expresses surprise.

> Hier ist es **aber** voll.   *It is really crowded here. (I
> didn't expect it.)*

The particle **mal** makes a statement very casual.

> Ich gehe **mal** dahin und   *I'll go there and ask. (Why
> frage.   don't I go and ask?)*

▣ Aktivität 3. Lückentext

Ergänzen Sie den Text mit Information aus dem Dialog.

Stefanie und Jens suchen _____[1] in einem _____[2]. Es ist ziemlich _____[3]. Jens sieht zwei _____[4] an einem _____[5]. Da ist noch _____[6] für zwei Leute. Er geht an den Tisch und fragt: „Ist _____[7]?" Die Antwort am ersten (*first*) Tisch ist: _____[8]. Die Antwort am zweiten Tisch ist: _____[9].

▣ Aktivität 4. Rollenspiel. Ist hier noch frei?

Bilden Sie mehrere Gruppen. Einige Personen suchen Platz.

A: Entschuldigen Sie. Ist hier noch frei?

B: Ja, hier ist noch _____.
A: Danke schön.

B: Nein, hier ist leider _____. Aber da drüben ist noch _____.
A: (*geht zu einem anderen Tisch*)

Aktivität 4. Suggestion: Set up the classroom so that half the class is sitting in groups of two or three. The other students individually approach a group and initiate a conversation.

Menu. (*page 174*). Spend time going over the dishes on this menu with students. The menu is from a Regensburg restaurant, D'Arch. That explains why several dishes have the word *Arch* in front, e.g., *Arch-Salatschüssel*. Among the Bavarian delicacies offered are *Pressack* (head cheese), *Kipferl* (a type of roll), *Leberknödelsuppe* (liver dumpling soup), and roasts prepared in many different ways. A *Zigeunerbraten* (gypsy roast) is spiced with paprika, and a *Jägerbraten* (hunter's roast) contains mushrooms. Typical Bavarian drinks are *Radler* (a mixture of beer and lemonade) and *Weinschorle* (a mixture of wine and soda water).

Die Speisekarte, bitte!

Lieber Gast!
Verschiedene Spezialitäten des Hauses
und unsere Riesenpizza sind auch zum
MITNEHMEN!

Kipferl . . . . . . –,50

Suppen

Leberknödlsuppe	3,60

Kleine Gerichte

1 x 6 Bratwürstl mit Kraut und Kipferl	7,20
1 x 8 Bratwürstl mit Kraut und Kipferl	8,60
1 x 10 Bratwürstl mit Kraut und Kipferl	9,80
Leberkäs mit Kartoffelsalat	6,90
Curry-Wurst mit Pommes frites	7,80
Tägl. frisch **Gyros** mit Brot und Salat	7,80

Kalte Speisen

Pressack sauer weiß und rot, mit Brot	6,90
Schweizer Wurstsalat mit Brot	6,90
Brotzeitteller verschiedene Wurst u. Butter mit Brot	9,80
Camembert mit Brot	5,50

Salate

Arch-Salatschüssel	8,80
grüner Salat, Gurken, Tomaten, Zwiebeln, Ei, Käse,Thunfisch	
Salatteller	8,80
verschiedene frische Salate, Ei und Schinken	

Für Kinder

Kleines Schnitzel mit Pommes frites und Ketchup	6,90
Schweinebraten mit Knödel	6,90

Tellergerichte

Schweinebraten mit Knödel und Salat	9,80
Jägerbraten mit Pommes frites und Salat	12,80
Zigeunerbraten mit Pommes frites und Salat	12,80
Schnitzel paniert mit Pommes frites und Salat	12,80
Zwiebelrostbraten mit Pommes frites und Salat	16,80

Vom Grill

Kotelett mit Kartoffelsalat	9,80
Grillteller	15,80
(versch. Fleischstücke vom Grill, Pommes frites, Salat und Gemüse)	
Räuberspieß	15,80
(Fleischstücke am Spieß, Pepperoni, Paprika, Champignons, Pommes frites und Salat)	
Kosakenspieß	15,80
(Fleischstücke am Spieß mit Chillysoße, Paprika, Pommes frites und Salat, pikant)	
Ritterspieß	16,80
(Schweinelendchen im Speckmantel, Pommes frites und Salat)	
Farmer-Steak	16,80
(Hüftsteak mit Kräuterbutter, Pommes frites und Salat)	
Madagaskar-Steak	17,80
(Hüftsteak mit Pfeffersoße, Pommes frites und Salat)	

Wasser / Säfte

Mineralwasser	0,4	2,80
Apfelsaft	0,4	3,80
Orangensaft	0,4	4,––
Coca-Cola	0,4	3,80
Fanta	0,4	3,80
Cola-Mix	0,4	3,80
Weinschorle	0,4	4,50

Bischofshof Bier
Das Bier das uns zu Freunden macht

Bischofshof Prälat Pilsener v. Faß	0,4	2,90
Angebot:		
1 Maß Bier oder Radler 5,20		

Eisspezialitäten

Gem. Eis	4,––
(Vanille, Schoko, Erdbeer)	
Gem. Eis mit Sahne	4,50
(Vanille, Schoko, Erdbeer)	
Schwarzwaldbecher	6,50
(Schoko, Vanille, Kirschen, Kirschwasser, Sahne)	
Arch-Becher	6,50
(Erdbeer u. Vanille, Früchte und Sahne)	
Eiskaffee	3,80

Kuchen

Apfelkuchen	2,80
Käsekuchen	2,80
Sahne	–,50

□□□□ *Kulturnotiz*

Every area of Germany has its own regional specialties. The menu on this page features some typically Bavarian dishes. Favorites are **Kipferl**, a type of roll, **Leberknödlsuppe,** liver dumpling soup, and **Weißwurst,** a type of veal sausage. Meat is frequently pork (**Schweinefleisch**). Beef (**Rindfleisch**) is served less frequently and is much more expensive.

Neue Wörter

die Bratwurst *sausage for frying or grilling*

das Kraut (Sauerkraut) *sauerkraut*

der Leberkäs *type of meat loaf typical for Southern Germany*

die Maß Bier *mug of beer holding about one liter*

das Schnitzel *cutlet*

die Suppe *soup*

der Teller *plate*

Aktivität 5. Welche Speisen gehören nicht in die Kategorie?

BEISPIEL: Wienerschnitzel, Schweinswürstl, 2 Stück Münchener Weißwürste, ~~Bouillon mit Ei~~

1. Leberknödlsuppe, Bouillon mit Ei, Rindsfilet, Gemüsesuppe
2. Sauerkraut, Kartoffeln, Gemüse, Emmentaler Käse
3. Diät-Bier, 0,25l Limonade, Tasse Kaffee, Apfelkuchen
4. Wurstsalat, Weißbier, Salatplatte, Tomatensalat
5. 1 Maß Bier, Apfelsaft, Mineralwasser, Orangensaft

Aktivität 5. **Suggestion:** Have students work in pairs, taking turns saying the items in each line aloud and deciding on the correct answer. When the activity is completed, check it by calling on individuals for responses.

Dialog. Im Restaurant

Was bestellen Jens und Stefanie im Restaurant?

JENS: Was möchtest du essen?

STEFANIE: Ich nehme Bratwürstl mit Kraut und Kipferl.

JENS: Nimmst du eine Vorspeise?

STEFANIE: Ich nehme Leberknödlsuppe. Und du?

JENS: Auch Leberknödlsuppe, und Schweinebraten mit Salat. Und was willst du trinken?

STEFANIE: Ich sehe hier Diät-Bier auf der Speisekarte. Das muß ich unbedingt mal probieren.

JENS: Ich nehme auch Bier, aber kein Diät-Bier. Herr Ober, wir möchten bestellen.

Dialog. **Suggestion:** Before students hear the dialogue, review the *Speisekarte* and *Neue Wörter*. Let them hear the dialogue once; then ask *Was bestellt Stefanie? Was bestellt Jens? Was trinken die beiden?* Then let students listen a second time, followed by role-playing.

Aktivität 6. Ergänzen Sie die Bestellung beim Ober.

Sie finden die Information in dem Gespräch zwischen Stefanie und Jens.

OBER: Bitte schön?

JENS: Zuerst möchten wir ____. Und dann ____ und für mich ____.

OBER: Und zu trinken?

STEFANIE: Zwei ____. Eins vom Faß und ein ____.

OBER: Sonst noch etwas?

JENS: Nein, danke, das ist alles.

Aktivität 6. **Suggestion:** Do this activity in pairs. After students have supplied the correct information from the previous dialogue, encourage them to substitute different foods and beverages.

Neue Wörter

das Hauptgericht *main dish*
die Nachspeise *dessert*
der Nachtisch *dessert*
die Vorspeise *appetizer*

▣ Aktivität 7. Interaktion

Was sollen wir bestellen? Schauen Sie sich die Speisekarte auf Seite 174 an, und besprechen Sie zu zweit oder zu dritt, was Sie bestellen möchten. Pro Person können Sie nur DM 25,- ausgeben.

BEISPIEL: Ich nehme Leberknödlsuppe als Vorspeise. Als Hauptgericht nehme ich 8 Bratwürstl mit Kraut und Kipferl. Ich trinke ein Bier. Und als Nachspeise nehme ich ein Stück Apfelkuchen.

Notieren Sie Ihre Bestellung:

Vorspeise: _____
Hauptgericht: _____
Nachspeise: _____
Getränk: _____

Aktivität 7. **Suggestion:** First have students scan the menu given earlier. Then have them jot down which foods and beverages they could order without exceeding 25 Marks. They then tell each other what they would like and how much it would cost.

▣ Aktivität 8. Rollenspiel

Im Restaurant: Ober/Kellnerin und Gäste. Bilden Sie kleine Gruppen. Eine Person spielt den Ober oder die Kellnerin und nimmt die Bestellungen an.

Aktivität 8. **Suggestion:** Group students in fours. Designate one to be the server. The server should act out the role-play with the other three. Talk about calling for a server in a restaurant: *Herr Ober!* or *Fräulein!*

OBER/KELLNERIN:	GAST:
Bitte schön? Was darf's sein? ⟶	Ich möchte gern _____.
Und zu trinken?	Bringen Sie mir bitte _____.
Sonst noch was?	Ja, _____.
	Nein, das ist alles.

▣ Dialog. Wir möchten zahlen, bitte!

JENS: Herr Ober, wir möchten zahlen.
OBER: Zusammen oder getrennt?
JENS: Zusammen, bitte.
OBER: Zwei Bier, einmal Bratwürstl, einmal Schweinebraten mit Salat. Hatten Sie auch Brot?
JENS: Ja, zwei Stück.
OBER: Das macht zusammen DM 30,70.

Dialog. **Note:** Students should role-play the dialogue. Encourage them to change items and prices.

□□□□   *Kulturnotiz*

When paying your restaurant bill, you do not have to add a fifteen-percent tip. The tip is always included in your bill. The menu (**Speisekarte**) sometimes indicates this by stating:

> Bedienungsgeld und Mehrwert-
> steuer enthalten.
> *Tip (service fee) and value-added
> tax (federal sales tax) included.*

It is customary to leave small change from your bill on the table or to have the waiter round off the figures on your bill to the next mark or two, but this is entirely up to the individual.

Aktivität 9.   Hören Sie zu.

Wir möchten zahlen, bitte. Was haben diese Leute bestellt? Wieviel kostet es? Kreuzen Sie an (X), was Sie hören.

Aktivität 9.   Remind students they are to listen specifically for what people in the dialogues ate and drank and what it cost them. Let students mark down the items as they hear each dialogue.

		GETRÄNKE		ESSEN		BETRAG
Dialog 1		2 Bier	X	Knackwürste		DM 9,50
		3 Cola		Weißwürste	X	19,50
	X	3 Bier		Bockwurst		29,50
			X	Sauerkraut		
				Brot		
Dialog 2		2 Tassen Tee		2 Stück Käsekuchen		DM 12,75
	X	2 Tassen Kaffee	X	1 Stück Käsekuchen		7,25
		1 Tasse Kaffee	X	1 Stück Obsttorte	X	17,45
Dialog 3		2 Bier	X	Leberknödlsuppe		DM 47,40
	X	5 Bier	X	Schweinskotelett		70,40
		3 Bier	X	5 Bretzel	X	74,40
			X	Weißwürste		
				Sauerkraut		

Im Theater

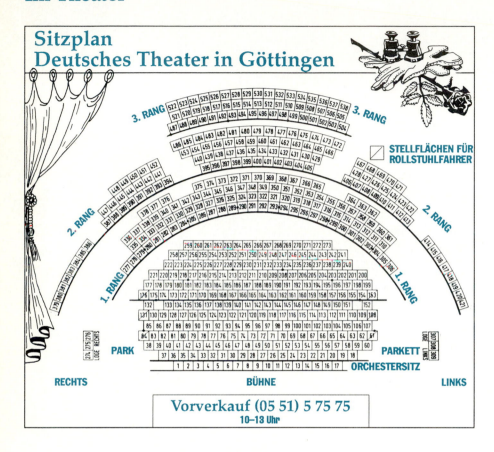

Analyse

Schauen Sie sich den Sitzplan für das Deutsche Theater in Göttingen an.

1. Das deutsche Wort für *stage* ist _____ .
2. Wenn man in der ersten Reihe sitzt, hat man einen _____ .
3. Wenn man im Theater unten sitzt, hat man einen Sitz im _____ .
4. Die Plätze ganz hoch oben sind im 3. (dritten) _____ .
5. Die besten und teuersten Plätze sind gewöhnlich in der _____ .

Neue Wörter

die Aufführung *performance*
die Bühne *stage*
die Karte *ticket*
die Loge *loge*
die Oper *opera*
das Parkett *main floor of a theater*

der Rang *circle, balcony*
  der erste Rang *mezzanine*
  der dritte Rang *upper balcony*
die Reihe *row*
der Stehplatz *standing room*

oben *above, upstairs*
unten *below, downstairs*

Aktivität 10. **Hören Sie zu.**

Aktivität 10. **Suggestion:** Have students scan the pictures of tickets before listening to the dialogue. Note that two ticket prices are in Austrian Shillings and one is in German Marks (1 Mark = 7 Austrian Shillings).

```
STADTTHEATER KLAGENFURT                          STTH. KLGFT.


DIENSTAG, 04.10.88                  19.30 UHR  04.10.88  19.30
RIGOLETTO                                        105


PLATZGATTUNG     I      LOGEN-NR:     LINKS
LOGE          11                      SITZ    1    1121101


KASSAPREIS      340,00   ZAHLBETRAG     0,00      0,00
REPRAESENTATION          INKL.10% MWST            6/04
```

```
            S T A A T S O P E R

           LE NOZZE DI FIGARO

   2.RANG LOGE 12          Reihe      Platz
   LINKS                              3
   FREITAG, 30.SEPTEMBER 88    19:00 UHR

                          Preis öS 1.280,-

   Bitte Rückseite beachten!  2309889948    einschl. Garderobegeb.
```

STAATSTHEATER AM GÄRTNERPLATZ

**Parkett rechts
Reihe 3**
24. April 1989
Bild- und Tonaufnahmen sind nicht gestattet.
Es gelten die Benutzungsbedingungen der Bayerischen Staatstheater.

** **72**   45.00

Ein Gespräch zwischen zwei Studenten, Andreas und Brigitte. Was erfahren Sie?

1. Brigitte war gestern abend ___d___ .
   a. im Kino
   b. im Theater
   c. im Jazzclub
   d. in der Oper
2. Sie hat eine(n) ___c___ bekommen.
   a. Platz im Parkett
   b. Freikarte
   c. Platz in der Loge
   d. Stehplatz

3. Die Karte hat ___b___ gekostet.
   a. nichts
   b. 10 Mark
   c. 45 Mark
   d. 340 Schilling
4. Die Aufführung war ___b___ .
   a. langweilig
   b. ausgezeichnet
   c. zu lang
   d. gut

GRAMMATIK IM KONTEXT

Two-Way Prepositions (*continued*)

In chapter five you learned three prepositions—**in, an,** and **auf**—that can take either the dative or the accusative case, depending on whether they indicate stationary location or movement towards a place. This chapter introduces six additional two-way prepositions:

hinter *behind*
neben *next to, beside*
über *above; across*
unter *under, below*
vor *in front of*
zwischen *between*

Like **in**, **an**, and **auf**, these prepositions take the dative case when they indicate where (**wo**) someone or something is located.

Wo ist das Restaurant Himmelsstube?   **Über den** Dächern von Wien.
Wo soll ich auf dich warten?   **Vor dem (Vorm)** Restaurant.
Wo steht die Kellnerin?   **Hinter der** Theke (*counter*).
Wo liegt die Tasche?   **Unter dem (Unterm)** Tisch.
Wo steht der Ober?   **Neben dem** Stuhl.
Wo sitzt die Dame?   **Zwischen den** zwei Herren.

RESTAURANT HIMMELSSTUBE[a]

TAGES-BAR

25 JAHRE ÜBER DEN DÄCHERN VON WIEN

Das Wienerlebnis in himmlischer Atmosphäre.

Einmaliger Panoramablick im Zentrum von Wien.

Eine Auswahl der Österreichischen Küche und gepflegte Weine im intimen Rahmen.

DEM HIMMEL EIN STÜCKCHEN NÄHER[b]

1., Gartenbauhochhaus, 12. Stock, Parkring 12.
Für Sie bereit: Montag bis Samstag 12–15 und 18–23 Uhr, Sonntag 12–16 Uhr. Tischbestellung: 52 43 88/17 DW.

RSM

a. der Himmel *heaven*
b. *closer*

The same prepositions take the accusative case when they indicate where (**wohin**) someone is going or where something is put.

> Wohin geht die Kellnerin?   **Hinter die** Theke.
> Wohin lege ich meine Tasche?   **Unter den (Untern)** Tisch
> Wohin stellt die Kellnerin das Glas?   **Neben den** Teller.
> Wohin legt sie die Rechnung?   **Auf den** Tisch **zwischen die** Dame und den Herrn.
> Wohin geht der Gast?   **Vor die** Tür.

The following contractions are commonly used.

unter dem → unterm	Die Tasche liegt **unterm** Tisch.
unter den → untern	Ich lege meine Tasche **untern** Tisch.
vor dem → vorm	Ich warte **vorm** Restaurant auf dich.

Parken! Problemlos!

3.000 kostenlose Parkplätze direkt vor der Tür. Dazu ein „Geheimtip"[a] zum (nicht) Weitersagen: Fahren Sie in unser großes Parkhaus an der Pelkovenstraße. Im 1. oder 2. OG[b] finden Sie da immer einen Platz.

OLYMPIA Einkaufszentrum

Hanauer Straße · Telefon 1 41 60 02

a. *secret tip*
b. Obergeschoß *upper level*

RSM

Restaurant
Schubert-Stüberln

Küchenchef
Franz Zimmer

hinter dem Burgtheater, vis-à-vis der Universität, beim Dreimäderlhaus

Schreyvogelgasse 4, 1010 Wien
Telefon für Tischreservierung 63 71 87

RSM

Mach' Dir ein paar schöne Stunden... geh' ins Kino

RSM

Kulinarische Notizen

Ein Brevier für Genießer.

Biergartenromantik im alten Forsthaus

Forsthaus Telegraph

Troisdorf
Nähe Flughafen
Mauspfad 3

Telefon 0 22 41/7 66 49
Inhaber Pilger und Daas

▣ Übung 1. Wo oder wohin?

Suchen Sie in den Anzeigen Präpositionen mit Dativ- oder Akkusativobjekten.

BEISPIEL: mit Dativ   mit Akkusativ

im alten Forsthaus   *ins Kino*

⊡ Übung 2. Geben Sie Auskunft° über die Anzeigen.

information

1. Wo kann man Biergartenromantik finden?
2. Wohin kann man fahren, wenn man problemlos parken will?
3. Wo gibt es 3000 kostenlose Parkplätze?
4. Wohin kann man für ein paar schöne Stunden gehen?
5. Wo arbeitet Küchenchef Franz Zimmer, und wo liegt dieses Restaurant?
6. Wo liegt das Restaurant Himmelsstube?

Übung 2. **Suggestion:** Have students work in pairs, taking turns asking questions and responding. Personalize the activity with questions such as *Kann man hier an der Uni problemlos parken?*

⊡ Übung 3. Wohin gehen Sie gern?

BEISPIEL: Ich gehe gern ins Café.

der Biergarten
das Café
das Kino
das Konzert
der Park

das Schwimmbad
die Stadt
das Restaurant
das Theater

Übung 3. **Suggestion:** Ask students to state two places they like to go. Encourage them to name places beyond the ones listed. You may have to supply the German for some of those places. Ask students to give reasons for their choices.

⊡ Übung 4. Die Theaterkarte

Andreas kann seine Theaterkarte nicht finden. Wo mag sie sein?

Übung 4. **Suggestion:** Have students describe the room before they say where the ticket could be.

BEISPIEL: Vielleicht ist die Karte unter der Zeitung.

▣ **Übung 5.** **Wo finden wir nur einen Parkplatz?**

BEISPIEL: **Park doch vor dem Museum.**

The Verbs *stehen, sitzen, liegen* and *stellen, setzen, legen*

The verbs **stehen, sitzen,** and **liegen** are intransitive verbs; that is, they do not take an accusative (direct) object. They describe where someone or something is located, answering the question **wo.**

> stehen (*to stand; to be located*)
> sitzen (*to sit; used only for people and animals*)
> liegen (*to lie; to be located*)
>
> Wo **steht** das Opernhaus?   Neben dem Stadtpark.
> Wo **sitzt** die Studentin?   Auf einer Bank im Park.
> Wo **liegt** der Park?   Zwischen dem Opernhaus und der
>   Universität.
> Wo **liegt** Wien?   An der Donau.

▣ **Übung 6.** **Liegen, stehen oder sitzen?**

1. Wo _____ Bonn?   Am Rhein.
2. Wo _____ euer Auto?   Vor dem Restaurant.
3. Wir _____ in einem Biergarten.
4. Der Ober _____ neben dem Tisch.
5. Die Rechnung _____ auf dem Tisch.
6. Vor mir _____ eine Maß Bier.
7. Um den Tisch _____ vier Stühle.
8. Unser Hund _____ unterm Tisch.

The verbs **stellen, legen,** and **setzen** indicate the movement of an object towards something, answering the question **wohin.** They are transitive verbs; that is, they need an accusative (direct) object to make a complete sentence.

> stellen (*to put, place*)
> setzen (*to put, set*)
> legen (*to lay, place*)

> Wohin **stellt** der Kellner das Bier?   Auf den Tisch vor den Gast.
> Wohin **setzt** die Kellnerin die Kaffeekanne?   Neben den Kuchen.
> Wohin **legt** der Kellner die Rechnung?   Auf den Tisch.

▣ Übung 7. Im Café Pipusch

Welches Verb paßt? Achten Sie auch auf die richtige Endung.

1. Im Café Pipusch _____ man sehr gemütlich. (setzen, sitzen)
2. Schnauzer, Monikas Hund, _____ vor dem Café. (stellen, sitzen)
3. Manchmal dürfen Hunde auch im Restaurant unter dem Tisch _____. (legen, liegen)
4. Herr Ober, bitte, _____ Sie meinen Regenschirm in die Ecke (*corner*). (liegen, stellen)
5. Warum _____ dein Mantel unter dem Stuhl? (legen, liegen)
6. Ich _____ den Mantel auf den Stuhl. (sitzen, legen)
7. _____ das alte Gasthaus noch? (sitzen, stehen)
8. Ich glaube, du _____ auf meiner Brille (*glasses*). (stellen, sitzen)
9. _____ Sie die Rechnung bitte auf meine Tasche. (liegen, legen)

Übung 7.   **Suggestion:** Students should work in pairs, taking turns responding.
Point out: In #2, mention is made of a dog in a restaurant. That is quite acceptable in many, but not all, restaurants and cafés in German-speaking countries.

▣ Übung 8. Partnerarbeit. Bitte, mach das!

Take turns asking a classmate to place an object somewhere in the room.

> BEISPIEL: A: Leg das Buch unter den Stuhl!
>   B: Stell den Stuhl ans Fenster!

Übung 8.   **Suggestion:** Have students work in groups of three. One student gives instructions; the others carry them out. Each student should get a turn giving instructions.
Follow-up: Groups give you instructions in order to practice the *Sie* imperative.

The Present Perfect Tense

The present perfect tense is used to talk about past events in spoken German and in informal written narratives. The simple past tense is used in most written and more formal German. A few verbs are used in the simple past tense in spoken German as well, notably the verbs **sein** and **haben.** There is no difference in meaning between the two tenses.

In this chapter you will learn the present perfect tense of strong and weak verbs, and the simple past tense of **sein** and **haben.** Consider the following dialogue.

INGE: Was hast du gestern abend gemacht?
HANS: Ich bin gestern abend ins Theater gegangen.
INGE: Was hast du denn gesehen?
HANS: Ich habe *Die Dreigroschenoper* von Brecht gesehen.
INGE: Wie war es denn?
HANS: Ausgezeichnet. Die Schauspieler haben phantastisch gespielt.

▣ Analyse

- List the verbs in each sentence of the preceding dialogue.

   BEISPIEL: hast gemacht

- Where are the verbs placed in each sentence?
- What part of the verb is the conjugated (finite) verb?
- What is the infinitive of each verb?

Analyse. **Suggestion:** This activity can be assigned for homework after you have previewed the present perfect tense. It can then be discussed in the next class.
Follow-up: Give students several additional short texts in which they must identify the present perfect tense.

As in English, the present perfect tense in German is a compound tense—that is, it consists of two parts: the present tense of an auxiliary verb and a past participle. Unlike English, the auxiliary verb in German can be either **haben** or **sein.** The auxiliary verb, the conjugated part of the verb, stands in second place in a statement; the past participle stands at the end of the sentence.

	AUXILIARY VERB		PAST PARTICIPLE
Gestern	bin	ich ins Theater	gegangen.
Ich	habe	eine Studentenkarte	gekauft.

Note that the auxiliary verb and the participle form a sentence bracket.

The Past Participle

German, like English, has two types of verbs: weak verbs (**schwache Verben**) and strong verbs (**starke Verben**). One way in which they differ from each other is in the way the past participle is formed.

Weak verbs form the past participle by placing the prefix **ge-** in front of the verb stem and by adding **-t** or **-et** to the stem. The **-et** ending facilitates pronunciation when the stem ends in **t**, **d**, or consonants that are difficult to pronounce without the additional **e**.

WEAK VERBS

INFINITIVE	PREFIX	STEM	ENDING	PAST PARTICIPLE
haben	ge-	hab	-t	gehabt
kaufen	ge-	kauf	-t	gekauft
öffnen	ge-	öffn	-et	geöffnet
tanzen	ge-	tanz	-t	getanzt
warten	ge-	wart	-et	gewartet

Strong verbs form the past participle by placing the prefix **ge-** before the (frequently altered) stem and adding the ending **-en**.

STRONG VERBS

INFINITIVE	PREFIX	STEM	ENDING	PAST PARTICIPLE
gehen	ge-	gang	-en	gegangen
nehmen	ge-	nomm	-en	genommen
sehen	ge-	seh	-en	gesehen
sitzen	ge-	sess	-en	gesessen
trinken	ge-	trunk	-en	getrunken

A few irregular verbs include aspects of both weak and strong verbs in the past participle.

IRREGULAR VERB	PAST PARTICIPLE
bringen	gebracht
kennen	gekannt
wissen	gewußt

Separable-prefix verbs insert the **ge-** prefix between the separable prefix and the stem of the verb.

SEPARABLE-PREFIX VERB	PAST PARTICIPLE
anrufen	angerufen
aufstehen	aufgestanden
ausgehen	ausgegangen
mitkommen	mitgekommen

Some verbs form the past participle without a **ge-** prefix:

- verbs ending in **-ieren**.
- verbs with inseparable prefixes like **be-**, **ver-**, **ge-**.*

INFINITIVE	PAST PARTICIPLE
passieren	passiert (*happened*)
probieren	probiert
reservieren	reserviert
bekommen	bekommen
bestellen	bestellt
gehören	gehört
gefallen	gefallen
verstehen	verstanden

---

*Inseparable prefixes are syllables like **be, er, ge, ver, zer** that are added to a verb, altering its meaning in some way. These prefixes are always unstressed, in contrast to separable prefixes, which are always stressed.

Following are some additional strong verbs and their past participles that you will find useful for this chapter. A complete list of strong and irregular verbs is in the appendix.

INFINITIVE	PAST PARTICIPLE
bleiben	geblieben
essen	gegessen
fahren	gefahren
geben	gegeben
laufen	gelaufen
liegen	gelegen
sein	gewesen
stehen	gestanden
werden	geworden

The Use of *haben* or *sein* in the Present Perfect Tense

Most verbs use **haben** as the auxiliary verb in the present perfect tense. **Sein** is used only when the main verb indicates a change in condition or location (movement from one place to another) *and* the verb is intransitive; that is, it takes no accusative (direct) object.

Wir **haben** gestern einen Film gesehen.

We saw a movie yesterday.

Dann **haben** wir in einer Disko getanzt.

Then we danced at a disco.

(**Tanzen** expresses movement, but not a change from one place to another.)

But:

Rudi **ist** ins Theater gegangen.	*Rudi went to the theater.*
Dann **ist** er nach Hause gefahren.	*Then he went home.*

(These sentences express change in location.)
    And:

Gestern **ist** er 21 geworden.	*Yesterday he turned 21.*
Ich **bin** um 7 Uhr aufgewacht.	*I woke up at 7 o'clock.*

(These sentences express change in condition.)
    Typically, the verbs **fahren, gehen,** and **laufen** use **sein** in the present perfect tense.
    In addition, two important verbs using **sein** in the present perfect tense are **sein** and **bleiben:**

Wo **ist** Sylvia gestern **gewesen**?	*Where was Sylvia yesterday?*
Warum **ist** sie so lange **dageblieben**?	*Why did she stay there so long?*

▣ Übung 9. Gestern sind wir zusammen ausgegangen.

Wählen Sie ein passendes Verb aus der Liste und ergänzen Sie die Sätze. (Alle Verben sind schwach.)

Übung 9. Suggestion: Have students work in pairs, taking turns responding.

bestellen	kosten	schmecken
bezahlen	probieren	suchen
haben	reservieren	warten

1. Wir haben ein gemütliches Restaurant in der Stadt _____.
2. In dem Haus, wo das Restaurant ist, hat früher Familie Mozart _____.
3. Wir haben keinen Tisch im Restaurant _____.
4. Wir haben 15 Minuten auf einen Platz _____.
5. Beate hat eine Salatplatte _____.
6. Ich habe Bratwurst mit Kartoffelsalat _____.
7. Die Bratwurst hat mir gut _____.
8. Peter hat für uns alle _____.
9. Ich habe nicht genug Geld _____.
10. Das Essen und die Getränke haben nicht zuviel _____.

▣ Übung 10. Gestern abend

Ergänzen Sie das Gespräch. Braucht man hier **haben** oder **sein**?

Übung 10. Suggestion: Have students work in pairs to complete the conversation. Call on several partners to role-play it for the class.

LINDA: Hallo, Hannes! _____ ihr gestern abend noch ins Kino gegangen?

HANNES: Ja, wir ____ einen alten Chaplin-Film im Rialto gesehen.

LINDA: Wie lange ____ der Film denn gedauert?

HANNES: Er ____ erst um 12.30 zu Ende gewesen. Und was ____ du gemacht?

LINDA: Ich ____ zu Hause geblieben und ____ gearbeitet.

▣ Übung 11. Interaktion

Fragen Sie einen Partner oder eine Partnerin: „Wann hast du zuletzt im Restaurant gegessen?" oder: „Wann bist du zuletzt im Kino (Konzert, usw.) gewesen?"

Wählen Sie einige Verben aus der folgenden Liste für Ihre Fragen und Antworten.

bestellt	geschmeckt
gefallen	gesehen
gegangen	getrunken
gegessen	vergessen

Übung 11. Suggestion: Review the participles listed with students first. Students should then role-play the activity several times with different partners. Call on several pairs to role-play for the class.
Point out: The question *Wann bist du zuletzt im Kino gewesen?* requires a number of changes in the sample dialogue.

A:

Wann hast du zuletzt im ⟶
  Restaurant gegessen?

Was hast du ____?

Und was ____?

Wie hat das Essen ____?

B:

Gestern.
Vor einer Woche.
Vor drei Wochen.

Ich habe Fisch mit Salat ____.

Ich habe nur Wasser ____.
Das habe ich ____.

____.

▣ Übung 12. Ein Nachmittag in der Stadt

Antje verbringt einen Nachmittag in der Stadt. Rekonstruieren Sie den Nachmittag. Bilden Sie Sätze im Perfekt.

Übung 12. Suggestion: Have students work in pairs. Check responses by calling on several individuals to give the entire story line.

BEISPIEL: Um vier Uhr ist Antje in die Stadt gefahren.

1. Im Kaufhaus Horten / ein Geschenk für ihren Freund / kaufen.
2. Die Rechnung an der Kasse / bezahlen.
3. Dann ins Café Huber / gehen.
4. Dort / das Geschenk für ihren Freund / auf einen Stuhl / legen.
5. Dann / Kaffee und Kuchen / bestellen.
6. Mit einer freundlichen Dame am Tisch / plaudern (*chat*).
7. Dann / im Café / die Tageszeitung / lesen.
8. Insgesamt 45 Minuten im Café / bleiben.
9. Vom Café aus eine Freundin / anrufen.
10. Um 5 Uhr / zur Bushaltestelle (*bus stop*) / laufen.

⊡ **Übung 13. Wo ist die Tasche?**

Im Bus hat Antje gemerkt, daß ihre Tasche weg (*gone*) war. Wo hat sie die Tasche zuletzt gesehen? Was ist alles möglich (*possible*)?

> BEISPIEL: Ich glaube, Antje hat die Tasche auf dem Weg zur Bushaltestelle verloren.

nützliche Verben:
verlieren (hat verloren) *to lose*
stehlen (hat gestohlen) *to steal*
nehmen (hat genommen)
legen (hat gelegt)

Expressing Time with Prepositions

The following two-way prepositions, when expressing time, always take the dative case.

vor drei Tagen	*three days ago*
vor dem Theater	*before the play*
in einer Stunde	*in one hour*
zwischen 5 und 7 Uhr	*between 5 and 7 o'clock*

You have learned several other prepositions expressing time—not two-way prepositions—that also take the dative case.

nach dem Theater	*after the theater*
seit einem Jahr	*for a year*
von 5 bis 7 Uhr	*from 5 to 7 o'clock*

The prepositions **um** and **gegen** always take the accusative.

bis (um) 5 Uhr	*until 5 o'clock*
(so) gegen 7 Uhr	*around 7 o'clock*

⊡ **Übung 14. Was machen Sie?**

Was machen Sie an diesem Tag um diese Zeit gewöhnlich?

> BEISPIEL: A: Montag morgen so gegen sieben?
> B: Ich stehe so gegen sieben Uhr auf.

von _____ bis	arbeiten
vor dem (Mittagessen)	in Vorlesungen gehen
nach _____	in der Mensa / zu Hause essen
um _____ Uhr	in der Bibliothek arbeiten
bis	zu Abend essen
zwischen	ins Bett gehen
so gegen	Kaffee trinken
	manchmal Karten spielen
	fernsehen

Vor und nach dem Theater an die schönste Bar in der Stadt

Paletti

direkt im Stadtkino

⊡ **Übung 15. Ein Bericht über das Wochenende**

„Was hast du letztes Wochenende gemacht?" Wählen Sie Verben aus der Liste unten.

Gebrauchen Sie folgende Wörter: dann (*then*), danach (*afterward*), vorher (*before that*), zuerst (*first*).

BEISPIEL: Letztes Wochenende habe ich gefaulenzt. Ich bin bis um 11 Uhr im Bett geblieben. Dann bin ich aufgestanden und habe die Zeitung gelesen. Danach habe ich meinen Bruder angerufen.

faulenzen
im Bett bleiben
schlafen
aufstehen
die Zeitung lesen
frühstücken
Freunde/Eltern anrufen
einen Brief schreiben
Zimmer/Wohnung aufräumen
Film sehen
Karten/Fußball usw. spielen
Freunde besuchen
zu einer Party gehen

Übung 15.   Note: This activity is designed to get students to link information. First review the meaning and use of *dann, danach, zuerst,* and *vorher.* Then let students jot down several things they did over the weekend. They can either report these to the whole class or tell a partner, who can share them with the class.

The Past Participle as a Predicate Adjective

As in English, the past participles of some German verbs can be used as predicate adjectives after the verb **sein.** As adjectives they describe a situation or condition.

Das Museum **ist** montags **geschlossen.**	*The museum is closed on Mondays.*
Die Geschäfte **sind** bis 6 Uhr **geöffnet.**	*Stores are open until 6 o'clock.*
Dieser Tisch **ist reserviert.**	*This table is reserved.*
Hier **ist** leider **besetzt.**	*Unfortunately, this seat is taken.*
Die Rechnung **ist** schon **bezahlt.**	*The bill is already paid.*
Der Kuchen **ist hausgemacht.**	*The cake is homemade.*

Note that this use of **sein** with a past participle has nothing to do with the present perfect tense. The preceding sentences all describe a situation in the present tense and not an action or event in the past.

⊡ Übung 16.   Welche Sätze passen zusammen?

Übung 16.   **Suggestion:** Have students work in pairs, taking turns initiating statements or questions and responding.

BEISPIEL: Die Bratwurst schmeckt gut. Die ist hausgemacht.

1. Wir müssen die Rechnung bezahlen.
2. Die Apfeltorte schmeckt sehr gut.
3. Ich möchte Montag ins Museum.
4. Ist hier noch frei?
5. Warum können wir nicht an diesem Tisch sitzen?
6. Ich muß noch einkaufen. Es ist schon 5 Uhr.

a. Die Geschäfte sind bis 6 Uhr geöffnet.
b. Hier ist leider besetzt.
c. Der ist reserviert.
d. An dem Tag ist es geschlossen.
e. Die ist hausgemacht.
f. Die ist schon bezahlt.

The Simple Past Tense of *haben* and *sein*

Several important verbs commonly use the simple past tense instead of the present perfect tense to express past time in spoken as well as in written German. These verbs include **haben** and **sein.** Others, like the modal verbs, will be introduced in chapter nine.

a. die Schwierigkeit(-en) *difficulty*

⊡ Analyse

Schauen Sie sich den Cartoon an.

Analyse.   **Suggestion:** Have students read the cartoon; then complete the *Analyse* as a whole-group activity. You might want to substitute a different city and a different language for variety and role-play the cartoon.

- Wo war das eine Mädchen?
- Wie gut war ihr Französisch?
- Wer hatte Schwierigkeiten mit ihrem Französisch?

RSM

sein		haben	
Singular	*Plural*	*Singular*	*Plural*
ich war	wir waren	ich hatte	wir hatten
Sie waren	Sie waren	Sie hatten	Sie hatten
du warst	ihr wart	du hattest	ihr hattet
er sie es } war	sie waren	er sie es } hatte	sie hatten

▣ Übung 17. **Partnerarbeit**

Wo warst du denn?

Übung 17. **Suggestion:** Encourage students to go beyond the possibilities listed here.

BEISPIEL: A: Wo warst du denn Montag abend?
B: Montag abend war ich im Theater.
A: Wie war es denn?
B: Es war sehr langweilig.

Andere Möglichkeiten:

WO:	WIE ES WAR:
bei Freunden	langweilig
im Kino	interessant
im Restaurant	nicht besonders gut
zu Hause	schön
auf dem Sportplatz	
im Theater	

▣ Übung 18. **Fragen und Antworten**

Warum bist du nicht mitgegangen? Wählen Sie passende Wörter aus jeder Spalte (*column*).

Übung 18. **Suggestion:** Students should work in pairs, first scanning the possibilities and then taking turns initiating questions and responding.

BEISPIEL: A: Warum bist du Samstag nicht mit zur Party gegangen?
B: Ich hatte keine Zeit.

WANN:	WOHIN:	WARUM NICHT:
Montag abend	ins Theater	keine Lust
Samstag nachmittag	auf den Sportplatz	kein Geld
Sonntag mittag	ins Restaurant	keine Theaterkarte
gestern	zur Party	keine Zeit
	ins Café	

LESEN IM KONTEXT

Vor dem Lesen

Aktivität 1. **Suggestion:** Give students several minutes to respond to the questionnaire. Poll opinions by asking *Wer ißt sehr gern* _____ ? Results of the poll can be listed on the board for a class profile.

▣ Aktivität 1. **Ins Restaurant gehen**

Kreuzen Sie die passenden Antworten an. Was essen Sie gern?

ICH ESSE	SEHR GERN	GERN	NICHT GERN	KENNE ICH NICHT
1. chinesisch	_____	_____	_____	_____
2. italienisch	_____	_____	_____	_____
3. mexikanisch	_____	_____	_____	_____
4. arabisch	_____	_____	_____	_____
5. deutsch	_____	_____	_____	_____
6. vietnamesisch	_____	_____	_____	_____
7. französisch	_____	_____	_____	_____
8. äthiopisch	_____	_____	_____	_____
9. thailändisch	_____	_____	_____	_____

Wie oft gehen Sie ins Restaurant?

Ich gehe   ein- oder zweimal im Monat.
            einmal in der Woche.
            zwei- bis viermal in der Woche.
            mehr als viermal in der Woche (im Monat).
            nie.
            jeden Tag.

Aktivität 2. Was ist Ihnen im Restaurant wichtig?

	SEHR WICHTIG	WICHTIG	NICHT SEHR WICHTIG	ÜBERHAUPT NICHT WICHTIG
1. die Atmosphäre	_____	_____	_____	_____
2. der Preis	_____	_____	_____	_____
3. die Bedienung (*service*)	_____	_____	_____	_____
4. das Essen	_____	_____	_____	_____
5. die Leute	_____	_____	_____	_____

Vergleichen Sie Ihre Antworten mit den Antworten eines anderen Studenten. Berichten Sie in der Klasse.

Aktivität 2.   Suggestions: Activity 2 should be done as pair work. Have students report about their partner.

Aktivität 3. (*page 195*).   **Suggestion:** Preview the restaurant page from the Vienna phone book's Yellow Pages by having students scan it and respond to #1. They can complete the table in pairs during class or as a homework assignment. Part #3 is based on the information gathered about restaurants in Vienna. Have students use this format to interview two students about different restaurants in Vienna.

Sprachnotiz

To indicate how many times something happens, add the word **mal** (*times*) to the number.

einmal *once*   zweimal *twice*   dreimal *three times*

▣ **Aktivität 3. Ein Restaurant auswählen°**

Schauen Sie sich den Text an.

Choosing a restaurant

RSM

---

992 Restaurant

CHINA HAUS
1030 Wien, Rennweg 62
KEIN RUHETAG   Tel. 78 15 83
KEIN PARKPROBLEM   78 15 84
Täglich: 11.30—14.30 und 17.30—23.30 Uhr

II. Bezirk

BERGER
Fischspezialitäten
Wiener Küche
Warme Küche 11—22 Uhr
KEIN RUHETAG
1020 Wien, (Handelskai) Dammhaufen 41
Tel. 218 19 10

Karl Kolarik's
Schweizerhaus
GesmbH.
Inh. seit 1920
Komm.-Rat. Karl Kolarik
1020 Wien, Prater 116
218 01 52
Restaurant, Biergarten,
Rohscheibenerzeugung

GASTHAUS
ZUM WILDEN MANN
1020 WIEN, IM PRATER 4
TEL. **26 21 93**

III. Bezirk

Pizzeria Ristorante
Da Bizi
WARME KÜCHE VON 11—23 UHR
(Sonntag geschlossen)
1030 WIEN, FASANG. 7   78 91 37
(PIZZA auch zum Mitnehmen)

Chinesisches Restaurant
FUNG-LING
Tägl. 11.30 bis 15 u. 17.30 bis 24 Uhr
1030 Wien, Löwengasse 24
Tischres.: **72 12 40 (712 12 40)**

Nikky's
Kuchlmasterei
N. KULMER

Unser Lokal bietet mit seiner
fürstlich-rustikalen
Atmosphäre den passenden Rahmen
für ein Essen mit Geschäftsfreunden
zu Mittag oder für einen
festlichen Abend zu zweit
Garten mit Stil u. Atmosphäre
III, Obere Weißgerberstr. 6
Tel. 72 44 18 (712 44 18)

Restaurant
STEIRERECK
1030 Wien,
Rasumofskygasse 2
(Ecke Weißgerberlände)
Tel. 0 22 2/713 31 68, 713 51 68
Samstag, Sonntag Ruhetag

IV. Bezirk

WIENER RESTAUTANT
Inh. Alfred Steinmetz
1040 Wien, Favoritenstr. 1
505 31 63

Zum
Land des Lächelns
Chinesische
Spezialitäten
1040 Wien
Paniglg. 15
65 63 44

V. Bezirk

RISTORANTE RIMINI
Italienische Spezialitäten
Warme Küche v. 12—15 u. 18.30—23 Uhr
1050 Wien, Hauslabgasse 23
Sonntag, Montag Ruhetag   Tel. **55 43 56**

---

1. Was für ein Text ist das? Wo findet man das gewöhnlich? Für welche Stadt ist das?
2. Ergänzen Sie die Tabelle mit Information aus dem Text.

KÜCHE	RESTAURANT	ADRESSE	TELEFONNUMMER
chinesisch	———	———	———
italienisch	———	———	———
Wiener-Küche	———	———	———
Fischspezialitäten	———	———	———

3. Fragen Sie jetzt einige Personen in Ihrer Klasse nach Restaurants in Wien.

- Wo kann man chinesisch essen?
- Wie ist die Adresse und Telefonnummer?
- Wann ist das Restaurant geöffnet?
- Wann ist das Restaurant geschlossen (Ruhetag)?

Auf den ersten Blick 1

1. The following text on cafés in Vienna contains many cognates and other words that look similar in English and in German. Scan the text and make a list of such words.

   BEISPIEL: traditionell, idyllisch

2. Now scan the text for compound words. Say these words out loud and try to identify their components.

   BEISPIEL: das Kaffeehaus = Kaffee + Haus

Neue Wörter

der Imbiß (Imbisse) *snack*
in Ruhe *at one's leisure*
der Treffpunkt *meeting place*

plaudern *to chat*
unterschätzen *to underestimate*

allerdings *however; to be sure*
stundenlang *for hours*

Auf den ersten Blick 1.
Suggestion: Have students do this for homework in preparation for discussion of the text. Students compare their lists of cognates and compound words in class with a partner. Go over the *Neue Wörter* first.

Im Kaffeehaus kann man stundenlang bei einem Kaffee sitzen und Zeitung lesen.

Kaffeehäuser

Das Kaffeehaus ist für den Wiener der traditionelle Treffpunkt untertags. Hier kannst du stundenlang in Ruhe bei einem Kaffee sitzen, Zeitung lesen (in fast allen „Alt-Wiener-Kaffeehäusern" liegen internationale Zeitungen auf), mit jemandem plaudern, Schach° oder—in manchen Kaffeehäusern—auch Billard spielen. Man trinkt natürlich Kaffee. Den großen oder den kleinen Braunen oder Schwarzen oder die Melange (ein Milchkaffee). Kleine Imbisse sind zu haben, aber auch die Kaffeehausküche sollte man nicht unterschätzen. Allerdings sind die Preise wegen° der kalkulierten langen Aufenthaltszeit° des Gastes höher als° im Beisl.°

chess

because of

stay / höher... higher than / restaurant (Austrian)

from *live Wien für junge Leute,* Vienna Tourist Board

Zum Text 1

1. Was kann man in einem Kaffeehaus machen? Steht das im Text?

Zum Text 1, #1.   Various students should formulate the questions for the rest of the class, e.g., *Kann man im Kaffeehaus Briefe schreiben?*

	JA	NICHT IM TEXT
a. Briefe schreiben	_____	_____
b. Kaffee trinken	_____	_____
c. Musik spielen	_____	_____
d. Zeitung lesen	_____	_____
e. etwas essen	_____	_____
f. Schach oder Billard spielen	_____	_____
g. Klavier (*piano*) spielen	_____	_____
h. stundenlang plaudern	_____	_____

2. Nennen Sie drei Kaffeegetränke.

3. **Vokabelübung:** Put the compound words back together. Choose parts from each column.

Zum Text 1, #3.   Suggestion: Have students work in pairs to complete this exercise. Check responses quickly and have students use the compound nouns in the *Lückentext* following.

BEISPIEL: Kaffee + -häuser = Kaffeehäuser

A	+	B
Kaffee		-punkt
Treff		-lang
Milch		-häuser
unter		-kaffee
stunden		-schätzen

Now complete the following text with the preceding words.

Lotte und ich treffen uns° jeden Dienstag in der Stadt. Unser normaler _____¹ ist ein Kaffeehaus im ersten Bezirk.* Es gibt sehr viele _____² in Wien. Dort kann man _____³ sitzen. Ich trinke immer einen _____⁴. Die Wiener sagen Melange dazu. Manchmal esse ich auch dort. Es ist nicht schlecht. Man soll das Essen in den Kaffeehäusern nicht _____⁵. Es kostet allerdings mehr als in einem Restaurant oder Beisl, weil die Aufenthaltszeit länger ist.

treffen... *meet (each other)*

Auf den ersten Blick 2

Überfliegen Sie den Text „Ein schwieriger [*difficult*] Tisch". Welche Wörter aus dem Text gehören zu folgenden Kategorien?

Aperitif	Hauptgericht	Nachspeise

Auf den ersten Blick 2. Suggestion: Give students several minutes to scan the text. Then write three columns on the board: *Aperitif, Hauptgericht,* and *Nachspeise.* Elicit responses from the whole group, listing each word under the appropriate category.

*Vienna is divided into districts called **Bezirke**. The first district (**der erste Bezirk**) is the center of Vienna.

◻◻◻◻ *Kulturnotiz*

Das Stammlokal is a pub where a group of people meets regularly on a set day and at a set time. These **Stammgäste** (*regular customers*) also have their own table, called a **Stammtisch.** This

Stammtisch is always available to **Stammgäste;** a stranger would not ask to be seated with **Stammgäste** at a **Stammtisch.**

Sprachnotiz.   Note: This section previews a grammar point for recognition only. It will be practiced actively in the next chapter.

Sprachnotiz

The pronoun **sich,** which occurs frequently in the following text, is a reflexive pronoun. It refers to the subject of the sentence. In the context of the following text it means (*for*) *himself or themselves.* Examples in this text are:

> sich treffen *to meet (each other)*
> sich bestellen *to order (for oneself or themselves)*
> sich entscheiden *to decide (for oneself or themselves)*
> sich fragen *to ask (himself)*

Ein schwieriger Tisch

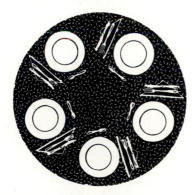

Fünf gute Freunde treffen sich wieder einmal zum Mittagessen in ihrem Stammlokal. Jedes ihrer Menüs° besteht aus° einem Aperitif, einer Hauptspeise und einem Dessert. Der Ober notiert:

Karl und Herr Raser bestellen sich Campari, Franz und Herr Flitz nehmen Sherry. Herr Schubert ist mit dem Auto gekommen und bestellt sich deshalb eine Cola.

Karl und Herr Glanz bestellen sich als Hauptgericht ein Schnitzel, Roland und Herr Schubert hingegen entscheiden sich für die Empfehlung° des Obers und essen Rehrücken.° Als Nachspeise wählen Roland und Herr Knall einen

Jedes... *Each of their menus*
besteht... *consists of*

recommendation
rack of venison

Pudding mit Vanillesoße, während Fritz und Herr Schubert ein Schälchen Obstsalat bevorzugen.° Der fünfte schließlich kann sich mit beiden Desserts nicht so recht anfreunden° und entscheidet sich für Schokoladeneis.

    Keiner der fünf Freunde verzehrt° das gleiche° wie seine Nachbarn°. Bei der Abrechnung° fragt sich der Ober: „Wer hat eigentlich den Fisch gegessen? Was hatte Hubert? Und überhaupt: Wie heißen die fünf Herren mit Vor- und Zunamen, was aß° und trank° jeder einzelne von ihnen und wie war die Sitzordnung° am Tisch?" Können Sie dem Ober helfen?

prefer

kann... does not like either of those two desserts
eats / the same / neighbors
Bei... Making out the bill

ate / drank
order of seating

Zum Text 2

1. Können Sie das Rätsel lösen? (*Can you solve the riddle?*) Versuchen Sie es zuerst auf einem Blatt Papier. Füllen Sie dann die Tabelle aus!

VOR- UND NACHNAME	APERITIF	HAUPTGERICHT	DESSERT
Karl _____	Campari	_____	_____
_____ Raser	Campari	_____	_____
Franz _____	_____	_____	_____
_____ Flitz	_____	_____	_____
_____ Schubert	_____	_____	_____

2. Wie ist die Sitzordnung? Wer sitzt neben wem? Niemand (*nobody*) ißt, was seine Nachbarn essen. Schreiben Sie die richtigen Namen auf die Teller in dem Bild.

Nach dem Lesen

▣ Aktivität. Schreiben Sie eine Anzeige!

Using the vocabulary about restaurants and foods and the ads used throughout this chapter as a guide, design and write an advertisement in German for an imaginary restaurant.

- Wie heißt das Restaurant?
- Was für ein Restaurant ist es?
- Was für Essen (Küche) kann man da bekommen?
- Wie ist die Adresse? Wann ist es geöffnet, und wann ist Ruhetag?
- Was ist ungewöhnlich an diesem Restaurant?
- Schreiben Sie einen Werbespruch (*ad slogan*).

BEISPIEL:

WORTSCHATZ

Substantive

Restaurants

der Gasthof (⸚e)	inn
die Gaststätte (-n)	restaurant
das Kaffeehaus (⸚er)	café
die Kneipe (-n)	pub
der Schnellimbiß (-imbisse)	fast-food restaurant
das Stammlokal (-e)	favorite restaurant where one goes regularly with a group of friends

Im Restaurant

die Bedienung	service (at a restaurant)
Bier vom Faß	beer on tap
die Bratwurst (⸚e)	special type of sausage
das Eis	ice cream
der Gast (⸚e)	guest
das Hauptgericht (-e)	main dish
der Imbiß (Imbisse)	snack
der Kellner (-), die Kellnerin (-nen)	waiter, waitress; server
die Küche (-n)	food, cuisine; kitchen
deutsche Küche	German food
bayerische Küche	Bavarian food
der Leberkäs	type of meatloaf (Bavarian)
die Maß Bier	a mug of beer, about one liter
die Nachspeise (-n)	dessert
der Nachtisch (-e)	dessert
der Ober (-)	waiter
Herr Ober!	Waiter!
Fräulein!	Waitress!
der Ruhetag (-e)	day when restaurant is closed
das Schnitzel (-)	cutlet
das Wienerschnitzel	veal cutlet
die Speise(n)karte (-n)	menu
die Spezialität (-en)	specialty
die Suppe (-n)	soup
die Leberknöd(e)lsuppe	liver dumpling soup (Bavarian)
der Teller (-)	plate
die Theke (-n)	counter

die Vorspeise (-n)	appetizer
die Weißwurst (⸚e)	veal sausage (Bavarian)

Im Theater

die Aufführung (-en)	performance
die Bühne (-n)	stage
die Karte (-n)	ticket
die Theaterkarte	theater ticket
die Loge (-n)	loge
die Oper (-n)	opera
das Opernhaus	opera house
das Parkett	main floor of a theater
der Rang (⸚e)	circle (in the theater), balcony
der erste Rang	mezzanine
der dritte Rang	upper balcony
die Reihe (-n)	row
der Stehplatz (⸚e)	standing room

Andere Substantive

die Ecke (-n)	corner
das Fenster (-)	window
der Platz (⸚e)	place, seat
die Schwierigkeit (-en)	difficulty
der Treffpunkt (-e)	meeting place

Verben

aufwachen (wacht auf), ist aufgewacht	to wake up
auswählen (wählt aus)	to choose
bezahlen (die Rechnung)	to pay (the bill)
bringen, gebracht	to bring
dauern	to last
entschuldigen	to excuse
legen	to lay, place
liegen, gelegen	to lie; to be located
öffnen	to open
passieren, ist passiert	to happen
plaudern	to chat
reservieren	to reserve
schließen, geschlossen	to close
setzen	to put, set
singen, gesungen	to sing

sitzen, gesessen	to sit
stehen, gestanden	to stand
stellen	to put, place
stehlen (stiehlt),	to steal
gestohlen	
treffen (trifft), getroffen	to meet
unterschätzen	to underestimate
verlieren, verloren	to lose
warten (auf, *acc.***)**	to wait (for)

Adjektive und Adverbien

allerdings	however
besetzt	occupied, taken
da	there
da drüben	over there
dahin	there
danach	afterward
dann	then
einmal	once
frei	free, unoccupied
Ist hier noch frei?	Is this seat taken?
Ist der Platz noch	Is this seat available?
frei?	
früher	formerly
genau	exact(ly)
geöffnet	open
getrennt	separate
hausgemacht	homemade
hoffentlich (*adverb*)	I hope

noch	still, yet
oben	above, upstairs
schwierig	difficult
stundenlang	for hours
täglich	daily
unbedingt	absolutely, really
unten	below, downstairs
voll	full, crowded
vorher	before that
vorne	in front
ganz vorne	way in front
wichtig	important
ziemlich	rather
zuerst (erst)	first, at first

Präpositionen

hinter	behind
neben	next to, beside
über	above; across
unter	under, below
vor	in front of; before, ago
zwischen	between

Sonstiges

niemand	nobody
in Ruhe	at one's leisure
zu Gast sein	to be a guest
Sie waren bei uns zu	They were our guests
Gast.	(guests at our place).

KAPITEL

7

WIE MAN FIT UND GESUND BLEIBT

Lernziele *In this chapter you will talk about fitness and health-related topics. You will learn to describe your symptoms when you don't feel well, ask for advice, and give advice.*

Schauen Sie sich die Anzeige für einen Drogeriemarkt an.

◻ **Alles klar?**

- Das Gegenteil von fit ist ___
- Wie kann man fit werden? Man soll
  a. Fußball spielen.
  b. schlapp im Sessel sitzen.
  c. Vitamine im Drogeriemarkt kaufen.

Schauen Sie sich jetzt den Cartoon „Herr Stierli" an. Wie ist Herr Stierli fit geworden?
  a. Er ist auf eine Party gegangen.
  b. Er hat viel Champagner getrunken.
  c. Er hat viel Vitamin B genommen.

Herr Stierli — von René Fehr

Und Sie? Nehmen Sie Vitamintabletten?
  a. nie
  b. manchmal
  c. regelmäßig

Warum nehmen Leute Vitamintabletten?
  a. Sie essen nicht gesund.
  b. Sie glauben, Vitamine verhüten Krankheiten.
  c. Sie glauben, Vitamine machen fit.
  d. Vitamine schmecken gut.

WÖRTER IM KONTEXT

Was tun Sie für Ihre Gesundheit?

Neue Wörter

die Bewegung *movement, motion; activity*
die Gesundheit *health*
gefährden *to endanger*
rauchen *to smoke*

Sport treiben *to engage in sports*
dick *fat*
krank *sick, ill*

"Ich rauche gern"

Ernährungsberaterin macht Vorschläge

Essen macht Spaß

Mozart gegen Streß

trimming
Bewegung ist die beste Medizin

SPORT-BILLY © DSB/SPORT-BILLY-PRODUCTIONS 1982

RSM

RSM

RSM

Der Bundesgesundheitsminister: Rauchen gefährdet Ihre Gesundheit. Der Rauch einer Zigarette dieser Marke enthält 0,4 mg Nikotin und 6 mg Kondensat (Teer). (Durchschnittswerte nach DIN).

Immer fit mit Brot und Schrot[a]

Wir backen für Sie täglich frisch verschiedene Sorten ballaststoff[b] und kalorienreiches Brot und Brötchen.

a. *whole wheat*
b. *roughage*

RSM

Jeder Deutsche trinkt im Leben 3060 Liter Bier

▣ Aktivität 1. Was ist gesund?

Schauen Sie sich die Texte und Bilder an. Was ist gut, und was ist schlecht für die Gesundheit?

BEISPIEL: Essen macht Spaß, aber zuviel Essen ist nicht gesund.

Zuviel _____ ist nicht gesund.
_____ macht dick/krank.
_____ schlecht/gut für die Gesundheit.
_____ gefährdet die Gesundheit.
_____ ist sehr gesund.

Sprachnotiz

You remember that you use the present tense with certain time phrases to express that a situation has been going on for some time.

Wie lange (Seit wann) bist du schon Vegetarier?	*How long (since when) have you been a vegetarian?*
Ich bin (**schon**) **seit zwei Jahren** Vegetarier. *or* Ich bin **schon zwei Jahre** Vegetarier.	*I have been a vegetarian for two years (already).*

When talking about a situation that used to exist in the past, but is no longer going on at the present time, use a past tense and an expression of time in the accusative case.

Du warst doch früher mal Vegetarier, nicht wahr?	*You used to be a vegetarian, isn't that right?*
Ich war mal **drei Jahre (lang)** Vegetarier.	*I was a vegetarian for three years.*

▣ Aktivität 2. Eine Umfrage in der Klasse: „Leben Sie gesund?"

Fragen Sie jemanden in Ihrer Klasse und berichten Sie im Plenum (*to the whole class*). Bilden Sie Ihre Fragen mit Hilfe der folgenden Kategorien:

Rauchen: Ja oder nein? Seit wann? Früher mal? Wie lange?
Sport treiben: Ja oder nein? Welchen Sport? Wie oft? Seit wann?
Essen: Ißt du gesund? zuviel? zu wenig? Vegetarier(in)? Seit wann?
Trinken: Alkoholische oder nicht-alkoholische Getränke? Warum oder
   warum nicht?

Aktivität 2.   Note: This is a somewhat lengthier interview than previous ones.
Suggestion: Go over the *Neue Wörter* first. Students should work in pairs interviewing each other and jotting down responses. Call on two or three individuals to report their findings.
Follow-up: A written profile of the person interviewed can be assigned for homework.

▣▣▣▣ *Kulturnotiz*

Germans of all ages often spend several weeks at a health resort after an illness or when they are run down from the strains and stresses of work. As the ad indicates, there are many health spas (**Heilbäder und Kurorte**) throughout Germany. The national health care system (**Krankenkasse**) pays for such a stay if rest and recuperation (**Kur und Erholung**) are recommended by a physician. At some health spas people go on a **Trinkkur**: at prescribed intervals they drink a glass of the healthful mineral waters for which some spas are famous.

GESUND-HEIT UND LEBENS-FREUDE

DIE KUR

IN DEUTSCHEN HEILBÄDERN UND KURORTEN

RSM

RSM

▣ Aktivität 3. Baden-Baden

Schauen Sie sich die Anzeige für Baden-Baden an, einen Kurort in
Deutschland. Was kann man in Baden-Baden unternehmen? Machen Sie
eine Liste.

	SPORT	UNTERHALTUNG	GESUNDHEIT
BEISPIEL:	schwimmen	ins Theater gehen	in die Sauna gehen

▣ Aktivität 4. Hören Sie zu.

Was machen diese Leute in Baden-Baden? Kreuzen Sie (X) die Aktivitäten an.

	HERR/FRAU LOHMANN	HERR KRANZLER	FRAU DIETMOLD
Golf		X	
Karten spielen	X		
Mini-Golf			X
Sauna		X	
Schwimmen		X	
Spazierengehen	X		
Tanzen			X
Theater			X
Thermalbad	X	X	X
Tischtennis			X
Trinkkur		X	X
Wandern		X	

Neue Wörter

der Arzt, die Ärztin *physician*
halten für *to consider*
  Ich halte Sport für wichtig. *I consider sports important.*
Urlaub machen *to go on vacation*

vegetarisch essen *to eat a vegetarian diet*
anstrengend *strenuous*
regelmäßig *regularly*

□ **Aktivität 5.** **Drücken Sie Ihre Meinung aus!**

Was halten Sie für sehr wichtig, und was halten Sie für nicht so wichtig?

  BEISPIEL: Sport treiben halte ich für sehr wichtig. Vegetarisch essen halte ich nicht für wichtig.

acht Stunden Schlaf bekommen
gesund essen und trinken
viel Wasser trinken
jeden Tag laufen
regelmäßig zum Arzt gehen

in die Sauna / in ein Fitness-Center gehen
regelmäßig Sport treiben
regelmäßig Urlaub machen
vegetarisch essen
Vitamintabletten nehmen

Aktivität 5. **Suggestion:** Have students do the activity in pairs. Students state two things they consider important and two that are not important to them. Partners jot down the other's responses. Call on several people to report their information.

□ **Aktivität 6.** **Interaktion**

Was tun Sie für Ihre Gesundheit—regelmäßig, manchmal, selten oder nie? Stellen Sie Fragen mit Hilfe der obigen (*preceding*) Liste. Berichten Sie dann über Ihren Partner oder Ihre Partnerin in der Klasse:

  BEISPIEL: A: Gehst du manchmal in ein Fitness-Center?
               B: Nein, nie.
               A: Warum nicht?
               B: Ich habe keine Zeit dazu.

mögliche Gründe:

macht (keinen) Spaß
keine Zeit dazu (*for that*)
nicht nötig

halte das für gesund/ungesund
kostet zuviel Geld
zu anstrengend

Aktivität 6. **Suggestion:** Review the list of items in *Aktivität 5* with students. Brainstorm several more with them, writing each one on the board. Students work in pairs, taking turns asking questions and responding. Call on several students to report what they have learned about their partner.

Wie fühlen Sie sich?

▣ **Aktivität 7.** **Hören Sie zu.**

Sie hören einen Aerobik-Lehrer beim Training im Aerobik-Kurs. Numerieren Sie auf der Liste auf Seite 208 alle Körperteile (*body parts*) in der Reihenfolge von 1–10, wie Sie sie hören. Einige Wörter auf der Liste kommen nicht im Hörtext vor.

Aktivität 7. **Suggestion:** Use the drawing of the body builder on the next page to practice vocabulary for parts of the body before doing *Aktivität 7*. To check comprehension you might call out words for parts of the body and have students point to them.
Suggestion: Let students hear the tape once. Then have students number the list while listening a second time.
Follow-up: Play tape again; this time you and the students actually perform the exercises you hear.

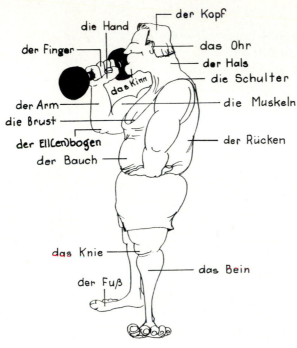

_1_ Arme
____ Bauch
____ Beine
_4_ Finger
_5_ Füße
_7_ Hals
____ Hände

_3_ Knie
_6_ Kopf
_9_ Ohren
_10_ Muskeln
_2_ Rücken
_8_ Schultern

□ **Aktivität 8. Das tut mir weh!°**

That hurts (me)!

Was tut dir manchmal weh? Und wann?

BEISPIEL: Die Füße tun mir weh, wenn ich zuviel laufe.

_____ tut/tun mir weh, wenn ich zuviel _____.

die Augen	arbeiten
die Beine	denken
die Finger	essen
die Füße	laufen
der Hals	lesen
der Magen (*stomach*)	schreiben
der Rücken	sitzen
	tanzen
	trinken

Dialog. **Ein Gespräch am Telefon**

Was ist denn los mit dir?

CHRISTOPH: Hallo.
UTA: Hallo, Christoph? Hier ist Uta.
CHRISTOPH: Ja, grüß dich, Uta.
UTA: Nanu! Was ist denn los? Du klingst ja so deprimiert.
CHRISTOPH: Ich liege im Bett. Ich fühle mich hundsmiserabel.
UTA: Was ist denn los?
CHRISTOPH: Ich habe eine Erkältung, vielleicht sogar die Grippe. Der Hals tut mir weh, ich kann kaum schlucken, mir ist schlecht. Ich habe Fieber. Und morgen muß ich eine Arbeit bei Professor Höhn abgeben.

UTA: So ein Pech. Warst du schon beim Arzt?
CHRISTOPH: Nein.
UTA: Wie lange bist du denn schon krank?
CHRISTOPH: Seit Sonntag.
UTA: Geh lieber gleich zum Arzt.
CHRISTOPH: Ich will noch einen Tag warten.
UTA: Also, ich wünsche dir gute Besserung.
CHRISTOPH: Ja, vielen Dank.

Neue Wörter

die Erkältung *cold*
die Grippe *flu*
Gute Besserung! *Get well soon!*
das Pech *bad luck*
  so ein Pech *what bad luck*
sich fühlen *to feel (a certain way)*
  ich fühle mich *I feel*
klingen *to sound*
schlucken *to swallow*

Was ist los? *What is the matter?*
weh tun *to hurt*
  Das tut mir weh. *That hurts (me).*
deprimiert *depressed*
gleich *right away, immediately*
hundsmiserabel *sick as a dog*
kaum *hardly*
krank *sick*

▣ Aktivität 9. Das Telefongespräch

Ergänzen Sie den Lückentext. Die Information finden Sie in dem Telefongespräch oben.

Christoph klingt sehr ____¹ am Telefon, denn er ____.² Er ____³ sich hundsmiserabel. Der ____⁴ tut ihm weh, und er kann kaum ____.⁵ Er ist ____⁶ Sonntag ____.⁷ Er war noch nicht beim ____.⁸ Er möchte noch einen Tag ____.⁹ Uta wünscht ihm ____¹⁰ ____.¹¹

Aktivität 9. Suggestion: Students can work in pairs, filling in the missing information in the *Lückentext.* Call on several individuals to check responses.

▪ Aktivität 10. Hören Sie zu.

Was fehlt diesen Leuten? (*What's wrong?*) Kreuzen Sie (X) Ihre Antwort an.

Aktivität 10. Suggestion: Students should look over all possibilities before listening to each dialogue. After each dialogue is played, pause to let students respond.

DIALOG 1:

| A hat: | Rückenschmerzen | x eine Erkältung | x Kopfschmerzen |
| B empfiehlt: | Geh zum Arzt. | x Leg dich ins Bett. | Nimm Aspirin. |

DIALOG 2:

| A hat: | Kopfschmerzen | x Magenschmerzen | Rückenschmerzen |
| B empfiehlt: | x Geh zum Arzt. | x Trink Kamillentee. | Leg dich ins Bett. |

DIALOG 3:

| Patient hat: | x keine Energie | Kopfschmerzen | x kann nicht schlafen |
| Arzt empfiehlt: | mehr Schlafen | x Kur im Schwarzwald | x Tabletten gegen Streß |

▣ Aktivität 11. Partnerarbeit. Was ist denn los mit dir?

Choose appropriate phrases from those given below with which to react to your partner's complaints.

BEISPIEL: A: Ich fühle mich so schlapp.
B: Geh nach Hause und leg dich ins Bett.

A:

Ich fühle mich so schlapp.
Der Hals tut mir weh.
Ich kann kaum schlucken.
Ich habe...
   Kopfschmerzen.
   Rückenschmerzen.
   Halsschmerzen.
   eine Erkältung.
   Fieber.
Ich kann nicht schlafen.
Mir ist schlecht.

B:

Nimm ein paar Aspirin.
Geh...
   in die Sauna.
   nach Hause.
   zum Arzt.
Warst du schon beim Arzt?
Trink viel Orangensaft.
Leg dich ins Bett.
Nimm mal Vitamin C.
Trink heißen Tee mit Rum.

Aktivität 11. Suggestion: Let students scan the range of possibilities first, and then work in pairs, taking turns saying what's wrong with them and giving advice. As a check, call on several students to voice a complaint and give advice.
Follow-up: Each student writes a complaint on a slip of paper (no names). Slips are collected and redistributed. As they are read by individuals, the others give advice.

EMSER PASTILLEN Naturkraft gegen Erkältung

In der Apotheke

Wunde Füße, Blasen? GEHWOL Fußkrem hilft.

EDUARD GERLACH GmbH D-4990 Lübbecke 1
GEHWOL Alles für das Wohl der Füße.

Eine „gute Nacht" Das Naturheilmittel mit besonders hohem Baldrian-Gehalt Zirkulin Baldrian
Zirkulin rote baldrian-dragées extra stark beruhigen die Nerven und fördern den Schlaf. Zirkulin Werke, Herdecke.
Zirkulin rote baldrian-dragées extra stark 45 In Apotheken und Drogerien

---

▣▣▣▣ *Kulturnotiz*

To purchase prescription drugs in Germany you have to go to an **Apotheke.** Nonprescription drugs may be purchased at an **Apotheke** or a **Drogerie.**

▣ Aktivität 12. Rollenspiel

Sie fühlen sich nicht wohl, wollen aber nicht zum Arzt. Sie gehen lieber zur Apotheke. Beschreiben Sie der Apothekerin Ihre Symptome. Die Apothekerin empfiehlt Ihnen dann etwas. (*Use the ads on page 211 for suggestions.*)

A:

Der _____ tut mir weh.
Ich habe/bin _____.
Haben Sie etwas gegen _____?

B:

Da empfehle ich Ihnen _____.
Gehen Sie _____.
Nehmen Sie doch _____.

die Symptome:

- Sie sind heiser (*hoarse*) und können kaum sprechen. (Heiserkeit)
- Der Kopf (Hals, Magen, usw.) tut Ihnen weh.
- Sie haben Husten und Schnupfen.
- Sie können nachts nicht schlafen. (Schlaflosigkeit)
- Sie sind immer so nervös. (Nervosität)
- Sie haben zuviel gegessen und fühlen sich hundsmiserabel.
- Die Füße tun Ihnen weh.

GRAMMATIK IM KONTEXT ▣▣▣▣

Reflexive Pronouns and Verbs

Sometimes the subject and the object of a sentence are the same person. In that case, a reflexive pronoun will be used for the object.

Ich informiere **mich** über Kurorte.	*I inform myself about spas.*
Herr Stierli hält **sich** fit.	*Mr. Stierli is keeping himself fit.*
Wie hältst du **dich** fit?	*How do you keep yourself fit?*
Machen Sie **sich** frei vom Streß.	*Free yourself from stress.*
Entspannen Sie **sich.**	*Relax.*

In the preceding sentences, the objects—**mich, dich,** and **sich**—are reflexive pronouns. Reflexive pronouns take their name from the fact that they "reflect" (refer to) the subject. Reflexive pronouns are identical to personal pronouns except for the third-person singular and plural and the polite **Sie** form of the reflexive pronoun, all of which are **sich**.

RSM

Geben Sie dem Streß keine Chance. Entspannen Sie sich so oft wie möglich. Dazu gehört auch ausreichender Schlaf und eine richtige Einteilung des Tagesablaufs.

Machen Sie sich frei vom Stress!!

The reflexive pronoun may be in the accusative or the dative case, depending on the verb. You will need to remember the distinction only for the **mich/mir** and **dich/dir** forms, the only forms of the reflexive pronoun to distinguish between the dative and accusative.

ACCUSATIVE: Ich informiere **mich** über Kurorte in Deutschland.
                Wie hältst du **dich** fit?
DATIVE: Ich wasche **mir** die Hände.
             Hast du **dir** weh getan? (*Did you hurt yourself?*)

Reflexive Pronouns

RSM

Wander-Vögel
informieren sich
jeden Samstag im
REISE-JOURNAL
der Rheinischen Post

ACCUSATIVE		DATIVE	
Singular	*Plural*	*Singular*	*Plural*
mich	uns	mir	uns
dich	euch	dir	euch
sich	sich	sich	sich

Ich halte mich fit.	*I am keeping myself fit.*
Sie halten sich fit.	*You (formal) are keeping yourself fit.*
Du hältst dich fit.	*You are keeping yourself fit.*
Er ⎫	*He is keeping himself fit.*
Sie ⎬ hält sich fit.	*She is keeping herself fit.*
Es ⎭	*It is keeping itself fit.*
Wir halten uns fit.	*We are keeping ourselves fit.*
Sie halten sich fit.	*You (formal) are keeping yourselves fit.*
Ihr haltet euch fit.	*You are keeping yourselves fit.*
Sie halten sich fit.	*They are keeping themselves fit.*

Reflexive Pronouns. **Suggestion:** Introduce reflexive pronouns and verbs by recycling some of the health vocabulary of the *Wörter im Kontext*, e.g., *Mein Gesundheitsprofil. Ich halte mich fit mit Laufen.* If possible, accompany your explanation with visuals or with gestures. **Point out:** The reflexive pronoun is not always translated in English: "Mr. Stierli is staying fit."

The reflexive pronoun is placed right behind the finite verb or behind the subject in inverted word order. It may also precede a noun subject in inverted word order.

Wie hast du **dich** so fit gehalten?	*How did you keep yourself so fit?*
Ich habe **mich** mit Yoga fit gehalten.	*I kept myself fit with yoga.*
Wie hält **sich** Herr Stierli fit?	*How does Mr. Stierli keep fit?*

Verbs that require an accusative (direct) object become reflexive verbs when the subject acts on itself rather than on someone or something else.

von Alex Graham

a. *unusual*
b. das Zeichen *sign*

Compare the following examples.

NONREFLEXIVE	REFLEXIVE
Irmgard legt ihre Brille auf den Tisch.	Irmgard legt sich auf das Sofa.
Irmgard lays her glasses on the table.	*Irmgard lies down on the sofa.*
Der Arzt setzt das Kind auf den Stuhl.	Der Arzt setzt sich auch hin.
The doctor puts the child on the chair.	*The doctor sits down as well.*
Der Arzt fühlt den Puls.	Der Patient fühlt sich nicht wohl.
The doctor checks (feels) the pulse.	*The patient does not feel well.*

Verbs with Accusative Reflexive Pronouns

German uses reflexive pronouns much more extensively than English does. Some verbs are always used with an accusative reflexive pronoun. Many of these verbs also take a special prepositional object.

INFINITIVE	PAST PARTICIPLE	
sich beschweren (über + acc.)	beschwert	*to complain about*
sich entspannen	entspannt	*to relax*
sich erholen	erholt	*to recuperate*
sich erkälten	erkältet	*to catch a cold*
sich freuen (auf + acc.)	gefreut	*to look forward to*
sich freuen (über + acc.)	gefreut	*to be happy about*
sich interessieren (für)	interessiert	*to be interested in*
sich unterhalten	unterhalten	*to have a conversation*
sich untersuchen lassen	untersuchen lassen	*to get a (physical) checkup*

◉ Übung 1. Beim Arzt

Ergänzen Sie die Reflexivpronomen und Verben.

1. Bitte, _____ Sie _____ . (sich setzen)
2. Herr Doktor, ich _____ _____ so schlapp. Ich kann _____ nicht _____ .
   (sich fühlen, sich konzentrieren)
3. Seit wann _____ Sie _____ schon so schlapp? (sich fühlen)
4. Sie müssen _____ mehr _____ . (sich entspannen)
5. Ich empfehle Ihnen eine Kur im Schwarzwald. Da können Sie _____
   vom Streß _____ . (sich erholen)
6. Ich _____ _____ auf vier Wochen Erholung im Schwarzwald. (sich
   freuen)
7. _____ Sie _____ für Sport? Mit Sport kann man _____ auch gut _____ .
   (sich interessieren, sich entspannen)
8. Leider _____ ich _____ nicht für Sport. (sich interessieren)
9. Mit Vitamintabletten können Sie _____ nicht _____ . (sich fit halten)

Übung 1. **Suggestion:** Students can work in pairs, taking turns responding. Check students' answers by calling on individuals after the activity has been completed.

◉ Übung 2. Wie war's im Urlaub?

Berichten Sie im Perfekt.

> BEISPIEL: ich / sich erholen / gut → Ich habe mich gut erholt.

1. wir / sich erholen / gut
2. ich / jeden Tag / sich legen / in die Sonne
3. wir / sich entspannen / in der Sauna
4. wir / sich fit halten / mit Aerobik
5. die meisten Leute / sich nicht interessieren / für Sport
6. viele Leute / sich beschweren über / das Essen
7. ich / sich freuen über / das schöne Wetter
8. die Kurgäste / sich unterhalten / auf der Terrasse

Übung 2. Review formation of the present perfect tense; all reflexive verbs use the auxiliary *haben*. **Suggestion:** Have students work in pairs, taking turns responding. **Follow-up:** Students can write a short report about what they did to stay fit while on vacation.

◉ Übung 3. Ratschläge

Was kann man in diesen Situationen sagen?

> BEISPIEL: A: Ich habe die Grippe und Fieber.
> B: Leg dich ins Bett.

Übung 3. Review imperatives with verbs and reflexive pronouns first. **Suggestion:** Students work in pairs, taking turns stating the friend's problem and giving advice. Spot-check several responses to ensure students' comprehension.

ein Freund oder eine Freundin:

1. hat sich erkältet
2. hat die Grippe
3. fährt vier Wochen zur Kur
4. fühlt sich hundsmiserabel
5. hat den ganzen Tag schwer
   gearbeitet
6. ist immer unter Streß

Ratschläge:

a. soll sich in den Sessel setzen
b. soll sich nicht immer beschweren
c. soll sich sofort ins Bett legen
d. soll sich gut erholen
e. soll sich öfter entspannen
f. soll sich vom Arzt untersuchen lassen

Trimm Dich am Feierabend

▣ Übung 4. Wie hältst du dich fit?

Fragen Sie in der Klasse: „Wie hältst du dich fit? Wie entspannst du dich?" Was machen andere Leute, die Sie kennen?

BEISPIEL: A: Jackie, wie hältst du dich fit?
   B: Ich halte mich mit Schwimmen fit. Wie entspannst du dich?
   A: Ich lege mich vor den Fernsehapparat. Meine Freundin macht Yoga.

SICH FIT HALTEN:	SICH ENTSPANNEN:
mit Aerobik	sich mit Freunden unterhalten
Tanzen	tanzen, schwimmen gehen
Schlafen	Yoga machen
Vitamintabletten	ins Kino, Café, in die Sauna gehen
Radfahren (*bicycling*)	sich vor den Fernsehapparat setzen
Wandern	lesen (Comics, einen Harlequin Roman)
Schwimmen	sich mit Freunden unterhalten
Yoga	sich (ins Bett, in die Sonne) legen

Übung 4. Suggestion: Before beginning this activity, brainstorm with students: *Wie halten Sie sich fit? Was machen Sie?* Then have students work in pairs, taking turns asking each other what they do to stay fit.
Suggestion: Have students interview several others in class and share their findings.

▣ Übung 5. Was machen Sie morgens?

Sie kämmt sich.

Sie schminkt sich.

Er rasiert sich.

Er zieht sich an.

Was machen Sie zuerst? Und dann?

BEISPIEL: Zuerst stehe ich auf. Dann strecke ich mich.

NÜTZLICHE WÖRTER:

zuerst *first*
dann *then*
danach *after that*
zuletzt *last*

Übung 5. Suggestion: Review the *Nützliche Wörter* and the expressions with the drawings first. Students choose the drawings that apply to them and link several items together, using *zuerst, dann, danach,* and *zuletzt.*

Sie streckt sich.

Sie wäscht sich.

*Er setzt sich an den Tisch
und liest die Zeitung.*

Er duscht sich.

Verbs with Reflexive Pronouns in the Dative

Verbs that take objects in the dative case can also be used with reflexive
pronouns. Compare the following examples.

DATIVE OBJECT: PERSONAL PRONOUN	DATIVE OBJECT: REFLEXIVE PRONOUN
Gabi, ich wünsche **dir** schöne Ferien.	Ich wünsche **mir** ein neues Auto.
Gabi, I wish you a nice vacation.	*I want a new car for myself.*
Ich kaufe **ihm** ein neues Auto.	Ich kaufe **mir** ein neues Auto.
I am buying him a new car.	*I am buying a new car (for myself).*
Herr Doktor, bitte helfen Sie **mir**!	Ich kann **mir** nicht helfen.
Doctor, please help me.	*I cannot help myself.*
Du tust **mir** weh.	Ich habe **mir** weh getan.
You are hurting me.	*I hurt myself.*

Note: Demonstrate these sample sentences with gestures.

One additional useful expression with a dative reflexive pronoun is:

Das kann ich mir nicht leisten.	*I can't afford that.*

The dative reflexive pronoun is also used with verbs like **anziehen, kämmen, putzen** (*to clean*), and **waschen** when the direct object is a body part or an item of clothing.

Ich ziehe **mir** ein Hemd an.	*I am putting on a shirt.*
Ich kämme **mir** die Haare.	*I am combing my hair.*
Ich wasche **mir** die Hände.	*I am washing my hands.*
Ich putze **mir** die Zähne.	*I am brushing my teeth.*

The Verb *lassen* with a Dative Reflexive Pronoun

The verb **lassen** is used with a dative reflexive pronoun and an infinitive to indicate that you are having something done for yourself.

Ich lasse mir das Auto reparieren.	*I am having my car repaired.*
Ich lasse mir die Haare waschen.	*I am having my hair washed.*
Er läßt sich einen Zahn ziehen.	*He has a tooth pulled.*

Note that in the expression **ich lasse mich untersuchen** (*I'm having a checkup*), the reflexive pronoun is in the accusative case.

The verb *lassen*. Suggestion: Emphasize *lassen* in the examples. Students often have trouble with English interference from "have" in learning this grammar point. This verb is usually listed with passive alternatives because the subject is having something done rather than acting on his or her own.

Neue Wörter

der Zahn *tooth*	**kaputt** *broken*
die Zahnschmerzen *toothache*	**schmutzig** *dirty*
ziehen *to pull*	

☐ Übung 6. Was paßt zusammen?

Kombinieren Sie.

1. Ich habe mich erkältet.
2. Ich habe kein Auto.
3. Ich habe Hunger.
4. Ich habe Kopfschmerzen.
5. Ich möchte mich fit halten.
6. Meine Hände sind schmutzig.
7. Vier Wochen Ferien kosten zuviel Geld.
8. Ich habe viel Kuchen gegessen.

a. Ich backe mir einen Kuchen.
b. Ich mache mir Tee mit Rum.
c. Das kann ich mir nicht leisten.
d. Ich muß mir die Hände waschen.
e. Ich hole mir Aspirin aus der Apotheke.
f. Ich muß mir die Zähne putzen.
g. Ich wünsche mir einen Maserati.
h. Ich kaufe mir ein Fahrrad.

Übung 6. Suggestion: Have students work in pairs combining the sentences. When the activity is completed, call on several individuals, to check comprehension.

◫ **Übung 7. Was machen sie nun?**

BEISPIEL: Frau Königs Auto ist kaputt. Sie läßt sich das Auto
reparieren.

1. Frau Webers Fotoapparat ist kaputt. (reparieren)
2. Meine Haare sind sehr lang. (schneiden *to cut*)
3. Unser Auto ist sehr schmutzig. (waschen)
4. Herr Lindblatt hat Zahnschmerzen. (einen Zahn ziehen)
5. Mein Vater fühlt sich nicht wohl. (vom Arzt untersuchen)

◫ **Übung 8. Wer kann sich das leisten?**

Fragen Sie Ihren Nachbarn in der Klasse.

BEISPIEL: eine Reise nach Hawaii
A: Kannst du dir eine Reise nach Hawaii leisten?
B: Nein, das kann ich mir nicht leisten.

1. einen Maserati
2. eine Tasse Kaffee
3. ein F in einem Kursus
4. eine Kinokarte
5. einen Hamburger bei McDonald's

Übung 7. Suggestion: Students can do this exercise in pairs. It is short enough to call on individuals for all items in order to check comprehension.
Follow-up: Sentence Pass. Each student writes a problem similar to the ones in the exercise on a slip of paper and passes it to the person on his or her right. This next person writes a solution, using the format in the exercise, and passes it back. Spot-check several students, who then tell the class both the problem and the solution given.

Übung 8. Suggestion: Students work in pairs, interviewing one another and keeping a record of their responses. Call on several individuals to say what their partners can and cannot afford.

da-Compounds

When a personal pronoun follows a preposition, it always refers to a person.

Der Patient wartet auf die Ärztin.	*The patient is waiting for the doctor.*
Er wartet schon lange **auf sie.**	*He has been waiting for her for a long time.*

When the object of the preposition is a thing or an idea, however, it is represented by a combination of the prefix **da-** and the preposition, a word referred to as a **da-**compound. **Da-** becomes **dar-** when the preposition begins with a vowel.

Die Ärztin wartet auf einen **Telefonanruf.**	*The doctor is waiting for a call.*
Sie wartet schon zwei Stunden **darauf.**	*She has been waiting for it for two hours.*
Wann hast du mit **Rauchen** aufgehört?	*When did you quit smoking?*
Ich habe vor einem Jahr **damit** aufgehört.	*I quit (it) a year ago.*

Frequently used **da**-compounds include:

dafür	Sport?	Heike interessiert sich dafür. *Heike is interested in it.*
dagegen	Rauchen?	Ich bin dagegen. *I am against it.*
damit	Rauchen?	Ich habe damit aufgehört. *I quit (it—smoking, that is).*
danach	Nach der Arbeit?	Danach gehen wir immer ins Fitness-Center. *Afterwards (after that) we always go to the gym.*
darauf	Urlaub?	Ich freue mich darauf. *I am looking forward to it.*
darüber	Viel Arbeit?	Die Studenten beschweren sich oft darüber. *The students often complain about it.*

🔲 Analyse

Schauen Sie sich die Bilder und den Text an. Suchen Sie in jedem Text ein **da**-Wort und geben Sie die richtige Information an.

Analyse. **Suggestion:** Have students scan the visuals first. Then go over the *Analyse* questions in the whole group.

1. Anneliese Rothenberger, eine bekannte Sängerin, fühlt sich prima
   a. nach einer Diätkur.
   b. nach der Oper.
   c. nach dem Radfahren.
2. Es ist immer die richtige Jahreszeit
   a. für Information.
   b. für die Arbeit.
   c. für eine Kur.
3. Jetzt ist Schluß (Ende) für Herrn Schulz
   a. mit dem Sport.
   b. mit dem Arbeiten.
   c. mit dem vielen Sitzen und Liegen.

Kur und Gesundheitsurlaub. Dafür ist immer die richtige Jahreszeit.

Den ganzen Tag sitzen und die ganze Nacht liegen. Jetzt ist Schluß damit. Ab heute wird Sport getrieben. Eins, zwei, eins, zwei.

RSM

Anneliese Rothenberger, Sopranistin:
„…und danach fühle ich mich einfach großartig."

Trimming 130 – Einfach zum Wohlfühlen. Schon 10 Minuten regel-
mäßiges Radfahren genügen, wenn das Herz dabei etwa 130
Schläge in der Minute erreicht. Wann starten Sie Ihr Trimming
130-Programm? Fordern Sie die kostenlose Broschüre „Gut für
die Figur – Trimming 130" an. DM −,80 Porto einsenden an
Deutscher Sportbund, Postfach 14 53, 6056 Heusenstamm.

trimming
Bewegung ist die beste Medizin

Deutscher Sportbund

RSM

☐ **Übung 9. Eine Umfrage in der Klasse**

BEISPIEL: Wer interessiert sich für Yoga? →
Drei Leute in der Klasse interessieren sich dafür.

1. Wer tut (viel, wenig, nichts) für die Gesundheit?
2. Wer interessiert sich für Yoga? Meditieren?
3. Wer beschwert sich im Restaurant über Rauchen?
4. Wer möchte mit Rauchen aufhören?
5. Wer unterhält sich (oft, nie, immer) über Diät und Essen.
6. Wer ist für oder gegen eine nationale Krankenversicherung (*health
   insurance*)? Wer soll dafür bezahlen? (der Staat, die Arbeitnehmer
   [*employees*], die Arbeitgeber [*employers*])

☐ **Übung 10. Interaktion. Situationen im Alltag**

Wie reagieren Sie darauf? Positiv oder negativ?

BEISPIEL: Jemand lädt Sie in die Sauna ein. →
A: Möchtest du in die Sauna gehen?
B: Nein, danke, ich interessiere mich leider nicht dafür.

SITUATIONEN

1. Sie haben gerade eine Stunde Aerobik gemacht. Sie sind fix und fertig (*exhausted*). Erzählen Sie einem Freund oder einer Freundin davon.
2. Jemand hat Ihnen ein Paket Tofu als Geschenk mitgebracht. Sie mögen Tofu (nicht).
3. Jemand schenkt Ihnen eine Karte für ein Rockkonzert. Sie bedanken sich für die Karte; Sie freuen sich sehr darüber.
4. Sie und andere Studenten haben sich schon über das Rauchen in der Mensa beschwert. Sie haben sich mit einigen Rauchern über dieses Problem unterhalten. Was kann man dagegen machen?
5. Sie brauchen dringend Erholung. Wo kann man sich gut erholen? Was ist die beste Jahreszeit dafür?

wo-Compounds

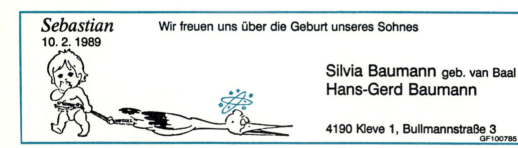

Sebastian
10. 2. 1989

Wir freuen uns über die Geburt unseres Sohnes

Silvia Baumann geb. van Baal
Hans-Gerd Baumann

4190 Kleve 1, Bullmannstraße 3
GF100785

Über was freuen sich Herr und Frau Baumann? **Worüber** freuen sich Herr und Frau Baumann?	*What are Mr. & Mrs. Baumann happy about?*
Sie freuen sich über die Geburt ihres Kindes.	*They are happy about the birth of their child.*

The interrogative pronoun **was** refers to things and ideas. A preposition and **was** are frequently replaced by a **wo-**compound, consisting of the prefix **wo-** and a preposition. When the preposition begins with a vowel, **wor-** is used instead.

Note that in informal English, this kind of question would call for the preposition to be placed at the end of the sentence.

Wofür (Für was) interessierst du dich?	*What are you interested in?*
Worauf (Auf was) wartest du?	*What are you waiting for?*
Worüber (Über was) hast du dich beschwert?	*What did you complain about?*

◻ Übung 11. Wofür? Womit? Worauf? Worüber?

Stellen Sie Fragen.

> BEISPIEL: Herr Huber tut nicht viel für seine Gesundheit. → Wofür tut er viel? (Für seine Familie.)

1. Herr Huber hat keine Zeit für Urlaub.
2. Er konzentriert sich nur auf seine Arbeit.
3. Frau Huber beschwert sich über Migräne.
4. Die Krankenkasse bezahlt für Frau Hubers Kur.
5. Sie freut sich sehr auf den Urlaub.
6. Sie unterhalten sich oft über ihre Gesundheit.
7. Sie tun nicht viel für ihre Gesundheit.
8. Frau Huber hält sich mit Schwimmen fit.
9. Herr Huber interessiert sich nicht für Sport.

Übung 11. Suggestion: Students work in pairs, taking turns asking questions. Call on several individuals to check students' comprehension.

◻ Übung 12. Eine Kettenreaktion

Fragen Sie eine Person in der Klasse. Wählen Sie Verben und Antworten aus der Liste (oder auch andere Antworten).

> BEISPIEL: A: Worauf freust du dich?
> B: Ich freue mich auf das Semesterende.

Übung 12. Suggestion: Have students work in pairs, initiating questions and responding. Encourage students to go beyond the list in their responses.

A:	B:
sich beschweren über	Kopfschmerzen
sich freuen auf	Rückenschmerzen
sich unterhalten über	die Arbeit
sich interessieren für	Sport und Fitness
warten auf	Reformkost (*health food*)
	die Ferien
	das Fitness-Training
	der Besuch beim Arzt
	das Semesterende

LESEN IM KONTEXT

In diesem Teil lesen Sie Texte zum Thema „Fitness".

Vor dem Lesen

◻ Aktivität 1. Sind Sie fit?

Beantworten Sie folgende Fragen zuerst selbst. Fragen Sie dann einen Studenten oder eine Studentin in der Klasse nach seinen oder ihren Antworten. Berichten Sie im Plenum.

Aktivität 1. Note: This activity is designed to link several pieces of information.
Suggestion: As students interview each other, they should jot down responses.

BEISPIEL: Judy spielt gern Korbball. Sie ist ziemlich gut in diesem Sport. Sie spielt ungefähr zweimal die Woche. Sie hat gestern zuletzt gespielt.

1. Was sind zwei oder drei Sportarten, die Sie gerne treiben?
2. Wie gut sind Sie darin? (z.B. sehr gut; es geht)
3. Wie oft treiben Sie Sport?
4. Wann haben Sie zuletzt Sport getrieben?
5. Für welchen Sport interessieren Sie sich überhaupt nicht?

Aktivität 2. Amerikaner und Deutsche

Vergleichen Sie sich mit den Deutschen.

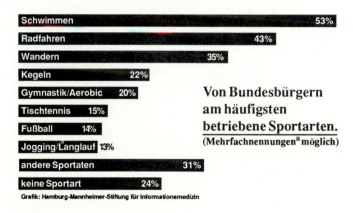

Schwimmen	53%
Radfahren	43%
Wandern	35%
Kegeln	22%
Gymnastik/Aerobic	20%
Tischtennis	15%
Fußball	14%
Jogging/Langlauf	13%
andere Sportaten	31%
keine Sportart	24%

Von Bundesbürgern am häufigsten betriebene Sportarten.
(Mehrfachnennungen[a] möglich)

Grafik: Hamburg-Mannheimer-Stiftung für Informationsmedizin

a. *duplication*

1. Welche Sportarten auf der Tabelle treiben Sie auch?
2. Machen Sie eine Umfrage in der Klasse, und schreiben Sie eine ähnliche Tabelle für Ihre Klasse an die Tafel.

Auf den ersten Blick 1

1. Schauen Sie sich die drei Zeichnungen im Text an. Welche Sätze beschreiben welche Aktivität auf den Zeichnungen?
   a. Joggen Sie fünf Minuten auf der Stelle.
   b. Legen Sie sich auf den Boden.
   c. Beide Arme in Schulterhöhe halten.
   d. Bewegen Sie die Arme im Laufrhythmus mit.
   e. Das Bein langsam in Richtung Nasenspitze heben.
   f. Heben Sie das Bein gestreckt hoch, und bleiben Sie so stehen.
2. Suchen Sie alle Wörter für Körperteile im Text.

Zehn Minuten Fitness-Test

Jetzt geht's los!

A.

B.

C.

Machen Sie die drei Übungen zügig nacheinander, und halten Sie dabei bitte die Reihenfolge ein, damit es nicht zu Muskel- oder Bänderzerrungen[a] kommt.

1. Kondition

Joggen Sie fünf Minuten auf der Stelle, und bewegen Sie die Arme im Laufrhythmus mit. Langsam anfangen, das Tempo allmählich steigern und nach drei Minuten die Knie kräftig hochziehen. Wie fühlen Sie sich danach?

- ☐ a) Bin fix und fertig.[b] Habe die Übung vorzeitig[c] abgebrochen.
- ☐ b) Mein Herz schlägt wie verrückt. Fünf Minuten mit Ach und Krach[d] geschafft.
- ☐ c) War gar nicht anstrengend. Könnte leicht noch weiterlaufen.

2. Kraft

Stellen Sie sich locker[e] hin, die Knie sind leicht gebeugt. Jetzt beide Arme in Schulterhöhe nach vorn nehmen, ganz feste Fäuste machen und die Spannung[f] halten. Eine Fußspitze anziehen und das Bein gestreckt heben—so hoch wie möglich. Wie weit können Sie in dieser Haltung zählen, ohne sich zu verkrampfen? (Dann bitte sofort aufhören.)

- ☐ a) Bei 20 mußte ich aufgeben.
- ☐ b) Bin bis 50 gekommen.
- ☐ c) Habe langsam bis 100 gezählt.

3. Beweglichkeit

Jetzt strecken Sie sich mal richtig: auf die Seite legen und den Ellenbogen aufstützen. Das untere Bein an den Bauch ziehen, das andere vorsichtig zur Decke strecken. Dann die Wade umfassen und das Bein langsam in Richtung Nasenspitze dehnen, das Knie dabei nicht beugen. Wie weit kommen Sie, ohne daß es weh tut?

- ☐ a) Ich kann das Bein zwar strecken, aber nicht weiter an den Körper ziehen.
- ☐ b) Mein Knie berührt die Nasenspitze.
- ☐ c) Ich habe das Knie bis ans Ohr gekriegt.

a. *torn muscles or ligaments*
b. fix... *totally exhausted*
c. *prematurely*
d. mit... *barely*
e. *relaxed*
f. *tension*

Zum Text 1

1. Wie fit sind Sie? Machen Sie den zehn Minuten Fitness-Test zu Hause! Kreuzen Sie (X) Ihre Antworten an. Dann lesen Sie „Hier finden Sie Ihr Testergebnis" (Seite 226), und bewerten Sie Ihre Leistung (*achievement*)! Berichten Sie in der Klasse über das Ergebnis.

Zum Text 1. Note: This fitness activity is meant to be done outside of class. Prepare students for the task by having them quickly scan each section and summarize it. Review the *Testergebnisse* on the following day to ensure student comprehension.

Hier finden Sie Ihr Testergebnis

—2 ODER 3MAL (A) ANGEKREUZT:

Sie sind ganz schön abgeschlafft—das wissen Sie selbst. Fangen Sie mit einem Minimal-Programm an, und tun Sie langsam immer etwas mehr.

—2 ODER 3MAL (B) ODER: JE EINMAL (A), (B) UND (C) ANGEKREUZT:

Das Ergebnis ist nicht schlecht. Es zeigt, daß Sie etwas für Ihren Körper tun oder zumindest° getan haben.   *at least*

—2 ODER 3MAL (C) ANGEKREUZT:

Sie sind gut in Form! Gehen Sie regelmäßig zum Sport? Weiter so!

---

2. **Was stimmt? Welche Sätze passen zusammen? Suchen Sie je einen Satz aus A, B und C, um zu beschreiben, was Sie gemacht haben.**

   A.

   1. Ich bin fünf Minuten gejoggt.
   2. Ich habe die Knie gebeugt.
   3. Ich habe mich auf die Seite gelegt und den Ellenbogen aufgestützt.

   B.

   1. Dann habe ich beide Arme in Schulterhöhe nach vorne genommen, feste Fäuste gemacht und die Spannung gehalten.
   2. Dann habe ich das untere Bein an den Bauch gezogen und das andere zur Decke gestreckt.
   3. Ich habe langsam angefangen und bin immer schneller gelaufen.

   C.

   1. Ich habe versucht, meine Nasenspitze mit meinem Knie zu berühren (*touch*).
   2. Am Ende bin ich ganz energisch gelaufen.
   3. Ich habe das Bein hochgestreckt und lange so gehalten.

Auf den ersten Blick 2

Scan the headings over the different sections of the text **Radfahren.** Brainstorm in small groups. For each section of the text think of some words in German that would fit under each heading.

> **BEISPIEL:**   Wer sollte radfahren? Kinder, junge Leute. Man muß fit sein.

Auf den ersten Blick 2.
Suggestion: Put students in groups of three. Write headings on the board and supply one example under each. Give students 5 minutes to brainstorm as many vocabulary items as they can.

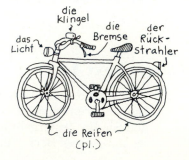

Radfahren

Radfahren

Wer sollte radfahren?

Wer sich auf dem Fahrrad sicher fühlt und wer die Regeln der Straßenver-kehrsordnung[a] kennt und beachtet[b]

Wo sollte man rad-fahren?

Suchen Sie sich eine abgasfreie[c] Strecke. Rad-wege sind besonders geeignet[d] aber auch auf Waldwegen und wenig befahrenen Straßen macht es Spaß.

Das Fahrrad

Das Fahrrad muß in Ord-nung sein: Bremsen, Licht, Klingel, Rückstrahler etc. müssen funktionieren. Ab-gefahrene oder brüchige[e] Reifen müssen aus-gewechselt werden.

Die Kleidung:

Sie soll praktisch und bequem sein. Unterwäsche oder ein Trikot, das den Schweiß aufsaugt, sowie ein Trainingsanzug sind ideal. Erst für lange Fahr-ten ist eine Fahrradhose zu empfehlen. Knallig bunte[f] Kleidung erhöht die Sicherheit[g] im Straßenver-kehr.

Wichtig für Anfänger:

Langsam beginnen. 2 bis 3 Mal in der Woche 4–6 km in mäßigem[h] Tempo sind genug. Später Strecken-längen erhöhen, Tempo beibehalten.

Auszeichnungen[i], Wett-bewerbe:

Wer schon gut trainiert ist, kann an Volksradfahren, Radtourenfahrten u. ä. teil-nehmen oder auch das Radabzeichen[j] erwerben.

Informationen:

Alle Infos rund um's Fahr-rad und auch den Breiten-sportkalender 1983 erhal-ten Sie beim

Bund Deutscher Radfahrer
Abt. Breitensport
Otto-Fleck-Schneise 4
6000 Frankfurt/Main 71

a. Regeln... *traffic rules*
b. *observes*
c. *free of exhaust fumes*
d. *suitable*
e. *defective*
f. Knallig... *very colorful*
g. *safety*
h. *moderate*
i. *awards*
j. *bicycle award*

Zum Text 2

Zum Text 2. **Suggestion:** Have students do #1 in pairs, taking turns asking the question *Steht im Text, wo (oder was) man... ?* After the activity is completed, call on individuals to check comprehension.

1. **Radfahren:** Kann man diese Information im Text finden? Kreuzen Sie **ja** oder **nein** an. Wenn Sie **ja** ankreuzen, notieren Sie auch die Information.

	JA	NEIN	INFORMATION
a. wo man in der BRD radfahren kann	____	____	_____
b. wo man radfahren sollte	____	____	_____
c. Teile eines Fahrrads	____	____	_____
d. wo man ein Fahrrad kaufen kann	____	____	_____
e. was man beim Radfahren tragen soll	____	____	_____
f. wo man Radbekleidung kaufen kann	____	____	_____
g. wo man mehr über Radfahren erfahren kann	____	____	_____

2. Richtig, falsch oder im Text nicht zu finden? Schreiben Sie **r** (richtig), **f** (falsch) oder **n** (nicht im Text). Wenn der Satz richtig oder falsch ist, finden Sie die Stelle im Text, wo die Information steht.

   a. _____ Radfahren ist nicht für alte Leute.
   b. _____ Wenn man radfährt, sollte man sich auf einem Fahrrad wohl fühlen, und die Regeln kennen.
   c. _____ In der BRD darf man nicht auf der Straße radfahren.
   d. _____ Bunte (*colorful*) Bekleidung ist sehr modisch.
   e. _____ Ein buntes Hemd ist empfehlenswert.
   f. _____ Wenn man anfängt, soll man vier- bis fünfmal in der Woche fahren.

3. Wie heißen die zusammengesetzten Wörter? Sie finden die fehlenden Wortteile im Text!

   a. _____verkehrs_____ (wie der Verkehr fährt)
   b. abgas_____ (ohne Abgase)
   c. Wald_____ (Wege im Wald, wo man radfahren kann)
   d. Unter_____ (die Kleidung, die man unter der oberen Kleidung trägt)
   e. Trainings_____ (was man beim Training oder Sporttreiben trägt)
   f. Straßen_____ (Autos, Busse, Fahrräder auf der Straße.)

Nach dem Lesen

▣ Aktivität 1. Macht mit!

Sagen Sie, was Ihre Klassenkameraden tun sollen.

BEISPIEL: Hebt das rechte Bein!

joggen   das rechte/linke Bein
berühren (*touch*)   der rechte/linke Arm
heben (*lift*)   die Fußspitze
strecken   die Schulter
bewegen (*move*)   der Kopf
                                usw.

Aktivität 1.   Suggestion: Form
groups of four. Students take turns
telling the group what to do.
Follow-up: Have students make up
an exercise routine in German consisting of five to seven different
moves. They can bring them to class
and try them out in small groups.

▣ Aktivität 2. Tagebuch führen

Führen Sie eine Woche lang Tagebuch (*diary*) über Ihre Aktivitäten.
Haben Sie etwas für Ihre Gesundheit getan? Haben Sie Sport getrieben?
Haben Sie zuviel gearbeitet? Haben Sie gesund gegessen? Machen Sie
eine Liste mit positiven und negativen Dingen.

BEISPIEL: POSITIV   NEGATIV

   Ich habe Tennis gespielt.   Ich habe nicht genug
                                   geschlafen.

Aktivität 2.   Suggestion: Students
should trade their *Tagebuch* with a
partner. The partner offers written
advice about what the other can do
to be more health conscious.

WORTSCHATZ

Substantive

Gesundheit und Krankheit	**Health and Sickness**
der Arzt (¨e), die Ärztin (-nen)	physician
die Apotheke (-n)	pharmacy
die Drogerie (-n)	drugstore
die Erholung	rest and recuperation
die Erkältung (-en)	cold
das Fieber	fever
die Gesundheit	health
die Grippe	flu
der Husten	cough
die Krankheit (-en)	sickness, ailment
die Krankenkasse	health insurance company

die Kur	health cure, treatment (at a spa)
der Kurort (-e)	health spa, resort
das Medikament (-e)	medicine (pills, etc.)
die Medizin	the field of medicine
der Patient (-en), die Patientin (-nen)	patient
die Reformkost	health food
der Schmerz (-en)	pain, ache
die Kopfschmerzen	headache
die Zahnschmerzen	toothache
Ich habe Kopfschmerzen.	I have a headache.
die Tablette (-n)	pill
der Vegetarier (-), die Vegetarierin (-nen)	vegetarian

Körperteile / Parts of the body

Körperteile	Parts of the body
der Arm (-e)	arm
das Auge (-n)	eye
der Bauch	abdomen, stomach
das Bein (-e)	leg
die Brust (¨e)	chest, breast
der Ell(en)bogen (¨)	elbow
der Finger (-)	finger
der Fuß (¨e)	foot
der Hals	neck
das Haar (-e)	hair
das Kinn	chin
das Knie (-)	knee
der Kopf (¨e)	head
der Magen (-)	stomach
der Mund	mouth
der Muskel (-n)	muscle
die Nase (-n)	nose
das Ohr (-en)	ear
der Rücken (-)	back
die Schulter (-n)	shoulder
der Zahn (¨e)	tooth

Andere Substantive

die Bewegung (-en)	exercise, movement
der Fotoapparat (-e)	camera
der Staat (-en)	state, government
das Wasser	water

Verben

sich anziehen (zieht an), angezogen	to get dressed
aufhören (hört auf) mit	to quit
sich bedanken	to thank
sich beschweren über (acc.)	to complain about
(sich) bewegen	to move about
denken, gedacht	to think
sich entspannen	to relax, take a rest
sich erholen	to recuperate; to rest
sich erkälten	to catch a cold
sich freuen auf (acc.)	to look forward to
sich freuen über (acc.)	to be happy about
sich fühlen	to feel
Ich fühle mich nicht wohl.	I am not feeling well.
gefährden	to endanger
sich fit halten (hält sich fit), gehalten	to keep fit
halten für	to consider
Ich halte das für wichtig	I consider that important
sich hinsetzen (setzt sich hin)	to sit down
sich informieren	to inform oneself
sich interessieren für	to be interested in
sich kämmen	to comb (one's hair)
lassen (läßt), gelassen	to let
sich (dat.) etwas leisten	to afford
Das kann ich mir nicht leisten.	I can't afford that.
putzen	to clean
Ich putze mir die Zähne.	I brush my teeth.
rauchen	to smoke
reparieren	to repair
schlucken	to swallow
Sport treiben, getrieben	to engage in sports
sich unterhalten (unterhält), unterhalten	to have a conversation
unternehmen (unternimmt), unternommen	to undertake
sich untersuchen lassen	to go for a checkup
verhüten	to prevent
(sich) waschen (wäscht), gewaschen	to wash (oneself)
(sich) weh tun (dat.), weh getan	to hurt (oneself)
ziehen, gezogen	to pull

Adjektive und Adverbien

anstrengend	strenuous
deprimiert	depressed
dick	plump, fat
gleich	right away, immediately
heiser	hoarse
hundsmiserabel (coll.)	sick as a dog
kaputt	broken
kaum	hardly
krank	sick
lang(e)	long
müde	tired
regelmäßig	regularly
schlapp	without energy, run-down, listless
schmutzig	dirty

wenig	little
zu wenig	too little
zuletzt	last
zuviel	too much

Ausdrücke

auf der Stelle	on the spot; immediately
fix und fertig sein (*coll.*)	to be completely exhausted
Gute Besserung!	Get well soon!

Ich gehe zum Arzt.	I am going to see the doctor.
Ich war beim Arzt.	I was at the doctor.
Was fehlt Ihnen?	What's wrong?
Was ist los?	What is the matter?
Mir ist nicht gut.	I'm not feeling well.
Mir ist schlecht.	I'm sick (to my stomach).
Das klingt nicht gut.	That doesn't sound good.
nicht wahr?	isn't that so?
So ein Pech!	What a shame! (What bad luck!)

FREIZEIT UND VERGNÜGEN

Lernziele *In this chapter you will learn to talk about what you do for fun and recreation. You will learn to plan an outing with friends and talk about the weather.*

▣ Alles klar?

Wie verbringen junge Deutsche ihre Freizeit?

- _____ % (Prozent) treiben Sport.
- _____ % verbringen ihre Freizeit mit _____.
- _____ % gehen gern _____.
- _____ % hören gern _____.
- _____ % fahren gern _____.
- _____ % _____ gern.

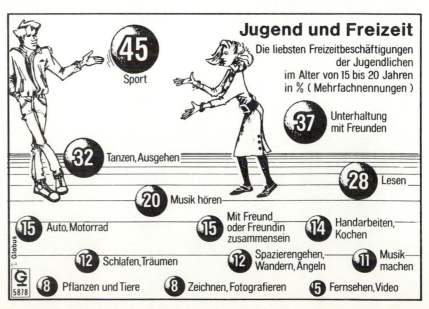

Jugend und Freizeit
Die liebsten Freizeitbeschäftigungen der Jugendlichen im Alter von 15 bis 20 Jahren in % (Mehrfachnennungen)

- **45** Sport
- **37** Unterhaltung mit Freunden
- **32** Tanzen, Ausgehen
- **28** Lesen
- **20** Musik hören
- **15** Auto, Motorrad
- **15** Mit Freund oder Freundin zusammensein
- **14** Handarbeiten, Kochen
- **12** Schlafen, Träumen
- **12** Spazierengehen, Wandern, Angeln
- **11** Musik machen
- **8** Pflanzen und Tiere
- **8** Zeichnen, Fotografieren
- **5** Fernsehen, Video

Globus

G 5878

Sie verbringen ihre Freizeit mit Freunden.

Und wie verbringen Sie Ihre Freizeit gewöhnlich?

- Meine Lieblingsbeschäftigung ist ＿＿.
- Ich ＿＿ gern.
- Ich verbringe meine Freizeit mit ＿＿.
- Ich interessiere mich für ＿＿.

Diese zwei angeln gern in ihrer Freizeit.

WÖRTER IM KONTEXT

Vergnügungen

Neue Wörter

sich beschäftigen mit *to occupy oneself with*
bummeln (sind gebummelt) *to stroll*
(herum)gammeln ([herum]gegammelt) *to goof off*

▣ **Aktivität 1.** **Wie verbringen diese Leute ihre Freizeit?**

Benutzen Sie folgende Verben, um die Bilder auf der nächsten Seite zu beschreiben: sich beschäftigen mit, bummeln, fernsehen, fotografieren, herumgammeln, Musik machen.

233

BEISPIEL: a. Er macht Musik.

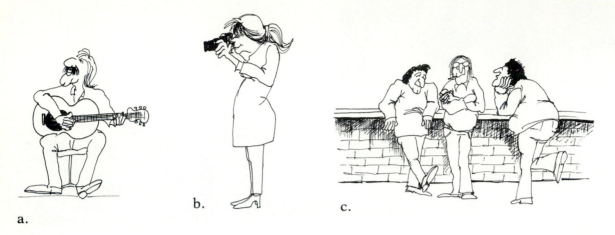

a.
b.
c.

d.

e.

f.

◻ Aktivität 2.   Partnerarbeit

Fragen Sie einen Partner: Wie hast du in den letzten acht Tagen deine Freizeit verbracht?

BEISPIEL: Ich habe Musik gehört und bin mit Freunden ausgegangen. Ich habe ein paarmal ferngesehen.

mit Freunden	ausgehen
mit einem Freund	in die Disko/ins Kino, usw.
mit einer Freundin	gehen
allein	diskutieren
	Musik hören
	Musik machen
	fernsehen
	herumgammeln
	sich mit dem Computer/
	Hobby beschäftigen
	durch Geschäfte / die Stadt,
	usw. bummeln

Aktivität 2.   Suggestion: First have students scan the range of possibilities. This activity can be done with the whole group. Encourage students to link several pieces of information together. Brainstorm other activities with the group, providing new vocabulary for them as needed.

Sport

Die Karte „Naherholung" (*nearby recreation*) zeigt, was für Sportmöglichkeiten es in Göttingen, einer deutschen Kleinstadt, gibt. Göttingen ist typisch für viele deutsche Städte.

RSM

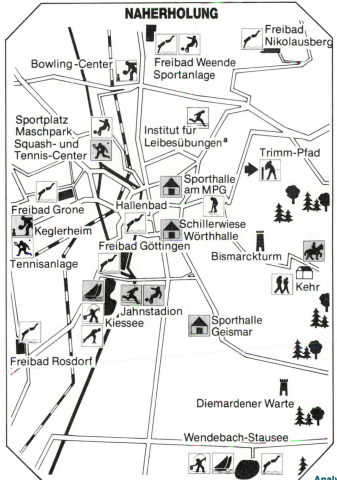

a. *sports*

🔲 Analyse

- Schauen Sie sich die Bildsymbole auf der Karte an. Welche verschiedenen Sportarten kann man in und um Göttingen treiben?
- Wo kann man schwimmen?
- Was ist ein Freibad? Was ist ein Hallenbad?

Analyse. This requires students to make a list of sports activities. Students can do this activity in pairs. Have partners exchange lists with others to compare and fill in missing items. Focus students' attention on the words *frei* and *Halle* to see if they can guess their meaning.

Neue Wörter

die Mannschaft *team*	das Stadion *stadium*
der Pfad *path*	angeln *to fish*
der See *lake*	kegeln *to bowl*
die Sporthalle *gymnasium*	segeln *to sail*
der Sportplatz *sports field*	tauchen *to dive*

⊡ Aktivität 3. Was braucht man für diese Sportarten?

BEISPIEL: Zum Angeln braucht man einen See.

1. Zum Angeln
2. Für Eishockey
3. Für Fußball
4. Für Golf
5. Zum Reiten   braucht man
6. Zum Segeln
7. Zum Tauchen
8. Zum Wandern

a. einen Ball
b. ein Pferd
c. einen See
d. Wege und Pfade in der Natur
e. ein Eisstadion
f. einen Sportplatz
g. eine Mannschaft
h. Sonstiges

⊡ Aktivität 4. Interaktion

Kommst du mit? Machen Sie eine Verabredung (*date*).

A: Ich gehe heute kegeln. Kommst du mit?
    ins Kino
    in ein Rockkonzert
    ins Stadtbad

B: Na gut, um wieviel Uhr denn?
A: Um _____ Uhr.
    Nach dem Abendessen um _____.
B: Wo wollen wir uns treffen?
A: Vor dem Kino.
    Im Studentenheim.
    Bei mir zu Hause.
B: Gut. Ich treffe dich dann.

B: Ich kann nicht.
A: Warum denn nicht?
B: Ich muß arbeiten.
    Ich habe kein Geld.
        keine Zeit.
        keine Lust.
A: Schade.

RSM

Sprachnotiz

To say how often you do something, use the following expressions:

jeden Tag	*every day*
einmal die Woche	*once a week*
zweimal die Woche	*twice a week*
dreimal im Monat	*three times a month*
einmal im Jahr	*once a year*

▣ Aktivität 5. Ein Gespräch über Sport

Bilden Sie kleine Gruppen, und diskutieren Sie. Für welchen Sport interessieren Sie sich? Wie oft treiben Sie Sport?

BEISPIEL: A: Ich jogge gern, und ich wandere auch gern.
B: Wie oft machst du das?
A: Ich gehe einmal im Jahr wandern, aber ich jogge jeden Tag.

Aktivität 5. Suggestion: Have students work in pairs. Remind them that they can either accept or reject the invitation. Have students repeat the conversation with several partners. Call on one or several pairs to role-play the conversation for the class.

▣ Aktivität 6. Freizeit-Budget

Schauen Sie sich das Freizeit-Budget einer deutschen Familie an.

1. Geben Sie auch Geld für diese Sachen aus?
2. Wofür geben die Deutschen viel aus?
3. Wieviel Geld geben Sie im Monat ungefähr für die Freizeit aus?
4. Wofür geben Sie wenig oder nichts aus?

Ich gebe ungefähr $20 im Monat fürs Kino aus. Ich gebe nichts für Garten und Haustiere aus.

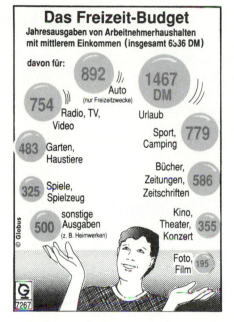

Das Freizeit-Budget
Jahresausgaben von Arbeitnehmerhaushalten mit mittlerem Einkommen (insgesamt 6336 DM)

davon für:

892 Auto (nur Freizeitzwecke)
754 Radio, TV, Video
1467 DM Urlaub
779 Sport, Camping
483 Garten, Haustiere
325 Spiele, Spielzeug
586 Bücher, Zeitungen, Zeitschriften
500 sonstige Ausgaben (z. B. Heimwerken)
355 Kino, Theater, Konzert
195 Foto, Film

© Globus

7267

RSM

Aktivität 6. Suggestion: First have students look at the Globus chart. Ask individuals to identify items they don't know; others—or you yourself—supply the answer. Then have students do the activity in pairs. They should jot down each other's responses and share the information with the class.

Pläne für einen Ausflug

▣ Dialog

Verena und Antje planen fürs Wochenende. Sie wohnen beide in Düsseldorf.

VERENA: Sag mal, wie wäre es mit einem Ausflug am Wochenende?
ANTJE: Prima Idee! Ich brauche unbedingt Abwechslung. Die Arbeit geht mir im Moment auf die Nerven. Was schlägst du denn vor?
VERENA: Warst du schon mal in Neandertal?
ANTJE: Nein, noch nie. Wie weit ist das von hier?
VERENA: Nicht zu weit. Wir können mit dem Rad dahin. Man kann bequem in zwei Stunden da sein. Der Weg führt fast nur durch Wald.
ANTJE: Soll ich Stefan auch einladen?
VERENA: Schön. Wenn er Lust hat.
ANTJE: Ich weiß, daß er gern mitkommt. Hoffentlich bleibt das Wetter schön.

Dialog. Suggestion: Preview the *Neue Wörter* on page 238 with students before they hear the dialogue. Let them hear it once (with books closed). Ask the class to give information on the content of the dialogue; then play it a second time as they read along in the book. Finally, have them role-play the dialogue.

Neue Wörter

die Abwechslung *change,*
   diversion
der Wald *forest*
führen *to lead*
  der Weg führt *the road goes*

weit von hier *far away from here*
wie wäre es mit... *how about . . .*

▣ **Aktivität 7. Was haben Verena und Antje vor?**

Was ist hier richtig, und was ist falsch? Worüber steht nichts im Text?

1. Verena und Antje planen einen Ausflug.
2. Sie wollen nach Neandertal wandern.
3. Es dauert nur eine Stunde bis nach Neandertal.
4. Der Weg führt durch den Wald.
5. Auf dem Wege dahin wollen sie picknicken.
6. Antje hat ihren Freund Stefan eingeladen.
7. Wenn das Wetter schlecht ist, bleiben sie zu Hause.

Aktivität 7. **Suggestion:** Students work in pairs, taking turns saying each statement and asking *Stimmt das?* Their partner should respond *Ja, Nein,* or *Das steht nicht im Text* and supply the correct information, as needed.

Sprachnotiz

Words like **daß** (*that*) and **wenn** (*if; when*) are conjunctions connecting a main clause and a dependent clause. These conjunctions cause the verb to be placed at the end of the dependent clause.

Ich weiß, **daß** er gern **mitkommt**.
Wenn es schön **ist**, können wir mit dem Rad fahren.

▣ **Aktivität 8. Interaktion**

Sie schlagen einen Ausflug für das Wochenende vor. Sagen Sie, wohin Sie wollen, wo und wie weit das ist, wann Sie dahin wollen, und was man da unternehmen kann.

Aktivität 8. **Note:** This interaction permits students to make many choices and to link more information. Students work in pairs to create the conversation. The activity can be repeated several times with different partners. Students should be encouraged to ad lib freely.
Follow-up: Assign pairs to write the script for such a conversation and role-play it during the next class.

A:

Wie wäre es mit einem Ausflug?

Nach ＿＿. Warst du schon mal da?

Ungefähr ＿＿ Meilen von hier.

＿＿

mit dem Wagen / Fahrrad / zu Fuß

picknicken / schwimmen / usw.

B:

Gute Idee! Wohin?

Ja/Nein. Wie weit ＿＿?

Wann ＿＿?

Wie ＿＿?

Was ＿＿?

Das Wetter

DIE JAHRESZEITEN

der Frühling

der Sommer

der Herbst

der Winter

Der Wetterbericht. Suggestion: Introduce weather expressions by asking questions of the whole group. *Wie ist das Wetter heute? Und wie war es gestern? Wie ist das Wetter in Süd-Florida? Und in Neu-England?*

DER WETTERBERICHT

DIE SONNE	**DIE WOLKEN**	**DER REGEN**	**DAS GEWITTER**	**DER SCHNEE**
Die Sonne scheint. Es ist sonnig; heiter; warm; angenehm (*pleasant*); heiß.	Es ist wolkig; bedeckt; bewölkt; kühl; kalt.	Es regnet. Es gibt Regen. Es gibt einen Schauer.	Es gibt ein Gewitter. Es blitzt. Es donnert. Es ist schwül (*muggy*).	Es schneit.

⬚⬚⬚⬚ *Kulturnotiz*

To convert Celsius into Fahrenheit: Divide by 5, multiply by 9, and add 32. To convert Fahrenheit into Celsius: Subtract 32, divide by 9, and multiply by 5.

F	C	
104°	40°	Es ist sehr heiß.
85°	30°	Es ist schön warm.
70°	20°	Es ist angenehm.
50°	10°	Es ist kühl.
32°	0°	Es ist sehr kalt.

Kulturnotiz. Ask students to give today's temperature in degrees Celsius.

⬚ Analyse

Ein Wetterbericht: wie ist das Wetter?

- Für welches Land und welche Stadt ist der Wetterbericht rechts?
- Wie ist das Wetter?
- Was ist die Höchsttemperatur? Wieviel ist das in Fahrenheit?
- Finden Sie das deutsche Wort für *forecast*. Wie ist das Wetter bis Samstag?

Analyse. Suggestion: Students can do this in pairs, taking turns asking questions and responding. They should also jot down the answers to each question.

Neue Wörter

der Nebel *fog*

draußen *outside*

regnerisch *rainy*

scheußlich *terrible*

wolkenlos *without clouds*

RSM

⬚ Aktivität 9. Wetter-Hugo meint.

Wetter-Hugo predicts and gives advice about the weather. He is also a poet: his reports and predictions rhyme! What does the text say?

1. Dieser Wetterbericht ist wahrscheinlich (*probably*) für einen Tag im
   a. Sommer   c. Winter
   b. Herbst   d. Frühjahr
2. Das Wetter war angenehm warm in
   a. Deutschland   c. Österreich
   b. der Schweiz   d. Spanien
3. In Deutschland war das Wetter
   a. kalt und scheußlich   c. schwül
   b. regnerisch   d. sehr windig

Aktivität 9.
Suggestion: Since the weather report is a "poem," read it aloud to students first. Students can also read it aloud after some practice, either individually or in chorus. Then have students work in pairs, taking turns saying each sentence and deciding on the correct response.
Follow-up: Ask students to create a two- or four-line weather poem.

a. *rain*

WETTER

Region
Zürich

Schöön![a]

Sonnig und warm. Temperaturmaximum um 28 °C.

Ganze
Schweiz

Strahlend schön

Schönes Wetter. Nullgradgrenze bei 4400 Metern. In den Bergen schwache bis mässige Südwestwinde.

Aussichten
bis Samstag

Sonnig und warm

Ziemlich sonnig und warm. Vor allem in der zweiten Tageshälfte Neigung zu Gewittern.

a. *actually* schön, *but the ö is drawn out for emphasis*

RSM

Wetter-Hugo meint:

HUHU!

Heute:
Nebel deckt zur Früh die Länder, und dann kommen Wolkenbänder. Vier Grad sind's am Tage rund, Nachtfrost drei ist ungesund. Äußerst selten Niederschläge[a] Wind aus West bläst eher träge.

Morgen:
Draußen bleibt es kalt und scheußlich, darum bleibe lieber häuslich.

Temperaturen gestern, 14 Uhr

Frankfurt	4	Rom	15
Hamburg	8	Riviera	16
München	3	Barcelona	20
Saarbrücken	3	Zürich	5
Berlin	6	Innsbruck	5

...und vor einem Jahr:

Frankfurt	8 wolkenlos

a. *rain*

4. Wetter Hugo meint, man soll
   a. nach Spanien reisen   c. sich warm anziehen
   b. zu Hause bleiben   d. draußen bleiben
5. In Frankfurt war das Wetter vor einem Jahr
   a. warm   c. bewölkt
   b. kühl   d. neblig

Aktivität 10. Hören Sie zu.

Sie hören fünf kurze Wetterberichte für fünf Städte in Europa. Kreuzen Sie die Information an, und notieren Sie die Temperatur (Grad Celsius).

	ZÜRICH	WIEN	BERLIN	PARIS	LONDON
sonnig	X				
warm	X				
heiter bis wolkig		X	X		
(stark) bewölkt					X
Schauer			X		
Regen					X
Wind				X	
Gewitter		X			
Grad Celsius	20–25	18	20	29	10

Aktivität 10. Suggestion: First have students scan the possibilities. Then let them hear the weather reports and fill in the information. Check students' responses by asking *Wie ist das Wetter in* _____? Students use the information on their chart in their responses.

Aktivität 11. Woher kommen Sie? Wie ist das Wetter da?

BEISPIEL: Ich komme aus San Franzisko. Da ist das Wetter im Sommer oft kühl und neblig. Im Frühling ist es meistens sonnig. Und im Winter regnet es.

Aktivität 11. Note: This activity combines seasons and weather descriptions. Encourage students to describe the weather during at least two seasons.
Suggestion: The activity can be done in pairs, with students jotting down what their partner says so they can report back to the whole group.

WETTER: Es wird kühler

Wetter behinderte den Osterverkehr
Sturm, Staus,[a] Regen – und am Montag 20 Grad Wärme

a. *traffic jams*

▣ **Aktivität 12. Ein Wetterbericht**

Was steht im Wetterbericht über diese Länder?

> BEISPIEL: In Frankreich ist es stark bewölkt. Es ist
> ziemlich warm. Es gibt auch Gewitter.

1. Griechenland
2. die Schweiz
3. Spanien
4. Dänemark
5. die Kanarischen Inseln
6. Italien

DAS WETTER:
Frühnebel, heiter bis wolkig,
um 28 Grad, schwachwindig

VORHERSAGE FÜR DAS AUSLAND, MORGEN:
Dänemark: Stark bewölkt, Schauer, um 24 Grad. **Frankreich:** Gebietsweise stark bewölkt, Gewitter, 28 bis 33 Grad. **Spanien:** Wolkig mit Aufheiterungen, einzelne Gewitter, über 30 Grad. **Kanarische Inseln:** Heiter bis wolkig, 24 bis 28 Grad. **Österreich/Schweiz:** Sonnig, einzelne Wärmegewitter, um 30 Grad. **Italien/Jugoslawien:** Sonnig, örtlich Gewitter, 29 bis 35 Grad. **Griechenland:** Sonnig, über 30 Grad.

▣ **Aktivität 13. Ihr Wetterbericht**

Schreiben Sie einen Wetterbericht für Ihr Gebiet.

> BEISPIEL: Das Wetter für Donnerstag: Schwül und heiß. Temperaturen: 30–35 Grad Celsius. Das Wetter für morgen: morgens Nebel, dann sonnig, um 30 Grad.

GRAMMATIK IM KONTEXT

Coordinating Conjunctions

Conjunctions are words that connect phrases or sentences. German has two types of conjunctions: coordinating conjunctions and subordinating conjunctions. Coordinating conjunctions link phrases and sentences that are of equal value. They can be stated independently of each other. The coordinating conjunctions are

> und
> aber
> oder
> denn (*because*)
> sondern (*but rather*)

> Die jungen Deutschen treiben gern Sport, **und** sie reisen viel.
> Ich lese gern, **aber** ich sehe auch gern fern.
> Wollen wir ins Kino gehen, **oder** wollen wir zu Hause bleiben?
> Ich möchte ins Kino gehen, **denn** im Kino läuft ein interessanter
>   Film.
> Wir wollen nicht zu Hause bleiben, **sondern** ins Kino gehen.

Coordinating conjunctions do not affect word order.

The conjunction **sondern** (*but rather*) implies a contrast and is used to juxtapose two mutually exclusive ideas. It always follows a negative statement.

▣ Übung 1. Freizeitpläne

Ergänzen Sie die fehlenden Konjunktionen.

   und, oder, aber, denn, sondern

Jörg ____[1] seine Freundin Karin planen einen Ausflug ____[2] ein Picknick. Die Frage ist: wohin ____[3] wann? Heute geht es nicht, ____[4] es regnet, ____[5] morgen haben beide keine Zeit. Also müssen sie bis zum Wochenende warten. Sie wollen diesmal nicht mit dem Auto ins Grüne fahren, ____[6] mit ihren Fahrrädern. Das macht bestimmt mehr Spaß, ____[7] ist gut für die Gesundheit. Sie wollen an einen See, ____[8] da können sie schwimmen gehen. Danach können Sie ein Picknick im Wald machen, ____[9] sie können am See bleiben. Karin ist nicht für die öffentlichen (*public*) Picknickplätze, ____[10] da sind meistens zu viele Leute, Kinder ____[11] Hunde, Onkel ____[12] Tanten. Jörg lädt auch seinen Freund Andreas ein, ____[13] der kann leider nicht mit. Es tut ihm leid, ____[14] er braucht unbedingt ein wenig Freizeit.

▣ Übung 2. Pläne für einen Ausflug

Bilden Sie Sätze mit den Konjunktionen. (*Choose elements from each column to form your sentences.*)

   und, oder, aber, denn, sondern

BEISPIEL: Ich will nicht zu Hause bleiben, sondern ins Grüne fahren.

Ich mache gern einen Ausflug,	zu Hause bleiben.
Wollen wir zu Fuß gehen,	ins Grüne fahren.
Ich will nicht zu Hause bleiben,	gern fernsehen.
Morgen kann ich nicht mit,	Tennis spielen.
Möchtest du schwimmen gehen,	mit dem Wagen fahren.
Ich muß zu Hause bleiben,	durch die Stadt bummeln.
Ich möchte nicht ins Kino gehen,	mein Wagen ist kaputt.

Subordinating Conjunctions

Subordinating conjunctions are words that connect a main clause with a dependent clause. Subordinating conjunctions include **weil** (*because*), **daß** (*that*), and **wenn** (*if*).

▣ Analyse

> Hans joggt gern, weil ihn das fit hält. Er läuft sogar, wenn es regnet. Ich weiß, daß Joggen schlecht für meine Knie ist.

- Finden Sie die Konjunktionen in den Sätzen.
- Wo steht das konjugierte Verb in den Sätzen mit Konjunktionen?

Analyse. Suggestion: Since the *Analyse* is very brief, do it quickly with the whole group. Focus on the importance of certain conjunctions "kicking" the finite verb to the end of the sentence.

In a dependent clause beginning with a subordinating conjunction, the conjugated verb appears at the end of the clause. In the present perfect tense, the auxiliary verb (**haben** or **sein**) comes last. Verbs with separable prefixes appear as one word at the end of the dependent clause.

Ich hoffe, **daß** wir bald eine Radtour ins Grüne **machen.**

Wir sind zu Hause geblieben, **weil** es geregnet **hat.**

Stefan kann nicht mit, **weil** er arbeiten **muß.**

Ich hoffe, **daß** du mich auch **einlädst.**

Word Order of Main Clause and Dependent Clause

You recall that the conjugated verb is always the second element in a statement.

	1	2	
Hans	**joggt**	gern am Wochenende.
Er	**ist**	zu Hause geblieben.

In a dependent clause, the conjugated verb is the last element of the sentence.

MAIN CLAUSE		DEPENDENT CLAUSE
1	2	
Wir	wissen,	daß Hans am Wochenende gern **joggt.**
Er	bleibt zu Hause,	weil es geregnet **hat.**

If the dependent clause precedes the main clause, the subject and verb in the main clause are inverted. Thus, the conjugated verb of the main clause is still the second element of the sentence.

DEPENDENT CLAUSE	MAIN CLAUSE	
1	2	
Weil es geregnet hat,	sind	wir zu Hause geblieben.
Wenn wir Zeit haben,	gehen	wir am Wochende ins Fitness-Center.

In a conditional sentence (**wenn**), the main clause stating the conclusion sometimes starts with the word **dann** (*then*). It does not affect word order.

> Wenn wir Zeit haben, dann besuchen wir euch.

▣ Übung 3. **Was haben Sie gehört?**

BEISPIEL: Ich habe gehört, daß es morgen kühler wird.

1. Es wird morgen kühler.
2. Ihr könnt nicht mitkommen.
3. Stefan geht auch segeln.
4. Das Freibad ist noch geschlossen.
5. Es hat auf der Autobahn (*freeway*) einen Stau (*traffic jam*) von 30 Kilometern gegeben.

Übung 3. Suggestion: Students can work in pairs, taking turns responding. Encourage them to extend the activity with several free responses to the question.

▣ Übung 4. **Was tun Sie, wenn...?**

BEISPIEL: Wenn ich nicht arbeite, fahre ich Motorrad.

Wenn	nicht Motorrad fahren	Fußball spielen
	nicht Fußball spielen	Krimis lesen
	usw.	in die Disko gehen
		mein Auto reparieren
		mit Freunden ausgehen
		einen Roman schreiben

Übung 4. Suggestion: Students can work in pairs or in small groups. **Follow-up:** Have students formulate questions such as: *Was tust du, wenn du nicht lernst?* Place questions on slips of paper in a box. Students draw one out and respond.

▣ Übung 5. **Warum gehst du nicht mit?**

Nennen Sie Gründe, warum sie nicht mitgehen.

BEISPIEL: Ich kann nicht mit, weil ich morgen eine Klausur habe. *oder auch:* Es tut mir leid, aber ich habe morgen eine Klausur.

1. Gehst du mit ins Kino?
2. Kommst du heute abend zur Party?
3. Wir wollen kegeln gehen. Kommst du mit?

Kopfschmerzen
kein Geld / keine Zeit /
   keine Lust
zu langweilig
arbeiten müssen

Übung 5. Suggestion: Divide the class in half. One half writes invitations; the other writes rejections or excuses. Call on students from each group to match up sentence halves. Encourage students to go beyond the suggestions in the activity.

▣ Übung 6. **Kleine Dialoge**

Was möchten Sie lieber? Geben Sie einen Grund dafür.

BEISPIEL: A: Möchtest du spazierengehen oder zu Hause bleiben?
B: Ich möchte zu Hause bleiben, weil ich ein Fußballspiel im Fernsehen sehen möchte.

Übung 6. Suggestion: Brainstorm several additional items with students. Have students circulate in the classroom, asking other students questions and responding to questions from others.

Möchtest du:

1. spazierengehen?
2. zu Hause bleiben?
3. ins Kino gehen?
4. schwimmen gehen?
5. reiten?
6. einen Ausflug machen?
7. ins Konzert gehen?

Indirect Questions

Question words such as **wann, warum, was, wie,** and **wer** can also act as subordinating conjunctions introducing an indirect question. The conjugated verb appears at the end of the indirect question.

DIRECT QUESTION	INDIRECT QUESTION
Wie wird das Wetter morgen?	Weißt du, **wie** das Wetter morgen wird?
Wann kommt der Wetterbericht im Fernsehen?	Ich möchte wissen, **wann** der Wetterbericht im Fernsehen kommt.
Wo ist die Fernsehzeitung?	Weißt du, **wo** die Fernsehzeitung ist?

▣ Übung 7. Ein Ausflug

Sie wollen etwas mit Freunden unternehmen. Machen Sie einen Vorschlag. Es gibt viele Fragen.

> BEISPIEL: ins Rockkonzert gehen:
> A: Weißt du, was das kosten soll?

Vorschlag: einen Ausflug nach _____ machen

- Wie lange wollen wir bleiben?
- Wie weit ist das?
- Wie ist das Wetter dort?
- Wann kommen wir zurück?
- Was soll das kosten?
- Was können wir dort unternehmen (*do*)?

Übung 7. Suggestion: Have students work in pairs, each making three suggestions and asking three questions.
Students can also circulate in the whole group.

LESEN IM KONTEXT ▣▣▣▣▣▣▣▣▣▣▣▣▣▣▣

In diesem Teil lesen Sie über Freizeitbeschäftigungen.

Vor dem Lesen

▣ Aktivität. Eine Umfrage in der Klasse

Was machen Sie und Ihre Klassenkameraden in Ihrer Freizeit? Füllen Sie die Tabelle aus!

Aktivität. Suggestion: Give students time first to respond to the questions and then to record their partner's responses. Call on individuals to give information about their partner, linking the various responses.

	SIE	IHR(E) GESPRÄCHSPARTNER(IN)

1. Was machen Sie am liebsten in Ihrer Freizeit? _____ _____
2. Welchen Film haben Sie zuletzt gesehen? _____ _____
3. Welches Buch haben Sie in letzter Zeit gelesen? _____ _____
4. Welche Hobbys hatten Sie als Kind? _____ _____
5. Wie viele Stunden in der Woche verbringen Sie vor dem Fernseher? _____ _____

Auf den ersten Blick 1

Überfliegen Sie den Text *Bestseller,* und beantworten Sie folgende Fragen!

1. Welche Informationen findet man hier?
2. Welche Buchtitel erkennen Sie?
3. Haben Sie Bücher auf dieser Liste gelesen?
4. Was ist der Unterschied zwischen Belletristik und Sachbüchern?
5. Lesen Sie lieber Belletristik oder Sachbücher?

Auf den ersten Blick 1.
Suggestion: Students work in pairs, taking turns asking each other the questions and responding. The activity is brief enough to check responses to all questions.

Bestseller

Die Bestseller des Monats

W. Hamburg

	BELLETRISTIK		SACHBUCH	
1	Benoite Groult: Salz auf unserer Haut Droemer; 34,– DM	(2)	Stephen Hawking: Eine kurze Geschichte der Zeit. Rowohlt; 34,– DM	(1)
2	Anna Wimschneider: Herbstmilch Piper; 22,– DM	(1)	Peter de Rosa: Gottes erste Diener Droemer; 42,– DM	(2)
3	Elfriede Jelinek: Lust Rowohlt; 32,– DM	(4)	Peter Scholl-Latour: Leben mit Frankreich DVA; 44,– DM	(4)
4	Isabel Allende: Eva Luna Suhrkamp; 38,– DM	(3)	Uta Ranke-Heinemann: Eunuchen für das Himmelreich. Hoffmann und Campe; 38,– DM	(3)
5	Frederic Forsyth: Der Unterhändler Piper; 42,– DM		Colette Dowling: Perfekte Frauen S. Fischer; 29,80 DM	(5)
6	Gita Mehta: Die Maharani Droemer; 39,80 DM	(5)	Michail Gorbatschow: Glasnost – Das neue Denken. Ullstein; 29,80 DM	
7	Patrick Süskind: Das Parfüm Diogenes; 29,80 DM	(7)	Gerhard Konzelmann: Allahs Schwert Herbig; 39,80 DM	(7)
8	James Michener: Alaska Econ; 48,– DM	(9)	Dian Fossey: Gorillas im Nebel Kindler; 39,80 DM	(8)
9	Utta Danella: Das Hotel im Park Hoffmann und Campe; 39,80 DM	(6)	Michail Gorbatschow: Perestroika Droemer; 36,– DM	(6)
10	Milan Kundera: Der Scherz Hanser; 19,80 DM		Robin Norwood: Wenn Frauen zu sehr lieben Rowohlt; 29,80 DM	

Auf den ersten Blick 2

Lesen Sie den Titel des nächsten Textes, und überfliegen Sie den Text (nicht mehr als zwei Minuten). Wovon handelt (*deals with*) der Text? Der Text handelt hauptsächlich von

a. Nicole Uphoff.
b. Reiten als Freizeitsport.
c. Reiten als Wettkampfsport (*competitive sport*).
d. Pferderassen in Deutschland.

Neue Wörter

das Abenteuer *adventure*
die Freiheit *freedom*
die Mehrzahl *majority*
die Schulferien *school holidays*
das Zelt *tent*

besitzen *to own*
entdecken *to discover*

erleben *to experience*
(sich) teilen *to share*
  Wir teilen uns ein Pony. *We share a pony.*
begeistert von *enthusiastic about*
jugendlich *young, youthful*

Reiten, das große Abenteuer

Nicole Uphoff ist Deutschlands Reiterin des Jahres 1988. In Deutschland gibt es heute weit über 500.000 aktive Reiter. Die Mehrzahl davon sind Mädchen und junge Frauen. Viele arbeiten genauso hart wie° Nicole. Sie zeigen auf nationalen und internationalen Wettbewerben sehr gute Leistungen°… Im Kampf um° Meter und hundertstel Sekunden sind sie harte Konkurrentinnen° der Männer.

    Deutschland ist eine international anerkannte Reiternation. Viele bekannte Rassen° kommen von den Gestüten° des Landes. Württemberger und Hannoveraner, Münsterländer und Trakehner… Deutschland ist aber vor allem das Land der jugendlichen Freizeit-Reiter. Sie reiten zum Spaß. Locker,° fröhlich und oft ohne Sattel. Warum sind sie so begeistert von diesem Sport? Die Jugendlichen suchen beim Reiten die Dinge, die sie woanders° nicht mehr finden: Freiheit und Abenteuer—das sagen die Fachleute.°

    Ein Beispiel von vielen ist Vera Ehmen aus Bergisch-Gladbach. Vera ist 15 Jahre und reitet seit sieben Jahren: „Für den Wettkampfsport interessiere ich mich nicht. Ich möchte nur einen intensiven Kontakt zu meinem Pony und täglich reiten."

    Vera hat ein eigenes Pferd. Es gehört zu einer Pferderasse, die man für die 12–18jährigen Reiterinnen gezüchtet° hat: Das „Deutsche Reitpony". Dieses Pony ist ein „ideales Pferd" für Jugendliche. Denn es hat einen guten Charakter und ein ruhiges Temperament.

genauso… *as hard as*

achievements / Im… *In the competition for*
competitors

breeds / stud farms

relaxed

elsewhere
experts

bred

Solche Ponys sind aber in der Anschaffung° und auch im Unterhalt° nicht billig. Darum teilen sich oft zwei oder drei junge Mädchen ein Pony. Die jungen Pferdebesitzer verbringen oft ihre ganze Freizeit mit ihren Tieren. Denn neben dem Reiten gibt es viel Arbeit: Sie müssen die Tiere füttern und pflegen° sowie den Stall säubern.° Viele Jugendliche besitzen kein eigenes Pferd. Darum entstanden° in den letzten Jahren zahlreiche Pony-Höfe.° Dort können Freizeit-Reiter in den Schulferien „Urlaub im Sattel" machen. In kleinen Gruppen erleben sie das „Abenteuer Pferd". Sie pflegen ihr Pferd und unternehmen gemeinsame Ausritte.° Reitkurse gibt es für Anfänger und für Fortgeschrittene°…

buying / upkeep

groom / sowie… as well as cleaning the stable
came into existence (opened up) / riding farms

gemeinsame… riding in a group
advanced (riders)

Besonders beliebt ist bei den Jugendlichen das Wanderreiten: Man reitet bei gutem und schlechtem Wetter… Mit ihren Pferden entdecken sie die Natur. Nachts schlafen sie in Zelten. Reiten in Deutschland ist nicht nur ein Spaß, es ist ein Abenteuer.

Jugend Magazin, March 1989

Zum Text 2

1. **Information suchen:** Was finden Sie im Text über:
   - Nicole Uphoff?
   - das deutsche Reitpony?
   - Wanderreiten?
   - Pony-Höfe?
2. **Beweise suchen** (*Looking for evidence*): Suchen Sie Beweise im Text für die folgenden Behauptungen.
   a. Die Deutschen interessieren sich für Pferde.
   b. Reiten ist vor allem bei Jugendlichen beliebt.
   c. Es gibt viele Reitmöglichkeiten.
3. **Das Wichtige zusammenfassen** (*Summarizing the important points*): The following sentences contain a number of facts—some important, others less important—about riding in Germany, based on the previous reading. Choose several statements for a brief summary.

   Before creating your summary, mark each sentence (a. through j.) as either **wichtig** or **nicht so wichtig**. Then arrange the important sentences in a logical sequence.

Zum Text 2.   Suggestion: Numbers 1, 2, and 3 can be assigned for homework, to serve as the basis for the next class discussion.
Suggestion for #1: You might assign individual items to students at random. Each student finds information about this item only. As he or she reads the information to the class, the others take notes.
Suggestion for #2: Have students work in pairs to find the evidence for each statement.
Note for #3: Here students evaluate the importance of details in a text by summarizing only what is absolutely essential.
Suggestion for #3: Have students work in pairs, taking turns reading the sentences to one another and determining their importance. As a follow-up, they arrange the sentences in a logical sequence. You might also assign #3 as homework. The importance of each statement can be discussed in the next class.

	WICHTIG	NICHT SO WICHTIG
a. Das Deutsche Reitpony ist ein ideales Pferd für junge Reiterinnen.	____	____
b. Beim Wanderreiten entdecken die Jugendlichen die Natur.	____	____
c. Die Mehrzahl der Reiter sind Mädchen und junge Frauen.	____	____
d. Die Jugendlichen suchen beim Reiten Freiheit und Abenteuer.	____	____
e. Viele bekannte Pferderassen kommen aus Deutschland.	____	____
f. Auch in Wettbewerben zeigen sie gute Leistungen.	____	____

g. Auf Pony-Höfen können Freizeit-Reiter in den Schulferien „das Abenteuer Pferd" erleben.

h. Neben dem Reiten gibt es viel Arbeit.

i. Es gibt Reitkurse für Anfänger und Fortgeschrittene.

j. Reiten ist in Deutschland ein beliebter Sport.

Auf den ersten Blick 3

Auf den ersten Blick 3.
Suggestion: Do these with the whole group. Write the association responses on the board as students give them.

1. **Text identifizieren:** Dieser Text ist:
    a. eine Wortliste.
    b. eine Geschichte.
    c. ein Gedicht (*poem*).
2. **Assoziationen:** Was fällt Ihnen zu den folgenden „Vergnügungen" ein? (*What comes to your mind with respect to the following pleasures?*)

    BEISPIEL: Schnee: Winter; Spaß; Schneemann; kalt

    a. Reisen   d. bequeme Schuhe
    b. Schwimmen   e. Hund
    c. freundlich sein

Neue Wörter

das Gesicht (-er) *face*   begreifen *to comprehend*
der Hund *dog*   pflanzen *to plant*
die Reise *trip*

Vergnügungen

Der erste Blick° aus dem Fenster am Morgen   *glance*
Das wiedergefundene alte Buch
Begeisterte Gesichter
Schnee, der Wechsel der Jahreszeiten
Die Zeitung
Der Hund
Die Dialektik°   *dialectics*
Duschen, Schwimmen
Alte Musik
Bequeme Schuhe
Begreifen
Neue Musik
Schreiben, Pflanzen
Reisen
Singen
Freundlich sein.

Bertolt Brecht

*Bertolt Brecht
(1898–1956)*

Zum Text 3

Zum Text 3. Suggestion: Discussion of #1 can be in English.

1. **Fragen zur Interpretation:**
    a. The words **Duschen, Pflanzen,** and **Reisen** can either be understood to be the plural forms of the nouns **Dusche, Pflanze,** and **Reise,** or they can be verbal nouns meaning traveling, planting, and showering. How do you think Brecht would want each of these words to be understood? Explain your reasoning.
    b. Are any of Brecht's **Vergnügungen** unusual? Why?
2. **Ein Gedicht schreiben:** Schreiben Sie Ihr eigenes Gedicht mit dem Titel „Vergnügungen". Tauschen Sie (*trade*) Ihr Gedicht mit jemand anders in der Klasse aus. Lesen Sie das Gedicht in der Klasse vor.

Nach dem Lesen

▣ Aktivität 1. Rätsel lösen

Aktivität 1. Suggestion: Keep track of some of the students' responses on the board.

Können Sie das folgende Rätsel lösen? Versuchen Sie es!

2		5	
	8	7	
	12		
			17

Magisches Quadrat

Tragen Sie in die Kästen[a] Zahlen zwischen 1 und 18 so ein, daß sich in den waagerechten,[b] senkrechten[c] und den beiden diagonalen Reihen jeweils die Summe 38 ergibt

Illustration: Schäfer

a. *boxes*
b. *horizontal*
c. *vertical*

▣ Aktivität 2. Stadt, Land...

Vielleicht kennen Sie das Spiel *Stadt, Land*... Hier ist eine Variation. Spielen Sie es in kleinen Gruppen.

-   Jemand (A) sagt das Alphabet, so daß niemand es hören kann.
-   Eine andere Person (B) sagt: „Halt".
-   A nennt den Buchstaben, wo er ist.
-   Das Ziel ist dann, eine Tabelle wie im Beispiel unten so schnell wie möglich mit Wörtern auszufüllen, die mit diesem Buchstaben anfangen.
-   Lesen Sie Ihre Antworten nach jeder Runde vor. Sie bekommen einen Punkt (*point*) für jede richtige Antwort, die nur Sie allein haben.

BEISPIEL: G

Buchstabe	Land	Stadt	berühmte° Person	Freizeit-beschäftigung
G	Griechenland	Greensboro	Goethe	Golf

famous

WORTSCHATZ

Substantive

Freizeit — Leisure Time

das Abenteuer (-)	adventure
die Abwechslung (-en)	change, diversion
die Ferien	vacation
die Schulferien	school holidays
das Freibad (¨er)	outdoor pool
die Freizeit	leisure time
das Hallenbad (¨er)	indoor pool
das Hobby (-s)	hobby
die Lieblingsbeschäftigung (-en)	favorite activity
die Mannschaft (-en)	team
der Pfad (-e)	path
das Rad (Fahrrad) (¨er)	bike
die Reise (-n)	trip
der See (-n)	lake
der Sport	sports
die Sportart (-en)	type of sport
die Sporthalle (-n)	gymnasium
der Sportplatz (¨e)	sports field, playing field
das Stadion (Stadien)	stadium
das Vergnügen (-)	pleasure
der Wald (¨er)	forest
der Weg (-e)	path
der Wettbewerb (-e)	competition
das Zelt (-e)	tent

Andere Substantive

die Autobahn (-en)	freeway
die Freiheit	freedom
das Gesicht (-er)	face
der Grund (¨e)	reason
der Hund (-e)	dog
der/die Jugendliche (-n)	young person, youth
die Mehrzahl	majority
der Stau(-s)	traffic jam

Verben

angeln	to fish
begreifen, begriffen	to comprehend
sich beschäftigen mit	to spend time with; to occupy oneself with
besitzen, besessen	to own
bummeln	to stroll
entdecken	to discover
erleben	to experience
fliegen, ist geflogen	to fly
führen	to lead
Der Weg führt durch den Wald.	The road goes through the forest.
(herum)gammeln	to fool around, be lazy
kegeln	to bowl, go bowling
pflanzen	to plant
reiten, ist geritten	to ride (horseback)
segeln	to sail
tauchen	to dive
(sich) teilen	to share

Das Wetter

Substantive

der Donner	thunder
das Gewitter (-)	thunderstorm
der Grad (-e)	degree
20 Grad Celsius	20 degrees Celsius
das Klima	climate
der Nebel	fog
der Regen	rain
der Schauer	rain shower
der Schnee	snow
die Sonne (-n)	sun
der Sturm (¨e)	storm
die Temperatur (-en)	temperature
die Höchsttemperatur	highest temperature, daily high
die Wärme	warmth
der Wetterbericht (-e)	weather report
der Wind (-e)	wind

Wie ist das Wetter?

angenehm	pleasant
bedeckt	cloudy, covered
bewölkt	cloudy
heiß	hot
heiter	pleasant
kühl	cool
kühler	cooler
neblig	foggy
regnerisch	rainy
scheußlich	horrible
schwül	muggy

sonnig	sunny
warm	warm
schön warm	nice and warm
wolkenlos	without clouds

Ausdrücke

Es blitzt und donnert.	There is thunder and lightning.
Es regnet.	It is raining.
Die Sonne scheint (hat geschienen).	The sun is shining.
Es schneit.	It is snowing.
Es gibt Regen.	It is going to rain.
Wie wäre es mit...	How about . . .

Jahreszeiten — Seasons

der Frühling	spring
der Herbst	fall
der Sommer	summer
der Winter	winter

Adjektive und Adverbien

anders	different
anstrengend	strenuous
begeistert von	enthusiastic about
beliebt	popular
draußen	outside
dort	there
fast	almost
gestern	yesterday
jugendlich	youthful
nichts	nothing
öffentlich	public
ungefähr	approximate(ly)
wahrscheinlich	probable, probably
weit von hier	far from here
woanders	elsewhere

Konjunktionen

daß	that
denn	for, because
sondern	but rather
weil	because
wenn	when, if

REISEN UND FERIEN

Lernziele *This chapter focuses on planning a trip, making travel preparations, and traveling by train. You will learn how to ask for travel information, express your preference with respect to travel plans, and narrate events in the simple past tense.*

▣ Alles klar?

- Was bieten (*offer*) die drei Anzeigen an?

Segeln lernen.
Ein tolles Ferien-Erlebnis

Bei uns lernen auch Ihre Kinder gleich richtig segeln – und haben viel Spaß dabei! In Glücksburg/Ostsee, am Chiemsee und auf Elba.

Wir schicken Ihnen gern unseren Farbkatalog mit dem aktuellen Ausbildungs- und Törnprogramm.

Deutscher Hochseesportverband 'Hansa' e.V.
Postfach 13 20 34, 2000 Hamburg 13
oder Telefon (040) 44 11 42 50.

Romantisch
reisen mit dem Fahrrad
Kultivierte Reisen abseits großer Straßen zu Küche, Kunst und Keller durchs **Elsaß**
Eine von 20 Radreisen. Kostenloser Katalog durch terranova, Hirschsprung 7 6078 Zeppelinheim, Tel.: 069/69 30 54
terranova

Diesmal Aktiv-Urlaub[a]

BAUMELER Wanderreisen: mehr sehen, mehr erleben.[b] Auf eigenen Füßen unterwegs[c] sein, dort wo wandern sich lohnt.[d] Kleine Gruppen. Kompetente Reiseleitung. Ausgewählte[e] Hotels. Linienflug oder Busreise.

a. *vacation*
b. *to experience*
c. *on the road*
d. *sich... is worth (it)*
e. *select*

- Die Reise durchs Elsaß führt „zu Küche, Kunst und Keller". Was bedeutet „Küche, Kunst und Keller"?
- Für wen sind Segel-Ferien besonders attraktiv? Wo gibt es Segelkurse?
- Was macht eine Wanderreise attraktiv?
- Was würde Ihnen persönlich in den Ferien besonders Spaß machen: eine Radtour, eine Wanderreise oder Segeln lernen? Warum?

WÖRTER IM KONTEXT ▫▫▫

Ich möchte verreisen.

Zu Fuß sieht man viel.

Mit dem Heißluftballon ist es romantischer.

> ### *Sprachnotiz*
>
> To form the comparative of an adjective or adverb add **-er** to the basic form.
>
> schnell → schneller (*faster*)
> romantisch → romantischer (*more romantic*)

Neue Wörter

der Autobus (Bus) *bus*
der Autostop *hitchhiking*
  per Autostop reisen *to hitchhike*
die Bahn *train, railroad*
das Flugzeug *airplane*
zu Fuß *on foot*

der Wagen *car*
der Zug *train*
gefährlich *dangerous*
langsam *slow*
schnell *fast*
sicher *safe*

▣ Aktivität 1. Reisen—aber wie?

Was sind Vorteile (*advantages*), was sind Nachteile (*disadvantages*)? Was meinen Sie?

BEISPIEL: Mit dem Fahrrad erlebt man viel, aber es ist anstrengend.
Mit dem Auto geht es schneller.

mit ____			
Bahn (Zug)			
Bus			bequem / anstrengend
Flugzeug	ist es		billig / teuer
Fahrrad	sieht man	nicht	romantisch / langweilig
Heißluftballon	erlebt man	sehr	schnell / langsam
Wagen (Auto)	kostet es	zu	sicher / gefährlich
zu Fuß (Wandern)	geht es		viel / wenig
per Autostop			
?			

Aktivität 1. Suggestion: First go over the *Neue Wörter* and the drawings on page 255 with students. Point out the *Sprachnotiz* about the comparative. Then have them scan the possibilities in the sentence builder before they complete the activity, working in pairs. Spot-check the answers by asking several students to state the advantages and disadvantages of various ways of traveling.

▣ Aktivität 2. Pläne für einen ungewöhnlichen° Urlaub

°unusual

Schauen Sie sich die Anzeigen für Urlaubsreisen an. Wohin möchten Sie gern? Wofür interessieren Sie sich? Machen Sie sich Notizen (negativ oder positiv) über jede Möglichkeit.

BEISPIEL: 25 Tage in der Wildnis finde ich toll.

nützliche Ausdrücke:

das möchte ich (nicht) machen
das gefällt mir nicht
das finde ich ungewöhnlich / toll / langweilig usw.
ich interessiere mich für

Aktivität 2. Suggestion: This activity can be done as a writing assignment for homework. It can then form the basis of discussion during the next class.
Suggestion: Have students scan the realia and choose two ads, about which they write a sentence each. These sentences are then exchanged with a partner, who shares this information with the class.

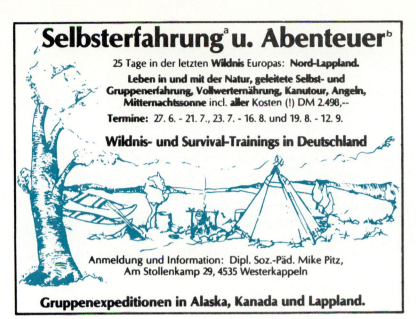

Selbsterfahrung[a] u. Abenteuer[b]

25 Tage in der letzten **Wildnis** Europas: **Nord-Lappland.**

Leben in und mit der Natur, geleitete Selbst- und Gruppenerfahrung, Vollwerternährung, Kanutour, Angeln, Mitternachtssonne incl. **aller** Kosten (!) DM 2.498,--

Termine: 27. 6. - 21. 7., 23. 7. - 16. 8. und 19. 8. - 12. 9.

Wildnis- und Survival-Trainings in Deutschland

Anmeldung und Information: Dipl. Soz.-Päd. Mike Pitz,
Am Stollenkamp 29, 4535 Westerkappeln

Gruppenexpeditionen in Alaska, Kanada und Lappland.

a. *finding yourself*
b. *adventure*

Sommerprogramm Griechenland — Italien — Portugal — Polen — Marokko. Info beim Buskollektiv „die wilde 13", Vor der Eichhecke, 3501 Fuldatal 1,

SPANISCHKURSE IN SEVILLA
3—4-wöchige Kurse mit Kultur- und Freizeitprogramm ab 365 DM. Unterkunft und Halbpension ab 145 DM. Prospekte und Information

„HORIZONTE"
Spanisch am Strand oder auf dem Land
Windsurf & Fahrräder & Tennis
Ab DM 555,--. Info: Lop Moliner, Marburgerstr. 9, 6000 Frankfurt 90

Traumurlaub auf modernen Motorsegeljachten in der türk. Ägäis. Segeln, Surfen, Ausflüge, Faulenzen uvm. Pers./Wo. ab 535 DM. VP

Südschweden, wie vermieten unser liebevoll renoviertes Ferienhaus, 4 Pers., Bad, WC, Heizung, 200 m von See, ab 22.8.

Sommerworkshops in SW-Frankreich: Französischkurse, Selbsterfahrung — Tiefenentspannung, Psychodrama, Experimentelles Theater, Tanztheater, Yoga, Shiatsu, Berg-und Kanuwandern, Freies Malen in Portugal. l'Atelier, Hansastr. 55, 4100 Duisburg 1,

ABENTEUERLAND SCHWEDEN
Kanu-Safari * Wandern
Survival für Anfänger
Ferienhäuser am See
2 Wochen Kanu-Safari
für 725,-- DM.
Sverige Reisen, Benzstr. 21
8400 Regensburg

Arbeiten Sie in kleinen Gruppen. Sagen Sie nun, wohin Sie in Urlaub möchten. Wer möchte mit?

BEISPIEL: A: Ich möchte mit dem Buskollektiv *die wilde 13* nach Marokko. Kommst du mit, Paul?

B: Marokko? Nein. Ich möchte lieber Spanisch in Sevilla lernen. Kommst du mit, Beth? usw.

 ## Dialog

Ein Gespräch im Reisebüro zwischen Frau Siemens und Herrn Bittner,
einem Reisebüroangestellten

FRAU S: Mein Mann und ich möchten dieses Jahr mal einen Aktivurlaub
machen. Können Sie uns etwas vorschlagen?

HERR B: Ja, gern. Wofür interessieren Sie sich denn? Es gibt so viele
Möglichkeiten. Sind Sie sportlich aktiv?

FRAU S: Nicht besonders. Manchmal spielen wir Tennis und fahren auch
schon mal° Rad.

HERR B: Wie wäre es mit einer Radreise durchs Elsaß?

FRAU S: Hm, klingt gut. Wie lange dauert so eine Reise denn?

HERR B: Wir haben ein Angebot für eine siebentägige Reise.

FRAU S: Und wie groß sind die Gruppen?

HERR B: Mit dem Reiseleiter° sind es höchstens elf Personen. Hier ist ein
Reiseprospekt.°

FRAU S: Ich sehe hier „Küche, Kunst und Keller".

HERR B: Es gibt viele gute Restaurants und ausgezeichnete Weine im
Elsaß. Und natürlich kulturelle Sehenswürdigkeiten.

FRAU S: Nicht schlecht. Und wo übernachtet man?

HERR B: Hauptsächlich in kleinen Gasthöfen auf dem Land.

FRAU S: Was kostet die Reise insgesamt?

HERR B: Pro Person, DM 750,-.

FRAU S: Das ist wirklich günstig. Ich will es mir überlegen. Ich gebe
Ihnen in zwei Tagen Bescheid. Ich hoffe, mein Mann ist damit
einverstanden.

schon... occasionally

travel guide
travel brochure

Dialog. **Suggestion:** Let students
hear the dialogue once with their
books closed. Ask them each to give
a single bit of information from the
dialogue. Write these items on the
board or overhead. Ask several students to summarize. Then go over
the *Neue Wörter* following the dialogue. Play the dialogue a second
time, this time with books open.
Finally have students role-play *Aktivität 3*, which is based on the
dialogue.

Neue Wörter

das Angebot *offer*
auf dem Land *in the*
countryside
die Möglichkeit *possibility*
das Reisebüro *travel agency*
die Sehenswürdigkeit *tourist*
attraction
der Urlaub *vacation*
Bescheid geben (*dat.*) *to inform,*
to let someone know

einverstanden sein *to agree*
(Das) Klingt gut. (*That*) *Sounds*
good.
sich (*dat.*) etwas überlegen *to*
think about
Ich will es mir überlegen.
I want to think about it.

hauptsächlich *mostly*
höchstens *at most*
insgesamt *all together*

Aktivität 3. Claudia Siemens berichtet.

Zu Hause berichtet Frau Siemens ihrem Mann über ihren Besuch im
Reisebüro. Ergänzen Sie die Sätze durch Informationen aus dem Gespräch
im Reisebüro und aus der Anzeige „Romantisch reisen" (Seite 254).

Aktivität 3. **Follow-up:** For homework, assign pairs the task of completing the role-play. Call on several
pairs to role-play the conversation
during the next class.

CLAUDIA: Ich war heute im Reisebüro. Ich schlage vor, wir machen
_____.

MANFRED: Was kann man da denn sehen und machen?

CLAUDIA: _____.

MANFRED: Was soll denn so eine Reise kosten?

CLAUDIA: _____.

MANFRED: Und wo übernachtet man? Hoffentlich nicht im Zelt.

CLAUDIA: Natürlich nicht. _____

MANFRED: Und wie viele Leute nehmen an so einer Reise teil?

CLAUDIA: _____.

MANFRED: Was meinst du denn, sollen wir das machen?

CLAUDIA: Also ich finde, das ist mal was anderes.°

MANFRED: Im Reiseprospekt heißt es: romantisch reisen. Was ist so
romantisch auf Straßen mit vielen Autos?

CLAUDIA: Aber nein, man fährt abseits° von _____.

MANFRED: Eigentlich ist das keine schlechte Idee. Also, ich bin damit
einverstanden.

was... *something different*

away

▣ Aktivität 4. Interaktion

Try to convince someone who is a little reluctant to join you on your
vacation trip this year. Choose a trip from the ads on page 257 or suggest
an idea of your own.

Aktivität 4. Suggestion: Before
beginning this activity, brainstorm
several exciting vacations with students. Have them work in pairs,
doing the activity twice and reversing
roles the second time. Encourage
students to bring in travel brochures
and ads (in English or German).

A:

Ich möchte dieses Jahr _____. Willst du mit? ⟶

Man kann da zum Beispiel _____.

Nein, man kann auch _____.

_____.

_____.

_____.

B:

Was kann man denn da unternehmen?

Ist das alles? Was sonst noch?

Wo übernachtet man denn?

Wieviel soll das kosten?

Wie lange soll die Fahrt dauern?

Ich will es mir überlegen.
Ich weiß nicht, das ist mir zu _____ (teuer,
langweilig, usw.).
Klingt prima. Ich komme mit.

Eine Fahrkarte, bitte!

Sprachnotiz

Schüler(in) oder Student(in)? A student (pupil) in primary school,
secondary school, or a trade school is called a **Schüler(in).** Only
someone attending a university or a university-level school (**Universität** or **Hochschule**) is considered a **Student(in).**

=== **Die neue Bahn** ===

Trampen zwischen Nordsee und Alpen.
Das Tramper-Monats-Ticket.

Tramper-Monats-Ticket   2. Klasse

Für 240 Mark fahren Sie einen ganzen
Monat lang, sooft und so weit Sie wollen.
Vorausgesetzt,[a] Sie sind unter 23 als
Schüler oder Student unter 27.

Wie man das Tramper-Monats-Ticket bekommt.

Ganz einfach: Man bringt seinen Ausweis und ein Paßbild mit. Und 240 Mark.

RSM

a. *under the condition that*

Neue Wörter

das Paßbild *passport photo*
der Schüler, die Schülerin *pupil, student (not at
   university)*

einfach *simple*
   ganz einfach *very simple*
gültig *valid*
weit *far*

▣ **Aktivität 5. Partnerarbeit: Fragen und Antworten**

Eine Person stellt Fragen, und die andere antwortet
mit Informationen aus dem Text, „Trampen zwischen
Nordsee und Alpen". Sie könnten, zum Beispiel, fragen:

- wie man ein Tramper-Monats-Ticket bekommt
- wer es bekommen kann
- wo es gültig ist

```
DB         10.04.87 13.04.87 -------- 455852

        2 EINFACHE FAHRT********* -------

        DUESSELDORF FLUGH.

        BAD HARZBURG
        DUESSELDORF*HANNOVER HBF*R1146

                   XX 0396      ***79,00
        DUESSELDORF
        FLUGHAFEN   15653951        ☺☺☺
```

RSM

 **Dialog**

Am Fahrkartenschalter im Bahnhof

MICHAEL: Eine Fahrkarte nach Bad Harzburg, bitte.
BEAMTER°: Hin und zurück?
MICHAEL: Nein, einfach, zweiter Klasse.
BEAMTER: Das macht DM 79,-.
MICHAEL: Wann geht der nächste Zug?
BEAMTER: In 30 Minuten geht ein Intercity nach Hannover. Da müssen
       Sie umsteigen.

Federal employee (here: ticket agent)

Einmal zweiter Klasse nach...

Dialog. Suggestion: Go over the *Neue Wörter* with students first. Then let them hear the dialogue once. Follow this with questions on the dialogue, e.g., *Wohin will Michael fahren? Was kostet die Karte?* Refer to the DB ticket. After eliciting information from the whole group, have students listen to and read the dialogue once more. Afterward they may role-play it.

MICHAEL: Habe ich da gleich Anschluß?
BEAMTER: Sie haben 20 Minuten Aufenthalt. Für den IC müssen Sie noch Zuschlag zahlen.
MICHAEL: Und wann komme ich in Bad Harzburg an?
BEAMTER: Um 18.07 Uhr.
MICHAEL: Und auf welchem Bahnsteig fährt der Zug ab?
BEAMTER: Bahnsteig drei, Gleis fünf.
MICHAEL: Danke schön.
BEAMTER: Bitte sehr.

Realia. Suggestion: Help students read the train schedule: *Df* stands for Düsseldorf. Note that there are two possible train connections between Hannover and Bad Harzburg.

Neue Wörter

der Anschluß *connection*
der Aufenthalt *stopover, layover*
der Bahnhof *train station*
der Bahnsteig *platform*
die Fahrkarte *ticket*
der Fahrkartenschalter *ticket window*
das Gleis *track (platform)*
die Hinfahrt *one-way trip*
die Rückfahrt *return trip*
der Zuschlag *surcharge*

einfach [*here*] *one way*
hin und zurück *round trip*

abfahren (fährt ab) *to leave, depart*
ankommen (kommt an) *to arrive*
umsteigen (steigt um) *to transfer, change trains*

Reiseverbindungen Connections Horaires des trains

Station		Reisetag date/day date/jour	🕐	🕐	🕐	🕐
Df	ab dep		14.29			
Hannover	an arr		16.49			
	ab dep		17.58		17.13	
Bad Harz	an arr		19.55	60	18.07	
	ab dep					
	an arr					
	ab dep					
	an arr					
	ab dep					
	an arr					

Bemerkungen notes observations

Auskunft ohne Gewähr, Information without guarantee, renseignement no garanties

DEUTSCHES REISEBÜRO (DER), Deutschlands große Reisebüro-Organisation mit über 900 Reisefachgeschäften in der Bundesrepublik und Berlin (West). Wir vermitteln Ihnen sämtliche Reisedienstleistungen. Für Ferien- und Geschäftsreisen. Mit individuellem Service. Durch langjährig erfahrene Fachleute.

Deutsches Reisebüro

60001 Merkzettel für Fahrplanauskünfte A6 Bk 100 5c–60 Mü 6.85 200000

RSM

▣ Aktivität 6. Michaels Pläne

Ergänzen Sie den Text mit Informationen aus dem Dialog.

Michael fährt mit dem _____[1] nach Bad Harzburg. Er kauft seine Fahrkarte am _____[2] im _____[3]. Er fährt zweiter _____[4]. Der nächste Zug nach
Bad Harzburg fährt in _____[5] ab. Michael muß in Hannover _____[6]. Für
den Intercity Zug muß er einen _____[7] zahlen.

▣ Aktivität 7. Was bedeuten die Zeichen? Was paßt zusammen?

1. _____
2. _____
3. _____
4. _____
5. _____
6. _____

a. Hier muß man den Reisepaß vorzeigen.
b. Es gibt Schlafwagen im Zug.
c. Der Zug ist ein Schnellzug.
d. Man braucht eine Platzkarte.
e. Der Zug verbindet Städte miteinander.
f. Hier gibt es ein Zugrestaurant.

RSM

Zeichenerklärung:		
⟋⟍ = Intercity-Zug		1
D = Schnellzug		2
E = Eilzug		
🕓 = DB-Schnellbahnzug		
ohne Buchstaben =	Zug des Nahverkehrs[a]	
✕ = Zugrestaurant		3
🍴 = Quick-Pick-Zugrestaurant		
🍷 = Speisen und Getränke im Zug erhältlich		
🚍 = Kurswagen[b]		
🚌 = Omnibuslinie		
Ⓤ = umsteigen		
🛏 = Schlafwagen		4
🏢 = Grenzstation[c]		5
Ⓡ = Sitzplatzreservierung erforderlich		6

a. *short distance*
b. *train car with a particular destination*
c. *border station*

▣ Aktivität 8. Ein Gespräch im Reisebüro

The following sentences—spoken by either a travel agent or a customer—are all out of sequence. Which ones are spoken by the travel
agent (A), and which ones are spoken by the customer (B)? Arrange the
sentences into a meaningful dialogue, ordered from one to ten. Role-play
this dialogue with a partner.

B _____ Samstag morgen.
_____ _____ Wann möchten Sie denn fahren?
_____ _____ Wie komme ich am schnellsten von hier nach
München?
_____ _____ Um 10.30 fährt ein IC Zug.
_____ *1* Kann ich Ihnen helfen?
_____ _____ Dann sind Sie um 16.03 in München.
_____ _____ Bitte sehr.
_____ _____ Ja, Sie müssen in Würzburg umsteigen.
_____ _____ Vielen Dank.
_____ _____ Muß ich umsteigen?

▣ Aktivität 9. Partnerarbeit

Mit dem Zug von der Schweiz nach Österreich. The timetable below is
part of an information pamphlet called **Zugbegleiter.** You find it in your

train compartment on long-distance trains. Take turns asking and answering questions about the Zugbegleiter.

BEISPIEL: A: Wie heißt der Zug?   B: Franz Schubert.

Basel · Zürich · Sargans · Buchs SG · Feldkirch · Bludenz · Langen am Arlberg · St. Anton am Arlberg · Landeck · Innsbruck · Jenbach · Wörgl · Kufstein · Salzburg · Attnang-Puchheim · Wels · Linz · St. Pölten · Wien Hütteldorf · Wien Westbf

Ex 65   Franz Schubert

Basel (IC 65)—Zürich—Buchs SG (Ex 65)—Innsbruck—Kufstein *(Korridorzug)*—Salzburg—Linz—**Wien**

1. 2. ✕   **Basel—Wien**

Buchs SG—Kufstein und Salzburg—Wien

an / arr	ab / dep			km
	10 12		**Basel** SBB	
11 12	11 26		**Zürich** HB	88
12 24	12 26		**Sargans**	178
12 38	12 48	🍴	**Buchs** SG	194
13 06	13 09		**Feldkirch** Ⓒ	213
	13 12		Feldkirch Dornbirn 13 42 Bregenz 13 58 Lindau Hbf 14 19	
13 24	13 26		**Bludenz** Ⓒ	234
	13 38		Bludenz Schruns 14 00	
13 54	13 55		**Langen am Arlberg** Ⓒ	259
14 04	14 06		**St. Anton am Arlberg** Ⓒ	270
14 30	14 32		**Landeck** Ⓒ	297
	14 50		Landeck Ötztal 15 21 Telfs - Pfaffenhofen 15 41	
15 27	15 35		**Innsbruck** Hbf Ⓒ	372

an / arr	ab / dep			km
15 54	15 55		**Jenbach** Ⓒ	407
	🚌 16 20		Jenbach Mayrhofen 17 27	
16 08	16 09		**Wörgl** Ⓒ	432
16 19	16 20		**Kufstein** Ⓒ	445
17 36	17 40		**Salzburg** Hbf Ⓒ	❶ 565
	18 04		Salzburg Hbf Hallein 18 20 Golling - Abtenau 18 29	
	🚌 18 15		Salzburg Hbf St. Gilgen 19 05	
18 25	18 27		**Attnang - Puchheim** Ⓒ	636
	18 37		Attnang - Puchheim Gmunden 18 49 Bad Ischl 19 31 Bad Aussee 20 15	
18 45	18 48		**Wels** Ⓒ	667
19 03	19 05		**Linz** Hbf Ⓒ	692
	19 10		Linz Hbf Enns 19 31 St. Valentin 19 39 Steyr 20 08	
20 11	20 12		**St. Pölten** Hbf Ⓒ	822
20 49	20 51		**Wien** Hütteldorf	876
21 00			**Wien** Westbf Ⓒ	882

Your questions should elicit some of the following information:

- was für ein Zug das ist (z.B. ein IC oder ein D-Zug)
- wo die Reise beginnt und endet
- ob es Schlafwagen und Zugrestaurant gibt (oder andere Dinge)
- wo die Grenzstation zwischen der Schweiz und Österreich ist
- wann der Zug abfährt und ankommt
- die Distanz (km) zwischen Basel und Wien Westbahnhof
- Sonstiges

Aktivität 10. Hören Sie zu.

Sie hören drei kurze Dialoge im Reisebüro und am Fahrkartenschalter.
Setzen Sie die richtige Information in die Tabelle.

INFORMATION	DIALOG 1	DIALOG 2	DIALOG 3
Fahrkarte nach:	Hamburg	Salzburg	Bonn
1. oder 2. Klasse	1.	keine Information	keine Information
einfach oder hin und zurück	hin und zurück	hin und zurück	einfach
für wie viele Personen	2	5	1
Platzreservierung (ja/nein)	ja	nein	nein

Aktivität 11. Rollenspiel

Sie wollen mit dem Franz Schubert nicht nach Wien, sondern nach St.
Gilgen. Schauen Sie sich den Zugbegleiter an und finden Sie St. Gilgen.
Wie kommt man dahin?

A:

B:

Ich möchte gern nach St. Gilgen. ⟶ Da können Sie mit _____ fahren.

Kann ich durchfahren, oder muß ich _____? In _____ müssen Sie umsteigen.

Wann komme ich in Salzburg an? Um _____.

Und wann habe ich Anschluß? Um _____ fährt ein _____ nach St. Gilgen.

Und wann komme ich in St. Gilgen an? Um _____. Ich schreibe Ihnen die Verbindung (*connection*) auf.

Vielen Dank. Bitte sehr.

Reisevorbereitungen°

Preparations for a trip

Aktivität 12. Partnerarbeit

Schauen Sie sich die persönliche Checkliste auf Seite 265 an. Nehmen
Sie diese Sachen auch gewöhnlich auf Reisen mit? Vergessen Sie manch-
mal etwas? Was finden Sie nötig oder unnötig? Machen Sie sich einige
Notizen.

Fragen Sie dann einen Partner oder eine Partnerin: Was nimmst du
gewöhnlich mit?

Ihre persönliche Checkliste vor der Reise – haben Sie nichts vergessen?

Bekleidung Wie lange dauert der Urlaub?
Mit welcher Witterung[a] ist am Ziel zu rechnen?

- ☐ Oberbekleidung und Wäsche
- ☐ Regenbekleidung
- ☐ Handschuhe
- ☐ Badesachen

- ☐ Schlafanzug
- ☐ Kopfbedeckung
- ☐ Schal
- ☐ Sportbekleidung

Schuhwerk

- ☐ Wanderschuhe
- ☐ Hausschuhe

- ☐ Turnschuhe[b]
- ☐ Hüttenschuhe[c]

Toilettensachen

- ☐ Hautcreme
- ☐ Sonnenschutzmittel
- ☐ Erfrischungstücher[e]

- ☐ Haarshampoo
- ☐ Rasierzeug[d]

Für Ihre Aktivitäten im Urlaub

- ☐ Kamera
- ☐ Zubehör (Filter, Wechselobjektive, Blitzgeräte, Belichtungsmesser)
- ☐ Filme

- ☐ Fernglas[f]
- ☐ Stadtpläne
- ☐ Wanderkarten
- ☐ Reiseführer[g]

Achtung! Ist die Lagerzeit der Filme abgelaufen?

Das sollte im Handgepäck nicht fehlen …

- ☐ Reiseapotheke
- ☐ Reiselektüre[h]

Auch das muß mit – aber nicht im Koffer![i]

- ☐ Bargeld[j] (auch Fremdwährung)
  Achtung! Höchstgrenzen bei der Deviseneinfuhr nach bestimmten Ländern!
- ☐ Reiseschecks, Euroschecks
  Achtung! Scheckkarte!
- ☐ Reisepaß, Personalausweis
  Achtung! Wann läuft die Geltungsdauer der Pässe ab?
- ☐ Fahrkarten
- ☐ Reiseproviant[m]

- ☐ Platzkarten
- ☐ Bettkarten
- ☐ Liegekarten
- ☐ Familienpaß
- ☐ Senioren-Paß
- ☐ Junior-Paß
- ☐ Fahrplan[k]
- ☐ Reiseversicherungspapiere[l]
- ☐ Kofferschlüssel
- ☐ Wohnungsschlüssel

RSM

a. *weather conditions*
b. *sneakers*
c. *slippers*
d. *shaving kit*
e. *towelettes*
f. *binoculars*
g. *travel guide*
h. *reading material*
i. *suitcase*
j. *cash*
k. *schedule*
l. *travel insurance papers*
m. Proviant = *Essen und Trinken*

⊡ Aktivität 13. Sie machen eine Reise.

Nennen Sie drei Dinge aus der Checkliste, die Sie unbedingt mitnehmen würden für:

- eine Wanderreise durch Europa
- eine Reise nach Hawaii
- eine Schiffsreise durch die Karibik
- eine Safari nach Afrika
- eine Reise nach _____

BEISPIEL: Ich möchte nach Hawaii. Ich nehme Badesachen, Sonnenschutzmittel und eine Kamera mit.

Aktivität 13. Suggestion: The list of destinations is only a suggestion. Brainstorm other exotic *Reiseziele* with students.
Note: This activity aims at getting students to be precise in their statements. There must be a fit between the *Reiseziel* and the items they take along.
Suggestion: Divide the class in half. Individuals in one half write *Reiseziele*; the others write *Was ich mitnehmen würde*. Pair students together at random; combinations will often be comical.

Sprachnotiz

The prefix **un-** can be added to many adjectives to describe the opposite of a quality. It is always stressed.

nötig → unnötig *unnecessary*
sicher → unsicher *unsafe, insecure*
günstig → ungünstig *disadvantageous*
gültig → ungültig *invalid*

GRAMMATIK IM KONTEXT ▣▣▣▣▣▣▣▣▣▣▣

Comparison of Adjectives and Adverbs

Adjectives and adverbs have three degrees to describe or compare people and things.

positive degree (*basic form*)	Der Fahrpreis ist **günstig.** *The regular travel price is favorable.*
comparative degree	Der Sparpreis ist **günstiger.** *The savings price is even more favorable.*
superlative degree	Der Super-Sparpreis ist **am günstigsten.** *The super-saver price is the most favorable* (*of all prices*).

> **Fahr & Spar. Die neuen Preise der neuen Bahn.**
>
> Günstig fahren Sie zum Fahrpreis. Er beträgt 20 Pfennig pro Kilometer. **–.20**
>
> **180.–** Günstiger fahren Sie zum Sparpreis von 180 Mark.
>
> Am günstigsten fahren Sie zum **120.–** Super-Sparpreis von 120 Mark.

RSM

Comparing Two Items: (*nicht*) *so... wie*

Use the basic form of an adjective or adverb and **so... wie** to express that one person or thing is as . . . (e.g. fast) as another.

Der Bus fährt **so schnell wie** der Zug.	*The bus goes as fast as the train.*
Mit dem Tramper-Monats-Ticket kann man **so oft** und **so weit** fahren, **wie** man will.	*With the hiker's ticket, you can travel as often and as far as you want.*

To express that someone or something is not as . . . (e.g. favorable) as another person or item, use **nicht so... wie.**

Der Sparpreis ist **nicht so günstig wie** der Super-Sparpreis.	*The savings price is not as favorable as the super-saver price.*

The Comparative of Predicate Adjectives and Adverbs

The comparative form of an adjective or adverb compares the qualities or quantities of dissimilar persons or things.

Der Schaffner war **freundlicher als** der Kellner im Zugrestaurant.	*The conductor was friendlier than the waiter in the train restaurant.*
Man reist **bequemer** mit der Bahn **als** mit dem Wagen.	*One travels more comfortably by train than by car.*

Comparison.   Suggestion: Point out the similarities between English and German when analyzing comparisons: fast, faster, fast**est**/ *schnell, schneller, schnellst.* Focus attention on the **-er/-est** endings, and the fact that German has no comparative forms equivalent to "more" and "most."

In German, the comparative is formed in only one way, by adding **-er** to the adjective or adverb: **schnell** → **schneller.** This is comparable to English: *fast* → *faster*. German has no equivalent for the English comparative form that uses *more* with an adjective or adverb (*more comfortably* = **bequemer**). The comparative is followed by **als** (*than*) to link the two parts of a comparison.

 Analyse

Billiger zur Arbeit. Billiger zur Schule

B & S-Karten: die Fahrkarten für Berufstätige[a]und Schüler 1. und 2. Klasse

Ist Ihr Weg zwischen Wohnort und Arbeits- oder Schulort weiter als 50 km? Dann fahren Sie mit der B & S-Karte auf dieser Strecke[b] etwa 15% billiger Bahn.

---

a. *working people*
b. *route*

- Find the comparatives in the illustrations.
- What is the basic form of each adjective or adverb?
- One of the forms is irregular and has a cognate in English. What is this comparative and what is its basic (positive) form?
- For whom is the **B & S Karte** advantageous? How does the text state the advantage of purchasing this type of ticket?
- The **Mitfahrzentrale** is a national ride-sharing agency. What comparison is implied when it states: Mitfahren...ist günstiger und...macht mehr Spaß?

mitfahr zentrale

Mitfahren[a]...

...ist günstiger

...ist sicher

...schont die Umwelt[b]

...macht mehr Spaß

a. *ride sharing*
b. schont... *protects the environment*

Most adjectives of one syllable with the vowels **a, o,** or **u,** as well as a few others, have an umlaut in the comparative form.

alt → älter *older*
nah → näher *nearer*
groß → größer *bigger*
oft → öfter *more often*
kurz → kürzer *shorter*
gesund → gesünder *healthier*

Use the adverb **immer** and an adjective or adverb in the comparative to express that someone or something is getting more and more . . . (e.g. "more and more convenient" or "faster and faster").

Mit der Bahn reisen wird **immer bequemer.**	*Traveling by train is getting more and more convenient.*
Die Züge fahren **immer schneller.**	*Trains are going faster and faster.*

The Superlative of Predicate Adjectives and Adverbs

The superlative indicates the highest degree of a quality or quantity.

Wie kommt man **am günstigsten** von Hamburg nach Köln?	*What is the best way to get from Hamburg to Cologne?*
Mit dem Flugzeug ist es **am schnellsten,** aber nicht **am billigsten.**	*Traveling by plane is the fastest way, but not the cheapest.*
Mit einem Heißluftballon ist es **am interessantesten.**	*Traveling by hot air balloon is the most interesting way.*

The superlative of predicate adjectives and adverbs uses the inflexible form

> **am** (*adjective/adverb*-**(e)sten**

The form **-esten** is used to facilitate pronunciation when an adjective or adverb ends in **t, d, ß,** or **z.**

> interessant → am interessantesten
> kurz → am kürzesten
> *but:* groß → am größten

Irregular Forms of the Comparative and the Superlative

A number of adjectives and adverbs in German have irregular forms for the comparative and/or the superlative. The most important ones are:

POSITIVE	COMPARATIVE	SUPERLATIVE
gern	lieber	am liebsten
gut	besser	am besten
hoch	höher	am höchsten
nah	näher	am nächsten
viel	mehr	am meisten

Was machen Berliner am liebsten?

Urlaub.

Beratung und Buchung bei uns im TUI Reisebüro.

Sie haben es sich verdient. Urlaub mit der TUI.

TUI

RSM

The adverbs **äußerst** (*extremely*), **möglichst** (*as much as possible*), and **höchstens** (*at most*) are used with adjectives and other adverbs to indicate the highest degree of a certain quality without reference to other things or people.

Buchen Sie Ihre Reise **möglichst** bald.	*Book your trip as soon as possible.*
Diese Reise ist **äußerst** preiswert.	*This trip is an extremely good bargain.*
Höchstens zehn Leute fahren mit.	*At most ten people are going along.*

Liegewagenplatz
Diese Plätze sind äusserst[a] preiswert und sehr bequem. Reservieren Sie ihn entweder bei den Fahrkartenausgaben, DER-Reisebüros oder anderen DB-Verkaufsagenturen.

a. *äusserst = äußerst*

▣ Übung 1. Vergleichen Sie diese Orte und Sachen.

Bilden Sie Sätze im Komparativ.

BEISPIEL: Los Angeles / San Franzisko →
Los Angeles ist größer als San Franzisko.

1. München / Bonn (groß)
2. Berlin / New York (interessant)
3. eine Reise mit dem Flugzeug / mit dem Auto (viel kosten)
4. nach Hawaii / nach Alaska (gern fahren)
5. der Rhein / der Mississippi (lang)
6. sich für das Meer / die Berge interessieren (viel)
7. Mount Everest / die Zugspitze (hoch)
8. Rom / Los Angeles (alt)

⊡ Übung 2. Interaktion

Was machst du lieber?

> BEISPIEL: A: Was machst du lieber, mit dem Zug oder mit dem
> Schiff reisen?
> B: Ich reise lieber mit dem Schiff.

1. Radfahren oder wandern?
2. Allein oder in einer Gruppe reisen?
3. Einen Aktivurlaub machen oder faul am Strand liegen?
4. Mit dem Zug oder mit dem Auto fahren?
5. Reisefilme sehen oder selbst reisen?

Übung 2. Suggestion: Have students work in pairs, writing down their partner's answers to each question. Then call on individual students to link the information describing their partner's preferences.

⊡ Übung 3. Was ist Ihre Meinung?

Was gefällt Ihnen besser? Warum?

> BEISPIEL: Eine Jugendherberge gefällt mir besser als ein Hotel. Eine
> Jugendherberge ist nicht so teuer wie ein Hotel.

1. radfahren / wandern   schön
2. wandern / per Autostop reisen   bequem
3. per Autostop reisen / fliegen   preiswert
4. einen Reisefilm sehen / ein Buch lesen langweilig
5. Flugzeug / Zug   schnell
6. Motorradfahren / zu Fuß gehen   teuer
7. Jugendherberge (*youth hostel*) / Hotel interessant
8. im Hotel / im Zelt übernachten   gefährlich

⊡ Übung 4. Kettenreaktion

Was machst du am liebsten im Urlaub?

> BEISPIEL: A: Was machst du am liebsten im Urlaub?
> B: Ich liege am liebsten am Strand (*on the beach*). Was
> machst du am liebsten?
> C: Ich . . .

Übung 4. Suggestion: Encourage students to address others in the class at random.

Nützliche Ausdrücke:

> einkaufen gehen
> faulenzen
> interessante Orte besuchen
> neue Leute kennenlernen
> surfen
> viel lesen
> wandern
> zu Hause bleiben

▣ **Übung 5.** **Eine Reise von Hamburg nach Köln**

The following chart shows information about trips from Hamburg to Cologne by car, by train, and by plane as reported by three people. Compare their experiences using the chart and the questions below as a guideline.

> BEISPIEL: Die Fahrt mit dem Auto war am billigsten.
> Mit dem Auto war es nicht so teuer wie mit
> dem Flugzeug.

1. Was hat die Reise gekostet? (viel, wenig, teuer, billig, preiswert)
2. Wie lange hat die Fahrt gedauert? (kurz, lang)
3. Wie war die Fahrt? (anstrengend, bequem)
4. Wie war das Essen? (teuer, billig, gut)
5. Waren der Zug und das Flugzeug pünktlich?
6. Wie war die Bedienung? (freundlich/unfreundlich)

Übung 5. **Suggestion.** Have students work in pairs. Each pair writes down two statements about each category and reports to the class. **Note:** The information is from an article in *Bild am Sonntag*.

Der Kölner Dom im Zentrum der Stadt beim Hauptbahnhof

	AUTO	BAHN	FLUGZEUG
Kosten	DM 92,- (Benzin)	DM 206,-	DM 490,-
Dauer	3 Stunden und 48 Minuten	4 Stunden und 4 Minuten	46 Minuten Flugzeit; insgesamt 2 Stunden und 5 Minuten, inklusive Taxifahrt vom Flughafen bis in die Stadt.
Bequemlichkeit	kostet viel Nerven, anstrengend	Gepäck schleppen; kann im Zug schlafen	sehr bequem
Essen/Trinken	DM 7,80 für Bockwurst, Pommes, Cola an Autobahnraststätte; Qualität: nicht besonders	Zugrestaurant Qualität: sehr gut; DM 9,90 für Kaffee, Rührei, Croissant, Brötchen	nur etwas zu trinken; nichts zu essen
Pünktlichkeit	keine Information	sehr pünktlich	sehr pünktlich
Service	Selbstbedienung	Schaffner: freundlich	Flugbegleiterin: freundlich

Simple Past Tense

Präteritum

German uses the simple past tense to narrate past events in writing or in formal speech. By using this tense, the narrator or writer generally establishes a distance from the events. Remember to use the present perfect tense to talk about past events in your everyday life. A few verbs are commonly used in the simple past tense in conversation as well as in writing; among them are **sein, haben,** and modal auxiliary verbs.

◻ Analyse

Scan the following excerpt from an article about a special offer by the German railway system (**Deutsche Bundesbahn**) to celebrate an environmental protection weekend. The article is written almost entirely in the simple past tense.

Fahrkarten gibt es auch am Automaten.

100 000 nutzten[a] Super-Angebot am Umweltwochenende[b]:

Umweltticket brachte Bahnrekord

Für 50 Mark in der zweiten und 75 Mark in der ersten Klasse konnte am Wochenende 3/4. Juni jedermann zu einem X-beliebigen[c] Ziel[d] im Bundesgebiet mit der Bahn fahren. Kalkuliert waren etwa 15 000 zusätzliche[e] Reisende, doch alle Rekorde waren bis Sonntagabend gebrochen, denn 100 000 fuhren zusätzlich Bahn.

Seit Jahren ist der 5. Juni "Tag der Umwelt".

Der Beitrag[f] der Bundesbahn war ein äußerst günstiges Sonderangebot. Mit 50 DM in der 2. und 75 DM in der 1. Klasse, Kinder zahlten jeweils nur 10 DM, konnte jedermann am 3. und 4. Juni ein Ziel seiner Wahl[g] ansteuern[h].

So hatte die Bahn an den beiden Tagen nicht die üblichen[i] 400 000 Reisenden, sondern stellte mit 500 000 einen neuen Rekord auf.

Der hauptsächliche[j] Zuspruch[k] war am Samstagmorgen und Sonntagnachmittag und -abend. Die Zeitungen schrieben von Massenandrang[l] und überfüllten[m] Zügen.

a. *used*
b. Umwelt = *environment*
c. *any*
d. *destination*
e. *additional*
f. *contribution*
g. Ziel... *destination of one's choice*
h. *head towards*
i. *usual*
j. *main*
k. *demand*
l. *crush*
m. *crowded*

- Underline all verbs or list them on a separate sheet of paper.
- What are the infinitives of the verbs?
- What pattern or patterns can you distinguish in the formation of the simple past tense?

Weak Verbs

Weak verbs form the simple past tense by adding **-(e)te** and a personal ending to the stem. The first- and third-person singular do not add a personal ending.

INFINITIVE: **reisen** STEM: **reis-**	
Singular	*Plural*
ich reiste	wir reisten
Sie reisten	Sie reisten
du reistest	ihr reistet
er sie reiste es	sie reisten

Verbs with stems ending in **t** or **d** add the ending **-ete** to the stem to facilitate pronunciation.

übernachten:	Wir **übernachteten** im Hotel.
	We stayed at a hotel.
reden:	Der Fahrer **redete** nicht viel.
	The driver did not talk much.

Other examples of weak verbs used in this chapter are

dauern:	Die Fahrt **dauerte** drei Stunden.
	The trip took three hours.
erleben:	Sie **erlebten** viel.
	They experienced a lot.
packen:	Er **packte** die Koffer.
	He packed the suitcases.
zahlen:	Sie **zahlten** nur DM 50,- für die Fahrt.
	They only paid 50 Marks for the trip.

Modal verbs drop the umlaut in the simple past tense.

dürfen → durfte
können → konnte
müssen → mußte

Verbs with separable prefixes place the prefix at the end of a sentence in the simple past tense

> auspacken: Sie **packten** ihre Koffer wieder **aus.**
> *They unpacked their suitcases again.*

When the entire separable-prefix verb stands at the end of a sentence, the prefix is attached again.

> Ich möchte wissen, warum sie ihre Koffer wieder **auspackten.**

🔲 Übung 6. Kleine Erlebnisse im Urlaub

Ergänzen Sie die Sätze durch passende Modalverben im Präteritum: **dürfen, können, müssen, wollen.**

1. Wir _____ per Autostop nach Spanien fahren.
2. Niemand _____ uns mitnehmen.
3. Wir _____ zwei Stunden an der Autobahn warten.
4. Ein Fahrer _____ uns bis nach Freiburg mitnehmen.
5. Wir _____ in der Jugendherberge übernachten, aber dort war kein Platz mehr.
6. Deshalb _____ wir im Park übernachten.
7. Im Park _____ man aber nicht übernachten.
8. Wir _____ aber noch ein Hotel finden.
9. Das _____ wir natürlich nicht, weil es teuer war.

Übung 6.   **Follow-up:** After doing the exercise with the entire class, use all or some of the sentences as the basis for a quick substitution exercise, giving students different subjects for each sentence, e.g., *ich, zwei Studentinnen, ein Freund von mir, eine amerikanische Studentin.* This will require not only changes in verb endings but also changes in personal pronouns.

🔲 Übung 7. Notizen von einer Reise

Familie Eppel took a trip last summer and is trying to remember everything they did in order to write an account of their trip for their family history (**Familienchronik**).

> BEISPIEL: Letztes Jahr machten wir im Juni eine Reise nach Österreich.

1. machen / letztes Jahr / wir / eine Reise / im Juni / nach Österreich.
2. planen / die Reise / mit Hilfe vom Reisebüro Kronen / ich
3. buchen / Hotel in Salzburg / für fünf Tage / wir
4. besuchen / dort / die Salzburger Festspiele / wir
5. reisen / von da / die Familie / mit dem Zug / nach Wien
6. sich amüsieren / dort / die Kinder / im Prater
7. sich interessieren für / auch / die Kinder / die spanische Hofreitschule
8. arrangieren / das Hotel / eine Schiffahrt auf der Donau
9. schicken / Ansichtskarten / wir / an alle Freunde
10. dauern / die Reise / insgesamt / drei Wochen
11. machen / wir / über 100 Aufnahmen von der Reise

Übung 7.   **Point out:** #6, the Prater, is a famous amusement park in Vienna. A picture of its enormous ferris wheel is on page 131. A picture of a horse and rider of the *Spanische Hofreitschule* in Vienna (#7) is on page 302.

☐ Übung 8. Geschichten

Erfinden Sie eine Geschichte über eine Reise. Jede Person in der Klasse setzt einen Satz dazu. Erzählen Sie so spezifisch wie möglich. Gebrauchen Sie Vorschläge aus der Liste unten oder auch andere Ideen.

BEISPIEL: A: Letztes Jahr machte ich eine Wanderreise durch die Schweiz.
　　　　　 B: Zuerst kaufte ich mir einen Reiseführer.

Vorschläge:

sich amüsieren über: die Leute
sich beschweren über: das Essen / der Reisebus / das Wetter
sich (*dat.*) etwas besorgen: die Videokamera, der Fotoapparat, das Zelt
besuchen: der Zoo / (10) Museen
haben: wenig Geld / Glück / Pech
sich (*dat.*) etwas kaufen: die Sonnenbrille / der Reiseführer
kennenlernen: interessante Leute
machen: eine Reise mit ＿＿ nach ＿＿ (z.B. Tahiti, zum Mond, auf die Bahamas)
packen: der Koffer / der Rucksack
reisen: allein / mit einem Freund / mit einer Reisegruppe
übernachten: im Hotel / im Zelt / unter freiem Himmel / im Zug
sich verabschieden von (auf Wiedersehen sagen): die Familie

Übung 8. Suggestion: Divide students into small groups. Set a ten-sentence limit for each story. Have one student in each group share the story with the rest of the class. **Suggestion:** This activity can be done as an in-class writing assignment. Use the same procedure as above. One student passes the story to the next, each adding a sentence for a maximum of ten sentences. **Suggestion:** As a variation, turn *Übung 8* into a whole-class writing activity. Divide the class into small groups. Each group begins by making up one sentence and writing it on a sheet of paper. The papers are then passed clockwise to the next group, which in turn adds a sentence. After the stories have circulated eight to ten times, one student in each group reads the story to the entire class.

Strong Verbs

Starke Verben

Strong verbs change their stem vowel in the simple past tense and add a personal ending. The first- and third-person singular do not add a personal ending. Many verbs that are strong in English have strong equivalents in German.

INFINITIVE: **geben**	
Singular	*Plural*
ich gab	wir gaben
Sie gaben	Sie gaben
du gabst	ihr gabt
er ⎫ sie ⎬ gab es ⎭	sie gaben

The following strong verbs exemplify different past stems. You will find a complete list of strong verbs in the appendix.

INFINITIVE	SIMPLE PAST
anfangen	fing an
fahren	fuhr
kommen	kam
schreiben	schrieb
sehen	sah
verlieren	verlor (*lost*)
verstehen	verstand

Irregular Weak Verbs

Unregelmäßige schwache Verben

Several verbs change their stem vowel *and* add **-te** to the changed stem in the simple past, combining aspects of both strong and weak verbs. These verbs include:

bringen → brachte *to bring*
denken → dachte *to think*
kennen → kannte *to know*
wissen → wußte *to know*

The simple past tense of **werden** (*to become*) is **wurde.**

Beginning with this chapter, the vocabulary section at the end of each chapter will list strong or irregular verbs with their principal parts, that is: infinitive, third-person singular present tense (if irregular), simple past tense, and past participle (with the auxiliary **ist** for verbs forming the perfect tense with **sein**). Regular weak verbs conjugated with **haben** will show only the infinitive.

BEISPIEL: bringen, brachte, gebracht
fahren (fährt), fuhr, ist gefahren
geben (gibt), gab, gegeben

Übung 9. Introduce this exercise by telling about the Baron von Münchhausen, also known as the *Lügenbaron* because of his implausible adventures. A recent (1989) movie about Münchhausen proves the lasting appeal of his stories. In one adventure, Münchhausen rides on a cannonball into the enemy camp during battle and returns safely. In another, Münchhausen and his horse are about to drown when he rescues them both by pulling himself up and out of the water by his own long ponytail.
Suggestion: Preview unknown strong verbs with students first. Then assign the exercise for homework.
Follow-up: Have students write a short summary of the Münchhausen story, using the simple past tense.

▣ Übung 9. Ein sonderbares Erlebnis°

Ein... *A strange event*

The Baron von Münchhausen lived in the 18th century and had amazing adventures. Read the following story about Münchhausen, underlining all verbs in the simple past tense. Try to guess the infinitive for each verb. A list of new strong verbs follows the story.

MÜNCHHAUSENS REISE NACH RUßLAND

Meine Reise nach Rußland begann im Winter. Ich reiste zu Pferde, weil das am bequemsten war. Leider trug ich nur leichte Kleidung und ich fror sehr. Da sah ich einen alten Mann im Schnee. Ich gab ihm meinen Reisemantel und ritt weiter. Ich konnte leider kein Dorf° finden. Ich war müde und stieg vom Pferd ab. Dann band ich das Pferd an einen Baum-

village

ast° im Schnee° und legte mich hin. Ich schlief tief und lange. Als° ich am anderen Morgen aufwachte, fand ich mich mitten in einem Dorf auf dem Kirchhof.° Mein Pferd war nicht da, aber ich konnte es über mir hören. Ich schaute in die Höhe° und sah mein Pferd am Wetterhahn des Kirchturms° hängen. Ich verstand sofort, was passiert war. Das Dorf war in der Nacht zugeschneit° gewesen. In der Sonne war der Schnee geschmolzen. Der Baumast, an den ich mein Pferd gebunden hatte, war in Wirklichkeit die Spitze des Kirchturms gewesen. Nun nahm ich meine Pistole und schoß nach dem Halfter.° Mein Pferd landete ohne Schaden° neben mir. Dann reiste ich weiter.

branch of a tree / snow / When

churchyard
in... up
am... on the weathervane on top of the churchtower
snowed under

halter / damage

absteigen → stieg ab (*to get down*)	frieren → fror (*to freeze*)
binden → band (*to tie, bind*)	schießen → schoß (*to shoot*)

▣ Übung 10. Ein typisches Wochenende

Beschreiben Sie ein typisches Wochenende. Folgende Verben kommen in den Sätzen vor:

anrufen (rief an)
aufstehen (stand auf)
bleiben (blieb)
einladen (lud ein)
essen (aß)
gehen (ging)
lesen (las)
schreiben (schrieb)
sehen (sah)
trinken (trank)
verbringen (verbrachte)
wach werden (wurde)

1. Ich _____ letztes Wochenende _____. (zu Hause, bei Freunden, am Ozean, usw.)
2. So gegen 9 Uhr _____ ich wach (*awake*).
3. Ich _____ aber noch bis ungefähr _____ Uhr im Bett.
4. Um _____ Uhr _____ ich endlich _____.
5. Dann _____ ich die Zeitung und _____ Frühstück.
6. Ich _____ auch _____ (zwei starke Tassen Kaffee, Tee, ein Glas Milch, Saft).
7. Dann _____ mein(e) (Freund, Freundin, Mutter, Bruder, usw.) _____ mich _____.
8. Sie (Er) _____ mich zu einer Party _____.
9. Nachmittags _____ ich _____ (zum Sportplatz, einkaufen, in die Bibliothek, usw.)
10. Später _____ ich _____ (eine Arbeit für Professor _____, einen Brief an _____)
11. Abends _____ ich einen alten Buster Keaton Film im Kino.

⊡ Übung 11. Gestern

Suchen Sie aus den Sätzen in Übung 10 mindestens fünf Dinge, die Sie gestern getan haben und sagen Sie auch, wann Sie das getan haben. Erzählen Sie im Präteritum.

BEISPIEL: Gestern stand ich um sieben Uhr auf. Um acht Uhr aß ich Frühstück in der Mensa. Um neun Uhr ging ich in eine Vorlesung.

Übung 11. **Suggestion:** Students can work in pairs, each taking notes on what the other says about his or her activities. Ask several students to report on their partners' activities, making sure they use the simple past tense for their narrative.

Sprachnotiz

The word **als** has several important functions in German. You have learned to use it in the comparison of adjectives.

Mit dem Zug fährt man bequemer **als** mit dem Bus.

Additionally, **als** can be used as a subordinating conjunction meaning *when*, referring to a one-time occurrence in the past. Sentences with the conjunction **als** are often in the simple past tense, even in conversation.

Be sure not to confuse the conjunction **als** (*when*) with the conjunction **wenn** (*when* or *if*, stating a condition) or the interrogative **wann** (*when*), asking for the time of an event.

Als ich in Wien wohnte, bin ich oft in die Oper gegangen.	*When I lived in Vienna I often went to the opera.*

⊡ Übung 12. Wann war das?

BEISPIEL: den Führerschein machen →
Ich war 17 Jahre alt, als ich meinen Führerschein machte.

1. in den Kindergarten kommen
2. das erste Geld verdienen
3. sich zum erstenmal verlieben (*to fall in love*)
4. den Führerschein machen
5. meine Familie umziehen (zog um) nach _____
6. _____ (Freund oder Freundin) kennenlernen
7. Sonstiges

Übung 12. **Suggestion:** Start this exercise by reviewing *wann*-questions. Model one question based on the suggestions for this exercise and then ask students to formulate additional questions. Ask for very brief answers only; e.g., to *Wann hast du den Führerschein gemacht?* the answer could be *Mit 16 Jahren* or simply the year, e.g., 1986. In a second phase, introduce the conjunction *als*, asking for answers in the form shown in the *Beispiel*. Have students add one item when something special happened in their lives, e.g., *Ich war acht Jahre alt, als ich meinen Hund zum Geburtstag bekam.*

Past Perfect

Plusquamperfekt

The past perfect describes an event that precedes another event in the past.

Bevor wir in Urlaub fuhren, **hatten** wir alle Rechnungen **bezahlt**.	*Before we went on vacation we had paid all the bills.*
Als wir auf Mallorca **ange-kommen waren**, gingen wir sofort an den Strand.	*When we had arrived in Mallorca, we immediately went to the beach.*

To form the past perfect, combine the simple past of **haben** (*hatte*) or **sein** (*war*) and the past participle of the main verb. Verbs using **sein** in the present perfect tense also use **sein** in the past perfect.

PRESENT PERFECT	PAST PERFECT
Ich bin gegangen.	Ich war gegangen. (*I had gone.*)
Wir haben bezahlt.	Wir hatten bezahlt. (*We had paid.*)

🔲 Analyse

These drawings and texts are from an ad for travel insurance. They describe the mishaps that a family on vacation might encounter.

- Find a sentence or sentences in the simple past tense.
- Find a sentence or sentences in the past perfect tense.

Analyse. **Suggestion:** This brief *Analyse* can be done with the whole group. Have students describe each scene of the ad.

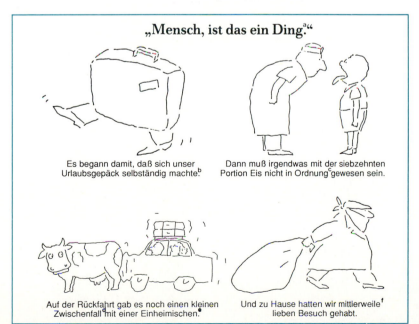

„Mensch, ist das ein Ding.[a]"

Es begann damit, daß sich unser Urlaubsgepäck selbständig machte.[b]

Dann muß irgendwas mit der siebzehnten Portion Eis nicht in Ordnung[c] gewesen sein.

Auf der Rückfahrt gab es noch einen kleinen Zwischenfall[d] mit einer Einheimischen.[e]

Und zu Hause hatten wir mittlerweile[f] lieben Besuch gehabt.

RSM

a. ist… (*idiom*) *that's really something*
b. selbständig… *took off on its own*
c. nicht… *wrong (not in order)*
d. *incident*
e. *local resident*
f. *in the meantime*

▣ Übung 13. **Die Fahrt hatte kaum begonnen.**

Ergänzen Sie die Sätze durch Verben im Plusquamperfekt.

1. Ich ⎯⎯ schon früh aus dem Haus ⎯⎯ (gehen), denn mein Flugzeug nach Frankfurt flog um 8 Uhr ab.
2. Ich ⎯⎯ ein Taxi ⎯⎯ (bestellen).
3. Am Flughafen fiel mir plötzlich ein (*I suddenly remembered*), daß ich die Schlüssel in der Haustür ⎯⎯ ⎯⎯. (vergessen)
4. Kein Wunder, denn letzte Nacht ⎯⎯ ich kaum ⎯⎯. (schlafen)
5. Sobald ich am Flughafen ⎯⎯ ⎯⎯ (ankommen), rief ich eine Nachbarin an.
6. Der Flug nach Frankfurt war verspätet (*late*). Nachdem wir drei Stunden ⎯⎯ ⎯⎯ (warten), konnten wir endlich abfliegen.

▣ Übung 14. **Nach der Reise**

BEISPIEL: A: Nachdem ich aus dem Urlaub zurückgekommen war, packte ich meinen Koffer aus.
B: Nachdem ich meinen Koffer ausgepackt hatte, ⎯⎯.

- Nachbarn/Freund/Freundin anrufen
- Post vom Postamt holen
- Katze/Hund aus dem Katzen-/Hundehotel abholen
- die Zeitung lesen
- ins Restaurant gehen
- einkaufen gehen
- ein Bad nehmen/duschen

Übung 14. **Suggestion:** Have students work in pairs, taking turns responding. This activity can also be done as a chain exercise in groups of five.

LESEN IM KONTEXT

Was muß man sich überlegen, bevor man eine Reise unternimmt? Was bieten deutsche Jugendherbergen ihren Besuchern? Diese Fragen beantworten die Texte in diesem Kapitel.

Vor dem Lesen

▣ Aktivität 1. **Planen Sie eine Traumreise.**

Überlegen Sie sich gemeinsam mit einem Partner oder einer Partnerin:

- wohin Sie reisen
- was Sie mitnehmen müssen
- wie Sie dahin kommen
- wie lange Sie bleiben wollen

- was Sie sehen und unternehmen wollen
- was Sie von Ihrer Traumreise nach Hause mitbringen wollen

Berichten Sie der Klasse über Ihre Pläne.

Aktivität 2. Suggestion: Preview new vocabulary with students. They can fill out the checklist by taking turns reading the items aloud. If some students don't own a bicycle, have them add this to the checklist. When the activity is completed, have students tally their results and share them with the rest of the class.

▣ Aktivität 2. Eine Fahrradtour planen

Sind Sie fit dazu?

1. Füllen Sie in kleinen Gruppen (nicht mehr als vier) den Fragebogen aus.

✓✓✓ Konditions-Checkliste für Mensch und Rad ✓✓✓

Meine Kondition — S1: S2: S3: S4:
- treibe keinen Sport — ☐ ☐ ☐ ☐ A
- treibe ab und zu Sport — ☐ ☐ ☐ ☐ B
- treibe regelmäßig Sport — ☐ ☐ ☐ ☐ C
- bin aktiver Sportler — ☐ ☐ ☐ ☐ D

Welcher Fahrradtyp steht mir zur Verfügung?[a]
- Klapprad — ☐ ☐ ☐ ☐ A
- Tourenrad ohne Gangschaltung[b] — ☐ ☐ ☐ ☐ B
- Tourenrad mit Gangschaltung — ☐ ☐ ☐ ☐ C
- Sportrad — ☐ ☐ ☐ ☐ D

In welchem Zustand[c] befindet sich[d] mein Fahrrad?
- für längere Strecken[e] nicht geeignet[f] — ☐ ☐ ☐ ☐ A
- benötigt[g] Reparatur — ☐ ☐ ☐ ☐ B
- benötigt leichte Reparatur, dann o.k. — ☐ ☐ ☐ ☐ C
- zuverlässig[h] — ☐ ☐ ☐ ☐ D

Was will ich?
- an die frische Luft, spielen, mich amüsieren — ☐ ☐ ☐ ☐ A
- an die frische Luft und etwas ansehen — ☐ ☐ ☐ ☐ B
- Sehenswürdigkeiten anfahren — ☐ ☐ ☐ ☐ C
- lang und schnell Radfahren — ☐ ☐ ☐ ☐ D

Meine Anforderungen[i] an die Strecke
- keine Berge — ☐ ☐ ☐ ☐ A
- möglichst wenig Berge — ☐ ☐ ☐ ☐ B
- ist egal[j], wie es kommt — ☐ ☐ ☐ ☐ C
- viele Steigungen[k], viele Berge — ☐ ☐ ☐ ☐ D
- nur asphaltierte Straßen — ☐ ☐ ☐ ☐ A
- befestigte Fahrwege[l] — ☐ ☐ ☐ ☐ B
- Fahrbahnbelag[m] ist egal — ☐ ☐ ☐ ☐ C
- Wald-[n], Feld- und Wiesenweg[o] — ☐ ☐ ☐ ☐ D

Wie lange wollen wir unterwegs[p] sein?
- Tagestour — ☐ ☐ ☐ ☐ A
- Wochenende — ☐ ☐ ☐ ☐ B
- einige Tage — ☐ ☐ ☐ ☐ C
- mehrere Wochen — ☐ ☐ ☐ ☐ D

Wie verpflegen[q] wir uns?
Tagestour:
- Gasthof/Restaurant — ☐ ☐ ☐ ☐ A
- Selbstverpflegung — ☐ ☐ ☐ ☐ B
Mehrtagesausflug:
- Gasthof/Restaurant — ☐ ☐ ☐ ☐ C
- Selbstverpflegung — ☐ ☐ ☐ ☐ D

Wo schlafen wir?
- keine Übernachtung — ☐ ☐ ☐ ☐ A
- Hotel, Pension — ☐ ☐ ☐ ☐ B
- Jugendherberge, Bauernhof — ☐ ☐ ☐ ☐ C
- Zelt — ☐ ☐ ☐ ☐ D

Anzahl der Kreuze pro Teilnehmer:

A ▭ ▭ ▭ ▭
B ▭ ▭ ▭ ▭
C ▭ ▭ ▭ ▭
D ▭ ▭ ▭ ▭

Wenn die meisten Kreuze (X) in die Buchstabengruppe A oder B fallen, so sollten Sie eine ruhige und nicht allzu anstrengende Fahrt absolvieren. Wenn die meisten Kreuze bei C und D der Liste sind, können Sie Ihre Tour etwas schwieriger gestalten.

a. steht... *is at my disposal*
b. *gears*
c. *condition*
d. befindet... *is*
e. *routes*
f. *suitable*
g. *needs*
h. *reliable*
i. *requirements*
j. *doesn't matter*
k. *slopes*
l. befestigte... *paved bike paths*
m. *road surface*
n. *forest*
o. *meadow roads*
p. *on the road*
q. *to get food*

---

2. Was sind die Ergebnisse? Was für eine Reise können Sie unternehmen?

   BEISPIEL: Ich kann nur eine leichte Tour machen. Ich treibe nämlich keinen Sport. Ich habe nur ein Klapprad (*collapsible bike*).

Neue Wörter

der Bauernhof *farm*
der Berg *hill, mountain*
die Jugendherberge *youth hostel*
die Pension *bed and breakfast inn*

der Weg *road*
sich amüsieren *to have fun*
egal *no matter*

Auf den ersten Blick

1. Read the title and the subtitle of the text. What is the theme of this reading?
2. What do you expect to find out by reading this article?

Neue Wörter

die Burg *fortress, castle*
die Erinnerung *memory*
der/die Erwachsene *adult*
die Jungen (*pl.*) [*here*] *young people*
das Mitglied *member*

mit Pfiff *with flair, style*
das Schloß (Schlösser) *castle, palace*
recht haben *to be correct*
vorbei *over, gone*

Jugendherbergen: Die alten Zöpfe sind ab°

Die... *The old ways are gone*

Fast unbemerkt° hat die gute alte Jugendherberge an einem neuen Image gebastelt.° Inzwischen kommt sie ganz flott° daher: Ferien mit Pfiff.

unnoticed
worked on / smartly

1. Wenn der Vater von früher erzählt, von damals,° als er mit dem Fahrrad an die Nordsee fuhr und in Büsum in der Jugendherberge übernachtete, hört die Tochter längst nicht mehr hin.° Das sind doch alles alte Hüte, ...Jugendherberge, nein danke: Tische decken° und um zehn das Licht aus!

a long time ago

hört...hin listens

set

Der resignierte Vater begräbt° wieder einmal seine romantischen Erinnerungen. Doch die Tochter hat nur zum Teil recht: Die Zeiten der Hausgewalt,° der kontrollierten Disziplin und des gestrengen Umgangstons°...sind in Jugendherbergen endgültig vorbei.

buries

house rules
gestrengen... strict manner

2. Heute ist man bei knapp° neun Millionen Übernachtungen in 557 bundesdeutschen Jugendherbergen angelangt,° und die Zahl der Mitglieder stagniert bei 1,2 Millionen. Schulklassen auf Wanderfahrt sind es meist, die in Jugendherbergen übernachten, und in den Städten junge Ausländer. Erwachsene über 25 bringen es gerade auf zwei Prozent. Im Sommer ist in den Jugendherbergen Nebensaison,° denn auch die Jungen reisen in den Ferien lieber in den Süden; das Wandern haben sie schon lange den Eltern überlassen.

barely
arrived

off-season

Jugendherberge in Baden-Baden: ein Treffpunkt für Jugendliche aus der ganzen Welt

3. Was die Jugendherbergen dennoch attraktiv macht, ist die unerhörte° Exklusivität mancher Häuser. In landschaftlich geschützten Gegenden° stehen sie überall dort, wo die Lage unvergleichlich° ist... Vierzig Jugendherbergen befinden sich in Burgen und Schlössern, eine ganze Reihe in Prunk- und Prachtbauten° quer durch die Architekturgeschichte.°

4. Bei den Jugendlichen, die allein etwas unternehmen wollen, ist „Äktschen"° angesagt, und die richtet° sich bei den Jugendherbergen heute auch danach, was gerade „in" ist. Die „unbegrenzten° Möglichkeiten des Computers" herauszufinden, gehört in der JH (Jugendherberge) Aschaffenburg dazu, mit BASIC-Kursen und Textverarbeitung. In der JH Wiesbaden sind es Grundkenntnisse° in Jiu-Jitsu für Mädchen. An einem Video-Seminar können Jugendliche ab 16 Jahren in der Jugendherberge Gersfeld teilnehmen.

Windsurfen auf dem Bodensee, Segeln, Kanuwandern, eine Radtour: Es gibt kaum einen Sport, den das Deutsche Jugendherbergswerk mit seinen verschiedenen Pauschalangeboten° ausläßt. Selbst Drachenfliegen° bieten verschiedene Jugendherbergen an: im Schwarzwald, in der Rhön, im Hochsauerland, in Bayern.

ADAC motorwelt, August 1988

incredible

landschaftlich... *scenically protected areas*
incomparable

sumptuous edifices / durch... *across architectural history*

action

focuses

unlimited

basic knowledge

comprehensive offerings / hang gliding

Zum Text

1. Lesen Sie die vier Abschnitte, und wählen Sie den passendsten Titel für jeden Abschnitt.

   1. _____
      a. Konflikte zwischen Eltern und Jugendlichen
      b. Jugendherbergen damals und heute
      c. Jugendherbergen sind unpopulär bei Jugendlichen
      d. Die alten Zeiten sind vorbei

   2. _____
      a. Jugendherbergen werden immer populärer
      b. Jugendherbergen stagnieren
      c. Hochsaison in Jugendherbergen

   3. _____
      a. Jugendherbergen werden exklusive Hotels
      b. Sie brauchen keine Prinzessin zu sein, um in einem Schloß zu übernachten

   4. _____
      a. Jugendherbergen—Schulen für morgen
      b. Aktivferien für Jung und Alt
      c. Jugendherberge in Aktion

Zum Text # 1. **Suggestion:** This activity can be done for homework, in preparation for class discussion. If it's done in class, have students work in pairs. They first read the paragraphs silently; then they take turns reading the headings to each other and deciding which is the most appropriate title for each segment.

2. **Richtig oder falsch?** Lesen Sie Abschnitt zwei und drei noch einmal. Welche Behauptungen sind richtig und welche falsch? Wenn falsch, geben Sie die richtige Information an.
   a. _____ Neun Millionen Deutsche sind Mitglieder des Jugendherbergwerks.
   b. _____ Erwachsene über 25 dürfen nicht in Jugendherbergen übernachten.
   c. _____ Sommer ist Nebensaison in den Jugendherbergen, weil die jungen Deutschen in den Süden reisen.
   d. _____ Man findet Jugendherbergen in Schlössern, Burgen und Kirchen.
   e. _____ In den Jugendherbergen in den Städten übernachten meistens Schulklassen.

3. **Wo kann man das machen?** Die Information finden Sie im vierten Abschnitt.

   1. _____ in Aschaffenburg   a. Video Seminar
   2. _____ im Schwarzwald   b. Jiu-Jitsu für Mädchen
   3. _____ in Gersfeld   c. Windsurfen
   4. _____ am Bodensee   d. Drachenfliegen
   5. _____ in Wiesbaden   e. Computer

Nach dem Lesen

Aktivität 1. Sie wollen eine Radtour mit Freunden unternehmen.

Aktivität 1. **Follow-up:** Have students suggest alternatives to a bicycle trip—e.g., a hiking trip or a hot air balloon trip.

Machen Sie mit Hilfe der Checkliste auf Seite 281 einen Plan. Teilen Sie die Klasse nach Leistung auf: die A in eine Gruppe, die B in eine andere Gruppe, usw. Was müssen Sie sich alles überlegen und planen (z.B.: wohin Sie wollen, wie lange Sie unterwegs sein wollen, wo Sie übernachten wollen)?

▣ Aktivität 2. Rollenspiel

Sie planen mit einem Freund oder einer Freundin eine Reise in den Schwarzwald. Der eine möchte nach Schramberg, der andere nach Triberg. Diskutieren Sie und treffen Sie eine Entscheidung (*make a decision*).

Aktivität 2. Note: The prompts in the two columns (A and B) are set up differently from most other student dialogues. Students must create their own dialogue, following the guidelines and searching the brief texts for information. Some choices for variations are provided.

Triberg im Schwarzwald 7600 Einwohner[a]

Staatlich anerkannter heilklimatischer Kurort, mit modernem Kurhaus, geeignet für Tagungen, Seminare und Veranstaltungen. Ausgangspunkt der schönsten Wanderungen, Wintersportort. Sehenswürdigkeiten: Deutschlands höchste Wasserfälle, holzgeschnitzter Rathaussaal, Heimatmuseum mit Uhren-, Trachten-[b], Gewerbe-[c] und Mineralienschau, Holzschnitzereien, Wallfahrtskirche[d] (1700).

Schramberg 20 000 Einwohner

Die Fünftäler-[e] und Burgenstadt im Herzen des Mittleren Schwarzwaldes. Gut markierte Spazier- und Wanderwege, Stadtpark, Minigolf, beheiztes Freischwimmbad, Hallenbad mit Sauna, Reiten, Tennis, Schießen und Angeln, Skilift, Skischule, Konzerte.

a. *inhabitants*
b. *costumes*
c. *crafts*
d. *pilgrimage church*
e. *five-valley*

A:

makes a suggestion:
   Wie wäre es mit _____? ⟶

B:

would like more information:
   Wo _____?
   Was _____?
   Wie _____?

gives additional information

makes a countersuggestion:
   Ich möchte lieber _____.
gives reasons

accepts or rejects suggestion:
   Na, gut!
   Ach nein, _____ gefällt mir besser.
   _____ finde ich interessanter.

▣ Aktivität 3. Schreiben Sie!

Sie gewinnen eine Reise. Die Möglichkeiten sind

1. eine Radtour durch Deutschland.
2. Ferien auf Tahiti.
3. eine Safari.

Was wählen Sie? Warum? Beschreiben Sie Ihre Reisevorbereitungen. Wie stellen Sie sich einen Tag auf dieser Reise vor?

WORTSCHATZ

Substantive

Reisen / Traveling

der Anschluß (ẍsse)	connection
der Aufenthalt	stopover, layover
der (Auto)bus (-se)	bus
der Autostop	hitchhiking
per Autostop reisen	to hitchhike
die Bahn (-en)	railroad
mit der Bahn	by train
der Bahnhof (ẍe)	railroad station
der Bahnsteig (-e)	(train) platform
die Fahrkarte (-n)	ticket
der Fahrkarten-schalter (-)	ticket window
die Fahrt (-en)	trip
die Hinfahrt	trip (first half of roundtrip)
die Rückfahrt	return trip
der Flughafen (ẍ)	airport
das Flugzeug (-e)	airplane
das Gepäck	luggage
das Gleis (-e)	platform, track
der Koffer (-)	suitcase
die Platzkarte (-n)	reserved seat ticket
das Reisebüro (-s)	travel agency
der Schaffner (-)	conductor
der Urlaub	vacation
der Wagen (-)	car
der Zug (ẍe)	train
der Zuschlag (ẍe)	surcharge

Andere Substantive

der Bauernhof (ẍe)	farm
der Berg (-e)	mountain
die Burg (-en)	fortress, castle
die Erinnerung (-en)	memory, remembrance
der/die Erwachsene (decl. adj)	adult
die Grenze (-n)	border
die Jugendherberge (-n)	youth hostel
das Mitglied (-er)	member
die Möglichkeit (-en)	possibility
das Paßbild (-er)	passport photo
die Pension (-en)	bed and breakfast inn (hotel)
das Schloß (ẍsser)	palace, castle
der Schüler (-), die Schülerin (-nen)	pupil, student in primary or secondary school
die Sehenswürdigkeit (-en)	(tourist) attraction
der Vorschlag (ẍe)	suggestion

Verben

abfahren (fährt ab), fuhr ab, ist abgefahren	to leave
abfliegen (fliegt ab), flog ab, ist abgeflogen	to depart by plane, leave
sich amüsieren	to have fun
ankommen (kommt an), kam an, ist angekommen	to arrive
Bescheid geben (gibt Bescheid), gab, gegeben	to inform, let someone know
besorgen	to (go) get
bieten, bot, geboten	to offer
halten (hält), hielt, gehalten	to stop
kennenlernen (lernt kennen)	to get to know
mitfahren (fährt mit), fuhr mit, ist mitgefahren	to drive along, come along
mitkommen (kommt mit), kam mit, ist mitgekommen	to come along
packen	to pack
auspacken (packt aus)	to unpack
recht haben	to be correct, right
teilnehmen (nimmt teil), nahm teil, teilgenommen	to participate
sich etwas überlegen	to think about something
Ich will es mir überlegen.	I want to think about it.
umsteigen (steigt um), stieg um, ist umgestiegen	to transfer, change

unternehmen (unternimmt), unternahm, unternommen	to undertake, to do
verreisen	to go on a trip
sich verabschieden (von)	to say good-bye (to)

Adjektive und Adverbien

äußerst	extreme(ly)
einfach	simple; one way (ticket)
ganz einfach	quite simple
einverstanden	in agreement
einverstanden sein	to be in agreement, agree
Ich bin damit einverstanden.	I agree with that.
geeignet	suitable, appropriate
gefährlich	dangerous
gültig	valid
hauptsächlich	mainly, mostly
hin und zurück	roundtrip
höchstens	at most
insgesamt	all together

kurz	short
langsam	slow
möglichst	as . . . as possible
möglichst bald	as soon as possible
nah	near, close by
nächst-	next
der nächste Zug	the next train
pünktlich	punctual, on time
schnell	fast
sicher	safe
unterwegs	on the road
vorbei	over, gone
weit	far

Sonstiges

als (*conj.*)	when
auf dem Land(e)	in the country
(Das) klingt gut.	(That) sounds good.
mit Pfiff	with style
nachdem (*conj.*)	after
ob (*conj.*)	whether (or not)
so . . . wie	as . . . as
zu Fuß	on foot

UNTERWEGS

Unterwegs. Introduce the chapter by telling students where you spent your last vacation or where you are planning to go. Ask students *Wo waren Sie letztes Jahr in den Ferien? Wo verbringen Sie Ihre Ferien am liebsten? In den Bergen, am Meer, zu Hause? Wohin würden Sie gern reisen?*

Lernziele *In this chapter you will be talking about places to stay when you are traveling, and you will learn to make hotel reservations and ask for directions. You will be describing objects and situations in greater detail.*

**Grindelwald/
Berner Oberland (1050 m)**

Zielbahnhof: Grindelwald via Basel Bf

Grindelwald, das gastliche[a] Gletscherdorf,[b] liegt in 1050 m Höhe in einem windgeschützten, sonnigen Talkessel[c] am Fuße der imposanten Bergriesen[d] Wetterhorn, Eiger und Jungfrau und ist als Ferien- und Sportort weltberühmt.[e]

RSM

a. *hospitable*
b. *glacier village*
c. *valley basin*
d. *mountain giants*
e. *world-famous*

a. städtisches Verkehrsamt = *municipal tourist bureau*

Dillingen

Historisches Stadtbild, viele Sehenswürdigkeiten, großes Freizeitangebot . . .

Info: Städt. Verkehrsamt[a] Pf. 1210, 8880 Dillingen, Tel. (09071) 54-109

Neuburger Schloßfest

Ein Fest der Renaissance

23. bis 25. Juni und 30. Juni bis 2. Juli 1989

St. Peter Ording

12 km Badestrand,[a] über 100 km Wanderwege, 350 ha Wald und bewaldete Dünen. Für sportlich Aktive: ideale Bedingungen für Reiten, Tennisspielen, Surfen und Golfen. Kommen Sie ins Nordseeheil- und Schwefelbad. Besuchen Sie unser Meerwasser-Thermalbad (32° C), unser Meerwasser-Wellenbad[d] (25° C) und unsere Sauna mit Meeresblick.

Auskunfte und Buchung: Kurverwaltung 15 , Postfach 100. 2252 St. Peter-Ording. Tel. 04863/1008

a. *beach for swimming*
b. *square acres*
c. *salt water*
d. das Meer = *ocean*; die Welle = *wave*

▣ Alles klar?

Zwischen der Nordsee und den Alpen gibt es zahlreiche (*numerous*) Möglichkeiten, etwas zu erleben. Schauen Sie sich die Anzeigen für einige Orte und Gegenden an. Wo kann man, zum Beispiel

- eine historische Stadt besuchen?
- Ferien am Meer verbringen?
- sich in den Bergen vom Alltagsstreß erholen?
- Spaß bei einem historischen Fest haben?

Wo liegen diese Orte?

1. das Berner Oberland   a. im Norden Deutschlands
2. St. Peter Ording   b. im Süden Deutschlands
3. Dillingen   c. in der Schweiz

WÖRTER IM KONTEXT

Auf der Suche nach Unterkunft°

Auf... *in search of accommodations*

☐ Aktivität 1. Was für ein Hotel?

Sie sind mit Freunden unterwegs. Leider haben Sie keine Unterkunft in der Jugendherberge bekommen. Was für ein Hotel suchen Sie?

BEISPIEL: Das Hotel muß eine Sauna haben. Und es soll in der Innenstadt liegen.

über 100,- Mark
in der Nähe des
    Bahnhofs
ein Restaurant im
    Haus
zu teuer

Es muß	in der Innenstadt	haben
Es darf (nicht)	Sauna/	kosten
Es soll	Schwimmbad	liegen
	Farbfernsehen und	sein
	Telefon	

zu laut
zu groß
Garage im Hause
Zimmer mit Bad
    und/oder Dusche

Aktivität 1. Suggestion: Do this activity with the whole group to get as much variety in the responses as possible. You might want to substitute a dollar amount for the price of a hotel, to make it more realistic for students.
Note: As one of the items (*in der Nähe des Bahnhofs*) includes a genitive expression and the following *Sprachnotiz* introduces the genitive for recognition before the chapter grammar explains it in detail, you may want to add *in der Mitte der Stadt* or *in der Nähe der Universität* to the list, for variety.

> ### Sprachnotiz
>
> Phrases like **die Lage des Hotels** (*the location of the hotel*), **in der Nähe des Bahnhofs** (*in the vicinity of the railroad station*) or **in der Mitte der Stadt** (*in the middle of the city*) use the genitive (possessive) case for noun attributes that modify another noun.

Neue Wörter

die Auskunft *information*
die Halbpension *room, breakfast, and lunch or dinner*

die Übernachtung *overnight stay*
die Vollpension *room and three meals a day*

Aktivität 2. Hören Sie zu.

Hotel-Restaurant „Stadt Hannover": was hat es zu bieten?
Richtig (R), falsch (F), oder keine Information (0) darüber?

1. __R__ Zum Hotel gehört auch eine Pension mit Bauernhof.
2. __R__ Das Hotel ist sehr klein.
3. __R__ Das Hotel liegt in der Nähe der Stadt Hannover.
4. __F__ Frühstück ist nicht im Preis enthalten.
5. __F__ Man kann im Hotel nur Frühstück essen.
6. __F__ Alle Zimmer haben Dusche und WC.
7. __R__ Das Hotel ist für Familien mit Kindern geeignet.
8. __0__ Jeden Tag gibt es Musik und Tanz im Hotel.
9 __R__ Der Preis für eine Übernachtung ist sehr günstig.

Neue Wörter

das Doppelzimmer *room with two beds*
die Dusche *shower*
das Einzelzimmer *room with one bed*
der Hafen *harbor*
der Hauptbahnhof *main railroad station*
die Innenstadt *center of town*
die Lage *location*
in der Nähe *in the vicinity*
die Unterkunft *accommodation*
im Preis enthalten *included in the price*

RSM

Aktivität 2. Point out: Students will hear a conversation between someone looking for a place for a family to spend a vacation and someone recommending a particular hotel, the Hotel-Restaurant „Stadt Hannover". Explain the meaning of *Halbpension* and *Vollpension*, listed in the *Neue Wörter*. These options are only for guests who spend their vacation at a hotel or *Pension*.
Point out: Smaller hotels, particularly *Pensionen*, do not always have a bathroom for each room. Guests share a bathroom and *WC* (toilet), located on the same floor as their room.
Suggestion: Have students scan the responses before you play the taped conversation for them.
Suggestion: Ask students to focus on additional details in the conversation by asking questions such as *Ist das Hotel alt oder modern? Wieviel kostet eine Übernachtung? Wie viele Personen können insgesamt im Hotel übernachten? Warum ist das Hotel ideal für Familien mit Kindern? Was für Essen gibt es im Hotel?*

Aktivität 3. Gruppenarbeit

Sie suchen eine Unterkunft in Hamburg und haben im Unterkunftsverzeichnis (*list of accommodations*) einige Hotels gefunden. Schauen Sie sich die Anzeigen auf Seite 292 an und überlegen Sie sich, welches Hotel für Sie geeignet ist. Bedenken Sie dabei, zum Beispiel,

- ob Sie Einzelzimmer, Doppelzimmer oder Mehrbettzimmer wollen
- wieviel Geld Sie ausgeben wollen
- welchen Komfort Sie brauchen: Luxushotel? Pension? Zimmer mit Bad, Dusche, Fernsehen?
- die Lage des Hotels (in zentraler Lage, in der Nähe des Bahnhofs, in der Mitte der Stadt)

Aktivität 3. Suggestion: First have students scan the ads for hotels in Hamburg. Encourage them to guess the meaning of words from the context, including the abbreviations used in one ad; e.g., they can guess that *EZ = Einzelzimmer* after they have seen *Einzelzimmer* and *Doppelzimmer* in the ad for the Hotel Westerland. Review the *nützliche Ausdrücke* that students can use in their discussion. Then have them do the activity in groups of three or four. Set a time limit for the discussions and ask the groups to report which hotel they chose and why they chose it.

Nützliche Ausdrücke:

Ich finde das Hotel _____ preiswert/preiswerter als _____.
Mir gefällt das Hotel _____.
Es gibt _____ (*z.B. eine Garage*) im Hotel.
Das Hotel liegt günstig _____ (*z.B. in zentraler Lage*).
Ja, aber _____.

Berichten Sie dann, für welches Hotel Sie sich entschieden haben, und warum.

Im Hotel

 **Dialog**

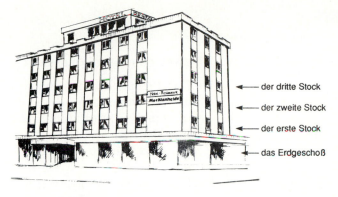

- der dritte Stock
- der zweite Stock
- der erste Stock
- das Erdgeschoß

RSM

Dialog. Note: This dialogue presents a typical situation that a visitor might encounter at a hotel. It recycles vocabulary from previous chapters and vocabulary already introduced in this chapter. New vocabulary and expressions can easily be guessed from the context.
Suggestion: Play the dialogue once, for students to get the gist. Ask a few basic questions: *Wer sind die Sprecher? Wie heißt der Gast? Wie lange möchte er bleiben?* Then ask students to scan the text once. Help them figure out the meaning of *Würden Sie bitte das Anmeldeformular ausfüllen?* by asking *Was muß ein Gast im Hotel machen, bevor er sein Zimmer bekommt?* To figure out the meaning of *im ersten Stock* and *Erdgeschoß*, refer to the realia showing the Hotel Mecklenheide.
Point out: The meaning of *Würden Sie... ausfüllen* corresponds to the English "Would you fill out . . . ," used for polite requests.
Point out: *erster Stock* corresponds to second floor; *zweiter Stock* is the third floor; *Erdgeschoß* is either the ground floor or the first floor.
Suggestion: Play the tape of the dialogue and have students complete *Aktivität 4* as a whole group. Then have them work in pairs, role-playing the dialogue.

An der Rezeption im Hotel Mecklenheide

REZEPTION: Guten Abend.
GAST: Guten Abend. Ich habe ein Zimmer für zwei Nächte bestellt.
REZEPTION: Auf welchen Namen, bitte?
GAST: Thompson.
REZEPTION: Ah, ja. Herr Thompson. Ein Einzelzimmer mit Bad. Würden Sie bitte das Anmeldeformular ausfüllen?
GAST: Möchten Sie auch meinen Reisepaß sehen?
REZEPTION: Nein, das ist nicht nötig. Ihr Zimmer liegt im ersten Stock, Zimmer 21. Hier ist der Schlüssel.
GAST: Danke.
REZEPTION: Wir bringen Ihr Gepäck aufs Zimmer. Der Lift ist hier rechts.
GAST: Übrigens, wann gibt es morgens Frühstück?
REZEPTION: Zwischen 7 und 10 Uhr im Frühstücksraum hier gleich links im Erdgeschoß.
GAST: Danke sehr.
REZEPTION: Bitte sehr. Ich wünsche Ihnen einen angenehmen Aufenthalt.

Neue Wörter

das Anmeldeformular *registration form*
der Aufenthalt *stay*
das Erdgeschoß *ground floor*
der Stock *floor*

links *left, to the left*
rechts *right, to the right*
ausfüllen *to fill out*

Aktivität 4. Welche Satzteile gehören zusammen?

1. _____ Ich wünsche Ihnen
2. _____ Ihr Zimmer liegt
3. _____ Wir bringen Ihr Gepäck
4. _____ Ich habe ein Zimmer
5. _____ Würden Sie bitte

a. bestellt.
b. das Anmeldeformular ausfüllen?
c. im ersten Stock.
d. einen angenehmen Aufenthalt.
e. aufs Zimmer.

Aktivität 5.   Hören Sie zu. Zwei telefonische Zimmerbestellungen

Was stimmt? Kreuzen Sie die richtige Antwort an.

ERSTES TELEFONGESPRÄCH

1. Der Gast braucht ein
   a. Einzelzimmer.
   b. Doppelzimmer. X
2. Er braucht das Zimmer für
   a. eine Nacht.
   b. mehrere (*several*) Nächte. X
3. Das Hotel hat ein Zimmer frei
   a. mit Bad.
   b. ohne Bad. X
4. Frühstück ist im Preis
   a. nicht enthalten.
   b. enthalten. X
5. Der Gast
   a. nimmt das Zimmer.
   b. muß ein anderes Hotel finden. X

ZWEITES TELEFONGESPRÄCH

1. Das Jugendgästehaus hat
   a. nur Doppelzimmer.
   b. nur Mehrbettzimmer. X
2. Das Haus ist
   a. ganz neu.
   b. sehr alt. X
3. Die Übernachtung kostet
   a. mehr als 20 Mark.
   b. weniger als 20 Mark. X
4. Jedes Zimmer hat
   a. WC und Dusche. X
   b. fünf Betten.
5. Das Gästehaus liegt
   a. in der Nähe der Stadt.
   b. in der Nähe der Innenstadt. X

Aktivität 5.   Suggestion: Have students first scan the information requested in the first telephone conversation. Then let them listen to it on the tape. Students can work in pairs, taking turns responding to each item. Repeat this procedure with the second conversation.
Follow-up: Exploit both conversations further through questions eliciting more detail, e.g., *Warum muß der Gast im ersten Gespräch ein anderes Hotel suchen? Wie alt ist das Jugendgästehaus genau?*
Point out: *Auf Wiederhören*—the final words of the first telephone conversation—is only used to end a telephone conversation.

Neue Wörter

auf Wiederhören *good-bye (only on the phone)*

erlaubt *permitted*
versuchen *to try, attempt*

Aktivität 6.   Rollenspiel

Sie sind im Hotel-Gasthof Roter Hahn, wo Sie übernachten möchten. Führen Sie ein Gespräch mit der Dame / dem Herrn an der Rezeption.

Das Hotel bietet:

> moderne Zimmer mit Dusche und WC
> Einzelzimmer DM 55,- pro Person
> Doppelzimmer DM 80,- für zwei Personen
> ein gemütliches Speiserestaurant
> Farbfernsehen und Telefon
> gute deutsche Küche

Aktivität 6.   Suggestion: Students work in pairs. Student A first looks at the items to be requested, jotting down notes in German. With book closed, student A then begins the conversation. Student B has the list of hotel amenities and responds accordingly. This activity should be repeated several times with different partners.

A:

State your need.
Ask about the price and what it includes.
Decide whether or not to take the room; if yes, for how long?

→

B:

Respond with appropriate information from the list.
Add additional information about the hotel that the guest did not ask about.

Nach dem Weg fragen

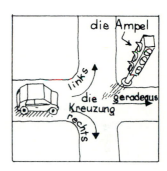

Aktivität 7. **Suggestion:** First go over the illustrations demonstrating new vocabulary in *Nach dem Weg fragen*. Then focus students' attention on the information grid, with the examples. Finally, let them hear each miniexchange once. Pause so they have time to jot down their responses.

Aktivität 7. Hören Sie zu.

Drei Leute fragen nach dem Weg. Wohin wollen sie? Wie müssen sie gehen?

	BEISPIEL	DIALOG 1	DIALOG 2	DIALOG 3
Wohin?	Bank	Markt	Hotel	Post
Auskunft	geradeaus, dann rechts	geradeaus, dann links	zwei Straßen geradeaus, dann rechts	keine Auskunft

Neue Wörter

Entschuldigung *pardon me*
die Haltestelle *stop (for bus, streetcar)*
die Kreuzung *intersection*

die Straßenbahn *street car*
die U-Bahn (Untergrund-bahn) *subway*

Aktivität 8. **Suggestion:** Have students first scan the possibilities on page 296 and add a few places in their own city or on campus. Working in pairs, students then practice a number of combinations, reversing roles each time.
Follow-up: Start a chain by having one student ask another how to get to a place from where he or she is right now. For instance, A: *Wie kommt man von hier zur Bibliothek?* B: *Geradeaus bis zur Mensa, dann rechts. Wie kommt man von der Bibliothek zur Post?*

Aktivität 8. Wie kommt man dahin?

Fragen Sie nach dem Weg in Ihrer Stadt oder auf Ihrem Campus. Wählen Sie passende Fragen und Antworten aus jeder Spalte auf Seite 296.

BEISPIEL: A: Entschuldigung, wo ist hier die Post?
B: Da nehmen Sie am besten den Bus.
A: Wo ist die Haltestelle?
B: Gleich da drüben.

FRAGEN:	ANTWORTEN:

Wie kommt man am besten
zum Supermarkt?
Wie weit ist es bis ins
Zentrum?
Entschuldigung, wo ist hier
die Post (Bank, Mensa)?

Wo ist die Haltestelle?

Immer geradeaus.
Nächste Kreuzung rechts/
links.
Da nehmen Sie am besten
_____ (den Bus, z.B. Linie 8)

Gleich da drüben.
Gleich an der Ecke.
5 Minuten zu Fuß.   **RSM**

☐ **Aktivität 9. Rollenspiel**

Sie sind in einer fremden Stadt. Erkundi-
gen Sie sich (*Inquire*) nach dem Weg. Benutzen Sie die Tabelle unten.

BEISPIEL: A: Ist der Bahnhof weit von
hier?
B: Er ist 15 Minuten von
hier, im Zentrum.
A: Wie komme ich am be-
sten dahin?
B: Nehmen Sie ein Taxi.

WOHIN	WIE WEIT	WO	WIE
Landesmuseum	6 km von hier	bei der Universität	Buslinie 7, am Rathaus in Linie 12 umsteigen
Bahnhof	15 Minuten	im Zentrum	mit dem Taxi
Post	nicht weit	in der Nähe vom Bahnhof	zu Fuß
Rathaus	3 km vom Hotel		mit der U-Bahn
Schloß	15 km	außerhalb der Stadt	mit dem Auto oder Bus in Richtung° Nürnberg
Opernhaus	ganz in der Nähe	rechts um die Ecke	zu Fuß, die Poststraße entlang

Aktivität 9.   Point out: Go over the
information in the chart with the
class, pointing out new expressions:
e.g., *in Richtung...* (Nürnberg is of
course only a suggestion) and *die
(Name) Staße entlang. Entlang* is an
accusative preposition that follows
the noun to which it belongs.
Suggestion: Students can combine
the items for their answer, either at
random or by reading across.

in... *in the direction*

Unterwegs auf der Autobahn

Wenn man mit dem Auto im fremden Land unterwegs ist, sollte man etwas über die Straßen und Verkehrszeichen (*traffic symbols*) des Landes wissen. Hier sehen Sie einige Verkehrszeichen.

Zulässige Höchst-
geschwindigkeit
1.

Autobahngasthaus
2.

Verbot für Kraftwagen
3.

Parkplatz
4.

Kinder
5.

Einbahnstraße
6.

Ende der Autobahn
7.

Tankstelle
8.

Zur Autobahn
9.

Zollstelle
10.   **RSM**

▣ Aktivität 10. Verkehrszeichen

Schauen Sie sich die Verkehrszeichen an, und finden Sie die passende Erklärung dafür.

1. *g*
2. _____
3. _____
4. _____
5. _____
6. _____
7. _____
8. _____
9. _____
10. _____

a. Dort bekommt man Benzin fürs Auto.
b. Auf dieser Straße fährt aller Verkehr nur in eine Richtung.
c. Hier soll man besonders vorsichtig fahren, denn Kinder überqueren oft die Straße.
d. Hier ist die Autobahn zu Ende.
e. Hier müssen Sie den Reisepaß vorzeigen.
f. Hier kann man etwas essen.
g. Hier darf man nicht schneller als 60 km die Stunde fahren.
h. Hier sind keine Autos erlaubt.
i. Nach rechts abbiegen zur Autobahn nach Berlin.
j. Hier darf man parken.

Neue Wörter

das Benzin *gasoline*
die Einbahnstraße *one-way street*
die Geschwindigkeit *speed*
   die Höchstgeschwindigkeit *maximum speed; speed limit*
die Tankstelle *gas station*
der Verkehr *traffic*

der Zoll *customs*
   die Zollstelle *customs station*
abbiegen (nach rechts) *turn (to the right)*
tanken *to get gas*
überqueren (die Straße) *to cross (the street)*
vorsichtig *careful*

▣ **Aktivität 11.** Tips für unterwegs

1. Autobahn Service gibt Tips für die Reise auf der Autobahn. Was sind diese drei Tips?
2. Schauen Sie sich den Cartoon *Auch das noch* an. Was hat Herr Schmitz alles falsch gemacht, laut (*according to*) den drei Tips?

Aktivität 11. **Suggestions:** For #1, ask students to come up with additional tips for traveling. For #2, ask them to work in pairs describing the cartoon frames. Call on several groups to explain their understanding of the cartoon.

▐▲▌1x1   Tips für unterwegs

Die Bundesautobahnen berühren[a] die schönsten deutschen Landschaften[b] und Sehenswürdigkeiten. Es lohnt sich,[c] die Reise sorgfältig vorzubereiten.

● **Die Reise planen**

Es ist zu empfehlen, nicht gleich im Anschluß an[d] einen vollen Arbeitstag in den Urlaub zu starten. Der erste Reisetag sollte zu einem schönen erlebnisreichen Ferientag werden.

● **Streß vermeiden**

Wer seine Reiseroute im voraus festlegt[f] und dabei vernünftige[g] Pausen einplant, kommt ausgeruht ans Ziel. Und er vermeidet Unfälle,[h] die durch Streß und Übermüdung entstehen.

● **Pause einlegen**

Spätestens[j] alle zwei Stunden sind Pausen einzulegen. Es gibt an der Autobahn genügend Rastplätze,[k] die für eine 10-Minuten-Entspannung geeignet sind. Gymnastische Übungen sind zu empfehlen.

RSM

a. *touch on*
b. *landscapes*
c. Es... *it's worth it*
d. nicht... *not right after*
e. *to avoid*
f. im... *plans in advance*
g. *reasonable*
h. *accidents*
i. Pause... *to take a break*
j. *at the latest*
k. *rest areas*

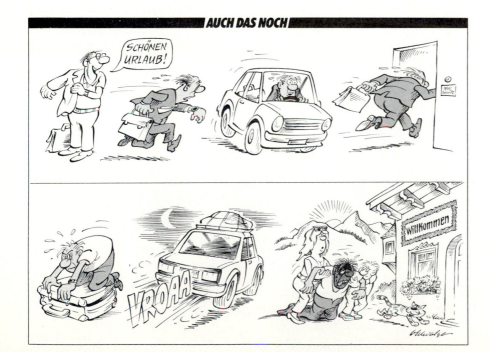

GRAMMATIK IM KONTEXT

The Genitive Case

der Genitiv

A noun phrase in the genitive case modifies another noun, functioning as an attribute—much the way an adjective does—further describing and defining the other noun. One important use of the genitive case is to indicate possession. For this reason the genitive is sometimes referred to as the possessive case.

das Hotel **meiner Familie**	*my family's hotel*
das Auto **meines Vaters**	*my father's car*
das Gepäck **der Gäste**	*the guests' luggage*

Genitive attributes can be omitted without altering the basic meaning of a sentence. Compare the following sentences:

Das Gepäck der Gäste steht im Zimmer.	*The guests' luggage is in the room.*
Das Gepäck steht im Zimmer.	*The luggage is in the room.*

The genitive phrase **der Gäste** functions as an attribute of the expression **das Gepäck**, providing detail about whose luggage it is. Note that English has two ways of expressing what German expresses with a genitive form:

die Lage **des Hotels**	*the location **of the hotel***
die Unterschrift **des Gastes**	*the **guest's** signature*

In the first example a prepositional phrase (*of . . .*) is used in English; in the second example a genitive (possessive) form (*guest's*) is used.

▣ Analyse

Analyse.   **Suggestion:** Have students prepare this as part of their homework; it can serve as a basis for a class discussion of the genitive.

- Scan the illustrations for genitive attributes and the nouns they modify.
- Where is the genitive attribute found? In front of or after the noun that it modifies? How does this compare with English?
- What endings do some of the nouns have in the genitive?
- What are the definite articles in the genitive case?
- How would you express the noun phrases in these illustrations in English?

RSM

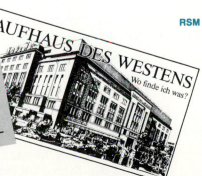

As in the other three cases, the **der-** and **ein-**words have special forms in the genitive case.

SINGULAR			PLURAL
Masculine	*Neuter*	*Feminine*	
des dieses eines unseres } Gastes	des dieses eines unseres } Hotels	der dieser einer unserer } Stadt	der dieser unserer } Gäste

Masculine and neuter nouns in the singular add **-(e)s** in the genitive case. Masculine and neuter nouns of one syllable usually add **-es.**

Die Lage **dieses Hotels**	*the location of this hotel*
die Unterschrift **des Gastes**	*the guest's signature*

Masculine nouns that add **-n** or **-en** in the dative and accusative also add **-n** or **-en** in the genitive case.

das Gepäck **des Studenten**	*the student's luggage*
der Koffer **des Herrn** aus Hannover	*the suitcase of the gentleman from Hanover*

A few common nouns that add **-en** to form the accusative and dative case form the genitive by adding **-ens.** Two important nouns of this type are **der Name** and **das Herz** (*heart*)

Nominative:	der Name	das Herz
Genitive:	**des Namens**	**des Herzens**

Nouns with this pattern will be listed in the vocabulary sections as follows: **das Herz (-ens, -en).**

The noun in the genitive always follows the noun it modifies, unless the genitive is a proper name. A proper name normally precedes the noun it modifies. Proper names in the genitive add **-s** without an apostrophe, in contrast to English.

Martinas Koffer	*Martina's suitcase*
Herrn Kramers Reisepaß	*Mr. Kramer's passport*
Mutters Tasche	*Mother's bag*

In the last example, **Mutter** is used as a proper name. Therefore, **-s** is added to the name **Mutter.** Compare the following examples:

Wo ist **Mutters** Tasche? (*Mutter is used as a proper name.*)
Wo ist die Tasche **meiner Mutter**? (*Mutter is used as a noun.*)

Nouns in the genitive.
Suggestion: For a quick practice of genitive forms, do a substitution exercise: *Wo liegt deine Wohnung? In der Nähe... (Universität, Bahnhof, Park, Theater, Post, Einkaufszentrum) Wie ist die Telefonnummer... ? (Freund, Freundin, Eltern, Familie, Polizei, Auskunft, Hotel)*

Masculine nouns ending in -n or -en. Suggestion: Review other nouns that fall into this category: *der Kunde, der Tourist, der Mensch.* For instance, *die Unterschrift des Kunden, (aber: die Unterschrift der Kundin), eines Touristen.*

Point out: A genitive *s* is added to names regardless of the gender of the person. Genitive endings are also added to both parts of a masculine proper name: *Herr Kramer → Herrn Kramers;* but *Frau Kramer → Frau Kramers.*

When the name of a country or a region is in the genitive case, it may precede or follow the noun it modifies.

Hessen: das Herz **Deutschlands**	*Hesse: the heart of Germany*
München, **Deutschlands** heimliche Hauptstadt	*Munich, Germany's secret capital*

The genitive case is sometimes replaced by the preposition **von** and the dative case, particularly in everyday speech. This is similar to using a prepositional phrase with *of* in English.

in der Nähe **vom Bahnhof**   *in the vicinity of the railroad station*

To ask for the owner of something, use the interrogative pronoun **wessen** (*whose*).

Wessen Koffer ist das?	*Whose suitcase is that?*
Wessen Unterschrift ist das?	*Whose signature is that?*

▣ Übung 1. Was für eine Stadt ist Wien?

You have just returned from Vienna and are describing the city to someone. Use genitive attributes in your description.

BEISPIEL: Wien ist eine Stadt der Tradition.

Wien ist eine Stadt _____
- die Kaffeehäuser
- die Tradition
- das Theater
- die Musik
- die Museen
- die Gärten
- der Jugendstil (*art nouveau*)

▣ Übung 2. Wo lag eure Pension?

Describe the location using a genitive phrase.

BEISPIEL: Unsere Pension lag in der Nähe eines Cafés.

Unsere Pension lag in der Nähe
- ein Café
- ein Schloß
- die Donau
- die Universität
- der Bahnhof
- die Ringstraße
- das Fremdenverkehrsamt
- die Stadt
- das Burgtheater
- der Stephansdom (*St. Stephen's Cathedral*)

Übung 2. Follow-up: Personalize the exercise by asking students *Wo liegt Ihre Wohnung / Ihr Studentenheim?* In addition to using *in der Nähe*, they might also use *in der Mitte*.

▣ **Übung 3. Aus einem Reisebericht**

Complete the sentences with a noun from the list. Each noun will be in the genitive case.

die Renaissance Deutschland
der Sommer der Bahnhof
die Stadt Regensburg die Ferien

1. Am Anfang _____ gab es 30 Kilometer lange Staus auf der Autobahn.
2. In der Nähe _____ kam es zu einigen schweren Unfällen (*accidents*) auf der Autobahn.
3. Auf Schloß Neuburg gibt es im Juni ein Fest _____ .
4. Die Museen _____ laden Sie zu einem Besuch ein.
5. Unser Hotel lag günstig in der Nähe _____ .
6. Hessen liegt im Herzen _____ .
7. Am Ende _____ besuchten wir noch Berlin.

Prepositions with the Genitive

A number of prepositions are used with the genitive case. Several common ones are:

außerhalb (*outside of*) → außerhalb der Stadt
trotz (*in spite of*) → trotz des Regens
während (*during*) → während des Sommers
wegen (*because of*) → wegen der hohen Kosten

Trotz, während, and **wegen** may also be used with the dative case, though that usage is still considered somewhat colloquial.

▣ **Übung 4. Notizen von einer Reise nach Wien**

Complete each sentence with an appropriate genitive preposition.

1. _____ unserer Reise nach Wien haben wir viel gesehen.
2. _____ der hohen Hotelpreise haben wir in einer kleinen Pension übernachtet.
3. Die Pension lag _____ der Stadt.
4. _____ der vielen Touristen war es in Wien schön.
5. _____ der vielen Besucher konnten wir keine Karten für die Spanische Reitschule bekommen.

Attributive Adjectives

Predicate adjectives—adjectives used with the verbs **sein** and **werden**—take no endings. Attributive adjectives—adjectives in front of nouns they modify—always take endings.

Ein Lippizaner und sein Reiter zeigen ihre Künste in der Spanischen Hofreitschule in Wien.

Genitive Prepositions.
Suggestion: Practice the preposition *wegen* individually, contrasting it with *weil*; students tend to mix these words up. Do a quick substitution exercise: *Warum studieren Sie hier? Wegen...* (*die Lage, das Wetter, der Ruf der Uni / des Colleges, der Preis, die Studenten, meine Freundin, meine Eltern, mein Vater,* etc.) Now ask students to rephrase their sentences using *weil*. Repeat the question *Warum studieren Sie hier?* Provide cues using the substitution nouns: *Der Ruf der Universität (das Wetter, die Lage,* etc.) *ist sehr gut.* Or: *Meine Freundin studiert hier; meine Eltern haben die Universität empfohlen.* Students say ...*weil der Ruf der Universität (das Wetter, die Lage,* etc.) *gut ist,* or *weil meine Freundin hier studiert,* etc.

Adjectives. **Point out:** Students have seen adjectives with endings in the many visuals and texts throughout this book. Adjective endings do not interfere with understanding a text, yet they are difficult to master. However, in scanning almost any German text, students will quickly discover that only two adjective endings are used with great frequency: *e* and *en*.

predicate adjective Die Pension Hubertus ist **preiswert.**
attributive adjective Diese **preiswerte** Pension liegt außerhalb der Stadt.

▣ Analyse

Das kleine historische Haus in der Innenstadt

HOTEL UND GASTSTÄTTE

Erholung

Karin und Reinhold Haferkorn
Dragonerstall 11 (Valentinskamp)
2000 Hamburg 36 · Telefon (040) 34 23 87
Gegenüber der Musikhalle

Regensburg

Schatzkammer[a] der Vergangenheit[b] mit über 1400 historischen Gebäuden[c], z. B. Dom[d] St. Peter, Steinerne Brücke[e] Altes Rathaus[f]. Zahlreiche Museen und Galerien, Stadtführungen, Schiffahrten auf der Donau, idyllische Biergärten, Einkaufsstadt, Kultureller Sommer „Kunst an historischen Stätten"

. . . **immer einladend**

Auskünfte:
Tourist-Information
Altes Rathaus
8400 Regensburg
Tel. 0941/507-2141

Gaststätte

Zur Brauschänke

Galgenbergstraße 3, Regensburg, Telefon 7 28 83

Bei schönem Wetter sitzen Sie in unserem gemütlichen Biergarten!

Es freut sich auf Ihren Besuch: **Familie Wild**

a. *treasure chest*
b. *past*
c. *buildings*
d. *cathedral*
e. *stone bridge*
f. *city hall*

- List all noun phrases with attributive adjectives in the illustrations. Include prepositions in the phrases.
- How many different adjective endings are used?

Several factors determine the ending of an attributive adjective in German.

1. the presence or absence of a **der-** or **ein**-word (also called the limiting word) before the adjective
2. the ending—or lack of an ending—of the limiting word
3. the case, gender, and number of the noun

In a noun phrase, either the limiting word (**der, ein, unser**) or the adjective itself must have a specific ending signaling the case, gender, and number of the noun. Consider the following examples:

no ending	specific ending	nonspecific ending	noun
1. —	der	schöne	Urlaub
2. —	schöner	—	Urlaub
3. ein	schöner	—	Urlaub
4. —	dieser	schöne	Urlaub

One word in each phrase has a specific ending signaling the case, gender, and number of the noun (**Urlaub**). Often the limiting word fulfills this function (1 and 4). In example 2, there is no limiting word; therefore, the adjective (**schön**) takes on the specific ending **-er,** signaling that **Urlaub** is masculine, singular, and in the nominative case. In example 3, the limiting word **ein** has no ending; therefore, the adjective following it takes on the specific ending **-er.**

In examples 1 and 4, the limiting words **der** and **dieser** signal the case, gender, and number of the noun. Therefore, the adjective following it takes the nonspecific ending **-e.** Nonspecific adjective endings—there are only two—are used when the adjective is preceded by a **der-** or **ein-** word with a specific ending. They will be taken up later in the chapter.

Specific Adjective Endings

You are already familiar with the specific endings an adjective can take. They are, with the exception of the genitive case endings, the same as the endings of **der-** words. Let's briefly review them, using **dies-** as a model:

der-WORD ENDINGS

	SINGULAR			PLURAL
	Masculine	*Neuter*	*Feminine*	
Nom.	dies**er**	dies**es**	dies**e**	dies**e**
Acc.	dies**en**	dies**es**	dies**e**	dies**e**
Dat.	dies**em**	dies**em**	dies**er**	dies**en**
Gen.	dies**es**	dies**es**	dies**er**	dies**er**

An adjective that is not preceded by a limiting word or that is preceded by an **ein-**word without any ending (nominative masculine and nominative and accusative neuter) takes a specific ending to signal the case, gender, and number of the noun.

Übung 5 (page 305). **Suggestion:** Have students work in pairs, taking turns creating short phrases and initiating "small talk." **Follow-up:** Divide class in half. Students in one half jot down nouns, students in the other, adjectives. Call on a student to name a noun, and another to combine it with an attributive adjective.
Note: The adjective *miserabel* drops the *e* before the *l* as an attributive adjective: *miserables Wetter.*

SPECIFIC ADJECTIVE ENDINGS

	SINGULAR			PLURAL
	Masculine	*Neuter*	*Feminine*	
Nom.	(ein) schön**er** Urlaub	(ein) schön**es** Wetter	schön**e** Stadt	schön**e** Ferien
Acc.	schön**en** Urlaub	(ein) schön**es** Wetter	schön**e** Stadt	schön**e** Ferien
Dat.	schön**em** Urlaub	schön**em** Wetter	schön**er** Stadt	schön**en** Ferien
Gen.	schön**en** Urlaubs	schön**en** Wetters	schön**er** Stadt	schön**er** Ferien

Note that the genitive singular masculine and neuter adds **-en** to the adjective.

⊡ Übung 5. Partnerarbeit: „*Small talk*"

BEISPIEL: A: Das Wetter ist schön.
B: Schönes Wetter, nicht wahr?
A: Ein schönes Wetter, wirklich.

das Auto	schön
der Urlaub	schnell
der Stau	bequem
das Bier	gemütlich
der Biergarten	toll
das Bett	langweilig
der Film	miserabel
das Wetter	ausgezeichnet

⊡ Übung 6. Was haben diese Plätze zu bieten?

Ergänzen Sie die Adjektive.

1. Gasthof Zum Bären: Warm_____ Küche von 10.30 bis 24.00 Uhr. Bayerisch_____ Spezialitäten. Selbstgebraut_____ Bier.
2. Adlersberg: Gemütlich_____ Biergarten am Stadtrand.
3. Penthaus-Restaurant Mecklenheide: Wir sorgen für Sie mit gut_____ deutsch_____ Küche und kulinarisch_____ Spezialitäten unseres Hauses.
4. Gasthaus Schneiderwirt: Die Hausmusik spielt für Sie! Rustikal_____ Gästezimmer mit Dusche, WC und Balkon.
5. Dillingen: historisch_____ Stadtbild, viel_____ Sehenswürdigkeiten.
6. Schön_____ Ferien im Berner Oberland.
7. Willkommen im Hotel Luitpold! Ihr „Zuhause" liegt günstig in zentral_____ Lage zur City. Doppel- und Einzelzimmer in familiär_____ Atmosphäre mit Dusche, WC, TV und Mini-Bar!
8. Regensburg: 1400 historisch_____ Gebäude, alt_____ Rathaus, idyllisch_____ Biergärten.

⊡ Übung 7. Frühstücksbestellung

Order a breakfast from the breakfast menu of the Baseler Hof. Add an attributive adjective to each item you order.

BEISPIEL: Kaffee → Ich hätte gern schwarzen Kaffee.

Übung 6. Follow-up: Ask students to create an ad—along the lines of those in the exercise—describing a popular place to go in their city or on campus.

Übung 7. Suggestion: Have students work in small groups. One student acts as recorder. The others order from the menu while the recorder writes down their orders. Call on the recorders to share with the class what their group ordered.

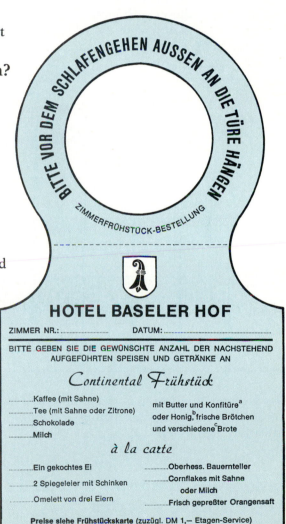

BITTE VOR DEM SCHLAFENGEHEN AUSSEN AN DIE TÜRE HÄNGEN

ZIMMERFRÜHSTÜCK-BESTELLUNG

HOTEL BASELER HOF

ZIMMER NR.:.............. DATUM:..............

BITTE GEBEN SIE DIE GEWÜNSCHTE ANZAHL DER NACHSTEHEND AUFGEFÜHRTEN SPEISEN UND GETRÄNKE AN

Continental Frühstück

.......Kaffee (mit Sahne)
.......Tee (mit Sahne oder Zitrone)
.......Schokolade
.......Milch

mit Butter und Konfitüre[a] oder Honig,[b] frische Brötchen und verschiedene[c] Brote

à la carte

.......Ein gekochtes Ei
.......2 Spiegeleier mit Schinken
.......Omelett von drei Eiern

.......Oberhess. Bauernteller
.......Cornflakes mit Sahne oder Milch
.......Frisch gepreßter Orangensaft

Preise siehe Frühstückskarte (zuzügl. DM 1,— Etagen-Service)
Besondere Wünsche: ....

a. *jam*   b. *honey*   c. *various*   **RSM**

Nonspecific Adjective Endings

An adjective preceded by a limiting word (**der**- or **ein**-word) with a specific ending takes a nonspecific **-e** or **-en**.

	SINGULAR		
	Masculine	*Neuter*	*Feminine*
Nom.	dieser schön**e** Urlaub	dieses schön**e** Wetter	diese schön**e** Reise
Acc.	diesen schön**en** Urlaub	dieses schön**e** Wetter	diese schön**e** Reise
Dat.	diesem schön**en** Urlaub	diesem schön**en** Wetter	dieser schön**en** Reise
Gen.	dieses schön**en** Urlaubs	dieses schön**en** Wetters	dieser schön**en** Reise

	PLURAL
Nom.	diese schön**en** Ferien
Acc.	diese schön**en** Ferien
Dat.	diesen schön**en** Ferien
Gen.	dieser schön**en** Ferien

SUMMARY OF NONSPECIFIC ADJECTIVE ENDINGS

	SINGULAR			PLURAL
	Masculine	*Neuter*	*Feminine*	
Nom.	e	e	e	en
Acc.	en	e	e	en
Dat.	en	en	en	en
Gen.	en	en	en	en

The adjective ends in **-e** in the nominative singular for all genders and in the accusative singular for neuter and feminine. In all other cases, the adjective ends in **-en**.

Indefinite Numerals and *alle*; Adjectives in a Series

The indefinite numerals **einige** (*some*), **mehrere** (*several*), **viele** (*many*), and **wenige** (*few*) are considered adjectives. They often appear in a series with other adjectives. Adjectives in a series all take the same ending.

Indefinite Numerals and *alle*.
Point out: Adjectives in a series means that the adjectives modify the same noun; therefore, they all have the same ending. This may need special emphasis because we have so far stressed the fact that only one word in a noun phrase has a specific ending showing the gender, case, and number of a noun. Use the example in the Instructor's Resource Kit: *Junge, alte, große, kleine, dicke und dünne Göttinger treffen sich in der umgebauten, vergrößerten Sauna.*
Note: Adjectives in a series sometimes do show different endings, as demonstrated by the common pattern em–en: *Bei nassem, kalten Wetter bleiben wir zu Hause.* It is, of course, also correct to say *bei nassem, kaltem Wetter.* You may want to mention several common patterns: e–e in the singular (*die alte Stadt*); e–en in the plural (*die alten Städte*); en–en (*diesen schönen Garten, in diesen schönen Gärten*); and em–en (*in diesem schönen Garten*).

Mehrere kleine Hotels bieten Halbpension an.	*Several small hotels offer a two-meal plan.*
In vielen kleinen Gasthäusern gibt es nur Frühstück.	*In many small inns, they only serve breakfast.*

The specific numeral **alle** (the plural of **jeder**) is considered a **der**- word. Adjectives following it take the nonspecific **-en** ending.

Alle großen Hotels haben ein Schwimmbad.	*All large hotels have a swimming pool.*
In allen großen Städten gibt es ein Verkehrsamt.	*There is a tourist office in all large cities.*

The Adjectives *teuer* and *hoch*

As attribute adjectives, **teuer** and **hoch** each drop a letter: **teu(e)r** drops the **e**; **ho(c)h** drops the **c**.

Das Hotel ist **teuer.** → Das ist ein **teures** Hotel.
Die Preise sind **hoch.** → Das ist ein **hoher** Preis für so ein kleines Zimmer!

Adjectives Referring to Cities

Haben Sie schon einmal im Hotel **Baseler** Hof übernachtet?
Das Hotel liegt in der **Frankfurter** Innenstadt.

Simply add **-er** to the name of the city. This is one of the rare instances where an adjective is capitalized in German. No further changes are made. One country name can also be used in this way: **die Schweiz.**

Essen Sie gern **Schweizer** Käse?

▣ Übung 8. Herzliche Grüße

Familie Peters aus Hannover verbringt ihren Urlaub in einem kleinen Ort in der Schweiz. Helga Peters schreibt einen Kartengruß an Freunde in Hannover. Ergänzen Sie die Adjektive.

Grindelwald, den 3. August

Lieb_____¹ Kerstin, lieb_____² Paul!

Wir sind jetzt schon eine ganz_____³ Woche hier im Bern_____⁴ Oberland.
Die Zeit vergeht wie im Flug.° Die hoh_____⁵ Berge, die frisch_____⁶ Luft°   *vergeht... flies by / air*
und das angenehm_____⁷ Klima gefallen uns sehr. Wir haben einig_____⁸
nett_____⁹ Leute im Hotel kennengelernt. Wir haben auch schon
mehrer_____¹⁰ Ausflüge in die Berge unternommen. Gestern haben wir
eine abenteuerlich_____¹¹,° wunderschön_____¹² Fahrt im Heißluftballon   *adventurous*
gemacht. Bei gut_____¹³ Wetter kann man das ganz_____¹⁴ Land überblicken, einfach toll. Jetzt sitzen Christoph und ich gemütlich auf der
Terrasse unseres Hotels, trinken Wein und genießen das herrlich_____¹⁵
Wetter.

Herzlich_____¹⁶ Grüße
Eure Helga und Christoph

☑ **Übung 9. Wo waren Sie letzten Sommer?**

Was hat Ihnen gefallen? Was hat Ihnen nicht gefallen?

BEISPIEL: Ich war letzten Sommer in Wien. Mir haben die gemüt-
            lichen Wiener Kaffeehäuser gefallen.

das Wetter	viel
die Museen	gemütlich
die Kaffeehäuser	fantastisch
die Preise	alt
die Gebäude (*buildings*)	elegant
die Atmosphäre	romantisch
die Geschäfte	berühmt (*famous*)
die Leute	hoch
der Dom (*cathedral*)	schön

☑ **Übung 10. Eine Reise an den Bodensee**

Machen Sie den Werbetext interessanter durch passende Adjektive aus der Liste.

exklusiv groß herrlich kalt modern schön warm weiß

Vier-Tage-Reise an den _____¹ Bodensee.
Unsere Leistungen: alles im Preis enthalten!

- Hin- und Rückfahrt in _____² Reisebussen
- Unterkunft in _____³ Gasthäusern und Pensionen
- Eine _____⁴ Rundfahrt auf dem Bodensee
- Einladung zu einer _____⁵ Modenschau
- Fahrt mit einem Schiff der _____⁶ Flotte (*fleet*) zur Tropeninsel Mainau
- Sommernachtsfest auf der Insel Mainau mit _____⁷ Büffett, Musik und Tanz.

Die Insel Mainau im Bodensee

Ordinal Numbers

Ordnungszahlen

Cardinal numbers (**eins, zwei, drei,** etc.) have no endings, with the exception of **eins,** which is the same as the indefinite article (**ein**) in front of a noun. Ordinal numbers, on the other hand, take the same endings as attributive adjectives.

Ordinal Numbers. **Suggestion:** To reinforce ordinal numbers, have students give the date at the beginning of each class period for the next couple of weeks. Ask students to make announcements of events, stating the date.
Suggestion: Have students ask their neighbor *Wann hast du Geburtstag?* Call on several students to say when someone has his or her birthday.

der **erste** Mai	*the first of May*
am **ersten** Mai	*on the first of May*
die **zweite** Woche	*the second week*
mein **zweites** Auto	*my second car*
zum **dritten** Mal	*for the third time*
im **dreizehnten** Stock	*on the thirteenth floor*

der (die, das) erste	*the first*	der sechste	*the sixth*
der zweite	*the second*	der siebte	*the seventh*
der dritte	*the third*	der achte	*the eighth*
der vierte	*the fourth*	der neunte	*the ninth*
der fünfte	*the fifth*	der zehnte	*the tenth*

Up to nineteen, the ordinal numbers end in **-te**. From twenty on, they end in **-ste**.

Heute ist der 20. (zwanzigste) November.
Am 25. (fünfundzwanzigsten) Juli waren wir in der Schweiz.

Note that in German a period follows ordinal numbers written as digits.

▣ **Übung 11.** **Hotelreservierungen**

Diese Leute brauchen eine Unterkunft. Geben Sie
das Datum an.

> BEISPIEL: Karin Merck braucht eine Unterkunft für den
> fünften Juni.

NAME	WANN
Karin Merck	5. Juni
Klaus Stephan	1. Mai
Familie Stratmann (2 Kinder)	25. August
Franz Müller	21. Februar
Susanne und Hans Niemöller	17. April

▣ **Übung 12.** **Partnerarbeit**

Sie sind zu Besuch in Berlin und schauen sich im Kaufhaus des Westens (KaDeWe) um. Wo kann man was
finden? (die Etage = der Stock)

> BEISPIEL: A: Wo gibt es Autoradios?
> B: Autoradios gibt es in der vierten Etage.
> *oder:* Die gibt es im vierten Stock.

LESEN IM KONTEXT ▣▣▣▣▣▣

In diesem Teil lesen Sie über deutsche Urlaubsziele und
über Kiel, eine Stadt in Norddeutschland. In Kiel spielt
auch die Geschichte, „Fahrkarte bitte," die Sie lesen werden.

Vor dem Lesen

▣ **Aktivität 1.** **Wohin im Urlaub?**

Schauen Sie sich das Schaubild und die Landkarte von Europa an. Das
Schaubild zeigt die Länder, wo die Deutschen ihren Urlaub verbringen.
Beschreiben Sie die geographische Lage der Länder.

> BEISPIEL: Portugal liegt westlich von Spanien.

KaDeWe Etagenplan

Erdgeschoß	= Ⓔ
1. Etage	= ①
2. Etage	= ②
3. Etage	= ③
4. Etage	= ④
5. Etage	= ⑤
6. Etage	= ⑥

A
Absatzbar Mister Minit	③
Alles für das Bad	④
Alles für das Kind	①
Ann Christine-Shop	①
Antiquitäten-Shop	⑤
Auslegeware	⑤
Autozubehör	④
Autoradios	④

B
Babybekleidung	①
Babywickeltisch	②
Bade- und Strandmoden	①
Bank (BHI)	①
Beleuchtungsabteilung	⑤
Berlinsouvenirs	①
Berufsbekleidung	①
Bettenabteilung	⑤
Bettwäsche	⑤
Bilder-Automat	③ Ⓔ
Bilder, Bilderrahmen	④
Bilderdienst	③
Bodenbeläge	⑤
Briefmarken- automat	① ③
Bücher	③
Bürotechnik	③

C
Café	Ⓔ
Campingartikel	①
CD-Platten	③
Charles Jourdan	Ⓔ
Christ (Uhren/Schmuck)	Ⓔ
Computer	③
Confiserie	Ⓔ

D
Damenbademoden	①
Damenhüte	②
Damenkonfektion	②
Damenlederbekleidung	②
Damenstrümpfe	Ⓔ
Damenwäsche	①
Davidoff	Ⓔ
Devisenschalter (BHI)	①

E
Echte Teppiche	⑤
Elektrogroß- und -kleingeräte	⑤
Erste Hilfe	②
Escada-Moden	Ⓔ
Esprit	②

F
Fahrräder	Ⓔ
Feinschmecker-Etage	⑥
Feinschmecker-Service	⑥
Fernseher	③
Fernsprecher	① ③ ⑤ ⑥
Fogal - Strümpfe	Ⓔ
Fotoabteilung	③
Fotokopierer	③
Frisiersalon	①
Frottierwaren	①
Fundbüro	①

G
Garderobe	②
Gardinen	⑤
Gardinenzubehör	⑤
Garne	①
Gartencenter	④
Geldautomat EC	②
Geschenkartikel	④
Glasabteilung	④

H
Handarbeiten	①
Handschuhe	Ⓔ
Haushaltwaren	④
Heimtextilien	⑤
Heimtierbedarf	④
Herrenartikel	Ⓔ
Herrenbademoden	①
Herrenhüte	Ⓔ
Herrenkonfektion	②

RSM

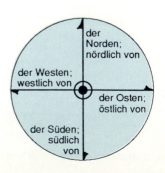
der Norden; nördlich von / der Westen; westlich von / der Osten; östlich von / der Süden; südlich von

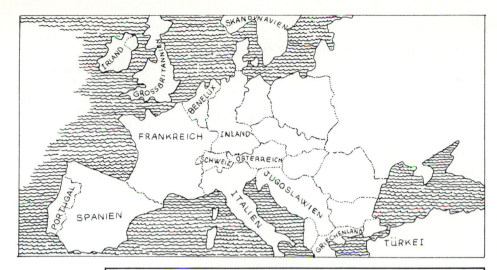

Beliebteste Urlaubsziele der Bundesdeutschen laut Globus Schaubild

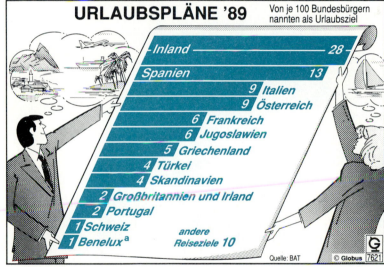

a. Benelux = Belgien, die Niederlande, Luxemburg

☑ **Aktivität 2. Was ist „in"?**

Das Schaubild *Urlaubspläne 89* enthält die Antwort. Ergänzen Sie folgenden Text.

Wohin geht die nächste Urlaubsreise? Diese Frage stellten Freizeitforscher in der Bundesrepublik Deutschland. Das Ergebnis: Der Urlaub im _____[1] (Inland, Ausland) bleibt „in". Nur etwa jeder vierte Deutsche sucht in Ferienorten zwischen Nordsee und Alpen Erholung. Drei Viertel (3/4) der Befragten reisen ins Ausland, vor allem in die Länder um _____[2] (die Nordsee, das Mittelmeer). Reiseziel Nummer eins unter der südlichen Sonne ist weiterhin _____[3] (Spanien, Italien). Der Norden lockt nur wenige: _____[4] (vier Prozent, fünf Prozent) der Befragten haben eine Reise in skandinavische Länder geplant.

Auf den ersten Blick 1

1. Überfliegen Sie den Text, und suchen Sie Wörter, die mit englischen Wörtern verwandt sind.

   BEISPIEL: Schiff = *ship*

2. Suchen Sie zusammengesetzte Wörter im Text. Was bedeuten sie auf englisch?

   BEISPIEL: die Hauptstadt: das Haupt = *head*, die Stadt = *city*; Hauptstadt = *capital*

Kiel

In Kiel endet der 53 km lange Nord-Ostsee Kanal, die Schiffsautobahn zwischen der Nord- und Ostsee.

Schon der Name klingt wie° ein Teil vom Schiff, und tatsächlich sind Schiffe für diese Stadt ein Symbol. Kiel, die Hauptstadt des Landes Schleswig-Holstein im nördlichsten Zipfel° der Bundesrepublik, lebt von und mit großen und kleinen „Pötten".° Die riesigen Kräne der Docks und Werftanlagen° am Hafen zeichnen die Skyline der Stadt. Hier endet der Nord-Ostsee-Kanal, die Schiffs-Autobahn zwischen den großen Meeren. Und so ist der Schiffbau° auch der wichtigste Industriezweig am „Tor des Nordens". Aber das ist der Alltag. Ein Höhepunkt im Leben der Stadt ist in jedem Sommer die „Kieler Woche", eines der attraktivsten internationalen Segelereignisse. Die Kieler Förde, eine enge Ostsee-Bucht° von etwa 15 Kilometern Länge, ist ein ideales Revier° für Segelsportler. Schon zweimal fanden hier die olympischen Wettbewerbe statt.

klingt... *sounds like*

tip
boats (lit. *pots*) / *shipyards*

shipbuilding

bay
area

Jugendscala, Sept. 1988

Zum Text 1

1. Was steht im Text?

	JA	NEIN	INFORMATION
• wo Kiel liegt	✓	____	*im Norden*
• wie viele Einwohner Kiel hat	____	____	_____
• was die Hauptindustrie in Kiel ist	____	____	_____
• wie eine bekannte Wasserstraße heißt	____	____	_____
• wie lang die Kieler Förde ist	____	____	_____
• welcher Sport für Kiel wichtig ist	____	____	_____

2. Was gehört zusammen?

1. ____ Der Nord-Ostsee-Kanal   a. ist die Hauptstadt von Schleswig-Holstein.
2. ____ Die „Kieler Woche"   b. ist eine enge Ostsee-Bucht.
3. ____ Die Kieler Förde   c. ist eine Schiffs-Autobahn.
4. ____ Kiel   d. ist ein internationales Segelereignis.

Auf den ersten Blick 2

1. Assoziationen: Was assoziieren Sie mit den Worten „Fahrkarte bitte"? Machen Sie eine Liste.

   BEISPIEL: der Bahnhof

Auf den ersten Blick 2 # 1. Assoziationen. **Suggestion:** Make this a whole-class project, recording students' responses on the board.

2. **Wer, was, wo, wann**? When you read, read with a goal in mind. Think of questions you want the text to answer. Two helpful questions are:

   Wer hat **was wann** und **wo** gemacht?
   Wie ist es passiert?

   To look for the answers to **wer, wo,** and **wann** questions, look for the following clues:

   FRAGE: ANTWORT:

   wer   Personennamen
   wo   Länder- und Städtenamen;
         Präpositionen wie: **an, in, vor, bei**
   wann   Jahr, Datum, Wochentage, Uhrzeiten;
          Adverbien wie: **morgen, vor einem Jahr**

   Now read the first ten lines of the following story by Helga M. Novak and answer the questions.

   a. Wer sind die Hauptfiguren?
   b. Wo findet die Geschichte statt? („Kiel" genügt nicht.)
   c. Wann findet die Geschichte statt?

   Add several questions of your own that you expect or want the story „Fahrkarte bitte" to answer. (After you finish reading the story, come back to these questions to see whether you can answer them.)

Fahrkarte bitte

HELGA M. NOVAK

Kiel sieht neu aus. Es ist dunkel.° Ich gehe zum Hafen. Mein Schiff ist   *dark*
nicht da. Es fährt morgen. Es kommt morgen vormittag an und fährt um
dreizehn Uhr wieder ab. Ich sehe ein Hotel. Im Eingang steht ein junger
Mann. Er trägt einen weinroten Rollkragenpullover.°   *turtleneck sweater*

Ich sage, haben Sie ein Einzelzimmer?

Er sagt, ja.

Ich sage, ich habe nur eine Handtasche bei mir, mein ganzes Gepäck
ist auf dem Bahnhof in Schließfächern.°   *lockers*

Er sagt, Zimmer einundvierzig. Wollen Sie gleich bezahlen? Ich sage,
ach nein, ich bezahle morgen.

Ich schlafe gut. Ich wache auf. Es regnet in Strömen.° Ich gehe hinunter.   *Es... It's pouring*
Der junge Mann hat eine geschwollene Lippe.

Ich sage, darf ich mal telefonieren?

Er sagt, naja.

Ich rufe an.

Ich sage, du, ja, hier bin ich, heute noch, um eins, ja, ich komme gleich,
doch ich muß, ich habe kein Geld, mein Hotel, ach fein, ich gebe es dir
zurück, sofort, schön.

Der junge Mann steht neben mir. Er hat zugehört.°   *listened*

Ich sage, jetzt hole ich Geld. Dann bezahle ich.

Er sagt, zuerst bezahlen.

Ich sage, ich habe kein Geld, meine Freundin.

Er sagt, das kann ich mir nicht leisten.°   *kann... I can't afford it*

Ich sage, aber ich muß nachher weiter.

Er sagt, da könnte ja jeder kommen.°   *da... anyone could say that*

Ich sage, meine Freundin kann nicht aus dem Geschäft weg.

Er lacht.

Ich sage, ich bin gleich wieder da.

Er sagt, so sehen Sie aus.°   *idiom: I bet you are (sarcastic)*

Ich sage, lassen Sie mich doch gehen. Was haben Sie denn von mir?

Er sagt, ich will Sie ja gar nicht.

Ich sage, manch einer wäre froh.°   *manch... many a man would be glad*

Er sagt, den zeigen° Sie mir mal.   *show*

Ich sage, Sie kennen mich noch nicht.

Er sagt, abwarten und Tee trinken.°   *idiom: abwarten... let's wait and see*

Es kommen neue Gäste.

Er sagt, gehen Sie solange° in die Gaststube.   *for the time being*

Er kommt nach.

Ich sage, mein Schiff geht um eins.

Er sagt, zeigen Sie mir bitte Ihre Fahrkarte.

Er verschließt° sie in einer Kassette.°   *locks / box*

Ich sitze in der Gaststube und schreibe einen Brief.

Liebe Charlotte, seit einer Woche bin ich im „Weißen Ahornblatt" Servererin. Nähe Hafen. Wenn Du hier vorbeikommst, sieh doch zu mir herein. Sonst geht es mir glänzend. Deine Maria.

„PALISADEN" Erzählungen, 1980

Zum Text 2

1. Is the narrative **ich** a man or a woman? What evidence do you have to prove your point?
2. Look for words and phrases that provide further information about the main characters. How much can you infer from some details, for instance, the mention of the young man having a **geschwollene Lippe**?
3. At what point does the reader learn about a major dilemma facing the characters? How would you act under such circumstances? What role does the **Fahrkarte** play?
4. The fictitious narrator ends by writing a letter to a friend. What does the letter reveal about the narrator? Is the friend the same person she calls up in the story? What evidence do you have?
5. Refer to the questions you were asked to create before reading the story: which questions did the story answer or not answer? What questions do you have about the story that the text does not answer?

Nach dem Lesen

▣ Aktivität 1. Ein Theaterstück

Führen Sie den Dialog zwischen den beiden Hauptfiguren in „Fahrkarte bitte" als Theaterstück in der Klasse auf.

▣ Aktivität 2. Wie könnte die Geschichte weitergehen?

Arbeiten Sie in kleinen Gruppen. Ein Monat ist vergangen. Was ist aus der Frau geworden? Schreiben Sie gemeinsam eine Fortsetzung (*continuation*) der Geschichte (7 bis 10 Sätze).

▣ Aktivität 3. Das war eine tolle Reise!

Bringen Sie ein Foto von einer tollen Reise, die Sie gemacht haben. Zeigen Sie Ihrer Partnerin oder Ihrem Partner das Foto, und erzählen Sie, was Sie erlebt haben. Wenn Sie keine tolle Reise gemacht haben, erfinden Sie eine Geschichte—wie der Baron von Münchhausen!

Zum Text 2.   Note: Discussion of these items will be primarily in English; however, encourage German whenever possible.
Suggestion: Explore with students what goes on between the two characters in the story and look for evidence showing distinct changes in their attitude toward each other. Some things are only clear by reading between the lines; others are ambiguous. Have students point out some ambiguities. Ask students how they would act in a similar situation. Students might be puzzled by this story, because there seems to be so little going on, leading to speculation that cannot be supported by the text. Question #5 provides an opportunity to explore any unease and to see if it can be resolved.

Aktivität 3.   Suggestion: Encourage students, when they listen to each other's stories, to interject or ask for clarification with expressions such as *Moment mal! Wie war das? Wie bitte? Na, so was! Das verstehe ich nicht. Mensch!*

WORTSCHATZ

Substantive

Im Hotel	**At the hotel**
das Anmeldeformular (-e)	registration form
das Doppelzimmer (-)	double room
die Dusche (-n)	shower
die Etage (-n)	floor
das Einzelzimmer (-)	single room
das Erdgeschoß (-sse)	ground floor
die Pension (-en)	bed-and-breakfast inn
die Halbpension	two meals per day included
die Vollpension	three meals per day included
der Stock	floor
im ersten Stock	on the second floor
die Übernachtung (-en)	overnight stay
die Unterkunft (¨e)	accommodations

Unterwegs	**On the road**
die Ampel (-n)	traffic light
das Benzin	gasoline
die Einbahnstraße (-n)	one-way street
das Fremdenverkehrsamt (¨er)	tourist information center
die Gegend (-en)	area, region
die Geschwindigkeit (-en)	speed
die Höchstgeschwindigkeit	maximum speed, speed limit
der Hafen (¨)	harbor
die Haltestelle (-n)	stop (bus or streetcar)
der Hauptbahnhof (¨e)	main railroad station
die Innenstadt (¨e)	center of town
die Kreuzung (-en)	intersection
die Landschaft (-en)	scenery
die Nähe	vicinity
in der Nähe	nearby, in the vicinity
der Norden	north
nördlich von	to the north of
der Osten	east
östlich von	to the east of
die Richtung (-en)	direction
in Richtung	in the direction of
die Straßenbahn (-en)	streetcar
der Süden	south
südlich von	to the south of

die Tankstelle (-n)	gas station
die U-Bahn (-en)	subway
der Verkehr	traffic
das Verkehrszeichen (-)	traffic sign
der Westen	west
westlich von	to the west of
der Zoll	customs

Andere Substantive	
der Anfang (¨e)	beginning
die Auskunft (¨e)	information
der Dom (-e)	cathedral
das Ende (-n)	end
das Fest (-e)	party, feast
das Gebäude (-)	building
das Herz (-ens, -en)	heart
die Insel (-n)	island
die Mitte	the middle
das Rathaus (¨er)	city hall
die Tasche (-n)	bag

Verben

abbiegen (biegt ab), bog ab, ist abgebogen	to make a turn
nach rechts abbiegen	to make a righthand turn
ausfüllen (füllt aus)	to fill out
besichtigen	to view, visit
buchen	to book a trip, to make a reservation
tanken	to get gas
überqueren	to cross a street
verpassen	to miss
den Zug verpassen	to miss the train
vorbereiten (bereitet vor)	to prepare
wechseln	to change

Adjektive und Adverbien

berühmt	famous
erlaubt	permitted
ganz	very
ganz in der Nähe von	very close to
geradeaus	straight ahead
gleich da drüben	right over there
links	left, to the left

mehrere	several	**außerhalb**	outside of
rechts	right, to the right	**entlang** (+ *acc.*)	along
spätestens	at the latest	**die Straße entlang**	along this street
viele	many	**Entschuldigung**	pardon me
vernünftig	reasonable	**geht in Ordnung**	that's all right; sure
vorsichtig	cautious, careful	**Schöne Ferien!**	Have a nice vacation!
wenige	a few, few	**Schönen Urlaub!**	Have a nice vacation!
zahlreich	numerous	**im Preis enthalten**	included in the price
		trotz	in spite of
		während	during
## Sonstiges		**wegen**	because of
		Die Zeit vergeht wie im Flug.	Time flies by.
auf Wiederhören	good-bye (only on the phone)		

DAS LIEBE GELD

Lernziele *This chapter focuses on money, budgets, income, and expenditures. You will learn about currencies and some banking practices in German-speaking countries, and you will compare the budgets of several German students with your own. You will learn to express wishes and requests politely, offer suggestions, and make hypothetical statements about what might be or might have been.*

▣ Alles klar?

- Tolle Haare für wenig „Mäuse"... Was ist bei diesem Frisör los?
- Was ist mit diesem Geldautomaten los? Warum springt eine Maus heraus?
- Warum ist der Geldautomat für die Kunden der Sparkasse praktisch?
- „Mäuse" ist ein Wort der Umgangssprache für _____ .

RSM

Allee Frisör

Tolle Haare für wenig "Mäuse". . .

Dauerwellen mit Komplett-Service
- Haarschnitt
- Waschen u. legen oder fönen
- Haar-Kur
- Dauerwelle
- Festiger ● Haarfestiger zum **Komplett-Preis**

von nur **39.99**

Damit unsere Kunden
sonntags wie alltags
von morgens bis abends
an ihre Mäuse kommen

NIXDORF
COMPUTER

Geldautomat
Weender Str. 69 von 7–22 Uhr

Geldautomat
Zentralmensa (GWZ)
während der Öffnungszeiten des Hauses

Städtische Sparkasse zu Göttingen $

RSM

WÖRTER IM KONTEXT

Monatliche Ausgaben

▣ Aktivität 1. Die Lage der Studenten

Die Information für Ihre Antworten finden Sie im Globus Schaubild auf
Seite 320.

1. Wieviel Geld brauchen deutsche Studenten durchschnittlich pro
   Monat?
2. Wofür geben deutsche Studenten das meiste Geld aus?
3. Wofür geben sie das wenigste Geld aus?
4. Wofür geben deutsche Studenten—im Vergleich zu amerikanischen
   Studenten—scheinbar überhaupt kein Geld aus?
5. Wo wohnen die meisten deutschen Studenten?
6. Wo wohnen die wenigsten Studenten?

Aktivität 1. Suggestion: Have students first scan the chart on page 320, identifying unfamiliar words and seeking clarification from you or from other students. Then have them work in pairs, asking each other questions and responding. Check information by calling on several students for responses.
Point out: German students pay no tuition, because all universities are state institutions. At a few private professional schools (notably business schools), tuition can be quite steep.

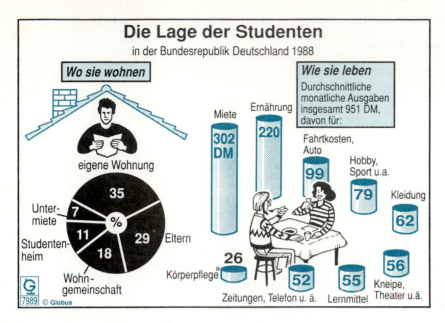

RSM

Die Lage der Studenten
in der Bundesrepublik Deutschland 1988

Wo sie wohnen

eigene Wohnung

Unter-
miete 7

Studenten-
heim 11

18

35

29 Eltern

%

Wohn-
gemeinschaft

© Globus 7989

Wie sie leben
Durchschnittliche monatliche Ausgaben insgesamt 951 DM, davon für:

Miete **302 DM**

Ernährung **220**

Fahrtkosten, Auto **99**

Hobby, Sport u.ä. **79**

Kleidung **62**

Körperpflege^a **26**

Zeitungen, Telefon u. ä. **52**

Lernmittel **55**

Kneipe, Theater u.ä. **56**

a. *toiletries*

Neue Wörter

die Ausgabe *expenditure*
der Durchschnitt *average*
  im Durchschnitt *on average*
  im Schnitt *on average*
  durchschnittlich *average*

die Ernährung *food*
die Untermiete *sublet*
  in/zur Untermiete wohnen *to rent a room*
ausgeben (gibt aus) *to spend*

Aktivität 2. Mein monatliches Budget

Notieren Sie: Wofür geben Sie monatlich Geld aus, und ungefähr wieviel im Durchschnitt? Wofür geben Sie das meiste Geld aus? Und das wenigste? Wofür geben Sie nur ab und zu oder gar kein Geld aus?

	$	
Miete	_____	
Nebenkosten	_____	(Strom, Heizung, Telefon)
Auto	_____	(Benzin, Reparaturen, Versicherung)
Fahrtkosten	_____	(öffentliche Verkehrsmittel, z.B. Bus; Fahrten nach Hause)
Ernährung	_____	(Essen und Trinken, auch Mensa, Restaurants)
Lernmittel	_____	(Bücher, Hefte, Bleistifte, Kugelschreiber, Papier, Sonstiges)
Freizeit	_____	(Kino, Theater, Partys)
Sparen	_____	
Sonstiges	_____	
Insgesamt:	_____	

Berichten Sie jetzt.

> Ich gebe das meiste Geld für _____ aus.
> Das wenigste Geld gebe ich für _____ aus.
> Ich gebe nur ab und zu oder gar kein Geld für _____ aus.

Neue Wörter

der Bleistift *pencil*
das Heft *notebook*
die Heizung *heat*
die Nebenkosten *additional costs*

der Strom *electricity*
die Versicherung *insurance*

sparen *to save*

Sprachnotiz

The particle **gar** makes a negation very emphatic. Even more emphatic is the use of the adverb **überhaupt** with negations. Both **gar** and **überhaupt** immediately precede the negation.

Ich habe **gar** kein Geld.	*I have no money at all.*
Ich gebe **überhaupt** nichts für Kleidung aus.	*I spend absolutely nothing on clothing.*

▣ Aktivität 3. Interaktion

Fragen Sie jemanden in Ihrer Klasse nach seinen oder ihren monatlichen Ausgaben, und woher er oder sie Geld bekommt. Berichten Sie kurz darüber.

BEISPIEL:

A:

Wofür gibst du Geld aus? ⟶
Woher bekommst du Geld?

B:

Ich bezahle $300 für Miete, usw.
Meine Eltern schicken mir Geld, und ich arbeite nebenbei (*on the side*).

▫▫▫▫ Kulturnotiz

BAFöG stands for **Bundesausbildungsförderungsgesetz!** This is the financial aid (loan) program sponsored by the government of the Federal Republic of Germany to assist university students with expenses. Tuition is free at universities, except for nominal fees (**Studiengebühren**).

▣ **Aktivität 4.** **Drei Heidelberger Studenten und ihre monatlichen Budgets**

Vergleichen Sie die Ausgaben, und beantworten Sie die Fragen.

	MARION	WOLFGANG	CLAUDIA	
Studienfach	Übersetzer°/ Dolmetscher°	Medizin	Romanistik/Politik	*translator* *interpreter*
Studiengebühren	keine	keine	keine	
Unterhalt	Eltern	BAFöG	Eltern	
Miete	200 DM (1 Zi, Studentenwohnheim)	300 DM (1 Zi, Küche, Bad außerhalb)	500 DM (1 Zi, Küche, Bad)	
Verkehrsmittel	keine (alles mit dem Fahrrad erreichbar)	40 DM	30 DM	
Lebensmittel und Mensa	260 DM	350 DM	280 DM	
Bücher/Arbeitsmittel	20 DM	100 DM	50 DM	
Telefon	10 DM	60 DM (eigenes Telefon)	70 DM (eigenes Telefon)	
Freizeit	80 DM	100 DM	100 DM	
Fahrt nach Hause	40 DM (Mitfahrgelegenheit) 68 DM (mit der Bahn)	—	20 DM	
Sonstiges	40 DM	30 DM	40 DM	

1. Wieviel Geld gibt jeder Student insgesamt monatlich aus?
2. Wofür geben sie das meiste Geld aus?
3. Wer bezahlt die höchste Miete? Wo ist die Miete billiger?
4. Warum bezahlt Marion weniger als die zwei anderen für Telefon?
5. Wer hat die höchsten Kosten für Bücher und Arbeitsmittel?
6. Was ist—außer (*besides*) Miete—günstig, wenn man im Studentenwohnheim wohnt?
7. Wer unterstützt die drei Studenten finanziell?
8. Warum hat Marion keine Ausgaben für Verkehrsmittel?

Aktivität 4. Suggestion: Have students work in pairs. Give them several minutes to scan the information and clarify any unfamiliar vocabulary for them. Have them take turns asking each other questions and responding. Check answers by having individual pairs respond to at least two or three questions each.

□ **Aktivität 5.** **Vorteile und Nachteile**

Kürzlich ist Marion von Heidelberg nach München umgezogen, wo sie jetzt an einer Fachakademie studiert. Der Vorteil: Sie findet die Ausbildung in München besser als in Heidelberg. Aber München bringt auch Nachteile mit sich. Vergleichen Sie Marions monatliche Ausgaben in München mit ihren Ausgaben in Heidelberg.

BEISPIEL: In Heidelberg hatte sie keine Studiengebühren, aber in München muß sie jeden Monat circa 50 Mark für Studiengebühren ausgeben.

Aktivität 5. **Note:** This exercise is linked with the previous one. **Suggestion:** Have students first go over the *Neue Wörter*. Then have them work in pairs, asking each other how much Marion spends in Munich for the various items listed and what she spent in Heidelberg. They should jot down the amounts under the headings *München* and *Heidelberg*. They can then compare her expenditures. **Suggestion:** With the whole group, have students choose two or three items to compare. Call on individuals to share their findings.

	MARIONS MONATLICHE AUSGABEN IN MÜNCHEN
Studiengebühren	ca. 50 DM
Miete	300 DM (1 Zi, Küche, Bad; außerhalb bei Bekannten°)
U-Bahn-Karte	40 DM
Sonstige Kosten für Verkehrsmittel	10 DM
Lebensmittel	280 DM
Bücher/Arbeitsmittel	20 DM
Telefon	10 DM (kein eigenes Telefon)
Freizeit	100 DM (Kino, Theater, Kaffee trinken, Essen gehen)
Fahrt nach Hause	20 DM (Mitfahrgelegenheit) 54 DM (mit der Bahn)
Sonstiges	40 DM (Kosmetikartikel, Wasch- und Putzmittel,° Reinigung, Post)

°*acquaintances*

Wasch- ... *laundry and cleaning materials*

Neue Wörter

die Ausbildung *training, education*

die Fachakademie *professional school (e.g. for interpreting or translation)*

der Nachteil *disadvantage*

die Reinigung *dry cleaning*

die Studiengebühren *study fees (e.g. tuition)*

der Unterhalt *support*

der Vorteil *advantage*

außerhalb *short for: outside of the city*

erreichbar mit *reachable, can be reached by*

kürzlich *recently*

umziehen (ist umgezogen) *to move*

Aktivität 6. Hören Sie zu.

Vier Studenten sprechen über ihre Einnahmen, wo sie wohnen und über ihre monatlichen Ausgaben für Miete. Kreuzen Sie die passende Spalte an. Was gibt jeder Student für Miete aus?

Aktivität 6. **Suggestion:** Students record their responses after they have heard each person's comments. **Follow-up:** Using the information students have marked in the grid, have them make several connecting statements about each of the four speakers in order to approach paragraph-length narration.

	STEFANIE	GERT	SUSANNE	MARTIN
Einnahmen von:				
Job während des Semesters			√	√
Job während der Semesterferien	√	√		√
Eltern			√	√
Stipendium/BAFöG		√		
Ausgaben für: *Zimmer (privat)*		300 DM		
Studentenwohnheim	200 DM			
eigene Wohnung				400 DM
Wohngemeinschaft			350 DM	

Dialog. **Andrea hat Geldsorgen.°**

money worries

ANDREA: Sag mal, könntest du mir einen Gefallen tun?
STEFAN: Was denn?
ANDREA: Würdest du mir bis Ende der Woche 50 Mark leihen? Ich bin total pleite.
STEFAN: Fünfzig Mark? Das ist viel Geld.
ANDREA: Ich mußte 150 Mark für Bücher ausgeben. Und jetzt habe ich keinen Pfennig mehr übrig. Ich warte auf einen Scheck von meinen Eltern.
STEFAN: Hm, ich würde es dir gern leihen. Aber 50 Mark habe ich selber nicht mehr. Ich kann dir höchstens 20 Mark leihen.
ANDREA: Ich zahle es dir bis Ende des Monats bestimmt zurück.
STEFAN: Eben hast du gesagt, bis Ende der Woche.
ANDREA: Ja, ja. Der Scheck von meinen Eltern kann jeden Tag kommen.
STEFAN: Na gut. Hier ist ein Zwanziger.
ANDREA: Vielen Dank.

Point out: *könntest du...* and *würdest du...* represent new verb forms that indicate a different mode of speaking: the subjunctive, used to express politeness and tentativeness, in the context of this dialogue. This generally presents no difficulties to students if you point out that the two expressions parallel *could* and *would*, which can also express politeness and tentativeness. Without going into further detail about the subjunctive, you can use this opportunity to preview the concept of the subjunctive mode in a simple and nonthreatening way.

Dialog. Suggestion: First have students go over the *Neue Wörter*. With their books closed, have them listen to the dialogue once. Ask individuals to supply one fact from the dialogue. Encourage students to summarize as much as they can; then have them complete *Aktivität 7* in pairs. Students read the statements aloud to one another and supply the missing information.

> ### Sprachnotiz
>
> The verb forms **Könntest du...?** (*Could you?*) and **Würdest du...?** (*Would you?*) are subjunctive forms that express a tentative attitude on the part of the speaker who can't be sure of the other person's response.

Neue Wörter

eben *just now*
pleite *broke*
selber *self (emphatic)*
übrig *left over*

einen Gefallen tun *to do a favor*
leihen *to lend; borrow*
zurückzahlen *to pay back*

◻ Aktivität 7. Andreas Dilemma

Ergänzen Sie die Sätze durch Informationen aus dem Gespräch zwischen Stefan und Andrea.

Andrea hat _____[1] mehr; sie ist total _____[2]. Sie möchte sich von Stefan _____[3]. Sie hat nämlich ihr ganzes Geld für _____[4]. Deshalb hat sie jetzt nichts mehr für Essen und Trinken _____[5]. Stefan kann ihr aber _____[6]. Andrea hofft, daß sie Stefan das Geld bis _____[7] zurückzahlen kann. Sie wartet auf _____[8].

◻ **Aktivität 8.** **Rollenspiel**

Sie sind pleite und müssen sich etwas Geld leihen.

A	B

A

Könntest du mir _____?
Ich bin nämlich _____.

B

⟶ Soviel? Wofür denn?

Für _____. Ich muß _____
kaufen.

Bis wann kannst du es
mir _____?

Ich kann es dir _____
zurückzahlen.
(in _____ Tagen)
(bis Ende der Woche)
(bis Ende des Monats)

Na gut, hier hast du _____.
Ich habe aber höchstens _____.
Tut mir leid, _____.

Es geht um Geld.°

Die Währungseinheiten in den deutschsprachigen Ländern:

Es... It's a question of money.

Deutschland	eine Mark	=	100 Pfennige
Schweiz	ein Franken	=	100 Rappen
Österreich	ein Schilling	=	100 Groschen

*Geldscheine und Münzen
aus der Schweiz, Österreich
und Deutschland*

◻◻◻◻ *Kulturnotiz*

Die Post hat in deutschsprachigen Ländern verschiedene Funktionen. Natürlich kann man dort Briefmarken (*stamps*) kaufen, Pakete aufgeben, Geldanweisungen (*money orders*) kaufen und telefonieren. Die Post hat außerdem in allen deutschsprachigen Ländern ein Banksystem für Girokonten und Sparkonten.

PostGiro. Das clevere Konto.

Eine kluge Entscheidung.

PostGiro: Start frei bei jedem Postamt.

Neue Wörter

das Bargeld *cash*
das Konto *account*
  das Girokonto *checking account*
  das Sparkonto *savings account*
die Sparkasse *savings bank*

bar zahlen *to pay cash*

Ihr erstes Konto – mit der Erfahrung[a] der Deutschen Bank.

RSM

a. *experience*

◻ **Aktivität 9.** Interaktion

Interviewen Sie einen Partner oder eine Partnerin in der Klasse. Machen Sie sich Notizen und berichten Sie. Sie möchten wissen:

- was für ein Konto er oder sie hat (ein Girokonto, ein Sparkonto, gar kein Konto)
- ob er oder sie Kreditkarten hat. Warum oder warum nicht?
- wie er oder sie gewöhnlich Rechnungen bezahlt. (bar, mit Kreditkarte, mit Schecks vom Girokonto)

Aktivität 9. Suggestion: Preview the *Neue Wörter* and explain about the currency and the role of the postal service. Use the picture showing German, Austrian, and Swiss currencies to demonstrate the various denominations; better yet, bring in some actual money from German-speaking countries. After talking about the currencies of these countries, students will interview a partner and share their findings with the rest of the class.

Neue Wörter

die Münze *coin*
der Schein *paper money*
  der Fünfzigmarkschein *fifty-mark bill*
  der Zwanziger *twenty-mark bill*
die Währung *currency*
der Wechselkurs *exchange rate*

fallen, ist gefallen *to fall, decline*
steigen, ist gestiegen *to climb, rise*
umtauschen (tauscht um) *to exchange*
unterschreiben *to sign*

Aktivität 10. Hören Sie zu. An der Bank beim Geldumtausch°

money exchange

Ein Tourist, unterwegs in einer deutschen Stadt, möchte an einer Bank Reiseschecks in deutsches Geld umtauschen.

Ist das richtig oder falsch? Korrigieren Sie falsche Aussagen.

1. Der Tourist möchte $40 in deutsches Geld umtauschen.   R
2. Der Tourist bekommt mehr deutsches Geld, als er gedacht hatte, weil der Dollar gestiegen ist.   R
3. Der Wechselkurs für den Dollar steht an diesem Tag auf 3 Mark.   F: 2 Mark
4. Der Kunde muß seinen internationalen Führerschein vorzeigen.   F: Reisepaß
5. Der Bankangestellte gibt dem Kunden 76,00 Mark.   R
6. Der Kunde möchte keine Münzen, sondern nur Geldscheine.   F: beides

Aktivität 10. Suggestion: Have students go over the *Neue Wörter* and the picture of the bank currency exchange statement; also have them scan the true/false statements before listening to the exchange at a bank counter. Have students answer *das stimmt* or *das stimmt nicht* to the statements.

DRESDNER BANK AG

340/40/06/B REISESCHALTER   BONN, 22.06.89

A N K A U F   SORTEN

WAEHRUNG	WAEHRUNGSBETRAG	KURS	DM-GEGENWERT	GEBUEHR	DM-GESAMTBETRAG	LFNR
400	40,00	1,90	76,00	0,00	76,00	0146
USD VEREIN.STAATEN						

AUSZAHLUNG DM   76,00

ONS 20 (1–2) 87.09.

Bitte Rückseite beachten! p. t. o.! tourner s.v.p.! Favor fijarse al dorso!

Note: Point out that the exchange rate fluctuates on a daily basis. Look up the current exchange rate and tell students, for example, *Der Dollar steht heute (stand gestern) auf DM 1,72.* It is generally more advantageous to exchange traveler's checks rather than cash, but there may be a hefty fee for exchanging checks.

RSM

Aktivität 11. Wechselkurse

Verfolgen Sie eine Woche lang die Wechselkurse für Deutschland, Österreich und die Schweiz in der Zeitung. Ist der Dollar gestiegen oder gefallen in dieser Zeit? Berichten Sie kurz.

Aktivität 11. Note: This activity can be facilitated by assigning different individuals the task of reporting the exchange rate of these currencies for different days. Students can take notes as the information is reported to them on a daily basis and write a report a week later, based on the information reported in class.

So könnten Sie anfangen:

Am Montag stand der Dollar auf _____ D-Mark, auf _____ Schweizer Franken und auf _____ österreichische Schillinge. Während der Woche _____ (ist _____ gestiegen/gefallen oder hat sich nichts verändert [*changed*]).

GRAMMATIK IM KONTEXT ⊡⊡⊡⊡⊡⊡⊡⊡⊡⊡

The Comparative and Superlative of Attributive Adjectives

Comparative and Superlative.
Note: There is essentially nothing new here grammatically. The reason for treating this topic separately is to give students additional practice with attributive adjectives and thereby keep them active.

Attributive adjectives in the comparative or superlative add regular adjective endings after the comparative and superlative forms.

POSITIVE	COMPARATIVE	SUPERLATIVE
ein alt**es** Haus	ein älter**es** Haus	das älteste Haus
die hoh**e** Miete	die höher**e** Miete	die höchst**e** Miete

Ich möchte lieber eine **größere** Wohnung als ein **größeres** Auto.

I would rather have a bigger apartment than a bigger car.

Ein Girokonto ist das **praktischste** Konto.

A checking account is the most practical account.

Die **meisten** Studenten haben ein Girokonto, aber kein Sparkonto.

Most students have a checking account, but no savings account.

Two important exceptions are **mehr** and **weniger**. They do not add adjective endings in the comparative.

Ich habe **mehr** Geld als mein Bruder, aber **weniger** Geld als meine Schwester.

I have more money than my brother, but less money than my sister.

⊡ Übung 1. Heidelberg und München

Vergleichen (*compare*) Sie die zwei Städte.

> BEISPIEL: In Heidelberg ist das Essen billiger. →
> In Heidelberg gibt es billigeres Essen.

1. Die Mieten sind niedriger in Heidelberg.
2. Die Cafés sind gemütlicher in Heidelberg.
3. Es gibt nicht so viele Studenten in Heidelberg.
4. Die Menschen sind freundlicher in Heidelberg.
5. In Heidelberg hat man nicht so viel Streß wie in München.
6. In München sind die Restaurants teurer.

▣ Übung 2. Die höchsten und niedrigsten Ausgaben

Übung 2. Suggestion: This exercise can be done in the whole group or as a pair activity. If it is done as pair work, have several groups report to the class.

Wofür geben Sie mehr oder weniger Geld aus? Was sind Ihre höchsten und niedrigsten Ausgaben?

BEISPIEL: Meine höchsten Ausgaben sind die Studiengebühren. Ich gebe mehr Geld für Bücher als für Essen aus.

Meine höchsten/niedrigsten Ausgaben sind (für) _____ .
Ich gebe mehr/weniger Geld für _____ als für _____ aus.

> Miete, Bücher, Essen, Trinken, Parties, Geschenke, Benzin, Autoreparatur, Bekleidung, Arbeitsmittel, Ernährung, Reinigung

▣ Übung 3. Wo gibt es das hier?

Stellen Sie einem Partner oder einer Partnerin Fragen.

BEISPIEL: A: Was ist hier das gemütlichste Café?
B: Das gemütlichste Café ist Café Pipusch.

Wo gibt es hier _____ ?
Was ist hier _____ ?

das Café	schön
der Park	preiswert
die Bank	hoch
das Restaurant	freundlich
der Buchladen	billig
das Lebensmittelgeschäft	gemütlich
das Gebäude	gut
?	

Adjectival Nouns

Substantivierte Adjektive

Adjectives can become nouns that designate people and things.

> **Deutsche** und US-Amerikaner unterscheiden sich deutlich, wenn sie Rechnungen bezahlen: Die meisten **Deutschen** bezahlen ihre Rechnungen in bar; die Amerikaner greifen lieber zur Plastik-Karte. In den USA ist die Kreditkarte nichts **Ungewöhnliches**.

Adjectival Nouns. Suggestion: Have students scan the brief text, showing three examples of adjectival nouns. Ask for the basic form of the adjectives.

ADJECTIVE	ADJECTIVAL NOUN
deutsch	1. der/die Deutsche (*the German man/woman*) 2. Deutsche (*Germans*)
bekannt	3. ein Bekannter (*a male acquaintance*) 4. eine Bekannte (*a female acquaintance*)
ungewöhnlich	5. nichts Ungewöhnliches (*nothing unusual*) 6. etwas (was) Ungewöhnliches (*something unusual*)
neu	7. viel Neues (*much [that is] new*) 8. wenig Neues (*little [that is] new*) 9. das Neue (*the new [thing]*)
sonstig	10. Sonstiges (*other [items]*)

When they function as nouns, adjectives are capitalized. In addition, adjectival nouns follow the rules that apply to attributive adjectives. The gender of adjectival nouns is determined by what they designate: people are masculine or feminine (examples 1 through 4), abstract concepts are neuter (examples 5 through 10). After **etwas, nichts, viel,** and **wenig** the adjectival noun is always neuter (examples 5 through 8).

🔲 **Übung 4. Wer sind diese Leute?**

Complete each sentence with an adjectival noun formed from the words in bold.

> BEISPIEL: Sind Sie aus **Deutschland,** Frau Huber?
 Ja, ich bin Deutsche.

1. Erich ist mir seit Jahren **bekannt.** Er ist ein guter _____ von mir.
2. Seine Mutter ist mir auch **bekannt.** Sie ist eine _____.
3. **Reich** und **arm:** Kennen Sie den Spruch: „Die _____ werden reicher, und die _____ werden ärmer"?
4. Wo ist Dieter **angestellt** (*employed*)? Er ist _____ bei der Post.
5. Seine Schwester ist bei der Bank **angestellt.** Sie ist Bank_____.
6. Herr Lindemann ist aus **Deutschland**. Er ist _____.

🔲 **Übung 5. Wie reagieren Sie darauf?**

Wählen Sie einen passenden Ausdruck und ein Adjektiv aus der Liste.

> BEISPIEL: Die Preise gehen immer höher.
 Das ist nichts Neues.

Suggestion: To practice using the word *deutsch* as a noun, do the following quick substitution: *Hans ist Amerikaner.* Students say *Hans ist Deutscher.* Likewise, *Irene ist Amerikanerin; Ich kenne...* (einen Amerikaner, eine Amerikanerin, viele Amerikaner, diese Amerikaner, diese Amerikanerin, diesen Amerikaner). *Ich habe gestern mit drei Amerikanern* (Amerikanerinnen, einer Amerikanerin, einem Amerikaner) *gesprochen.* This can be further expanded by using the adjectives *bekannt* or *angestellt.*

Etwas, nichts, viel, wenig.   Note: It is sufficient for students to actively master *etwas* and *nichts* with an adjectival noun using only the nominative and accusative cases. *Viel* and *wenig* plus an adjectival noun are less common; students should be able to recognize them in writing, though.

Übung 5.   First go over the sentences on page 332 to which students are to express their reaction. Have them work in pairs. Check comprehension and reaction by calling on several students in class. **Follow-up:** Working in pairs, students make up several statements similar to those in the exercise. Have them read their statements to the whole class and ask for reactions.

Besides expressing politeness, other important functions of the subjunctive are to express wishes and hypotheses, speculating about matters that are contrary to fact. Consider the following sentence:

> If I **had** the money, I **would buy** myself a new car now.

Clearly, the implication is that the speaker does not have enough money to buy a new car right now. The conjunction *if* and the verbs *had* and *would . . . buy*, in this particular case, convey the hypothetical nature of the statement. The past-tense form *had* is used here as a subjunctive expressing present time. German also uses the subjunctive in a contrary-to-fact sentence.

> Wenn ich Geld **hätte, würde** ich mir einen neuen Wagen **kaufen.**

Present Subjunctive of Weak Verbs and Modals

The subjunctive in German has only two tenses: the present and the past tense. The present subjunctive forms of weak verbs are identical with the simple past tense.

INFINITIVE: **sparen** PAST STEM: **sparte**	
Singular	*Plural*
ich sparte	wir sparten
Sie sparten	Sie sparten
du spartest	ihr spartet
er sie sparte es	sie sparten

An deiner Stelle **sparte** ich mehr.	*If I were you (in your place), I would save more (money).*
Wenn du nur mehr **spartest!**	*If only you saved more!*

Modal verbs take the stem vowel of the infinitive in the present subjunctive.

INFINITIVE	SIMPLE PAST	PRESENT SUBJUNCTIVE
dürfen	ich durfte	ich dürfte
können	ich konnte	ich könnte
mögen	ich mochte	ich möchte
müssen	ich mußte	ich müßte
wollen	ich wollte	ich wollte
sollen	ich sollte	ich sollte

Könntest du mir etwas Geld leihen?	*Could you lend me some money?*
Du **solltest** vorsichtiger sein.	*You ought to be more careful.*
Ich **müßte** eigentlich mehr sparen.	*I really ought to save more.*
Wir **möchten** ein Girokonto eröffnen.	*We would like to open a checking account.*

Present Subjunctive of Irregular Weak Verbs

Irregular weak verbs add an umlaut to the stem vowel of the simple past to form the present subjunctive.

INFINITIVE	SIMPLE PAST	PRESENT SUBJUNCTIVE
bringen	ich brachte	brächte
haben	ich hatte	hätte
werden	ich wurde	würde
wissen	ich wußte	wüßte

Wenn ich Talent **hätte, würde** ich Schauspieler.	*If I had talent, I would become an actor.*
Ach, wenn ich nur **wüßte,** wie ich mehr Geld verdienen könnte!	*Oh, if I only knew how I could earn more money!*

RSM

Ein Telefon müßte man haben …

Jetzt können Sie Ihr Telefon bestellen …

BERLINER VOLKSBANK

Mit Computer-Service

Alles was[a] Sie über Geld wissen sollten.

a. Alles… *Everything*

Present Subjunctive of Strong Verbs

The present subjunctive of strong verbs is also derived from the simple past stem. When the past stem vowel is **a, o,** or **u,** it changes to an umlaut. In addition, personal endings are added.

INFINITIVE: **sein**	
PAST STEM: **war**	
Singular	*Plural*
ich wäre	wir wären
Sie wären	Sie wären
du wär(e)st	ihr wär(e)t
er	
sie } wäre	sie wären
es	

		PRESENT
INFINITIVE	SIMPLE PAST	SUBJUNCTIVE
gehen	ich ging	ich ginge
fahren	ich fuhr	ich führe
fliegen	ich flog	ich flöge
kommen	ich kam	ich käme

Wenn wir zu Fuß **gingen,** **kämen** wir zu spät ins Kino.
An deiner Stelle **führe** ich mit dem Taxi.

If we walked, we would be late for the movie.
If I were you, I would take a cab.

würde plus Infinitive

The regular present subjunctive forms are replaced more and more by **würde** plus the infinitive of the main verb, a construction paralleling the English *would* plus an infinitive.

Ich **gäbe** nicht soviel Geld für Luxusartikel aus.
Ich **würde** nicht soviel Geld für Luxusartikel **ausgeben**.

I would not spend so much money on luxury items.

An deiner Stelle **sparte** ich mehr.
An deiner Stelle **würde** ich mehr **sparen**.

If I were you, I would save more.

The subjunctive forms of the modals and of **wissen, haben,** and **sein** are normally not replaced by **würden** plus the infinitive, though you will occasionally see **würde... sein** instead of **wäre** and **würde... haben** instead of **hätten**.

The expression **an deiner Stelle** means *if I were you* (lit. *in your place*) and is always used with verbs in the subjunctive. The possessive article changes depending on the person to whom advice is being given.

An **seiner** Stelle würde ich nicht mit Kreditkarte bezahlen.	*If I were in his place, I would not pay with a credit card.*
An **deiner** Stelle würde er alles bar bezahlen.	*If he were in your place, he would pay cash.*

Contrary-to-Fact Conditions

A sentence that states a condition that is contrary to fact begins with the conjunction **wenn** and uses subjunctive forms in both the **wenn**-clause and the conclusion clause.

Wenn ich Geld **brauchte, ginge** ich zur Bank.	If I needed money, I would go to the bank.

Würde forms are frequently used in the conclusion clause. Only in colloquial speech, however, are **würde** forms used in the **wenn**-clause.

Wenn ich Geld **brauchte, würde** ich zur Bank **gehen**.	If I needed money, I would go to the bank.

When a conditional sentence states a fact, no subjunctive forms are used at all.

Wenn ich Geld **brauche, gehe** ich zur Bank.	Whenever I need money, I go to the bank.

Note the position of the finite (conjugated) verbs in sentences that begin with a **wenn**-clause followed by a conclusion.

The two finite verbs appear right next to each other, separated by a comma. The comma is essential in this case. The entire subordinate clause (**Wenn ich...**) counts as the first element of the sentence. It is followed in second position by the finite verb of the main clause.

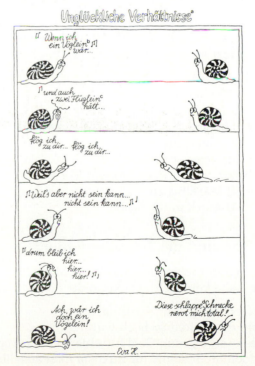

RSM

Unglückliche Verhältnisse[a]

🔲 **Analyse**

Die Schnecke in diesem Cartoon, „Unglückliche Verhältnisse", singt ein bekanntes deutsches Volkslied (*folk song*).

- What would the snail like to be?
- What verbs express the snail's wishful thinking? How do these forms differ from the standard subjunctive forms? What could be the reasons for this?

a. Unglückliche... *Unhappy conditions*
b. *little bird*
c. *little wings*
d. *lame*

Wishes: *wenn ich doch nur; ich wünschte; ich wollte*

Sentences expressing wishes often begin with **wenn** and frequently contain the particles **doch** and **nur** (used individually or combined). These particles intensify wishes.

Wenn ich **doch nur** wüßte, wo mein Autoschlüssel ist.	*If I only knew where my car key is.*
Wenn der Zug **doch** endlich käme.	*If only the train would finally come.*

Ich wünschte and **ich wollte** (*I wish*) are fixed expressions in the present subjunctive. They are always followed by a sentence in the subjunctive.

Ich wollte, die Geschäfte in Deutschland wären länger offen.	*I wish (that) stores in Germany were open longer.*
Frau Schiff wünschte, sie könnte auch abends einkaufen.	*Mrs. Schiff wishes she could shop in the evening, too.*

▣ Übung 7. Etwas höflicher, bitte!

Using a modal verb in the present subjunctive, or **würde** plus an infinitive, express each of the following sentences more politely.

> BEISPIEL: Leih mir bitte DM 50,-! →
> Würdest du mir bitte DM 50,- leihen? *or*
> Könntest du mir bitte DM 50,- leihen?

1. Gib mir mein Geld zurück!
2. Können Sie mir 100 Mark wechseln (*change*)?
3. Geben Sie mir Reiseschecks für DM 500,-.
4. Wie steht der Dollar heute? (*Would/Could you please tell me how . . .*)
5. Unterschreiben Sie hier, bitte!
6. Darf ich Ihren Ausweis sehen?
7. Ich will ein Girokonto eröffnen. (*I would like to . . .*)
8. Kannst du mir 50 Mark bis zum Monatsende leihen?
9. Ich will $100 in D-Mark umtauschen.

Übung 7.   Note: Because subjunctive forms to express politeness are commonly used in German, use this exercise to elicit as many variations of individual sentences from students as possible. Rephrase imperatives with *würde* or *könnte* plus an infinitive; questions requesting something, with *würde* or *könnte*; rephrase sentences with *will* using *möchte* (*gern*).
Suggestion: One student requests something of another, who in turn says *Etwas höflicher bitte: Würdest du bitte...*, etc.
Suggestion: Have students make up additional requests in the imperative. Ask individual students to rephrase the requests more politely.

▣ Übung 8. Was sind die Tatsachen° hier?

facts

> BEISPIEL: Ich wünschte, ich könnte dir 50 Mark leihen. →
> Ich habe kein Geld. Ich kann dir nichts leihen.

1. Ich wünschte, ich hätte eine Kreditkarte.
2. Wenn die Miete doch nicht so hoch wäre.
3. Ich wollte, ich könnte genug Geld für eine Weltreise sparen.
4. Wenn Klaus doch nicht soviel für Luxusartikel ausgäbe.

Übung 8.   Note: This exercise checks students' comprehension of nonreality by having them state facts.
Follow-up: Have students state their own wishes and then give the facts.

5. Ich wünschte, ich könnte in München eine Wohnung finden.
6. Mein Freund hätte gern einen BMW.
7. Ich wünschte, mein Freund oder meine Freundin führe nicht so schnell Auto.
8. Ich wünschte, das Semester wäre zu Ende.

▣ **Übung 9. Partnerarbeit**

Würdest du das machen?

> BEISPIEL: einem Fremden auf der Straße Geld geben →
> A: Würdest du einem Fremden auf der Straße Geld geben?
> B: Ja, ich würde einem Fremden Geld geben. *oder auch:* Ich würde ihm kein Geld geben.

1. einem Freund oder einer Freundin dein Auto leihen
2. einem Freund oder einer Freundin die Miete bezahlen
3. für sehr schlechtes Essen im Restaurant bezahlen
4. mehr ausgeben, als du verdienst
5. eine Stunde vor dem Kino auf einen Freund oder eine Freundin warten
6. allein in Ferien fahren

▣ **Übung 10. Wie würden Sie in diesen Situationen handeln?**

Beschreiben Sie die Situation auf jedem Bild. Suchen Sie einen passenden Ausdruck aus der Liste, und sagen Sie, was Sie an seiner oder ihrer Stelle täten.

1.

2.

3.

> BEISPIEL: An ihrer Stelle würde ich AAA anrufen. *oder:* An ihrer Stelle riefe ich AAA an.

1. weggehen (ging weg); guten Tag sagen; freundlich sein; nichts sagen; böse sein; nicht mit ihm reden; freundlich lächeln,
2. eine Reparaturwerkstatt anrufen; sich ins Auto setzen und warten, bis der Regen aufhört; Hilfe anbieten; um Hilfe bitten; nach Hause gehen; weitergehen; den Reifen wechseln (*change the tire*)
3. nicht länger warten; allein ins Kino gehen; ungeduldig sein; bei Harry anrufen

◘ **Übung 11.** **Was würden Sie machen, wenn...?**

BEISPIEL: Wenn ich Talent hätte, würde ich Opernsängerin.

Wenn ich Zeit hätte, ein großer / eine große _____(z.B. Sänger[in])
  Geld interessante Leute kennenlernen
  Talent eine Insel im Pazifik kaufen
  Präsident(in) wäre, jeden Tag die Zeitung lesen
    ?

◘ **Übung 12.** **Rat geben**

Ein Freund oder eine Freundin hat ein Problem. Geben Sie Rat.

BEISPIEL: A: Ich bin total pleite. Was soll ich machen?
  B: Wenn ich total pleite wäre, würde ich mir eine Arbeit
    suchen.

Mögliche Probleme:

- kann keine Wohnung finden
- zahlt zuviel Miete
- langweilt sich
- hat Probleme mit Zimmerkollegen, Freundin, Eltern
- hat kein Geld

Übung 11. **Note:** This exercise focuses on two verbs: *hätte* and *wäre*. Because they are so common, exploit this exercise to the fullest. **Suggestion:** Have one student ask another *Was würden Sie (würdest du) machen, wenn Sie (du) Zeit hätten (hättest)?* The second student answers with a complete sentence: *Wenn ich Zeit hätte, würde ich eine Reise machen.*
Follow-up: Half the class writes *wenn*-clauses, the other half result-clauses only. Call on students to combine clauses; the attempt might produce some odd and amusing combinations!

The Past Subjunctive

The past subjunctive is used to express wishes, hypotheses, and conjecture concerning events in the past.

Wenn ich in der Lotterie *If I had won the lottery, I*
  gewonnen hätte, wäre ich *would have been ecstatic.*
  überglücklich gewesen.

The hypothesis (*If I had . . .*) speculates about an event in the past: The speaker did not win the lottery. Both English and German require the past subjunctive in this case.

The past subjunctive forms are derived from the past perfect tense. Use the subjunctive forms **hätte** or **wäre** plus the past participle of the main verb.

INFINITIVE	PAST PERFECT	PAST SUBJUNCTIVE
kaufen	ich hatte gekauft	ich hätte gekauft (*I had bought / would have bought*)
sein	ich war gewesen	ich wäre gewesen (*I had been / would have been*)

Roter Fü[...]

der Mosel.° Sie
Schwerpunkt a[...]
Vom Parkplatz
Burgtore bleibe[...]
November bis 1[...]

Zum Text

1. **Richtig oder**
   a. ____ Deu[...]
   b. ____ Den[...]
      meis[...]
   c. ____ Das[...]
   d. ____ Die l[...]
      zigm[...]
      Heus[...]
   e. ____ Den[...]
   f. ____ Die 8[...]
   g. ____ Der l[...]

2. **Was paßt zusa**[...]
   Spalte.

   BEISPIEL: Das[...]
   ist a[...]

   1[...]

   Das Bild „Unbe[...]
   Venezianerin'[...]

   Das Gemälde „[...]
   Kind",

   Die Geige und [...]

   Der Dom von Li[...]

   Burg Eltz,

   Die „Gorch Fock[...]

LESEN IM KONTEXT

In diesem Teil lesen Sie über deutsches[...]
Bilder auf den deutschen Geldscheinen[...]

Vor dem Lesen

▣ **Aktivität.** Wie gut kennen Si[...]

Wer ist auf diesen Dollarscheinen?

1. ____ $1,00	a. Grant
2. ____ $2,00	b. Washington
3. ____ $5,00	c. Lincoln
4. ____ $10,00	d. Franklin
5. ____ $20,00	e. Jefferson
6. ____ $50,00	f. Hamilton
7. ____ $100,00	g. Jackson

Auf den ersten Blick

Schauen Sie sich den Titel, den Untert[...]
„Weg vom schönen Schein" an. Was sag[...]
kels aus?

Abschied° vom schönen Sch[...]

AB° 1990 GIBT ES NEUE GELDNOTEN°: WEG° M[...]
MEHR FRAUENKÖPFE. UND ZUM ERSTENMAL:[...]

Der Schnellste: der Zehner. Mit dem k[...]
am häufigsten. Deshalb wird er am sc[...]
Nach 16 Monaten gehört er zum Altpa[...]
„Gorch Fock", Schulschiff der Bundesm[...]

Ich wünschte, ich **hätte** den neuen Porsche nicht **gekauft**.	*I wish I had not bought the new Porsche.*
Ein gebrauchter Wagen **wäre** billiger **gewesen**.	*A used car would have been cheaper.*

Use **hätte** or **wäre** according to the same rules that determine the use of **haben** or **sein** in the perfect tense: intransitive verbs that indicate a change of place (**gehen, fahren**) or a change of condition (**werden**), as well as **bleiben** and **sein**, take **wäre** (**sein**); all others take **hätte** (**haben**). No **würde** plus infinitive form is used in the past subjunctive.

▣ **Analyse**

Schauen Sie sich den Cartoon „Ewige Fragen" an.

- Find the verb forms in the past subjunctive and give their infinitives.
- What variation from the standard form do you see?
- What is the woman speculating about?
- What stereotype does the cartoon allude to? Formulate a conclusion to the hypothesis **„Wenn ich als Blondine geboren wäre,…"**
- What is the reality of her life?

Usually, a clause stating a hypothetical situation starts with the conjunction **wenn**. The conjunction is sometimes omitted. In that case, the conjugated verb is placed at the beginning of the sentence.

RSM

Hätte sie doch die Zeitansage angerufen.

Ruf doch mal an! Post

☑ **Übung 13.   Was hätten Sie a**

BEISPIEL: Christoph hat seinem Fr
ihm die DM 500,- nicht g

1.   Mein Bruder hat eine Rockband g
2.   Er hat sein ganzes Geld von der Ba
3.   Dann hat er sein Studium aufgege
4.   Meine Freundin ist aus dem Stude
5.   Sie ist zu ihren Eltern zurückgezo

☑ **Übung 14.   Bruce ist total p**

Wie ist das passiert? Sie sehen hier B
Lesen Sie die Liste zuerst. Was hätten
Ihrer Meinung nach zuviel Geld ausge
Vorschläge, was Sie anders machen w

Geburtstagsgeschenk, Buch und E
drei Sporthemden
Karten für *Cats* (zum zweiten Mal
zweimal im Kino
Briefmarken
zweimal mit Freunden in der Kne
Bücher für Biologie und Compute
Benzin fürs Auto
zwei CD Platten
dreimal zum Essen ausgegangen
   Schnellimbiß)
Spende für Amnesty Internationa
Visakarte

Nützliche Ausdrücke:

An seiner Stelle hätte ich nic
Das wäre wirklich nicht nötig
Braucht er wirklich...?
Zweimal...? Einmal wäre ge
An seiner Stelle würde ich w

Der Gehei
ben, daß er sc
Woher kommt
„Der kleine Sc
Mark." Da hat
Millionen Stüc

De
lau

Werk. Denn ke
Linien formen F

Der Älteste
dieser Grüne. Er
Zwanzigers Geig
oberhaupt° Theo
hen für die deut

Der braune
Tausender:
20 Mio. Stück
im Umlauf,
fast sechs
Jahre Lebens-
dauer

Limburg. Die zw
gehört zu den be

3.   **Das sind die Neuen**. Was erfahren Sie über die neuen Geldscheine?

DAS SIND DIE NEUEN

 Von einem Fachgremium[a] ausgewählt.[b] Die Köpfe für die neuen Scheine.   Auf dem Tausender die Märchen-Brüder Jacob (1785–1863) und Wilhelm Grimm (1786–1859).

 Auf dem Fünfhunderter: Maria Sibylla Merian (1647–1717), Tochter des Mathias Merian d. Ä.[c], Malerin,[d] Kupferstecherin[e] und Naturforscherin.[f]

 Auf dem Hunderter: Clara Schumann (1819–1896). Pianistin, berühmt als beste Interpretin der Werke ihres Mannes Robert Schumann.

 Auf dem Fünfziger: Balthasar Neumann (1687–1753). Barockbaumeister, Schöpfer[g] des berühmten Treppenhauses[h] der Würzburger Residenz.

 Auf dem Zwanziger: Annette Freiin von Droste-Hülshoff (1797–1848). Eine der bedeutendsten Dichterinnen[i] des 19. Jahrhunderts – „Die Judenbuche"![j]

 Auf dem Zehner: Carl Friedrich Gauß (1777–1855), begnadeter[k] Mathematiker, Astronom und Physiker. Er schuf[l] die Grundlage[m] der modernen Zahlentheorie.

Zum Text # 3.   Note: The new money, showing Germans significant in fields from science to the arts, features an almost equal number of men and women.
Suggestion: Have students think of other Germans they know who made significant contributions in their fields; e.g., *Johann Sebastian Bach war ein großer deutscher Musiker. Johann Wolfgang von Goethe war ein großer deutscher Dichter. Er hat das Drama „Faust" geschrieben.*
Suggestion: Have students work in small groups to choose whom they would put on the new German bills. Have each group report its choices to the class.

a.   *committee of experts*
b.   *chosen*
c.   *d. Ä = der Ältere*
d.   *painter*
e.   *copper engraver*
f.   *natural scientist*
g.   *creator*
h.   *staircase*
i.   *female poets*
j.   *The Jew's Beechtree (title of a novella)*
k.   *gifted*
l.   *created*
m.   *foundation*

Auf dem Fün-
fer: Bettina von
Arnim
(1785–1859). Die Dichterin
schrieb u. a.ⁿ das berühmte
Werk „Goethes Briefwechsel°
mit einem Kinde".

Auf dem neu-
en Zweihunderter:
Paul Ehrlich
(1854–1915). Der Arzt und No-
belpreisträger erfand die
Chemotherapie zur Krebsbe-
kämpfung.ᵖ

n. u.a. = unter anderem = *among
other things*
o. *correspondence*
p. *fight against cancer*

- Wer sind die Leute auf den Scheinen? Welche Namen sind Ihnen bekannt?
- Welche Bereiche (*areas*) repräsentieren diese berühmten Deutschen?
- Was ist wirklich „neu" an den Geldscheinen? Denken Sie zum Vergleich (*comparison*) an die „Köpfe" auf amerikanischen Scheinen.
- Finden Sie, daß das Fachgremium eine gute Wahl getroffen hat? Hätten Sie andere berühmte Deutsche auf die Geldscheine gesetzt? Wen?

Nach dem Lesen

▣ Aktivität 1. Gruppenarbeit

Sie sind auf einem Fachgremium und schlagen neue Ideen und Motive für die Geldscheine Ihres Landes vor. Bilden Sie kleine Gruppen und berichten Sie, wen oder was Ihr Fachgremium ausgewählt hat. Geben Sie auch Gründe für Ihre Wahl an.

▣ Aktivität 2. Ein Interview

Stellen Sie jemandem in Ihrer Klasse Fragen über folgende Themen. Machen Sie sich Notizen dabei, und schreiben Sie einen Bericht darüber.

- Taschengeld als Kind? Wieviel? Wie oft?
- erste bezahlte Arbeit
- was er oder sie mit dem Geld gemacht hat
- ob er oder sie sparen kann oder alles Geld sofort ausgibt, und wofür
- was er oder sie mit einer Million Dollar machen würde

WORTSCHATZ

Substantive

Über Geld	About Money
die Ausgabe (-n)	expense
die Bank (-en)	bank
das Bargeld	cash
die Einnahme (-n)	income
die Gebühr (-en)	fee
die Studiengebühren (*pl.*)	study fees, tuition
der Geldautomat (-n *masc.*)	automatic teller
der Geldschein (-e) (auch: der Schein)	bank note, paper money
das Konto (-s *or* Konten)	account
das Girokonto	checking account
das Sparkonto	savings account
die Kreditkarte (-n)	credit card
die Münze (-n)	coin
die Nebenkosten (*pl.*)	incidental expenses
der Reisescheck (-s)	travelers' check
die Sparkasse (-n)	savings bank
die Spende (-n)	donation, contribution
der Unterhalt	support
die Währung (-en)	currency
der Wechselkurs (-e)	exchange rate

Andere Substantive

der Abschied	farewell
die Ausbildung (-en)	training, education
der Bleistift (-e)	pencil
die Briefmarke (-n)	stamp
der Durchschnitt	average
im Durchschnitt	on the average
im Schnitt	on the average
durchschnittlich	on average
die Erfahrung (-en)	experience
die Ernährung	food, nutrition
die Fachakademie (-n)	professional school (university level)
der Gefallen	favor
die Hälfte (-n)	half
das Heft (-e)	notebook
die Heizung (-en)	heating
der Nachteil (-e)	disadvantage
das Paket (-e)	package

das Portemonnaie (-s)	wallet
die Post	mail
die Reinigung	dry cleaning
die Reparatur (-en)	repair
die Stelle (-n)	place
an seiner Stelle	in his place
die Steuer (-n)	tax
der Strom	electricity
die Untermiete	sublet
in/zur Untermiete wohnen	to rent a room
der Vergleich (-e)	comparison
im Vergleich	in comparison
die Versicherung (-en)	insurance
der Vorteil (-e)	advantage
die Zukunft	future

Verben

ausgeben (gibt aus), gab aus, ausgegeben	to spend
benutzen	to use
sich entscheiden, entschied, entschieden	to decide
fallen (fällt), fiel, ist gefallen	to fall; decline (money)
finanzieren	to finance
einen Gefallen tun, tat, getan	to do a favor
leihen, lieh, geliehen	to borrow; lend
Ich leihe mir Geld	I borrow money
Ich leihe ihm Geld	I lend him money
sparen	to save
steigen, stieg, (ist) gestiegen	to rise, climb
umtauschen (tauscht um)	to exchange
umziehen (zieht um), zog um, ist umgezogen	to move
unterschreiben, unterschrieb, unterschrieben	to sign
verdienen	to earn

vergleichen, verglich, verglichen	to compare
zurückgeben (gibt zurück), gab zurück, zurückgegeben	to give back
zurückzahlen (zahlt zurück)	to pay back

Adjektive und Adverbien

angestellt	employed
der/die **Angestellte** (*declined adj.*)	employee
ärgerlich	annoying
arm	poor
ausschließlich	exclusively
außerhalb	(here short for) at a distance from, outside of the city
bar	in cash
bekannt	known, acquainted
der/die **Bekannte** (*declined adj.*)	acquaintance
deshalb	therefore

eben	just
eigen	own, of one's own
erreichbar mit	can be reached by, reachable with
höflich	polite
kürzlich	recently
leicht	easy
mehrmals	on several occasions
möglicherweise	possibly
monatlich	monthly
nebenbei	on the side
pleite (*coll.*)	broke
reich	rich
selber	self (emphatic)
selten	rare
sonstig	other, additional
soviel	so much
überhaupt	at all
übrig	left over
unglaublich	unbelievable

Sonstiges

außer (+ *dat.*)	besides; except for
Es geht um	It's a question of

KAPITEL 12

DIE VIER WÄNDE

Lernziele *This chapter takes a closer look at housing and what's inside a home, the* vier Wände. *You will learn to describe your housing needs and where you prefer to live, and to make recommendations regarding housing.*

▣ Alles klar?

Schauen Sie sich die verschiedenen Angebote für Häuser und Wohnungen an.

RSM

10 Einfamilienhäuser
(als Doppelhaushälfte)

Kaufpreis

z. B. 1 Haus mit ca. 418 m² Grundstücksfläche,[a] 110 m² Wohnfläche[b]
5 Zimmer, Küche, 2 Bäder, Sitzterrasse, Balkon und ca. 76 m² Nutzfläche[c]

DM 321 000,- Festpreisgarantie

a. *property area*
b. *living area*
c. *usable area*

RENOV. ALTB., 3 ZI., KÜ., BAD, BALK., INKL. NK.[a]

Nichts gegen Neubauwohnungen. Aber so ein renovierter Altbau hat nun mal einen besonderen Charme. . . Kein Wunder also, daß Altbauwohnungen vor allem bei jungen Leuten sehr begehrt[b]sind. . . Obendrein[c] sind sie im allgemeinen auch noch leichter erschwinglich[d] als die meisten Neubauwohnungen.

a. Renovierter Altbau, 3 Zimmer, Küche, Bad, Balkon, inklusive Nebenkosten
b. *in demand*
c. *on top of everything*
d. *affordable*

5 attraktive Reihenhäuser in Müllheim-Niederweiler

ca. 2 km vom bekannten Kurort Badenweiler

Kaufpreis

z. B. 1 Haus mit ca. 300 m² Grundstücksfl., 133 m² Wohnfläche, 5 Zimmer, Küche, 2 Bäder, Balkon, Sitzterrasse.

DM 358 000,- Festpreisgarantie

Baden-Baden

Eigentumswohnungen

in besonders schö. Halbhöhenlage. 10 Gehmin. z. Zentr., guter Schnitt, gehobene Ausstattung, Garage.

3 Zi.,	113 m²,	**DM 486 000,-**
2 Zi.,	78 m²,	**DM 356 000,-**
Penth.,	110 m²,	**DM 514 000,-**

Sichern Sie sich jetzt Ihr Domizil in Baden-Baden, denn gute Lagen werden immer seltener.

Immobilien Kientz

Sonnenpl. 2, 7570 Baden-Baden
Tel. 0 72 21/2 52 53 + 27 14 56

- Was bedeutet Eigentumswohnung? (das Eigentum = *possession*)
- Was ist ein Reihenhaus?
- Was für Räume hat das Einfamilienhaus? das Reihenhaus?
- Was macht eine Altbauwohnung attraktiv für junge Leute?
- Wo sind die Preise am höchsten? Warum wohl?

a. *real estate*

WÖRTER IM KONTEXT

Mieten und Vermieten

Aktivität 1. Zwei Mietgesuche°

Lesen Sie die folgenden zwei Mietgesuche, und beantworten Sie die Fragen auf der nächsten Seite.

ads for a place to rent

Neue Wörter

der Hinweis *tip, clue*
der Teppichboden *wall-to-wall carpet*
die Umgebung *surroundings*
nähere Umgebung *vicinity*

Wir suchen für einen Angestellten unseres Werkes Regensburg zum 1. Juli oder später eine

2- bis 3-Zimmer-Wohnung

ca. 70 m², mit Küche, Bad, Garage, Zentralheizung, wenn möglich mit Teppichböden, in ruhiger Lage in Regensburg oder Umgebung.

Schriftliche Angebote senden Sie bitte an:

vH
von Heyden

**Personalabteilung
von Heyden GmbH
Donaustaufer Straße 378
8400 Regensburg**

Welche der folgenden Wörter beziehen sich auf (*refer to*) das Mietgesuch von Mathias und Brigitte? Welche Wörter beziehen sich auf das Mietgesuch für den Angestellten eines Werkes?

BEISPIEL: mit Garage → der Angestellte

Wohngemeinschaft
in der Stadt
auf dem Lande
günstige Wohnung
ruhige Lage
Hündin Sarah
2-3 Zimmer Wohnung
mit Teppichböden
kleines Haus
Zimmer
Umgebung von Regensburg
in der Nähe von Göttingen
mit Garage

Aktivität 2.   Note: This activity builds on the previous one. Students first read the two *Mietangebote* and then recommend which apartment would be appropriate for the three people introduced in *Aktivität 1*. (Mathias and Brigitte and the *Angestellter einer Firma*).

RSM

a. Wohngemeinschaft
b. Göttingen (*university town in northwest Germany*)
c. *community*
d. möglichst
e. *since*

▣ **Aktivität 2. Mietangebote°**   *rental offers*

Lesen Sie folgende zwei Mietangebote. Welches Angebot würden Sie Brigitte und Mathias empfehlen? Welches Angebot wäre etwas für den Angestellten?

Nützliche Ausdrücke:

Ich finde _____ ideal für _____, denn da gibt es _____.
_____ ist praktisch, weil _____.
Ich empfehle dem Angestellten / Brigitte und Mathias _____.
Es gibt jedoch ein Problem: _____.

1.

Land-WG sucht Mitbewohner(in)!

Wir, Bruno (26) und Britta (21), Hund und Katze, vermieten eine ganze obere Etage in einem älteren Bauernhaus, 2 1/2 Zimmer, ca 38 qm. Benutzbar sind Küche, Bad, großer Garten. Die Miete beträgt monatlich 300.- DM, plus 30.- DM Nebenkosten. 20 km von Göttingen. Ab 1. Juni.

2.

Mieter gesucht für große, helle 3 Zimmer in Neubau, ab 1. August, ca. 70 qm. Balkon, eingerichtete Küche (Spülmaschine, Eisschrank), Waschraum mit Maschine, Zentralheizung, Teppichboden, Bad und WC, Garage. Zu Fuß ca. 15 Minuten von der Universität, 5 Minuten vom Bahnhof, 10 Minuten vom Zentrum. Miete DM 680.- Nebenkosten DM 83.-

Suggestion: First go over the two ads to clarify new vocabulary. Then have students work in pairs to discuss their recommendations. Ask several individuals to report their recommendations. Encourage students to use some or all of the *nützliche Ausdrücke* to express the pros and cons. The goal is to present close to a paragraph-length narration.

Neue Wörter

der Boden *the floor*
der Eisschrank (der
  Kühlschrank) *refrigerator*
der Neubau *new building*
die Spülmaschine *dishwasher*
ab 1. (erstem) Juni *from June
  first on*

benutzbar *usable*
ganz *entire, whole*
möglichst bald *as soon as
  possible*
ober *upper*
einrichten *to furnish*
vermieten *to rent (out), to
  sublet*

▣ Aktivität 3. Vokabelübung

Was paßt zusammen?

1. _____ Die stellt man im Winter an.
2. _____ Die gehören zu den Nebenkosten.
3. _____ Man stellt den Wagen dahin.
4. _____ Dort kocht man.
5. _____ Dort wäscht man sich.
6. _____ Die ist praktisch zum Wäschewaschen.
7. _____ Der liegt auf dem Boden.
8. _____ Das steht gewöhnlich auf dem Lande.

a. Strom, Heizung, Telefon
b. der Teppich
c. die Waschmaschine
d. die Zentralheizung
e. die Garage
f. das Bauernhaus
g. die Küche
h. das Bad

Aktivität 3. Suggestion: Have students work in pairs. Check comprehension by asking questions such as *Was stellt man im Winter an? Was gehört zu den Nebenkosten? Wo kocht man gewöhnlich? Was ist praktisch zum Wäschewaschen? Wo steht ein Bauernhaus gewöhnlich?*

▣ Aktivität 4. Rollenspiel

Rollen: Brigitte und Mathias (suchen eine Wohnung)
      Bruno und Britta (vermieten eine Wohnung)
Situation: Sie treffen sich im Café. Was möchten sie alles wissen?

Aktivität 4. Suggestion: Have students work in groups of four to create a script for the characters, who are the four people in two of the previous ads. Some additional items have been added to provide further ideas for this *Rollenspiel*. Students should use the suggestions in the two columns, but should also feel free to add or change them. Groups role-play their conversation to the rest of the class.

BRIGITTE UND MATHIAS:

Sind Studenten in Göttingen
haben kein Auto
müssen dreimal die Woche
  zur Uni
möchten wissen, wie man zur
  Uni kommt
möchten möglichst bald
  einziehen
haben eine Hündin, Sara
möchten mal vorbeikommen

BRUNO UND BRITTA:

möchten etwas über die zwei
  wissen
haben viel Arbeit im Garten
fahren mit dem Zug in die
  Stadt
vermieten die Wohnung im
  Juni
haben ein Bauernhaus
mögen Tiere, haben selbst
  zwei
laden sie zum Wochenende
  ein vorbeizukommen

Dialog. Ein Gespräch am Telefon. Ist die Wohnung noch frei?

FRAU KRENZ: Hier Krenz.

HERR BRUNNER: Brunner. Guten Tag. Ich rufe wegen der Anzeige in der Zeitung an. Ist die Wohnung noch frei?

FRAU KRENZ: Ja, die ist noch frei.

HERR BRUNNER: Ich hätte einige Fragen. Ist Heizung in den Nebenkosten eingeschlossen?

FRAU KRENZ: Nein, Heizung ist extra.

HERR BRUNNER: In welchem Stock liegt die Wohnung?

FRAU KRENZ: Im vierten Stock.

HERR BRUNNER: Gibt es denn einen Aufzug im Haus?

FRAU KRENZ: Aber natürlich. Sind Sie alleinstehend, oder haben Sie Familie?

HERR BRUNNER: Ich bin alleinstehend. Kann ich mir die Wohnung mal ansehen?

FRAU KRENZ: Ja, gerne. Wann können Sie vorbeikommen?

HERR BRUNNER: Möglichst bald. Am besten direkt nach der Arbeit.

FRAU KRENZ: Schön, wie wäre es mit morgen so um 18.00 Uhr?

HERR BRUNNER: Das ist mir recht. Übrigens, bevor ich es vergesse, wie ist die Adresse?

FRAU KRENZ: Augustinerstraße 27. Es ist ganz leicht zu finden. Das Haus steht nämlich direkt gegenüber vom Museum.

HERR BRUNNER: Vielen Dank. Bis morgen dann. Auf Wiederhören.

FRAU KRENZ: Auf Wiederhören.

Neue Wörter

der Aufzug *elevator*

alleinstehend *single*

sich (*dat.*) **etwas ansehen** *to look at something*

eingeschlossen *included*

gegenüber von *across from*

Das ist mir recht. *That's fine with me.*

Aktivität 5. Anruf bei Frau Krenz

Herr Brunner hat auf die Anzeige hin angerufen: Mieter gesucht für große, helle 3 Zimmer (Seite 352). Er weiß also schon, wie groß die Wohnung ist und wie hoch die Miete ist. Was wollte er sonst noch von der Vermieterin, Frau Krenz, wissen? Was wollte sie von ihm wissen? (Mehrere Antworten sind möglich.)

1. Herr Brunner wollte wissen,
    a. ob Heizung im Preis der Nebenkosten eingeschlossen ist.
    b. ob die Küche einen Mikrowellenherd hat.
    c. wie er vom Haus zur Innenstadt kommt.
    d. wo die Wohnung liegt.
    e. ob es einen Aufzug gibt.
    f. wo man parken kann.
2. Frau Krenz wollte von Herrn Brunner wissen,
    a. wie viele Kinder er hat.
    b. ob er verheiratet ist.
    c. ob er eine gutbezahlte Stellung hat.
    d. wann er vorbeikommen kann.

⊡ **Aktivität 6.** **Rollenspiel. Ist die Wohnung noch frei?**

Sie interessieren sich auch für die Wohnung, die Herr und Frau Krenz zu vermieten haben. Sie rufen deshalb an.

ANRUFER(IN):	VERMIETER(IN):
nennt Namen $\longrightarrow$	nennt Namen
fragt, ob die Wohnung noch frei ist	ja
möchte wissen, wie hoch die Miete ist	nennt Preis
fragt, ob Nebenkosten eingeschlossen sind	alles, außer Heizung
möchte die Adresse wissen	gibt Adresse und Lage an
nennt Tag und Zeit, um die Wohnung zu sehen	macht einen Vorschlag, wann Anrufer vorbeikommen kann

Aktivität 6. **Suggestion:** Ask students for additional suggestions to add to the list: *Was möchten Sie noch wissen, wenn Sie eine Wohnung suchten? Was möchten Sie als Vermieter oder Vermieterin noch wissen?*
Note: Encourage students to use phrases such as: *Wenn ich eine Wohnung suchte, möchte ich wissen,... (ob das Haus alt oder neu ist.) Wenn ich der Vermieter wäre, möchte ich wissen,... (ob die Person eine Arbeit hat).* Incorporate these questions into the list to be used for the *Rollenspiel.*

⊡ **Aktivität 7.** **Meine Wohnsituation—damals und heute**

Interviewen Sie einen Partner oder eine Partnerin.

Mögliche Fragen:

Wo hast du vor _____ Jahr(en) gewohnt?
Wo wohnst du jetzt?
Gefällt es dir da? Warum oder warum nicht?

⊡ **Aktivität 8.** **Hören Sie zu.**

Drei Leute berichten, was für eine Wohnung sie suchen, und was ihnen in der Wohnung wichtig oder unwichtig ist. Schreiben Sie A, B oder C neben die passende Antwort. (Eine Lücke bleibt frei, weil keiner so etwas sucht.)

Wer sucht:

ein Zimmer in einer Wohngemeinschaft? ____
eine Neubauwohnung in der Innenstadt? __A__
ein älteres Haus in der Nähe der Stadt? __B__
eine gemütliche Altbauwohnung in der Stadt? __C__

Was ist den drei Sprechern wichtig (**w**), was ist ihnen unwichtig (**uw**)? Schreiben Sie **w** oder **uw** in die Tabelle unter A, B, und C. (*If no information is given, leave blank.*)

WICHTIG/UNWICHTIG:			
Lage	w	w	w
Zentralheizung	w	w	w
Balkon	w		
Garage	uw		uw
Garten		w	
Teppichboden		uw	uw
Waschmaschine			w

Aktivität 9. Sie suchen eine neue Wohnung.

Sagen Sie, was Ihnen wichtig oder unwichtig ist.

BEISPIEL: Die Wohnung muß in der Nähe der Uni liegen. Ein Balkon wäre nett, ist aber nicht so wichtig. Eine Garage ist nicht wichtig, ich habe nämlich kein Auto.

die Lage:

Nähe Uni/Arbeit
Innenstadt
auf dem Land

die Wohnung:

Balkon
großer Garten
Neubau/Altbau
Zentralheizung
moderne Küche
Teppichboden
Waschraum mit Waschmaschine
Bad und WC
Garage
Miete und Nebenkosten ziemlich niedrig

Aktivität 9. Suggestion: To make the activity as realistic as possible, you might suggest the following situation: *Stellen Sie sich vor, Sie müßten nächsten Monat aus Ihrer Wohnung / Ihrem Zimmer im Studentenwohnheim ausziehen.* Give students time to scan the list of suggestions before they each tell a partner what they would look for and what is important and not so important. The example shows one of many different ways of doing this. Call on several students to report what their partner told them.

Aktivität 10 (page 357). Note: The purpose of this exercise is vocabulary building geared toward expressing opinions in different ways. It also reviews expressions using subjunctive forms.

Suggestion: Brainstorm with the whole group to find adjectives that could be used to describe the options listed, e.g., *Schloß: romantisch, unpraktisch, teuer; Zelt: ungemütlich, billig, unpraktisch.* Write these on the board to help students formulate their opinions.

Suggestion: Have students work in small groups, encouraging them to express different opinions and to contradict each other.

◻ **Aktivität 13.** Der Grun

Unsere Eig

für e

Sie sehen hier einen Grundriß. Be
Wohnzimmer, die Küche, das Sch
Beschreiben Sie dann, wo die Zin

Nützliche Ausdrücke:

Zuerst kommt man in _____ .
Von _____ (der Küche) kommt
Links von / Neben / Rechts nel
Eine Tür / Eine Treppe führt ___
die Terrasse, auf den Balkon

◻ **Aktivität 10.** **Zukunftspläne**

Wie möchten Sie später mal wohnen? Wo möchten Sie nicht wohnen?
Reagieren Sie auf die Vorschläge.

BEISPIEL: A: Ich möchte in einem Hochhaus in der Stadt wohnen.
            B: In einem Hochhaus? Nein. Das wäre mir zu ungemüt-
               lich. Ich möchte in einer renovierten Altbauwohnung
               wohnen.
            C: Das wäre mir zu unbequem. Ich möchte am liebsten...
               (usw.)

Vorschläge:

Schloß   Haus am Rande einer
Gartenhaus   Großstadt
renovierte Altbauwohnung   eine Villa in Spanien
Wohnwagen   Zelt
Bauernhaus

Neue Wörter

die Insel *island*   sauber *clean*
die Luft *air*   träumen von *to dream of*
die Steuern *taxes*

◻ **Aktivität 11.** **Mein Wunschtraum**

In was für einer Umgebung oder in was für einem Land möchten Sie am
liebsten leben? Wovon träumen Sie?

BEISPIEL: Ich träume von einer Insel, wo ich den ganzen Tag in der
            Sonne faulenzen kann.

Großstadt   den ganzen Tag in der Sonne faulenzen
Kleinstadt   die Menschen / freundlich
Dorf   keine Autos / kein Verkehr
Berg   die Luft / sauber
Insel   das Leben / nicht so hektisch
am Ozean   ins Theater / in die Oper / ins Konzert gehen
Land   keine Steuern zahlen
?   ?

RSM

„In so einem Hochhaus möchte ich nicht wohnen!"

Unsere eigenen vier W

Neue Wörter

der Abstellraum *storage room*
die Diele *entrance way, hallway*
der Eingang *entrance*
die Garderobe *wardrobe, closet*

Liebe Mart

Wir wohnen
in unseren
Wänden. V
sind wir
Haus einge
schicken E
und eine
Grundrisse
sehr glückl
uns bald

▣ Aktivität 12. Familie H

Schauen Sie sich den Grundriß v
an. Ergänzen Sie dann folgende S

Das Haus hat zwei Stockwerke: ___
man zuerst in ___³. Rechts nebe
ein ___⁵. Von der Diele führt ei
liegt links. Neben der Küche ist n
gang in der Diele führt eine ___
sind drei Schlafzimmer, eins für
___¹³. Leider gibt es nur ein ___
schlafzimmer führt eine Tür dire
geschoß noch ___¹⁶.

Gemütlich muß es sein.

▣▣▣▣ *Kulturnotiz*

To call a home, a room, or a public place like a restaurant **gemütlich** is a compliment everyone appreciates. **Gemütlichkeit** means that one feels at ease and comfortable in a place. Furnishings, decorative touches, as well as the congeniality of the people in it, all combine to bring about **Gemütlichkeit.**

Gemütlich sitzen bei einer Tasse Kaffee im Wohnzimmer

▣ Aktivität 14. Beschreiben Sie diese Studentenbude.

Nützliche Ausdrücke:

Links/Rechts neben der Tür / neben dem Fenster steht ___.
Rechts an der Wand hängt ___.
Davor/Daneben liegt/steht ___.
Auf dem Boden liegt/liegen ___.

In this last case, **lassen** plus an infinitive express
to, or on behalf of, the subject of the sentence. No
pronouns (**uns, mir**) in two of the preceding sente
person for whom the action is intended.

When **lassen** is used with a dependent infiniti
modal, forming the perfect tense with a double in

Herr Bauer hat den Wagen
 reparieren lassen.

Mr. Ba

Wir haben uns ein Haus auf
 dem Land bauen lassen.

*We had
 coun*

Neue Wörter

die Blume (-n) *flower*

anstreichen (streicht an) *to
 paint (e.g. a house)*

aufstellen (stellt auf) *to put, set
 up*

einbauen (baut ein) *to build in*

pflanzen *to plant*

tapezieren *to wallpaper*

▣ Übung 3. Bekannte von Ihnen ziehen u

Ihre Bekannten erklären Ihnen, was sie selbst (selber
und was jemand anders für sie machen wird.

BEISPIEL: Die Blumen im Garten pflanzen wir s
 Die Küche lassen wir modernisieren.

- das Haus renovieren
- die Möbel aufstellen
- das Badezimmer modernisieren
- die Zimmer anstreichen
- das Wohnzimmer und Eßzimmer tapezieren
- die Garderobe in der Diele einbauen
- die neue Waschmaschine aufstellen
- Gemüse im Garten pflanzen

▣ Übung 4. Einen Monat später

Ihre Bekannten sind jetzt umgezogen. Sie berichten Ihr
ten sie selbst gemacht haben, und welche Arbeiten jem
gemacht hat. (*Refer to the list in the previous activity for*

BEISPIEL: Wir haben das Haus renovieren lassen. D
 haben wir selbst tapeziert.

▣ Aktivität 15. Was ist Ihre Meinung?

Finden Sie das gemütlich oder ungemütlich? Geben Sie auch den Grund
an.

BEISPIEL: Ich finde die Mensa sehr ungemütlich. Sie ist zu groß und
 zu laut.

Wie finden Sie:

Ihr eigenes Zimmer
das Klassenzimmer
die Bibliothek

die Mensa
das Wohnzimmer zu Hause
?

Aktivität 15. Suggestion: Before
doing this activity, brainstorm with
the whole group to expand the list of
places named, to personalize this
activity.
Note: This activity reviews how to
state the reason for an opinion (or
action), a topic that is presented in
the grammar section of this chapter.
The example sentence states a reason in the simplest way. Ask students for different ways to say the
same thing, e.g., by using a conjunction (*weil, denn*).

GRAMMATIK IM KONTEXT ▣▣▣▣▣▣▣▣▣▣▣▣

The Interrogative Pronoun: *was für (ein)*

To ask what kind of person someone is, or what kind of thing something
is, use the interrogative pronoun **was für (ein)**. The case of the noun that
follows **was für (ein)** depends on its function in the sentence. **Für** does
not function as a preposition here and does not, therefore, determine the
case of the noun.

NOMINATIVE:

Was für eine Stadt ist das?

What kind of city is this?

ACCUSATIVE:

Was für eine Wohnung sucht
 ihr?

*What kind of apartment are
 you looking for?*

Was für einen Sessel habt ihr
 gekauft?

*What sort of easy chair did you
 buy?*

DATIVE:

In **was für einem** Sessel sitzt
 man am bequemsten?

*In what kind of easy chair can
 one sit most comfortably?*

Mit **was für einem** Wagen
 seid ihr gefahren?

*With what kind of car did you
 drive?*

PLURAL:

Was für Möbel wollt ihr
 kaufen?

*What kind of furniture do you
 want to buy?*

Was für Leute wohnen da?

What kind of people live there?

Note that **ein** is omitted in the plural.

Was für ein. Note: No example
sentence is provided for the genitive
case because it has little, if any,
practical application.
Suggestion: Do a substitution exercise for a quick practice of forms. For
the nominative case: *Was für eine
Stadt ist das? (Haus, Wohnung,
Wagen, Auto, Straße, Film, usw.);* for
the accusative case: *Was für eine
Wohnung sucht (habt) ihr? (Haus,
Wagen, Sessel, Lampe, Tisch, Sofa);*
for the dative case: *In was für einem
Haus wohnst du? (Stadt, Zimmer,
Wohnung, Studentenwohnheim)*
Suggestion: Have students ask
each other *was für ein* questions
pertaining to people or objects in the
class to personalize the exercise;
e.g., *Was für ein Buch hast du da?
Was für einen Wagen hast du?* The
classmate addressed answers the
question as it applies to him or her.

☐ **Übung 2.** Probleme mit der Wohnun...
Vermieter

Jan ist ausgezogen, weil er Probleme mit dem Ve...
Sie Sätze im Perfekt.

> BEISPIEL: durfte keine Musik spielen.→
> Er hat keine Musik spielen dürfen.

1. mußte hohe Nebenkosten zahlen
2. durfte nur einmal in der Woche ein Bad nehm...
3. konnte dort nicht in Ruhe (*peace and quiet*) an...
4. sollte bei der Gartenarbeit helfen, wollte aber...
5. wollte manchmal Musik hören, durfte aber ni...
6. durfte nach 22.00 Uhr keine Besucher haben
7. mußte bis spätestens 24.00 Uhr im Hause sein...
8. konnte sich einfach nicht mit dem Vermieter v...

The Verb *lassen*

The verb **lassen (läßt, ließ, gelassen)** has a numbe...
meanings:

1. *to leave, leave behind*

Laß mich bitte in Ruhe.	*Please le...*
Er läßt den Wagen immer auf der Straße (stehen).	*He alwa...* *street.*
Hast du die Schlüssel im Auto gelassen?	*Did you...* *car?*

2. *to let, allow, permit* (with a dependent infinitive)

Gerd, laß uns doch aufs Land ziehen.	*Gerd, let'...*
Nein, laß uns lieber in der Stadt bleiben.	*No, let's...*
Schuberts haben ihre Tochter nicht in eine WG ziehen lassen.	*The Schu...* *daught...* *munal...*

3. *to have something done* (with a dependent infinit...

Wir lassen uns ein Haus auf dem Land bauen.	*We are ha...* *the cou...*
Herr Bauer läßt seinen Wagen reparieren.	*Mr. Bauer...*
Ich habe mir die Wohnung zeigen lassen.	*I had som...* *apartme...*

☐ **Übung 5.** Fragen und Antworten

Finden Sie eine passende Antwort auf jede Frage.

> BEISPIEL: A: Wo ist deine Kamera?
> B: Die habe ich zu Hause gelassen.

1. Wo ist der Hausschlüssel denn schon wieder?
2. Woher hast du den neuen Sessel?
3. Seit wann geht die Kuckucksuhr wieder?
4. Wo ist deine alte Couch?
5. Habt Ihr das Badezimmer selbst renoviert?
6. Wo ist deine Kamera?

a. vom Geschäft schicken lassen
b. zu Hause lassen
c. beim Uhrmacher reparieren lassen
d. in der alten Wohnung lassen
e. machen lassen
f. abholen lassen

The Verbs *brauchen* and *scheinen*

The verbs **brauchen** and **scheinen** are sometimes used with a dependent infinitive preceded by **zu**.

Brauchen is used with a negative plus an infinitive with **zu** to express what someone does not have to do. It replaces the modal **müssen**, which is generally not used with a negation.

Ich **brauche** heute **nicht zu arbeiten.** Gestern **habe** ich auch **nicht zu arbeiten brauchen.**	*I don't have to work today.* *Yesterday I did not have to work either.*

Note the double infinitive preceded by **zu** in the perfect tense.

The verb **scheinen** with an infinitive that is preceded by **zu** expresses what seems to be the case.

Er **scheint** nicht zu Hause **zu sein.** Das Haus **scheint** neu **zu sein.**	*He doesn't seem to be at home.* *The house seems to be new.*

☐ **Übung 6.** Interaktion

Fragen Sie einen Partner oder eine Partnerin: Was mußt du heute noch machen, was brauchst du nicht zu machen?

> BEISPIEL: A: Mußt du heute arbeiten?
> B: Nein, heute brauche ich nicht zu arbeiten.

1. mit deinem Professor reden
2. deinen Freund oder deine Freundin besuchen
3. das Auto / die Wäsche waschen
4. einkaufen gehen
5. die Miete bezahlen
6. arbeiten

Brauchen and scheinen. **Note:** These verbs are similar to modal verbs, except of course that the dependent infinitive is preceded by *zu.* Students need to actively master only the present tense and be able to recognize other tenses in reading. **Point out:** Even though *brauchen... zu* is used instead of *müssen* when a sentence contains *nicht* or *kein*, *müssen* can be used in a sentence with a negative when the verb is stressed. A good example of this is seen in the ad on page 370, *Sie müssen kein Fisch sein....*

Neue Wörter

aus sein *to be off/out*
sich am Telefon melden *to answer the phone*
  Niemand meldet sich (am Telefon). *No one is answering the phone.*
verreist sein *to be on a trip*

▣ Übung 7. Was ist denn los?

Finden Sie eine passende Reaktion.

BEISPIEL: Die Kuckucksuhr geht nicht mehr. (kaputt sein) →
          Sie scheint kaputt zu sein.

1. Bei Meiers meldet sich niemand am Telefon.
2. Die Lampe ist aus.
3. Ich habe jemanden in der Wohnung gesehen.
4. Müllers haben sich neue Möbel gekauft.
5. Ich habe meine Nachbarn lange nicht gesehen.

a. kaputt sein
b. wieder vermietet sein
c. verreist sein
d. nicht zu Hause sein
e. viel Geld haben

Infinitive Clauses

Infinitive clauses often function as necessary complements of verbs, adjectives, and nouns; that is, without them the sentence would be incomplete. The infinitives used in these clauses are always preceded by **zu**.

Familie Schulz hat sich entschlossen, aufs Land **zu ziehen.**	*The Schulz family decided to move to the country.*
Es macht ihnen Spaß, im Garten **zu arbeiten.**	*They are having fun working in the garden.*
Es ist nicht leicht **zu sparen.**	*It is not easy to save money.*

The infinitive with **zu** is always the last element of the sentence. Separable-prefix verbs place **zu** in between the separable prefix and the verb stem.

Ich habe gestern versucht, dich **anzurufen.**	*I tried calling you up yesterday.*
Du hast doch versprochen **vorbeizukommen.**	*You promised to come by.*

A comma sets off an infinitive clause that includes more than just the infinitive with **zu**. No comma is used otherwise.

Here are additional examples of nouns, adjectives, and verbs that are typically followed by an infinitive clause.

Zeit haben:	Ich habe keine Zeit umzuziehen.
Geld haben:	Wir haben kein Geld, ein Haus zu bauen.
Lust haben:	Herr Bauer hat keine Lust, mit dem Wagen zur Arbeit zu fahren. (*Mr. Bauer doesn't feel like driving to work.*)
Spaß machen:	Es macht Spaß, in ein neues Haus einzuziehen.
schwierig:	Es ist schwierig, eine preiswerte Wohnung zu finden.
günstig:	Es ist günstig, in der Stadt zu wohnen.
schön:	Es ist schön, ein eigenes Haus zu haben.
sich entschließen:	Er hat sich entschlossen auszuziehen.
vergessen:	Ich habe vergessen, die Miete zu zahlen.
versprechen:	Ich habe ihm versprochen, ihn zu besuchen.

Zeit haben. Suggestion: As you go over the expressions in class, ask students to come up with additional examples for each expression. You might also want to ask for the English equivalents.
Note: *Es macht Spaß, mit Freunden zu reisen.* Students previously learned *Lesen macht Spaß; Schwimmen macht Spaß.* When the infinitive is at the beginning of the sentence, it is the subject (the *-ing* form in English). As a verbal complement, the infinitive is used with *zu* and placed at the end of the sentence: *Es macht Spaß, im Garten zu arbeiten.* The infinitive clause generally contains more than just the infinitive with *zu*. Otherwise you would simply say *Essen macht Spaß.*

▣ Übung 8. Wie ist das?

Ist es schön, schwierig, anstrengend oder langweilig?

> BEISPIEL: ein preiswertes Zimmer finden →
> Es ist schwierig, ein preiswertes Zimmer zu finden.

1. ein neues Haus bauen
2. in einem Hochhaus in New York wohnen
3. mit dem Wohnwagen durchs Land fahren
4. mit Freunden in einer WG wohnen
5. im Garten arbeiten
6. in eine andere Stadt umziehen
7. meine Wohnung / mein Zimmer aufräumen
8. ?

▣ Übung 9. Interaktion

Fragen Sie einen Partner oder eine Partnerin: Was hast du versprochen? Was hast du vergessen?

> BEISPIEL: Ich habe versprochen, meine Freundin anzurufen.

	Rechnung bezahlen
	einen Scheck unterschreiben
	Geld zurückzahlen
Ich habe versprochen	tanken
Ich habe vergessen	Freund oder Freundin besuchen
	einkaufen
	am Wochenende vorbeikommen
	?

▣ **Übung 10.** **Macht das Spaß? Macht das keinen Spaß?**

Schauen Sie sich an, was die Leute auf den Bildern machen. Hätten Sie
Lust oder keine Lust dazu?

BEISPIEL: Es macht Spaß, in der Sonne zu liegen.

Infinitive Clauses with *um... zu* and *ohne... zu*

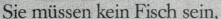

Sie müssen kein Fisch sein, um Meerwasser trinken zu können.

Bessere Dinge für ein besseres Leben **DU PONT**

German uses many different ways to explain the reasons for an action. You have already learned a number of them. Compare the following sentences.

1. Stefan spart für einen neuen CD Player. (*prepositional phrase:* **für einen neuen CD Player.**)
2. Stefan will einen neuen CD Player kaufen. Deswegen spart er jetzt. (*adverb:* **deswegen** *therefore*)
3. Stefan spart. Er will nämlich einen neuen CD Player kaufen. (*adverb:* **nämlich** [*no English equivalent*])
4. Stefan spart, denn er will einen neuen CD Player kaufen. (*coordinating conjunction:* **denn**)
5. Stefan spart, weil er einen neuen CD Player kaufen will. (*subordinating conjunction:* **weil**)

There is yet another way to explain one's reasons for an action—that is, with an infinitive clause with **um... zu**.

Stefan spart, **um** einen neuen CD Player **zu kaufen**.
Familie Huber spart seit Jahren, **um** ein Haus auf dem Lande **zu bauen**.

Stefan is saving money in order to buy a new CD player.
The Hubers have been saving for years in order to build a house in the country.

Auf den

- kulturelles Leben
- die Umgebung: Schönheit der Natur und Möglichkeiten, vie
  nen zu sein
- Freunde und Familie in der Nähe
- Sportmöglichkeiten
- Sonstiges

1. Inform
   Partne
   a. Ha
   b. Wa
   c. Wo
      ter
2. Sehen
   republ
3. Schau
   Artikel
4. Welche

Auf den ersten Blick 1

Schauen Sie sich den Titel und den ersten Satz des folgenden Te

1. Das Wort „Nest" im Titel steht für
   a. das Nest eines Vogels (bird).   b.   das Elternhaus.   c.   d
2. Die „Alten" sind
   a.   die Großeltern.   b.   die Eltern.   c.   alle Leute über drei
3. „Raus aus dem Nest" bedeutet hier:
   a.   die Eltern wollen ausziehen.   b.   die Jungen kommen na
   verlassen (leave) das Elternhaus.

Stadt

Raus aus dem Nest! Was nun?

Weg von zu Hause, Neues ausprobieren, anders leben als die „Alte
davon träumen Töchter und Söhne. Über die Hälfte aller jungen Leute zwis
21 und 24 Jahren lebt nicht mehr bei den Eltern. Sie tun sich mit Fr
oder Freundin zusammen, leben in Wohngemeinschaften, teilen° Wohn
Ansichten° und in manchen Fällen auch die Arbeit miteinander, nisten
in unbewohnten Häusern oder alten Werkstätten° ein.

KEINER WILL IN DIE STADT ZURÜCK

Katrin, Logopädin° von Beruf, bewohnt mit drei Freun
zusammen einen alten Bauernhof. Sie haben Garten und Kle
vieh° und einen Vertrieb von Naturprodukten.°

Katrin, Rike, Peter und Martin haben einen Beruf oder studieren. Sie p
deln° zwischen Stadt und Dorf hin und her. Nur wegen des Geldes? Katr
„Ich finde es auch anstrengend nur zu Hause. Da gibt es sehr viel zu tu
Draußen und im Haus… Trotz Doppelbelastung° will keiner in die Sta
zurück." Katrins Freundin Rike, eine Medizinstudentin: „Wir haben Auslau
hier. Wir sehen was wachsen.° Wir fangen auch was an damit. Das ist sch
ein wichtiger Teil° für unser Leben hier, auch für die Gruppe. Nach so eine
Uni-Tag komme ich wenigstens in ein Zuhause zurück, wo frische Luft is
wo ich im Garten wühlen° oder einfach weit gucken° kann. In der Stadt gibt
doch nur Straßen und kleine Zimmer mit großen Schreibtischen. Da füh
ich mich wie in einer Kaninchenbox."

Brigitte Sonderheft, 198

Statistisc
rad. 26(
Keller. E
bei den
Doktore
Kliniken
rieren.
auf schw
nen rad

Use **ohne… zu** plus an infinitive to express that you do something without doing something else.

Hubers wollen ein Haus bauen, **ohne** große Schulden **zu machen.**	*The Hubers want to build a house without going into heavy debt.*
Er ist an mir vorbeigegangen, **ohne** mich **zu erkennen**.	*He passed by me without recognizing me.*

⊡ Übung 11. Was sind ihre Gründe dafür?

State the reasons for their actions in several different ways.

1. Familie Huber spart regelmäßig. Die Familie will ein Haus auf dem
   Land bauen.
2. Ich spare auch. Ich will nach dem Studium eine Reise um die Welt
   machen.
3. Hans und Erika sind jungverheiratet (newlywed). Sie sparen auch. Sie
   wollen neue Möbel für ihre Wohnung kaufen.
4. Herr und Frau Koch gehen zu einem Immobilienmakler (real-estate
   agent). Sie wollen sich mehrere Eigentumswohnungen in München
   ansehen.
5. Frau Sommer ist zu einem Immobilienmakler gegangen. Sie will ein
   kleines Haus in der Nähe der Stadt kaufen.
6. Michael will ins Studentenwohnheim ziehen. Er will mit anderen
   Studenten zusammen wohnen und Spaß haben.
7. Susan will aus dem Studentenwohnheim ausziehen. Sie will ihre
   Ruhe haben und arbeiten können.

⊡ Übung 12. Woran haben diese Leute nicht gedacht?

Bilden Sie Sätze mit **ohne… zu.**

BEISPIEL: Erich und Katja haben den Altbau gekauft, ohne an die
          hohen Renovierungskosten zu denken.

1. Erika hat die Wohnung gemietet.	a. hat nicht an die Zahl 13 gedacht
2. Hans ist in die Wohnung im 13. Stock eingezogen.	b. haben die Miete nicht gezahlt
3. Schuberts sind in die Altbauwohnung eingezogen.	c. hat nicht nach den Nebenkosten gefragt
4. Erich und Katja haben einen Altbau gekauft.	d. haben sie nicht renoviert
5. Herr Wegener hat den Vermieter angerufen.	e. hat nicht nach der Adresse der Wohnung gefragt
6. Die Schmidts sind ausgezogen.	f. haben nicht an die hohen Renovierungskosten gedacht
	g. hat/haben die Wohnung nicht gesehen

Übung 12. Suggestion: Begin this
exercise by asking several students
Warum sparen Sie? Allow for different ways of expressing their reasons,
but be sure to include *um… zu.*

Special Use of *möchte* and *will*

Compare the following German sentences:

1. Ich möchte aufs Land ziehen. (*I would like to move to the c*
2. Ich will dort ein Haus kaufen. (*I want to buy a house there.*)
3. Mein Freund möchte, daß ich in der Stadt bleibe. (*My boyf* *would like me to stay in the city.*)
4. Ich will, daß er auch umzieht. (*I want him to move too.*)

In sentences 1 and 2, the subject (**ich**) wishes to do something. tences 3 and 4, the subject (**mein Freund, ich**) wants someone something. In this latter case, the modal **möchte** or **will** must b lowed by a dependent clause introduced by **daß**.

▣ Übung 13. Was möchten sie? Was wollen sie?

BEISPIEL: Mein Freund möchte, daß ich mit ihm ins Kino g

Ich	will, daß	unser Haus renovieren lass
Meine Familie	möchte, daß	einen gebrauchten Wagen
Mein Freund		möglichst bald aus dem St
Meine Freundin		wohnheim ausziehen
?		in ein Studentenwohnheim
		ein Haus mieten
		ins Kino gehen
		?

LESEN IM KONTEXT

In diesem Teil lesen Sie über Leben und Wohnen in Deutschland, die Wohnsituation einiger junger Menschen und über eine deutsch Stadt, wo Fahrräder die Autos verdrängen (*replace*).

Vor dem Lesen

▣ Aktivität. Sie ziehen um.

Was ist Ihnen wichtig im neuen Wohnort? Was steht an erster Stelle an letzter Stelle?

- gute Arbeitsmöglichkeiten
- preiswerte Wohnmöglichkeiten
- gute Restaurants

Zum T

1. Welch

   a. M
      BI

   b. ei

2. Fasse
   ben u

   J

3. Finde
   steht

4. Wie
   Stad
   (Bau

   a. _
   b. _
   c. _
   d. _
   e. _
   f. _

5. Wäh
   besc

Täglich radeln 1000 Pendler° in die Stadt

Einer von den vielen ist Erich Walbaum, Vater von sechs Kindern. Seit zwölf Jahren schwingt er sich an jedem Arbeitstag um 6.10 Uhr aufs Rad, ist eine Viertelstunde später am Bahnhof des Dörfchens Davensberg, fährt im Zug zwölf Minuten bis Münster, steigt° dort auf sein am Hauptbahnhof abgestelltes zweites Fahrrad und sitzt pünktlich um Viertel vor sieben an seinem Schreibtisch in einer Versicherungsgesellschaft.°

Auch der Baurat° ist ein Fahrrad-Fan

Verkehrsplaner Heinrich Wacker: „Ich muß den Münsteranern ja sehr dankbar sein, daß sie soviel radeln." Er will die Stadt den Radfahrern versüßen.° Überdachte° und bewachte° Parkanlagen, schnelle, hindernisfreie Radwege im Stadtkern° und Privilegien an den Kreuzungen gehören zu seinem Sonderangebot. Schon jetzt hat die Westfalen-Metropole Radwege, die zusammen über zweihundert Kilometer lang sind.

In den letzten zehn Jahren ist das Klima für Radfahrer in der Bundesrepublik Deutschland deutlich angenehmer geworden. Der Anteil° der Zweiräder am innerstädtischen Verkehr stieg in dieser Zeit um fast dreißig Prozent. Nicht nur in Münster, sondern auch anderswo in deutschen Städten denken Stadtplaner auch an die Radfahrer. Aber so weit wie die Münsteraner sind sie noch lange nicht. Denn nicht jede Stadt hat auch so günstige Voraussetzungen:° Das Land ist flach,° und die Stadt drängt sich° um einen kleinen Kern, so daß wichtige Behörden° und Geschäfte schnell zu erreichen sind. Am Bahnhof etablierte sich eine „Radwache";° hier kann man für 1,50 Mark am Tag seinen zweirädrigen Liebling bewachen lassen.

Scala, Nov./Dec. 1988

commuters

climbs

insurance company

building inspector

make attractive
covered / guarded
center

share

preconditions / flat / clusters
offices
bike guard

Zum Text 2

Finden Sie Informationen zu folgenden Aussagen:

1. Viele Einwohner von Münster fahren Rad.
   - wer radfährt
   - Zahl der Räder
2. Ein Beispiel für die vielen Pendler ist Erich Walbaum.
   - Familiensituation
   - aus welcher Stadt
   - Weg zur Arbeit (wie, wie lange)
3. Münster ist besonders günstig zum Radfahren.
   - Sonderangebote für Radfahrer
   - Geographie der Stadt
   - Radwache am Bahnhof
4. Radfahren in Deutschland ist im allgemeinen sehr beliebt.
   - Klima für Radfahrer
   - Statistik

Der Rauch°

smoke

Das kleine Haus unter Bäumen am See.
Vom Dach steigt Rauch.
Fehlte er,°
wie trostlos° dann wären
Haus, Bäume und See.

Fehlte... If it were missing

desolate

> *Bertolt Brecht*

Zum Text 3

1. Brecht „zeichnet" eine Landschaft in seinem Gedicht. Was gehört zum Bild dieser Landschaft?
2. Warum ist der Rauch in dieser Landschaft wichtig? Was bedeutet er für den Dichter?

Der Rauch.   Note: This short poem by Brecht consists of just three sentences. The first is really only a sentence fragment: two simple statements and a hypothesis. The poem shows the influence of an Asian verse form—Japanese Haiku poetry—in its stark simplicity and evocative nature imagery.
Suggestion: You might lead students toward discussion of the mood of the poem and the presence or absence of man in this image of nature.

Nach dem Lesen

▣ Aktivität 1. Stadtbroschüre

Sie arbeiten beim Fremdenverkehrsamt in Münster und schreiben eine Broschüre für Besucher und Leute, die eventuell nach Münster ziehen wollen.

▣ Aktivität 2. Ihre Heimatstadt

Sie arbeiten beim Fremdenverkehrsamt Ihrer Heimatstadt und müssen eine Broschüre entwerfen über die positiven Aspekte Ihrer Stadt oder Ihrer Gegend. Die Werbung richtet sich an Besucher. Können Sie Ihre Heimatstadt empfehlen?

Aktivität 1, 2.   Suggestion: Both activities can be done in class with students working in pairs; or assign them as written homework to be presented in class the following day.

▣ Aktivität 3. Ein Brief nach Deutschland

Schreiben Sie einen Brief an einen imaginären deutschen Bekannten und beschreiben Sie, wie man in Ihrer Heimatstadt lebt. Beschreiben Sie unter anderem:
- die Umgebung : flach, Berge, am Ozean
- Wohnmöglichkeiten: Einfamilienhäuser, Hochhäuser
- Verkehr
- Freizeitbeschäftigungen.

Können Sie diese Stadt oder diesen Platz zum Besuch oder als Wohnort empfehlen?

WORTSCHATZ

Substantive

Wohnen

der Altbau (Altbauten)	old building (built before World War II)
das Dorf (¨er)	village
die Eigentumswohnung (-en)	condominium
das Einfamilienhaus (¨er)	single-family house
die Großstadt (¨e)	large city
der Grundriß (-sse)	blueprint
das Hochhaus (¨er)	high rise
die Kleinstadt (¨e)	small city
der Neubau (Neubauten)	new building (built after World War II)
das Reihenhaus (¨er)	town house
die Umgebung	surroundings, vicinity
nähere Umgebung	in the vicinity, close to
die Vorstadt (¨e)	suburb
der Wohnwagen (-)	trailer, camper

Im Haus

der Aufzug (¨e)	elevator
der Balkon (-e)	balcony
der Boden (¨)	floor (of a room)
das Dachgeschoß	floor right below the roof (often with slanted walls)
die Diele (-n)	entranceway, hallway
die Dusche (-n)	shower
der Eingang (¨e)	entrance
die Garderobe (-n)	wardrobe, closet
der Schrank (¨e)	closet, cupboard
der Bücherschrank	bookshelf, cabinet
der Eisschrank	refrigerator
der Kleiderschrank	clothes closet
der Kühlschrank	refrigerator
der Raum (¨e)	room
der Abstellraum	storage room
die Spülmaschine (-n)	dishwasher
der Teppich (-e)	carpet
der Teppichboden (¨)	wall-to-wall carpet
die Terrasse (-n)	terrace
die Treppe (-n)	staircase
die Tür (-en)	door
die Eingangstür	entrance door

die Wand (¨e)	wall
die vier Wände	(fig.) one's home
die Waschmaschine (-n)	washing machine
das WC	toilet
die Zentralheizung (-en)	central heating

Andere Substantive

die Blume (-n)	flower
der Hinweis (-e)	tip, clue
der Immobilienmakler (-), die Immobilienmaklerin (-nen)	real-estate agent
die Insel (-n)	island
die Luft	air
der Mieter (-), die Mieterin (-nen)	renter, tenant
der Ozean (-e)	ocean
die Schulden (pl.)	debts
Schulden machen	to go into debt
der Vermieter (-), die Vermieterin (-nen)	landlord, landlady

Verben

ansehen (sieht an), sah an, angesehen	to look at
anstreichen (streicht an), strich an, angestrichen	to paint (a wall)
aufstellen (stellt auf)	to set up, put up
aus sein	to be off/out
bauen	to build
einbauen (baut ein)	to build in
betragen (beträgt), betrug, betragen	to amount to, come to
die Miete beträgt	the rent comes to
bedeuten	to mean
einrichten (richtet ein)	to furnish
sich entschließen, entschloß, entschlossen	to decide
erkennen, erkannte, erkannt	to recognize
führen	to lead
hängen, hing, gehangen	to hang

sich (am Telefon) melden	to answer the phone
Niemand meldet sich.	No one is answering (the phone).
modernisieren	to modernize
pflanzen	to plant
renovieren	to renovate
scheinen, schien, geschienen	to seem
tapezieren	to wallpaper
träumen von	to dream of
vermieten	to rent (out)
verreist sein	to be on a trip
versprechen (verspricht), versprach, versprochen	to promise
ziehen, zog, ist gezogen	to move
ausziehen (zieht aus)	to move out
einziehen (zieht ein)	to move in
umziehen (zieht um)	to move (from one place to another)

Adjektive und Adverbien

alleinstehend	single
außerdem	in addition, besides that

benutzbar	usable, can be used
damals	formerly
ganz	entire, whole
jungverheiratet	newlywed
laut	loud
ober	upper
sauber	clean

Sonstiges

ab	from . . . on
ab erstem Juni	from June first on
bevor (*conj.*)	before
gegenüber von	across from
in Ruhe	in peace and quiet
jemand	somebody, someone
jemand anders	somebody else
selbst (*emph. pronoun*)	self
um...zu	in order to
Das geht nicht.	That doesn't work.
Die Uhr geht nicht.	The clock isn't working.
Das ist mir recht.	That's fine with me.

DER START IN DIE ZUKUNFT

Lernziele *In this chapter you will learn about German schools and talk about career choices and training for young people in German-speaking countries. You will also discuss your own future plans.*

▣ Alles klar?

Was möchten Sie werden? Die Berufswahl und die Berufsausbildung gehören zu den wichtigsten Entscheidungen im Leben. Hier sehen Sie einige typische Anzeigen und Stellenangebote aus deutschen Zeitungen.

RSM

Ihr Start in die Zukunft
mit einer Ausbildung als
Versicherungskaufmann/-frau[a]

a. *insurance sales-man/woman*

Wir hätten einen tollen Job für eine

nette Telefonistin

RSM

EURO MARKT

Abiturientenausbildung[a] beim Euro Waren Verbrauchermarkt[b]

a. Abiturienten *graduates of the* Gymnasium
b. Verbraucher *consumer*

Was stimmt?

- Die Stellenangebote sind für
  a. Arbeitslose.
  b. junge Leute, die eine Ausbildungsstelle suchen.
  c. alle Leute, die eine Arbeit suchen.
- Schulabgänger in Frankfurt am Main (*see ad below*) können
  a. beim Arbeitsamt arbeiten.
  b. beim Arbeitsamt mit einem Berufsberater über ihre Zukunft sprechen.
  c. mit der Wahl einer Ausbildungsstelle noch warten.

IHRE ZUKUNFT

Schulabgänger[a] 1989: Jetzt keinen Tag mehr warten!

Es ist höchste Zeit, einen Termin[b] mit Ihrer Berufsberatung[c] zu vereinbaren: wir helfen bei der Wahl[d] der Ausbildungsstelle[e].

Sprechen Sie jetzt mit uns über Ihre berufliche Zukunft.

Arbeitsamt[f]
Frankfurt a. M.
Fischerfeldstraße 10—12
6000 Frankfurt a. M.
Telefon 069/21 71-1

Ihre Berufsberatung

RSM

a. der Schulabgänger *school graduate*
b. der Termin *appointment;* einen Termin vereinbaren *to make an appointment*
c. die Berufsberatung *career counseling*
d. die Wahl *choice*
e. die Ausbildungsstelle *training position*
f. das Arbeitsamt *employment office*

WÖRTER IM KONTEXT

Was erwartet man vom Beruf?

▣ Aktivität 1. Wer macht was?

BEISPIEL: Eine Architektin entwirft Häuser.

1. Detektiv(in)
2. Schauspieler(in)
3. Astronaut(in)
4. Sekretär(in)
5. Kellner(in)
6. Arzt/Ärztin
7. Architekt(in)
8. Musiker(in)
9. Automechaniker(in)
10. Programmierer(in)

a. untersucht Patienten
b. arbeitet mit Computern
c. spielt eine Rolle im Film oder auf der Bühne
d. arbeitet für die Polizei und löst Verbrechen
f. fliegt mit einem Weltraumschiff durch das Weltall
g. repariert Autos
h. serviert Essen und Trinken im Restaurant
i. spielt in einem Orchester
j. schreibt Geschäftsbriefe

Aktivität 1. **Suggestion:** Have students work in pairs, taking turns matching the name of an occupation to its description. Check comprehension and reinforce vocabulary by asking questions such as *Wer repariert Autos?* and *Wer entwirft Häuser?*

Photo.   Suggestion: Ask students *Was für Musik spielt dieser Straßenmusikant? Gibt es Straßenmusikanten in Ihrer Stadt? Nennen Sie einige Vorteile und Nachteile dabei?*

Für DM 15,- spielt dieser Straßenmusikant Beethovens Mondscheinsonate.

🔲 **Aktivität 2. Vorteile und Nachteile**

Was meinen Sie dazu?

Drawing.   Suggestion: Ask students *Was macht dieser Mann von Beruf? Gibt es diesen Beruf in Ihrem Land?*
Point out: Seeing a chimney sweep is considered to bring good luck!

BEISPIEL: Ein Astronaut hat die gefährlichste Arbeit.

1. Wer hat die gefährlichste Arbeit?
2. Welcher Beruf hat das meiste Prestige?
3. Wer arbeitet meistens an der frischen Luft?
4. Wer arbeitet meistens in einem Büro?
5. Wer verdient das meiste Geld?
6. Für welche Berufe muß man studieren?
7. Welche Arbeit bringt viel Streß mit sich?
8. Wer hat die längsten Arbeitsstunden?
9. Wer hat die langweiligste Arbeit?

Ein Schornsteinfeger arbeitet meistens an der frischen Luft.

Neue Wörter

die Aufstiegsmöglichkeit *opportunity for advancement*
die Gelegenheit *opportunity*
die Luft *air*
  an der frischen Luft *in the open air; outside*

die Stelle *place; position*
  an erster Stelle *in first place*
erwarten *to expect*
selbständig *independent*

Aktivität 2.   Note: Use the list of professions and occupations from *Aktivität 1* but expand it with others that students come up with.
Suggestion: Write the two or three most common answers to each question on the board. Call on individuals to summarize the characteristics of professions. For instance, *Ein Astronaut hat die gefährlichste Arbeit, aber er hat auch das meiste Prestige.*

🔲 **Aktivität 3. Interaktion. Berufswünsche**

Fragen Sie einen Partner oder eine Partnerin: „Was erwartest du von deinem Beruf? Was ist dir nicht so wichtig?" Verwenden Sie einige der unten folgenden Redemittel.

BEISPIEL: A: Mir ist ein sicherer Arbeitsplatz wichtig.
           B: Ein sicherer Arbeitsplatz ist mir nicht so wichtig, aber ich erwarte, daß ich Gelegenheit zum Reisen habe.

Aktivität 3.   Suggestion: Go over the lists of *Redemittel* and *Erwartungen* first. Then have students work in small groups, stating two or three important expectations for their future professions and contradicting what others have said. Ask one student in each group to summarize the most frequently mentioned expectations.

REDEMITTEL

Mir ist ____ (nicht) wichtig.
Ich erwarte, daß ____ .
Ich möchte gern ____ .
An erster Stelle steht für
  mich ____ .
____ interessiert mich
(nicht).

ERWARTUNGEN

möglichst viel Geld verdienen
viel Kontakt mit Menschen
anderen Menschen helfen
Spaß an der Arbeit
Gelegenheit zum Reisen
möglichst viel Freizeit
Prestige (Ansehen)
sicherer Arbeitsplatz
selbständig arbeiten
gute Aufstiegsmöglichkeiten
an der frischen Luft arbeiten

Aktivität 4. Suggestion: Have students scan the *Schaubild* first; then have them work in pairs to complete the activity.
Follow-up: Take a class survey. Read the items from the *Schaubild* to the class; students raise their hand whenever an item applies to them. Have the class create statistics similar to those of the *Schaubild*.
Aktivität 5 (below). Suggestion: Prepare this activity by asking *Was sind typische Berufe, von denen Kinder manchmal romantische Vorstellungen haben?* For ideas, refer to the drawing accompanying the activity. Then have students circulate in the classroom, talking to several classmates and jotting down their responses. Ask several students to share their findings with the whole class.

◻ **Aktivität 4. Was wollen junge Deutsche vom Beruf?**

Die Information finden Sie in dem Schaubild.

RSM

a. **künftig** *future*
b. *to advance*
c. **der Schmutz** *dirt*
d. *suitability*
e. **das Prestige**

Das wollen junge Leute vom Beruf
Von je 100 Jugendlichen sagten über ihre Berufswahl:
Das wichtigste bei meinem künftigen[a] Beruf ist...

35 ...daß ich aufsteigen[b] kann
32 ...daß ich Menschen helfen kann
46 ...Sicherheit des Arbeitsplatzes
26 ...mit interessanten Menschen zu tun haben
57 ...daß ich einen Ausbildungsplatz bekomme
25 ...keine Schmutzarbeit[c]
75 ...Eignung[d]
17 Hobbys verwirklichen
16 ...guter Verdienst
90 ...Spaß am Beruf
14 ...Ansehen[e]

© Globus 5660

1. Die meisten jungen Deutschen glauben, daß ____ das wichtigste ist.
2. Ungefähr ein Drittel der jungen Leute will ____ .
3. Ein Viertel der Jugendlichen will ____ machen.
4. 35% der jungen Leute erwarten, daß ____ .
5. Für 16% ist ____ wichtig.
6. Die wenigsten jungen Leute erwarten ____ von ihrem künftigen (*future*) Beruf.
7. Einen sicheren Arbeitsplatz haben ist wichtig für ____ .

◻ **Aktivität 5. Traum und Wirklichkeit**

Fragen Sie einen Partner oder eine Partnerin: „Was wolltest du als Kind immer werden? Was willst du jetzt werden? Was sind die Gründe?"

BEISPIEL: Früher wollte ich immer Astronaut werden. Jetzt will ich Ingenieur werden. Man braucht wenige Astronauten, aber viele Ingenieure.

MAURER
TECHNIKER
ARCHITEKT
INGENIEUR
MILLIONÄR
CLOWN
BAUCHREDNER

Schuljahre

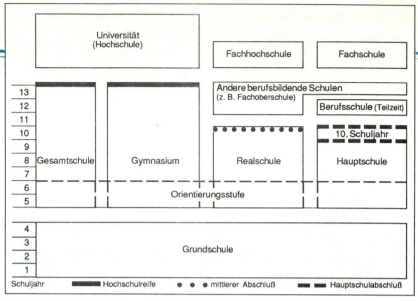

Universität (Hochschule)	Fachhochschule · Fachschule

Andere berufsbildende Schulen (z. B. Fachoberschule)

Berufsschule (Teilzeit)

Schuljahr				
13 12 11 10 9 8 7	Gesamtschule	Gymnasium	Realschule	10. Schuljahr / Hauptschule
6 5		Orientierungsstufe		
4 3 2 1		Grundschule		

Schuljahr ▬▬▬ Hochschulreife   • • • • mittlerer Abschluß   ▬ ▬ ▬ Hauptschulabschluß

◻◻◻◻ *Kulturnotiz*

Mit sechs Jahren beginnt für Kinder in Deutschland die Schule. Alle Kinder gehen zuerst vier Jahre lang gemeinsam auf **die Grundschule.** Danach trennen sich die Wege.

Ein großer Teil der Schüler und Schülerinnen geht dann auf **die Hauptschule,** die nach dem neunten oder zehnten Schuljahr mit dem Hauptschulabschluß endet. Danach suchen sich die meisten Schulabgänger eine Ausbildungsstelle für einen praktischen Beruf. An zwei Tagen in der Woche müssen die „Azubis" (**Auszubi**ldenden oder Lehrlinge) auf **die Berufsschule** gehen. Dort lernen sie vor allem praktische Fächer, die für den künftigen Beruf wichtig sind.

Ein kleinerer Teil der Schüler und Schülerinnen geht von der Grundschule auf die **Realschule.** Sie endet nach dem zehnten Schuljahr mit dem Abschluß der **mittleren Reife.** Danach geht man auf eine **Fachschule** oder auch auf eine Berufsschule.

Als dritte Möglichkeit gibt es **das Gymnasium.** Das Gymnasium umfasst neun Klassen, vom fünften bis zum dreizehnten Schuljahr. Am Ende von neun Jahren machen Schüler **das Abitur.** Ohne Abitur (in Österreich und in der Schweiz **die Matura** genannt) kann man nicht studieren.

Als Alternative für die drei verschiedenen Schultypen gibt es in Deutschland heutzutage auch **die Gesamtschule.** Ähnlich wie an amerikanischen Schulen gehen alle Schüler zur selben Schule bis zum Abschluß; daher der Name Gesamtschule.

Wer trifft die Entscheidung, auf welche Schule ein Schüler oder eine Schülerin nach den ersten vier Jahren geht? Gewöhnlich empfiehlt der Klassenlehrer oder die Klassenlehrerin—aufgrund der Leistungen (*achievements*)—auf welche Schule ein Schüler oder eine Schülerin gehen sollte. In einigen Ländern der Bundesrepublik gibt es eine sogenannte Orientierungsstufe (*lit. orientation level*) für das fünfte und sechste Schuljahr. Erst danach entscheidet sich, ob ein Schüler oder eine Schülerin aufs Gymnasium, auf die Realschule oder auf die Hauptschule geht.

Der erste Schultag: der Ernst des Lebens beginnt.

Aktivität 9. Ein Zeugnis

Schauen Sie sich die Fächer und Noten in dem deutsch[...]
(11. Klasse Gymnasium) an und beantworten Sie die F[...]

Leistungen[a]			
Religionslehre(rk[b])	gut	Geschichte. . . .	
Deutsch.	befriedigend	Erdkunde	
Latein (2 . Fremdspr.)	befriedigend	Sozialkunde . . .	
Griechisch (__. Fremdspr.)	------------	Ethik	
Englisch (1 . Fremdspr.)	gut	Wirtschafts- u. Rechtsleh	
Französisch (3 . Fremdspr.)	ausreichend	Kunsterziehung . . .	
Mathematik	befriedigend	Musik.	
Physik	befriedigend	Sport. . . .	
Chemie	sehr gut	Handarbeiten . . .	
Biologie	------------		

1. Wie viele Fächer hat diese Schülerin? Vergleichen Sie [...]
   Fächern, die Sie in der *high school* hatten.
2. In welchen Fächern hat sie die besten Noten? In welch[...]
   hatten Sie die besten Noten?
3. Wie viele Fremdsprachen lernt sie? In welcher Sprache [...]
   beste Note? Wie viele Fremdsprachen hatten Sie in der [...]

Eine Bewerbung

Neue Wörter

der Abiturient, die Abiturientin
*person who has passed the
Abitur*
**der Bewerber, die
Bewerberin** *applicant*
die Bewerbung *application*
das Büro *office*
der Kaufmann, die Kauffrau
*businessman,
businesswoman*
der Laborant, die Laborantin
lab technician
der Lebenslauf *résumé*
**handschriftlicher Lebens-
lauf** *handwritten résumé*
tabellarischer Lebenslauf
résumé in outline form

das Lichtbild *photo[...]*
die Unterlagen *pape[...]
(documentation)*
**abhängen von (häng[...]
depend on*
ausbilden zu *to train[...]
ausgebildet werden[...]
trained*
**bestehen (hat bestand[...]
pass*
sich bewerben um *to [...]*
erfolgreich *successful[...]*

Aktivität 6. Schuljahre

Berichten Sie über Ihre eigenen Schuljahre, indem Sie den folgenden
Lückentext mit Information über Ihre Schuljahre ergänzen. Gibt es sonst
noch Interessantes über Ihre Schuljahre zu berichten?

Ich bin mit ____ Jahren zuerst auf die Schule gekommen. Diese Schule
habe ich ____ Jahre besucht. Danach bin ich ____ gegangen. Mit ____
Jahren habe ich den ____ Abschluß gemacht. Meine beste Zeit war, als
ich ____ .

Neue Wörter

die Erdkunde *geography*
das Fach *subject (in school)*
　das Hauptfach *major subject*
　das Nebenfach *minor subject*
die Handarbeit *crafts*
die Kunst *art*
die Sprache *language*

die Fremdsprache *foreign
language*
die Wirtschaft *economy,
economics*
malen *to draw*
ähnlich *similar*
anders *different*

Aktivität 7. Stundenpläne

Sie sehen hier die Stundenpläne von drei deutschen Schülern. Ein
vierter Stundenplan für die 13. Klasse im Gymnasium steht auf Seite 109
dieses Buches. Schauen Sie sich die verschiedenen Stundenpläne an, und
vergleichen Sie dann das deutsche und amerikanische Schulsystem.

- Was für Fächer haben die Schüler in Deutschland? Ist das ähnlich an
  amerikanischen Schulen? Was ist anders?
- Was halten Sie für besser oder schlechter? Begründen Sie Ihre Meinung.

Hanjo (9 Jahre alt): 3. Klasse, Grundschule

Zeit	Montag	Dienstag	Mittwoch	Donnerstag	Freitag	Samstag
				Mathematik	--	Mathe
8-8.45	Sprache	Sprache	Religion	Sprache	Mathe	Mathe
8.45-9.30	Mathe	Sachunterricht[a]	Sprache	Sachunterricht	Sprache	
10-10.45	Sprache	Mathe	Mathe	Malen	Musik	
10.45-11.30	Sachunterricht	Religion	Handarbeiten	Malen	Religion	
11.45-12.30	--	Sport	--	Sport	Schwimmen	
12.30-13.15	--	--	--			

Saskia (12 Jahre alt): 6. Klasse, Orientierungsstufe fürs Gymnasium

	Montag	Dienstag	Mittwoch	Donnerstag	Freitag	Samstag
				Englisch	Mathe	(2 Tage
1.	Mathe	Englisch	Mathe	Englisch	Englisch	im Monat)
2.	Musik	Deutsch	Englisch	Mathe	PC[b]	
3.	Erdkunde	Erdkunde	Deutsch	Geschichte	Deutsch	
4.	Biologie	Biologie	Deutsch	Geschichte	AG[c]	
5.	Deutsch	Religion	Religion	Schwimmen	AG	
6.	Sport	--	--			

a. *social studies*
b. *personal computer*
c. AG = Arbeitsgemeinschaft
　(*group project activities*)

Nicolas (15 Jahre alt): 9. Klasse, Realschule

	Montag	Dienstag	Mittwoch	Donnerstag
1.	Technik	Deutsch	Deutsch	Arbeit/Wirtschaft
2.	Technik	Mathe	Religion	Physik
3.	Mathe	Erdkunde	Englisch	Mathe
4.	Englisch	Englisch	Musik	Englisch
5.	Deutsch	Geschichte	Kunst	Technik
6.	Chemie	Physik	Geschichte	--
7.	Spanisch	--	Arbeit/Wirtschaft	--

REDEMITTEL

Hier / Bei uns gibt / gab es kein(e) _____ .
Als ich zur Schule ging, _____ .
Die Schule dauert _____ .
Die deutschen / amerikanischen Schüler haben m
Ich halte das _____ System für besser / schlechter.
Meiner Meinung nach _____ .

▣ Aktivität 8. Ein Interview

Fragen Sie jemanden in der Klasse nach seinen oder ihren
in der Schule. Berichten Sie dann darüber.

1. Welches Fach war
   a. dein Lieblingsfach? b. das langweiligste Fach?
2. Wer war
   a. der oder die beste Lehrer(in)? b. der oder die net
   (War der netteste auch der beste?)
3. Für welches Fach hast du
   a. am meisten gearbeitet? b. nur wenig getan?
4. Sonstige Fragen: _____ .

▣▣▣▣ *Kulturnotiz*

Es gibt folgende sechs Noten oder Zensuren (*grades*) für S

1 (die Eins, der Einser) = sehr gut *excelle*
2 (die Zwei, der Zweier) = gut *good (*
3 (die Drei, der Dreier) = befriedigend *satisfa*
4 (die Vier, der Vierer) = ausreichend *suffici*
5 (die Fünf, der Fünfer) = mangelhaft *deficie*
6 (die Sechs, der Sechser) = ungenügend *inadequ*

Man sagt, zum Beispiel: Ich habe eine Eins, und eine V
drei Zweier und fünf Vierer im Zeugnis habe ich ke
(*report card*). Ich habe eine Eins in Religion

ASTA PHARMA
Ein Unternehmen der Degussa

Ausbildung 1989[a]

Wir gehören zu den führenden Arzneimittelherstellern[a] mit eigener Forschung.[b]
Für den Ausbildungsbeginn am 1. September 1989 suchen wir noch Bewerber
und Bewerberinnen für die Ausbildung zum/zur

Biologielaboranten/in Chemielaboranten/in und Bürokaufmann/-frau

Als Abiturient/in können Sie bei uns Biologielaborant/in werden; wenn Sie
einen mittleren Bildungsabschluß[c] vorweisen können, bilden wir Sie – je nach
Ihren Neigungen und Interessen – zu Chemielaboranten/innen oder Bürokauf-
leuten aus.

Wenn Sie Interesse haben in einer erfolgreichen, zukunftsorientierten Konzern-
tocher der Degussa ausgebildet zu werden, dann schicken Sie uns umgehend[d]
Ihre Bewerbungsunterlagen (handschriftlicher Lebenslauf, Lichtbild und die
letzten beiden Zeugnisse), damit wir Sie zu unseren Eignungstests einladen
können.

a. *producers of pharmaceuticals*
b. *research*
c. *mittleren... mid-level school diploma (from a Realschule)*
d. *immediately*

▣▣▣▣ *Kulturnotiz*

Es ist nicht ungewöhnlich, bei einer Bewerbung einen handschriftlichen Lebenslauf zu
verlangen. Die Handschrift ermöglicht einen
Einblick in persönliche Qualitäten eines
Bewerbers oder einer Bewerberin. Oft ist ein
Lebenslauf noch in Form eines Berichtes
(*narrative*). Ein tabellarischer Lebenslauf
nach amerikanischem Muster (*model*) ist
auch möglich.

▣ Analyse: Ein Stellenangebot

- Welche Wörter oder Ausdrücke in der Anzeige deuten an, daß die Firma junge Leute sucht, die gerade einen Schulabschluß gemacht haben?
- Wie zeigt die Firma, daß sie Männer und Frauen sucht?
- Welchen Unterschied macht die Firma zwischen Bewerbern mit Abitur und Bewerbern ohne Abitur?
- Wie beschreibt sich die Firma selbst, damit sie gute Bewerber anzieht (*attracts*)?
- Wie unterscheidet sich die Bewerbung bei einer deutschen Firma von der Bewerbung bei einer Firma in Ihrer Heimat?

Kulturnotiz (page 388). It is illegal nowadays to accept or reject a candidate on the basis of a graphologist's analysis of his or her handwriting. Nonetheless, handwritten résumés are still widely required to determine the legibility and neatness of an applicant's handwriting.

▣ Aktivität 10. Ausbildung 1989

Wählen Sie passende Wörter aus der Liste, um die Sätze zu ergänzen.

Abitur	handschriftlichen Lebenslauf
ausgebildet	Lichtbild
Bewerber	Unterlagen
Bewerberinnen	die zwei letzten Zeugnisse
Eignungstest (*aptitude test*)	
erfolgreichen	

Aktivität 10. **Note:** This activity is a follow-up to the *Analyse*, to highlight new vocabulary students should learn.
Suggestion: This activity can be assigned for homework, or students can work in pairs, taking turns responding.

1. Die Firma sucht ＿＿ für die Ausbildung zum/zur Biologielaboranten / in.
2. Um Biologielaborant(in) zu werden, muß man ＿＿ haben.
3. Wenn man einen mittleren Bildungsabschluß hat, wird man als Chemielaborant(in) ＿＿.
4. Um sich zu bewerben, muß man folgende ＿＿ schicken: ＿＿.
5. Die Firma lädt alle Bewerber und Bewerberinnen zu einem ＿＿ ein.
6. Die Ausbildung ist in einer ＿＿ und zukunftsorientierten Firma für Arzneimittel.

▣ Aktivität 11. Hören Sie zu. Ein Gespräch unter Freunden

Aktivität 11. **Suggestion:** Let students listen to the entire dialogue once. Ask them to give the gist of the conversation. Then have them scan the true/false statements before listening to a second playing of the conversation. Finally, students respond to the statements, making any necessary corrections.

Was stimmt? Was stimmt nicht? Korrigieren Sie falsche Aussagen.

1. Peter sucht einen Ausbildungsplatz. Stimmt.
2. Peter ist noch nicht zum Arbeitsamt gegangen. Stimmt nicht. Er ist gestern hingegangen.
3. Peter hat ein interessantes Stellenangebot in der Zeitung gefunden. Stimmt.
4. Er hat sich um eine Ausbildungsstelle beworben. Stimmt.
5. Er hat die Firma sofort angerufen. Stimmt nicht. Er wartet noch.
6. Peter ist sehr enthusiastisch, weil er die Firma gut kennt. Stimmt nicht. Er kennt sie nicht.
7. Die Firma verlangt, daß Bewerber Biologie studiert haben. Stimmt nicht. Nicht für seine Stelle.

▣ **Aktivität 14.** **Interaktion. Ein Gespräch über eine Stellensuche**

	A		B

A

Was willst du ____ machen? ⟶ Ich will mir eine Stelle ____ suchen.

nach dem   bei einer Bank
   Studium   in einem Büro
nach der Schule   bei einer Firma
im Sommer   auf einem Schiff
?

Wie ____ ?   Man muß/kann ____ .

die Stellenangebote in der Zeitung
   durchlesen
zur Arbeitsvermittlung an der Uni
   gehen
Freunde, Familie, Bekannte fragen
zum Arbeitsamt/zur Berufsberatung
   gehen
Glück haben

Wie lange dauert es, bis ____ ?   ____ geht es schnell.
                               ____ dauert es ____ .

Manchmal   ein paar Wochen
Meistens   ____ Monate

Na, dann wünsche ich dir ____ .   Vielen Dank.
       alles Gute
       viel Glück
Ich drücke dir die Daumen.

Aktivität 14. **Note:** Now that students have practiced the material of the *Wörter im Kontext* in various formats, they are asked to use it actively in a controlled format. Have them do the activity with two or three different partners, creating different versions with each. Call on several pairs to model a dialogue for the class.

GRAMMATIK IM KONTEXT ▣▣▣▣▣▣▣▣▣▣▣▣

Future Tense

You recall that in German the present tense can also refer to future action, particularly when an adverb of time is present.

Nächstes Jahr macht Sabine ein Praktikum in den USA.
Morgen schickt sie mehrere Bewerbungen ab.

Next year Sabine is going to do an internship in the U.S.A.
Tomorrow she will send off several applications.

5. Sie haben Ihr letztes Geld fü…
   total pleite und bekommen …
6. Sie haben einen wichtigen G…
   Vaters) vergessen. Eine Woch…
   daran.

▣ Übung 2. Partnerarbeit

Stellen Sie Ihrem Partner oder Il…
über die Zukunft. Schreiben Sie …

> BEISPIEL: A: Wo wirst du in …
> B: Ich werde wahr…
> sein.

Sagen Sie etwas über:

Familie	Geld ver…
Kinder	Beruf
Autos	Hobby
Haus	

Relative Clauses

A relative clause provides additiona…
object, much like an adjective does.

> XYZ Company is looking for…
> are interested in a career i…
>
> XYZ Company is looking for…
> a degree in computer scien…
>
> XYZ Company is looking for…
> limit.

▣ Analyse

- Identify the main clause and the …
  three ads.
- About whom or what do the depe…
- What words are at the beginning …
  or what do these words refer?
- Where is the finite verb placed in …
- How would you express these sent…

The actual future tense form is used to express future time when there is no specific time reference to the future.

Read the following cartoon.

Poesie[a] von Erich Rauschenbach   RSM

a. *poetry*
b. das Gedicht *poem*
c. der Erfolg *success*
d. der Himmel *sky, heaven*
e. *to lift*
f. *famous*
g. der Wunsch *wish*
h. *probably*
i. weitermachen *to continue*
j. wie… *as before*
k. ausgewählt *select*
l. die Leserschaft *readership*

▣ Analyse: *Poesie*

- Underline the verbs in each sentence. Which verbs clearly refer to the present?
- Find three sentences that express the poet's wishful thinking.
- What verb forms are used to express his wishful thinking? Where are the verbs placed?
- For each sentence expressing the poet's hopes for the future, state the reality of his present life.

In German, the future tense is formed with the auxiliary verb **werden** and the infinitive of the main verb. The infinitive is placed at the end of the sentence.

Eines Tages **werde** ich Erfolg **haben**.

Someday I will be successful.

Millionen **werden** meine Bücher **kaufen**.

Millions will buy my books.

FUTURE TENSE FORM…

ich werde kaufen

Sie werden kaufen

du wirst kaufen

er wird ⎫
sie wird ⎬ kaufen
es wird ⎭

Expressing Probability

The future tense is frequently use…
often in conjunction with the adv…
(*probably*).

Consider the following hypot…
cessful poet of the cartoon *Poesie.*

> Zehn Jahre später: Der Di…
> einen Mercedes 500 SL mi…
> in einer Villa in Spanien. A…
> trifft sich die Prominenz d…

What is probably true about Ansel…

> Er **wird wohl** jetzt erfolgre…
> **sein.**
> Millionen **werden** jetzt
> **wahrscheinlich** seine
> Bücher **kaufen.**
> Er **wird wohl** sehr reich sei…

☐ **Übung 1.   Partnerarbeit:** …

Notieren Sie, wie Ihr Gesprächspar…
Sie darüber in der Klasse. Verwend…

BEISPIEL: Sie haben eine Verab…
            Ich werde ihn anrufe…

1. Sie haben eine Verabredung mit…
   fürs Kino, aber Sie müssen unb…
   morgen fertig schreiben.
2. Sie essen im Restaurant. Als Sie…
   Sie Ihr Portemonnaie (*wallet*) ni…
3. Sie beobachten (*observe*) in eine…
4. Ihr Auto bleibt mitten auf der St…

Forms of the Relative Pronoun

In German, a relative clause is always introduced by a relative pronoun. The forms of the relative pronoun are the same as those of the definite article, except in the genitive singular and the genitive and dative plural.

The indefinite relative pronouns **wer** (*whoever*) and **was** (*that, which, what*) will be discussed in chapter fourteen. (**Was** was used in the ad for **Handelsblatt: was Leute lesen.**)

	Masculine	*Neuter*	*Feminine*	*Plural*
Nom.	der	das	die	die
Acc.	den	das	die	die
Dat.	dem	dem	der	denen
Gen.	dessen	dessen	deren	deren

Relative pronouns take the gender and number of their antecedent—that is, of the noun they modify. The case of the relative pronoun, however, is determined by its function within the relative clause; it can be the subject, an object, or a prepositional object.

SUBJECT

Wir suchen eine junge Frau, **die** Kreativität besitzt.

*We are looking for a young woman **who** possesses creativity.*

ACCUSATIVE OBJECT

Wie heißt der junge Mann, **den** du gestern kennengelernt hast?

*What is the name of the young man **whom** you met yesterday?*

DATIVE OBJECT

Gehören Sie zu den Menschen, **denen** ein sicherer Arbeitsplatz wichtig ist?

*Are you one of those people to **whom** a secure position is important?*

GENITIVE OBJECT

Wir sind eine Firma, **deren** Produkte weltbekannt sind.

*We are a company **whose** products are known worldwide.*

PREPOSITIONAL OBJECT

Laborant ist ein Beruf, **für den** ich mich interessiere.

*Being a lab technician is an occupation **in which** I am interested.*

Note that the relative clause in German is always preceded by a comma. The finite verb is placed at the end of the relative clause. The relative pronoun must always be expressed in German; it cannot be omitted as it sometimes can in English, nor can a preposition be separated from the relative pronoun to which it belongs.

Der Mann, **den** ich kürzlich kennenlernte,...

The man I met recently . . .
(*The man whom I met recently . . .*)

Die Frau, **mit der** ich sprach,...

The woman I spoke with . . .
(*The woman with whom I spoke . . .*)

⊡ **Übung 3.** Wir suchen.

Übung 3. Suggestion: Assign *Übung 3*, numbers 1 to 3, for homework and number 4 as an in-class exercise.

Wir suchen eine modisch interessierte, gepflegte[a] junge Dame, die nach einem Praktikum[b] in unserem Hause eine Lehre als

Einzelhandels-kauffrau

absolvieren[c] möchte.

Horn

Kurfürstendamm 213
1000 Berlin 15
Telefon 8 81 40 55

RSM

a. gepflegt *well groomed*
b. *internship*
c. eine Lehre absolvieren *to serve an apprenticeship*

Wir suchen für unsere Brigade einen **Jungkoch** der mit Freude und Interesse seinen Beruf ausübt. Beginn 21. 7. 87, 5-Tage-Woche, geregelte Arbeitszeit, guter Verdienst. Hotel Restaurant zur Post in OF-Bürgel. ☎ 069 / 86 13 37

RSM

a. Dipl.-Ing. = Diplom-Ingenieur *graduate in engineering*
b. *communications technology*
c. *mind, intellect*
d. *professional schools or colleges*
e. *employer*

Kommen Sie als Dipl.-Ing. Nachrichtentechnik[b] (FH) zur Post!

DESHALB SUCHEN WIR SIE:

Junge Diplom-Ingenieurinnen und -Ingenieure, mit Herz und Verstand.[c] Junge Menschen, die von den Fachhochschulen[d] kommen und bei uns ihren Weg machen wollen.

WIR SIND DER GRÖSSTE ARBEITGEBER[e] IN DER BUNDESREPUBLIK.

RSM

1. Each of these ads contains a relative clause. Identify the relative clauses, and determine which nouns the relative pronouns refer to.
2. Are the relative pronouns subjects or objects?
3. Express each sentence in English.
4. Restate each sentence by substituting a different antecedent noun, as shown below, and making the necessary changes in the relative pronoun.
   a. Jungkoch → Jungköchin
   b. Dame → Herr; Einzelhandelskauffrau → Einzelhandelskaufmann
   c. junge Menschen → eine junge Frau, einen jungen Mann

▣ **Übung 4. Was suchen sie?**

Beschreiben Sie, wer die Firmen sind, und was sie wollen. Suchen Sie zwei Möglichkeiten für jeden Satz.

BEISPIEL: Wir suchen einen jungen Mann, der gern kocht.

1. Unsere Firma sucht eine junge Dame,
2. Wir suchen einen jungen Mann,
3. Die Post sucht junge Leute,
4. Wir sind ein erfolgreiches Unternehmen,
5. Wir sind ein junger Betrieb,

der/die eine Ausbildung als Bürokaufmann/-frau möchte.

der/das Ihnen gute Aufstiegsmöglichkeiten bietet.

der/die nicht nur Briefe tippen kann.

der/die Herz und Verstand hat.

die bei uns Karriere machen möchten.

der/die gern kocht.

denen ein gutes Gehalt wichtig ist.

die/das eine solide Ausbildung bietet.

dem/der/denen interessante Mitarbeiter wichtig sind.

dessen Produkte weltbekannt sind.

der/dem eine gute Ausbildung wichtig ist.

▣ **Übung 5. Qualifikationen**

Ergänzen Sie die passenden Relativpronomen.

1. Unsere Firma sucht Abiturienten, _____ Kreativität und Flexibilität besitzen.
2. Wenn Sie eine junge Dame sind, _____ sich für technische Berufe interessiert, schicken Sie uns Ihre Bewerbung.
3. Wir suchen einen Auszubildenden, _____ das Bäckerhandwerk lernen möchte.
4. Elektroniker ist ein Beruf, für _____ sich viele junge Leute interessieren.
5. Wir sind eine Firma, mit _____ Sie über Ihre Zukunft reden sollten.
6. Ist Ihnen die Umwelt, in _____ Sie leben, wichtig? Dann werden Sie doch Umwelt-Wart (*environmental analyst*), ein neuer Beruf für engagierte Menschen, _____ unsere Umwelt wichtig ist.
7. Wir suchen junge Leute, _____ ein gesundes Selbstbewußtsein haben.
8. Wir sind eine progressive Firma, _____ Produkte weltbekannt sind.
9. Der Personalchef, mit _____ Susanne kürzlich sprach, hat ihr einen Ausbildungsplatz angeboten.
10. Wir suchen junge Leute, _____ Herz und Verstand haben und _____ bei der Post Karriere machen wollen.

TIME MANNER PLACE

Petra fährt heute allein in die Stadt.

The Position of *nicht*

You recall that the adverb **nicht** is used when the negative
cannot be used. The position of **nicht** varies according to th
the sentence.

When **nicht** negates a specific sentence element, thereb
it, it precedes this sentence element.

> Ich komme **nicht heute,** sondern morgen.
> Wir haben **nicht viel Geld.**

When **nicht** negates an entire sentence, its position varies:
Nicht follows:

1. *the finite verb:*
2. *adverbs of time:*   Petra **kommt nicht.**
3. *most other adverbs:*   Petra kommt **morgen ni**
4. *dative and accusative objects:* Petra kommt morgen **lei**
                                    Sie gibt mir **das Buch n**

Nicht precedes:

1. *predicate adjectives:*   Petras Bewerbungsbrief i
                                    lang.
2. *predicate nouns:*   Das ist **nicht Petras Brie**
3. *verbal complements at the end of the sentence:*
   a. *separable prefixes:*   Sie schickt den Brief **nic**
   b. *past participles:*   Sie hat sich **nicht bewor**
   c. *infinitives:*   Sie will sich **nicht bewer**
                                    Sie braucht sich **nicht zu**
                                    bewerben.
4. *prepositional phrases:*   Sie hat sich **nicht um die**
                                    beworben.
5. *place or direction:*   Klaus ist **nicht nach Haus**
                                    gegangen.

◉ Übung 9. Das stimmt nicht!

Sagen Sie das Gegenteil.

1. Hans hat die Prüfung bestanden.
2. Er kennt den Personalchef der Firma Wüstenrot.
3. Er hat seine Bewerbung zur Post gebracht.
4. Er hat den Personalchef gestern angerufen.

◉ Übung 6. Berufswünsche

Was für einen Beruf wünschen Sie sich? Was für eine Firma suchen Sie?

> BEISPIEL: Ich wünsche mir einen Beruf, bei dem ich selbständig
> arbeiten kann. Ich suche eine Firma, die progressiv ist.

eine gute Ausbildung / gute Aufstiegsmöglichkeiten bieten
gut bezahlen
mir Spaß machen
progressiv/erfolgreich sein
(bei der Firma gibt es) ein gutes Arbeitsklima
(in der Firma) mit netten Kollegen zusammenarbeiten
selbständig arbeiten können

Übung 6. Suggestion: Encourage students to choose several items describing the kind of profession they'd like to have and the kind of firm they would like to work for. They should also add their own ideas.

Neue Wörter

der Briefträger *mail carrier*   beißen (hat gebissen) *to bite*
die Nachbarin *neighbor*   böse *annoyed, angry*
die Tatsache *fact*

◉ Übung 7. Das kann passieren.

Beschreiben Sie, was Sie auf dem Bild sehen. Einige Tatsachen:

> Der Hund, Fritz, gehört dem Jungen, Niko.
> Die Nachbarin, Frau Kluge, hat alles genau gesehen.
> Der Vater des Jungen, Herr Krüger, ist sehr böse.
> Der Briefträger, Herr Grimm, hat die Polizei geholt.

Übung 7. Suggestion: Focus students' attention on the first drawing and the *Neue Wörter*. Working in small groups, students first scan the *Tatsachen* and the second drawing on the next page. Each student in a group states a fact about one of the characters portrayed. One person in each group summarizes the facts for the whole class.

Wer ist wer? Beschreiben Sie, indem Sie Relativsätze bi[...]

BEISPIEL: Herr Grimm ist der Briefträger, der die P[...]

1. Fritz
2. Frau Kluge
3. Herr Krüger
4. Niko
5. Herr Grimm

⊡ Übung 8. Was wünschen Sie sich?

Nennen Sie mindestens drei Wünsche.

BEISPIEL: Ich wünsche mir einen Freund, der tolerant [...]
voll ist.

REDEMITTEL

Ich wünsche mir
ich suche
ich möchte
ich hätte gern

Word Order: Expressions of Time, Manner, and Place; *nicht*

Expressions of Time, Manner, and Place

When expressions of time, manner, and place occur in a sen[...]
order is as follows: time, manner, place. Few sentences, how[...]
contain all three types of expressions.

⊡ Übung 12. Wann?

Ergänzen Sie: **eines Morgens, eines Tages, eines Abends, eines Nachts.**

1. Ich werde _____ berühmt sein.
2. Kennen Sie Kafkas Erzählung *Die Verwandlung* (*The Metamorphosis*)? Der Protagonist, Gregor Samsa, wachte _____ als ungeheures Ungeziefer (*huge bug*) auf.
3. Rotkäppchen (*Little Red Riding Hood*) ging _____ in den Wald.
4. Ich hatte Klaus lange nicht gesehen. Dann sah ich ihn _____ nach dem Theater in der Stadt.
5. Ich konnte _____ nicht schlafen und las um ein Uhr noch ein Buch. Plötzlich hörte ich draußen laute Stimmen.

Übung 12. **Suggestion:** Have students work in pairs, taking turns responding.
Follow-up: Extend this activity by encouraging students to add something to each statement, e.g., *Ich hatte Klaus lange nicht gesehen. Dann sah ich ihn eines Abends nach dem Theater in der Stadt. Er wollte gerade ins Restaurant gehen.*

⊡ Übung 13. Partnerarbeit

Wann war das? Wann wird das sein? Eines Morgens, eines Tages, eines Abends, eines Nachts? Schreiben Sie die Sätze Ihres Partners auf.

BEISPIEL: A: Eines Tages
B: Eines Tages werde ich perfekt Deutsch sprechen.

Übung 13. **Suggestion:** Encourage students to be as creative as possible.

LESEN IM KONTEXT

In diesem Teil lesen Sie über die Arbeitswelt und Menschen mit ungewöhnlichen Karrieren.

Vor dem Lesen

⊡ Aktivität 1. Assoziationen

Stellen Sie eine Liste mit Berufen zusammen, für die Sie sich interessieren. Was fällt Ihnen bei diesen Berufen ein?

BEISPIEL: Astronaut: Abenteuer, Mond, fliegen, gefährlich

Aktivität 1. **Suggestion:** List the different careers students come up with on the board. Then ask them *Was fällt Ihnen dabei ein?*
Suggestion: Students can also work in small groups. One group suggests an occupation, and another gets one minute to come up with associations.

⊡ Aktivität 2. Ein Interview

Fragen Sie einen Partner oder eine Partnerin: „Erinnerst du dich an deine erste Stelle?" Sie möchten wissen,

- was er oder sie gemacht hat.
- wo die Stelle war.
- wer der/die Chef(in) war.
- was er oder sie verdient hat.
- was er oder sie mit dem Geld gemacht hat.

Geben Sie einen kurzen Bericht in der Klasse darüber.

☐ **Aktivität 3. Ihre Berufspläne**

Interviewen Sie eine Person in Ihrer Klasse, und berichten Sie darüber. Sie möchten wissen,

- was er oder sie werden möchte, und warum.
- was für eine Ausbildung man dafür braucht.
- was für persönliche Qualitäten man dafür braucht.

Auf den ersten Blick 1

1. Was wissen Sie darüber: Welche Jugendlichen haben Schwierigkeiten, nach der Schule eine Stelle (Lehrstelle) zu bekommen? Bedenken Sie dabei: Junge/Mädchen, Schulnoten, Schulabschluß, Ausländer, Rasse, Sprachkenntnisse.

    BEISPIEL: Ein Jugendlicher, der die Landessprache nicht gut spricht, hat Schwierigkeiten, eine Stelle zu bekommen.

2. Schauen Sie sich den Titel und die fettgedruckten Teile des Textes auf Seite 406 an. Dieser Text ist:
    a. eine Anzeige vom Arbeitsamt.
    b. eine Anzeige von Betrieben (Firmen), die Lehrlinge suchen.
    c. eine Anzeige der Berufsberatung an einer Schule.
3. Lesen Sie die ersten vier Zeilen der Anzeige. Die Wörter **gestern** und **heute** weisen (point) auf eine Veränderung (change) und ein künftiges Problem. Was hat sich von gestern auf heute geändert? (Mehrfachnennung ist möglich.)
    a. Es gibt heute mehr Lehrlinge als gestern.
    b. Es gibt heute weniger Lehrlinge als gestern.
    c. Für einige Lehrstellen gibt es heute nicht genug Lehrlinge.
4. Schauen Sie sich die fettgedruckten Sätze im Text an: „**Denken Sie deshalb um.**" „**Verhalten Sie sich marktgerecht.**" Diese Sätze sind:
    a. Aussagesätze (statements).
    b. Fragesätze.
    c. Imperativsätze.
    Diese Sätze richten sich spezifisch an (are directed to):
    a. Lehrlinge.
    b. das Arbeitsamt.
    c. Betriebe, die Lehrlinge einstellen.

Auf den ersten Blick 1. Suggestion: Assign numbers 2, 3, and 4 for homework to be discussed in the next class. Number 1 can be done in class in two ways: (1) students respond individually or (2) students create sentences on the board.

☐☐☐☐ *Kulturnotiz*

People moving to the Federal Republic of Germany are grouped according to their country of origin. Until 1990, when this became unnecessary, citizens of the German Democratic Republic (**Übersiedler**) were always automatically entitled to full citizenship on arrival. Others entitled to immediate citizenship are so-called **Aussiedler.** These are ethnic Germans from eastern countries, e.g., Poland, Czechoslovakia, Rumania, and

the USSR man. The "guest" we instance, invited in ties when Many hav their chil and face

Zum Text 1

1. Beantworten Sie folgende Fragen zum Text.
    a. Die Anzeige erwähnt (mentions) vier Kategorien von J lichen, die oft Schwierigkeiten haben, eine Lehrstelle weil es Vorurteile gegen sie gibt. Wer sind diese Jugen
    b. Was will das Arbeitsamt mit dieser Anzeige erreichen (accomplish)?
2. **Manche Arbeitgeber glauben...** Bilden Sie Sätze mit eine **ment** und dem passenden **Gegenargument** für jede Grup Jugendlichen. Suchen Sie passende Satzteile aus der Tab

    BEISPIEL: Manche Arbeitgeber (employers) glauben, daß A nicht so gut arbeiten wie deutsche Arbeiter. Ab Ausländer sind hochmotiviert und können mei Deutsch.

GRUPPE	VORURTEIL (*PREJUDICE*)
Jugendliche mit schlechten Schulnoten	haben kein Talent für tech nische Berufe
Mädchen	sprechen kein Deutsch
Ausländer	leisten schlechte Arbeit
Aussiedler	sind nicht so gut wie deutsche Arbeiter

Lehrlinge°—gibt's die noch?

Lehrlinge – gibt's die noch?

Gestern konnte Ihr Betrieb° unter vielen Bewerb[...]
Heute ist der Lehrling gesucht. In einigen Wirtschafts[...]
Gegenden° können schon heute nicht alle Ausbildungs[...]
werden. Das kann in der Zukunft ernste Schwierigkeit[...]

Denken Sie deshalb um.° Verhalten Sie sich marktgerecht.°

Beurteilen° Sie die Jugendlichen° nicht nur nach den S[...]
Auch Einstein war kein Musterschüler. Fragen Sie sich, ob [...]
Zeug zu einer erfolgreichen Ausbildung hat. Allein dara[...]
Viele warten auf eine Chance. Viele entwickeln° sich erst [...]
Können°.

Lassen Sie auch Mädchen an technische Berufe hera[...]
Damen können das genauso gut wie die jungen Männe[...]
oft genug bewiesen.° Ohne Frauen geht es nicht – das g[...]
auch für die Arbeitswelt.

Denken Sie an die jungen Aussiedler, die zur Zeit in [...]
kommen. Sie sind hoch motiviert. Holpriges° Deutsch mu[...]
grund sein. Erfahrungsgemäß eignen sich junge Leute s[...]
an, wenn sie damit täglich umgehen müssen.

Nutzen Sie den Ehrgeiz° junger Ausländer. Sie warte[...]
Mittlerweile können sie meist gut Deutsch. In der Schule [...]
bewiesen, daß sie mithalten° können.

Bedenken Sie, daß Ihr Betrieb mit anderen um Lehr[...]
Je qualifizierter Ihr Ausbildungsangebot ist, desto größe[...]
Chancen, den Lehrling Ihrer Wahl zu finden.

Ein Gespräch mit der Berufsberatun[...] lohnt sich.

RSM

Auf den ersten Blick 2

Die folgenden Texte, Ausschnitte aus vier verschiedenen Artikeln, berichten über vier Deutsche und ihre ungewöhnlichen Tätigkeiten.

Welcher Titel (1–4) gehört zu welchem Text (a–d)?

1. _____ Herr Pfarrer predigt auch Heavy-Metal
2. _____ Das ist Deutschlands jüngster Bürgermeister
3. _____ Die Frau mit dem heißen Draht nach Entenhausen
4. _____ Wunderkind

Interessante Menschen und ungewöhnliche Tätigkeiten

a. Es war keineswegs Liebe° auf den ersten Blick. Doch sie hält inzwischen seit mehr als 30 Jahren. Als Dr. Erika Fuchs 1949 erstmals die amerikanischen Hefte mit bunten° Bildergeschichten von Micky Maus und Donald Duck sah, konnte sie sich nicht vorstellen,° daß diese Phantasiefiguren aus Walt Disneys Trickkiste auch bei uns Erfolg haben würden. Die damals 43jährige promovierte Kunsthistorikerin° war auf der Suche nach einem Job. „Meine Kinder brauchten mich nicht mehr 24 Stunden am Tag, und ich langweilte mich tödlich°", erinnert sie sich. „Offenbar kam ich im richtigen Moment ins richtige Büro. Denn trotz anfänglicher Skepsis habe ich die ‚Leutchen' aus Entenhausen inzwischen richtig liebgewonnen.°"

Seit jenem denkwürdigen Tag legt Frau Doktor den berühmten Enten° und ihren Freunden das (deutsche) Wort in die Schnäbel.°

Frau im Spiegel, April 1982

°love

°colorful

°imagine

°promovierte... art historian with a Ph.D.

°langweilte... was bored to death

°habe... I have become fond of the little people from Ducksburg.
°ducks
°beaks

b. Er ist 40facher Dollarmillionär. Doch diesen Wohlstand° sieht man ihm nicht an. Denn Andreas „Andy" Bechtolsheim trägt mit 31 Jahren immer noch am liebsten seine Studentenkluft: Jeans, Pullover und Sandalen. Auch das Chefbüro dieses Deutschen im kalifornischen Mountain View ist klein und karg,° seine Bedeutung° in der amerikanischen Computerwelt dafür aber um so größer: Der Zuwanderer vom Bodensee,° der Deutschland verließ, weil ihm hier die Studienbedingungen zu primitiv waren, entwickelte eine

°wealth

°sparse / importance
°Lake Constance

die Handarbeit (-en)	crafts
der Ingenieur (-e), die Ingenieurin (-nen)	engineer
der Kaufmann (Kaufleute), die Kauffrau (-en)	businessman, businesswoman
die Kunst	art
der Laborant (-n *masc.*) die Laborantin (-nen)	lab technician
der Lebenslauf (-e)	résumé
handschriftlicher Lebenslauf	handwritten résumé
tabellarischer Lebenslauf	résumé in outline form
der Lehrling (-e)	apprentice
das Lichtbild (-er)	photograph
der Nachbar (-n *masc.*), die Nachbarin (-nen)	neighbor
die Note (-n)	grade (on a report card)
der Praktikant (-n *masc.*), die Praktikantin (-nen)	job intern
das Praktikum (Praktika)	internship
die Sprache (-n)	language
die Fremdsprache	foreign language
die Stelle (-n)	position, place
an erster Stelle	in first place
eine feste Stelle	permanent position
der Stundenlohn (-e)	hourly wage
die Tätigkeit (-en)	occupation, activity
die Tatsache (-n)	fact
der Termin (-e)	appointment
die Unterlagen (*pl.*)	papers, documentation
das Vorstellungsgespräch (-e)	job interview
die Wirtschaft	economy; economics
das Zeugnis (-se)	report card
die Zensur (-en)	grade (on a report card)

Verben

abhängen von (hängt ab), hing ab, abgehangen	to depend on
abschicken (schickt ab)	to send off
ausbilden zu (bildet aus)	to train as
ausgebildet werden zu	to be trained as
beißen, biß, gebissen	to bite

Rechnerfamilie,° die nicht nur in den USA, sondern weltweit° zu einem Renner° wurde.

Das High-Tech-Märchen° von Sun Microsystems, wie Bechtolsheim seine Firma taufte, begann im Winter 1982 in einem kalifornischen McDonald's Restaurant. Dorthin hatte der Inder Vinod Khosla seine gleichaltrigen Studienkollegen Bechtolsheim und Scott McNealy eingeladen, um mit ihnen die Gründung eines eigenen Unternehmens zu besprechen. Der kaufmännisch begabte° Khosla… konnte den damals 26jährigen Bechtolsheim dafür gewinnen, den Prototyp eines Wundercomputers zu vermarkten, den er an der Stanford University entworfen hatte.

Capital, March 1987

c. „Verschiedene° Realitäten" nennt das Christian Hoppe. Der 30jährige Kölner legt gerade sein Examen in evangelischer Theologie ab° und will Pfarrer° werden. „Und abends laß' ich richtig Dampf ab°", sagt der junge Theologe. Wie? Als Bassist der Heavy-Metal-Band „Trans Am", die schon zwei LPs herausbrachte.

Hoppe: „Diese Rhythmik erzeugt° eine Portion von Gefühlen,° geht an die essentiellen Nerven. Das ist… eine andere Art° von Bestätigung,° die ich brauche."

In seinem späteren Beruf als Pfarrer hält Christian Hoppe sein ungewöhnliches Hobby sogar für wichtig. „Heute genügt° es nicht mehr, seinen starken Glauben° zu verteidigen.° Man muß auch zeigen, wie man selber in der Welt° steht."

Bild am Sonntag, Aug. 27, 1989

d. Er studiert Jura,° fährt einen knallgelben VW Käfer, Baujahr 1979, spielt in der zweiten Mannschaft TuS Hachenburg Handball und trägt am liebsten Jeans. Zur Zeit leistet er seinen Zivildienst ab und pflegt einen Querschnittgelähmten,° wenn er sich nicht gerade um seinen zweiten Job kümmern muß: Hendrik Hering (25) ist Deutschlands jüngster ehrenamtlicher Bürgermeister.

Hachenburg im Westerwald hat 5500 Einwohner und keine Schulden. Die vielen Klein- und Mittelbetriebe, eine Brauerei und ein Geschenkartikelvertrieb bringen das Geld. Dem jungen Bürgermeister unterstehen 17 Beschäftigte: Sekretärinnen, Sachbearbeiterinnen, Forstbeamte, Straßenreinigungsleute und auch der Verwalter der Bibliothek. Für fünf Jahre haben die Hachenburger ihn gewählt. Hendrik Hering, jüngstes von fünf Kindern, in Hachenburg geboren, lächelt: „Die Sache beginnt jetzt, mir richtig Spaß zu machen."

Bild am Sonntag, Aug. 27, 1989

hit
fairy tale
talented
different
legt… is taking his exams in protestant theology
pastor / laß… I really let off steam
generates / feelings
kind / confirmation
is sufficient
faith / defend
world
law
paraplegic

Zum Text 2

1. Lesen Sie die vier Ausschnitte, und sammeln Sie Information über die vier Leute. Tragen Sie diese Information in Stichwörtern (*key words*) in eine Tabelle nach folgendem Muster ein:

Zum Text 2. **Suggestion:** Assign number 1 for homework. Using the grid format suggested on page 410, students summarize the information in class (for number 2).

Aktivität 2. Was bin ich?

Eine Person denkt an einen Beruf, und die ande_
erraten. Die Teilnehmer dürfen nur **ja oder nein**
sen mindestens fünf Fragen stellen, bevor Sie rat

BEISPIELSFRAGEN: Muß man für diesen Beru_
Arbeitet man in einem Bü_
Luft / auf der Bühne / in
Ist die Arbeit gefährlich?
Verdient man viel Geld?
Arbeitet man mit den Händ_
Arbeitet man allein / mit Ma_
Menschen zusammen?

Aktivität 3. Lebenslauf

Schreiben Sie einen tabellarischen Lebenslauf, den S_
bung gebrauchen könnten. In Deutschland gehören fo_
tionen zu einem tabellarischen Lebenslauf:

- Name und Adresse
- Geburtsort und Geburtsdatum
- Namen der Eltern
- Daten und Orte aller Schulen und Hochschulen
- Arbeitserfahrungen
- Familienstand (verheiratet, ledig, Kinder)

WORTSCHATZ

Substantive

der Abiturient (-n
masc.), **die Abitu-
rientin (-nen)**

graduate of the **Gymna-
sium,** person who
has passed the
Abitur

das Arbeitsamt (¨er)

employment (develop-
ment) office

**die Aufstiegsmöglich-
keit (-en)**
die Ausbildung
der Ausbildungsplatz
(¨e)
**die Ausbildungsstelle
(-n)**
der/die Auszubildende
(decl. adj.), abbr.
Azubi (-s)

opportunity for
advancement

training
training position

training position

trainee, apprentice

der I_
die B_
der B_
B_
die Be_
der Br_
Bri_
das Bü_
die Erd_
der Erf_
das Fach_
das Ha_
das Ne_
das Geha_
die Geleg_
der Grund_

KAPITEL 14

WIE MAN AUF DEM LAUFENDEN BLEIBT

*Wie man auf dem Laufenden
bleibt.* **Suggestion:** Introduce the
chapter by asking students to name
any German newspapers or magazines they know of.

Lernziele *In this chapter you will be
talking about German mass media:
newspapers, television, and radio. You
will learn to express your preferences
about programs, comment on events,
and present different sides of an
argument.*

Alles klar?

Hier sehen Sie einige deutsche Zeitungsnamen. Einige davon sind regio-
nale Zeitungen, andere sind überregional; das heißt, man liest sie überall
im Land. Welche Zeitung:

- ist wahrscheinlich überregional?
- ist regional?
- erscheint morgens?
- spezialisiert sich auf Wirtschaft und Finanzen?
- nennt sich überparteilich (*nonpartisan*) und unabhängig?

Alles klar. **Point out:** *Regional*
refers to a local newspaper; *überregional* refers to a national newspaper. *Handelsblatt* is the German
equivalent of the *Wall Street Journal.*

Süddeutsche Zeitung
MÜNCHNER NEUESTE NACHRICHTEN AUS POLITIK, KULTUR, WIRTSCHAFT UND SPORT

BERLINER MORGENPOST
Überparteilich · Berlins größte Abonnementzeitung · Unabhängig

DIE WELT
UNABHÄNGIGE TAGESZEITUNG FÜR DEUTSCHLAND

Was gibt's im Fernseh...

☐ **Aktivität 5. Das Fernse...**

Suchen Sie im Fernsehprogram...

BEISPIEL: 1. Um 15.00 Uhr ...

1. Sport
2. Nachrichten
3. Spielfilm
4. Geschichte/Dokumentarfilm...
5. Sendung für Kinder
6. Spiele und Quiz

RSM

SA 11. Juli AF...

16.40 Johannes

Eine Familiengeschichte vor 100 Jahren im Hunsrück, 1. Teil

Familie Selzer aus dem Hunsrück hofft auf Arbeit und Brot, weil eine Eisenbahn gebaut werden soll. Johannes, der 12jährige Sohn der Selzers, schaut lieber bei den Sprengungen zu, statt Kühe zu hüten. (ca. 50 Min.)
Es spielen: Johannes (Michal Dlouhy), Julius (Herbert Stass), Marie (Brigitte Janner), Anna (Marie-Luise Marjan), Wilhelm (Rüdiger Vogler), Franzek (Peter Skarke), Paul (Peter Bongartz) und andere

Johannes (M... die Sprengu...

20.15 Vom Broad... bis nach Holly...

George Gershwins Musik: Gala-Abend zu s...

Dem Erfolgskomponisten George Gershwin (1898–1937, „R... sody in Blue") ist der Abend gewidmet. Peer Augustinski p... rell (M.), Sylvia Vrethammar, Ron Williams, Slava Kantch... Eugene Holmes, Catherine Swanson, Gabriele Rossmanith...

Neue Zürcher Zeitung
und schweizerisches Handelsblatt

Frankfurter Rundschau
Unabhängige Tageszeitung

Handelsblatt
WIRTSCHAFTS⁰ UND FINANZZEITUNG

a. der Handel *trade, commerce*
b. die Wirtschaft *economy*

Frankfurter Allgemeine
ZEITUNG FÜR DEUTSCHLAND

WÖRTER IM KONTEXT

Was steht heute in der Zeitung?

☐ **Aktivität 1. In dieser Ausgabe**

Sie sehen hier das Verzeichnis einer Berliner Zeitung.

1. Welche Kategorien sind Ihnen bekannt?
2. Gibt es etwas, was man in amerikanischen Zeitungen im allgemeinen nicht findet?
3. Vermissen Sie eine Kategorie, die man regelmäßig in den meisten amerikanischen Zeitungen findet, aber hier nicht?

IN DIESER AUSGABE

Anzeigen-Wegweiser .... Seite 2	Ratgeber 30	Freizeit 86
Politik 2, 11, 12	Sport 31–34	Reise 87–97
Berlin, Bezirke ... 3–10	Feuilleton 41–43	Rätsel 94
Rußland-Serie 12	Leserbriefe ... 47, 79	Horoskop 96
Fernsehen 16–18	Roman 47	Humor 98
Wirtschaft 19–21	Auto 48, 49, 51	Dazu in Farbe
Kurzkrimi 28	Aus aller Welt ... 59, 60	Berliner Illustrirte Zeitung
	Reportage 61	

RSM

Neue Wörter

das Abonnement *subscription*
abonnieren *to subscribe*
die Ausgabe *edition, issue*
das Feuilleton (*French:*) *part of a newspaper dealing with articles on literature, culture, and science*

der Ratgeber *advice (column), advisor*
das Rätsel *riddle, puzzle*
der Roman *novel*

falls *in case*

☐ **Aktivität 2.** Interaktio…

Fragen Sie einen Partner oder e…
gewohnheiten. Sie möchten unt…

- ob er oder sie regelmäßig Ze…
- wieviel Zeit er oder sie tägli…
- was er oder sie zuerst in der…
- was er oder sie immer ganz…
- wann er oder sie gewöhnlich…
- ob er oder sie ein Abonneme…
  welche Zeitung? Falls er ode…
  welche Zeitung würde er ode…

☐ **Aktivität 3.** Schlagzeile…

Was steht heute in der Zeitung? …
anfänge in die passende Kategor…

BEISPIEL: 1. Das gehört zum…

Verkehrsprobleme
Wetterbericht
Wirtschaft
Lokalnachrichten

1.
**Schauer, zunächst wolkig oder bedeckt
und gelegentlich Regen**

3. **Köln: Grizzlybär spa…**

4. **53 Kilometer langer Stau auf
der Autobahn München—Salzburg**

☐ **Aktivität 4.** Hören Sie…

Sie hören fünf kurze Berichte. We…
welchem Bericht? Für eine Schla…
Sie die passende Zahl (1–5) vor d…

a. __3__ Kluges Köpfchen vorm …
b. __4__ Spender der Woche
c. __2__ Unbekanntes Dorf in Ira…
d. __5__ Massenflucht aus der DI…
e. __1__ Autodieb auf Surfbrett g…
f. _____ Wartezeiten an den Gren…

☐☐☐☐ *Kulturnotiz*

Bis vor kurzem verbreiteten nur öffentlich-rechtliche Rundfunkanstalten (*public broadcasting institutions*) Hörfunk- und Fernsehprogramme in der Bundesrepublik. Die ARD (Arbeitsgemeinschaft der Rundfunkanstalten Deutschlands) und das ZDF (das Zweite Deutsche Fernsehen) verbreiten das erste und zweite Programm des Fernsehens. Heutzutage gibt es auch eine wachsende Zahl an Kabel- und Satellitenprogrammen.

In der Bundesrepublik Deutschland muß jeder Haushalt für Radio und Fernsehen eine Gebühr (*fee*) zahlen. Auch für ein Radio im Auto oder für ein Kofferradio muß man zahlen. Man zahlt die Gebühr an die GEZ (Gebühreneinzugszentrale der Rundfunkanstalten).

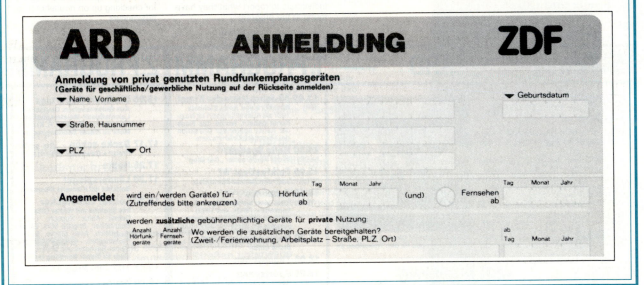

Neue Wörter

das Programm *channel, network; program*
der Rundfunk *radio; broadcast*
die Sendung *program*
die Übertragung *broadcasting; live show*

aktuell *current*
aufregend *exciting*
ermüdend *tiring*
oberflächlich *shallow, superficial*
spannend *exciting*
unterhaltsam *entertaining*

☐ **Aktivität 6.** **Das sehe ich gern!**

Was ist Ihre Lieblingssendung im Fernsehen? Warum? Was finden Sie nicht besonders gut im Fernsehen? Geben Sie Beispiele.

BEISPIEL: Ich mag Serien, zum Beispiel *L.A. Law.* Diese Sendung finde ich meistens spannend und unterhaltsam. Aber Familienserien finde ich schrecklich langweilig.

Krimis	gewöhnlich	aktuell
Nachrichten	immer	aufregend
Dokumentarfilme	meistens	ermüdend
Quizsendungen	schrecklich	unterhaltsam
Talkshows	sehr	langweilig
Sport		komisch
Serien		spannend
Musik		oberflächlich
Sonstiges		schlecht

□□□□ *Kulturnotiz*

Eine Sendung im ARD (dem ersten Fernsehprogramm) heißt *Wunschfilm der Woche.* In der Fernsehzeitung stehen drei Filmtitel, von denen man einen auswählt. Dann ruft man eine besondere Telefonnummer an, um einen Film zu wählen. Der Film, der die meisten Telefonstimmen bekommt, wird an dem Tag gezeigt.

20.15 Wunschfilm der Woche
Drei Spielfilme zur Auswahl
So wählen Sie: bundesweit zum Ortstarif die **Tel.-Nr. 01 81 91** (Ausnahme Berlin: 19 11), dahinter dann die Nr. 1, 2 oder 3 für den gewünschten Film
Nr. 1: Auch die Engel mögen's heiß (Italien, 1974)
Regie: E. B. Clucher
Nr. 2: Der große Eisenbahnraub (England, 1978)
Regie: Michael Crichton
Nr. 3: Die Höllenfahrt der Poseidon (USA, 1972)
Regie: Ronald Neame
Mehr zu dieser Sendung rechts   **RSM**

Dialog. Was gibt's denn im Fernsehen?

THOMAS: Was gibt es denn heute abend im Fernsehen?

BARBARA: Im ersten Programm kommt direkt nach der Tagesschau um 20 Uhr eine Sendung über George Gershwin und seine Musik.

THOMAS: Und was gibt's im zweiten Programm?

BARBARA: Wunschfilm der Woche.

THOMAS: Also, mal wieder nichts Gescheites (*nothing good*).

BARBARA: Was möchtest du denn lieber?

THOMAS: Einen guten Dokumentarfilm oder eine Sportsendung.

BARBARA: Das Sport-Extra kommt später. Ich möchte mir heute aber den Wunschfilm ansehen.

THOMAS: Wie heißen die Filme denn?

BARBARA: Moment mal eben. Ich kenne nur den einen Titel. Ein Film ist aus Italien, einer aus England und einer aus den USA. Ich würde gern den englischen Film sehen, *Der große Eisenbahnraub.*

THOMAS: Ruf doch schnell an.

BARBARA: Ich habe noch nie Glück damit gehabt.

THOMAS: Wie wäre es denn mit der Sendung über Gershwin?

BARBARA: Na gut. Aber falls *Der große Eisenbahnraub* kommt, möchte ich den lieber sehen.

▣ **Aktivität 7. Stimmt das?**

Verbessern Sie falsche Aussagen. Die Information finden Sie im Gespräch zwischen Barbara und Thomas.

1. Barbara und Thomas interessieren sich für dieselben Sendungen.
2. Thomas interessiert sich nur für Musik und Spielfilme.
3. „Wunschfilm der Woche" bietet drei deutsche Filme an.
4. Barbara ruft die Nummer für den Wunschfilm sofort an.
5. Die beiden entscheiden sich für eine Musiksendung.

> *Sprachnotiz*
>
> derselbe Film   dieselbe Sendung
> dasselbe Programm   dieselben Sendungen
>
> The word **derselbe** (*the same*) combines the definite article and the adjective (**selb-**) in one word. The appropriate article and adjective endings are both used.

▣ **Aktivität 8. Interaktion. Eine Sendung auswählen**

Besprechen Sie mit einem Partner oder einer Partnerin, was Sie sehen oder hören könnten. Wählen Sie eine Sendung aus Fernsehen oder Hörfunk (Radio).

Aktivität 8. Suggestion: Have students scan the TV and radio program before they create a dialogue with a partner. Students select whatever fits their dialogue from the items suggested. Call on several pairs to role-play their dialogue in class. This can also be assigned for homework, to be performed in class the next day.

RSM

Die große Programmübersicht vom 11. Juli bis 17. Juli 87

Mit Spieldauer in Minuten zum Aufzeichnen von Fernseh- und Hörfunksendungen

FERNSEHEN

Spielfilme

Wunschfilm der Woche
Drei Spielfilme zur Auswahl — ca. 105 Minuten
Samstag, 20.15, ZDF
Die vier Gesellen (sw)
Deutscher Spielfilm von 1938 — 88 Minuten
Samstag, 21.20, RB/NDR/SFB III
Die Toten sterben nicht
mit George Hamilton, Ray Milland — 70 Minuten
Samstag, 22.05, ARD
Wer erschoß Salvatore G.?
mit Salvo Randone, Frank Wolff — 115 Minuten
Samstag, 23.15, ARD
Wirbelwind der Liebe (sw)
USA 1941 — Mit Gary Cooper — 110 Minuten
Freitag, 23.25, ARD
Schmutziges Spiel
Australischer Spielfilm von 1980 — 94 Minuten
Freitag, 23.40, ZDF

Krimis, Serien

Der Schachzug
Kriminalkomödie mit Gerlinde Locker, Ernst Stankovski — 90 Minuten
Samstag, 23.20, ZDF
Lindenstraße
84. Das Mädchen mit den roten Haaren
30 Minuten
Sonntag, 18.40, ARD

Umwelt, Natur, Technik

Bilder aus der Wissenschaft
von Hans Lechleitner — 30 Minuten
Sonntag, 16.45, ARD
Istanbul — Die Mauer lebt
45 Minuten
Sonntag, 19.30, ZDF

Kultur

Dietrich Fischer-Dieskau
Vom Gewissen der Stimme — 60 Minuten
Samstag, 22.50, RB/NDR/SFB III
Musik im Dritten
Lorin Maazel dirigiert das Sinfonieorchester des NDR: Barber und Strauss — 70 Minuten
Sonntag, 21.15, RB/NDR/SFB III
Professor Bernhardi
Komödie von Arthur Schnitzler — 155 Minuten
Sonntag, 21.35, ZDF

Sport

Sportschau
u.a. Tour de France, Leichtathletik — 55 Minuten
Samstag, 18.05, ARD

HÖRFUNK

Hörspiele und Krimis

Wochenend-Krimi
»Indizien« von Louis C. Thomas
Samstag, 17.05 Uhr, NDR 3 — 55 Minuten
Metamorphose der Stille
von Martin Burckhardt und Johannes Schmölling. Mit Hans Madin, Anne Haenen
Samstag, 21.00 Uhr, NDR 3 — 60 Minuten

Klassische Musik

Großer Opernabend
Zum 50. Todestag von George Gershwin:
»Porgy and Bess«, Leitung: John Demain
Samstag, 19.10 Uhr, Bremen 2 — 205 Minuten
Internationale Musikfestspiele
Wiener Festwochen: ORF-Symphonie-Orchester, Leitung: Eliahu Inbal. Mahler: Sinfonie Nr. 7
Montag, 20.15 Uhr, NDR 3 — 135 Minuten

A:	B:

Was gibt es heute abend im
   Fernsehen/im Radio? ⟶ Um ____ Uhr gibt es ____.

Was ist denn das? Das ist ____.
Wovon handelt das denn?° Ich weiß es nicht.   Wovon... *What's it about?*

Wer spielt mit? ____.

Wie lange ____? ____ Stunden/Minuten.

Was gibt es sonst noch? Magst du ____?
   Wie wäre es mit ____?

Ja, das finde ich ____.
Ich lese heute lieber die
   Zeitung.

GRAMMATIK IM KONTEXT

The Subjective Use of Modals

Modal verbs can be used to express the speaker's subjective opinion or to identify what is considered hearsay by the speaker.

Es **soll** morgen Regen **geben.**	*It's supposed to rain tomorrow.*
Es **soll** einen 53 km langen Stau auf der Autobahn **gegeben haben.**	*Supposedly, (I heard) there was a traffic backup of 53 kilometers on the freeway.*
Das **muß** vorgestern **passiert sein.**	*That must have happened the day before yesterday.*
Das **kann** nur an der Grenze zwischen Deutschland und Österreich **gewesen sein.**	*That can only have been at the border between Germany and Austria.*

In the example sentences, the modals **sollen, müssen,** and **können** express the opinion of the speaker or the writer: what the speaker heard or read somewhere and what he or she concludes on the basis of some evidence. This subjective use of the modals in German parallels the use of modals in English. The modal itself is usually in the present tense; the dependent infinitive, however, will be in one of two different forms:

1. If the event or situation talked about involves something going on in the present or the future, the (present) infinitive of the main verb is used.

   Present Infinitive: Es soll morgen Regen **geben.**

2. If th
infir

In t
the
still

The
verb an
verb tal

□ Übu

Report
equivale
tive to u

BEIS

1. Die
2. Ein
3. Ein
vert
4. Am
5. Für
6. Die
7. Taus

□ Übu

Schauen
und wie
können,

Indirect Discourse

When you report to someone what another person has said, you can quote that person verbatim, using the direct discourse method. In writing, this is indicated by the use of quotation marks.

DIRECT DISCOURSE

Der Autofahrer behauptete: „Ich habe den Radfahrer nicht gesehen."

The automobile driver claimed, "I did not see the bicyclist."

Note that in German, opening quotation marks are placed just below the line.

Another way of reporting what someone said to a third person uses the indirect discourse method—something commonly done in newspapers. In this case, German often uses subjunctive verb forms, especially the indirect discourse subjunctive—special subjunctive forms which differ from the subjunctive forms you learned in chapter eleven.

INDIRECT DISCOURSE

Der Autofahrer behauptete, er **habe** den Radfahrer nicht **gesehen.**

The driver claimed (that) he had not seen the bicyclist.

In using the indirect discourse subjunctive in German, a speaker or writer clearly indicates that the information transmitted does not necessarily reflect the speaker's own knowledge or views. The indirect discourse subjunctive tends to establish distance between the reporter and the subject. This is useful when you want to be objective or neutral.

With the exception of the verb **sein,** the indirect discourse subjunctive, or subjunctive I, is used only in a few forms. Only in the third-person singular is the indirect discourse subjunctive commonly used. This is because the third-person singular is the only form in which the indirect discourse subjunctive is different from the regular present-tense forms of most verbs. Increasingly, Germans use the more common subjunctive II forms instead of the indirect discourse subjunctive. In everyday conversation, people avoid subjunctive forms and use regular indicative verb forms for indirect discourse.

The Indirect Discourse Subjunctive: Present Tense

The present tense of the indirect discourse subjunctive (subjunctive I) is used to express present and future time. It is formed from the stem of the infinitive.

Der Autofahrer
durch rotes L
rechtzeitig **st**

▣ Übung 5.   Unge

Restate the following se
or subjunctive II expres

Heute habe ich im

1. Im Südwesten Irans
2. Ein Mann im Gorill
    Scheine an Fußgäng
3. Im Jahre 1875 habe
    tet. Im Jahre 1988 h
    gearbeitet.
4. Bei einer Verkehrsk
    gesprungen. Er ist i
    voller Uniform hat s
    Dieb nach zehn Min
5. Gestern ist auf einer
    det. Die Leute, die a
    gewesen. Nach kurz

▣ Übung 6. Grupp

Schreiben Sie in mehrer
vor. Ihre Klassenkamera

BEISPIEL: Gruppe A
rant ein G
Kuchen g

OHNE KAFFEESATZ[a] LES

sein	
Singular	*Plural*
ich sei	wir seien
Sie seien	Sie seien
du sei(e)st	ihr sei(e)t
er	
sie ⎱ sei	sie seien
es ⎰	

> Und wie war's heute in der Schule?
>
> Prima. Frau Koch hat gesagt, wenn alle so wären wie ich, könnten sie die Schule dichtmachen!

The verbs **haben, wissen,** and all modals use the following singular forms:

haben	können	wissen
ich -	ich könne	ich wisse
er	er	er
sie ⎱ habe	sie ⎱ könne	sie ⎱ wisse
es ⎰	es ⎰	es ⎰

All other verbs just add **-e** to the stem of the infinitive to form the third-person singular. Use the subjunctive II for all forms other than the third-person singular.

	INDIRECT DISCOURSE	
INFINITIVE	SUBJUNCTIVE	SUBJUNCTIVE II
bringen	⎧ bringe	⎧ brächte
fahren	er/sie/es ⎨ fahre	ich ⎨ führe
sehen	⎪ sehe	⎪ sähe
tun	⎩ tue	⎩ täte

Meine Freunde schrieben mir, das Land **sei** in einer großen Krise. Niemand **wisse**, wie es weitergehen **solle**. Niemand **habe** eine Antwort.

My friends wrote to me that the country is in a deep crisis. Nobody knows how it ought to continue. Nobody has an answer.

Übung 3. Hör

Immer diese Ausreden

Dialog 1 Verab
Dialog 2 Semin
Dialog 3 50 Ma

Erzählen Sie dann mit H
für Ausreden die Perso

BEISPIEL: Dialog 1

Übung 4. Klug

Report the following in
discourse subjunctive,

In der Zeitung stan
funden hätten,

1. der Mensch denkt a
2. schwierige Problem
3. die Sinne funktioni
4. deshalb schmeckt
5. deshalb sind wir al
   empfänglichsten (*m*
6. für den Sport ist de
7. nachmittags ist das
   Höhepunkt.
8. man schwitzt (*swe*
   schnell.

The Indirect Dis

The past tense of the in
past time. It is formed
the main verb.

INFINITIVE

haben
sein
fahren   er,
sehen
wissen

Indefinite Relative Pronouns:
wer and *was*

The pronouns **wer** (*whoever*) and **was** (*what; whatever; that which*) are used as indefinite relative pronouns whenever there is no specific noun serving as an antecedent for a relative clause.

Wer das Leben liebt, denkt auch an morgen.	*Whoever loves life also thinks of tomorrow.*
Was er sagt, stimmt nicht.	*What he says is not true.*

Sichern Sie Ihre Zukunft!

Wer das Leben liebt, denkt auch an morgen.

●-Girokonto: gebührenfrei für Schüler, Azubis und Studenten

WER SCHWIMMEN WILL, MUSS SCHWIMMEN LERNEN

After the words **alles, nichts, etwas,** and **viel,** use the indefinite relative pronoun **was.**

Alles, was in der Zeitung steht, habe ich schon im Fernsehen gehört.	*Everything that is in the paper I have already heard on TV.*
Das ist **etwas, was** uns alle angeht.	*That is something that concerns us all.*
Nichts, was er sagt, stimmt.	*Nothing (that) he says is true.*
Vieles, was ich gelernt habe, habe ich schon wieder vergessen.	*Much of what I have learned I have already forgotten again.*

Alles was Sie über Geld wissen sollten.

◘ **Übung 7. Wer oder was?**

Ergänzen Sie **wer** oder (**alles, etwas, nichts, viel**) **was.**

1. _____ am Wochenende auf der Autobahn über die Grenze von Deutschland nach Österreich fährt, muß mit langen Staus rechnen.
2. Ich habe _____ gesehen, _____ ich sehen wollte.
3. In der Zeitung steht _____, _____ man nicht im Fernsehen hört oder sieht.
4. _____, _____ du sagst, habe ich schon gehört.
5. Die Öffnung der Mauer in Berlin ist _____, _____ man nicht so schnell vergessen wird.
6. _____ den Unfall an der Ecke Leipzigerstraße gesehen hat, rufe mich bitte an.
7. _____ schwimmen will, muß schwimmen lernen.

ein-Words as Pronouns

ein-Words as Pronouns.
Suggestion: Briefly review all forms of *ein*-words, including *unser* and *ihr*. You might want to do a quick substitution exercise: *Das ist mein/e (unser, ihr, sein) Wagen / Auto / Bleistift / Zeitung = Das ist meiner, unserer, ihrer, seiner, usw.*

Ein-words can be used as pronouns to avoid unnecessary repetition of nouns. As pronouns, **ein**-words take the endings of **der**-words.

Das ist ein toller Wagen. Ist das **deiner?** —Ja, das ist **meiner.**	*That is a fabulous car. Is it yours? —Yes, it is mine.*
Ist das dein Radio? —Nein, ich habe **keins.** Wo ist denn **deins?**	*Is that your radio? —No, I don't have one. Where is yours?*
Hast du einen Fernseher? —Nein, ich habe **keinen.** Hast du **einen?**	*Do you have a TV? —No, I don't have one. Do you have one?*
Ich suche eine Zeitung. Wo kann ich **eine** finden?	*I am looking for a newspaper. Where can I find one?*

◘ **Übung 8. Wem gehört das?**

Sammeln Sie irgendetwas von jeder Person in der Klasse ein. Jemand fragt, wem das gehört, und der Besitzer antwortet.

> BEISPIEL: A: Wem gehört das Buch?
> B: Das ist meins.

Sachen, die man einsammeln könnte:

> Kugelschreiber, Tasche, Geld, Brille, Foto, Zeitung, Buch, Ring, Portemonnaie, Rucksack

Übung 8. Suggestion: Have students take turns distributing the things again, asking first *Wem gehört...* The student to whom the item belongs should answer, e.g., *(Buch) Das ist meins.*

Zum Text

1. Richtig oder falsch? Wenn falsch, verbessern Sie die Aussagen.
   a. _____ Der Fernseher ist kaputt. Aber es ist kein Problem, denn die zwei Leute haben einen zweiten Apparat im Schlafzimmer.
   b. _____ Der Mann behauptet, daß er sowieso nicht gern fernsieht.
   c. _____ Die zwei bleiben aber vor dem Fernseher sitzen und starren ihn einfach an.
   d. _____ Die Frau schlägt eine Alternative zum Fernsehen vor.
   e. _____ Der Mann meint, er darf hinschauen, wohin er will, auch wenn er den dunklen Fernseher anschaut.
   f. _____ An diesem Abend gibt es Sport im Fernsehen.
   g. _____ Der Mann behauptet, daß es normalerweise ausgezeichnete Sendungen im Fernsehen gibt.
   h. _____ Die zwei unterhalten sich und gehen dann früh ins Bett.

2. Finden Sie Stellen im Text
   a. wo das Ehepaar sich über den kaputten Fernseher beklagt (*complains*).
   b. wo das Ehepaar eine kleine Auseinandersetzung (*dispute*) hat.
   c. wo das Ehepaar über das Programm redet.
   d. wo das Ehepaar über Alternativen zum Fernsehen spricht.

3. Finden Sie Beweise (*evidence*) im Text für oder gegen folgende Behauptung:

   > Auch wenn der Fernseher kaputt ist, dominiert er den Ablauf des Abends.

4. **Worträtsel.** Sie finden die Wörter für das Rätsel im Text. Die Buchstaben in den □ (Quadraten) ergeben ein Wort.

   Zum Text #4. Note: The answer is *glotzen (...man glotzt auf dieses blöde Fernsehprogramm).*

   a. □ _ _ _ _ _   ein anderes Wort für Fernseher
   b. _ _ _ _ _ _ _ _ □ _ _ _ _   miteinander reden, sich _____
   c. _ _ _ □ _ _ _ _   normal, üblich
   d. _ _ _ _ □ _ _ _   Beachtung schenken
   e. □ _   eine Dativpräposition
   f. _ _ _ _ _ □ _ _ _ _ _ _ _ _   eine Alternative zum Fernsehen
   g. _ _ _ _ _ _ □   sehen, schauen

Nach dem Lesen

▣ Aktivität 1. Rollenspiel

Führen Sie mit einem Partner oder einer Partnerin ein Gespräch über einen typischen Fernsehabend:

1. im Studentenwohnheim.
2. zu Hause bei Ihrer Familie.

Wie verläuft so ein Gespräch? Sind Sie gewöhnlich einer Meinung? Spielen Sie es der Klasse vor.

▣ **Aktivität 2. Das heutige Programm...**

Beschreiben Sie kurz ein Radioprogramm oder eine Fernsehsendung. Tragen Sie diese Beschreibung, ohne den Titel zu nennen, in der Klasse vor. Lassen Sie die anderen raten (*guess*), welche Sendung Sie meinen.

▣ **Aktivität 3. Gruppenarbeit: Ein Skript für eine Fernsehsendung**

Sie möchten einem deutschen Publikum eine typisch amerikanische Sendung vorstellen. Schreiben Sie gemeinsam ein Skript, und tragen Sie es als Rollenspiel in der Klasse vor (z.B. eine Nachrichtensendung, Werbung (*ads*) im Fernsehen, usw.).

Die Plakate auf dieser Litfaßsäule informieren über kulturelle Veranstaltungen in München.

WORTSCHATZ

Substantive

Die Medien

das Abonnement (-s)	subscription
die Anmeldung (-en)	registration
die Ausgabe (-n)	edition, issue
der Bericht (-e)	report
der Dokumentarfilm (-e)	documentary
das Feuilleton	newspaper section on art, culture and science
das Gerät (-e)	apparatus; device; equipment
das Fernsehgerät	television set
der Krimi (-s)	detective story/show
die Nachrichten (*pl.*)	news
das Programm (-e)	(TV) channel, program
der Rundfunk	broadcasting, radio
die Schlagzeile (-n)	headline
die Sendung (-en)	TV or radio program
die Übertragung (-en)	(live) show, broadcast

Andere Substantive

die Behauptung (-en)	assertion
der Beweis (-e)	evidence
der Dieb (-e)	thief
das Ehepaar (-e)	married couple
die Flucht	flight, escape
die Massenflucht	mass flight
der Flüchtling (-e)	refugee
die Polizei	police
der Polizist (-en)	policeman
der Ratgeber (-)	advisor; *here:* advice column
das Rätsel (-)	riddle, puzzle
der Roman (-e)	novel
der Sinn (-e)	sense
der Unfall (¨e)	accident
der Zeuge (-n), die Zeugin (-nen)	witness

Verben

abonnieren	to subscribe
achten auf	to pay attention to
anregen (regt an)	to stimulate
sich (*dat.*) etwas ansehen (sieht an), sah an, angesehen	to watch
Ich sehe mir das an.	I'm watching that.
befürchten	to fear
behaupten	to claim; to assert
bemerken	to notice
beschreiben, beschrieb, beschrieben	to describe
bezweifeln	to doubt
erscheinen, erschien, ist erschienen	to appear
fangen (fängt), fing, gefangen	to catch
funktionieren	to function, to work
gucken	to look at
handeln von	to be about, deal with
Wovon handelt es?	What is it about?
lösen (ein Problem)	to solve
(sich) nennen	to name, to be called
raten	to guess
sitzenbleiben (bleibt sitzen), blieb sitzen, ist sitzengeblieben	to fail a class, to be left behind
spazieren	to take a walk
überfliegen, überflog, überflogen	to skim (a reading)
verdummen	to become stupid, to make stupid
sich verlassen auf (verläßt), verließ, verlassen	to depend on
verteilen	to distribute

Adjektive und Adverbien

absichtlich	intentional
aktuell	current
aufregend	exciting
deshalb	therefore
derselbe, dieselbe, dasselbe	the same
ermüdend	tiring
gewohnt	accustomed, usual
klug	smart
möglich	possible

nachher	afterward
oberflächlich	superficial
schädlich	harmful
spannend	exciting
trotzdem	nevertheless
überparteilich	nonpartisan
überregional	national (for a newspaper)
unterhaltsam	entertaining
vorher	before

Sonstiges

auf dem Laufenden bleiben	to stay current
falls	in case
Gott sei Dank	thank God
hin und her	back and forth
im allgemeinen	in general
Moment (mal)	just a moment
obwohl	although

DIE ÖFFENTLICHE MEINUNG

Lernziele *In this chapter you will discuss some issues of public concern, such as the environment and traffic congestion in cities, and also how people are dealing with these issues. You will learn to state your opinions in more complex ways, to evaluate and justify an opinion, to express reservations, and to make suggestions.*

▣ Alles klar?

Buttons—so heißen sie auch auf deutsch—oder Aufkleber (*stickers*) sind eine beliebte Form, die eigene Meinung zu äußern. Schauen Sie sich die Sprüche (*sayings*) auf der nächsten Seite an.

* Welcher Spruch ist für oder gegen:

Krieg	Atomenergie
Umweltschutz	Gesundheit
Energie sparen	Menschen
Chemikalien (Pestizide) in Lebensmitteln	Tiere

* Welche Probleme sind global? Welche sind regional?
* Welche Sprüche sind humorvoll? Welche reimen sich?
* Für welche Probleme interessieren Sie sich persönlich? Warum?

a. Allgemeine Ortskrankenkasse
name of a health insurance company
b. *pigeon*

Neue Wörter

der Frieden *peace*
das Gift *poison*
die Kernenergie *nuclear energy*
die Kraft *power*
der Krieg *war*
die Meinung *opinion*
   die Meinung äußern *to voice an opinion*
das Tier *animal*

mitmachen (macht mit) *to participate*
retten *to save, rescue*
sauberhalten (hält sauber) *to keep clean*
schaffen *to create, to succeed*
schützen *to protect*

WÖRTER IM KONTEXT

Stellung nehmen°

Taking a stand

▣ Aktivität 1. Um welche Probleme geht es hier?

Wählen Sie für jedes Bild einen passenden Titel aus der Liste.

Aktivität 1. Suggestion: Ask students to describe each picture before going over the list of possible titles. Students can work in pairs to find

_____ Schützt die Umwelt
_____ Abfälle vermeiden; aber wie?
_____ Nicht genug Geld für Atomkraft
_____ Rettet die Autos
_____ Atomraketen verschrotten

_____ Fußgänger: nein, danke
_____ Autos raus aus der Stadt
_____ Mehr Geld für alternative Energie
_____ Aktion saubere Landschaft

titles, or the activity can be done quickly with the whole class. Not all titles can be used. Ask students to come up with additional headings.

1.

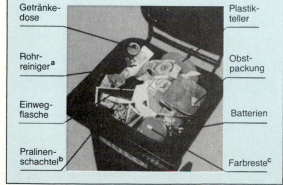

2.

3.

a. *pipe-cleaning fluid*
b. *chocolate box*
c. *paint remains*

4.

5.

Neue Wörter

der Abfall *garbage*
die Ansicht *opinion, view*
  meiner Ansicht nach *in my*
   opinion
der Fußgänger *pedestrian*
der Quatsch (*coll.*) *nonsense*
der Unsinn *nonsense*

bedauern (ich bedaure) *to*
  regret
übertreiben *to exaggerate*
  übertrieben *exaggerated*
vermeiden *to avoid*
verschrotten *to scrap*

☐ **Aktivität 2.**　Interaktion. Was meinen Sie dazu?

Äußern Sie Ihre Meinung zu einigen Problemen. Was könnte man dagegen machen?

BEISPIEL:　A: Ich bin der Meinung, daß Atomkraft gefährlich ist.
           B: Ich halte das für übertrieben. Atomenergie ist sauber und billig.
           C: Man sollte mehr alternative Energie entwickeln, z.B. Solarenergie oder Windenergie.

EINIGE PROBLEME:

Autos	Es gibt zuviel / zu viele _____ .
Atomraketen	die Umwelt verschmutzen
Abfall	zu Krieg führen
Atomkraft	_____ gefährden (Fußgänger / die Umwelt / die
Rauchen	Menschen)
?	_____ sein (gefährlich / sauber / billig)

WAS MAN VORSCHLAGEN KÖNNTE:

Man sollte (mehr / weniger):
  zu Fuß gehen / Rad fahren
  alternative Energie (Windenergie / Solarenergie) entwickeln
  öffentliche Parkplätze / Verkehrsmittel benutzen / schaffen
  Geld für _____ ausgeben
  dagegen protestieren / demonstrieren
  vermeiden
  verschrotten
  zum Recycling bringen

REDEWENDUNGEN, UM IHRE MEINUNG ZU ÄUSSERN:

Ich halte das für übertrieben / falsch / nötig / wichtig
Ich bin der Meinung / Ansicht, daß
meiner Meinung / Ansicht nach
Ich finde es (nicht) richtig / schade, daß
Ich glaube, daß
Ich bin dafür / dagegen, daß
Ich bedaure, daß
Es ist mir egal, ob
Das ist Unsinn / Quatsch

Aktivität 2.　Suggestion: This activity consists of two phases: (1) formulate sentences with the help of the sentence builders to state problems and write them on the board, and (2) go over the list of suggestions and expressions before dividing the class into small groups of three or four. Following the example provided, each student is asked to express his or her opinion about the problems. Encourage students to use the expressions listed. Spot-check by stating a problem and calling on individuals to give one sentence expressing their opinion.

Wie man Energie sparen kann

RSM

Neue Wörter

beschleunigen *to accelerate*
bremsen *to brake*
schalten *to shift* (*gears*)
rechtzeitig *in time*

▣ **Aktivität 3.**   **Mehr Kilometer mit weniger Geld**

Wie kann man Benzin sparen? Die Antworten finden Sie auf dem Bild.

> BEISPIEL: Man kann Benzin sparen, indem man unnötiges Beschleu-
> nigen vermeidet.
> *oder:* Man sollte nicht unnötig beschleunigen.

Aktivität 3.   **Suggestion:** This activity is integrated with the realia *Mehr Kilometer mit weniger Benzin.* Go over the picture and the new vocabulary first. Then go over the example, including the *Sprachnotiz,* to explain the function of *indem.* Encourage students to use this new conjunction, as well as *man sollte.* **Point out:** The suggestions in the picture all use impersonal imperative forms, i.e., an infinitive at the end of the phrase.

Unnötiges **Bremsen +
Beschleunigen**
vermeiden

Keine
**Höchstgeschwindigkeit
fahren** (Bleifuß)[a]

**Kein
Kavalierstart**[b]

**Rechtzeitig
schalten**

**Mehr
KILOMETER
mit weniger
BENZIN**

Motor nicht
im Leerlauf[c]auf
Temperatur bringen[d]

a. *lit. lead foot*
b. *sudden spurt*
c. *neutral*
d. auf... *warm up*

Sprachnotiz

The conjunction **indem** introduces a subordinate clause that explains how something is accomplished. In English, a gerund (participial phrase) is used for this purpose.

Man kann Benzin sparen, **indem** man unnötiges Bremsen vermeidet.	*One can save gasoline by avoiding unnecessary braking.*
Man vermeidet Unfälle, **indem** man vorsichtig fährt.	*One avoids accidents by driving cautiously.*

◻◻◻◻ *Kulturnotiz*

In allen Ländern Europas außer in der Bundesrepublik gibt es eine Höchstgeschwindigkeit auf der Autobahn. In der BRD ist die Richtgeschwindigkeit (*suggested speed*) 130 km pro Stunde auf der Autobahn. Natürlich gibt es streckenweise (*for certain stretches*) Geschwindigkeitsbegrenzungen, zum Beispiel an Baustellen (*road construction sites*). Über der Autobahn sind manchmal Kameras angebracht, die einen Wagen, der zu schnell fährt, aufnehmen. Man bekommt dann ein Protokoll (*ticket*) mit dem Bild des Fahrers im Wagen und dem Nummernschild ins Haus geschickt. Niemand kann dann sagen: Das war jemand anders.

Tempogrenzen in Europa ... auf Autobahnen	
Norwegen, Rumänien, Türkei, UdSSR	90
Dänemark, DDR, Griechenland	100
ČSSR, Polen, Schweden*	110
Großbritannien	112
Belgien, Bulgarien, Finnland, Jugoslawien, Luxemburg, Niederlande, Portugal, Schweiz, Spanien, Ungarn	120
Frankreich, Italien,** Österreich	130
BR Deutschland (Richtgeschwindigkeit: 130 km/h)	⊘

*90 km/h vom 20.6. bis 20.8.
**110 km/h an Wochenenden, Feiertagen, in der Ferienzeit

Kulturnotiz. **Point out:** The cameras above the *Autobahnen* use infrared light to take pictures of speeding drivers even after dark.

Dialog. Auf der Autobahn von Frankfurt nach Nürnberg

Ein deutscher Autofahrer im Gespräch mit einer amerikanischen Besucherin, die er gerade am Flughafen in Frankfurt abgeholt hat

JENNIFER: Sag mal, fliegen wir eigentlich oder fahren wir?
ANDREAS: Wieso?
JENNIFER: Wie kannst du mit 200 Sachen durch die Landschaft fahren? Mir stehen die Haare zu Berge.

Dialog. **Suggestion:** While students have their books closed, play the tape once for them to get the gist of the conversation. Then go over the *Neue Wörter* and play the dialogue a second time as students follow the text in their books.
Point out: Driving on a German *Autobahn* tends to be a hair-raising experience for American drivers. Tailgating at high speeds, honking horns, and blinking headlights are among the tactics employed by speeding drivers to rapidly clear the lane ahead of them. A newspaper once reported that a local airport for small planes had voiced concern that cars driving at extremely high speeds along a nearby *Autobahn* were showing up as low-flying aircraft on its radar screens.

Verkehr auf der Autobahn

ANDREAS: Keine Angst. Mein BMW schafft das spielend. Der liegt doch
           wie ein Brett auf der Straße.°

JENNIFER: Ich bin an so ein Tempo nicht gewöhnt. Bei uns ist die Höchst-
           geschwindigkeit nur etwa 100 km pro Stunde.

ANDREAS: Dann kann man ja gleich zu Fuß gehen.

JENNIFER: Das ist ja nun auch übertrieben. Diese Raserei ist doch
           gefährlich.

ANDREAS: Mein Wagen ist doch für hohe Geschwindigkeiten gebaut.

JENNIFER: Du, schau mal, da ist ein Schild über der Autobahn: Höchst-
           geschwindigkeit 100 km.

ANDREAS: Wahrscheinlich eine Baustelle in der Nähe.

JENNIFER: Also doch ein Tempolimit. Gott sei Dank. Bei 100 km fühle ich
           mich direkt wie zu Hause.

Der... (Figurative:) The car is very stable on the road.

Neue Wörter

die Angst *fear*
  Keine Angst. *Don't be afraid.*
der Flughafen *airport*
die Geschwindigkeit *speed*
die Raserei *driving too fast*
das Schild (-er) *road sign*
das Tempo *speed*

abholen (holt ab) *to pick up*
aufnehmen (nimmt auf) *to take a picture*
gewöhnt an *accustomed to*
mit 200 Sachen *(coll.)* *200 km/h (approx. 130 mph.) (used only for high speeds)*

▣ Aktivität 4.   Fragen und Antworten

Die Information finden Sie im Dialog oben.

1. Wie läßt Jennifer Andreas wissen, daß er zu schnell fährt?
2. Wie rechtfertigt (*justifies*) Andreas sein schnelles Fahren?
3. Welchen Ausdruck gebraucht Jennifer, um Andreas zu sagen, daß so schnelles Fahren sie nervös macht?
4. Warum fährt Andreas schließlich doch langsamer?

Aktivität 4.   **Suggestion:** Have students work in pairs to do this activity, which is designed mainly for vocabulary reinforcement. Students should come up with several phrases for numbers 1 and 2. Work with several of the idiomatic expressions by asking students, for example, *Wann stehen Ihnen die Haare zu Berge?*

▣ Aktivität 5.   Interaktion. Ein Gespräch im Auto

Wählen Sie einige Ausdrücke aus beiden Spalten. Führen Sie dann Ihren Dialog in der Klasse vor.

BEISPIEL: A: Sag mal, warum fährst du denn so langsam?
            B: Wieso? Bei dem Verkehr geht es nicht schneller.
            A: Alle Autos fahren schneller als du. Du hältst den ganzen Verkehr auf, usw.

Aktivität 5.   **Suggestion:** Working in pairs, students are asked to create a short dialogue using vocabulary from the previous *Dialog* and some of the phrases listed with this activity. Have them choose a starting situation for their dialogue: the driver is going either too slowly or too fast on a freeway.

A:

Sag mal, warum fährst du
  denn so langsam / schnell?
Könntest du vielleicht etwas
  schneller / langsamer / vor-
  sichtiger fahren?
Mir stehen die Haare zu
  Berge.
Du hältst den ganzen Verkehr
  auf.
Du machst mich nervös.
Du hast einen richtigen
  Bleifuß.
Das Tempolimit ist ⎯⎯.

B:

Wieso?
Warum fragst du?
Hast du Angst?
Keine Angst.
Der Wagen schafft das
  spielend.
Bei dem Verkehr geht es nicht
  schneller.
Ich muß mich beeilen.
Hier gibt es kein Tempolimit.

Bürgerinitiative

□□□□ *Kulturnotiz*

Grass roots movements **(Bürgerinitia-tiven)** are a popular way for private citizens to band together to defend or promote the interests of their community. Interest groups are formed around environmental issues and the quality of life in cities, for instance, as is the case with the flyer on page 450, distributed by a citizens' group in the city of Göttingen. The flyer published by the **Bürgerinitiative Göttingen** ends with the initials **V.i.S.d.P.,** followed by the name of an individual. The letters stand for **Verantwortlich im Sinne des Pressegesetzes,** meaning that the flyer is published in accordance with the law (press act) regulating the publication of materials distributed to the public. These letters appear at the bottom of all flyers approved by public ordinance.

Neue Wörter

die Abgase (*pl.*) *exhaust fumes*
der Bürger *citizen*
die Folge *consequence*
die Gefahr *danger*
im Gegenteil *on the contrary*
der Lärm *noise*
Schluß *stop, end*
  Schluß mit der Verkehrsbelästigung. *Stop the traffic
  nuisance.*
empfinden *to feel, consider*
erkennen *to recognize*
fordern *to demand*

rechnen mit (*here*) *to count on,
  expect*
zunehmen (nimmt zu), zugenommen *to increase*
sich zusammenschließen zu
  (*dat.*) *to form*
bzw. = beziehungsweise *or*
da (*conj.*) *since*
augenblicklich *momentary,
  current*
unerträglich *unbearable*

> ### *Sprachnotiz*
>
> The verb **sein** is used in conjunction with an infinitive preceded by **zu** to say what can (or cannot) be done.
>
> Verbesserungen sind nicht zu erwarten.
>
> *Improvements cannot be expected.*
>
> Mit einer Zunahme des Verkehrs ist zu rechnen.
>
> *An increase in traffic can be counted on (expected).*

Schluß mit der Verkehrsbelästigung[a]

- Der Verkehr in der Innenstadt und den angrenzenden[b] Wohnbereichen[c] hat in den letzten Jahren drastisch zugenommen; das hat unerträgliche Folgen[d] für die Bewohner: zugeparkte Straßen, Verkehrslärm und −abgase, Gefahren für Fußgänger u. Radfahrer, Gefährdung für Jung u. Alt.

- In den nächsten Monaten steht die Abstimmung über das PLANUNGSLEITBILD INNENSTADT bevor[e]:

  in diesem sind keine wirklichen Verbesserungen für die Bevölkerung zu erkennen bzw. in der Zukunft zu erwarten,   im Gegenteil ist mit einer deutlichen Zunahme[f] des Park−Such−Verkehrs zu rechnen!

- Da auch wir die augenblickliche Situation als unerträglich empfinden, haben wir uns zu einer Interessengemeinschaft zusammengeschlossen.

  Wir fordern eine angemessene[g] Beteiligung[h] und Information aller betroffenen[i] Bürger vor den politischen Entscheidungen.

Bı**G** **BÜRGERINITIATIVE GÖTTINGEN**

V.i.S.d.P. Klaus Richter

Bürgerinitiative. Note: There is a lot of unknown vocabulary in this flyer; some is glossed in the margin (for recognition only) and some listed in the *Neue Wörter* (for active knowledge). Guide students through this (refer also to the *Kulturnotiz*) and ask them to list or underline the important idea for each item.

RSM

a. die Belästigung *annoyance*
b. *adjoining*
c. der Bereich *area*
d. die Folge *consequence*
e. steht... *the vote on the plans for the inner city is coming up*
f. *increase*
g. angemessen *appropriate*
h. *participation*
i. betroffen *concerned*

Expressing the A

As already noted, the age
ever, when it is stated, th

In einer Stunde wer
von Deutschen ge

When the action is caused

Die Umwelt wird **du
zung** zerstört.

Sentences in the passive
active voice. There is no d

Passive: In einer Stunde
subject (agent)

Active: **Die Deutschen**

Note that the subject in th
sentence, and the subject i
passive-voice sentence.

☐ Übung 2.   60 Minu

The following facts and fig
during sixty minutes of an
attention to sentences in th
of all sentences in the pass

- 77 Kinder werden gebore
- 79 Menschen sterben.
- 419 Menschen werden art

The Passive Voice

German and English sentences use either the active or the passive voice. In the active voice—which you have been using in German so far—the subject of the sentence carries out the action indicated by the verb. In the passive voice, on the other hand, the subject of the sentence is acted on; it is the "passive" recipient of an action. The agent or cause of the action often remains unnamed, either because it is not important or because it is unknown. Compare the following sentences:

ACTIVE VOICE	PASSIVE VOICE
Viele Leute lesen täglich eine Zeitung. *Many people read a newspaper daily.*	In Deutschland werden viele Zeitungen gelesen. *Many newspapers are read in Germany.*
Welche Zeitung lesen die Deutschen am häufigsten? *Which paper do Germans read most often?*	Welche Zeitung wird am häufigsten gelesen? *Which newspaper is read most often?*

The active voice emphasizes the subject carrying out an activity. In the passive voice, the emphasis shifts from the subject to the activity. For this reason, the passive voice tends to be more impersonal. It is commonly used in newspapers, scientific writing, and in descriptions of procedures.

Formation of the Passive Voice

In German, the passive is formed with the auxiliary verb **werden** and the past participle of the main verb. (English uses the auxiliary verb *to be* and the past participle.)

The passive voice has the same tenses as the active voice. Although it can be used in all personal forms, the passive occurs most frequently in the third-person singular or plural.

Following are the commonly used tenses of the passive.

PRESENT:

Die Zeitung **wird verkauft.**	The newspaper is (*being*) sold.
Die Zeitungen **werden verkauft.**	The newspapers are (*being*) sold.

SIMPLE PAST:

Sie **wurde verkauft.**	It was (*being*) sold.
Sie **wurden verkauft.**	They were (*being*) sold.

☐ Aktivität 6.   Schluß mit der Verkehrsbelästigung!

Fassen Sie die wichtigen Aspekte der Bürgerinitiative Göttingen zusammen, indem Sie passende Satzteile miteinander verbinden. Lesen Sie die Sätze dann in einer logischen Reihenfolge.

1. _____ Deshalb haben sich einige Bürger der Stadt Göttingen
2. _____ Die Folgen für die Bevölkerung sind
3. _____ In den nächsten Monaten steht
4. _____ Der Verkehr in der Innenstadt
5. _____ Die Bürgerinitiative fordert

a. hat in den letzten Jahren drastisch zugenommen.
b. Schluß mit der Verkehrsbelästigung.
c. zu einer Interessengemeinschaft zusammengeschlossen.
d. eine Abstimmung (*vote*) über die Planung für die Innenstadt bevor.
e. zugeparkte Straßen, Lärm, Abgase und Gefahren für Jung und Alt.

☐ Aktivität 7.   Hören Sie zu.

Vier Leute (A–D) sprechen über Probleme in ihrer Stadt und wie man sie lösen könnte. Schreiben Sie den passenden Buchstaben (A–D) vor das Problem, über das der Sprecher redet, und kreuzen Sie auch die Lösung an, die er oder sie vorschlägt. (*One space will remain blank.*)

SPRECHER	PROBLEM	LÖSUNG (KREUZEN SIE **a** ODER **b** AN)
B	Atomkraft	a. Solarenergie b. Windenergie x
D	Gift im Essen	a. strenge Staatskontrolle x b. keine Pestizide
A	Verkehr	a. Tempolimit b. Wagen am Stadtrand parken x
	Atomraketen	a. verschrotten b. zum Recycling bringen
C	Lärm	a. weniger Flugzeuge x b. Autos verbieten

☐ Aktivität 8.   Gruppenarbeit

Entwerfen Sie eine „Bürgerinitiative" zu einem Problem, das die Bewohner Ihres Ortes oder die Studenten betrifft. Benutzen Sie die Bürgerinitiative Göttingen als Modell.

- Beschreiben Sie das Problem.
- Was fordern die Bürger?
- Schlagen Sie eine Lösung (*solution*) vor.

Tragen Sie Ihre Bürgerinitiative vor.

GRAMMATIK IM KONTEXT

The Present Participle

The present participle (ending in *-ing* in English) is used in a more limited way in German than it is in English. In German it functions primarily as an adjective or an adverb. As an attributive adjective (preceding a noun), the participle takes appropriate adjective endings.

The present participle of a German verb is formed by adding **-d** to the infinitive.

INFINITIVE	PRESENT PARTICIPLE
angrenzen	angrenz**end** (*adjoining, bordering*)
kommen	komm**end** (*coming*)
steigen	steig**end** (*climbing, increasing*)

PRESENT PARTICIPLE AS ADJECTIVE

der **angrenzende** Wohn-bereich	*the adjoining housing area*
steigender Benzinverbrauch	*increasing gasoline consumption*
im **kommenden** Sommer	*in the coming (next) summer*

PRESENT PARTICIPLE AS ADVERB

Jennifer spricht **fließend** Deutsch.	*Jennifer speaks German fluently (lit. flowingly).*

No ending is added to the present participle when it is used as an adverb. (German adverbs never take endings.)

▣ Übung 1. Worüber liest man fast täglich in der Zeitung?

Expand each noun with an adjective derived from a suitable verb in the list.

BEISPIEL: Man liest täglich über den wachsenden Verkehr.

1. die Menschen — steigen
2. die Preise — flüchten (*to flee*)
3. die Bürger — streiken
4. die Studenten — wachsen (*to grow*)
5. der Verkehr — protestieren
6. das Problem — sterben
7. der Wald — demonstrieren
8. die Arbeiter

PRESENT P...

Sie **ist verkauft w...**
Sie **sind verkauft...**

PAST PERF...

Sie **war verkauft...**
Sie **waren verkau...**

Note that in the perfect t...
to **worden.** The presence...
the sentence is in the pas...
You now know three...

1. **werden** as independe...
2. **werden** + infinitive (...
3. **werden** + past partici...

▣ Analyse

In jeder Minute werde...

Schon in wenigen Jahren wir...

RSM

DIESE WOCHE IN BERLIN
SED-Zeitung: „Die Mauer[a] wird nicht niedergelegt[b]"
BM/AP Berlin, 13. Aug...

a. *wall*
b. *taken down*

Analyze these headlines a...

- how the verb **werden**...
- where the past partici...
  a. a main clause in th...
  b. a subordinate clau...

Realia: In jeder Minute... Point out: *21 Hektar Regenwald: ein Hektar* = 2.47 *acres.*

EINKOMMEN:

- Die Deutschen verdienen 188 534 240 Mark, 3,11 Mark pro Kopf. Boris Becker verdient mit seinem Tennisschläger 368 Mark an Preisgeldern, Steffi Graf „nur" 299 Mark. Bundeskanzler Kohl verdient dagegen nur 41,53 Mark.

PRODUKTION:

- Deutschlands Kühe produzieren 2 789 498 Liter Milch.
- 102 283 Pfund Butter werden erzeugt.
- 458 neue Autos laufen vom Band, allein 98 davon bei VW in Wolfsburg, dem größten deutschen Automobilwerk.
- 329 neue Fahrräder werden zusammengeschraubt.° — *assembled*
- 404 Fernsehgeräte werden hergestellt.

MEDIEN:

- 1,05 Millionen Tageszeitungen werden gekauft.
- 887 000 Zeitschriften werden gekauft.
- 12 000 Menschen sind im Kino und bezahlen dafür 89 600 Mark.
- 457 neue Fernsehgeräte werden gekauft, 274 Video-Recorder, 42 Video-Kameras, 160 CD-Player und 434 Autoradios.

VERKEHR:

- Auf Deutschlands Straßen ereignen sich 231 Unfälle,° vier davon unter Alkoholeinfluß. 16 Autofahrern wird der Führerschein entzogen. 39 Menschen werden verletzt, 13 davon schwer. Einer wird getötet (weltweit: 46 Tote im Straßenverkehr). — *accidents*
- 5563 Passagiere starten oder landen auf deutschen Flughäfen...

VERBRAUCH/KONSUM:

- 333 Bürger kaufen sich einen Neuwagen, 105 davon entscheiden sich für ein ausländisches Fabrikat.
- 682 242 Liter Milch werden verbraucht.
- 721 Tonnen Fleisch werden gegessen.
- 1 006 221 Liter Bier fließen durch deutsche Kehlen. 1,27 Millionen Liter Bier werden gebraut.
- 756 233 Liter Limonade und Fruchtsäfte werden getrunken.
- In den 295 deutschen McDonald's-Restaurants werden 28 995 Menschen abgefüttert.

UMWELT:

- 9 827 968 Kilo Müll° landen auf Deutschlands Müllhalden (161 Gramm pro Kopf). Das entspricht einem Güterzug° mit 491 Waggons, der 5,4 Kilometer lang ist. — *garbage* / *freight train*
- 3586 Kilo Pflanzenschutzmittel werden versprüht.
- Emissionen: 251 142 Kilo Schwefeldioxid werden in die Atmosphäre gepustet.° — *blown*

Bevölkerung one might say *In Deutschland werden weniger Kinder geboren als Menschen sterben. Das heißt, es gibt weniger Menschen in Deutschland.* Accept responses in either the active or the passive voice.

◫ Übung 3. **Was passiert alles in 60 Minuten in Deutschland?**

Bilden Sie Sätze im Passiv Präsens.

1.	1,5 Millionen Briefe	essen
2.	Mehr als eine Million Liter Bier	verletzen
3.	77 Kinder	kaufen
4.	484 Autos	trinken
5.	404 Fernsehgeräte	schreiben
6.	Über eine Million Zeitungen	gebären (geboren)
7.	39 Menschen / in Unfällen auf der Straße	herstellen
8.	721 Tonnen Fleisch	produzieren

Übung 3. **Suggestion:** Ask students to give the past participles of all verbs listed before they formulate their sentences.
Point out: To say "I was born" in German, one says *Ich bin geboren.* (*Ich bin am 15. Dezember geboren. Wo / Wann Sind Sie geboren?*) Avoid talking about the statal passive; it tends to confuse students. The function of the past participle as an adjective was introduced in chapter six, so students should be accustomed to seeing sentences such as: *Das Buch ist geöffnet. Die Tür ist geschlossen. Ich bin geboren.*

◫ Übung 4. **Was ist in einer Stunde in Deutschland geschehen?**

Restate the sentences of the previous exercise in the present perfect tense of the passive voice.

  BEISPIEL: In einer Stunde sind 77 Kinder geboren worden.

◫ Übung 5. **Achtung, Uhren umstellen!**

Read the following article about daylight saving time in Germany. Find a sentence or sentences in the

- present tense of the passive.
- simple past tense of the passive.
- past perfect tense of the passive.

Give the English equivalent for each sentence in the passive voice.

Übung 5. **Suggestion:** This exercise asks students to analyze a short but fairly complex text. Give them time to scan it for the gist before you do the exercise with the whole class.

RSM

Achtung, Uhren umstellen:
Die Sommerzeit beginnt

BM/dpa Hamburg, 26. März

Der Osterhase bringt in diesem Jahr auch die Sommerzeit: In der Nacht zum Sonntag um 2 Uhr werden die Uhren auf 3 Uhr vorgestellt; die Nacht wird um eine Stunde verkürzt. Die Sommerzeit endet am 24. September – traditionsgemäß wieder eine Sonntag-Nacht.

Die Sommerzeit war in der Bundesrepublik Deutschland – nach 30 Jahren Unterbrechung – erstmals 1980 wieder eingeführt worden. Das eigentliche Ziel, Energie einzusparen, wurde jedoch nicht erreicht. Dafür genießen viele ihre Freizeit an den langen hellen Abenden.

a. *attention*
b. *change*
c. *Easter Bunny*
d. *set ahead*
e. *shortened*
f. *interruption*
g. *introduced*
h. *real*
i. *reached*
j. *enjoy*

Expressing a General Activity

Sometimes a sentence in the passive voice will express a general activity or a process without stating a subject at all. The finite verb always appears in the third-person singular. This grammatical feature has no equivalent in English. Even though no subject appears in the German sentence, an impersonal **es** is generally understood.

Hier wird gerudert.	*These people are rowing.*
Wann wird gewählt?	*When are elections held?*

Eins – und eins – und eins . . .

Hier wird mächtig gerudert! **Jochen** sitzt zwischen **Peter** und **Stefan, Armin** sitzt zwischen **Martin** und **Thomas**. Vorn in einem Boot sitzt **Peter**, während **Martin** hinten sitzt. **Kalli** und **Stefan** rudern nicht in demselben Boot. Wer ist wer?

Lösung: 1. Stefan, 2. Jochen, 3. Peter, 4. Martin, 5. Armin, 6. Thomas, 7. Kalli

Realia. Suggestion: Give students several minutes to figure out who sits where.

RSM

Übung 6. Suggestion: Have students work in pairs, describing in general terms what is going on in the pictures. Call on several pairs to describe a drawing, using as many verbs as possible.

▣ Übung 6. Was ist hier los?

Describe what is going on in the pictures by using passive voice sentences without a subject.

BEISPIEL: Hier wird gefeiert.

Schü

Flüsse u...

Diese Lebensräume vieler
Pflanzenarten dürfen nicht

Spendenkonto: 1703-203...
werden Sie Mitglied im Bun...

Deutscher Bund für Vog...

Ja, ich möd...

Name:

Straße

Habichtstr....

1. möglichst viele Menschen über Umweltschutz i...
2. mehr Energie sparen (können)
3. Zeitungen und anderes Papier zum Containerste...
4. Altglas wie Flaschen und Gläser sammeln (könn...
5. Abfälle wie Plastiktüten und Einwegflaschen ve...
6. Altbatterien nicht in den Müll werfen (sollen)
7. die Luftverschmutzung vermindern (können)
8. Wegwerfprodukte (wie z.B. Einmal-Rasierer, Ein...
9. Wälder und Flüsse schützen (müssen)

▣ Übung 10. **Was ist das Problem damit?**

Was soll, kann oder darf damit (nicht) gemacht werd...

BEISPIEL: Digitaluhren können nicht repariert w...

1. Billiguhren (Digitaluhren)	vom Umweltbus ab...
2. Einmal-Fotoapparate	in fast alle Apothek...
3. alte Batterien	nur für einen Film g...
4. Einwegflaschen	nicht in den Müll w...
5. alte Medikamente	nicht wiederfüllen (...
6. Gifte	nicht reparieren

▣ Übung 7. **Reiseerinnerungen**

Wie war das—oder ist das—in Ihrer Familie? Nennen Sie einige Dinge, die bei Ihnen gewöhnlich vor oder während einer Reise gemacht wurden.

BEISPIEL: Zuletzt wurde unser Hund zu Freunden gebracht.

zuerst	im Reisebüro eine Reise buchen
dann	das Auto saubermachen
danach	Koffer packen
schließlich	Koffer ins Auto bringen
zuletzt	Hund / Katze ins Hunde-/Katzenhotel / zu Freunden bringen
	Fahrkarten / Landkarten kaufen
	Schlüssel beim Nachbarn abgeben
	die Post / die Zeitung abbestellen
	Benzin tanken
	Postkarten an alle Freunde schreiben
	Sonstiges

Übung 7. **Suggestion:** Do this exercise with the whole group to create a story. Call on one student to start a chain with one opening sentence. This student in turn calls on another, who adds another sentence. Continue until all phrases fit into the story.

▣ Übung 8. **Traditionen**

Nennen Sie einige Dinge, die bei Ihnen und Ihrer Familie regelmäßig gemacht werden (oder auch nicht). Wann wird das gemacht?

BEISPIEL: Bei mir zu Hause wird morgens immer gefrühstückt (an der Uni nie). Am Wochenende wird lange geschlafen. Einmal im Jahr wird eine Reise gemacht.

morgens
abends
am Wochenende
einmal im Jahr
zu Thanksgiving (oder an anderen Festtagen)

Übung 8. **Follow-up:** Call out a time or a day of the week and ask a student to form a sentence by saying what might be going on at that time. For instance, you say *Am Wochenende*; a student continues *wird lange geschlafen*. Ask this student in turn to say a time and to call on another student, who continues the chain.

The Passive with Modal Verbs

Modal verbs are used with a passive infinitive to convey something that should, must, or can be done. Only the present tense and the simple past tense of modals are commonly used in the passive.

Die Bomben **sollen zerstört werden.**	*The bombs should be destroyed.*
Umweltschutz **kann** nicht **befohlen werden;** er **muß gelebt werden.**	*Environmental protection cannot be ordered, it must be lived.*
Die Tiere **konnten gerettet werden.**	*The animals could be saved.*

The passive infinitive consists of the past partici

ACTIVE INFINITIVE	PASSIVE INFINIT
befehlen	befohlen werden (*to b*
leben	gelebt werden (*to be l*
retten	gerettet werden (*to be*
zerstören	zerstört werden (*to be*

Neue Wörter

die Flasche *bottle*
die Luftverschmutzung *air pollution*
der Müll *garbage*

gebrauchen
sammeln *to*
vermindern
werfen *to th*
wegwerfen

Beispiele für Gefahrensymb

Gifte

Leicht entzündlich

Ätzend

▣ Übung 9. Was kann für die Umwelt ge

Bilden Sie Sätze mit Modalverben im Passiv.

BEISPIEL: Die Natur darf nicht weiter zerstört

> ▣▣▣▣ *Kulturnotiz*
>
> In einigen Orten Deutschlands kann man alte Medikamente in die Apotheke zurückbringen, damit sie nicht in den Abfall geworfen werden und als Giftstoffe (*poisonous substances*) die Umwelt gefährden. Andere potentiell gefährliche Substanzen wie alte Batterien und Farben werden von „Umweltbussen" abgeholt.

Alternatives to the Passive

Generally, the passive voice is used whenever the agent of an action is unknown. There are, however, a number of common active-voice alternatives that can be used even when the agent of an action is not expressed. Some of these are shown below.

PASSIVE VOICE

Die Gefahr ist nicht erkannt worden.
The danger was not recognized.

Die Zerstörung der Altstadt ist verhindert worden.
The destruction of the old city was prevented.

ACTIVE-VOICE ALTERNATIVE:
man

Man hat die Gefahr nicht **erkannt.**
People (one) did not recognize the danger.

Man hat die Zerstörung der Altstadt **verhindert.**
They (one) prevented the destruction of the old city.

PASSIVE VOICE

Eine Verbesserung für Fußgänger kann nicht erwartet werden.
An improvement for pedestrians cannot be expected.

Wie kann die Umwelt geschützt werden?
How can the environment be protected?

ACTIVE-VOICE ALTERNATIVE:
sein + **zu** + *infinitive*

Eine Verbesserung für Fußgänger **ist** nicht **zu erwarten.**
An improvement for pedestrians is not to be expected.

Wie **ist** die Umwelt **zu schützen**?

How is the environment to be protected?

PASSIVE VOICE

Wie kann das Problem gelöst werden?
How can the problem be solved?

Papier kann wiedergebraucht werden.
Paper can be reused.

ACTIVE VOICE ALTERNATIVE:
sich lassen + *infinitive*

Wie **läßt sich** das Problem **lösen**?
How can the problem be solved?

Papier **läßt sich** wiedergebrauchen.
Paper can be reused.

Auf den ersten Blick 1

1. Was sagen die Überschriften und die Zeichnung über das Thema des Informationsblattes aus?
2. Welche weiteren Informationen erwarten Sie vom Text?
   a. etwas über Atomreaktoren in der UdSSR
   b. welche Lebensmittel man nicht essen sollte, weil sie radioaktiv sind
   c. wie es zur Katastrophe in Tschernobyl kam
   d. wie man gegen Atomkraft demonstrieren kann

3 Jahre nach Tschernobyl

Verbraucher-Zentrale Hambu

Große Bleichen 23 · Hamburg 36   26.4.1989

3 Jahre nach Tschernobyl:

STRAHLUNG SIEHT. MAN NICHT

Am 26. April 1986 um
begann die wohl größt
Katastrophe, die Euro
heimgesucht[a] hat. Ein
geriet bei Tschernoby
Sowjetunion außer Kon
Teil seines radioakti
gelangte[c] in die Umwelt
wird es dauern - also
Jahre 2116 - bis sich
des in der Umwelt befi
Cäsium-137 durch radio
Zerfall[d] auch nur halbi

Einige Lebensmittel
immer radioaktiv be

a. *befallen*
b. *geriet... went out of control*
c. *reached*
d. *decay*
e. *reduced by half*
f. *as a precaution*
g. *do without*
h. *deer*
i. *reindeer meat*
j. *mushrooms*
k. *sage tea*
l. *lentils*
m. Preiselbeeren *cranberries*
n. *inland lakes*
o. *venison*
p. *moorland sheep*

Ernährungs–Empfehlungen:

Zur Zeit vorsorglich[f]
verzichten[g] auf:
- Reh[h], Rentierfleisch[i]
- wildwachsende Pilze[j]
- Paranüsse
- Salbeiblättertee[k]
- schwarzer Tee aus der Türkei

Vorsorglich weniger essen u
- rote Linsen[l] aus der Türke
- Haselnußkerne
- Wildpreiselbeeren[m]
- Fisch aus Binnenseen[n] (insbesondere Hecht, Bars
- italienische Nudeln
- Hirschfleisch[o], Heidschnuc

☐ **Übung 11.** **Was kann man für den Umweltschutz machen?**

Sagen Sie die Sätze anders mit **man.**

> BEISPIEL: Wegwerfprodukte sollen vermieden werden. →
> Man soll Wegwerfprodukte vermeiden.

1. Umweltschutz muß gelebt werden; er kann nicht befohlen werden.
2. Die Umwelt darf nicht weiter zerstört werden.
3. Altpapier und Glas sollten zum Recycling gebracht werden.
4. In Göttingen ist Geld für den Umweltschutz gesammelt worden.
5. Mehr Containerstellplätze sind aufgestellt worden.
6. Chemikalien im Haushalt sollen vermieden werden.
7. Batterien sollen nicht in den Hausmüll geworfen werden.
8. Der Wald muß besonders geschützt werden.

☐ **Übung 12.** **Probleme**

Was läßt sich machen? Was läßt sich nicht machen?

> BEISPIEL: Flugzeuglärm läßt sich vermindern, aber nicht vermeiden.

Schmutz (*dirt*) auf den Straßen	verbieten (*to forbid*)
Luftverschmutzung	vermindern (*to lessen*)
Häßliche moderne Architektur	vermeiden
Verkehr und Staus auf den Straßen	
Kriege	
Drogen	
Umweltkatastrophen (z.B. Tschernobyl)	
Bevölkerungsexplosion	
Sonstiges	

☐ **Übung 13.** **Lebensqualität**

Was kann man tun, um die Lebensqualität zu verbessern? Bilden Sie Sätze mit **sein** + **zu** + Infinitiv.

> BEISPIEL: Alte Zeitungen →
> Alte Zeitungen sind zum Recycling zu bringen.

Plastiktüten	bauen
Windenergie	vermeiden
Kinderspielplätze	sammeln
Solarautos	entwickeln
Atomwaffen	schützen
Altpapier	verschrotten
öffentliche Verkehrsmittel	
Wälder	

Natur- und Umweltschutz ist Liebe zum Leben

LESEN IM KONTEXT ▫▫▫▫▫▫▫▫▫▫

Vor dem Lesen

▣ Aktivität. Gesellschaftliche Probleme

1. Was halten Sie für die drei wichtigsten Probleme in der folgenden Liste? Erklären Sie, warum Sie diese gewählt haben. Welche Probleme hält Ihr Partner oder Ihre Partnerin für die wichtigsten? Welches Problem hält die ganze Klasse für das wichtigste Problem? Diskutieren Sie.

	SIE	IHR(E) PARTNER(IN)
Arbeitslosigkeit	___	___
Umweltverschmutzung	___	___
Obdachlosigkeit°	___	___
Terrorismus	___	___
Drogen / Drogenhandel / Alkoholismus	___	___
Inflation	___	___
Welthunger	___	___
AIDS	___	___
sonstige Probleme	___	___

2. Wo gibt es diese Probleme?
   a. hauptsächlich in Städten
   b. weltweit
   c. in der westlichen Welt
   d. auf dem Land
   e. in den Ländern der dritten Welt

3. Sind Sie aktiv in einer Organisation?
   a. Mitglied in Greenpeace
   b. Mitglied in Amnesty International
   c. Geld sammeln für ____
   d. andere Organisation: ____

4. Wie umweltbewußt sind Sie? Was machen Sie?
   a. Altglas und Altpapier sammeln
   b. Benzin sparen
   c. keine Treibgasdosen (*spray cans*) gebrauchen
   d. Sonstiges

5. Welches Problem halten Sie überhaupt nicht für wichtig?

Der Preis für den Luxus

STEFFI, 19 Jahre: Ich habe mein Auto verkauft. Das ist mein Beitrag gegen die Luftverschmutzung durch Autoabgase. Das war nicht der einzige Grund, aber doch der wichtigste. Denn ich bin vom Ammersee nach München gezogen. Und in der Stadt brauche ich kein Auto. Mit dem Fahrrad komme ich viel besser voran.

Ich glaube nicht, daß die Leute in Zukunft umweltbewußter° werden. Jeder schiebt die Verantwortung° auf den anderen. Man sollte vielleicht mehr Bürgerinitativen gründen. Denn jeder einzelne° bildet mit den anderen zusammen den Staat. So müssen alle im kleinen bei sich selbst anfangen.

ECKI, 22 Jahre: Ich werfe° kein Papier auf die Straße. Ich fahre auch wenig Auto. Im Haushalt allerdings tue ich wenig. Das Baumsterben,° radioaktiver Abfall und die Verschmutzung der Meere sind wohl die größten Umweltprobleme. Ich hoffe, daß sich da bald was ändert.°

SUSANNE, 26 Jahre: Ich trenne zum Beispiel den Hausmüll.° Ich sammle Aluminium, Altpapier und Plastik. Das bringe ich dann zu den Sammelstellen. Davon gibt es leider zu wenig. Auch meine Familie und meine Freunde sammeln.

Das Hauptumweltproblem, denke ich, ist der Hausmüll. Natürlich auch die Autoabgase. Es gibt ja auch immer mehr Autos. Leider wird gerade da nicht viel getan. Man könnte doch endlich auf Methanol umsteigen. Aber das eigentliche Problem ist die Industrie, die dahintersteckt.

ERWIN, 21 Jahre: Ich kaufe Spraydosen ohne Treibgas, sammle Alufolien, Glas, Papier und werfe das Zeug in die entsprechenden Container. Außerdem spende ich im Monat 30 Mark für Greenpeace. Mein Freund macht es ähnlich, er ist genauso umweltbewußt wie ich. Meine Eltern, wie überhaupt die ältere Generation, sind das weniger. Das Hauptproblem sehe ich darin, daß sich unsere Lebensweise geändert hat. Wir leben von der Industrie. Also nicht mehr so natürlich wie früher. Das belastet° die Umwelt. Doch ich sehe Chancen, damit fertig zu werden.° Alle müssen mithelfen. Umweltschutz kann nicht befohlen werden, er muß gelebt werden.

Jugendscala, September 1988

more conscious of the environment
responsibility
individual
throw
der Baum tree; *sterben* to die
changes
household garbage
burdens
damit... *to cope with that*

Zum Text 3

1. Einer der vier jungen Leute sagt: „Umweltschutz kann nicht befohlen werden, er muß gelebt werden." Wie „leben" die vier jungen Leute Umweltschutz?
2. Wer leistet Ihrer Meinung nach den größten Beitrag zum Umweltschutz?
3. Was halten Sie für die größten Umweltprobleme?
4. Was machen Sie persönlich oder was macht Ihre Familie gegen Umweltverschmutzung?

Auf den ersten Blick 4

1. Was sagen der Titel und die Überschriften über das Thema des Artikels aus?

2. Welche weiteren Informationen erwarten Sie?

3. Raten Sie die Bedeutung der folgenden Wörter. Suchen Sie die Wörter zuerst im Text. Wenn Sie sie nicht gleich verstehen, lesen Sie weiter. (Manchmal hilft es, vorwärts und rückwärts [*forward and backward*] zu lesen.

   a. **Nulltarif** heißt:
      1. ein Park in Hamburg
      2. ohne Kosten
      3. eine Firma für Pflanzen
   b. **Ein Bürger** ist:
      1. etwas zu essen
      2. ein Mann, der bei der Behörde arbeitet
      3. (hier) eine Person, die in Hamburg wohnt
   c. **Der Teich** ist:
      1. ein Gewässer
      2. ein Park
      3. eine Straße
   d. **einen Vertrag schließen** heißt:
      1. die Tür zumachen
      2. einen Kontrakt unterschreiben
      3. ein Geschenk machen
   e. **geeignet sein** heißt:
      1. der Stadt gehören
      2. (dort) gut passen
      3. gefährlich sein
   f. **Brutplätze** sind:
      1. Plätze, wo man Fußball spielt
      2. Plätze, wo Vögel ihre Eier legen
      3. Plätze, wo man schwimmen kann

4. Manchmal machen kleine Wörter das Lesen schwierig, wenn man sie nicht kennt. Welche Funktion spielen die folgenden Wörter im Satz?

   a. **indem** bedeutet (Er [der Pate] hält das Gewässer sauber, **indem**...):
      - **wie** man etwas macht
      - **warum** man etwas macht
      - **wo** man etwas macht

   b. **damit** heißt (Wir schließen mit den Bachpaten einen Vertrag, **damit**...):
      - **sodaß**
      - **weil**
      - **oder**

WORTSCHATZ

Substantive

der Abfall (¨e)	garbage
die Abgase (*pl.*)	exhaust fumes
die Angst (¨e)	fear
keine Angst	don't be afraid
die Ansicht (-en)	opinion
meiner Ansicht nach	in my opinion
der Bach (¨e)	creek, stream
der Bürger (-), die Bürgerin (-nen)	citizen
die Flasche (-n)	bottle
der Flughafen (¨)	airport
die Folge (-n)	consequence
der Frieden	peace
der Fußgänger (¨), die Fußgängerin (-nen)	pedestrian
die Gefahr (-en)	danger
das Gegenteil	opposite
im Gegenteil	on the contrary
die Geschwindigkeit (-en)	speed
das Gift (-e)	poison
die Kernenergie	nuclear energy
die Kraft (¨e)	power
der Krieg (-e)	war
der Lärm	noise
die Lösung (-en)	solution
die Luftverschmutzung	air pollution
die Meinung (-en)	opinion
der Müll	garbage
der Quatsch	nonsense
die Raserei	driving too fast
das Schild (-er)	sign, road sign
der Schluß	end
der Schluß	end
Schluß mit ____!	Stop ____!
der Schmutz	dirt
der Teich (-e)	pond
das Tempo (-s)	speed
das Tier (-e)	animal
das Ufer (-)	bank (of a body of water)
der Umweltschutz	environmental protection
der Unfall (¨e)	accident
der Unsinn	nonsense
der Vogel (¨)	bird

Verben

abholen (holt ab)	to pick up
aufnehmen (nimmt auf), nahm auf, aufgenommen	to take a picture
die Meinung äußern	to voice an opinion
bedauern (ich bedaure)	to regret
befehlen (befiehlt), befahl, befohlen	to order
beschleunigen	to accelerate
bremsen	to brake, put on the brakes
empfinden, empfand, empfunden	to feel, consider
erkennen, erkannte, erkannt	recognize
flüchten	to flee
fordern	to demand
gebrauchen	to use
glauben	to believe
geschehen (geschieht), geschah, ist geschehen	to happen
herstellen (stellt her)	to manufacture
meckern	to gripe
mitmachen (macht mit)	to participate
pflegen	to take care of
rechnen mit	to count on, expect
retten	to save, rescue
sammeln	to collect
sauberhalten (hält sauber), hielt sauber, saubergehalten	to keep clean
schaffen, schuf, geschaffen	to create, succeed
schalten	to shift gears
schützen	to protect
sterben (stirbt), starb, ist gestorben	to die
übertreiben, übertrieb, übertrieben	to exaggerate
verkaufen	to sell
verhindern	to prevent
vermeiden, vermied, vermieden	to avoid

vermindern	to lessen
verschrotten	to scrap
wachsen (wächst), wuchs, ist gewachsen	to grow
wählen	to vote, elect; choose
wegwerfen (wirft weg), warf weg, weggeworfen	to throw away
zunehmen (nimmt zu), nahm zu, zugenommen	to increase
sich zusammen-schließen zu (schließt zusammen), schloß zusammen, zusammenge-schlossen	to form (a group)

Adjektive und Adverbien

augenblicklich	momentary, current
geboren	born
gewöhnt an	accustomed to
rechtzeitig	in time
unerträglich	unbearable

Sonstiges

beziehungsweise (bzw.)	or
da (*conj.*)	since
mit 200 Sachen (*coll.*)	speeding at 200 km an hour
Mir stehen die Haare zu Berge.	My hair stands on end.

GESTERN UND HEUTE

Gestern und heute. Suggestion: Since this chapter concludes with the dramatic events of November 9, 1989, when the GDR government announced the opening of all borders, introduce it by focusing on that event as an example of *Geschichte erleben*. Ask students to recall another significant event that will one day feature prominently in history books.

Lernziele *This chapter presents a brief overview of recent German history culminating in the events of November 1989. You will experience history through the personal recollections and spontaneous responses of everyday people to events around them, and then formulate your own responses to these events.*

Alles klar? Point out: German cities are extremely proud of their individual histories and like to celebrate their "birthdays" as civic occasions, often with an eye toward attracting visitors.

▣ Alles klar?

Geschichte spielt eine wichtige Rolle in unserem Leben. Je älter (*the older*) und traditionsreicher ein Land, ein Ort oder eine Institution, umso

RSM

Hamburg kommt.
Sie auch?

1989. Hamburgs Hafen wird 800.

VIERZIG JAHRE BUNDESREPUBLIK DEUTSCHLAND

750 JAHRE BERLIN 1987

40 JAHRE DDR

10 DDR

Das Festprogramm der Stadt Bonn

Düsseldorf
700 Jahre Stadt – 1988

ca. 500 vor Christus, Erste Besiedlung durch die Kelten.

stolzer (*the prouder*) sind die Menschen darauf. Diesen Stolz auf Tradition und Geschichte drücken die Namen und Daten auf Seite 474 aus.

- Welcher Ort wurde zuerst durch die Kelten besiedelt (*settled*)?
- Worauf ist Bonn stolz?
- Was erfahren (*find out*) Sie über einige andere Städte?
- Was ist 1989 vierzig Jahre alt geworden?

Suggestion: Personalize this by recalling your own experiences when you visited a German-speaking country. Show the location of Rothenburg along the *Romantische Straße* extending from Würzburg to Füssen in the Alps. Focus on the contrast between the age of individual cities and the short history of the Bundesrepublik and the DDR, both of which celebrated their 40th birthday in 1989.

WÖRTER IM KONTEXT

Gestern

KLEINE CHRONIK DEUTSCHER GESCHICHTE VON 1939–1989

Gestern. Suggestion: If it is available, show the film *Triumph des Willens* by filmmaker Leni Riefenstahl, which documents Hitler's effect on the German people, as shown in the annual ritual of the *Parteitag* in Nürnberg.
Suggestion: Assign the *Kleine Chronik* reading as homework. Discuss and elaborate on dates and events the following day, bringing in additional pictures and slides.

1. September 1939	Der Zweite Weltkrieg beginnt um 5.45 Uhr mit der Invasion Polens durch deutsche Truppen. Zwei Tage später, am 3. September, erklären England, das Commonwealth (Australien, Indien, Neuseeland, Canada) und Frankreich Deutschland den Krieg.
9. Mai 1945	Um null Uhr eins endet der Zweite Weltkrieg in Europa offiziel mit der Kapitulation der Deutschen Wehrmacht.° Durch diesen Krieg verloren insgesamt 55 Millionen Menschen ihr Leben als Opfer° der nationalsozialistischen (Nazi) Rassenpolitik, als Soldaten, als Zivilisten, als Flüchtlinge° und Vertriebene.°

armed forces

victims

refugees
expelled people

Das zerbombte Reichstagsgebäude in Berlin 1945

475

17. Juni 1953	Volksaufstand° in Ost-Berlin und der DDR gegen das kommunistische Regime.	*popular uprising*
13. September 1961	Bau der Mauer in Berlin.	
26. Juni 1963	Besuch Präsident John F. Kennedys in Berlin. Seine Rede über den Wert° der Freiheit und seine Erklärung der Solidarität mit den Berlinern endet mit den oft zitierten Worten: „Ich bin ein Berliner."	*worth*
3. September 1971	Die Sowjetunion garantiert den ungehinderten Zugang° nach West-Berlin im Viermächteabkommen° über Berlin.	*access* / *four-power agreement*
17. Mai 1972	Die Bundesrepublik Deutschland und die Deutsche Demokratische Republik unterzeichnen einen Grundlagenvertrag,° in dem sie sich zu gutnachbarlicher Beziehung verpflichten.°	*basic agreement* / *oblige themselves*
9. November 1989	Die Grenzen zwischen der DDR und der BRD werden geöffnet. Die Mauer zwischen Ost- und West-Berlin hat genau 10 315 Tage gehalten.	

Volksaufstand. Suggestion: Discuss Bertolt Brecht's famous poem *"Die Lösung,"* which deals with this uprising. Brecht had been openly supportive of the goals of the communist party in suppressing the uprising; yet this poem, found after his death, showed that Brecht understood what was essentially at stake.

▫▫▫▫ *Kulturnotiz*

Die Präambel des Grundgesetzes der Bundesrepublik betont den provisorischen Charakter des Grundgesetzes bis zu dem Tag einer neuen (gesamtdeutschen) Verfassung, „die von dem deutschen Volke in freier Entscheidung beschlossen worden ist." Die Hoffnung auf einen einheitlichen deutschen Staat drückt sich in den Worten der Präambel aus: „Das gesamte deutsche Volk bleibt aufgefordert, in freier Selbstbestimmung [*self-determination*] die Einheit und Freiheit Deutschlands zu vollenden."

Die zwei höchsten Ämter (*offices*) in der Bundesregierung sind der Bundeskanzler und der Bundespräsident.

Neue Wörter

der Aufstand *rebellion, uprising*
die Besatzung (*military*) *occupation*
die Einheit *unity*
das Gesetz *law*
die Gründung *founding*
die Mauer *wall*
die Regierung *government*
die Trümmer (*pl.*) *rubble, ruins*

die Vereinigten Staaten *United States*
die Verfassung *constitution*
das Volk *people*
die Wahl *election*
aufteilen (teilt auf) *to divide up*
versorgen *to supply*
wählen *to vote, to elect, to choose*

□ **Aktivität 1.** Welches Datum und welcher Satz passen zu welchem Bild?

Am 17. Juni 1953	feierte ganz Deutschland die Öffnung der Grenze zwischen Ost- und West-Berlin und zwischen der DDR und der BRD.
Am 9. Mai 1945	gab es in der DDR einen Aufstand gegen das kommunistische Regime.
Am 13. Sept. 1961	als der Zweite Weltkrieg in Europa endete, lag ganz Deutschland in Trümmern.
Am 9. Nov. 1989	wurde die Grenze zwischen Ost- und West-Berlin durch den Bau der Mauer geschlossen.

Aktivität 1. Suggestion: Have students match dates and appropriate phrases first before matching the completed statements with the pictures.

Aktivität 7. Hören Sie zu.

Sie hören einige Erinnerungen aus der Zeit zwischen 1945 und 1989. Notieren Sie das Jahr, von dem der Sprecher redet, und machen Sie sich ein paar Notizen über das Thema des Berichtes.

BEISPIEL: 1. Jahr: 1945; Thema: keine Schule

Nachdem Sie alle Berichte gehört haben, fassen Sie den Inhalt der Berichte mit Hilfe Ihrer Notizen zusammen. Folgende neue Wörter kommen in den Berichten vor.

Neue Wörter

das Bettuch *bed sheet*
der Panzer *tank*
der Soldat *soldier*

anstehen (steht an) *to stand in line*

begrüßen *to greet*
kaputtmachen (macht kaputt) *to break*

Westberliner begrüßen einen ostdeutschen Trabi (Trabant Auto) und seine Insassen nach Öffnung der Grenzen.

Heute

Dialog. So erlebten die Berliner Geschichte

Die folgenden spontanen Reaktionen von Menschen aus Ost und West nach dem „Fall" der Mauer am 9. November 1989 dokumentieren, wie der „kleine Mann" und die „kleine Frau" auf den Straßen Berlins den historischen Moment empfanden.

2. Jahr: 1948; Thema: Schokolade, Bananen
3. Jahr: 1947; Thema: Suppe in der Schule
4. Jahr: 1989; Thema: Checkpoint Charlie; singen
5. Jahr: 1961; Thema: Flucht in den Westen

Aktivität 7. Suggestion: Play each segment twice, pausing long enough for students to write down the information. When they have listened to all segments and finished their notes, have them work in pairs to summarize the content of each segment. Call on individual students to read one summary.
Note: The texts are all based on actual experiences; number 4 is based on a newspaper report.

Dialog. Note: All sentences are taken from German newspapers published right after the Berlin wall was opened.
Suggestion: Ask students to write the numbers, in the order in which these sentences are spoken on tape, next to each sentence on the page.
Point out: The Café Kranzler is probably the most famous and elegant of the cafés on the Kurfürstendamm in Berlin. With regard to the Ka-De-We *(Kaufhaus des Westen)*, students may remember that they used its floor plan in an exercise in chapter ten. This department store is known for the size of its food department. Bananas were hard to get in East Berlin, which explains the comment from one onlooker that "The Ka-De-We is going to run out of bananas."

Kulturnotiz (page 482). Point out: A few memorials to the destruction of World War II have been left standing in Germany. Dresden has preserved the ruins of a church in the center of town as a reminder of the war; in West Berlin the blackened tower of the Kaiser-Wilhelm-Gedächtniskirche is right next to the new church.

REPORTER: Volksfeststimmung überall. An der Gedächtniskirche umarmen (*hug*) sich wildfremde Leute. Bier und Sekt werden ausgeschenkt. Vor dem Café Kranzler tanzen die Menschen. Dazwischen immer wieder die Rufe „Wahnsinn" und „Das tollste Ding seit 100 Jahren".

Erst mal Ku'damm.

Bloß mal den Fuß auf die andere Seite setzen, mal gucken, wie es hier ist.

Ich glaube, morgen gehen im Ka-De-We[a] die Bananen aus.

Das ist der Tag, auf den wir so lang warten mußten, ich kann es nicht fassen.

Auf den Tag hab ich 28 Jahre lang gewartet. Ich will nur mal sehen, ob meine Straße auch im Westen weitergeht.

Ich war gerade bei meiner Oma in der Grunewaldstraße. Die war so perplex, daß die gar nichts mitgekriegt[b] hat.

Wir saßen alle schon in Schlafanzügen vor dem Fernsehen, als die Nachricht durchkam. Dann ging alles ruck zuck.[c]

Junge Ostberlinerin in einer Westberliner Disco: „Diese Nacht werde ich mein Leben lang nicht vergessen —jetzt weiß ich, daß wir alle zusammengehören."

Ick fass mir pausenlos an Kopp.[d]

Ich bin der erste Japaner, der die Ostseite der Mauer berührt hat.

Junge Frau am Checkpoint Charlie: „Guten Abend, ich werd' verrückt."

Berliner aus Ost und West feiern auf dem Ku'damm ein Fest des Wiedersehens.

a. Kaufhaus des Westens
b. (*coll.*) verstanden
c. ruck... (*coll.*) *in a flash*
d. Berlinerisch für: Ich fasse mir pausenlos an den Kopf.

◻◻◻◻ *Kulturnotiz*

Die Kaiser-Wilhelm-Gedächtniskirche liegt am Ku'damm (Kurfürstendamm), dem großen Einkaufsboulevard Westberlins. Die Kirche lag am Ende des Zweiten Weltkriegs in Trümmern. Man baute eine neue, moderne Kirche auf, ließ aber die schwarze Ruine des Turms stehen als Mahnmal (*memorial*) an die dunklen Jahre des Krieges.

Die Kaiser-Wilhelm Gedächtniskirche in Berlin

Neue Wörter

das Fest *party*	**zusammengehören** *to belong together*
die Kirche *church*	
die Stimmung *mood*	**lustig** *funny*
der Wahnsinn *madness*	**nachdenklich** *reflective, thoughtful*
fassen *to comprehend, to grasp*	**pausenlos** *continuously*
Das (Es) ist nicht zu fassen. *That (It) is unbelievable.*	**verrückt** *crazy, mad*
umarmen *to hug*	**wildfremd** *totally strange*

▣ Analyse

- Suchen Sie Wörter und Ausdrücke in den Aussagen der Berliner, die ihre Gefühle ausdrücken.
- Warum redet der Reporter von einem Volksfest?
- Wie verbringen einige Leute die ersten Stunden ihrer neugewonnenen Freiheit?
- Manche Reaktionen scheinen oberflächlich, andere sind nachdenklicher. Welche scheinen Ihnen oberflächlich? Welche nachdenklicher?
- Welche Reaktion finden Sie humorvoll oder lustig?
- Welche Reaktionen sind typisch für die etwas älteren Menschen?

▣ Aktivität 8. **Was halten Sie davon?**

Können Sie die Reaktionen der Berliner verstehen? Drücken Sie Ihre eigene Reaktion aus.

BEISPIEL: Ich hätte nicht gedacht, daß die Mauer eines Tages fällt. Ich konnte es kaum fassen.

Nützliche Redemittel:

Zustimmung (*agreement*) ausdrücken:	Ich kann das verstehen. Ich finde es schön, daß Ich freue mich, daß
Überraschung (*surprise*):	Ich war überrascht, als Das ist wirklich eine Überraschung. Ich konnte es kaum fassen. Wer hätte das gedacht? Ich hätte nicht gedacht, daß Na, so was!
Zweifel (*doubt*):	Ich frage mich, Ich weiß nicht, Ich bezweifle, daß

Aktivität 8. Suggestion: Go over all *Redemittel* first before asking students to choose one expression from each category to express their views.

Aktivität 9. Eine Überraschung

Erinnern Sie sich an etwas, was Sie überrascht hat? Wie haben Sie reagiert?

> BEISPIEL: A: Ich war überrascht, als ich zu meinem 21. Geburtstag ein Auto bekam. Ich konnte es kaum fassen.

GRAMMATIK IM KONTEXT

Verbs with Prepositions Used Figuratively

Many German and English verbs require prepositional objects. The prepositions used with these verbs often take on a figurative meaning that is different from their original spatial or temporal meaning. You already know a few such verbs; for instance:

> sich beschweren über (+ *acc.*) (*to complain about*)
> sich erinnern an (+ *acc.*) (*to remember*)
> sich freuen auf (+ *acc.*) (*to look forward to*)
> sich freuen über (+ *acc.*) (*to be happy about*)
> sich interessieren für (+ *acc.*) (*to be interested in*)
> warten auf (+ *acc.*) (*to wait for*)

The prepositions used with the German verbs often do not correspond to the prepositions used in English. Sometimes a German verb requires a prepositional object when English requires a direct object to express the same thing. The verb **sich erinnern an** is a case in point.

> Ich erinnere mich noch gut **an meine Kindheit.**
>
> I remember **my childhood** well.

Since the prepositions used with verbs are unpredictable, you should memorize the prepositions together with the verbs. Here are some additional verbs with prepositions used figuratively:

> achten auf (+ *acc.*) (*to pay attention to*)
> Angst haben vor (+ *dat.*) (*to be afraid of*)
> sich ärgern über (+ *acc.*) (*to be annoyed about*)
> bitten um (+ *acc.*) (*to ask for, to request*)
> fragen nach (+ *dat.*) (*to ask about, to inquire after*)
> glauben an (+ *acc.*) (*to believe in*)
> hoffen auf (+ *acc.*) (*to hope for*)
> reagieren auf (+ *acc.*) (*to react to*)
> stolz sein auf (+ *acc.*) (*to be proud of*)
> warnen vor (+ *dat.*) (*to warn against*)
> wissen von (+ *dat.*) (*to know about*)

▣ **Übung 1.** Nachrichten aus Berlin: Aus einem Brief von Freunden in Berlin

So ein Wahnsinn! Ergänzen Sie die fehlenden Präpositionen.

Wir haben lange nichts mehr von euch gehört. In der Zwischenzeit ist hier soviel passiert. Die Mauer ist gefallen! Wir haben 28 Jahre _____[1] diesen Tag gewartet. Wir hoffen jetzt alle _____[2] eine bessere Zukunft.

Die Leute hier haben mit großer Freude _____[3] die Nachricht von den offenen Grenzen reagiert. Ich erinnere mich noch gut _____[4] die Tage kurz vor dem Bau der Mauer im Jahre 1961.

Einige Leute haben allerdings auch Angst _____[5] der neuen Zeit. Alles ist so plötzlich gekommen... Nur wenige Leute wollen noch _____[6] den Kommunismus glauben.

Man sieht die unglaublichsten Szenen auf der Straße. Ein Mann hat einen Volkspolizisten am Checkpoint Charlie _____[7] ein Autogramm gebeten. So ein Wahnsinn!

Bei dem ersten Besuch in den Geschäften im Westen haben viele Kunden _____[8] Bananen und Apfelsinen gefragt.

▣ **Übung 2.** Wer könnte das sein?

Machen Sie mit einem Partner oder einer Partnerin einen Fragebogen mit Fragen, in denen Sie die Verben aus der Liste unten gebrauchen. (Keine ja/nein Fragen, bitte!) Verteilen Sie die fertigen Fragebögen in der Klasse. Jeder sollte einen Fragebogen bekommen und die Fragen darauf schriftlich beantworten. Verteilen Sie dann die beantworteten Fragebögen an andere Personen.

Jeder berichtet kurz über die Person, deren Fragebogen er hat, ohne den Namen zu nennen. Lassen Sie die Klasse raten.

sich (gern oder ungern) erinnern an   sich freuen auf
Angst haben vor   stolz sein auf
sich ärgern über   glauben an
hoffen auf   sich beschweren über

BEISPIEL: Woran erinnerst du dich gern? → an meinen ersten Freund
            Wovor hast du als Kind Angst gehabt? → vor Hunden

Übung 2. **Suggestion:** Assign the design and formulation of questions for a *Fragebogen* as homework, to be distributed in class the next day. Then proceed as suggested in the exercise.

Anticipatory *da*-Compounds

You have already learned to use **da**-compounds such as **dafür, dagegen, damit, daran,** and **darauf** as pronouns standing for prepositional phrases referring to a thing or an idea. **Da**-compounds do not refer to human beings.

Was halten die Deutschen von Wiedervereinigung? —Die meisten sind **dafür.** Einige sind **dagegen.**

What do Germans think about reunification? —Most are for it. Some are against it.

Erinnerst du dich an die Nachkriegszeit? —Ich erinnere mich gut **daran.**

Do you remember the postwar period? —I remember it well.

Seid ihr stolz auf euer Land? —Ja, wir sind stolz **darauf.**

Are you proud of your country? —Yes, we are proud of it.

Da-compounds are also used in another, related function. Sometimes a verb that requires a prepositional phrase is not followed by a preposition and a noun, but instead by a dependent clause or an infinitive phrase. In that case, a **da-**compound frequently appears in the main clause, anticipating the following dependent clause or infinitive phrase.

Eine Zeitung fragte eine Gruppe junger Deutscher: „Seid ihr stolz **darauf, Deutsche zu sein?"**

A newspaper asked a group of young Germans, "Are you proud to be Germans?"

The infinitive phrase **Deutsche zu sein** completes the question **Seid ihr stolz?** Since the verb **stolz sein** requires a prepositional object with **auf,** the **da-**compound **darauf** appears in the main clause and is followed immediately by the infinitive phrase.

The anticipatory **da-**compound in the main clause precedes a past participle, an infinitive, or a separable prefix which is part of the verb of the main clause.

Ich habe nicht **daran** gedacht, daß heute sein Geburtstag ist.

I did not think about the fact that today is his birthday.

Ich kann mich nie **daran** erinnern, wann sein Geburtstag ist.

I can never remember when his birthday is.

Kannst du zu meinem Geburtstag kommen? —Es kommt **darauf** an, an welchem Tag.

Can you come to my birthday party? —It depends what day it is.

In many instances, the anticipatory **da-**compound is optional. Several important idiomatic expressions, however, are always used with an anticipatory **da-**compound.

Ich kann nichts **dafür,** daß du den Termin verpaßt hast.

I can't help it that you missed the appointment.

Wann kommst du mich besuchen? —Es kommt **darauf** an, wann ich Zeit habe.

When can you come for a visit? —It depends (on) when I have the time.

Anticipatory *da*-Compounds.
Suggestion: Reinforce the review of *da*-compounds by asking additional questions using the verbs from the previous list: *Ärgern Sie sich über schlechtes Wetter? Freuen Sie sich auf das Ende des Semesters? Haben Sie Angst vor einem Erdbeben?* Ask for brief answers incorporating *da*-compounds. Also remind students that personal pronouns or demonstrative pronouns must be used when talking about people; e.g., *Haben Sie Angst vor Ihrem Chef? (Ja, ich habe große Angst vor ihm.)*
Point out: In English, whenever the object of a preposition is more than a short noun phrase, a participial phrase (gerund) must be used; e.g., the verb "to warn against": "The mayor warned Berliners against climbing on the wall." German has no such construction, but uses a dependent clause or an infinitive clause with *zu* instead: *Der Bürgermeister hat davor gewarnt, auf die Mauer zu klettern.*

◻ **Übung 3. Aus der Zeitung**

Add an appropriate anticipatory **da**-compound to each main clause.

1. Bürgermeister Momper (Westberlin) hat gestern _____ gewarnt, auf die Mauer zu klettern.
2. Wir haben 28 Jahre _____ gewartet, daß wir zusammen einen Ku'dammbummel machen können.
3. Berliner waren immer schon stolz _____, Berliner zu sein.
4. Einige Leute haben Angst _____, arbeitslos zu werden oder ihr erspartes Geld zu verlieren.
5. Die meisten jungen Leute können sich nicht mehr _____ erinnern, wie Berlin vor der Mauer ausgesehen hat.

◻ **Übung 4. Fragen und Antworten**

Wählen Sie einen passenden Ausdruck aus der rechten Spalte, um Ihre Antworten zu formulieren.

BEISPIEL: A: Ich sehe dich bald wieder, nicht wahr?
            B: Ja, ich freue mich schon darauf, dich wiederzusehen.

1. Wir sehen uns bald wieder, nicht wahr?
2. Warum bist du zu spät zur Vorlesung gekommen?
3. Die DDR-Bürger können jetzt endlich in den Westen reisen, nicht wahr?
4. Hast du die Fahrprüfung gleich beim erstenmal bestanden?
5. Hat dein Freund dir bei der Arbeit geholfen?
6. Wie alt warst du, als du dein erstes Geld verdient hast?

a. Ja, ich bin ihm sehr dankbar dafür,...
b. Sie haben lange darauf gewartet,...
c. Ich kann nichts dafür,...
d. Ja, wir freuen uns schon darauf,...
e. Ich kann mich nicht mehr daran erinnern,...
f. Ja, ich war sehr stolz darauf,...

◻ **Übung 5. Interaktion: Wußtest du das schon?**

Stellen Sie einander Fragen mit Hilfe der Verben aus der Liste unten. Antworten Sie frei oder mit Hilfe der Vorschläge. Machen Sie sich Notizen, und berichten Sie darüber.

BEISPIEL: A: Worauf mußt du immer achten?
            B: Ich muß immer darauf achten, daß ich nicht zuviel esse.

Wie stolz sind junge Deutsche?

Junge Deutsche sind nicht sehr stolz

„Sind Sie stolz, Deutscher zu sein?" Auf diese Frage des Instituts für Demoskopie Allensbach antworteten im Januar 1988 die jüngsten Befragten am seltensten[a] mit einem klaren Ja. 14 Prozent der jungen Leute im Alter von 16 bis 29 gaben an, „sehr stolz" zu sein. Eine relative Mehrheit der Befragten im Alter von 16 bis 29 ist „ziemlich stolz": nämlich 37 Prozent. Ein Fünftel fühlt sich „nicht sehr stolz". 18 Prozent sagten, sie seien „überhaupt nicht stolz". 11 Prozent äußerten keine konkrete Meinung.

a. selten *rarely*

Dies

Ich bin nich
sein. Korre
nicht. Ohn
Patriotismu
war ein sc
deshalb die
Reichs[c] zu
dammt sei
England wu
gegenüber
und die Zei
geben[e] weil
germanoph
habe. Es sti
als vierzig Ja
nationalsozi
Folgen eine
nichts zu tu
dem Gefühl
ist. Ich will
Kontakt au
Aufschrift
tragen zu mi

Zum Text 1

1. Lesen Sie nun *Dies ist mein Land* genauer. Wel
   sagen stimmen? Welche nicht? Fassen Sie den
   den Sätzen zusammen.

   Der Autor des Artikels
   _____ will die deutsche Vergangenheit ve
   _____ ist ein junger Neonazi.
   _____ möchte gern stolz darauf sein, ein
   _____ ist traurig, daß er immer noch die
       spüren muß.
   _____ hatte in England Probleme mit eng

2. Was empfindet der Autor als problematisch? W

Auf den ersten Blick 2

Der folgende Text, ein kurzer Ausschnitt aus der A
Zigeunerin (*gypsy*) Ceja Stojka, *Wir leben im Verbo
einer Rom-Zigeunerin*, ist im Jahre 1989 erschienen

VORSCHLÄGE:

achten auf:
    genug Schlaf bekommen
    nicht zuviel Geld für _____ ausgeben
Angst haben vor:
    ein F in einer Prüfung / einem Kurs bekommen
    keine interessante Arbeit finden
sich ärgern über:
    etwas kaufen, was gleich kapputt geht oder schlechte Qualität hat
    lange auf jemanden warten müssen
stolz sein auf:
    eine Prüfung mit A bestehen
    etwas sehr gut können, z.B. ein Instrument spielen
sich erinnern an:
    was Sie zum _____ gegessen haben
    wie alt Sie waren, als Sie Ihr erstes Geld verdient haben
    wann Sie sich zum erstenmal verliebt haben

LESEN IM KONTEXT

Wie berührt Geschichte unser Leben? In diesem Teil des Kapitels erleben Sie Geschichte, indem Sie persönliche Dokumente, Auszüge aus einer Autobiographie und aus einem Tagebuch und Briefe lesen. Diese persönlichen Erfahrungen bringen historische Ereignisse auf ungewöhnliche Weise näher.

Vor dem Lesen

Aktivität. Historisches Bewußtsein° und Selbstbewußtsein°

Wie groß sind Ihr Selbstbewußtsein und Ihr historisches Bewußtsein? Beantworten Sie die folgenden Fragen, und vergleichen Sie dann Ihre Antworten mit den Antworten anderer in Ihrer Klasse. Was ist das Resultat?

1. Sind Sie stolz auf Ihre Nationalität?
   a. Ja. / Nein, ich bin (nicht) stolz darauf, _____ zu sein.
   b. Wenn ja, warum sind Sie stolz darauf?
   c. Wenn nein, warum sind Sie nicht stolz darauf?

consciousness

self-confidence

2. Was halten Sie für positive Aspekte des ame
   halten Sir für negativ? (Setzen Sie P oder N
   Kategorie.)
   _____ die vielen Autos
   _____ das Leben in den Großstädten
   _____ die Landschaft
   _____ persönliche Freiheit
   _____ Demokratie
   _____ soziale Leistungen (services)
   _____ Sonstiges: _____

3. Welche Ereignisse in der amerikanischen G
   positiv? Welche finden Sie negativ? Warum
   _____ der Unabhängigkeitskrieg
   _____ der Bürgerkrieg
   _____ die Landung auf dem Mond 1969
   _____ Atombomben auf Hiroshima und Nag
   _____ die Inhaftierung amerikanischer Bürg
   mung im Zweiten Weltkrieg
   _____ Sonstiges: _____

4. Was wissen Sie über folgende Ereignisse? W
   den? Unter welchem Präsidenten?
   a. Watergate
   b. der Vietnam Krieg
   c. die Iran Geisel Affäre
   d. die Challenger Raumschiffkatastrophe

Auf den ersten Blick 1

Wie steht es mit dem Selbstbewußtsein und his
ger Deutscher?

1. Suchen Sie im folgenden Text Information,
   worten: Wie stolz sind junge Deutsche dara

   sehr stolz: _____%
   ziemlich stolz: _____%
   nicht sehr stolz: _____%
   überhaupt nicht stolz: _____%
   keine konkrete Meinung: _____%

2. Überfliegen Sie den Text Dies ist mein Land.
   a. eine statistische Untersuchung zum The
   b. einen Bericht über die Nazizeit.
   c. eine persönliche Meinung zum Thema N

3. Suchen Sie Wörter im Text, die mit persönli
   haben.

4. Suchen Sie Wörter im Text, die sich auf die
   beziehen.

über das Schicksal der Zigeuner unter Hitler geschrieben worden. Ceja Stojka wurde 1933 in einem Gasthaus in der Steiermark in Österreich geboren. Während des Dritten Reiches wurde sie als Zigeunerin—sie gehörte zu der Rom Gruppe—aus rassistischen Gründen verfolgt (*persecuted*). Sie kam zusammen mit ihrer Mutter und ihren Schwestern in die Konzentrationslager in Ausschwitz und in Ravensbrück.

Überfliegen Sie den ersten Abschnitt des Textes. Welche der folgenden Namen und Wörter stehen im Text?

_____ Ausschwitz	_____ SS-Soldaten
_____ Hitler	_____ sterilisieren
_____ experimentieren	_____ Ravensbrück
_____ nach Hause gehen	_____ SS-Frauen
_____ Berlin	

Kulturnotiz. **Note:** The *SS (Schutzstaffel)* was created by Hitler in 1925 as a military organization within his party and was totally loyal to him. It became the most feared party organization during the Nazi years.

⬛⬜⬜⬜ *Kulturnotiz*

Die Aufseherinnen (*female guards*) in den Konzentrationslagern wurden automatisch zu Mitgliedern der SS. Daher die Bezeichnung SS-Frauen, die Ceja Stojka benutzt.

Für „arische" Frauen waren Verhütungsmittel (*birth control*), Abtreibungen (*abortions*) und Sterilisation gegen das Gesetz; aber für andere Frauen, die nicht der Norm entsprachen, gab es Zwangssterilisation (*forced sterilization*). In den Konzentrationslagern wurden Zwangssterilisationen an vielen Frauen vorgenommen, um mit neuen Methoden der Sterilisation zu experimentieren.

Wir leben im Verborgenen

Ja, es war nicht einfach in diesem Frauenlager Ravensbrück. Die SS-Frauen waren schlechter als jeder Satan. Eines Tages kamen zwei von ihnen und sagten zu uns: „Hört alle gut zu, was wir euch sagen. Es ist ein Schreiben aus Berlin gekommen und das sagt, alle Frauen und Kinder, die sich sterilisieren lassen, können bald nach Hause gehen." Und weiter sagten sie: „Na, ihr braucht ja keine Kinder mehr, also kommt morgen und unterschreibt,° daß ihr freiwillig dazu bereit seid. Der Oberarzt wird euch diesen Eingriff° machen. In ein paar Tagen könnt ihr dann das Lager verlassen." (Das war alles eine Lüge.° Ja, es war eine Lüge, denn wir standen alle schon auf der Liste.)

Die SS-Frauen wurden immer böser. So verging° ein Tag um den anderen. Täglich warf man Frauen in den Bunker und sie kamen nicht mehr zurück. So ging es wochenlang.

Die Tage wurden nun schon länger und manchesmal war es nicht mehr

sign

operation

lie

passed

versorgung aufgehört hat, gibt es auch fast k
sich vor, überhaupt kein elektrisches Licht. Ke
einmal angestellt,° und gerade erklingt Musik
die Geigen,° als sei der schönste Friede auf d

23. April — Es geht jetzt immer mehr dem
am Stadtrand von Hamburg, die Russen vor
Alarm. Überall stehen die Menschen vor der
noch alles, was man irgend bekommen kann,
daß in nächster Zeit die Brücken gesprengt we
der die weiße Fahne hißt,° wird „ausgerottet".

2. Mai — Eben höre ich, der Führer° sei
Radio bekannt gegeben worden. Auch Goebb
Lebenden weilen°... Ob's wahr ist? Vielleicht geh
zu Ende.

Ja, es ist wahr: der Führer ist tot. Unser F
danken haben,° unseren Aufstieg,° unseren N
pfend an der Spitze° seines Volkes in der Reich

8. Mai — Nun ist unser Land endgültig bese
an diesem Krieg? Wo sind diejenigen, die al
Jammer° verursacht° haben? Sie haben sich du
tung entzogen.° — Man erzählt sich, Deutsc
kapituliert.

Zum Text 3

1. Welche Ereignisse beschreibt die Autorin?
   Suchen Sie die passende Reaktion auf die

   EREIGNISSE:

   _____ Im Lazarett liegen junge   a
   Menschen stöhnend und
   schreiend vor Schmerz   b
   und verkrüppelt fürs
   Leben.
   _____ Die Sowjets kommen immer   c
   näher an Danzig heran, wo
   ihr Vater Soldat ist.   d
   _____ Eben höre ich, der Führer
   sei gefallen.
   _____ Nun ist unser Land   e
   endgültig besetzt.
   _____ Heute war ich zum letztenmal mit Helmut zusammen.
   Er muß zum Fronteinsatz.

---

so kalt. Ich, Mama, Kathi, Chiwe mit Burli und Rupa mußten in die Waschküche. Wir machten dort unsere Arbeit und als wir zurückkamen, sahen
wir, wie zwei Häftlinge° einen Bretterwagen° vor unsere Baracke zogen. [*inmates / wooden wagon*]
Viele Frauen waren darauf, wie Schweine lagen sie übereinander. Ganz oben
lag unsere kleine liebe Resi. Sie waren sterilisiert worden, alle hatten große
Schmerzen, sie konnten nicht einmal ein einziges Wort sagen. Die kleine
Resi starb gleich, auch die anderen kamen nicht mehr durch. Alle waren
tot. Die SS-Frauen sagten dann zu uns: „Ihr braucht keine Angst zu haben,
der Oberarzt hat ein neues Gerät bekommen, das alte hatte einen Kurz-
schluß,° also ein Versehen.°" Wir wußten ganz genau, daß sie uns nur [*short circuit / accident*]
besänftigen° wollten, aber wir wußten auch, daß wir ihnen nicht entkom- [*quiet*]
men.° Eines Tages kamen Binz und Rabl und holten Mama, Kathi und mich [*escape*]
ab. Sie sprachen nicht viel und sagten nur: „Marsch, Marsch". Wir gingen
sehr schnell. In diesem Moment war uns alles egal. Wir kamen zu einem
richtigen Haus. Es ging stockaufwärts. Die SS-Frauen machten im Vorraum
dem Oberarzt ihre Meldung.° Nun warteten wir. Mama zeigte uns mit ihren [*report*]
blauen Augen, daß wir mutig° sein sollten, sprechen durften wir ja nicht. [*brave*]
Die Zeit verging und es geschah nichts. Plötzlich kam der Oberarzt und
sagte: „Heute ist nichts mehr, wir haben leider keinen Strom." Er schaute
uns mit großen Augen an und machte seine Tür zu. Zwei SS-Frauen brachten
uns wieder in das Lager zurück. Unterwegs sahen wir eine Baracke. Drinnen
waren viele Frauen mit Schreibmaschinen. Das war die Schreibstube. Nun
waren wir wieder in unserer Baracke. Alle fragten, was geschehen war, und
alle Frauen weinten vor Freude.

Mama sagte: *„O swundo Dell gamel awer wariso de gerel amenza."* (Der
liebe Gott hat was anderes mit uns vor.)

Ceja Stojka, *Wir leben im Verborgenen: Erinnerungen einer Rom-Zigeunerin*

Zum Text 2

1. Wie wurden Ceja und ihre Familie durch die Rassenpolitik der Nazis
   betroffen?
2. Welche Erfahrungen beschreibt die Autorin?
   - Die SS-Frauen versprachen den Häftlingen, wenn sie sich freiwillig
     sterilisieren lassen,
     a. bekommen sie besseres Essen.
     b. brauchen sie eine Woche nicht zu arbeiten.
     c. werden sie bald freigelassen.
   - Der Sterilisationsprozeß im Lager war
     a. freiwillig.
     b. eine Lüge.
     c. nicht freiwillig.
   - Die Autorin erinnert sich daran, daß sie
     a. im Konzentrationslager zur Schule ging.
     b. in der Waschküche arbeitete.
     c. auf der Schreibstube arbeitete.

- Die ersten Frauen, die sterilisiert w
  a. starben an den Folgen der Steri
  b. kamen nie in die Baracken zurü
  c. durften nach Hause fahren.
- Die Autorin und ihre Familie wurde
  a. der Oberarzt Mitleid (*sympathy*)
  b. man sie in der Waschküche brau
  c. es keine Elektrizität gab.

Auf den ersten Blick 3

Der folgende Text besteht aus Auszügen aus
zehnjährigen deutschen Mädchens, das die
Norddeutschland, in Schleswig-Holstein, er

Schauen Sie sich den Anfang von jedem
wann sind die Tagebucheintragungen?

„Daß es soviel Traurigkeit gibt"

AUS DEN TAGEBUCH-AUFZEICHNUNGEN D

20. Januar — Heute war ich in unserer
eingerichtet worden ist und in der sich scho
Wenn man sie so sieht, die jungen Menschen,
verkrüppelt fürs ganze Leben daliegen, stöhne
krampft sich einem das Herz zusammen°…

22. Januar — Immer näher schieben sich
Warschau, Lodz, Krakau sind eingenommen
Opplen. 80 Kilometer von Breslau entfernt.
Herr Gott, schütze° unseren Vater in Danzig.

7. Februar — Heute bekamen wir Post vo
Er ist in der Stadt eingeschlossen, und sie wiss
men sollen.

24. März — Heute war ich zum letztenmal
militärische Ausbildung ist beendet, er muß z
betäubt,° ich kann an gar nichts anderes denk

26. März — Vor einer Stunde ist eine Komp
mit Gasmasken, Tornistern°, Kochgeschirren°
dabei. Und sie sangen, sangen! Sie marschier
sagt: Dein Schmerz um deinen Freund schei
deinen Vater. Ja, im Augenblick ist es wirklich

28. März — Eigentlich müßte ich Schulan
Tagen kein Heft angerührt, mich um nichts gel
Ferien für eine Woche. „Ferien", wie herrlich

8. April — Unsere Lage wird immer katas

---

2. Wie beschreibt die Autorin die ständig wachsenden Probleme? Fassen
   Sie das Wichtige für jedes Datum zusammen.

   BEISPIEL: 20. Januar: Im Lazarett liegen viele junge Verwundete, die
   fürs Leben verkrüppelt sind.

3. Am 30. April beging Hitler in seinem Bunker in der Reichskanzlei in
   Berlin Selbstmord (*suicide*). Was hörte die Autorin über den Tod Hit-
   lers im Radio? Warum wurde nicht die Wahrheit berichtet?

Auf den ersten Blick 4

Im Frühjahr 1947 reiste der frühere Präsident Herbert Hoover nach
Deutschland und nach Österreich, um die katastrophale Ernährungssi-
tuation zu untersuchen (*investigate*). Das Resultat war die Hoover-
Speisung für Schulkinder in beiden Ländern. Kinder schickten Hoover
hunderte von Briefen, um ihm für seine Hilfe zu danken. Sie lesen hier
drei dieser Briefe, die jetzt in den Archiven des Hoover Instituts in Stanford, Kalifornien, gesammelt sind.

Neue Wörter

die Heimat *home (-town, -land)*
die Puppe *doll*
der Schwarzhandel *black
    market*
  Schwarzhandel treiben *to
    deal on the black market*
die Tafel Schokolade *chocolate
    bar*
entweder… oder *either … or*
satt *full (with food)*
  satt werden *to get enough to
    eat*
unterernährt *malnourished*

Auf den ersten Blick 4. Point out:
The letters reprinted here belong to
a large collection of letters in the
Hoover Institution Archives sent by
German and Austrian children. The
children's letters were, for the most
part, the result of a nationwide effort
to thank Hoover and the American
people for their help. For many children, the *Schulspeisung* was the
only regular meal of the day.

DANK
FÜR ALLE SPENDEN
AUS AMERIKA!
DIE DANKBAREN
KINDER AUS
WIEN.

ABLEITINGER ANGELA.
V. KL. W.N. ASPERN.

RSM

Überfliegen Sie die drei Briefe kurz.

1. Wer hat die Briefe geschrieben? (Namen und Alter)
2. Aus welchem Jahr stammen die Briefe?
3. Wie reden die Kinder Herbert Hoover an? Wie enden ihre Briefe?

Briefe an Herbert Hoover

Heike Leopold.   Note: The style, spelling *(Aberica),* and handwriting show this to be the youngest of the three writers. Heike is a refugee child who lost her home in Upper Silesia, now a part of Poland. Her keen interest in a doll with long hair, very typical for young girls of that time, reflects a child's capacity to block out the harsh realities of survival. Those realities are only hinted at by her mention of her mother frequently standing in line for bread for a long time, leaving Heike and her sister by themselves.

THE HERBERT HOOVER ARCHIVES

Eckernförde, den 26.3.47.
Lieber Onkel Hoover!
Ich habe Dich neulich im Kino gesehen und da Du so lieb und gut aussiehst, will ich Dir heute schreiben. Wir sind aus Oberschlesien hierher gekommen und haben dort unsre schönen Sachen lassen müssen.

Giebt es in Aberika schon Puppen mit langen Haaren zu kaufen? Wir sind so oft allein, weil unsre Mutti nach Brot anstehen muß. Werden bei euch alle Leute satt? Nun willst Du uns ja hier helfen in Deutschland. Viele Grüße, von Heike Leopold.

Margot Fränkel

Bayreuth, den 28.5. 1947.

Sehr geehrter Herr Hoover!

Wir freuten uns sehr, als uns verkündet[a] wurde, daß alle die Auslandsspeisen bekommen. Denn es wurde durch Wiegen und Messen festgestellt,[b] daß viele unterernährt[c] sind. Wir sind schon immer auf die Minute gespannt,[d] wenn es läutet[e] und wir unser Essen bekommen. Heute gibt es Teigwaren[f] mit Obsttunke.[g] Wenn manchmal ein Rest übrig bleibt, freuen wir uns am meisten, wenn wir es bekommen. Es gibt jetzt schon 24 Wochen Essen. Am meisten aber freuen wir uns, wenn es am Ende der Wochen Eiscrempaste gibt. Als es das erstemal die Auslandsspeisen gab,

bekamen wir am Ende der Woche eine Tafel Schokolade. Wir mußten sie gleich anbeißen,[h] damit wir nicht Schwarzhandel trieben.[i] Jeder geht jetzt gerne in die Schule.

Ich danke Ihnen nochmals dafür, für die guten Gaben.[j]

Mit dankbarem Gruß
eine ergebene Schülerin
Margot Fränkel

a. *announced*
b. *es... it was found by weighing and measuring*
c. *malnourished*
d. *eager*
e. *the bell rings*
f. *baked goods*
g. *fruit syrup*
h. *bite into it*
i. *deal on the black market*
j. *gifts*

Margot Fränkel. **Point out:** The writer shows her awareness of the value of chocolate on the black market; the teacher prevents the children from bartering with the chocolate bars by having them all take a bite out of theirs.

Frauenau, den 5. Mai 1947.

Sehr geehrter Herr Präsident Hoover!

Am Montag bekamen wir in der Schule Schokolade. Das war eine große Freude, denn wir haben schon lange keine mehr gehabt. Darum möchten wir Ihnen herzlich danken. Wir dürfen jetzt jeden Tag zur Kinderspeisung gehen. Darüber sind wir sehr froh, denn bei uns im Bayrischen Wald gibt es wenig zum Essen. Leider dürfen zur Speisung nicht alle gehen. An unserer Schule sind nämlich 650 Kinder und für 380 bekommen wir nur Speisung. Also gibt es nur zwei Möglichkeiten. Entweder dürfen die einen Kinder überhaupt nicht gehen oder wir müssen jede Woche wechseln. So bekommen wir alle nicht viel. Dennoch freuen wir uns sehr darüber und danken Ihnen von Herzen.

Im Namen der 3. Klasse
Ihre dankbare Gisela Thiemann 3. Klasse
Volksschule Frauenau Bayrischer Wald.

THE HERBERT HOOVER ARCHIVES

Zum Text 4

1. Was erfahren wir über die Folgen des Krieges für die Kinder?
2. Welche Probleme erwähnen die Kinder? Wer schreibt davon, daß
   * die meisten Kinder unterernährt sind?
   * die Kinder wissen, wie man Schwarzhandel treibt?
   * die Familie aus ihrer Heimat geflüchtet ist?
   * sie oft allein ist, weil die Mutter nach Brot anstehen muß?
   * es nicht genug Essen für alle Kinder in der Schule gibt?

Auf den ersten Blick 5

Das Jahr 1989 sah viele Veränderungen in Osteuropa und in der DDR. Der folgende Text ist ein Auszug aus dem Brief einer Familie aus der DDR an amerikanische Freunde. Am 3. Dezember 1989 geschrieben, dokumentiert dieser Brief die Gedanken (*thoughts*) und Überlegungen von zwei Bürgern der DDR in den ersten Wochen nach der Öffnung der Grenzen zwischen den zwei deutschen Staaten.

1. Was wissen Sie über die Ereignisse im Herbst 1989 in der DDR?
2. Wie haben Sie hauptsächlich über diese Ereignisse erfahren?
   a. durch die Zeitung
   b. durchs Fernsehen
   c. durchs Radio
   d. durch Besucher
   e. Sonstiges
3. Wie haben Sie selbst darauf reagiert?

Ein Brief aus der DDR.   Note: The two grown children of this family, a son and a daughter, had taken advantage of the possibility of traveling to Hungary to leave East Germany for West Germany. At the time this letter was written, the writer (the father) could have no idea of the sweeping changes about to take place, though he expresses his opinion that only German unification can save his country from ruin.

The amount of *D-Mark* made available to visitors from the DDR consisted of DM 100.-, given outright by the West German government. The East German government made available an additional DM 15.- at an exchange rate of 1:1.

Ein Brief aus der DDR

… Seitdem wir uns zuletzt gesehen haben, hat sich sehr viel bei uns verändert,° familiär und politisch. Ihr habt von Steffi und Jörg [Tochter und Sohn der Familie] inzwischen selbst erfahren, daß sie beide die Konsequenzen aus einer 40jährigen verfehlten° Politik gezogen haben°. Wir hoffen und wünschen, daß sie im anderen Teil Deutschlands glücklich und zufrieden° werden… Steffi schreibt viel und versucht auch oft bei uns anzurufen. Inzwischen haben wir unsere Kinder auch schon per Bahn… vom 18. bis 20. November besucht und uns bei dieser Gelegenheit die schöne Stadt München angesehen. Es war ein glückliches Wiedersehen… Wir haben uns überzeugen können, daß es ihnen gut geht und sehr gefällt. Wir hätten nie geglaubt, daß wir uns so schnell wiedersehen. Dafür hat unser Land einen hohen Preis bezahlt. Einige hunderttausend Menschen, meistens junge Leute, haben dieses Land in letzter Zeit verlassen. Immer noch protestieren im ganzen Land viele hunderttausend Menschen fast täglich auf Plätzen und Straßen für ein menschenwürdiges° Leben. Auch wir waren einige Male

changed

failed / Konsequenzen gezogen haben = *have drawn the conclusions*
satisfied

decent

dabei… Vierzig Jahre lang ist ein ganzes Volk belogen,° betrogen° und eingesperrt° gewesen. Der Sozialismus ist gescheitert.° Er kann nur noch mit kapitalistischer Hilfe existieren. Wir stecken in einer tiefen Krise. Unsere Wirtschaft ist am Boden.° Die alte Regierung ist zurückgetreten. Nun träumt unsere neue Führung schon wieder von einem besseren Sozialismus. Aber nur wenige wollen noch daran glauben. Uns kann nur noch die Einheit Deutschlands retten. Das gesamte° Volk sollte darüber entscheiden. Wir haben nach so vielen Jahren der Demütigung° in Ost-Deutschland ein Recht darauf. Doch leider sind im In- und Ausland noch viele skeptisch, zurückhaltend oder sogar ablehnend° gegenüber einem geeinten Deutschland.

Zunächst haben wir aber schon große Erfolge errungen. Jeder Bürger der DDR hat das Recht, jederzeit in das Ausland zu reisen. Mauer und Stacheldraht° stehen noch, sind aber durchlässig° geworden. Wegen der nötigen Zahlungsmittel machen sich die Finanzexperten noch Gedanken. Zur Zeit erhält jeder Bürger, der die Bundesrepublik besucht, ein Begrüßungsgeld von 100, - DM, sowie bei uns 15, - DM. Man kommt sich dabei sehr armselig° vor. Mit unserem guten Geld haben sich unsere arroganten und korrupten Spitzenfunktionäre in den vergangenen 40 Jahren des Bestehens dieses Staates ein schönes Leben in Luxus nach westlichem Stil gemacht. Sie sind Volvo gefahren, und die kleinen Leute fahren in 40 Jahren vielleicht immer noch Trabant°…

Trotz der Aufregungen in letzter Zeit sind wir noch alle gesund… Nach Steffis und Jörgs spontaner und unerwarteter Ausreise hatten wir sehr viel Arbeit. Die Wohnung haben wir ausgeräumt… Wenn es gestattet° wird, wollen Steffi und Jörg zu Weihnachten° nach Auerbach kommen. Wir würden uns alle sehr darüber freuen. Wir hätten Oma zu Weihnachten nicht allein lassen können. Silvester° möchten beide aber wieder in der Bundesrepublik feiern, und irgendwann besuchen wir sie auch wieder. Es ist kein Problem mehr.

Private letter

Margin glosses:
lied to / cheated
locked in / failed

am… on the ground; i.e. ruined

entire
humiliation

disapproving

barbed wire / porous

pitiful

small East German car

permitted
Christmas

New Year's Eve

Zum Text 5

1. Wie hat sich das Leben der Briefschreiber „familiär" geändert durch die Krise in der DDR?
2. Was ist die Haltung der Briefschreiber gegenüber der Situation ihres Landes? Waren sie aktiv beteiligt? Geben Sie konkrete Beispiele.
3. Was sehen sie als Lösung für die Probleme ihres Landes?
4. Kommentieren Sie den Satz: „Vierzig Jahre lang ist ein ganzes Volk belogen, betrogen und eingesperrt gewesen." Suchen Sie im Text Information, die sich darauf bezieht, wie das Volk der DDR „belogen, betrogen und eingesperrt" gewesen war.

APPENDIX

GR

TA

1. Personal Pronouns

		S
NOMINATIVE	ich	du (Sie)
ACCUSATIVE	mich	dich (Sie)
DATIVE	mir	dir (Ihnen)

2. Definite Articles

	SI
	MASCULINE
NOMINATIVE	der
ACCUSATIVE	den
DATIVE	dem
GENITIVE	des

3. Indefinite Articles and *ein*-Wo

	SIN
	MASCULINE
NOMINATIVE	ein
ACCUSATIVE	einen
DATIVE	einem
GENITIVE	eines

5. Partnerarbeit. Fassen Sie die Hauptgedanken des Briefes in etwa sechs bis zehn Sätzen zusammen. Schauen Sie sich den Text noch einmal gemeinsam genau an und entscheiden Sie zuerst, welche Information wichtig oder unwichtig für eine Zusammenfassung ist.

BEISPIEL: Wichtig: Sohn und Tochter der Familie sind in die Bundesrepublik gezogen.
Unwichtig (allerdings interessant): Es gefällt ihnen gut in der Bundesrepublik.

Lesen Sie Ihre Zusammenfassung in der Klasse vor.

Nach dem Lesen

⊡ Aktivität 1. Wer sind diese Personen?

Suchen Sie in einem deutschsprachigen Nachschlagewerk (*reference work*), z.B. im *Brockhaus*, in Ihrer Bibliothek Information über bedeutende Persönlichkeiten aus deutschsprachigen Ländern.

Vorschläge:

Heinrich Pestalozzi   Heinrich Böll
Bertha von Suttner   Rosa Luxemburg
General von Hindenburg   Sophie und Hans Scholl
Helene Lange   Claus von Stauffenberg

Berichten Sie kurz über:

- die Lebensdaten.
- wichtige biographische Tatsachen.
- warum er oder sie berühmt oder bekannt ist.

⊡ Aktivität 2. Erinnerungen

Interviewen Sie ein älteres Familienmitglied oder einen älteren Menschen über sein Leben. Konzentrieren Sie sich auf eine Phase oder ein Ereignis, z.B. wie er oder sie in der Jugend gelebt hat, oder auf Erinnerungen an ein historisches Ereignis. Schreiben Sie dann das Interview als eine mündliche Geschichte (*oral history interview*) auf.

⊡ Aktivität 3. Meine Memoiren

Schreiben Sie über Ihre eigenen Kindheitserinnerungen. Was hat sich in der Zwischenzeit in Ihrer Heimat geändert?

WORTSCHATZ

Substantive

der Aufstand (¨e)	rebellion, u
die Besatzung (-en)	(military) c
das Bettuch (¨er)	bed sheet
das Bewußtsein	consciousn
die Brücke (-n)	bridge
der Bundeskanzler	chancellor
	Repub
die Einheit	unity
das Fest (-e)	party
die Freude (-n)	joy
vor Freude	with joy
das Gesetz (-e)	law
die Grundlage (-n)	basis, foun
die Gründung	founding
die Heimat	homeland,
die Kirche (-n)	church
die Mauer (-n)	wall
der Panzer (-)	tank
die Puppe (-n)	doll
die Regierung (-en)	government
der Schwarzhandel	black marke
das Selbstbewußtsein	self-confide
der Soldat (-n *masc.*)	soldier
die Stimmung (-en)	mood
das Tagebuch (¨er)	diary
die Trümmer (*pl.*)	rubble, ruin
die Überraschung (-en)	surprise
die Vereinigten Staaten	United Stat
die Verfassung	constitution
das Volk (¨er)	people
die Wahl (-en)	election
der Wahnsinn	madness
das Weihnachten	Christmas
der Wiederaufbau	reconstructi

Verben

(sich) ändern	to change
anstehen (steht an),	to stand in l
stand an,	
angestanden	
sich ärgern über (+	to be annoye
acc.)	
aufteilen (teilt auf)	to divide
begrüßen	to greet

4. Relative and Demonstrative Pronouns

	SINGULAR			PLURAL
	MASCULINE	NEUTER	FEMININE	
NOMINATIVE	der	das	die	die
ACCUSATIVE	den	das	die	die
DATIVE	dem	dem	der	denen
GENITIVE	dessen	dessen	deren	deren

5. Principal Parts of Strong and Irregular Weak Verbs

The following is a list of the most important strong and irregular weak verbs that are used in this book. Included in this list are modal auxiliaries with irregular forms. Since the principal parts of compound verbs follow the forms of the base verb, compound verbs are generally not included, except for a few high-frequency compound verbs whose base verb is not commonly used. Thus you will find **anfangen** and **einladen** listed, but not **zurückkommen** or **ausgehen**.

INFINITIVE	(PRESENT)	SIMPLE PAST	PAST PARTICIPLE	MEANING
anbieten		bot an	angeboten	*to offer*
anfangen	(fängt an)	fing an	angefangen	*to begin*
backen	(backt)	backte	gebacken	*to bake*
beginnen		begann	begonnen	*to begin*
begreifen		begriff	begriffen	*to comprehend*
beißen		biß	gebissen	*to bite*
bitten		bat	gebeten	*to ask, beg*
bleiben		blieb	(ist) geblieben	*to stay*
bringen		brachte	gebracht	*to bring*
denken		dachte	gedacht	*to think*
dürfen	(darf)	durfte	gedurft	*to be allowed*
einladen	(lädt ein)	lud ein	eingeladen	*to invite*
empfehlen	(empfiehlt)	empfahl	empfohlen	*to recommend*
entscheiden		entschied	entschieden	*to decide*
essen	(ißt)	aß	gegessen	*to eat*
fahren	(fährt)	fuhr	(ist) gefahren	*to drive*
fallen	(fällt)	fiel	(ist) gefallen	*to fall*
finden		fand	gefunden	*to find*
fliegen		flog	(ist) geflogen	*to fly*
geben	(gibt)	gab	gegeben	*to give*
gefallen	(gefällt)	gefiel	gefallen	*to like; to please*
gehen		ging	(ist) gegangen	*to go*
genießen		genoß	genossen	*to enjoy*
geschehen	(geschieht)	geschah	ist geschehen	*to happen*
gewinnen		gewann	gewonnen	*to win*

INFINITIVE	(PRESENT)	SIMPLE PAST	PAST PARTICIPLE	MEANING
haben	(hat)	hatte	gehabt	*to have*
halten	(hält)	hielt	gehalten	*to hold; to stop*
hängen		hing	gehangen	*to hang*
heißen		hieß	geheißen	*to be called*
helfen	(hilft)	half	geholfen	*to help*
kennen		kannte	gekannt	*to know*
kommen		kam	(ist) gekommen	*to come*
können	(kann)	konnte	gekonnt	*to be able*
lassen	(läßt)	ließ	gelassen	*to let; to allow*
laufen	(läuft)	lief	(ist) gelaufen	*to run*
leihen		lieh	geliehen	*to lend; borrow*
lesen	(liest)	las	gelesen	*to read*
liegen		lag	gelegen	*to lie*
mögen	(mag)	mochte	gemocht	*to like*
müssen	(muß)	mußte	gemußt	*must; to have to*
nehmen	(nimmt)	nahm	genommen	*to take*
nennen		nannte	genannt	*to name*
raten	(rät)	riet	geraten	*to advise*
reiten		ritt	(ist) geritten	*to ride*
scheinen		schien	geschienen	*to seem; to shine*
schlafen	(schläft)	schlief	geschlafen	*to sleep*
schließen		schloß	geschlossen	*to close*
schreiben		schrieb	geschrieben	*to write*
schwimmen		schwamm	(ist) geschwommen	*to swim*
sehen	(sieht)	sah	gesehen	*to see*
sein	(ist)	war	(ist) gewesen	*to be*
singen		sang	gesungen	*to sing*
sitzen		saß	gesessen	*to sit*
sprechen	(spricht)	sprach	gesprochen	*to speak*
stehen		stand	gestanden	*to stand*
steigen		stieg	ist gestiegen	*to rise; to climb*
sterben	(stirbt)	starb	(ist) gestorben	*to die*
tragen	(trägt)	trug	getragen	*to carry; to wear*
treffen	(trifft)	traf	getroffen	*to meet*
trinken		trank	getrunken	*to drink*
tun		tat	getan	*to do*
umsteigen		stieg um	(ist) umgestiegen	*to change; to transfer*
vergessen	(vergißt)	vergaß	vergessen	*to forget*
vergleichen		verglich	verglichen	*to compare*
verlieren		verlor	verloren	*to lose*
wachsen	(wächst)	wuchs	(ist) gewachsen	*to grow*
waschen	(wäscht)	wusch	gewaschen	*to wash*
werden	(wird)	wurde	(ist) geworden	*to become*
wissen	(weiß)	wußte	gewußt	*to know*
wollen	(will)	wollte	gewollt	*to want*
ziehen		zog	(ist/hat) gezogen	*to move; to pull*

Present Tense: Subjunctive II

	fragen	**sein**	**haben**	**werden**	**fahren**	**wissen**
ich	fragte	wäre	hätte	würde	führe	wüßte
du	fragtest	wär(e)st	hättest	würdest	führ(e)st	wüßtest
er/sie/es	fragte	wäre	hätte	würde	führe	wüßte
wir	fragten	wären	hätten	würden	führen	wüßten
ihr	fragtet	wär(e)t	hättet	würdet	führ(e)t	wüßtet
sie/Sie	fragten	wären	hätten	würden	führen	wüßten

Past Tense: Subjunctive I (Indirect Discourse)

	fahren		**wissen**	
ich	sei		-	
du	sei(e)st		habest	
er/sie/es	sei	gefahren	habe	gewußt
wir	seien		-	
ihr	sei(e)t		habet	
sie/Sie	sei(e)n		-	

Past Tense: Subjunctive II

	sein		**geben**		**fahren**	
ich	wäre		hätte		wäre	
du	wär(e)st		hättest		wär(e)st	
er/sie/es	wäre	gewesen	hätte	gegeben	wäre	gefahren
wir	wären		hätten		wären	
ihr	wär(e)t		hättet		wär(e)t	
sie/Sie	wären		hätten		wären	

Passive Voice

einladen

	PRESENT		**SIMPLE PAST**		**PRESENT PERFECT**	
ich	werde		wurde		bin	
du	wirst		wurdest		bist	
er/sie/es	wird	eingeladen	wurde	eingeladen	ist	eingeladen worden
wir	werden		wurden		sind	
ihr	werdet		wurdet		seid	
sie/Sie	werden		wurden		sind	

Imperative

	sein	**geben**	**fahren**	**arbeiten**
FAMILIAR SINGULAR	sei	gib	fahr	arbeite
FAMILIAR PLURAL	seid	gebt	fahrt	arbeitet
FORMAL	seien Sie	geben Sie	fahren Sie	arbeiten Sie

VOCABULARY

This vocabulary contains German words used in the text, with the following exceptions: (1) compound words whose meaning can be easily guessed from their component parts; and (2) most identical or very close cognates (frequently used cognates are included so students can verify their gender).

Active vocabulary, in the end-of-chapter *Wortschatz* lists, is indicated by the number of the chapter in which it first appears. The letter E refers to the introductory chapter, *Einführung*.

The following abbreviations are used:

acc.	accusative
adj.	adjective
coll.	colloquial
coord. conj.	coordinating conjunction
dat.	dative
decl. adj.	declined adjective
form.	formal
gen.	genitive
indef. pron.	indefinite pronoun
-n masc.	masculine noun ending in **-n** or **-en** in all cases but the nominative singular
pl.	plural
sg.	singular
subord. conj.	subordinating conjunction

GERMAN-ENGLISH

A

ab (+ *dat.*) as of, from . . . on **ab erstem Juni** from June 1 on (12)
ab und zu now and then (3)

abbestellen (bestellt ab) to cancel
abbiegen (biegt ab), bog ab, ist abgebogen to make a turn (10); **nach rechts abbiegen** to make a right-hand turn

abbrechen (bricht ab), brach ab, abgebrochen to break off; to end
der Abend (-e) evening; **guten Abend** good evening (E); **heute abend** tonight (4)

das Abendessen (-) dinner, supper; **zum Abendessen** for dinner, supper

abends (in the) evenings (4); **eines Abends** one evening

das Abenteuer (-) adventure (8)

abenteuerlich adventurous

aber but, however (1)

abfahren (fährt ab), fuhr ab, ist abgefahren to depart, leave (9)

der Abfall (⁻e) garbage (15)

abfliegen (fliegt ab), flog ab, ist abgeflogen to depart by plane; to leave

die Abgase (*pl.*) exhaust fumes (15)

abgeben (gibt ab), gab ab, abgegeben to deliver, hand in

abhängen von (hängt ab), hing ab, abgehangen to depend on (13)

abholen (holt ab) to pick up (15)

das Abitur examination at the end of secondary school (Gymnasium)

der Abiturient (-n *masc.***) / die Abiturientin (-nen)** graduate of the Gymnasium, person who has passed the Abitur (13)

die Abkürzung (-en) abbreviation

ablaufen (läuft ab), lief ab, ist abgelaufen to expire

ablegen (legt ab): ein Examen ablegen to take an exam

ablehnen (lehnt ab) to reject, refuse

abliefern (liefert ab) to hand in, deliver

abnehmen (nimmt ab), nahm ab, abgenommen to lose weight

das Abonnement (-s) subscription (14)

abonnieren to subscribe (14)

abschicken (schickt ab) to send off, mail (13)

der Abschied (-e) farewell (11); **zum Abschied** saying good-bye (E)

der Abschluß (Abschlüsse) termination, completion

der Abschnitt (-e) paragraph, section

abseits (+ *gen.*) aside; away from (9)

absichtlich intentional (14)

absteigen (steigt ab), stieg ab, ist abgestiegen to dismount, get off

der Abstellraum (⁻e) storage room (12)

das Abteil (-e) compartment

die Abwechslung (-en) diversion; change (8)

Ach: mit Ach und Krach with great difficulty

Ach so! I see!

acht eight (E)

achten auf (+ *acc.*) to pay attention to (14)

Achtung! attention!

achtzehn eighteen (E)

achtzig eighty (1)

die Adresse (-n) address (E)

Ah so! (*coll.*) (*also:* **Ach, so!**) Oh, I get it! (E)

ähnlich similar (13)

die Aktion (-en) (political) action

die Aktivität (-en) activity

aktuell current (3)

all all; **vor allem** above all; **alle zwei Wochen** every other week (4)

allein alone (4)

alleinstehend single, unattached (12)

allerdings however; to be sure (6, 13)

alles everything; **alles Gute** best wishes (3); **alles klar** everything (is) all right (E); **Das ist alles.** That is all. (5)

allgemein general; **im allgemeinen** in general

allmählich gradually

der Alltag everyday routine; workday; **alltags** workdays

als when; as; than (9)

also thus; so (1); well

alt old; (1) used; **Alt und Jung** old and young people

der Altbau, die Altbauten old building (built before World War II) (12)

die Altbauwohnung (-en) apartment in pre–World War II building

das Alter (-) age; **im Alter von** at the age of

altmodisch old-fashioned

die Altstadt (⁻e) old part of town

die Alufolie (-n) aluminum foil

(das) Amerika America

der Amerikaner (-) / die Amerikanerin (-nen) American (person) (1)

amerikanisch American

die Ampel (-n) traffic light (10)

sich amüsieren to amuse oneself, have fun (9)

an (+ *acc./dat.*) at; near (5); up to; to

der Analphabeth (-n *masc.***) illiterate**

die Analyse (-n) analysis

anbieten (bietet an), bot an, angeboten to offer (5)

(sich) ändern to change (16)

anders different (8); else; other; **der, die, das andere** the other one; **unter anderem** among other things; **etwas anderes** something different (5); **jemand/niemand anders** somebody/nobody else (12)

anderswo somewhere/anywhere else

anerkannt recognized, acknowledged

der Anfang (⁻e) beginning, start (10)

anfangen (fängt an), fing an, angefangen to begin, start (4)

anfänglich initially

anfordern (fordert an) to request; to write away for

die Angabe (-n) declaration information (1); **persönliche Angaben** personal information

das Angebot (-e) offer; supply

angehen: Das geht mich nichts an. That is none of my concern.

angeln to fish (8)

angenehm pleasant (8)

angestellt employed; **der/die Angestellte** (*decl. adj.*) employee (11)

angrenzend adjacent

die Angst (⁻e) fear (15); **keine Angst** don't be afraid; **Angst haben** to be afraid

ankommen (kommt an), kam an, ist angekommen to arrive (9); **Es kommt darauf an.** It depends. (16)

ankreuzen (kreuzt an) to mark; to check off

anlangen (langt an) to arrive

der Anlaß (Anlässe) occasion

das Anmeldeformular (-e) registration form (10)

die Anmeldung (-en) registration (14)

anprobieren (probiert an) to try on (5)

anregen (regt an) to stimulate (14)

anrufen (ruft an), rief an, angerufen to call (on the phone) (4); **ruf mal an** why don't you call

die Ansage (-n) announcement

anschauen (schaut an) to look at

die Anschauung (-en) opinion, conviction

anscheinend apparently

der Anschluß (⁻sse) connection (9); **im Anschluß an** following

sich (+ *dat.*) **etwas ansehen (sieht an), sah an, angesehen** to watch, look at (14); **Ich sehe mir das an.** I'm watching that.

die Ansicht (-en) opinion; **meiner Ansicht nach** in my opinion (15)

die Ansicht (-en) opinion; **meiner Ansicht nach** in my opinion (15)

(an)statt instead of (16)

anstehen (steht an), stand an, angestanden to stand in line (12)

anstreichen (streicht an), strich an, angestrichen to paint (a wall) (12)

anstrengend strenuous (7)

die Antwort (-en) answer (E)

antworten to answer (1)

die Anzahl amount; number

die Anzeige (-n) (newspaper) advertisement (2)

(sich) anziehen (zieht an), zog an, angezogen to get dressed (7)

der Anzug (¨e) man's suit (5)

der Apfelsaft apple juice (6)

die Apfelsine (-n) orange

die Apotheke (-n) pharmacy (7)

der Apparat (-e) machine, set

(der) April April (3)

die Arbeit (-en) work; job (1)

arbeiten to work (1)

der Arbeitgeber (-) / die Arbeitgeberin (-nen) employer (7)

der Arbeitnehmer (-) employee (7)

das Arbeitsamt (¨er) employment (development) office (13)

arbeitslos unemployed (13)

die Arbeitslosigkeit unemployment

der Arbeitsplatz (¨e) place of work

der Arbeitstag (-e) workday

die Arbeitszeit (-en) working hours

ärgerlich annoying (11); annoyed

sich ärgern (über + *acc.*) to be annoyed about (16)

der Arm (-e) arm (7)

arm poor (11)

das Armband (¨er) bracelet

die Armbanduhr (-en) wristwatch

die Art (-en) kind, type; manner

der Artikel (-) article

das Arzneimittel (-) medication

der Arzt (¨e) / die Ärztin (-nen) physician, doctor (7)

asphaltiert paved

assoziieren to associate

die Atmosphäre atmosphere

die Atomenergie nuclear energy

die Atomkraft nuclear power; **das Atomkraftwerk** nuclear power plant

die Atomrakete (-n) nuclear-powered rocket

die Atomwaffe (-n) nuclear weapon

auch also, too (1)

auf (+ *acc./dat.*) on, upon; on top of (5)

der Aufenthalt stay; delay, stopover, layover (9)

auffordern (fordert auf) to call upon; to urge, encourage

die Aufführung (-en) performance (6)

die Aufgabe (n) task, duty

aufgeben (gibt auf), gab auf, aufgegeben to give up; **ein Paket aufgeben** to mail a package

aufgrund (+ *gen.*) based on; because of

aufhalten (hält auf), hielt auf, aufgehalten to delay, hold up

aufhören (hört auf) mit to quit, stop (doing something) (7)

der Aufkleber (-) sticker

aufmerksam attentive

aufnehmen (nimmt auf), nahm auf, aufgenommen to take a picture (15)

aufräumen (räumt auf) to straighten up (a room) (4)

aufregend exciting (14)

die Aufregung (-en) excitement

der Aufschnitt cold cuts (5)

der Aufstand (¨e) rebellion, uprising (16)

aufstehen (steht auf), stand auf, ist aufgestanden to get up (4)

aufstellen (stellt auf) to set up, put up (12)

die Aufstiegsmöglichkeit (-en) opportunity for advancement (13)

aufteilen (teilt auf) to divide (16)

aufwachen (wacht auf), ist aufgewacht to wake up (6)

der Aufzug (¨e) lift, elevator (12)

das Auge (-n) eye (7)

der Augenblick (-e) moment, instant

augenblicklich momentary, current (15); instantly

(der) August August (3)

aus (+ *dat.*) out of; from (5); **aus sein** to be off/out (12)

ausbilden zu (bildet aus) to train as (13); **ausgebildet werden zu** to be trained as (13)

die Ausbildung (-en) education (11); schooling, training (13)

der Ausbildungsplatz (¨e) training position (13)

die Ausbildungsstelle (-n) training position (13)

der Ausdruck (¨e) expression (1)

ausdrücken (drückt aus) to express

die Auseinandersetzung (-en) altercation, argument

die Ausfahrt (-en) exit; off-ramp

der Ausflug (¨e) excursion

ausführlich detailed

ausfüllen (füllt aus) to fill out (10)

die Ausgabe (-n) expense (11); edition, issue (14)

der Ausgangspunkt (-e) starting point

ausgeben (gibt aus), gab aus, ausgegeben to spend (11)

ausgehen (geht aus), ging aus, ist ausgegangen to go out (4)

ausgewählt select, chosen (13)

ausgezeichnet excellent, great (E)

auskommen (kommt aus), kam aus, ist ausgekommen to get by with (money)

die Auskunft (¨e) information (10)

das Ausland foreign country; **im Ausland** abroad

der Ausländer (-) / die Ausländerin (-nen) foreigner (1)

ausländisch foreign

auslassen (läßt aus), ließ aus, ausgelassen to leave out

die Ausnahme (-n) exception

auspacken (packt aus) to unpack (9)

ausprobieren (probiert aus) to try out

ausräumen (räumt aus) to empty, clean out

die Ausrede (-n) excuse

ausreichend sufficient (13)

ausrichten (richtet aus) to give a message

ausrotten (rottet aus) to eradicate

sich ausruhen (ruht aus) to rest up; to recuperate

die Aussage (-n) statement

ausschließlich exclusively

der Ausschnitt (-e) excerpt, section

aussehen (sieht aus), sah aus, ausgesehen to look, appear (4); **gut aussehend** good-looking

das Aussehen appearance, looks
der Außenminister (-) Secretary of
State
außer (+ *dat.*) except for, besides (16)
außerdem besides, in addition (12)
außerhalb (+ *gen.*) outside of (10); at
a distance from, outside of the city
(11)
äußern: die Meinung äußern to
voice an opinion (15)
äußerst extremely (9)
die Aussicht (-en) view; prospect
ausspannen (spannt aus) to rest,
relax
der Austauschstudent (-n *masc.***) /**
die Austauschstudentin (-nen)
exchange student (3)
(das) Australien Australia
der Ausverkauf (¨e) sale (5)
die Auswahl (-en) choice; selection
auswählen (wählt aus) to choose,
select (6)
der Ausweis (-e) ID card (1)
ausziehen (zieht aus), zog aus, ist
ausgezogen to move out
der/die Auszubildende (*decl. adj.*)
(*abbr.* **Azubi (-s)**) trainee,
apprentice (13)
der Auszug (¨e) excerpt, extract
das Auto (-s) car, automobile (1)
die Autobahn (-en) freeway (8)
der (Auto)bus (-sse) bus (9)
der Automat (-n *masc.***)** vending
machine; **der Geldautomat**
automatic teller (11)
automatisch automatic
der Automechaniker (-) / die
Automechanikerin (-nen) car
mechanic
der Autor (-n *masc.***) / die Autorin**
(-nen) author
autoritär authoritarian
der Autostop hitchhiking (9); **per**
Autostop reisen to hitchhike
Azubi = der/die Auszubildende (13)

B

der Bach (¨e) creek, stream (15)
backen, backte, gebacken to bake
der Bäcker (-) / die Bäckerin (-nen)
baker
die Bäckerei (-en) bakery (5)
die Backwaren (*pl.*) baked goods (5)
das Bad (¨er) bath; bathroom (2); spa
baden to bathe; to swim

die Badesachen (*pl.*) beach wear;
beach accessories
der Badestrand (¨e) beach with
swimming area
das Badezimmer (-) bathroom
die Bahn (-en) train; railroad (9);
mit der Bahn by train
der Bahnhof (¨e) railroad station
die Bahnstation (-en) train station
(9)
der Bahnsteig (-e) (train) platform
bald soon; **bis bald** see you later
der Balkon (-e) balcony (12)
der Ball (¨e) ball; **der Fußball** soccer
ball (1)
die Banane (-n) banana
die Bank (-en) bank (11)
die Bank (¨e) bench
der/die Bankangestellte (*decl. adj.*)
bank employee
bar in cash (11)
der Bär (-n *masc.***)** bear
das Bargeld cash (11)
basteln to tinker; to build (as a
hobby) (9)
die Batterie (-en) battery
der Bau (die Bauten) construction;
building
der Bauch (¨e) belly, abdomen,
stomach (7)
bauen to build
das Bauernbrot (-e) farmer's bread
das Bauernhaus (¨er) farmhouse
der Bauernhof (¨e) farm (9)
das Baujahr (-e) year of
construction; car model year
der Baum (¨e) tree
die Baumwolle cotton (5)
die Baustelle (-n) construction site
bayerisch Bavarian
(das) Bayern Bavaria
beachten to notice; **Beachtung**
schenken to pay attention to
der/die Beamte (*decl. adj.*) official;
civil employee
beanworten to answer
der Becher (-) beaker; container
sich bedanken to thank, say "thank-
you" (7)
bedauern to regret (15)
bedeckt covered; overcast (8)
bedenken, bedachte, bedacht to
consider, think about
bedeuten to mean, signify (12)
bedeutend important, distinguished

die Bedeutung (-en) meaning,
significance
bedienen to serve
die Bedienung service (at a
restaurant) (6)
das Bedienungsgeld service charge
die Bedingung (-en) condition
bedingungslos unconditional
bedrohen to threaten
sich beeilen to hurry (up)
beeindruckt impressed
beenden to complete, finish, end
sich befassen mit to occupy oneself
with
befehlen (befiehlt), befahl, befohlen
to order (15)
sich befinden, befand, befunden to
be located, to be
das Befinden well-being (E)
befriedigend satisfactory (13)
befürchten to fear (14)
begabt gifted, talented
begehen, beging, begangen to
commit
begeistert von enthusiastic about (8)
beginnen, begann, begonnen to
begin, start (4)
begraben (begräbt), begrub,
begraben to bury
begreifen, begriff, begriffen to
understand, comprehend (8)
begründen to substantiate
begrüßen to greet, welcome (16)
behaglich comfortable
behaupten to assert, claim (14)
behindern to handicap, hinder
die Behörde (-n) regulatory
authority, agency
bei (+ *dat.*) near; at; at the place of;
with (1, 5)
beide both
das Bein (-e) leg (7)
beinahe almost
das Beispiel (-e) example, model;
zum Beispiel (*abbr.* **z.B.**) for
example
beißen, biß, gebissen to bite (13)
beitragen (trägt bei), trug bei,
beigetragen to contribute
der Beitrag (¨e) contribution
bekannt acquainted; known (11)
der/die Bekannte (*decl. adj.*)
acquaintance (11)
bekanntgeben (gibt bekannt), gab
bekannt, bekanntgegeben to
announce, report

ernähren to feed; to support
die Ernährung food, nutrition (11)
erneut renewed
eröffnen to open up
erraten (errät), erriet, erraten to guess
erreichbar mit able to be reached by, reachable via (11)
erreichen to reach
erscheinen, erschien, ist erschienen to appear, come out (14)
ersetzen to replace
erst only, not until; first
erstaunt amazed
der/die Erwachsene (*decl. adj.*) adult, grownup (9)
erwähnen to mention
erwarten to expect; to wait for (13)
die Erwartung (-en) expectation
erzählen to tell, narrate (2)
die Erzählung (-en) story, narration
erzeugen to produce
es it
essen (ißt), aß, gegessen to eat (2)
das Essen (-) food; meal; eating (1); **zum Essen** for dinner; **Essen und Trinken** food and drinks (5)
die Etage (-n) floor, story (10)
etwa approximately, about
etwas something; anything; a little bit (1); **etwas anderes** something different (5)
euer your (*inform. pl.*)
(das) Europa Europe
evangelisch Protestant
eventuell perhaps
das Examen (-) examination
existieren to exist
experimentieren to experiment
explodieren to explode

F

die Fabrik (-en) factory
das Fach (¨er) subject (in school) (13); **das Hauptfach** major subject; **das Lieblingsfach** favorite subject (3); **das Nebenfach** minor subject
die Fachakademie (-n) professional school (*university level*) (11)
das Fachgeschäft (-e) specialty store
die Fachkraft (¨e) specialist, expert
die Fachleute (*pl.*) experts
die Fachschule (-n) technical school
die Fahne (-n) flag
fahren (fährt), fuhr, ist gefahren to drive, ride, travel, go (2)

die Fal
der Fa
    wind
der Fal
der Fal
das Fal
der Fal
die Fah
die Fah
    expen
der Fall
fallen (f
    to dec
fallenla
    fallen
falls in c
falsch fa
familiär
die Fami
die Fami
    family
das Fam
    celebra
der Fami
    last nar
der Fami
fangen (f
    catch (1
fantastisc
die Farbe
das Farbf
fassen to
    nicht zu
    (16)
das Faß (
    vom Fa
fast almos
faul lazy (
faulenzen
    (2)
die Faust (
(der) Febr
die Feder (
fehlen to b
    Was fehlt
    (7)
der Feierab
feiern to ce
der Feiertag
fein fine, de
das Feld (-e
das Fenster
die Ferien (
    Ferien! Ha
fern distant
fernsehen (s
    ferngesehe

sich beklagen to complain
die Bekleidung clothing, attire (5)
das Bekleidungsstück (-e) piece of clothing, garment
bekommen, bekam, bekommen to receive, get (4)
belasten to burden
(das) Belgien Belgium
beliebig any; arbitrary; **x-beliebig** (*coll.*) any old
beliebt popular (8)
die Belohnung (-en) reward (2)
belügen, belog, belogen to tell a lie to someone
bemerken to observe; notice (14)
die Bemerkung (-en) remark, comment
benötigen to need
benutzbar usable (12)
benutzen to use (11)
das Benzin gasoline (10)
beobachten to observe
bequem comfortable; easy (2)
beraten (berät), beriet, beraten to advise, counsel
berechnen to calculate; to charge
bereit ready; available
bereits already
der Berg (-e) mountain (9)
der Bericht (-e) report (14)
berichten to report, narrate (16)
der Beruf (-e) profession, occupation; **von Beruf** by occupation (1)
der Berufsberater (-) / die Berufsberaterin (-nen) job counselor (13)
die Berufsberatung job counseling (13)
die Berufspläne (*pl.*) career plans
der/die Berufstätige (*decl. adj.*) working person
beruhigen to calm, soothe
berühmt famous (10)
berühren to touch (7)
besänftigen to appease, placate
die Besatzung (-en) (military) occupation; occupation force (16)
sich beschäftigen mit to occupy oneself with; to spend time with
die Beschäftigung (-en) activity
Bescheid geben (gibt Bescheid) to inform, let someone know (9)
beschleunigen to accelerate, speed up (15)

beschließen, beschloß, beschlossen to decide
beschreiben, beschrieb, beschrieben to describe (14)
sich beschweren über (+ *acc.*) to lodge a complaint, complain about (7)
besetzen to occupy (16)
besetzt occupied, taken (6)
besichtigen to view, see (10)
besitzen, besaß, besessen to own, possess (8)
besonders especially, particularly; **nicht besonders (gut)** not particularly (well) (E)
besorgen to purchase, procure, get (9)
besprechen (bespricht), besprach, besprochen to discuss, talk about
besser better
die Besserung improvement; **Gute Besserung!** Get well soon! (7)
bestätigen to confirm, verify
bestehen, bestand, bestanden to pass (an exam) (13); **bestehen aus** to consist of
bestellen to order; to reserve (5)
die Bestellung (-en) order; reservation
bestimmen to determine, decide
bestimmt certainly, to be sure, for certain (2)
bestreichen, bestrich, bestrichen to spread on
der Besuch (-e) visit; visitor; guest(s)
besuchen to visit (1)
beteiligt sein (**an** + *dat.*) to participate (in)
betonen to stress, emphasize
betragen, (beträgt), betrug, betragen to amount to, come to (12); **die Miete beträgt** the rent comes to
betreffen (betrifft), betroff, betroffen to concern
der Betrieb (-e) enterprise, business
betrügen, betrog, betrogen to deceive, cheat
das Bett (-en) bed (2)
das Bettuch (¨er) bed sheet (16)
die Bevölkerung population
bevor before (12)
bevorstehen (steht bevor), stand bevor, bevorgestanden to lie ahead, be in store
bewachen to guard, watch over

bewahren to preserve, keep
sich bewegen to move, move about (7)
die Bewegung (-en) exercise, movement; **Bewegung brauchen** to need exercise (7)
der Beweis (-e) proof, evidence
sich bewerben um (bewirbt), bewarb, beworben to apply for (13)
der Bewerber (-) / die Bewerberin (-nen) applicant (13)
die Bewerbung (-en) application; application form (13)
bewerten to evaluate
bewohnen to reside in; to occupy
der Bewohner (-) / die Bewohnerin (-nen) resident, tenant
bewölkt cloudy, overcast (8)
das Bewußtsein consciousness; awareness (16)
bezahlen to pay (5)
die Bezeichnung (-en) label, term
sich beziehen auf (+ *acc.*) to refer to
die Beziehung (-en) relationship; connection
beziehungsweise (bzw.) respectively, or (15)
der Bezirk (-e) district, area
bezweifeln to doubt (14)
die Bibliothek (-en) library (2)
das Bier beer (4); **Bier vom Faß** beer on tap; **die Maß Bier,** a mug of beer, about one liter (6)
bieten, bot, geboten to offer, present (9)
das Bild (-er) picture (4)
bilden to form
billig cheap, inexpensive (2)
binden, band, gebunden to tie; to tape
bis (+ *acc.*) until (3); up to; as far as; **bis bald** see you later
bisher so far, up to now
ein bißchen a little (bit); somewhat
bitte please; you are welcome; here you are (E); **bitte schön** please; **Bitte sehr?** May I help you? (in a store) (2)
bitten um, bat, gebeten to ask for, request (16)
das Blatt (¨er) sheet (of paper); leaf
blau blue (5); **in Blau** in blue
bleiben, blieb, ist geblieben to stay, remain (1)
der Bleistift (-e) pencil (11)

die Einheit unity; unit (16)
einheitlich in unison; as one
einholen (holt ein) to catch up with
einige several, some
einkaufen (kauft ein) to shop, go shopping (4)
das Einkaufszentrum (Einkaufszentren) shopping center (5)
der Einkaufszettel (-) shopping list
das Einkommen (-) income
einladen (lädt ein), lud ein, eingeladen to invite (3)
die Einladung (-en) invitation
einlegen (legt ein): eine Pause einlegen to take a break
einmal once (6)
einmalig unique
die Einnahme (-n) income (11)
einnehmen (nimmt ein), nahm ein, eingenommen to take (a medicine)
einrichten (richtet ein) to furnish (12), equip
eins (numeral) one (E)
einsammeln (sammelt ein) to gather, collect
einschicken (schickt ein) to send in; to forward
einschließlich including, inclusive
einsenden (sendet ein), sandte ein, eingesandt to send in, forward
einst formerly
einstellen (stellt ein) to employ
einverstanden: einverstanden sein to be in agreement (9); to agree, approve; **Ich bin damit einverstanden.** I agree with that.
der Einwohner (-) / die Einwohnerin (-nen) resident, inhabitant
einzahlen (zahlt ein) to pay in; to deposit
der Einzelhandel retail trade
einzeln individual; single; **jeder einzelne** every single one
das Einzelzimmer (-) single room (10)
einziehen (zieht ein), zog ein, ist eingezogen to move in
einzig only, sole
das Eis ice cream (6); ice
das Eisbein pork hock
der Eisschrank (¨e) refrigerator (12)
elektrisch electrical
die Elektrizität electricity
das Elend misery, need

elf ele...
**der El...
**(das) ...
**die El...
**empfe...
   **emp...
**empfe...
**die En...
   reco...
**empfi...
   feel,...
**das En...
   the e...
   (4)
**enden
**endgül...
   all
**endlich...
**die Ene...
**energis...
eng nar...
**engagie...
**der Eng...
   **(-n)...
**englisch...
   Englis...
**der Enk...
   grands...
**entdeck...
**entferne...
   away f...
**die Entf...
**enthalte...
   enthal...
   Preis e...
   price (...
**entlang (...
   alongsi...
   along t...
**(sich) en...
   entschi...
**die Entsc...
   eine En...
   a decisi...
**sich entsc...
   entsch...
   one's m...
**entschuld...
**entschu...
**Entschu...
   me, ple...
**die Entsc...
   excuse;...
   (10)
**sich entsp...
   (7)

---

gut good; well; **Es geht mir gut.** I am fine; **alles Gute** best wishes; **guten Abend** good evening (E); **guten Morgen** good morning (E); **guten Tag** hello, good day (E); **gute Nacht** good night (E)
das Gymnasium (Gymnasien) secondary school (3)
die Gymnastik gymnastics

H

das Haar (-e) hair (7); **Mir stehen die Haare zu Berge.** My hair stands on end. (15)
haben (hat), hatte, gehabt (2); **Durst haben** to be thirsty (5); **Hunger haben** to be hungry; **Lust haben** to feel like doing something (2)
der Hafen (¨) harbor, port (10)
halb half
halbieren to divide in half
die Halbpension accommodation with two meals per day included (10)
die Hälfte (-n) half; fifty percent (11)
das Hallenbad (¨er) indoor swimming pool (8)
hallo hello (E)
der Hals neck; throat (7)
die Halsschmerzen (pl.) sore throat
Halt! Stop
halten (hält), hielt, gehalten to hold, keep; stop (9); **halten für** to consider (7); **halten von** to think of; **sich fit halten (hält sich fit)** to keep fit (7)
die Haltestelle (-n) stop (bus or streetcar) (10); **die Bushaltestelle** bus stop
die Hand (¨e) hand (7)
die Handarbeit (-en) handicraft (13)
handeln to act; **handeln von** to be about, deal with (14); **Wovon handelt es?** What is it about?
handschriftlich handwritten (13)
der Handschuh (-e) glove
die Handtasche (-n) handbag
hängen, hing, gehangen to hang (12); **Es hängt davon ab . . .** It depends (on) . . . (13)
hart hard
häßlich ugly (2)
häufig frequently, often; **am häufigsten** most often; most widely (7)
der Hauptbahnhof (¨e) main railroad station (10)

das Hauptfach (¨er) major subject (13)
die Hauptfigur (-en) main character; protagonist
das Hauptgericht (-e) main dish; entrée (6)
die Hauptmahlzeit (-en) main meal of the day
hauptsächlich mainly, mostly (9)
die Hauptschule (-n) junior high school (grades 5–9/10)
die Hauptspeise (-n) main dish, entrée
die Hauptstadt (¨e) capital
das Haus (¨er) house; home (1); **nach Hause** home (indicating going home) (3); **zu Hause** at home
hausgemacht homemade (6)
der Haushalt (-e) household
die Hausnummer (-n) street address (number) (E)
das Haustier (-e) pet
die Haut skin
heben, hob, gehoben to lift
das Heft (-e) notebook (11)
die Heimat homeland, home town (16)
heimlich secret
heiraten to marry, get married (3)
heiser hoarse (7)
heiß hot (8)
heißen, hieß, geheißen to be called (1)
der Heißluftballon(s) hot-air balloon
heiter pleasant, fair (8)
die Heizung (-en) heating (11)
helfen (+ dat.) (hilft), half, geholfen (5)
hell light; bright (5)
das Hemd (-en) shirt (5)
her this way, here; **hin und her** back and forth (14)
herauf up; upstairs
heraufkommen (kommt herauf), kam herauf, ist heraufgekommen to come upstairs
herausbringen (bringt heraus), brachte heraus, herausgebracht to publish
herausgehen (geht heraus), ging heraus, ist herausgegangen to go outside
der Herbst autumn, fall (8)
hereinkommen (kommt herein), kam herein, ist hereingekommen to come inside
herkommen (kommt her), kam her, ist hergekommen to come here

Herr; der Herr (-n masc.) Mr.; gentleman; (E)
herrlich wonderful, magnificent
herstellen (stellt her) to manufacture (15)
herüberkommen (kommt herüber), kam herüber, ist herübergekommen to come over
herum around
herumgammeln (coll.) **(gammelt herum)** to fool around, be lazy (8)
herunter (runter) down; downstairs
das Herz (-ens, -en) heart (4)
herzhaft hearty; strong
herzlich cordial; heartfelt; **herzlichen Glückwunsch** congratulations; **herzliche Grüße** kind regards
heute today (1); **heute abend** tonight (4); **heute morgen** this morning (4); **heute mittag** today at noon
heutzutage nowadays
hier here (1)
hiermit herewith
die Hilfe help, assistance (2)
der Himmel (-) sky; heaven
himmlisch heavenly, delightful
die Hin- und Rückfahrt (-en) round-trip
hin und her back and forth (14); **hin und zurück** roundtrip (9)
hinaufgehen (geht hinauf), ging hinauf, ist hinaufgegangen to go upstairs
hinauskommen (kommt hinaus), kam hinaus, ist hinausgekommen to come out; get out
die Hinfahrt (-en) trip there; first portion of roundtrip (9)
hingegen on the other hand
hingehen (geht hin), ging hin, ist hingegangen to go there
sich hinsetzen (setzt sich hin) to sit down (7)
hinten in the back
hinter (+ acc./dat.) behind (6)
hinterher afterwards
der Hinweis (-e) tip, clue (12)
historisch historic(al)
das Hobby (-s) hobby (8)
hoch (hoh-) high; tall (2)
das Hochhaus (¨er) high rise building (12)
hochmotiviert highly motivated
die Hochschule (-n) university, college

der Nachmit
  nachmitta
der Nachnar
  (1)
die Nachrich
  Nachrichte
die Nachspei
nächst- next,
  nearest (9)
die Nacht (-e)
  (4); gute Na
der Nachteil (
der Nachtisch
nah close by, n
die Nähe vicin
  nearby, in th
  der Nähe vo
  Umgebung
die Nahrung n
das Nahrungs
der Name (-ns
  the name of
nämlich namel
die Nase (-n) n
die Nationalitä
die Natur natur
natürlich natur
der Nazi (-s) (a
  member of th
  Socialist Part
der Nebel (-) fo
neben (+ acc./d
die Nebenarbei
  (4)
nebenbei on the
das Nebenfach (
  (at school) (13)
die Nebenkoster
  expenses (11)
die Nebensaison
neblig foggy (8)
der Neffe (-n ma
nehmen (nimmt)
  to take (2); Plat
  seat (5)
nein no (1)
nennen, nannte,
  to be called (14)
nervös nervous
nerven (coll.) to ge
  irritate; Das ner
  on my nerves. (3
nett nice, pleasant
neu new (1); nicht
  new

höchstens at most (9)
die Höchstgeschwindigkeit (-en)
  maximum speed, speed limit (10)
die Höchsttemperatur (-en) highest
  temperature, daily high
die Hochzeit (-en) wedding
hoffen auf (+ acc.) to hope for (16)
hoffentlich I hope; hopefully (6)
die Hoffnung (-en) hope
höflich courteous, polite (11)
der Höhepunkt (-e) climax;
  highlight
holen to get, fetch (5)
die Hölle hell
das Holz (-er) wood, timber
der Honig honey
hören to listen to, hear (1)
die Hose (-n) pants, trousers, slacks
  (5)
das Hotel (-s) hotel (10); im Hotel at
  the hotel
humorvoll humorous; full of humor
der Hund (-e) dog (3)
(ein) hundert one hundred (1);
  Hunderte von . . . hundreds of . . .
der Hunderter (-) one hundred mark
  note
hundsmiserabel (coll.) sick as a dog
  (7)
der Hunger hunger (2); Hunger
  haben to be hungry
hungrig hungry
husten to cough
der Husten (-) cough (7)
der Hustensaft (-e) cough syrup
der Hut (-e) hat (5)

I

IC = Intercity train
ich I
die Idee (-n) idea
identifizieren to identify
Ihr your (form.)
ihr you (inform. pl.); her; its; their
der Imbiß (-sse) snack (6)
immer always; ever (2)
der Immobilienmakler (-) real estate
  agent (12)
in (+ acc./dat.) in, into; inside
indem by (+ gerund)
(das) Indien India
individuell individual
die Industrie (-n) industry
sich informieren to inform oneself
  (7)

der Ingenieur (-e) / die Ingenieurin
  (-nen) engineer (13)
der Inhalt content(s)
Inland: Inland und Ausland at home
  and abroad
die Innenstadt (-e) center of town
  (10)
die Insel (-n) island (10)
insgesamt altogether (9)
interessant interesting (1)
das Interesse (-n) interest
sich interessieren für to be
  interested in (7)
interpretieren to interpret
interviewen to interview
inzwischen in the meantime,
  meanwhile
irgend any at all, some (13);
  irgendetwas anything at all;
  something (13); irgendjemand
  anybody at all; irgendwann
  anytime at all; irgendwo
  somewhere
(das) Italien Italy
italienisch Italian

J

ja yes (1)
die Jacke (-n) jacket (5)
das Jahr (-e) year (1, 4); nächstes
  Jahr next year; einmal im Jahr
  once a year; mit 10 Jahren at age
  10
jahrelang for years and years
die Jahreszeit (-en) season (8)
das Jahrhundert (-e) century
(ein)jährig (one) year old
jährlich annual
das Jahrzehnt (-e) decade
(der) Januar January (3)
der Japaner (-) / die Japanerin
  (-nen) Japanese person
japanisch Japanese
jawohl yes, of course
je ever, always; je (+ comparative)
  desto/umso (+ comparative) the
  (+ comparative) the (+
  comparative)
jeder, jede, jedes each, every;
  everybody; jeden Tag every day (4)
jedoch however, but
jemand somebody, someone (12);
  jemand anders somebody else
jetzt now, immediately (1)
die Jugend youth; young people

die Jugendherberge (-n) youth
  hostel (9)
jugendlich youthful; juvenile (8)
der/die Jugendliche (decl. adj.) young
  person; teenager (8)
(der) Juli July (3)
jung young (1); jungverheiratet
  newlywed (12)
der Junge (-n masc.) boy
(der) Juni June (3)
die Jura law

K

der Käfer (-) bug, beetle
der Kaffee coffee (3); Tasse Kaffee
  cup of coffee (4); der Schonkaffee
  low-acid decaffeinated coffee (5)
das Kaffeehaus (-er) café (6)
die Kaffeekanne (-n) coffee pot (6)
das Kalbfleisch veal
(das) Kalifornien California
kalifornisch Californian
kalkulieren to calculate
kalt cold
die Kamera (-s) camera
der Kamillentee camomile tea
sich kämmen to comb one's hair (7)
der Kampf (-e) battle, fight
kämpfen to fight, struggle
(das) Kanada Canada
das Kaninchen (-) rabbit
das Kapitel (-) chapter
kaputt broken (7)
kaputtgehen (geht kaputt), ging
  kaputt, ist kaputtgegangen to
  break (by itself)
kaputtmachen (macht kaputt) to
  (cause to) break (16)
die Karibik the Caribbean
kariert checkered, plaid (5)
die Karriere (-n) career; Karriere
  machen to be successful in a career
  (13)
die Karte (-n) card; ticket (6)
die Kartoffel (-n) potato (5); der
  Kartoffelsalat potato salad
der Käse cheese (5)
die Kasse (-n) cash register; cashier
  (5); vorne an der Kasse up front at
  the cash register
der Kasten (-) box
die Katze (-n) cat
kaufen to buy (5)
die Kauffrau (-en) businesswoman
  (13)

der Markt (
  market pl
die Marmel
marschiere
(der) März
die Maschir
die Massen
  (14)
die Maß Bie
  one liter (
materialistis
die Mathem
die Mauer (
die Maus (¨e
meckern (co
die Medien (
das Medikar
  etc.), medi
die Medizin
das Meer (-e
  Meer at th
mehr more
das Mehrbet
  with more
mehrere sev
die Mehrheit
mehrmals of
  several occa
die Mehrwer
  added tax;
die Mehrzahl
mein my
meinen to me
die Meinung (
  meiner Mei
  opinion
meist, meister
der, die, das
sich (am Telef
  the phone (1
  sich. No one
  phone).
die Mensa (-s)
der Mensch (-
  person (1)
das Menü (-s)
merken to noti
merkwürdig st
das Messer (-)
der/das Meter
der Metzger (-)
die Metzgerei (
die Miete (-n)
  beträgt the r
mieten to rent

die Schallplatte (-n) record
schalten to shift gears (15)
das Schaubild (-er) diagram
schauen to look; Schau mal! Look!
  (2)
der Schauer (-) (rain) shower (8)
der Schauspieler (-) / die
  Schauspielerin (-nen) actor,
  actress (1)
der Scheck (-s) check
die Scheibe (-n) slice
der Schein (-e) bank note, paper
  money (11)
scheinbar apparently
scheinen, schien, geschienen to
  shine (8); to appear, seem (12); Die
  Sonne scheint. The sun is shining.
schenken to give (a gift) (5)
scheußlich horrible (8)
schick stylish
schicken to send (5)
das Schicksal (-e) fate
schieben, schob, geschoben to push
schießen, schoß, geschossen to
  shoot
das Schiff (-e) ship
das Schild (-er) sign, road sign (15)
der Schilling (-e) Austrian monetary
  unit
der Schinken (-) ham
der Schirm (-e) umbrella
der Schlaf sleep
der Schlafanzug (¨e) pajama
schlafen (schläft), schlief,
  geschlafen to sleep (2); schlafen
  gehen to go to bed
der Schlafsack (¨e) sleeping bag
das Schlafzimmer (-) bedroom
schlagen, schlug, geschlagen to beat
der Schlager (-) hit song; hit
die Schlagzeile (-n) headline (14)
schlank slender
schlapp without energy, rundown,
  listless (7)
schlecht bad (E); Mir ist schlecht. I
  feel sick to my stomach. (7)
schleppen to drag, lug
schließen, schloß, geschlossen to
  close (6); einen Vertrag schließen
  to sign a contract
das Schließfach (¨er) locker
schließlich finally, in the end
der Schlips (-e) tie (5)
das Schloß (¨sser) castle; palace (9)
schlucken to swallow (7)

der Schluß end (15); jetzt ist Schluß
  this is it; Schluß mit . . . ! Stop
  . . . ! (15)
der Schlüssel (-) key (3)
schmecken to taste; Das schmeckt
  (mir) gut. That tastes good (to me).
  (5)
der Schmerz (-en) pain, ache (7); die
  Kopfschmerzen headache (7); die
  Zahnschmerzen toothache
(sich) schminken to put on makeup
der Schmuck jewelry
der Schmutz dirt
schmutzig dirty (7)
die Schnecke (-n) snail
der Schnee snow (8)
schneiden, schnitt, geschnitten to
  cut
schneien to snow (8); Es schneit. It
  is snowing. (8)
schnell quick; fast (9)
der Schnellimbiß (-sse) fast-food
  restaurant (6)
der Schnellzug (¨e) express train
Schnitt: im Schnitt on the average
  (11)
das Schnitzel (-) cutlet; das
  Wienerschnitzel veal cutlet (6)
der Schnupfen cold; sniffle
die Schokolade chocolate
schon already; yet; ever (3)
schön beautiful; bitte schön please;
  danke schön (many) thanks (E);
  schön warm nice and warm
die Schönheit (-en) beauty
der Schonkaffee low-acid
  decaffeinated coffee (5)
der Schornsteinfeger (-) chimney
  sweep
der Schrank (¨e) cupboard; closet;
  wardrobe (12)
schrecklich horrible
schreiben, schrieb, geschrieben to
  write (2)
die Schreibmaschine (-n) typewriter
der Schreibtisch (-e) desk (2)
die Schreibwaren (pl.) stationery
  goods
schreien, schrie, geschrien to
  scream
schriftlich in writing
der Schuh (-e) shoe (5)
der Schulabgänger (-) / die
  Schulabgängerin (-nen) school
  graduate (1)

der Schulabschluß
  (Schulabschlüsse) school diploma
die Schularbeiten (pl.) homework
die Schulden (pl.) debts (12);
  Schulden machen to go into debt
schuldig guilty
die Schule (-n) school (1)
der Schüler (-) / die Schülerin
  (-nen) pupil, student in primary or
  secondary school (9)
die Schulferien (pl.) school vacation,
  holidays (8)
die Schulspeisung meal provided at
  school
die Schulter (-n) shoulder (7)
die Schüssel (-n) bowl
schützen to protect (15)
schwach weak
schwarz black (5)
das Schwarzbrot black bread
der Schwarzhandel black market
  (16)
der Schwarzwald Black Forest
(das) Schweden Sweden
der Schweinebraten (-) pork roast
das Schweinefleisch pork
die Schweiz Switzerland (E)
schwer heavy; difficult
die Schwester (-n) sister (3)
schwierig difficult (6)
die Schwierigkeit (-en) difficulty (6)
das Schwimmbad (¨er) swimming
  pool
schwimmen, schwamm, ist
  geschwommen to swim (2)
schwitzen to sweat
schwül muggy (8)
sechs six (E)
sechzehn sixteen (E)
sechzig sixty (1)
der See (-n) lake (8); am See at the
  lake
die See ocean; seaside
segeln to sail (8)
sehen (sieht), sah, gesehen to see (2)
die Sehenswürdigkeit (-en) (tourist)
  attraction (9)
sehr very (1); Bitte sehr? May I help
  you? (in a store) (2)
die Seide silk (5)
sein (ist), war, ist gewesen to be (1)
sein his, its
seit (+ dat.) since; for (5); seit wann
  since when (1)
seitdem since then
die Seite (-n) side; page

die **Temperatur** (-en) temperature
(8); die **Höchsttemperatur** highest
temperature, daily high
das **Tempo** (-s) speed (15)
die **Tempogrenze** (-n) speed limit
der **Tennisschläger** (-) tennis racket
der **Teppich** (-e) carpet, rug (12)
der **Teppichboden** (⁻) wall-to-wall
carpet (12)
der **Termin** (-e) appointment (13)
die **Terrasse** (-n) terrace (12)
testen to test
das **Testergebnis** (-se) test result
teuer expensive (2)
die **Textverarbeitung** word
processing
thailändisch Thai
das **Theater** (-) theater (6)
die **Theaterkarte** (-n) theater ticket
(6)
die **Theaterkasse** (-n) box office
das **Theaterstück** (-e) play
die **Theke** (-n) counter (6)
das **Thema** (**Themen**) theme; topic
tief low; deep
das **Tier** (-e) animal (15)
der **Tip** (-s) hint, piece of advice
tippen to type
der **Tisch** (-e) table (2); **den Tisch
decken** to set the table
der **Titel** (-) title
die **Tochter** (⁻) daughter (3)
der **Tod** death
tödlich deathly; to death
die **Toilette** (-) toilet
die **Toilettensachen** (*pl.*) toiletries
toll (*coll.*) great (2)
die **Tomate** (-n) tomato (5)
die **Tonne** (-n) ton
das **Tor** (-e) gate; goal (*soccer*)
die **Torte** (-n) torte, pie, cake
tot dead
der **Tourist** (-n *masc.*) / die **Touristin**
tourist (E)
traditionell traditional
tragen (**trägt**), **trug**, **getragen** to
wear (5); to carry
die **Tragik** tragedy
trainieren to train; to practice
der **Trainingsanzug** (⁻e) jogging suit
trampen to hitchhike
der **Traum** (⁻e) dream
träumen (**von**) to dream (of) (12)
traurig sad (13)
die **Traurigkeit** sadness
treffen (**trifft**), **traf**, **getroffen** to
meet (3, 6); **eine Entscheidung**

treffen to make a d[...]
der **Treffpunkt** (-e) m[...]
treiben, trieb, getrieb[...]
treiben to engage in[...]
sich trennen to separa[...]
die **Treppe** (-n) stairca[...]
das **Treppenhaus** (⁻er[...]
treu loyal, faithful (1)
sich trimmen to exerc[...]
lose weight
trinken, trank, getrun[...]
(2)
trotz (+ *gen.*) in spite[...]
trotzdem nevertheless[...]
die **Trümmer** (*pl.*) rub[...]
die **Truppen** (*pl.*) trou[...]
tschüß (*coll.*) so long ([...]
tun, tat, getan to do, [...]
leid. I am sorry. (2)
die **Tür** (-en) door (12)[...]
Eingangstür entranc[...]
die **Türkei** Turkey
der **Turm** (⁻e) tower
die **Turnschuhe** (*pl.*) g[...]
sneakers
typisch typical

U

die **U-Bahn** (-en) subw[...]
übel nauseated; **Mir is**[...]
nauseated.
üben to practice
über (+ *acc./dat.*) over,[...]
überall everywhere
überarbeitet overhaule[...]
überblicken to overloo[...]
view of
übereinander one on t[...]
überfliegen, überflog,[...]
quickly read, skim (1[...]
überfüllt overcrowded[...]
überglücklich overjoye[...]
überhaupt at all (11); ü[...]
nicht not at all
überholen to pass (a ve[...]
überlassen, überließ, ü[...]
leave to
sich etwas überlegen t[...]
something (9); **Ich wi**[...]
überlegen. I want to [...]
übernachten to stay ov[...]
die **Übernachtung** (-en[...]
stay (10)
übernehmen (**übernim**[...]
übernahm, übernom[...]
over

der **Sekretär** (-) / die **Sekretärin**
(-nen) secretary
der **Sekt** champagne
die **Sekunde** (-n) second
selb- (*adj.*) same; **derselbe, dieselbe,
dasselbe** the same
selber self (11); **selber machen** to do
it oneself
selbst self (12)
selbständig independent; on one's
own (13)
die **Selbstbedienung** self-service
das **Selbstbewußtsein** self-confidence
(16)
selten seldom; rare (11)
das **Seminar** (-e) university
department, seminar (2)
die **Seminararbeit** (-en) paper to be
written for a seminar
die **Semmel** (-n) type of bread roll
senden, sandte, gesandt to send
die **Sendung** (-en) TV or radio
program (14)
(der) **September** September (3)
die **Serie** (-n) series
servieren to serve
der **Sessel** (-) armchair, easy chair (2)
setzen to set, put (6); **sich setzen** to
sit down
sicher for sure, certain (3); safe (9)
sichern to secure
Sie you (*form.*)
sie she; it; they
sieben seven (E)
siebzehn seventeen (E)
siebzig seventy (1)
singen, sang, gesungen to sing (6)
der **Sinn** (-e) sense (14); meaning;
feeling
sinnlos senseless
sitzen, saß, gesessen to sit (6)
sitzenbleiben (**bleibt sitzen**), **blieb
sitzen, ist sitzengeblieben** to be
left behind; to fail a class (14)
der **Sitzplatz** (⁻e) seat
skeptisch skeptical
slawisch Slavic
so so; like that; **so . . . wie** as . . . as
(9)
sobald as soon as
das **Sofa** (-s) sofa, couch (2)
sofort immediately
sogar even
sogenannt so-called
der **Sohn** (⁻e) son (3)
solange as long as

der **Soldat** (-n *masc.*) / die **Soldatin**
(-nen) soldier (16)
sollen shall; to be supposed to (4);
said to be
der **Sommer** (-) summer (8)
das **Sonderangebot** (-e) special offer
(at a store) (2)
sonderbar strange
sondern but rather (8)
(der) **Sonnabend** Saturday (3);
sonnabends Saturdays
die **Sonne** (-n) sun (8)
sonnig sunny (8)
(der) **Sonntag** Sunday (3); **sonntags**
Sundays
sonst (noch) otherwise; else (3, 4);
Sonst noch was? Anything else? (5)
sonstig other, additional (11)
Sonstiges other items, miscellaneous
sooft as often (as)
die **Sorge** (-n) worry; **sich Sorgen
machen** to worry
sorgfältig careful
die **Sorte** (-n) kind; variety
sowieso anyway
die **Sowjetunion** Soviet Union
der **Sozialismus** socialism
die **Sozialkunde** social science (4)
die **Soziologie** sociology
die **Spalte** (-n) (printed) column
(das) **Spanien** Spain
spanisch Spanish
spannend exciting, suspenseful (14)
sparen to save (11)
der **Spargel** (-) asparagus (5)
die **Sparkasse** (-n) savings bank (10)
das **Sparkonto** (**Sparkonten**) savings
account (11)
der **Spaß** fun; **Das macht mir Spaß.**
That's fun, I enjoy that.; **Viel Spaß!**
Have fun! (1)
spät late (4)
spätestens at the latest (10)
spazieren to go for a walk, stroll (14)
spazierengehen (**geht spazieren**),
**ging spazieren, ist
spazierengegangen** to go for a
walk (4)
der **Spaziergang** (⁻e) walk; stroll
der **Speck** bacon (5)
die **Speise** (-n) meal
die **Speise(n)karte** (-n) menu (6)
der **Speisewagen** (-) dining car
die **Spende** (-n) donation,
contribution (10)

spenden to donate
die **Spezialität** (-en) speciality (6)
spezifisch specific
das **Spiegelei** (⁻er) fried egg
das **Spiel** (-e) play; game
spielen to play (1)
der **Spielplatz** (⁻e) playground
die **Spielwaren** (*pl.*) toys
der **Spinat** spinach (5)
die **Spitze** (-n) tip; (pointed) top
spontan spontaneous
der **Sport** sports (8)
Sport treiben, trieb, getrieben to
engage in sports (7)
die **Sportart** (-en) type of sport (8)
die **Sporthalle** (-n) gymnasium (8)
der **Sportler** (-) / die **Sportlerin**
(-nen) athlete
sportlich athletic; casual; **sportlich
aktiv** active in sports
der **Sportplatz** (⁻e) athletic field,
stadium (8)
die **Sprache** (-n) language (13); die
Fremdsprache foreign language
(13)
die **Sprachkenntnisse** (*pl.*)
knowledge of foreign languages
sprechen (**spricht**), **sprach,
gesprochen** to speak (4)
die **Sprechstunde** (-n) office hour
springen, sprang, ist gesprungen to
jump
der **Spruch** (⁻e) saying; message
der **Sprudel** (-) carbonated water,
soft drink (5)
die **Spülmaschine** (-n) dishwasher
(7)
der **Staat** (-en) state, nation
die **Staatsprüfung** (-en) examination
administered by a national board
der **Stacheldraht** barbed wire
das **Stadion** (**Stadien**) stadium (8)
die **Stadt** (⁻e) city; town (1)
die **Stadtführung** (-en) city tour
der **Stadtplan** (⁻e) city street map
stagnieren to stagnate
der **Stammbaum** (⁻e) family tree (3)
stammen aus to come from; to
originate
der **Stammgast** (⁻e) regular guest
das **Stammlokal** (-e) favorite
restaurant where one goes
regularly with a group of friends (6)
der **Stammtisch** (-e) permanently
reserved table

ständig always; permanent
stark strong
starren to stare
die Statistik (-en) statistics
(an)statt (+ *gen.*) instead of (16);
　statt dessen in lieu of that
stattfinden (findet statt), fand statt,
　stattgefunden to take place
der Stau (-s) traffic jam (8)
staunen to be amazed
steckenbleiben (bleibt stecken),
　blieb stecken, ist
　steckengeblieben to be stuck
stehen, stand, gestanden to stand (4,
　6); look good; **Das steht dir gut.**
　That looks good on you. (5); **zur**
　Verfügung stehen to be available,
　be at one's disposal
stehlen (stiehlt), stahl, gestohlen to
　steal (6)
der Stehplatz (-e) standing room (6)
steigen, stieg, ist gestiegen to climb,
　go up, rise (11)
steigern to increase
der Stein (-e) stone
die Stelle (-n) place, position (11, 13);
　an seiner Stelle in his place; **auf**
　der Stelle right away, immediately;
　on the spot (7); **an erster Stelle** in
　first place (13); **eine feste Stelle**
　permanent position
stellen to place, put (upright) (6);
　eine Frage stellen to ask a
　question
das Stellenangebot (-e) job offer
die Stellensuche job search
die Stellung (-en) position
sterben (stirbt), starb, ist gestorben
　to die (15)
das Steuer (-) steering wheel (11)
die Steuer (-n) tax (11)
das Stichwort (-er) key word, cue
der Stiefel (-) boot (5)
die Stimme (-n) voice; vote
stimmen to be correct; **(Das)**
　stimmt. That's correct. (4)
die Stimmung (-en) mood,
　atmosphere (16)
der Stock floor, story (10); **im ersten**
　Stock on the first floor
das Stockwerk (-e) = Stock
stöhnen to moan, sigh
der Stolz pride
stolz proud (16); stolz sein auf (+
　acc.) to be proud of (16)

der Strand (-e) beach
die Straße (-n) street
　entlang along this s
　der Straße in the st
die Straßenbahn (-er
die Strecke (-n) stret
(sich) strecken to str
streiken to go on stri
streng strict (3)
der Strom (-e) stream
　electricity (11)
der Strumpf (-e) stoc
die Stube (-n) room
das Stück (-e) piece (
　each, per piece
der Student (-n *masc*
　Studentin (-nen) st
das Studentenheim (
das Studentenwohnh
　dormitory
der Studienanfänger
　Studienanfängerin
　freshman
das Studienfach (-er)
　subject
die Studiengebühren
　tuition (11)
der Studienplatz (-e)
　university (3)
studieren to study (a
　university) (1)
das Studium (Studie
　studies
der Stuhl (-e) chair (
die Stunde (-n) hour
stundenlang for hour
der Stundenlohn (-e)
　(13)
der Stundenplan (-e)
　schedule (4)
der Sturm (-e) (wind
suchen to look for (1)
der Süden south (10)
　the south of (10)
die Summe (-n) sum,
der Supermarkt (-e)
die Suppe (-n) soup (
das Surfbrett (-er) su
süß sweet; **etwas Süß**
　sweet (7)
die Süßigkeiten (*pl.*)
sympathisch likable,
　(1)

ENGLISH-GERMAN

This list contains all the words from the end-of-chapter vocabulary sections.

A

abdomen der Bauch (-e)
to be able to, can können (kann),
　konnte, gekonnt
about über (+ *acc.*); **to be about**
　handeln von; **How about . . . ?**
　Wie wäre es mit . . . ?
above oben; über (+ *acc./dat.*)
absolutely unbedingt
to accelerate beschleunigen
accident der Unfall (-e)
accommodations die Unterkunft (-e);
　accommodations with two meals
　die Halbpension; **with three**
　meals die Vollpension
account das Konto (Konten);
　checking account das Girokonto;
　savings account das Sparkonto
accustomed gewohnt
accustomed to gewöhnt an (+ *acc.*)
ache der Schmerz (-en); **headache**
　die Kopfschmerzen (*pl.*);
　toothache die Zahnschmerzen
　(*pl.*)
acquaintance der/die Bekannte (*decl.*
　adj.)
acquainted bekannt; **getting**
　acquainted bekannt werden
to be acquainted with kennen,
　kannte, gekannt
across from gegenüber von (+ *dat.*)
actor/actress der Schauspieler (-) /
　die Schauspielerin (-nen)
addition: in addition außerdem
additional sonstig
address die Adresse (-n)
adult der/die Erwachsene (*decl. adj.*)
advancement der Aufstieg
advantage der Vorteil (-e)
adventure das Abenteuer (-)
advertisement die Anzeige (-n)
advisor (*also*: **advice column in**
　newspaper) der Ratgeber (-)
to afford sich (+ *dat.*) etwas leisten; **I**
　can't afford that. Das kann ich
　mir nicht leisten.
to be afraid of Angst haben vor
after nach (+ *dat.*); nachdem (*conj.*)

afternoon der Nachmittag (-e); **in the**
　afternoon(s) nachmittags
afterward nachher; danach
again wieder; **yet again** (*emphatic*)
　schon wieder
against gegen (+ *acc.*)
ago vor (+ *dat. with time*); **one week**
　ago vor einer Woche
to agree einverstanden sein; **I agree**
　with that. Ich bin damit
　einverstanden.
ahead: straight ahead geradeaus
ailment die Krankheit (-en)
air die Luft
air pollution die Luftverschmutzung
airplane das Flugzeug (-e)
airport der Flughafen (-)
alarm clock der Wecker (-)
all alles; alle (*pl.*); **all right** in
　Ordnung
to be allowed to dürfen (darf),
　durfte, gedurft
almost fast
alone allein
along entlang (+ *acc.*); **along this**
　street die Straße entlang
already schon
also auch
although obwohl
altogether insgesamt
always immer
American (person) der Amerikaner (-)
　/ die Amerikanerin (-en)
to amount to betragen (beträgt),
　betrug, betragen
and und
angry böse
animal das Tier (-e)
annoyed böse
to be annoyed about sich ärgern
　über (+ *acc.*)
annoying ärgerlich
answer die Antwort (-en)
to answer antworten; **to answer (the**
　phone) sich (am Telefon) melden
anything etwas; **Anything else?**
　Sonst noch etwas?
apartment die Wohnung (-en)
apparatus das Gerät (-e)

to appear erscheinen, erschien, ist
　erschienen; scheinen, schien,
　geschienen
appetizer die Vorspeise (-n)
applicant der Bewerber (-) / die
　Bewerberin (-nen)
application die Bewerbung (-en)
to apply for sich bewerben um
　(bewirbt), bewarb, beworben
appointment der Termin (-e)
apprentice der Lehrling (-e)
appropriate geeignet
approximate(ly) ungefähr
April (der) April
area die Gegend (-en)
arm der Arm (-e)
around um (+ *acc.*)
to arrive ankommen (kommt an),
　kam an, ist angekommen
art die Kunst
as . . . as so . . . wie; **as soon as**
　possible möglichst bald
to ask fragen; **to ask for** bitten um,
　bat, gebeten
asparagus der Spargel
to assert behaupten
assertion die Behauptung (-en)
at an (+ *acc./dat.*); bei (+ *dat.*); **at 10**
　o'clock um 10 Uhr
at all überhaupt
at most höchstens
to pay attention to achten auf
　(+ *acc.*)
attraction: (tourist) attraction die
　Sehenswürdigkeit (-en)
August (der) August
aunt die Tante (-n)
Austria (das) Österreich
automatic teller der Geldautomat
　(-en)
automobile das Auto (-s)
available frei; **Is this seat available?**
　Ist der Platz noch frei?
average der Durchschnitt; **on (the)**
　average im Durchschnitt, im
　Schnitt, durchschnittlich
to avoid vermeiden, vermied,
　vermieden

peace der Frie...
quiet in Ru...
peculiar merk...
pedestrian de...
Fußgänger...
pencil der Ble...
people das Vo...
people (indef....
man sagt...
pepper der Pf...
performance...
perhaps viell...
permitted erl...
person die Pe...
(-n masc.);
Jugendlich...
personal per...
pharmacy di...
phone das Te...
phone sic...
to phone an...
angerufen...
physician de...
(-nen)
to pick up a...
pickle die Gu...
picnic das Pi...
basket de...
picture das l...
picture a...
piece das St...
pro Stück...
pill die Table...
place der Or...
Stelle (-);
Stelle; in
Stelle; m
Treffpunk...
der Wohn...
to place lege...
(upright)
to plan vorh...
vorgehab...
plane das Fl...
to plant pfla...
plate der Te...
platform de...
(-e)
to play spie...
at ... De...
pleasant sy...
angeneh...
heiter (w...
please bitte...
How's th...
pleasure da...

to lea...
ab...
ab...
ab...
lectu...
left li...
left o...
leg d...
leisu...
leisu...
leisu...
to le...
to les...
to let...
to let...
(g...
lettu...
libra...
to lie...
life o...
light...
light...
light...
to lil...
g...
g...
I...
to lis...
z...
listle...
little...
to liv...
liver...
liver...
to b...
loge...
long...
t...
to lo...
s...
n...
to lo...
(...
to lo...
to lo...
(...
to lo...
T...
to lo...
a lo...
loud...
loya...
luck...
luck...
O...
luck...
lugg...

freeway die Autobahn (-en)
fresh frisch
Friday (der) Freitag
friend der Freund (-e) / die Freundin (-nen)
friendly freundlich
from von (+ dat.)
from ... on ab (+ dat.); from June 1 on ... ab erstem Juni ...
from ... to von ... bis
in front vorne; way in front ganz vorne
in front of vor (+ acc./dat.)
fruit das Obst
full voll; satt
fun der Spaß; That's fun. Das macht (mir) Spaß.; Have fun! Viel Spaß!; to have fun sich amüsieren, Spaß haben
to function funktionieren
funny komisch, lustig
to furnish einrichten (richtet ein)
furnished möbliert
furnishings die Möbel (pl.)
future die Zukunft, künftig (adj.)

G
garage die Garage (-n)
garbage der Abfall, der Müll
garden der Garten (-)
gas(oline) das Benzin; to get gas tanken
gas station die Tankstelle (-n)
gears: to shift gears schalten
general: in general im allgemeinen
gentleman der Herr (-n masc.)
geography die Erdkunde
German deutsch; in German auf deutsch
German (person) der/die Deutsche (decl. adj.)
German Democratic Republic die Deutsche Demokratische Republik (DDR)
German mark die Deutsche Mark (DM)
to get: to fetch holen; to go get besorgen; to receive bekommen, bekam, bekommen; I get it! Ach so! (Ah so!); Get well soon! Gute Besserung! to get acquainted, get to know kennenlernen (lernt kennen); bekannt werden (wird), wurde, geworden
to get up aufstehen (steht auf), stand auf, ist aufgestanden

gift das Geschenk (-e)
girl das Mädchen (-)
to give geben (gibt), gab, gegeben
to give a gift schenken
to give back zurückgeben (gibt zurück), gab zurück, zurückgegeben
given name der Vorname (-n masc.)
gladly gern(e)
to go gehen, ging, ist gegangen; to go for a walk spazierengehen (geht spazieren), ging spazieren; to go on a trip verreisen; to go on an outing Grüne fahren (fährt), fuhr, ist gefahren; einen Ausflug machen
God: thank God! Gott sei Dank!
good gut; good-bye auf Wiedersehen; auf Wiederhören (only on the phone); good day guten Tag; (in Austria) grüß Gott; good evening guten Abend; good morning guten Morgen; good night gute Nacht
to say good-bye (to) sich verabschieden (von)
government die Regierung (-en), der Staat
grade (on a report card) die Note (-n), die Zensur (-en)
graduate (from a school) der Schulabgänger(-) / die Schulabgängerin (-nen)
graduate (of the Gymnasium) der Abiturient (-n masc.) / die Abiturientin (-nen)
granddaughter die Enkelin (-nen)
grandfather der Großvater (-); grandpa Opa
grandmother die Großmutter (-); grandma Oma
grandparents die Großeltern (pl.)
grandson der Enkel (-)
to grasp fassen; It is unbelievable. Es ist nicht zu fassen.
grass-roots movement die Bürgerinitiative (-n)
gray grau
great ausgezeichnet; prima, toll (coll.)
great-grandfather der Urgroßvater (-)
great-grandmother die Urgroßmutter (-)
green grün
to greet begrüßen
greetings die Grüße (pl.); (kind) regards herzliche Grüße

cupboard der Schrank (-...)
curd cheese der Quark
currency die Währung (-...)
current aktuell; to stay c... dem Laufenden bleib...
customer der Kunde (-n... Kundin (-nen)
customs der Zoll
cute niedlich
cutlet das Schnitzel (-); v... das Wienerschnitzel

D
to dance tanzen; dancing...
danger die Gefahr (-en)
dangerous gefährlich
dark dunkel
date das Datum (Daten);... Verabredung (-en); dat... das Geburtsdatum
daughter die Tochter (-)
day der Tag (-e); good day... every day jeden Tag; d... restaurant is closed d...
to deal with handeln von...
debts die Schulden (pl.);... debt Schulden mache...
December (der) Dezembe...
to decide sich entscheide... entschied, entschieden... entschließen, entschlo... entschlossen
deficient mangelhaft
degree der Grad (-e)
to demand fordern
to depart abfliegen (fliegt... ab, ist abgeflogen; abfa... ab), fuhr ab, ist abgefa...
department store das Ka...
to depend on abhängen v... ab), hing ab, abgehang... verlassen auf, verließ,... depends. Es kommt da...
depressed deprimiert
to describe beschreiben, b... beschrieben
to design entwerfen (entw... entwarf, entworfen
desk der Schreibtisch (-e)
dessert die Nachspeise (-... Nachtisch
detective story/show der...
to develop entwickeln
diary das Tagebuch (-er)

B
back der Rücken (-)
back zurück; to give back zurückgeben (gibt zurück), gab zurück, zurückgegeben; to pay back zurückzahlen (zahlt zurück)
back and forth hin und her
bacon der Speck
bad schlecht; too bad schade
bag die Tasche (-n)
bakery die Bäckerei (-en)
balcony der Rang (-e) (in the theater); der Balkon (-e)
ballpoint pen der Kugelschreiber (-)
bank die Bank (-en); das Ufer (-) (of a body of water); savings bank die Sparkasse (-n)
bank note der (Geld)schein (-e)
to barbecue grillen
a bargain preiswert
basis die Grundlage (-n)
bath(room) das Bad (-er)
Bavarian bayerisch
to be sein (ist), war, ist gewesen
beautiful schön
because denn (coord. conj.); weil (subord. conj.); because of wegen (+ gen.)
to become werden (wird), wurde, ist geworden; to become stupid verdummen
bed das Bett (-en)
bed-and-breakfast inn die Pension (-en)
bed sheet das Bettuch (-er)
beer das Bier (-e); beer on tap Bier vom Faß
before vor (+ acc./dat.); bevor (subord. conj.); before that vorher
to begin anfangen (fängt an), fing an, angefangen; beginnen, begann, begonnen
beginning der Anfang (-e)
behind hinter (+ acc./dat.); to be left behind in class sitzenbleiben (bleibt sitzen), blieb sitzen, ist sitzengeblieben
to believe in glauben an (+ acc.)
to belong gehören (+ dat.)
to belong together zusammengehören (gehört zusammen)
below unten; unter (+ acc./dat.)
belt der Gürtel (-)
beside neben (+ acc./dat.)

besides außer (+ dat.); außerdem
between zwischen (+ acc./dat.)
bicycle das Fahrrad (-er), das Rad
big groß
bill die Rechnung (-en)
bird der Vogel (-)
birth die Geburt (-en); date of birth das Geburtsdatum (Geburtsdaten); place of birth der Geburtsort (-e)
birthday der Geburtstag (-e); Happy birthday! Herzlichen Glückwunsch zum Geburtstag!
to bite beißen, biß, gebissen
black schwarz
black market der Schwarzhandel
blouse die Bluse (-n)
blue blau; in blue in Blau
blueprint der Grundriß (-sse)
body der Körper (-)
body part der Körperteil (-e)
book das Buch (-er); notebook das Heft (-e)
to book (a trip) buchen
bookcase der Bücherschrank (-e)
bookshelf das Bücherregal (-e)
boot der Stiefel (-)
border die Grenze (-n)
boring langweilig
born geboren
to borrow sich (etwas) leihen, lieh, geliehen
bottle die Flasche (-n)
to bowl kegeln
to brake bremsen
bread das Brot (-e)
to break kaputtmachen (macht kaputt)
breakfast das Frühstück; to eat breakfast frühstücken
breast die Brust (-e)
bridge die Brücke (-n)
bright hell
to bring bringen, brachte, gebracht
to bring along mitbringen (bringt mit), brachte mit, mitgebracht
broadcast die Übertragung (-en)
broadcasting der Rundfunk
broke pleite (coll.)
broken kaputt
brother der Bruder (-)
brown braun
to brush one's teeth sich die Zähne putzen
to build bauen;
to build in einbauen (baut ein)

building das Gebäude (-); new building der Neubau (Neubauten); old building der Altbau (Altbauten)
bus der Autobus / Bus (-se)
businessman/businesswoman der Kaufmann (Kaufleute) / die Kauffrau (-en)
but aber; but rather sondern
butcher shop die Metzgerei (-en)
to buy kaufen
by von (+ dat.)
by the way übrigens

C
cabinet der Schrank (-e)
café das Café
cafeteria (for students) die Mensa (Mensen)
cake der Kuchen (-)
to call rufen, rief, gerufen; to be called sich nennen; heißen; to call (on the phone) anrufen (ruft an), rief an, angerufen
calm ruhig
camera der Fotoapparat (-e)
camper der Wohnwagen (-)
can können (kann), konnte, gekonnt
car das Auto (-s), der Wagen (-)
carbonated water der Sprudel
card die Karte (-n); credit card die Kreditkarte; ID card der Ausweis (-e); report card das Zeugnis (-se)
care: I don't care. Das ist mir egal.
career die Karriere (-en); to be successful in a career Karriere machen
careful vorsichtig
carpet der Teppich (-e); wall-to-wall carpet der Teppichboden (-)
in case falls
cash das Bargeld; in cash bar
cash register die Kasse (-n)
castle die Burg (-en), das Schloß (-sser)
to catch fangen (fängt), fing, gefangen
to catch a cold sich erkälten
cathedral der Dom (-e)
cauliflower der Blumenkohl
cautious vorsichtig
to celebrate feiern
celebration das Fest (-e)

center das Zentrum (Zent...
  shopping center das
    Einkaufszentrum; tou...
  information center da...
    Fremdenverkehrsamt...
  of town die Innenstad...
centigrade Celsius
central heating die Zentr...
  (-en)
certainly bestimmt, siche...
chair der Stuhl (-e); easy...
    Sessel (-)
chancellor der Kanzler (-...
    Kanzlerin (-nen); chan...
    the Federal Republic...
    Bundeskanzler
change (diversion) die Ab...
to change sich ändern; to...
    trains umsteigen (steig...
    um, ist umgestiegen; t...
    money wechseln
channel (TV) das Progra...
to chat plaudern
cheap billig
check der Scheck (-s); tra...
    check der Reisescheck
checkered kariert
checking account das Gi...
    (Girokonten)
checkup die Untersuchun...
    go for a checkup sich...
    untersuchen lassen
cheerful fröhlich, lustig
cheese der Käse; curd ch...
    Quark
chest die Brust
child das Kind (-er)
chin das Kinn
to choose wählen; auswäl...
    aus)
Christmas (das) Weihnach...
church die Kirche (-n)
citizen der Bürger (-) / die...
    (-nen)
city die Stadt (-e); large c...
    Großstadt; small town...
    Kleinstadt
city hall das Rathaus (-er)
to claim behaupten
clean sauber
to clean putzen; to keep...
    sauberhalten (hält sau...
    sauber, saubergehalten...
(dry) cleaning die Reinig...
climate das Klima
to climb steigen, stieg, ist...

every jeder, jede, jedes; every day
    jeden Tag; every other week alle
    zwei Wochen
everything alles; everything (is) all
    right alles klar
evidence der Beweis (-e)
exact genau
to exaggerate übertreiben, übertrieb,
    übertrieben
exam die Prüfung (-en)
example das Beispiel (-e); for
    example zum Beispiel (abbr. z.B.)
excellent ausgezeichnet
except for außer (+ dat.)
to exchange umtauschen (tauscht
    um); umwechseln (wechselt um)
exchange rate der Wechselkurs
exchange student der
    Austauschstudent (-n masc.) / die
    Austauschstudentin (-nen)
exciting aufregend, spannend
exclusively ausschließlich
excursion der Ausflug (-e)
to excuse (sich) entschuldigen;
    Excuse me. Entschuldigung.
exercise die Bewegung (-en)
exhaust fumes die Abgase (pl.)
exhausted: to be completely
    exhausted fix und fertig sein
to expect erwarten; rechnen mit
expense die Ausgabe (-n); incidental
    expenses die Nebenkosten (pl.)
expensive teuer
experience die Erfahrung (-en)
to experience erfahren (erfährt),
    erfuhr, erfahren
expression der Ausdruck (-e)
extreme(ly) äußerst
eye das Auge (-n)

F

face das Gesicht (-er)
fact die Tatsache (-n)
to fail a class sitzenbleiben (bleibt
    sitzen), blieb sitzen, ist
    sitzengeblieben
false falsch
family die Familie (-n); family name
    der Familienname (-n masc.), der
    Nachname
family celebration das Familienfest
    (-e)
family tree der Stammbaum (-e)

famous berühmt
fantastic phantastisch
far weit; far from here weit von hier
farewell der Abschied
farm der Bauernhof (-e)
fashion die Mode (-n)
fast schnell
fast-food restaurant der
    Schnellimbiß (-sse)
fat dick
father der Vater (-)
fault: It is not my fault. Ich kann
    nichts dafür.
favor der Gefallen (-); to do a favor
    einen Gefallen tun
favorite: favorite activity die
    Lieblingsbeschäftigung (-en);
    favorite subject in school das
    Lieblingsfach (-er)
fear die Angst (-e)
to fear befürchten
February (der) Februar
Federal Republic of Germany die
    Bundesrepublik Deutschland
    (BRD)
fee die Gebühr (-en)
to feed füttern
to feel (sich) fühlen; empfinden,
    empfand, empfunden; I don't feel
    well. Ich fühle mich nicht wohl. to
    feel like doing something Lust
    haben
to fetch holen
fever das Fieber
few wenige
field das Feld; sports field, playing
    field der Sportplatz (-e)
fifteen fünfzehn
fifty fünfzig
to fill out ausfüllen (füllt aus)
to fill up (the gas tank) volltanken
    (tankt voll)
film der Film
finally endlich
to finance finanzieren
to find finden, fand, gefunden
to find out erfahren (erfährt), erfuhr,
    erfahren
fine gut, prima (coll.); I'm fine. Es
    geht mir gut/prima. That's fine
    with me. Das ist mir recht.
finger der Finger (-); to keep one's
    fingers crossed die Daumen
    drücken
first erst; at first zuerst; in first
    place an erster Stelle

her ih...
here h...
high h...
highe...
    Hö...
to hik...

natural natür...
near nah; nex...
    train der...
nearby in der...
neat ordentli...
necessary nö...
neck der Hal...
to need brau...
nephew der...
never nie
nevertheless...
new neu; not...
new buildin...
    (Neubaute...
newlywed ju...
news die Na...
newspaper d...
newspaper s...
    Feuilleton...
next to nebe...
nice nett, syr...
    warm sch...
niece die Nic...
night die Na...
    good nigh...
nine neun
nineteen ne...
ninety neun...
no nein
no one nie...
nobody nie...
noise der Lä...
nonpartisan...
nonsense d...
noon der M...
    today at...
noontime d...
north der N...
    nördlich
house...
    h...
    t...
nose die Na...
not nicht
note: bank...
notebook d...
nothing nic...
to notice be...
novel der R...
November...
now jetzt;...
nuclear en...
number die...
    (-en); st...
    Hausnu...
    die Telefo...
numerous...
nutrition...

subscription das Abonnement (-s)
suburb die Vorstadt (-e)
to succeed (in something) (etwas)
    schaffen, schuf, geschaffen
success der Erfolg (-e)
successful erfolgreich; to be
    successful in a career Karriere
    machen
sufficient ausreichend
sugar der Zucker
to suggest vorschlagen (schlägt vor),
    schlug vor, vorgeschlagen
suggestion der Vorschlag (-e)
suit der Anzug (-e)
suitable geeignet
suitcase der Koffer (-)
summer der Sommer (-)
sun die Sonne; The sun is shining.
    Die Sonne scheint.
Sunday (der) Sonntag
sunny sonnig
superficial oberflächlich
supermarket der Supermarkt (-e)
to supply versorgen; in short supply
    knapp
support der Unterhalt
to be supposed to sollen
surcharge der Zuschlag (-e)
sure bestimmt, sicher; geht in
    Ordnung; to be sure allerdings
surprise die Überraschung (-en)
to surprise überraschen
surroundings die Umgebung
to swallow schlucken
to swim schwimmen, schwamm, ist
    geschwommen
Switzerland die Schweiz

T

table der Tisch (-e)
to take nehmen (nimmt), nahm,
    genommen; to take along
    mitnehmen (nimmt mit)
to take a rest sich entspannen, sich
    erholen
to take care of pflegen
taken besetzt; The seat is taken. Der
    Platz ist besetzt.
to talk about reden über (+ acc.)
tall groß
tank der Panzer (-)
to taste schmecken (+ dat.); That
    tastes good (to me). Das
    schmeckt (mir).
tax die Steuer (-n)

teacher der Lehrer (-) / die Lehrerin
    (-nen)
team die Mannschaft (-en)
telephone das Telefon
telephone number die
    Telefonnummer (-n)
television (TV) das Fernsehen; to
    watch television fernsehen (sieht
    fern), sah fern, ferngesehen
television channel das Programm
    (-e)
television program die Sendung
    (-en), das Programm
television set der Fernsehapparat
    (-e), das Fernsehgerät (-e)
to tell erzählen
teller: automatic teller der
    Geldautomat (-n masc.)
temperature die Temperatur (-en);
    highest temperature die
    Höchsttemperatur
ten zehn
tenant der Mieter (-) / die Mieterin
    (-nen)
tent das Zelt (-e)
terrace die Terrasse (-n)
than als
to thank danken (+ dat.), sich
    bedanken; Thank God. Gott sei
    Dank.
thanks danke, danke schön, danke
    sehr; many thanks vielen Dank
that das; daß (conj.); isn't that so?
    nicht wahr? that's all right geht in
    Ordnung
the der, die, das
the ... the ... je ... umso ...; the
    older, the prouder je älter umso
    stolzer
their ihr
then dann; now and then ab und zu
there da, dort; over there da drüben;
    there is, there are es gibt
therefore deshalb
they sie; man (indef. pron.)
thief der Dieb (-e)
thing das Ding (-e), die Sache (-n)
to think denken, dachte, gedacht
to think about something sich
    (+ dat.) etwas überlegen
to think of finden, fand, gefunden;
    What do you think of Berlin? Wie
    finden Sie Berlin?
thirst der Durst
thirsty: to be thirsty Durst haben
thirteen dreizehn

thirty d...
this dies...
    morn...
thoughtf...
three dre...
through...
to throw...
    weg), v...
thumb de...
thunder d...
    thunde...
thunderst...
Thursday (...
ticket die K...
    (ticket)...
    ticket di...
    ticket di...
    ticket di...
ticket windo...
    Fahrkarte...
tie die Krawa...
tight eng
time die Zeit...
    kurz; in ti...
    time die Fr...
    Die Zeit ve...
What time...
    Wieviel Uh...
tip der Hinweis...
tired müde
tiring ermüden
to nach (+ dat.);...
today heute; tod...
    mittag
together gemein...
toilet das WC
tomato die Toma...
tomorrow morge...
    morning morg...
tonight heute abe...
too zu; too bad s...
    wenig
tooth der Zahn (-e...
toothache die Zah...
top: on top of auf...
tourist der Tourist...
    Touristin (-nen)...
tourist attraction...
    Sehenswürdigke...
tourist information...
    Fremdenverkehrs...
town die Stadt (-e);...
    die Innenstadt; h...
    Heimat(stadt)
town house das Reih...

ANITA: Wir gehen heute abend tanzen. Kommst du mit?
BRIGITTE: Ja, gern! Ich tanze nämlich gern. Wann gehen wir denn?
ANITA: Um neun.

Kapitel 3

▣ Aktivität 8. Hören Sie zu. Seite 90

TOM: Tom McKay.
HEIKE: Hallo, Tom? Hier ist Heike.
TOM: Tag, Heike.
HEIKE: Du, Tom, ich mache eine kleine Party zu Hause. Ich habe nämlich Geburts-
tag. Ich möchte dich einladen.
TOM: Vielen Dank für die Einladung. Ich komme gern. Wann ist die Party denn?
HEIKE: Am Samstag.
TOM: Schön. Wer kommt sonst noch?
HEIKE: Du kennst doch die Gabi? Die kommt auch. Und vielleicht Jürgen. Sonst
sind nur meine Eltern und Geschwister da.
TOM: Also gut, bis Samstag dann.
HEIKE: Mach's gut. Tschüß.

Kapitel 4

▣ Aktivität 3. Hören Sie zu. Seite 107

1. Die Zeit ist 17 Uhr 35.
2. Die Zeit ist 3 Uhr 6.
3. Die Zeit ist 14 Uhr 15.
4. Die Zeit ist 11 Uhr 25.
5. Die Zeit ist 19 Uhr 45.
6. Die Zeit ist 13 Uhr 40.
7. Die Zeit ist 0 Uhr 15.
8. Die Zeit ist 21 Uhr 50.

▣ Aktivität 10. Hören Sie zu. Seite 112

Dialog 1
PETER: Möchtest du heute abend ins Kino?
KARLA: Leider kann ich nicht. Ich habe nämlich am Montag eine Klausur.
PETER: Eine Klausur?
KARLA: Ja, in Physik. Ich muß noch dafür arbeiten.
PETER: Na, dann wünsche ich dir viel Glück.
KARLA: Danke, ich kann es brauchen.

Dialog 2
GABI: Hallo, Hans. Hast du heute abend Zeit? Im Olympia läuft ein toller Film,
Ich und Er.

HERR X: Nein.
KELLNERIN: Das macht zusam

2. FRAU X: Herr Ober, wir möcht
OBER: Zwei Tassen Kaffee, ei
Das macht zusammen

3. HERR Y: Fräulein, wir möc
KELLNERIN: Dreimal Leberknc
einmal zwei Stücl
HERR Y: Und fünf Brezel.
KELLNERIN: Ja, und fünf Bier ı
zusammen 74 Ma

▣ Aktivität 10. Hören Si

BRIGITTE: Ich war gestern abend in
ANDREAS: So? Was hast du denn ge
BRIGITTE: Rigoletto.
ANDREAS: Wie war's denn?
BRIGITTE: Ausgezeichnet. Pavarotti
ANDREAS: Hattest du einen guten Pl
BRIGITTE: Ich hatte wirklich Glück.
bekommen, für nur 10 M.

Kapitel 7

▣ Aktivität 4. Hören Sie

Herr Lohmann
Jeden Tag gehen wir ins Therma
sage. In die Sauna gehen wir nie. Mi
tags spielen wir manchmal Karten ı
lich gehen wir viel spazieren.

Herr Kranzler
Ich bin allein hier. Meine Famili
auch gern wandern und schwimmer
ins Thermalbad. Und dann mache ic
ein Glas Wasser.

Frau Dietmold
Ja, ich mache auch eine Trinkku
bekomme Massagen. Tischtennis ma
ins Theater. Ich spiele auch Mini-Gol

▣ Aktivität 7. Hören Sie z

Strecken Sie die Arme nach obe
Die Knie gerade halten. Mit den Fing
wiederhochkommen.

HANS: Ich möchte schon mitgehen. Wann fängt er denn an?
GABI: Um 17 Uhr.
HANS: Das ist mir zu früh. Ich habe nämlich noch eine Vorlesung bis fünf.
GABI: So spät am Freitag noch?
HANS: Ja, leider.

▣ Übung 15. Hören Sie zu. Seite 124

Studenten haben oft große Probleme, eine Wohnung zu finden. Viele Student-en müssen schon in ihren Autos schlafen, so heißt es in einer Berliner Zeitung.

Gwenola Martelot ist 21 Jahre alt. Sie stammt aus Paris und möchte in Ber-lin Germanistik studieren. Sie findet die Mieten sehr hoch. Als Studentin kann sie 300 Mark für Miete ausgeben.

Kamal Louh ist 19 Jahre alt und studiert Medizin an der Universität in Ber-lin. Seit zwei Monaten muß er bei Freunden schlafen. Den Tag verbringt er an der Universität. Ohne Wohnung muß er bald in eine andere Stadt nach West-deutschland gehen.

Oliver Kortenkamp ist 23 Jahre alt und kommt aus Westdeutschland. Er stu-diert Sport und Biologie in Berlin. Jetzt hat er für zwei Monate bis Ende Januar eine Wohnung. Was er dann macht, weiß er noch nicht.

Kapitel 5

▣ Aktivität 6. Hören Sie zu. Seite 139

A. (*male customer*)

o: Bitte schön, kann ich Ihnen helfen?
x: Ich brauche ein paar Schuhe.
o: Welche Größe bitte?
x: Größe 44.
o: Und welche Farbe?
x: Schwarz bitte.

B. (*female customer*)

o: Guten Tag. Kann ich Ihnen helfen?
x: Ich möchte gern eine Hose.
o: Welche Größe brauchen Sie?
x: Ich glaube Größe 38. Aber ich bin nicht sicher.
o: Und welche Farbe soll es sein?
x: Haben Sie etwas in Blau-weiß gestreift?

C. (*male customer*)

o: Guten Tag, kann ich Ihnen helfen?
x: Ja, ich suche ein Geschenk für meine Freundin. Eine Bluse vielleicht.
o: Und welche Größe hat Ihre Freundin?
x: Hmm, ich weiß nicht, sie ist ziemlich klein. Ich glaube ungefähr Größe 44.
o: Das ist aber ziemlich groß. Sie sagen, sie ist ziemlich klein?
x: Ja.

O: Ich empfehle Ihnen Größe
X: Vielen Dank. Also, Größe 3
O: Und welche Farbe?
X: Rot.

D. (male customer)

X: Bitte schön. Kann ich Ihne
O: Ich suche einen Winterman
X: Und welche Größe brauche
O: Größe 44.
X: Und welche Farbe?
O: Haben Sie was in Dunkelbl
X: Ja, da bin ich ganz sicher.

▣ Aktivität 12. Hören Si

1. VERKÄUFERIN: Bitte schön. Wa
   KUNDE: Ich möchte ger
   VERKÄUFERIN: Sonst noch etw
   KUNDE: Ja, ein Pfund A
   VERKÄUFERIN: Und sonst noch
   KUNDE: Nein, danke. Da
   VERKÄUFERIN: Das macht zusa

2. VERKÄUFERIN: Guten Morgen,
   KUNDIN: Guten Morgen.
   VERKÄUFERIN: Ja, natürlich. Ga
   Sie?
   KUNDIN: Sechs Brötchen,
   VERKÄUFERIN: Sonst noch etw
   KUNDIN: Nein, danke.
   VERKÄUFERIN: Das macht zusa

3. VERKÄUFERIN: Bitte schön?
   KUNDIN: Haben Sie frisch
   VERKÄUFERIN: Ja, Tomaten hab
   KUNDIN: Wieviel kosten d
   VERKÄUFERIN: 10 Mark das Kilo
   KUNDE: Das ist aber teu
   VERKÄUFERIN: Erdbeeren sind s
   KUNDIN: Na, dann nehme
   Tomaten.
   VERKÄUFERIN: Das macht zusa

Kapitel 6

▣ Aktivität 9. Hören Sie

1. HERR X: Fräulein, ich möcht
   KELLNERIN: Jawohl. Drei Bier, z
   Sie auch Brot?

PAGE 129
Was ist los in Wien? is a page from a cultural calendar giving information about summer events in Vienna.

Kapitel 5

PAGE 134
Einkaufen mit Spaß is from a flyer advertising a shopping area called **die Rutschbahn** off the Hamburg street of the same name.

PAGE 136
1. **Martens moden** is an ad from a small local newspaper, the *Klever Wochenblatt*.

2. **Leyendeckers herrenmoden** is an ad from the daily newspaper *Bonner Generalanzeiger*.

3. **Schön, chic . . .** is an ad for the fashion magazine *neue mode*.

PAGE 137
1. **Das neue Jahr . . .** is from an ad for a store (**Straub**) in Oberursel.

2. **Sonderangebot** is from the *Klever Wochenblatt*.

PAGE 138
Koffermemo appeared in the *Frankfurter Rundschau*, as an advertisement for the clothing chain **C&A.**

PAGE 139
This is from the *Süddeutsche Zeitung*, of Munich, advertising the **Hirmer** department store.

PAGE 142
This ad for the West German grocery chain **Edeka** is from the *Klever Wochenblatt*.

PAGE 144
The ad for **Mühlbacher Bauernbrot,** offered by the West German grocery chain **Tengelmann,** is from the *Süddeutsche Zeitung*.

PAGE 148
1. **Herr Professor . . .** is a regular column in the German tabloid *Bild am Sonntag*.

---

2. The ad for **Restaurant Haus Kuckuck** appeared in the weekly *Klever Wochenblatt*.

PAGE 154
This ad for **Mühlenbäckerei Borgmann** shows a windmill, a typical sight in this area of the German Niederrhein close to the Dutch border.

PAGE 155
Café Derks is located in Kleve. The ad is from the *Klever Wochenblatt*.

PAGE 156
This ad is from the *Frankfurter Rundschau*.

PAGE 157
1. **Sag Ja zu Yes** appears on the back of a form for train connections (**Reiseverbindungen**) used by the travel agency (**DER**) of the West German **Bundesbahn**.

2. This ad for **Hertie,** a German department store chain, appeared in a daily newspaper, the *Bonner Generalanzeiger*.

PAGE 158
The cartoon **Moppel** is from *Bildwoche*, a German TV magazine.

PAGE 160
Sei weiser: This slogan for **Kaiser** beer is on a beer mat (**Bierdeckel**).

PAGE 161
1. **Parkhaus Altstadt:** This is a ticket for a parking garage in the town of Limburg an der Lahn. The customer pays before picking up the car.

2. **Schon probiert:** This recipe is from the *Klever Wochenblatt*. Putting lettuce on a sandwich is considered unusual in Germany.

Kapitel 6

PAGE 168
This leaflet advertising **Hagenauerstuben,** a restaurant in the house where Mozart was born, was distributed in Salzburg.

2. **Jungkoch:** This ad

3. This ad for the Gern
was in *Welt am Sonn*

PAGE 406
This ad for the employm
Frankfurt is from *Welt an*

PAGE 411
This ad for newspaper de
ich's *Süddeutsche Zeitung*

Kapitel 14

PAGE 415
This index is from the *Be*

PAGE 416
This cartoon is from a pa
**zur politischen Bildung,
zentrale für politische B**

PAGE 417
The program listings are f
Fernsehwoche.

PAGE 419
The program listings are f

PAGE 420
This is an excerpt of TV ar
magazine *Fernsehwoche.*

PAGE 427
This is a postcard that read
to the *Volkszeitung.*

PAGE 428
1. This headline comes fr
investment firm **DWS
für Wertpapiere).** It a
become part of an inve
fixed amount of their r
firm. (**Der Kunde "der**

2. **Wer schwimmen will**
man **Sparkasse** saving
ple to open a checking
charge, while they are
ad was placed in the *A*

PAGE 169
The restaurant and café ads on this page and the next represent the cities of Munich, Regensburg, Berlin, and an obscure Bavarian town, Rieden.

PAGE 172
Restaurant Käuzchen is located in Regensburg.

PAGE 178
The seating arrangement for the **Deutsches Theater** is from the yellow pages of the Göttingen phone directory.

PAGE 180
This ad is a segment of a larger leaflet for **Restaurant Himmelsstube** in Vienna.

PAGE 181
1. **Kulinarische Notizen** is a regular newspaper section in the *Bonner Generalanzeiger*. It features an article describing what **Forsthaus Telegraph,** a restaurant near Bonn, has to offer in the way of scenic beauty as well as gastronomic delicacies.

2. The **Olympia Einkaufszentrum** is located in Munich.

3. **Schubert-Stüberln** is located in Vienna.

PAGE 187
Reserviert für 5 Personen: This is a place card reserving a table at the restaurant **Nürnberger Bratwurstglöckl** in Munich.

PAGE 192
Humor: This cartoon appeared in *Bunte* magazine.

PAGE 195
These restaurant ads are from the yellow pages of the Vienna phone directory.

Kapitel 7

PAGE 202
Kaisers Drogeriemarkt is a chain of drugstores in Bavaria. The ad demonstrates the pervasive influence of American terms in German advertising.

PAGE 203
The cartoon **Herr Stierli** appeared in the Swiss magazine **Brückenbauer,** published by **Migros-Genos-**
senschaft. **Migros** is a large department store chain selling everything from food to clothing.

PAGE 204
1. **Immer fit mit Brot und Schrot** is a portion of an advertisement for **Bäckerei-Konditorei Ehren** in Kleve. A concern for nutritious bread is stressed; however, it is advertised as rich in roughage and calories—thus, not exactly desirable for weight-conscious people!

2. **Mozart gegen Streß** is the title of an article in *Bunte* magazine explaining how music helps people stay younger longer.

3. **Der Gesundheitsminister. . . :** By law, this warning is printed on every cigarette package.

4. A daily newspaper, the *Bonner Rundschau*, reported in 1988 that each German drinks an average of 3060 liters of beer in a lifetime.

5. **Ich rauche gern** is a widespread slogan for a brand of cigarettes.

6. **Trimming:** These cartoon ads are frequently found in German newspapers and magazines. Published by the national organization **Deutscher Sportbund,** they encourage all people to engage in physical activities.

7. **Essen macht Spaß** is the title of an article from a small local newspaper, the *Klever Wochenblatt*. Its topic reflects modern Germans' concern for good nutrition.

PAGE 205
Die Kur is an ad placed in the weekly magazine *Der Spiegel* by the national organization **Deutscher Bäderverband.**

PAGE 206
Baden Baden: This is a segment of an ad by the **Bäder-und Kurverwaltung** of the city of Baden Baden, which is world famous for its spas and gambling casinos. Note the word **Casino** in one of the ad's activities squares.

PAGE 211
These three ads for common ailments and complaints appear often in various papers and magazines.

PAGE 212
Machen Sie sich frei. . . : This page from a pamphlet titled **Gesundheits Tips** is distributed by the **Krankenkassen Vereinigung** of Baden-Württemberg.

PAGE 327
Ihr erstes Konto: This l
people, to encourage the
Bank.

PAGE 328
This is a currency excha
Dresdner Bank.

PAGE 333
These statistics are from

PAGE 335
These two ad slogans are
bank and the **Deutsche**
the German federal telep

PAGE 337
Wenn ich ein Vöglein w
book by Eva Haue, *Vielle*
verschieden.

PAGE 341
1. This drawing is from
    leicht sind wir doch z

2. This was published b
    post to advertise its

Kapitel 12

PAGES 350–351
Renovierter Altbau is an
and loan bank, **Sparkasse**
remodeling. This type of a
German newspapers and
for various properties are

PAGE 351
The ad for an apartment i
Zeitung of Regensburg.

PAGE 352
This student flyer seeks a
Göttingen. It was found on
istic bulletin board, the so

PAGE 357
This cartoon is from the n

published in the *Berliner Morgenpost* 3 months
before the dramatic turn of events in Germany
in November 1989.

2. **Muß unser Dorf so häßlich werden** is in a pam-
    phlet published by the **Deutsches Nationalkom-
    itee für Denkmalschutz** in Bonn, which seeks to
    preserve the integrity and beauty of older build-
    ings and monuments.

PAGES 455–456
The headlines and article are excerpted from an article in the TV magazine *Hörzu*.

PAGE 457
This article appeared in the *Berliner Morgenpost.*

PAGE 458
This puzzle appeared in *Hörzu.*

PAGE 460
The drawing is from *Bunte* magazine.

Kapitel 16

PAGE 474
The drawing of Rothenburg is in a pamphlet published by that city to advertise its historical sites.
The other official city logos were designed specifically for the occasion of their various birthday
celebrations.

PAGE 496
This drawing by a Viennese child is part of a collection of letters sent to Herbert Hoover that is now in
the archives of the Hoover Institution at Stanford
University.